87%
of college students report that access to learning analytics can positively impact their learning experience.

75%
of students using adaptive technology report that it is "very helpful" or "extremely helpful" in aiding their ability to retain new concepts.

"I can honestly say that the first time I used SmartBook after reading a chapter I understood what I had just read better than I ever had in the past."
– Nathan Herrmann, Oklahoma State University

"I really enjoy how it has gotten me engaged in the course and it is a great study tool without having to carry around a heavy textbook."
– Madeline Uretsky, Simmons College

Professors spend:

Less time on administrative tasks

72%

90%
More time on active learning

"Connect keeps my students engaged and motivated. Requiring Connect assignments has improved student exam grades."
– Sophia Garcia, Tarrant County College

Mc Graw Hill Education

Because learning changes everything.™

To learn more about Connect History visit the McGraw-Hill Education American History page: www.mhhe.com/history

THE UNFINISHED NATION

A Concise History of the
American People
Volume 2: From 1865

Ninth Edition

ALAN BRINKLEY
Columbia University

JOHN GIGGIE
University of Alabama

ANDREW HUEBNER
University of Alabama

Mc
Graw
Hill
Education

THE UNFINISHED NATION: A CONCISE HISTORY OF THE AMERICAN PEOPLE
VOLUME 2: FROM 1865, NINTH EDITION

2 3 4 5 6 7 8 9 LCR 21 20 19

ISBN   978-1-260-16485-5 (bound edition)
MHID   1-260-16485-3 (bound edition)

ISBN   978-1260-16486-2 (loose-leaf edition)
MHID   1-260-16486-1 (loose-leaf edition)

Senior Portfolio Manager: *Jason Seitz*
Lead Product Developer: *Dawn Groundwater*
Product Developer: *Elisa Odoardi*
Marketing Manager: *Will Walter*
Lead Content Project Manager: *Susan Trentacosti*
Content Project Managers: *Emily Windelborn, Sandra Schnee*
Senior Buyer: *Susan K. Culbertson*
Design: *Jessica Cuevas*
Lead Content Licensing Specialist: *Carrie Burger*
Cover Images: *Background:* ©Curly Pat/Shutterstock; *Map (left):* ©Vector Icon Flat/Shutterstock; *Map (right):*
        Source: Library of Congress Geography and Map Division [G3301.R2 1767 .P3 Vault.]
Compositor: *Aptara®, Inc.*

Library of Congress Cataloging-in-Publication Data
Names: Brinkley, Alan, author. | Giggie, John Michael, 1965- contributor. |
  Huebner, Andrew, contributor.
Title: The unfinished nation : a concise history of the American people /
  Alan Brinkley, Columbia University ; with contributions from John Giggie,
  University of Alabama, Andrew Huebner, University of Alabama.
Description: Ninth edition. | New York, NY : McGraw-Hill Education, [2019]
Identifiers: LCCN 2018025712 | ISBN 9781259912535 (alk. paper)
Subjects: LCSH: United States—History.
Classification: LCC E178.1 .B827 2019 | DDC 973—dc23 LC record available at https://lccn.loc.gov/2018025712

mheducation.com/highered

ABOUT THE AUTHORS

ALAN BRINKLEY is the Allan Nevins Professor of History at Columbia University. He served as university provost at Columbia from 2003 to 2009. He is the author of *Voices of Protest: Huey Long, Father Coughlin, and the Great Depression*, which won the 1983 National Book Award; *American History: Connecting with the Past; The End of Reform: New Deal Liberalism in Recession and War; Liberalism and Its Discontents; Franklin D. Roosevelt;* and *The Publisher: Henry Luce and His American Century.* He is board chair of the National Humanities Center, board chair of the Century Foundation, and a trustee of Oxford University Press. He is also a member of the Academy of Arts and Sciences. In 1998-1999 he was the Harmsworth Professor of History at Oxford University, and in 2011-2012 the Pitt Professor at the University of Cambridge. He won the Joseph R. Levenson Memorial Teaching Award at Harvard and the Great Teacher Award at Columbia. He was educated at Princeton and Harvard.

JOHN GIGGIE is associate professor of history and African American studies at the University of Alabama where he also serves as director of the Summersell Center for the Study of the South. He is the author of *After Redemption: Jim Crow and the Transformation of African American Religion in the Delta, 1875-1917,* editor of *America Firsthand,* and editor of *Faith in the Market: Religion and the Rise of Commercial Culture.* He is currently preparing a book on civil rights protests in west Alabama. He has been widely honored for his teaching, most recently with a Distinguished Fellow in Teaching Award and Excellence in Community Engagement Award from the University of Alabama. He received his PhD from Princeton University.

ANDREW HUEBNER is associate professor of history at the University of Alabama. He is the author of *Love and Death in the Great War* (2018) and *The Warrior Image: Soldiers in American Culture from the Second World War to the Vietnam Era* (2008). He has written and spoken widely on the subject of war and society in the twentieth-century United States. In 2017, he was named an Organization of American Historians (OAH) Distinguished Lecturer. He received his PhD from Brown University.

BRIEF CONTENTS

PREFACE xxiii

15 RECONSTRUCTION AND THE NEW SOUTH 352

16 THE CONQUEST OF THE FAR WEST 381

17 INDUSTRIAL SUPREMACY 405

18 THE AGE OF THE CITY 427

19 FROM CRISIS TO EMPIRE 453

20 THE PROGRESSIVES 486

21 AMERICA AND THE GREAT WAR 516

22 THE NEW ERA 541

23 THE GREAT DEPRESSION 561

24 THE NEW DEAL ERA 586

25 AMERICA IN A WORLD AT WAR 612

26 THE COLD WAR 642

27 THE AFFLUENT SOCIETY 668

28 THE TURBULENT SIXTIES 698

29 THE CRISIS OF AUTHORITY 730

30 FROM "THE AGE OF LIMITS" TO THE AGE OF REAGAN 761

31 THE AGE OF GLOBALIZATION 784

APPENDIX 821
GLOSSARY 842
INDEX 868

PREFACE   xxiii

15 RECONSTRUCTION AND THE NEW SOUTH   352

THE PROBLEMS OF PEACEMAKING   353
The Aftermath of War and Emancipation   353
Competing Notions of Freedom   353
Plans for Reconstruction   355
The Death of Lincoln   358
Johnson and "Restoration"   359

RADICAL RECONSTRUCTION   359
The Black Codes   359
The Fourteenth Amendment   361
The Congressional Plan   361
The Impeachment of Andrew Johnson   363

THE SOUTH IN RECONSTRUCTION   363
The Reconstruction Governments   363
Education   365
Landownership and Tenancy   365
Incomes and Credit   365
The African American Family in Freedom   366

THE GRANT ADMINISTRATION   367
The Soldier President   367
The Grant Scandals   368
The Greenback Question   368
Republican Diplomacy   369

THE ABANDONMENT OF RECONSTRUCTION   369
The Southern States "Redeemed"   369
Waning Northern Commitment   370
The Compromise of 1877   370
The Legacy of Reconstruction   372

THE NEW SOUTH   372
The "Redeemers"   372
Industrialization and the New South   373
Tenants and Sharecroppers   374
African Americans and the New South   374
The Birth of Jim Crow   375

Debating the Past: Reconstruction   356

Consider the Source: Southern Blacks Ask for Help (1865)   360

Patterns of Popular Culture: The Minstrel Show   376

CONCLUSION   379
KEY TERMS/PEOPLE/PLACES/EVENTS   380
RECALL AND REFLECT   380

Source: Library of Congress, Prints and Photographs Division [LC-USZC4-5759]

16 THE CONQUEST OF THE FAR WEST   381

THE SOCIETIES OF THE FAR WEST   382
The Western Tribes   382
Hispanic New Mexico   383

Hispanic California and Texas   383
The Chinese Migration   384
Anti-Chinese Sentiments   386
Migration from the East   386

THE ROMANCE OF THE WEST   387
The Western Landscape and the Cowboy   387
The Idea of the Frontier   387

**THE CHANGING WESTERN
ECONOMY   390**
Labor in the West   390
The Arrival of the Miners   391
The Cattle Kingdom   392

Source: NPS photo by JR Douglas

THE DISPERSAL OF THE TRIBES   394
White Tribal Policies   394
The Indian Wars   394
The Dawes Act   397

**THE RISE AND DECLINE
OF THE WESTERN FARMER   398**
Farming on the Plains   399
Commercial Agriculture   402
The Farmers' Grievances   402
The Agrarian Malaise   403

Debating the Past: The Frontier and
the West   **388**

Consider the Source: Walter Baron Von Richthofen, *Cattle Raising On The
Plains In North America* (1885)   **400**

CONCLUSION   403
KEY TERMS/PEOPLE/PLACES/EVENTS   404
RECALL AND REFLECT   404

17 | INDUSTRIAL SUPREMACY   405

**SOURCES OF INDUSTRIAL
GROWTH   406**
Industrial Technologies   406
The Technology of Iron and Steel Production   407
The Automobile and the Airplane   408
Research and Development   409
Making Production More Efficient   409
Railroad Expansion and the Corporation   410

Source: Library of Congress, Prints and
Photographs Division [LC-USZC4-435]

CAPITALISM AND ITS CRITICS   413
Survival of the Fittest   413
The Gospel of Wealth   414
Alternative Visions   415
The Problems of Monopoly   415

THE ORDEAL OF THE WORKER   420
The Immigrant Workforce   420
Wages and Working Conditions   420
Emerging Unionization   421
The Knights of Labor   422

The American Federation of Labor 422
The Homestead Strike 423
The Pullman Strike 424
Sources of Labor Weakness 424

Consider the Source: Andrew Carnegie Explains "The Gospel
Of Wealth" (1889) 416

Patterns of Popular Culture: The Novels of Horatio Alger 418

CONCLUSION 425
KEY TERMS/PEOPLE/PLACES/EVENTS 425
RECALL AND REFLECT 426

18 THE AGE OF THE CITY 427

THE NEW URBAN GROWTH 428
The Migrations 428
The Ethnic City 429
Assimilation and Exclusion 432

THE URBAN LANDSCAPE 433
The Creation of Public Space 433
The Search for Housing 434
Urban Technologies: Transportation and
  Construction 435

STRAINS OF URBAN LIFE 436
Health and Safety in the Built
  Environment 436
Urban Poverty, Crime, and Violence 437
The Machine and the Boss 439

THE RISE OF MASS CONSUMPTION 439
Patterns of Income and Consumption 439
Chain Stores, Mail-Order Houses, and Department Stores 441
Women as Consumers 442

LEISURE IN THE CONSUMER SOCIETY 442
Redefining Leisure 443
Spectator Sports 443
Music, Theater, and Movies 444
Patterns of Public and Private Leisure 445
The Technologies of Mass
  Communication 446
The Telephone 446

HIGH CULTURE IN THE URBAN AGE 447
Literature and Art in Urban America 447
The Impact of Darwinism 448
Toward Universal Schooling 449
Universities and the Growth of Science and Technology 449
Medical Science 450
Education for Women 451

©Corbis

America in the World: Global Migrations 430

Consider the Source: John Wanamaker, The Four Cardinal Points Of The Department Store (1874) 440

CONCLUSION 451
KEY TERMS/PEOPLE/PLACES/EVENTS 452
RECALL AND REFLECT 452

19 FROM CRISIS TO EMPIRE 453

THE POLITICS OF EQUILIBRIUM 454
The Party System 454
The National Government 455
Presidents and Patronage 456
Cleveland, Harrison, and the Tariff 457
New Public Issues 458

THE AGRARIAN REVOLT 459
The Grangers 459
The Farmers' Alliances 459
The Populist Constituency 461
Populist Ideas 461

THE CRISIS OF THE 1890s 462
The Panic of 1893 462
The Silver Question 463
"A Cross of Gold" 464
The Conservative Victory 465
McKinley and Recovery 466

STIRRINGS OF IMPERIALISM 467
The New Manifest Destiny 467
Hawaii and Samoa 470

WAR WITH SPAIN 471
Controversy over Cuba 471
"A Splendid Little War" 474
Seizing the Philippines 475
The Battle for Cuba 475
Puerto Rico and the United States 476
The Debate over the Philippines 478

THE REPUBLIC AS EMPIRE 479
Governing the Colonies 481
The Philippine War 481
The Open Door 483
A Modern Military System 484

America in the World: Imperialism 468

Patterns of Popular Culture: Yellow Journalism 472

Consider the Source: Platform of the American Anti-Imperialist League (1899) 480

CONCLUSION 484
KEY TERMS/PEOPLE/PLACES/EVENTS 485
RECALL AND REFLECT 485

GETTING HOT ENOUGH FOR HIM.

Source: Library of Congress, Prints and Photographs Division [LC-DIG-ppmsca-28490]

20 THE PROGRESSIVES 486

THE PROGRESSIVE IMPULSE 487
The Muckrakers and the Social Gospel 489
The Settlement House Movement 490
The Allure of Expertise 491
The Professions 491
Women and the Professions 492

WOMEN AND REFORM 492
The "New Woman" 492
The Clubwomen 492
Woman Suffrage 493

THE ASSAULT ON THE PARTIES 495
Early Attacks 495
Municipal Reform 495
Statehouse Progressivism 496
Parties and Interest Groups 496

SOURCES OF PROGRESSIVE REFORM 497
Labor, the Machine, and Reform 497
Western Progressives 499
African Americans and Reform 500

CRUSADES FOR SOCIAL ORDER AND REFORM 501
The Temperance Crusade 501
Immigration Restriction 502
The Dream of Socialism 502
Decentralization and Regulation 503

THEODORE ROOSEVELT AND THE MODERN PRESIDENCY 503
The Accidental President 503
The "Square Deal" 504
Roosevelt and the Environment 505
Panic and Retirement 508

THE TROUBLED SUCCESSION 508
Taft and the Progressives 508
The Return of Roosevelt 509
Spreading Insurgency 510
Roosevelt versus Taft 510

WOODROW WILSON AND THE NEW FREEDOM 511
Woodrow Wilson 511
The Scholar as President 511
Retreat and Advance 514

America in the World: Social Democracy 488
Debating the Past: Progressivism 498
Consider the Source: John Muir On The Value Of Wild Places (1901) 506
CONCLUSION 514
KEY TERMS/PEOPLE/PLACES/EVENTS 515
RECALL AND REFLECT 515

Source: Library of Congress, Prints and Photographs Division [LCUSZ62-70382]

21 AMERICA AND THE GREAT WAR 516

THE "BIG STICK": AMERICA AND THE WORLD, 1901–1917 517
Roosevelt and "Civilization" 517
Protecting the "Open Door" in Asia 518
The Iron-Fisted Neighbor 519
The Panama Canal 519
Taft and "Dollar Diplomacy" 520
Diplomacy and Morality 521

THE ROAD TO WAR 522
The Collapse of the European Peace 522
Wilson's Neutrality 522
Preparedness versus Pacifism 523
Intervention 523

"OVER THERE" 525
Mobilizing the Military 525
The Yanks Are Coming 527
The New Technology of Warfare 528
Organizing the Economy for War 530
The Search for Social Unity 531

THE SEARCH FOR A NEW WORLD ORDER 533
The Fourteen Points 533
The Paris Peace Conference 534
The Ratification Battle 534

A SOCIETY IN TURMOIL 535
The Unstable Economy 535
The Demands of African Americans 536
The Red Scare 538
Refuting the Red Scare 538
The Retreat from Idealism 539

For Home and Country

VICTORY LIBERTY LOAN

Source: Library of Congress, Prints and Photographs Division [LC-USZC4-9884]

Consider the Source: Race, Gender, And World War I Posters 526

Patterns of Popular Culture: George M. Cohan, "Over There" (1917) 532

CONCLUSION 539
KEY TERMS/PEOPLE/PLACES/EVENTS 540
RECALL AND REFLECT 540

22 THE NEW ERA 541

THE NEW ECONOMY 542
Technology, Organization, and Economic Growth 542
Workers in an Age of Capital 543
Women and Minorities in the Workforce 545
Agricultural Technology and the Plight of the Farmer 547

THE NEW CULTURE 548
Consumerism and Communications 548

©Bettmann/Corbis

Women in the New Era 548
The Disenchanted 553

A CONFLICT OF CULTURES 554
Prohibition 554
Nativism and the Klan 554
Religious Fundamentalism 555
The Democrats' Ordeal 556

REPUBLICAN GOVERNMENT 556
The Harding Administration 557
The Coolidge Administration 558
Government and Business 558

Consider the Source: American Print Advertisements 552

America in the World: The Cinema 550

CONCLUSION 560
KEY TERMS/PEOPLE/PLACES/EVENTS 560
RECALL AND REFLECT 560

23 THE GREAT DEPRESSION 561

THE COMING OF THE DEPRESSION 562
The Great Crash 562
Causes of the Depression 562
Progress of the Depression 565

THE AMERICAN PEOPLE IN HARD TIMES 566
Unemployment and Relief 566
African Americans and the Depression 567
Hispanics and Asians in Depression America 568
Women and Families in the Great Depression 571

THE DEPRESSION AND AMERICAN CULTURE 572
Depression Values 572
Radio 572
The Movies 573
Literature and Journalism 575
The Popular Front and the Left 577

THE ORDEAL OF HERBERT HOOVER 579
The Hoover Program 579
Popular Protest 580
Hoover and the World Crisis 582
The Election of 1932 583
The "Interregnum" 584

America in the World: The Global Depression 564

Consider the Source: Mr. Tarver Remembers The Great Depression (1940) 570

Patterns of Popular Culture: The Golden Age of Comic Books 574

CONCLUSION 585
KEY TERMS/PEOPLE/PLACES/EVENTS 585
RECALL AND REFLECT 585

Source: Library of Congress, Prints and Photographs Division [LC-USF34-009872-E]

24 THE NEW DEAL ERA 586

LAUNCHING THE NEW DEAL 587
Restoring Confidence 587
Agricultural Adjustment 588
Industrial Recovery 589
Regional Planning 590
The Growth of Federal Relief 592

THE NEW DEAL IN TRANSITION 593
The Conservative Criticism of the
New Deal 593
The Populist Criticism of the New Deal 595
The "Second New Deal" 597
Labor Militancy 597
Organizing Battles 598
Social Security 599
New Directions in Relief 600
The 1936 "Referendum" 601

©Fotosearch/Archive Photos/Getty Images

THE NEW DEAL IN DISARRAY 601
The Court Fight 601
Retrenchment and Recession 602

ISOLATIONISM AND INTERNATIONALISM 603
Depression Diplomacy 603
The Rise of Isolationism 604
The Failure of Munich 605

LIMITS AND LEGACIES OF THE NEW DEAL 606
African Americans and the New Deal 606
The New Deal and the "Indian Problem" 607
Women and the New Deal 607
The New Deal and the West 609
The New Deal, the Economy, and Politics 609

Debating the Past: The New Deal 594

Consider the Source: Eleanor Roosevelt on Civil Rights (1942) 608

CONCLUSION 610
KEY TERMS/PEOPLE/PLACES/EVENTS 611
RECALL AND REFLECT 611

25 AMERICA IN A WORLD AT WAR 612

FROM NEUTRALITY TO INTERVENTION 613
Neutrality Tested 613
The Campaign of 1940 615
Neutrality Abandoned 615
The Road to Pearl Harbor 616

WAR ON TWO FRONTS 617
Containing the Japanese 617
Holding Off the Germans 618
America and the Holocaust 619
The Soldier's Experience 621

THE AMERICAN ECONOMY IN WARTIME 621
Prosperity and the Rights of Labor 622
Stabilizing the Boom and Mobilizing Production 622
Wartime Science and Technology 623

RACE AND ETHNICITY IN WARTIME AMERICA 624
Minority Groups and the War Effort 624
The Internment of Japanese Americans 625
Chinese Americans and the War 627

ANXIETY AND AFFLUENCE IN WARTIME CULTURE 627
Home-Front Life and Culture 628
Love, Family, and Sexuality in Wartime 628
The Growth of Wartime Conservatism 630

THE DEFEAT OF THE AXIS 631
The European Offensive 631
The Pacific Offensive 634
The Manhattan Project and Atomic Warfare 636

Consider the Source: The Face of The Enemy 626

Debating the Past: The Decision to Drop the Atomic Bomb 638

CONCLUSION 640
KEY TERMS/PEOPLE/PLACES/EVENTS 640
RECALL AND REFLECT 641

Source: Library of Congress, Prints and Photographs Division [LC-USZC4-1047]

26 THE COLD WAR 642

ORIGINS OF THE COLD WAR 643
Sources of Soviet–American Tension 643
Wartime Diplomacy 645
Yalta 646

THE COLLAPSE OF THE PEACE 647
The Failure of Potsdam 647
The China Problem and Japan 648
The Containment Doctrine 648
The Conservative Opposition to
   Containment 650
The Marshall Plan 650
Mobilization at Home 651
The Road to NATO 651
Reevaluating Cold War Policy 653

AMERICA AFTER THE WAR 653
The Problems of Reconversion 653
The Fair Deal Rejected 654
The Election of 1948 655
The Fair Deal Revived 656
The Nuclear Age 657

THE KOREAN WAR 660
The Divided Peninsula 660
From Invasion to Stalemate 660
Limited Mobilization 662

Source: U.S. Office for Emergency Management. Office of Civilian Defense. 5/20/1941-6/30/1945/NARA (38174)

THE CRUSADE AGAINST SUBVERSION 662
HUAC and Alger Hiss 663
The Federal Loyalty Program and the
    Rosenberg Case 663
McCarthyism 664
The Republican Revival 665

Debating the Past: The Cold War **644**

Consider the Source: "Bert The Turtle
(*Duck And Cover*)" (1952) **658**

CONCLUSION 666
KEY TERMS/PEOPLE/PLACES/EVENTS 666
RECALL AND REFLECT 667

27 THE AFFLUENT SOCIETY 668

THE ECONOMIC "MIRACLE" 669
Economic Growth 669
The Rise of the Modern West 671
Capital and Labor 671

**THE EXPLOSION OF SCIENCE AND
TECHNOLOGY 672**
Medical Breakthroughs 672
Pesticides 673
Postwar Electronic Research 674
Postwar Computer Technology 674
Bombs, Rockets, and Missiles 675
The Space Program 675

PEOPLE OF PLENTY 677
The Consumer Culture 677
The Suburban Nation 677
The Suburban Family 678
The Birth of Television 678
Travel, Outdoor Recreation, and Environmentalism 679
Organized Society and Its Detractors 682
The Beats and the Restless Culture of Youth 682
Rock 'n' Roll 683

THE OTHER AMERICA 684
On the Margins of the Affluent Society 684
Rural Poverty 685
The Inner Cities 685

THE RISE OF THE CIVIL RIGHTS MOVEMENT 686
The *Brown* Decision and "Massive Resistance" 686
The Expanding Movement 687
Causes of the Civil Rights Movement 688

EISENHOWER REPUBLICANISM 689
"What Was Good for . . . General Motors" 689
The Survival of the Welfare State 690
The Decline of McCarthyism 690

Source: NASA

EISENHOWER, DULLES, AND THE COLD WAR 691
Dulles and "Massive Retaliation" 691
France, America, and Vietnam 691
Cold War Crises 692
The U-2 Crisis 695

Patterns of Popular Culture: Lucy and Desi 680

Consider the Source: Eisenhower Warns of
The Military–Industrial Complex (1961) 694

CONCLUSION 696
KEY TERMS/PEOPLE/PLACES/EVENTS 697
RECALL AND REFLECT 697

28 THE TURBULENT SIXTIES 698

EXPANDING THE LIBERAL STATE 699
John Kennedy 699
Lyndon Johnson 701
The Assault on Poverty 702
Cities, Schools, and Immigration 703
Legacies of the Great Society 704

**THE BATTLE FOR RACIAL
EQUALITY 704**
Expanding Protests 704
A National Commitment 705
The Battle for Voting Rights 709
The Changing Movement 710
Urban Violence 711
Black Power 714

©John Orris/New York Times Co./
Getty Images

"FLEXIBLE RESPONSE" AND THE COLD WAR 715
Diversifying Foreign Policy 715
Confrontations with the Soviet Union 716
Johnson and the World 716

THE AGONY OF VIETNAM 717
America and Diem 717
From Aid to Intervention 718
The Quagmire 719
The War at Home 721

THE TRAUMAS OF 1968 723
The Tet Offensive 725
The Political Challenge 725
Assassinations and Politics 726
The Conservative Response 727

Debating the Past: The Civil Rights Movement 706

Consider the Source: Fannie Lou Hamer on the Struggle for
Voting Rights (1964) 712

Patterns of Popular Culture: The Folk-Music Revival 722

America in the World: 1968 724

CONCLUSION 728
KEY TERMS/PEOPLE/PLACES/EVENTS 729
RECALL AND REFLECT 729

29 THE CRISIS OF AUTHORITY 730

THE YOUTH CULTURE 731
The New Left 731
The Counterculture 733

THE MOBILIZATION OF MINORITIES 735
Seeds of Native American Militancy 735
The Indian Civil Rights Movement 735
Latino Activism 737
Gay Liberation 738

WOMEN AND SOCIAL CHANGE 739
Modern Feminism 739
Expanding Achievements 740
The Abortion Issue 741

©Michael Rougier/The LIFE Images
Collection/Getty Images

ENVIRONMENTALISM IN A TURBULENT SOCIETY 741
The New Science of Ecology 741
Environmental Advocacy 742
Earth Day and Beyond 743

NIXON, KISSINGER, AND THE VIETNAM WAR 743
Vietnamization 743
Escalation 744
The End of the War 745
Defeat in Indochina 745

NIXON, KISSINGER, AND THE WORLD 747
The China Initiative and Soviet-American Détente 747
Dealing with the "Third World" 750

POLITICS AND ECONOMICS IN THE NIXON YEARS 751
Domestic Initiatives 751
From the Warren Court to the Nixon Court 752
The 1972 Landslide 753
The Troubled Economy 753
The Nixon Response 754

THE WATERGATE CRISIS 755
The Scandals 755
The Fall of Richard Nixon 757

Consider the Source: Demands of the New York High School
Student Union (1970) **732**

America in the World: The End of Colonialism **748**

Debating the Past: Watergate **756**

CONCLUSION **759**
KEY TERMS/PEOPLE/PLACES/EVENTS **760**
RECALL AND REFLECT **760**

30 FROM "THE AGE OF LIMITS" TO THE AGE OF REAGAN 761

POLITICS AND DIPLOMACY AFTER WATERGATE 762
The Ford Custodianship 762
The Trials of Jimmy Carter 764
Human Rights and National Interests 765
The Year of the Hostages 765

THE RISE OF THE NEW CONSERVATIVE MOVEMENT 766
The Sunbelt and Its Politics 766
Religious Revivalism 766
The Emergence of the New Right 769
The Tax Revolt 769
The Campaign of 1980 770

THE "REAGAN REVOLUTION" 771
The Reagan Coalition 771
Reagan in the White House 774
"Supply-Side" Economics 775
The Fiscal Crisis 776
Reagan and the World 776

THE WANING OF THE COLD WAR 777
The Fall of the Soviet Union 778
The Fading of the Reagan Revolution 779
The Presidency of George H. W. Bush 780
The Gulf War 780
The Election of 1992 781

Consider the Source: Ronald Reagan On The Role Of Government (1981) 772

CONCLUSION 782
KEY TERMS/PEOPLE/PLACES/EVENTS 783
RECALL AND REFLECT 783

©Dirck Halstead/The LIFE Images Collection/Getty Images

31 THE AGE OF GLOBALIZATION 784

A RESURGENCE OF PARTISANSHIP 785
Launching the Clinton Presidency 785
Republican Wins and Losses 786
Clinton Triumphant and Embattled 787
Impeachment, Acquittal, and Resurgence 788
The Election of 2000 789
The Presidency of George W. Bush 790
The Election of 2008 791
Obama and His Opponents 793
Obama and the Challenge of Governing 797
The Election of 2016 and President Trump 797

Source: Official White House Photo by Pete Souza

SCIENCE AND TECHNOLOGY IN THE NEW ECONOMY 799
The Digital Revolution 799
The Internet 800
Breakthroughs in Genetics 801

A CHANGING SOCIETY 802
A Shifting Population 802
African Americans in the
    Post–Civil Rights Era 803
The Abortion Debate 804
AIDS and Modern America 805
Gay Americans and Same-Sex
    Marriage 806
The Contemporary Environmental
    Movement 807

AMERICA IN THE WORLD 812
Opposing the "New World Order" 812
The Rise of Terrorism 813
The War on Terror 815
The Iraq War 815
New Challenges in the Middle East 817
Diplomacy and Threats in East Asia 818
A New Cold War? 819

Patterns of Popular Culture: Rap 794

Consider the Source: Same-Sex Marriage, 2015 808

America in the World: The Global Environmental Movement 810

CONCLUSION 820
KEY TERMS/PEOPLE/PLACES/EVENTS 820
RECALL AND REFLECT 820

APPENDIX 821
GLOSSARY 842
INDEX 868

The title *The Unfinished Nation* is meant to suggest several things. It is a reminder of America's exceptional diversity—of the degree to which, despite all the many efforts to build a single, uniform definition of the meaning of American nationhood, that meaning remains contested. It is a reference to the centrality of change in American history—to the ways in which the nation has continually transformed itself and continues to do so in our own time. And it is also a description of the writing of American history itself—of the ways in which historians are engaged in a continuing, ever unfinished process of asking new questions.

Like any history, *The Unfinished Nation* is a product of its time and reflects the views of the past that historians of recent generations have developed. The writing of our nation's history—like our nation itself—changes constantly. It is not, of course, the past that changes. Rather, historians adjust their perspectives and priorities, ask different kinds of questions, and uncover and incorporate new historical evidence. There are now, as there have always been, critics of changes in historical understanding who argue that history is a collection of facts and should not be subject to "interpretation" or "revision." But historians insist that history is not simply a collection of facts. Names and dates and a record of events are only the beginning of historical understanding. Writers and readers of history interpret the evidence before them, and inevitably bring to the task their own questions, concerns, and experiences.

This edition brings two new authors and therefore a revised and broadened set of ambitions to *The Unfinished Nation.* John Giggie is a historian of race and religion, Andrew Huebner is a historian of war and society, and both more generally study and teach American social and cultural history. Their interests join and complement Alan Brinkley's expansive base of knowledge in the history of American politics, society, and culture. Alan's scholarship inspired John and Andrew as graduate students and they are honored to join him as authors of *The Unfinished Nation.* They endeavor to bring their own scholarly interests and sensitivities to an already vibrant, clear, concise, and balanced survey of American history. The result, we hope, is a text that explores the great range of ideas, institutions, individuals, and events that make up the fabric of society in the United States.

It is a daunting task to attempt to convey the history of the United States in a single book, and the ninth edition of *The Unfinished Nation* has, as have all previous editions, been carefully written and edited to keep the book as concise and readable as possible. It features most notably an enlarged focus on the history of Native Americans, the meaning of the American Revolution, the transformative effects of modern warfare on everyday life, the far-reaching effects of the civil rights movement, and dramatic political and technological change in the twenty-first century. Across these subjects, we recognize that to understand the full complexity of the American past it is necessary to understand both the forces that divide Americans and the forces that draw them together. Thus we've sought to explore the development of foundational ideals like democracy and equality as well as the ways that our nation's fulfillment of those ideals remains, like so much else, unfinished.

AMERICA'S HISTORY IS STILL UNFOLDING

Is American History finished? Not yet! *The Unfinished Nation* shows that as more details are uncovered, dates may not change—but perceptions and reality definitely can. America and her history are in a constant state of change.

Just like America, this edition evolves with two new authors to further Alan Brinkley's established tradition. John Giggie and Andrew Huebner bring expertise and new voices, shedding light on perspectives that will shape an examination of the past. Their aim is to help you, the reader, ask new questions. By doing so, you will find your own answer to the question: is American History finished?

PRIMARY SOURCES HELP STUDENTS THINK CRITICALLY ABOUT HISTORY

Primary sources help students think critically about history and expose them to contrasting perspectives of key events. The Ninth Edition of *The Unfinished Nation* provides three different ways to use primary source documents in your course.

Power of Process for Primary Sources is a critical thinking tool for reading and writing about primary sources. As part of Connect History, McGraw-Hill Education's learning platform Power of Process contains a database of over 400 searchable primary sources in addition to the capability for instructors to upload their own sources. Instructors can then select a series of strategies for students to use to analyze and comment on a source. The Power of Process framework helps students develop essential academic skills such as understanding, analyzing, and synthesizing readings and visuals such as maps, leading students toward higher order thinking and writing.

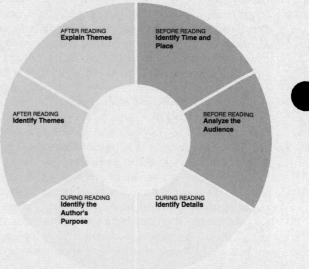

Features that offer contrasting perspectives or showcase historical artifacts. Within the print or eBook, the Ninth Edition of *The Unfinished Nation* offers the following features:

CONSIDER THE SOURCE

In every chapter, Consider the Source features guide students through careful analysis of historical documents and prompt them to closely examine the ideas expressed, as well as the historical circumstances. Among the classic sources included are Benjamin Franklin's testimony against the Stamp Act, the Gettysburg Address, a radio address from FDR, and Ronald Reagan on the role of government. Concise introductions provide context, and concluding questions prompt students to understand, analyze, and evaluate each source.

DEBATING THE PAST

Debating the Past essays introduce students to the contested quality of much of the American past, and they provide a sense of the evolving nature of historical scholarship. From examining specific differences in historical understandings of the Constitution, to exploring the causes of the Civil War and the significance of Watergate, these essays familiarize students with the interpretive character of historical understanding.

AMERICA IN THE WORLD

America in the World essays focus on specific parallels between American history and those of other nations and demonstrate the importance of the many global influences on the American story. Topics such as the global Industrial Revolution, the abolition of slavery, and the global depression of the 1920s provide concrete examples of the connections between the history of the United States and the history of other nations.

PATTERNS OF POPULAR CULTURE

Patterns of Popular Culture essays bring fads, crazes, hangouts, hobbies, and entertainment into the story of American history, encouraging students to expand their definition of what constitutes history and gain a new understanding of what popular culture reveals about a society.

McGraw Hill Education create **Select primary source documents that meet the unique needs of your course.** No two history courses are the same. Using McGraw-Hill Education's Create allows you to quickly and easily create custom course materials with cross-disciplinary content and other third-party sources.

- **CHOOSE YOUR OWN CONTENT:** Create a book that contains only the chapters you want, in the order you want. Create will even renumber the pages for you!
- **ADD READINGS:** Use our American History Collections to include primary sources, or Taking Sides: Annual Editions. Add your own original content, such as syllabus or History major requirements!
- **CHOOSE YOUR FORMAT:** Print or eBook? Softcover, spiral-bound, or loose-leaf? Black-and-white or color? Perforated, three-hole punched, or regular paper?
- **CUSTOMIZE YOUR COVER:** Pick your own cover image and include your name and course information right on the cover. Students will know they're purchasing the right book—and using everything they purchase!
- **REVIEW YOUR CREATION:** When you are all done, you'll receive a free PDF review copy in just minutes! To get started, go to create.mheducation.com and register today.

MAP TOOLS TO PROMOTE STUDENT LEARNING

Using Connect History and more than 100 maps, students can learn the course material more deeply and study more effectively than ever before.

Interactive maps give students a hands-on understanding of geography. *The Unfinished Nation* offers over 30 interactive maps that support geographical as well as historical thinking. These maps appear in both the eBook and Connect History exercises. For some interactive maps, students click on the boxes in the map legend to see changing boundaries, visualize migration routes, or analyze war battles and election results. With others, students manipulate a slider to help them better understand change over time. New interactive maps feature advanced navigation features, including zoom, as well as audio and textual animation.

SMARTBOOK

Available within Connect History, SmartBook has been updated with improved learning objectives to ensure that students gain foundational knowledge while also learning to make connections to help them formulate a broader understanding of historical events. SmartBook 2.0 personalizes learning to individual student needs, continually adapting to pinpoint knowledge gaps and focus learning on topics that need the most attention. Study time is more productive and, as a result, students are better prepared for class and coursework. For instructors, SmartBook 2.0 tracks student progress and provides insights that can help guide teaching strategies.

CONTEXTUALIZE HISTORY

Help students experience history in a whole new way with our **Podcast Assignments**. We've gathered some of the most interesting and popular history podcasts currently available and built assignable questions around them. These assignments allow instructors to bring greater context and nuance to their courses while engaging students through the storytelling power of podcasts.

CHAPTER-BY-CHAPTER CHANGES

We have extensively revised the narrative and features in this ninth edition to bring in new scholarship, particularly as it relates to the experiences and perspectives of Native Americans, African Americans, and women throughout American history. On the advice of other professors using the book, we have removed the former Chapter 25 on global events from 1921 to 1941 and instead integrated the coverage within chapters on the 1920s, 1930s, and World War II. Another major change in this edition is pedagogical—boldfacing within each chapter all words in the end-of-chapter Key Terms/People/Places/Events list, and creating glossary entries for these boldfaced words. (In the Connect eBook, these definitions will pop up when students click on bolded words; in print, students can find them in the end-of-book glossary.) We have also revised every chapter in response to heat map data that pointed to passages where students were struggling. On a chapter-by-chapter basis, major changes include:

Chapter 15, Reconstruction and the New South

- Revised discussion of Special Field Order No. 15.
- Revised explanation of Lincoln's plans for Reconstruction.
- Fuller description of the rise to power of the Radical Republicans.
- More nuanced view of Grant's presidency and his efforts to protect democracy for black Americans.
- Revised explanation of the rise of Jim Crow.

Chapter 16, The Conquest of the Far West

- Sequence of chapter topics modified for improved connection and flow.
- More clarification regarding nineteenth-century terms.
- Revised description of the military advantages of U.S. forces versus Indians.

Chapter 17, Industrial Supremacy

- Revised section "Making Production More Efficient" (previously titled "The Science of Production") for greater clarity.
- Revised section "Railroad Expansion and the Corporation," with an improved discussion of the importance of government subsidies.

Chapter 18, The Age of the City

- Expanded chapter introduction previewing the problems and attractions of cities in the late nineteenth and early twentieth centuries.
- Revised discussion of the importance of cultural ties to ethnic communities.
- Added to references in America in the World, "Global Migrations" feature.
- More cohesive discussion in "Health and Safety in the Built Environment" (previously headed "Fire and Disease" and "Environmental Degradation").

Chapter 19, From Crisis to Empire

- Improved explanation of the "free silver" debate.
- Thoroughly revised narrative in "The Battle for Cuba."
- Greater attention to the effects of the Philippine War on Filipinos.

Chapter 20, The Progressives

- Fuller explanation for the decline of party influence, including disfranchisement.
- Expanded discussion of McKinley's assassination and the creation of the Secret Service.
- Revised map of national parks, adding ten sites that have been designated since 1992.

Chapter 21, America and the Great War

- Expanded chapter introduction to offer a fuller preview of chapter topics.
- Revised description of Pershing's expedition in Mexico.
- Fuller treatment of African American veterans and the interwar civil rights movement.

Chapter 22, The New Era

- New Consider the Source box titled "American Print Advertisements."
- Thoroughly revised section on the Republican administrations of Harding and Coolidge, now including coverage of the major foreign policy initiatives of the 1920s.

Chapter 23, The Great Depression

- Expanded chapter introduction previewing the effects of the Great Depression and Hoover's response.
- Added discussion of the international context in "The Popular Front and the Left."
- Revised explanation of the limitations of the Reconstruction Finance Corporation.
- "Hoover and the World Crisis" on the rise of fascism added to the discussion of Hoover's presidency.

Chapter 24, The New Deal Era

- Expanded chapter introduction previewing the phases of the New Deal and how it was received.
- New Consider the Source box on Eleanor Roosevelt and civil rights.
- "Isolationism and Internationalism" on Roosevelt's foreign policy and U.S. attitudes toward fascist aggression added to the chapter.

Chapter 25, America in a World at War

- New chapter introduction on the evolution of American foreign policy in the interwar period as a context for World War II.

- New first section "From Neutrality to Intervention" on the events leading up to the American declaration of war.
- Revised narrative of the Allied invasion of Italy.
- New discussion "The Soldier's Experience" under "War on Two Fronts," including the experiences of African American, Native American, and Chinese American soldiers.
- New section "Minority Groups and the War Effort" focusing on the home front.
- Revised discussion of the internment of Japanese Americans.
- Thoroughly revised and updated Debating the Past box on the decision to drop the atomic bomb.

Chapter 26, The Cold War

- Expanded chapter introduction on the context for and main ideas of the Cold War.
- Updated Debating the Past box on how historians have viewed the Cold War.
- Fuller discussion of the implications of the civil war in China.
- Greater context on Soviet expansion and the containment doctrine.
- New Consider the Source box using the "Bert the Turtle (Duck and Cover)."

Chapter 27, The Affluent Society

- Expanded chapter introduction on the forces shaping domestic affairs in the 1950s and early 1960s.
- Fuller explanation of the connection between economic growth and government spending in the postwar period.
- Revised discussion of the reasons for the rise of the modern West.
- Patterns of Popular Culture box "Lucy and Desi" replaces "On the Road."
- Thoroughly revised and expanded section, "The Rise of the Civil Rights Movement," including new material on the Woman's Political Committee and the history of bus boycotts prior to Montgomery.

Chapter 28, The Turbulent Sixties

- Expanded chapter introduction on the social and political issues defining the decade.
- Clearer contrast of JFK's and Nixon's visions of the role of government and of Kennedy's strengths as a candidate.
- Fuller explanation of the New Frontier.

- Revised discussion of how Johnson was able to win support for domestic reform, including the role of Martin Luther King Jr.
- Thoroughly revised section "The Battle for Racial Equality," including vivid accounts of the attack on Freedom Riders in May 1961, the standoff over integration at the University of Alabama, the March on Washington, and the battle for voting rights during Freedom Summer.
- Expanded discussion of the black power movement, the Black Panthers, and Malcolm X. Added discussion regarding Malcolm X's murder.
- Added explanation of the Cold War context for foreign aid initiatives during the Kennedy administration.
- New coverage of the experience of the Vietnam War for the people of South Vietnam.

Chapter 29, The Crisis of Authority

- Expanded chapter introduction previewing the social and cultural revolutions of the 1960s and 1970s.
- Fuller account of the Free Speech Movement and its philosophy.
- Revised section now titled "Women and Social Change," with improved coverage of modern feminism and the abortion issue.
- More accessible explanations of *Furman v. Georgia* and *Roe v. Wade*.
- Revised narrative of the 1972 presidential contest.
- Updated Debating the Past box on Watergate.
- New material on Barbara Jordan's role in calling for Nixon's impeachment.

Chapter 30, From "the Age of Limits" to the Age of Reagan

- Revised description of Ford's pardon of Nixon.
- Added material on Carter's civil rights record.
- Revised discussions of the Sunbelt and religious revivalism in "The Rise of the Conservative Movement."

Chapter 31, The Age of Globalization

- Thoroughly updated chapter on the contemporary period, including the Obama and Trump presidencies and new social, cultural, technological, environmental, and diplomatic trends.
- New coverage of Black Lives Matter and the AIDS epidemic.

ACKNOWLEDGMENTS

We would like to express our deep appreciation to the following individuals who contributed to the development of *The Unfinished Nation, Ninth Edition*:

Academic Reviewers

Kenna Archer, *Angelo State University*
Peter Belser, *Ivy Tech Community College of Indiana*
Kevin W. Caldwell, *Blue Ridge Community College*
Annette Chamberlin, *Virginia Western Community College*
Cara Crowley, *Amarillo College*
Barbara Dunsheath, *East Los Angeles College, Monterey*
Marilyn Howard, *Columbus State Community College*
Katherine Jewell, *Fitchburg State University*
Donald F. Johnson, *North Dakota State University*
Michael Kinney, *Calhoun Community College*
Jordan O'Connell, *Howard College, Big Spring*
Carey Roberts, *Liberty University*
Todd Romero, *University of Houston*
David Snead, *Liberty University*
Dennis Spillman, *North Central Texas College, Gainesville*
Shawna Williams, *Houston Community College, Southeast*

THE
UNFINISHED
NATION

15 | RECONSTRUCTION AND THE NEW SOUTH

THE PROBLEMS OF PEACEMAKING

RADICAL RECONSTRUCTION

THE SOUTH IN RECONSTRUCTION

THE GRANT ADMINISTRATION

THE ABANDONMENT OF RECONSTRUCTION

THE NEW SOUTH

LOOKING AHEAD

1. What were the various plans for Reconstruction proposed by Lincoln, Johnson, and Congress? Which plan was enacted and why?
2. What were the effects of Reconstruction for blacks and whites in the South?
3. What were the political achievements and failures of the Grant administration?

FEW PERIODS IN THE HISTORY of the United States have produced as much bitterness or created such enduring controversy as the era of Reconstruction—the years following the Civil War during which Americans attempted to reunite their shattered nation. To many white Southerners, Reconstruction was a vicious and destructive experience—a period when vindictive Northerners inflicted humiliation and revenge on the defeated South. Northern defenders of Reconstruction, in contrast, argued that their policies were the only way to prevent unrepentant Confederates from restoring Southern society to what it had been before the war.

To most African Americans at the time, and to many people of all races since, Reconstruction was notable for other reasons. Neither a vicious tyranny, as white Southerners charged, nor a thoroughgoing reform, as many Northerners hoped, it was instead an important first step in the effort to secure civil rights and economic power for the former slaves. Reconstruction did not provide African Americans with either the enduring legal protections or the material resources to ensure anything like real equality. Most black men and women still had little formal power to overturn their oppression for many decades.

And yet for all its shortcomings, Reconstruction did help African Americans create new institutions and some important legal precedents that helped them survive and that ultimately, well into the twentieth century, became the basis of later efforts to win greater freedom and equality.

THE PROBLEMS OF PEACEMAKING

Although it was clear in 1865 that the war was almost over, the path to actual peace was not yet clear. Abraham Lincoln could not negotiate a treaty with the defeated government; he continued to insist that the Confederacy had no legal right to exist. Yet neither could he simply readmit the Southern states into the Union.

THE AFTERMATH OF WAR AND EMANCIPATION

The South after the Civil War was a desolate place. Towns had been gutted, plantations burned, fields neglected, bridges and railroads destroyed. Many white Southerners—stripped of their slaves through emancipation and of capital invested in now worthless Confederate bonds and currency—had almost no personal property. More than 258,000 Confederate soldiers had died in the war, and thousands more returned home wounded or sick. Some white Southerners faced starvation and homelessness.

If the physical conditions were bad for Southern whites, they were far worse for Southern blacks—the 3.5 million men and women now emerging from bondage. As soon as the war ended, hundreds of thousands of them left their plantations in search of a new life in freedom. But most had nowhere to go, and few had any possessions except the clothes they wore.

COMPETING NOTIONS OF FREEDOM

For blacks and whites alike, Reconstruction became a struggle to define the meaning of the war and, above all, the meaning of freedom. But the former slaves and the defeated whites had very different conceptions of what freedom meant.

For most white Southerners, freedom meant the ability to control their own

TIME LINE

1863
Lincoln announces Reconstruction plan

1864
Lincoln vetoes Wade-Davis Bill

1865
Confederacy surrenders

Lincoln assassinated; Johnson is president

Freedmen's Bureau

1866
Republicans gain in congressional elections

Joint Committee on Reconstruction

1867
Congressional Reconstruction begins

1868
Johnson impeached and acquitted

14th Amendment ratified

1869
Congress passes 15th Amendment

Grant elected president

1872
Grant reelected

1873
Panic and depression

1877
Hayes wins disputed election

Compromise of 1877 ends Reconstruction

1883
Supreme Court upholds segregation

1890s
Jim Crow laws in South

1895
Atlanta Compromise

1896
Plessy v. Ferguson

(Source: Library of Congress, Prints and Photographs Division [LC-USZC4-4593])

RICHMOND, 1865   By the time Union forces captured Richmond in early 1865, the Confederate capital had been under siege for months and much of the city lay in ruins, as this photograph reveals. On April 4, President Lincoln, accompanied by his son Tad, visited Richmond. As he walked through the streets of the shattered city, hundreds of former slaves emerged from the rubble to watch him pass. "No triumphal march of a conqueror could have equalled in moral sublimity the humble manner in which he entered Richmond," a black soldier serving with the Union army wrote. "It was a great deliverer among the delivered. No wonder tears came to his eyes."

destinies without interference from the North or the federal government. And in the immediate aftermath of the war, this meant trying to restore their society to its antebellum form. When these white Southerners fought for what they considered freedom, they were fighting above all to preserve local and regional autonomy and white supremacy.

For African Americans, freedom meant independence from white control. In the wake of advancing Union armies, millions of black Southerners sought to secure that freedom with economic opportunity, which for many meant landownership. An African American man in Charleston told a Northern reporter, "Gib us our own land and we take care ourselves."[1] For a short while during the war, Union generals and federal officials cooperated, awarding confiscated land to the former slaves who had worked it.

In November 1862, when Union forces occupied the Sea Islands of South Carolina and their main harbor, Port Royal, the islands' white property owners fled to the mainland. Ten thousand former slaves seized control of the vacated land, marking the beginning of the "Port Royal Experiment" in which formerly enslaved blacks were permitted to farm and raise crops for sale. Some saved enough money to purchase the land they worked from the federal government, totaling about 33,000 acres. Union officials and Northern missionaries recruited teachers, nurses, and doctors to build schools and hospitals for the newly freed people of the Sea Islands. Later in the war saw a broader redistribution of land. At the urging of black leaders, General William Sherman issued Special Field Order No. 15 on January 16, 1865; the order granted former Confederate land in coastal Georgia and South Carolina (including the Sea Islands) to the region's ex-slaves. Within five months, nearly 400,000 acres had been distributed to newly freed people, most of it in 40-acre plots.

In the war's immediate aftermath, the federal government attempted to help ex-slaves forge independent lives by establishing the Bureau of Refugees, Freedmen, and Abandoned Lands, which Congress authorized in March 1865. The **Freedmen's Bureau**, as it became known, helped feed, clothe, educate, and provide medical care for ex-slaves. It also settled land disputes and set labor contracts between freedmen and white property owners. Headed by General Oliver O. Howard, the Freedman's Bureau operated on a shoestring budget with fewer than 1,000 agents, some of whom were corrupt, yet it still emerged as a key federal institution shaping black and white life in the South after the war.

The Freedmen's Bureau, for a while at least, also supported the redistribution of land, overseeing the allocation of 850,000 acres of confiscated land to former slaves. General Howard instructed his agents in his famous "Circular 13" to lease the land in 40-acre plots to former slaves with the intention of eventually selling it to them. A small number of freedmen purchased land outright under the Southern Homestead Act of 1866 that Howard had championed; the act made 46 million acres of public land for sale in 160-acre plots in Alabama, Arkansas, Florida, Louisiana, and Mississippi. (The law was repealed before many ex-slaves were able to take advantage of it.) Some of Howard's officials and other army personnel secured mules for freed people as well, fulfilling the common wisdom that 40 acres and a mule were the building block of any stable household. The bureau also settled land disputes and set labor contracts between freedmen and white property owners.

PLANS FOR RECONSTRUCTION

Political control of **Reconstruction** rested in the hands of the Republicans, who were deeply divided in their approach to the issue. There were three major groups of Republicans. Conservatives insisted that the South accept abolition, but they proposed few other conditions for the readmission of the seceded states. The **Radicals**, led by Representative **Thaddeus Stevens** of Pennsylvania and Senator **Charles Sumner** of Massachusetts, urged a much harsher course, including disenfranchising large numbers of Southern whites, protecting black civil rights, confiscating the property of wealthy whites who had aided the Confederacy, and distributing the land among the freedmen. Finally the Moderates rejected the most stringent demands of the Radicals but supported extracting at least some concessions from the South on black rights.

Ultimately two major plans for Reconstruction in the South emerged under President Lincoln. Lincoln himself favored a lenient policy, believing that Southern Unionists (mostly former Whigs) could become the nucleus of new, loyal state governments. He announced his vision in December 1863, more than a year before the war ended. It came to be known as the "Ten Percent Plan" because it declared that any Southern state could be readmitted to the Union once 10 percent of eligible voters—defined as those present on the voter roles of the 1860 election—pledged an oath of loyalty to the government and accepted the abolition of slavery. These loyal voters could then elect representatives to fashion new state constitutions and governments. At the same time, Lincoln offered full amnesty to all Southerners except high-ranking military officers and government leaders of the Confederacy. He also proposed extending suffrage to African Americans who were educated, owned property, or had served in the Union army. Three Southern states—Louisiana, Arkansas, and Tennessee, all under Union occupation—reestablished loyal governments under the Lincoln formula in 1864.

Outraged at the mildness of Lincoln's program, the Radical Republicans refused to admit representatives from the three "reconstructed" states to Congress. In July 1864, they pushed

RECONSTRUCTION

Debate over the nature of Reconstruction has been unusually intense. Indeed, few issues in American history have raised such deep and enduring passions.

Beginning in the late nineteenth century and continuing well into the twentieth, a relatively uniform and highly critical view of Reconstruction prevailed among historians. William A. Dunning's *Reconstruction, Political and Economic* (1907) was the principal scholarly expression of this view. Dunning portrayed Reconstruction as a corrupt and oppressive outrage imposed on a prostrate South by a vindictive group of Northern Republican Radicals. Unscrupulous carpetbaggers flooded the South and plundered the region. Ignorant and unfit African Americans were thrust into political offices. Reconstruction governments were awash in corruption and compiled enormous levels of debt. The Dunning interpretation dominated several generations of historical scholarship and helped shape such popular images of Reconstruction as those in the novel and film *Gone with the Wind*.

W. E. B. Du Bois, the great African American scholar, offered one of the first alternative views in *Black Reconstruction* (1935). To Du Bois, Reconstruction was an effort by freed blacks (and their white allies) to create a more democratic society in the South, and it was responsible for many valuable social innovations. In the early 1960s, John Hope Franklin and Kenneth Stampp, building on a generation of work by other scholars, published new histories of Reconstruction that also radically revised the Dunning interpretation. Reconstruction, they argued, was a genuine, if inadequate, effort to solve the problem of race in the South. Congressional Radicals were not saints, but they were genuinely concerned with protecting the rights of former slaves. Reconstruction had brought important, if temporary, progress to the

(©Corbis)

A FREEDMEN'S BUREAU SCHOOL African American students and teachers stand outside a school for former slaves, one of many run by the Freedmen's Bureau throughout the defeated Confederacy in the first years after the war.

South and had created no more corruption there than was evident in the North at the same time. What was tragic about Reconstruction, the revisionists claimed, was not what it did to Southern whites but what it failed to do for Southern blacks. It was, in the end, too weak and too short-lived to guarantee African Americans genuine equality.

In more recent years, some historians have begun to question the assessment of the first revisionists that, in the end, Reconstruction accomplished relatively little. Leon Litwack argued in *Been in the Storm So Long* (1979) that former slaves used the protections Reconstruction offered them to carve out a certain level of independence for themselves within Southern society: strengthening churches, reuniting families, and resisting the efforts of white planters to revive the gang labor system.

Eric Foner's *Reconstruction: America's Unfinished Revolution* (1988) and *Forever Free* (2005) also emphasized how far African Americans moved toward freedom and independence in a short time and how important they were in shaping the execution of Reconstruction policies. Reconstruction, he argues, "can only be judged a failure" as an effort to secure "blacks' rights as citizens and free laborers." But it "closed off even more oppressive alternatives. . . . The post-Reconstruction labor system embodied neither a return to the closely supervised gang labor of antebellum days, nor the complete dispossession and immobilization of the black labor force and coercive apprenticeship systems envisioned by white Southerners in 1865 and 1866. . . . The doors of economic opportunity that had opened could never be completely closed." •

UNDERSTAND, ANALYZE, & EVALUATE

1. What are the popular interpretations of Reconstruction today? Do romanticized ideals of a benighted Old South, as seen in *Gone with the Wind*, still persist?

2. A new view of Reconstruction began to emerge in the 1960s, the end of the civil rights movement. Why do you think the civil rights movement might have encouraged historians and others to reexamine Reconstruction?

their own plan through Congress: the **Wade-Davis Bill**. Named for Senator Benjamin Wade of Ohio and Representative Henry Davis of Maryland, it called for the president to appoint a provisional governor for each conquered state. In contrast to Lincoln's Ten Percent Plan, the Wade-Davis Bill specified that only when 50 percent of eligible voters in a state declared loyalty to the Union could the process of readmission begin. At that point the provisional governor could summon a state constitutional convention, whose delegates were to be elected by voters who had never borne arms against the United States. The new state constitutions would be required to abolish slavery, disenfranchise Confederate civil and military leaders, and repudiate debts accumulated by the state governments during the war. Only then would Congress formally readmit the states to the Union. Like the president's proposal, the Wade-Davis Bill left the question of political rights for blacks up to the states.

Congress passed the bill a few days before it adjourned in 1864, but Lincoln disposed of it with a pocket veto, meaning that he killed the bill by refusing to sign it—keeping it "in his pocket" until it was too late for Congress to act on it during the legislative session. Predictively, Lincoln's pocket veto enraged Radical leaders and set up a showdown with the president over the future of Reconstruction policy. The debate between Congress and Lincoln over the proper course of Reconstruction and its purpose and objectives was one that scholars would soon pick up. Indeed, beginning in the latter stages of Reconstruction, historians struggled to make sense of its meaning to America. They continue to do so today. (See "Debating the Past: Reconstruction.")

THE DEATH OF LINCOLN

What plan the president might have produced no one can say. On the night of April 14, 1865, Lincoln and his wife attended a play at Ford's Theater in Washington. John Wilkes Booth, an actor fervently committed to the Southern cause, entered the presidential box from the rear and shot Lincoln in the head. Early the next morning, the president died.

The circumstances of Lincoln's death earned him immediate martyrdom. They also produced something close to hysteria throughout the North, especially because it quickly became clear that Booth had been the leader of a conspiracy. One of his associates shot and wounded Secretary of State **William H. Seward** on the night of the assassination, and another abandoned at the last moment a plan to murder Vice President Andrew Johnson. Booth himself escaped on horseback into the Maryland countryside, where, on April 26, he was cornered by Union troops and shot to death in a blazing barn. Eight other people were convicted by a military tribunal of participating in the conspiracy. Four were hanged.

To many Northerners, however, the murder of the president seemed evidence of an even darker conspiracy—one masterminded and directed by the unrepentant leaders of the defeated South to challenge the very authority of the nation's elected officials. Militant Republicans exploited such suspicions relentlessly in the ensuing months.

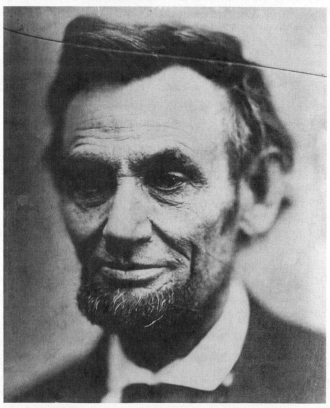

(Source: Library of Congress, Prints and Photographs Division
[LC-USZ62-12380])

ABRAHAM LINCOLN This haunting photograph of Abraham Lincoln, showing clearly the weariness and aging that four years as a war president had created, was taken in Washington only four days before his assassination in 1865.

Johnson and "Restoration"

Leadership of the Moderates and Conservatives fell immediately to Lincoln's successor, **Andrew Johnson** of Tennessee. A Democrat until he had joined the Union ticket in 1864, he became president at a time of growing partisan passions.

Johnson revealed his plan for Reconstruction—or "Restoration," as he preferred to call it—soon after he took office and implemented it during the summer of 1865 when Congress was in recess. Like Lincoln, he offered some form of amnesty to Southerners who would take an oath of allegiance. In most other respects, however, his plan resembled the Wade-Davis Bill. The new president appointed a provisional governor in each state and charged him with inviting qualified voters to elect delegates to a constitutional convention. To win readmission to Congress, a state had to revoke its ordinance of secession, abolish slavery and ratify the Thirteenth Amendment, and repudiate Confederate and state war debts.

By the end of 1865, all the seceded states had formed new governments—some under Lincoln's plan, others under Johnson's—and awaited congressional approval of them. But Radicals in Congress vowed not to recognize the Johnson governments, for, by now, Northern opinion had become more hostile toward the South. Delegates to the Southern conventions had angered much of the North by their apparent reluctance to abolish slavery and by their refusal to grant suffrage to any blacks. Southern states had also seemed to defy the North by electing prominent Confederate leaders to represent them in Congress, such as Alexander Stephens of Georgia, the former vice president of the Confederacy.

RADICAL RECONSTRUCTION

Reconstruction under Johnson's plan—often known as "presidential Reconstruction"—continued only until Congress reconvened in December 1865. At that point, Congress refused to seat the representatives of the "restored" states and created a new Joint Committee on Reconstruction to frame a policy of its own. The period of "congressional," or "Radical," Reconstruction had begun.

The Black Codes

Meanwhile, events in the South were driving Northern opinion in still more radical directions. Throughout the South in 1865 and early 1866, state legislatures enacted sets of laws known as the **Black Codes**, which authorized local officials to apprehend unemployed blacks, fine them for vagrancy, and hire them out to private employers to satisfy the fines. Some codes forbade blacks to own or lease farms or to take any jobs other than as plantation workers or domestic servants, jobs formerly held by slaves. Former slaves raised an alarm immediately and called for swift intervention by the federal troops and for new legislation to protect them. (See "Consider the Source: Southern Blacks Ask for Help.")

Congress first responded to the Black Codes by passing an act extending the life and expanding the powers of the Freedmen's Bureau so that it could nullify work agreements forced on freedmen under the Black Codes. Then, in April 1866, Congress passed the first Civil Rights Act, which declared blacks to be fully fledged citizens of the United States and gave the federal government power to intervene in state affairs to protect the rights of citizens. Johnson vetoed both bills, but Congress overrode him on each of them.

SOUTHERN BLACKS ASK FOR HELP (1865)

Even before the war ended, groups of former slaves gathered in conventions to petition the federal government for steady support for black civil rights, including the use of the U.S. Army to subdue unrepentant ex-Confederates. In this example, African Americans from Virginia publicly air their hopes and fears only three months after Appomattox.

We, the undersigned members of a Convention of colored citizens of the State of Virginia, would respectfully represent that, although we have been held as slaves, and denied all recognition as a constituent of your nationality for almost the entire period of the duration of your Government, and that by your *permission* we have been denied either home or country, and deprived of the dearest rights of human nature; yet when you and our immediate oppressors met in deadly conflict upon the field of battle—the one to destroy and the other to save your Government and nationality, we, with scarce an exception, in our inmost souls espoused your cause, and watched, and prayed, and waited, and labored for your success. . . .

When the contest waxed long, and the result hung doubtfully, you appealed to us for help, and how well we answered is written in the rosters of the two hundred thousand colored troops now enrolled in your Service; and as to our undying devotion to your cause, let the uniform acclamation of escaped prisoners, "whenever we saw a black face we felt sure of a friend," answer.

Well, the war is over, the rebellion is "put down," and we are *declared* free! Four fifths of our enemies are paroled or amnestied, and the other fifth are being pardoned, and the President has, in his efforts at the reconstruction of the civil government of the States, late in rebellion, left us entirely at the mercy of these subjugated but unconverted rebels, in *everything* save the privilege of bringing us, our wives and little ones, to the auction block. *We know* these men—know them well—and we assure you that, with the majority of them, loyalty is only "lip deep," and that their professions of loyalty are used as a cover to the cherished design of getting restored to their former relations with the Federal Government, and then, by all sorts of "unfriendly legislation," to render the freedom you have given us more Intolerable than the slavery they intended for us.

We warn you in time that our only safety is in keeping them under Governors of the *military persuasion* until you have so amended the Federal Constitution that it will prohibit the States from making any distinction between citizens on account of race or color. In one word, the only salvation for us besides the power of the Government, is in the *possession of the ballot*. Give us this, and we will protect ourselves. . . . But, 'tis said we are ignorant. Admit it. Yet who denies we *know* a traitor from a loyal man, a gentleman from a rowdy, a friend from an enemy? . . . All we ask is an *equal chance* with the white *traitors* varnished and japanned with the oath of amnesty. Can you deny us this and still keep faith with us? . . .

We are "sheep in the midst of wolves," and nothing but the military arm of the Government prevents us and all the *truly* loyal white men from being driven from the land of our birth. Do not then, we beseech you, give to one of these "wayward sisters" the rights they abandoned and forfeited when they rebelled until you have secured our rights by the aforementioned amendment to the Constitution.

UNDERSTAND, ANALYZE, & EVALUATE

1. What did the authors of this petition emphasize in the first two paragraphs, and why did they feel this was important?
2. Why did the authors emphasize that they had been "declared" free? What dangers to their prospect of freedom did they observe?
3. What federal legal responses did they propose? Can you recognize these suggestions in the constitutional changes that came with Reconstruction?

Source: "Proceedings of the Convention of the Colored People of Virginia, Held in the City of Alexandria, August 2, 3, 4, 5, 1865," Alexandria, Va., 1865, in W. L. Fleming (ed.), *Documentary History of Reconstruction*. Cleveland, Ohio, 1906, vol. 1, 195–196; located in "Southern Blacks Ask for Help (1865)," in Thomas A. Bailey and David M. Kennedy (eds.), *The American Spirit*, vol. 1, 7th ed., Lexington, Mass., 1991, 466–467.

THE FOURTEENTH AMENDMENT

In April 1866, the Joint Committee on Reconstruction proposed the **Fourteenth Amendment** to the Constitution. Without the support of Johnson, Congress approved it in early summer and sent it to the states for ratification. It offered the first constitutional definition of American citizenship. Everyone born in the United States, and everyone naturalized, was automatically a citizen and entitled to all the "privileges and immunities" guaranteed by the Constitution, including equal protection of the laws by both the state and national governments. There could be no other requirements for citizenship. For the first time in the nation's history, race or a prior condition of servitude was discarded as a barrier to full citizenship. The amendment also prohibited former members of Congress or other former federal officials who had aided the Confederacy from holding any state or federal office unless two-thirds of Congress voted to pardon them.

Congressional Radicals offered to readmit to the Union any state whose legislature ratified the Fourteenth Amendment. Only Tennessee did so. All the other former Confederate states, along with Delaware and Kentucky, refused, leaving the amendment temporarily without the necessary approval of three-fourths of the states.

Radicals, however, were undeterred and even began to grow in confidence and determination as they anticipated gaining new levels of support in the upcoming congressional election in the fall. And they were right. Bloody race riots in New Orleans and other Southern cities swiftly drew attention to the need for more vigorous legal and physical protection for African Americans and to the failure of Johnson's policies to restore peace and order. Johnson himself undercut his own popularity and that of his party by delivering intemperate and mean-spirited speeches in which he openly disparaged the Radicals, blamed the recent violence on them, and accused them of treating blacks like pawns. He nearly fell off the stage delivering several speeches, which gave rise to rampant speculation that he was drinking too much. In the 1866 congressional elections, the voters returned an overwhelming majority of Republicans, most of them Radicals, to Congress. In the Senate, there were now 42 Republicans to 11 Democrats; in the House, 143 Republicans to 49 Democrats. Congressional Republicans were now strong enough to enact a plan of their own even over the president's objections.

THE CONGRESSIONAL PLAN

The Radicals passed three Reconstruction bills early in 1867 and overrode Johnson's vetoes of all of them. Nearly two years after the end of the war, these bills finally established a coherent plan for Reconstruction.

Under the congressional plan, Tennessee, which had ratified the Fourteenth Amendment granting the franchise to all male citizens over twenty-one, was promptly readmitted. But Congress rejected the Lincoln–Johnson governments of the other ten Confederate states and, instead, combined those states into five military districts. A military commander governed each district and had orders to register qualified voters (defined as all adult black males and those white males who had not participated in the war). Once registered, voters would elect conventions to prepare new state constitutions, which had to include provisions for black suffrage. And once voters ratified the new constitutions, they could elect state governments. Congress had to approve a state's constitution, and the state legislature itself had to ratify the Fourteenth Amendment. Once enough states ratified the amendment to make it part of the Constitution, the former Confederate states could be restored to the Union.

By 1868, seven of the ten remaining former Confederate states had fulfilled these conditions and were readmitted to the Union. Conservative whites held up the return of Virginia and Texas until 1869 and Mississippi until 1870. By then, Congress had added an additional requirement for readmission—ratification of the **Fifteenth Amendment**, which forbade the states and the federal government to deny suffrage on account of "race, color, or previous condition of servitude." This opened the ballot box of all male citizens regardless of color, but kept it shut to all women. Ratification by the states was completed in 1870.

To stop Johnson from interfering with their plans, the congressional Radicals passed two remarkable laws of dubious constitutionality in 1867. One, the Tenure of Office Act, forbade the president to remove civil officials, including members of his own cabinet, without the consent of the Senate. The principal purpose of the law was to protect the job of Secretary of War Edwin M. Stanton, who was cooperating with the Radicals. The other

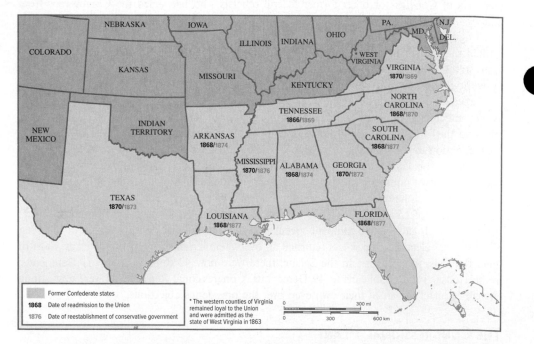

RECONSTRUCTION, 1866–1877 This map provides the date when each former Confederate state was readmitted by presidential order to the Union, as well as the date when a traditional white conservative elite took office as a majority in each state—an event white Southerners liked to call "redemption." • *What had to happen for a state to be readmitted to the Union? What had to happen before a state could experience "redemption"?*

law, the Command of the Army Act, prohibited the president from issuing military orders except through the commanding general of the army (General Grant), who could not be relieved or assigned elsewhere without the consent of the Senate.

The congressional Radicals also took action to stop the Supreme Court from interfering with their plans. In 1866, the Court had declared in the case of *Ex parte Milligan* that military tribunals were unconstitutional in places where civil courts were functioning. Radicals in Congress immediately proposed several bills that would require two-thirds of the justices to support any decision overruling a law of Congress, would deny the Court jurisdiction in Reconstruction cases, would reduce its membership to three, and would even abolish it. The justices apparently took notice. Over the next two years, the Court refused to accept jurisdiction in any cases involving Reconstruction.

THE IMPEACHMENT OF ANDREW JOHNSON

President Johnson had long since ceased to be a serious obstacle to the passage of Radical legislation, but he was still the official charged with administering the Reconstruction programs. As such, the Radicals believed, he remained a major impediment to their plans. Early in 1867, they began looking for reasons to begin formal efforts that would result in his **impeachment**. Republicans found it, they believed, when Johnson dismissed Secretary of War Stanton despite Congress's refusal to agree. Elated Radicals in the House quickly impeached the president for violating the recently passed Tenure of Office Act and sent the case to the Senate for trial.

The trial lasted throughout April and May 1868 but things eventually broke Johnson's way. The Radicals put heavy pressure on all the Republican senators, but the Moderates vacillated. On the first three charges to come to a vote, seven Republicans joined the Democrats and independents to support acquittal. The Senate vote was 35 to 19, one vote short of the constitutionally required two-thirds majority needed to remove Johnson from office. After that, the Radicals dropped the impeachment effort.

THE SOUTH IN RECONSTRUCTION

Reconstruction may not have immediately accomplished what its framers intended, but it did have profound effects on the South.

THE RECONSTRUCTION GOVERNMENTS

Critics branded Southern white Republicans with the derogatory terms **scalawags** and **carpetbaggers**. Scalawags, the slang term for "scoundrels," were former Whigs who had never felt comfortable in the Democratic Party or farmers who lived in remote areas where there had been little or no slavery. Carpetbaggers were white men originally from the North, most of them veterans of the Union army, who looked on the South as a more promising frontier than the West and had traveled there at war's end as hopeful planters, businessmen, or professionals. The term refers to their use of a cheap travel bag made from carpeting material.

The most numerous Republicans in the South were the black freedmen, few of whom had any previous experience in politics. They tried to build institutions through which they could learn to exercise their power. In several states, African American voters held their own conventions to chart their future course. Their newfound religious independence from white churches also helped give them unity and self-confidence.

THE "STRONG" GOVERNMENT 1869-1877.

(Source: Library of Congress, Prints and Photographs Division
[LC-DIG-ppmsca-15783])

CRITICS' VIEW OF RECONSTRUCTION   This Reconstruction-era cartoon expresses the view held by Southern white Democrats that they were being oppressed by Northern Republicans. President Grant (whose hat bears Abraham Lincoln's initials) rides in comfort in a giant carpetbag, guarded by bayonet-wielding soldiers, as the South staggers under the burden in chains. Evidence of military occupation is in the scarred background.

African Americans played significant roles in the politics of the Reconstruction South. They served as delegates to the constitutional conventions and held public offices of practically every kind. Between 1869 and 1901, twenty blacks served in the U.S. House of Representatives, two in the Senate. Blacks served, too, in state legislatures and in various other state offices. Southern whites complained loudly about "Negro rule," but in the South as a whole, the percentage of black officeholders was small—and always far lower than the percentage of blacks in the population.

The record of the Reconstruction governments is mixed. Critics at the time and later denounced them for corruption and financial extravagance, and there is some truth to both charges. But the corruption in the South, real as it was, was hardly unique to the Reconstruction governments. Corruption had been rife in some antebellum and Confederate governments, and it was at least as rampant in the Northern states. And the large state expenditures of the Reconstruction years were huge only in comparison with the meager budgets of the antebellum era. They represented an effort to provide the South with desperately needed services that antebellum governments had never provided.

EDUCATION

Perhaps the most important accomplishment of the Reconstruction governments was a dramatic improvement in Southern education. Much of the impetus for educational reform in the South came from outside groups—the Freedmen's Bureau, Northern private philanthropic organizations, the many Northern white women who traveled to the South to teach in freedmen's schools—and from African Americans themselves. Over the opposition of many Southern whites, who feared that education would give blacks "false notions of equality," these reformers established a large network of schools for former slaves—4,000 schools by 1870, staffed by 9,000 teachers (half of them black), teaching 200,000 students. In the 1870s, Reconstruction governments began to build a comprehensive public school system. By 1876, more than half of all white children and about 40 percent of all black children were attending schools in the South (although almost all such schools were racially segregated). Several black "academies," offering more advanced education, also began operating. Gradually, these academies grew into an important network of black colleges and universities.

LANDOWNERSHIP AND TENANCY

The most ambitious goal of the Freedmen's Bureau, and of some Republican Radicals in Congress, was to reform landownership in the South. The effort failed. By June 1865, the bureau had settled nearly 10,000 black families on their own land—most of it drawn from abandoned plantations in areas occupied by the Union armies. By the end of that year, however, Southern plantation owners were returning and demanding the restoration of their property. President Johnson supported their demands, and the government eventually returned most of the confiscated lands to their original white owners.

Even so, the distribution of landownership in the South changed considerably in the postwar years. Among whites, there was a striking decline in landownership, from 80 percent before the war to 67 percent by the end of Reconstruction. Some whites lost their land because of unpaid debt or increased taxes; others left the marginal lands they had owned to move to more fertile areas, where they rented. Among blacks, during the same period, the proportion of landowners rose from virtually none to more than 20 percent.

Still, most blacks, and a growing minority of whites, did not own their own land during Reconstruction and, instead, worked for others in one form or another. Many black agricultural laborers—perhaps 25 percent of the total—simply worked for wages. Most, however, became tenants of white landowners—that is, they worked their own plots of land and paid their landlords either a fixed rent or a share of their crops (hence the term **sharecropping**). As tenants and sharecroppers, blacks enjoyed at least a physical independence from their landlords and had the sense of working their own land, even if in most cases they could never hope to buy it. But tenantry also benefited landlords in some ways, relieving them of the cost of purchasing slaves and of responsibility for the physical well-being of their workers.

INCOMES AND CREDIT

In some respects, the postwar years were a period of remarkable economic progress for African Americans in the South. The per capita income of blacks (when the material benefits of slavery are counted as income) rose 46 percent between 1857 and 1879, while the per capita income of whites declined 35 percent. African Americans were also able to work less than they had under slavery. Women and children were less likely to labor in the fields, and adult men tended to work shorter days. In all, the black labor force worked about one-third fewer hours during Reconstruction than it had been compelled to work under slavery—a reduction that brought the working schedule of blacks roughly into accord with that of white farm laborers.

But other developments limited these gains. While the black share of profits was increasing, the total profits of Southern agriculture were declining. Nor did the income redistribution of the postwar years lift many blacks out of poverty. Black per capita income rose from about one-quarter of white per capita income (which was itself low) to about one-half in the first few years after the war. After this initial increase, however, it rose hardly at all.

Blacks and poor whites alike found themselves virtually imprisoned by the **crop-lien system.** Few of the traditional institutions of credit in the South—the "factors" and banks—returned after the war. In their stead emerged a new credit system, centered in large part on local country stores—some of them owned by planters, others owned by independent merchants. Blacks and whites, landowners and tenants—all depended on these stores. And since most who made their livelihood from the land did not have the same steady cash flow as other workers, they usually had to rely on credit from these merchants to purchase what they needed. Most local stores had no competition and thus could set interest rates as high as 50 or 60 percent. Poor farmers had to give the merchants a lien (or claim) on their crops as collateral for the loans (thus the term *crop-lien*). Those who suffered a few bad years in a row, as many did, could become trapped in a cycle of debt from which they could never escape.

As a result of this burdensome credit system, some blacks who had acquired land during the early years of Reconstruction, and many poor whites who had owned land for years, gradually lost it as they fell into debt. Southern farmers also became almost wholly dependent on cash crops—and most of all on cotton—because only such marketable commodities seemed to offer any possibility of escape from debt. The relentless planting of cotton ultimately contributed to soil exhaustion, which undermined the Southern agricultural economy over time.

THE AFRICAN AMERICAN FAMILY IN FREEDOM

A major reason for the rapid departure of so many blacks from plantations was the desire to find lost relatives and reunite families. Thousands of African Americans wandered through the South looking for husbands, wives, children, or other relatives from whom they had been separated. Former slaves rushed to have their marriages, previously without legal standing, sanctified by church and law.

Within the black family, the definition of male and female roles quickly came to resemble that within white families. Many women and children at first ceased working in the fields. Such work, they believed, was a badge of slavery. Instead, many women restricted themselves largely to domestic tasks. Still, economic necessity often compelled black women to engage in income-producing activities: working as domestic servants, taking in laundry, even helping their husbands in the fields. By the end of Reconstruction, half of all black women over the age of sixteen were working for wages.

(Source: Library of Congress, Prints and Photographs Division [LC-USZC4-5759])

LABORING OVER LAUNDRY One of the most common occupations of women recently emancipated from slavery was taking in laundry from white families who no longer had enslaved servants. This photograph illustrates how arduous a task laundry was.

THE GRANT ADMINISTRATION

American voters in 1868 yearned for a strong, stable figure to guide them through the troubled years of Reconstruction. They turned trustingly to General **Ulysses S. Grant**.

THE SOLDIER PRESIDENT

Grant could have had the nomination of either party in 1868. But believing that Republican Reconstruction policies were more popular in the North, he accepted the Republican nomination. The Democrats nominated former governor Horatio Seymour of New York. The campaign was a bitter one, and Grant's triumph was surprisingly narrow. Indeed, without the 500,000 new black Republican voters in the South, he would have had a minority of the popular vote.

Grant entered the White House with no formal political experience, relying instead on his slow but steady rise through the ranks of the army and his recent years as a general. The new president did not pick the best advisers, surrounding himself with wealthy friends intent on protecting their interests and appointing ineffective cabinet members, with the exception of secretary of state Hamilton Fish. Grant also relied heavily on established party leaders—the group most ardently devoted to patronage, and his administration used the spoils system even more blatantly than most of its predecessors. It was a choice of counsel that would eventually come back to haunt him.

Although his selection of colleagues was suspect, Grant steadily supported the citizenship of former slaves and the policies of Radical Reconstruction even as such a position increasingly posed political risk. Refusing to compromise much on matters of racial politics, he alienated the many Northerners who were growing disillusioned with the prolonged federal presence in the South and effort to protect and extend democracy to black Americans.

By the end of Grant's first term, therefore, members of a substantial faction of the party—who referred to themselves as Liberal Republicans—had come to oppose what they derisively called "Grantism." Some Republicans suspected, correctly as it turned out, that there was corruption in the Grant administration itself. In 1872, hoping to prevent Grant's reelection, they bolted the party and nominated their own presidential candidate: Horace Greeley, veteran editor and publisher of the *New York Tribune*. The Democrats, somewhat reluctantly, named Greeley their candidate as well, hoping that the alliance with the Liberals would enable them to defeat Grant. But the effort was in vain. Grant won a substantial victory, polling 286 electoral votes to Greeley's 66.

The Grant Scandals

During the 1872 campaign, the first of a series of political scandals came to light that would plague Grant and the Republicans for the next four years. It involved the French-owned Crédit Mobilier construction company, which had helped build the Union Pacific Railroad. The heads of Crédit Mobilier had used their positions as Union Pacific stockholders to steer large fraudulent contracts to their construction company, thus bilking the Union Pacific of millions. To prevent investigations, the directors had given Crédit Mobilier stock to key members of Congress. But in 1872, Congress conducted an investigation that revealed that some highly placed Republicans—including Schuyler Colfax, now Grant's vice president—had accepted stock.

One dreary episode of malfeasance followed another in Grant's second term. Benjamin H. Bristow, Grant's third Treasury secretary, discovered that some of his officials and a group of distillers operating as a "whiskey ring" were cheating the government out of taxes by filing false reports. Then a House investigation revealed that William W. Belknap, secretary of war, had accepted bribes to retain an Indian-post trader in office (the so-called Indian ring). Other, lesser scandals also added to the growing impression that "Grantism" had brought rampant corruption to government.

The Greenback Question

Compounding Grant's problems was a financial crisis, known as the Panic of 1873. It began with the failure of a leading investment banking firm, Jay Cooke and Company, which had invested too heavily in postwar railroad building. There had been panics before—in 1819, 1837, and 1857—but this was the worst one yet.

Debtors now pressured the government to redeem federal war bonds with greenbacks, which would increase the amount of money in circulation. But Grant and most Republicans wanted a "sound" currency—based solidly on gold reserves—that would favor the interests of banks and other creditors. There was approximately $356 million in paper currency issued during the Civil War that was still in circulation. In 1873, the Treasury issued more in response to the panic. But in 1875, Republican leaders in Congress passed the Specie Resumption Act, which provided that after January 1, 1879, greenback dollars would be redeemed by the government and replaced with new certificates, firmly pegged to the price of gold. The law satisfied creditors, who had worried that debts would be repaid in paper currency of uncertain value. But "resumption" made things more difficult for debtors because the gold-based money supply could not easily expand.

In 1875, the "Greenbackers" formed their own political organization: the National Greenback Party. It failed to gain widespread support, but the money issue was to remain one of the most controversial and enduring issues in late-nineteenth-century American politics.

REPUBLICAN DIPLOMACY

The Johnson and Grant administrations achieved their greatest successes in foreign affairs as a result of the work not of the presidents themselves but of two outstanding secretaries of state: William H. Seward and Hamilton Fish.

An ardent expansionist, Seward acted with as much daring as the demands of Reconstruction politics and the Republican hatred of President Johnson would permit. He accepted a Russian offer to buy Alaska for $7.2 million, despite criticism from many who derided the purchase as "Seward's Folly." In 1867, Seward also engineered the American annexation of the tiny Midway Islands, west of Hawaii.

Hamilton Fish's first major challenge was resolving the long-standing controversy over the American claims that Britain had violated neutrality laws during the Civil War by permitting English shipyards to build ships (among them the *Alabama*) for the Confederacy. American demands that England pay for the damage these vessels had caused became known as the "*Alabama* claims." In 1871, after a number of failed efforts, Fish forged an agreement, the Treaty of Washington, that provided for international arbitration.

THE ABANDONMENT OF RECONSTRUCTION

As the North grew increasingly preoccupied with its own political and economic problems, interest in Reconstruction began to wane. By the time Grant left office, Democrats had taken back seven of the governments of the former Confederate states. For three other states—South Carolina, Louisiana, and Florida—the end of Reconstruction had to wait for the withdrawal of the last federal troops in 1877.

THE SOUTHERN STATES "REDEEMED"

In the states where whites constituted a majority—the states of the upper South—overthrowing Republican control was relatively simple. By 1872, all but a handful of Southern whites had regained suffrage. Now a clear majority, they needed only to organize and elect their candidates.

In other states, where blacks were a majority or where the populations of the two races were almost equal, whites used outright intimidation and violence to undermine the Reconstruction regimes. Secret societies—the **Ku Klux Klan**, the Knights of the White Camellia, and others—used terrorism to frighten or physically bar blacks from voting. Paramilitary organizations—the Red Shirts and White Leagues—armed themselves to "police" elections and worked to force all white males to join the Democratic Party. Strongest of all, however, was the weapon of economic pressure. Some planters simply refused to rent land to Republican blacks; storekeepers refused to extend them credit; and employers refused to give them work or, when they did, pay them fairly.

The Republican Congress responded to this wave of repression with the **Enforcement Acts** of 1870 and 1871 (better known as the Ku Klux Klan Acts), which prohibited states from discriminating against voters on the basis of race and gave the national government the authority to prosecute crimes by individuals under federal law. The laws also authorized the president to use federal troops to protect civil rights—a provision President Grant used in 1871 in nine counties of South Carolina. The Enforcement Acts, although seldom enforced, discouraged Klan violence, which declined by 1872.

Waning Northern Commitment

But this Northern commitment to civil rights did not last long. After the adoption of the Fifteenth Amendment in 1870, some reformers convinced themselves that their long campaign on behalf of black people was now over, that with the vote blacks ought to be able to take care of themselves. Former Radical leaders such as Charles Sumner and Horace Greeley now began calling themselves Liberals, cooperating with the Democrats, and even denouncing what they viewed as black-and-carpetbag misgovernment. Within the South itself, many white Republicans now moved into the Democratic Party as voters threw out Republican politicians whom they blamed for the financial crisis.

The Panic of 1873 further undermined support for Reconstruction. In the congressional elections of 1874, the Democrats won control of the House of Representatives for the first time since 1861. To appeal to Southern white voters, Grant even reduced the use of military force to prop up the Republican regimes in the South.

The Compromise of 1877

Grant had hoped to run for another term in 1876, but most Republican leaders—shaken by recent Democratic successes and scandals by the White House—resisted. Instead, they settled on Rutherford B. Hayes, three-time governor of Ohio and a champion of civil service reform. The Democrats united behind Samuel J. Tilden, the reform governor of New York, who had been instrumental in overthrowing the corrupt Tweed Ring of New York City's Tammany Hall.

Although the campaign was a bitter one, few differences of principle distinguished the candidates from one another. The election produced an apparent Democratic victory. Tilden carried the South and several large Northern states, and his popular margin over Hayes was nearly 300,000 votes. But disputed returns from Louisiana, South Carolina, Florida, and Oregon, whose electoral votes totaled 20, threw the election in doubt. Hayes could still win if he managed to receive all 20 disputed votes.

The Constitution had established no method to determine the validity of disputed returns. The decision clearly lay with Congress, but it was not obvious with which house or through what method. (The Senate was Republican, and the House was Democratic.) Members of each party naturally supported a solution that would yield them the victory. Finally, late in January 1877, Congress tried to break the deadlock by creating a special electoral commission composed of five senators, five representatives, and five justices of the Supreme Court. The congressional delegation consisted of five Republicans and five Democrats. The Court delegation would include two Republicans, two Democrats, and the only independent, Justice David Davis. But when the Illinois legislature elected Davis to the U.S. Senate, the justice resigned from the commission. His seat went instead to a Republican justice. The commission voted along straight party lines, 8 to 7, awarding every disputed vote to Hayes.

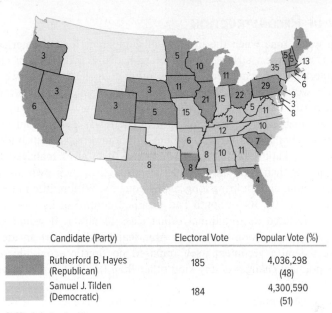

Candidate (Party)	Electoral Vote	Popular Vote (%)
Rutherford B. Hayes (Republican)	185	4,036,298 (48)
Samuel J. Tilden (Democratic)	184	4,300,590 (51)

81.8% of electorate voting

THE ELECTION OF 1876 The election of 1876 was one of the most controversial in American history. As in the elections of 1824, 1888, 2000, and 2016, the winner of the popular vote—Samuel J. Tilden—was not the winner of the electoral vote, which he lost by one vote. The final decision as to who would be president was not made until the day before the official inauguration in March. • *How did the Republicans turn this apparent defeat into a victory?*

Behind this seemingly partisan victory, however, lay a series of elaborate and sneaky compromises among leaders of both parties. When a Democratic filibuster threatened to derail the electoral commission's report, Republican Senate leaders met secretly with Southern Democratic leaders. As the price of their cooperation, the Southern Democrats exacted several pledges from the Republicans, which became known as the **Compromise of 1877**: the appointment of at least one Southerner to the Hayes cabinet, control of federal patronage in their areas, generous internal improvements, federal aid for the Texas and Pacific Railroad, and most important, withdrawal of the remaining federal troops from the South.

In his inaugural address, Hayes announced that the South's most pressing need was the restoration of "wise, honest, and peaceful local self-government," and he soon withdrew the troops and let white Democrats take over the remaining Southern state governments. That produced charges that he was paying off the South for acquiescing in his election—charges that were not wholly untrue. The outcome of the election created such bitterness that not even Hayes's promise to serve only one term could mollify his critics.

The president and his party hoped to build up a "new Republican" organization in the South committed to modest support for black rights. Although many white Southern leaders sympathized with Republican economic policies, resentment of Reconstruction was so deep that supporting the party became politically impossible. The "solid" Democratic South, which would survive until the mid-twentieth century, was taking shape.

THE LEGACY OF RECONSTRUCTION

Reconstruction was a time when the promise of democracy for all Americans, regardless of race or color, made great strides. Never before had the civil rights of citizens become so clearly enumerated and extended to those other than landholding white men; never before had the power of the federal government been marshaled so vigorously to protect these rights. In particular, African Americans achieved a new level of dignity and power in America unimaginable only a few years earlier. There was a significant redistribution of income among the races and a more limited but still noteworthy redistribution of landownership. Perhaps most important, African Americans themselves managed to carve out a society and culture of their own and to create or strengthen their own institutions.

Still, Reconstruction did not bring long-lasting equality. Within little more than a decade after a devastating war, the white South had regained control of its own institutions and, to a great extent, restored its traditional ruling class to power. It would soon dismantle many of the legal freedoms won by African Americans and support an ideology of white supremacy. The federal government itself imposed no drastic economic reforms on the region, and few political changes of any kind other than the abolition of slavery would stay in effect after the 1870s.

Reconstruction was notable, finally, for its limitations. For in those years, the United States failed in its first serious effort to resolve its oldest and deepest social problem—the problem of racial injustice.

Given the odds confronting them, however, African Americans had reason for considerable pride in the gains they were able to make during Reconstruction. And future generations would be grateful for the two great charters of freedom—the Fourteenth and Fifteenth Amendments to the Constitution—which, although widely ignored at the time, would one day serve as the basis for a "Second Reconstruction" that would renew the fight to bring freedom to all Americans.

THE NEW SOUTH

The Compromise of 1877 was supposed to be the first step toward developing a stable, permanent Republican Party in the South. In that respect, at least, it failed. In the years following the end of Reconstruction, white southerners established the Democratic Party as the only viable political organization for the region's whites. Even so, the South did change in some of the ways that the framers of the Compromise had hoped.

THE "REDEEMERS"

Many white southerners rejoiced at the restoration of what they liked to call "home rule." But in reality, political power in the region was soon more restricted than at any time since the Civil War. Once again, most of the South fell under the control of a powerful, conservative ruling class, whose members were known variously as the "**Redeemers**" or the "Bourbons."

In some places, this post-Reconstruction ruling class was much the same as it was in the antebellum period. In Alabama, for example, the old planter elite retained much of its former power. In other areas, however, the Redeemers constituted a genuinely new ruling class of merchants, industrialists, railroad developers, and financiers. Some of them were former planters, some of them northern immigrants, some of them ambitious, upwardly mobile white southerners from the region's lower social tiers. They combined a defense of "home rule" and social conservatism with a commitment to economic development.

The various Bourbon governments of the New South behaved in many respects quite similarly. Virtually all the new Democratic regimes lowered taxes, reduced public spending, and drastically diminished state services. One state after another eliminated or cut its support for public school systems.

INDUSTRIALIZATION AND THE NEW SOUTH

Many white southern leaders in the post-Reconstruction era hoped to see their region develop a vigorous industrial economy, a "**New South**." Henry Grady, editor of the *Atlanta Constitution,* and other New South advocates seldom challenged white supremacy, but they did promote the virtues of thrift, industry, and progress—qualities that prewar southerners had often denounced in northern society.

Southern industry did expand dramatically in the years after Reconstruction, most visibly in textile manufacturing. In the past, southern planters had usually shipped their cotton to manufacturers in the North or in Europe. Now textile factories appeared in the South itself—many of them drawn to the region from New England by the abundance of water power, the ready supply of cheap labor, the low taxes, and the accommodating conservative governments. The tobacco processing industry similarly established an important foothold in the region. In the lower South, and particularly in Birmingham, Alabama, the iron (and, later, steel) industry grew rapidly.

Railroad development also increased substantially in the post-Reconstruction years. Between 1880 and 1890, trackage in the South more than doubled. And in 1886, the South changed the gauge (width) of its trackage to correspond with the standards of the North. No longer would it be necessary for cargoes heading into the South to be transferred from one train to another at the borders of the region.

Yet southern industry developed within strict limits, and its effects on the region were never even remotely comparable to the effects of industrialization on the North. The southern share of national manufacturing doubled in the last twenty years of the century, but it was still only 10 percent of the total. Similarly, the region's per capita income increased 21 percent in the same period, but average income in the South was still only 40 percent of that in the North; in 1860 it had been more than 60 percent. And even in those industries where development had been most rapid—textiles, iron, railroads—much of the capital had come from, and many of the profits thus flowed to, the North.

The growth of southern industry required the region to recruit a substantial industrial workforce for the first time. From the beginning, a high percentage of the factory workers were women. Heavy male casualties in the Civil War had helped create a large population of unmarried women who desperately needed employment. Hours were long (often as much as twelve hours a day), and wages were far below the northern equivalent; indeed, one of the greatest attractions of the South to industrialists was that employers were able to pay workers there as little as one-half of what northern workers received. Life in most mill towns was rigidly controlled by the owners and managers of the factories, who rigorously suppressed attempts at protest or union organization. Company stores sold goods to workers at inflated prices and issued credit at exorbitant rates (much as country stores did in agrarian areas), and mill owners ensured that no competing merchants were able to establish themselves in the community.

Some industries, such as textiles, offered few opportunities to African American workers. But many did, like tobacco, iron, and lumber. In towns hosting these industries black and white cultures came into close contact, which fueled the determination of local white leaders to take additional measures to protect white supremacy.

TENANTS AND SHARECROPPERS

The most important economic problem in the post-Reconstruction South was the impoverished state of agriculture. The 1870s and 1880s saw an acceleration of the process that had begun in the immediate postwar years: the imposition of systems of tenantry and debt peonage on much of the region; the reliance on a few cash crops rather than on a diversified agricultural system; and increasing absentee ownership of valuable farmlands. During Reconstruction, perhaps a third or more of the farmers in the South were tenants; by 1900, the figure had increased to 70 percent.

AFRICAN AMERICANS AND THE NEW SOUTH

The "New South creed" was not the property of whites alone. Many African Americans were attracted to the vision of progress and self-improvement as well. Some former slaves (and, as the decades passed, their offspring) succeeded in elevating themselves into the

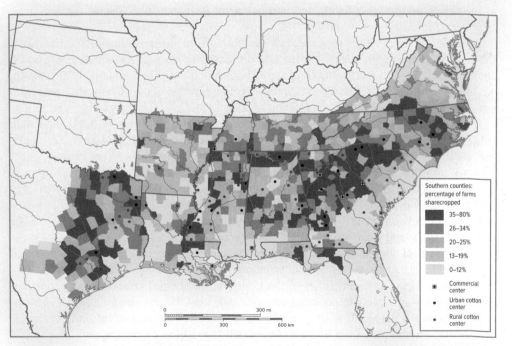

THE CROP-LIEN SYSTEM IN 1880 In the years after the Civil War, more and more southern farmers—white and black—became tenants or sharecroppers on land owned by others. This map shows the percentage of farms that were within the so-called crop-lien system, the system by which people worked their lands for someone else, who had a claim (or "lien") on part of the farmers' crops. Note the high density of sharecropping and tenant farming in the most fertile areas of the Deep South, the same areas where slaveholding had been most dominant before the Civil War. • *How did the crop-lien system contribute to the shift in southern agriculture toward one-crop farming?*

middle class, acquired property, established small businesses, or entered professions. Believing strongly that education was vital to the future of their people, they expanded the network of black colleges and institutes that had taken root during Reconstruction into an important educational system.

The chief spokesman for this commitment to education was **Booker T. Washington**, founder and president of the Tuskegee Institute in Alabama. Born into slavery, Washington had worked his way out of poverty after acquiring an education (at Virginia's Hampton Institute). He urged other blacks to follow the same road to self-improvement.

Washington's message was both cautious and hopeful. African Americans should attend school, learn skills, and establish a solid footing in agriculture and the trades. Industrial, not classical, education should be their goal. Blacks should, moreover, refine their speech, improve their dress, and adopt habits of thrift and personal cleanliness; they should, in short, adopt the standards of the white middle class. Only thus, Washington claimed, could they win the respect of the white population.

In a famous speech in Georgia in 1895, Washington outlined a controversial philosophy of race relations that became widely known as the **Atlanta Compromise**. Blacks, he said, should forgo agitation for political rights and concentrate on self-improvement and preparation for equality. Washington offered a powerful challenge to those whites who wanted to discourage African Americans from acquiring an education or winning any economic gains. But his message was also intended to assure whites that blacks would not challenge the emerging system of segregation.

The Birth of Jim Crow

Few white southerners had ever accepted the idea of racial equality. That the former slaves acquired any legal and political rights at all after emancipation was in large part the result of their own efforts and crucial federal support. That outside support all but vanished after 1877, when the last federal troops withdrew and the Supreme Court stripped the Fourteenth and Fifteenth Amendments of much of their significance. In the so-called civil rights cases of 1883, the Court ruled that the Fourteenth Amendment prohibited state governments from discriminating against people because of race but did not restrict private organizations or individuals from doing so. Popular culture reflected these frightening political developments. The rise of **minstrel shows**—slapstick dramatic representations of black culture—typically embodied racist ideas. "Corked-up" whites (a reference to the black makeup made by burning cork) grossly caricatured African American culture as silly, unintelligent, sensual, and immoral. Late in the 1800s, however, blacks founded their own minstrel shows in part to modify these stereotypes, though with only modest success. (See "Patterns of Popular Culture: The Minstrel Show.")

Eventually, the Court also validated state legislation that institutionalized the separation of the races. In *Plessy v. Ferguson* (1896), a case involving a Louisiana law that required segregated seating on railroads, the Court held that separate accommodations did not deprive blacks of equal rights if the accommodations were equal. In *Cumming v. County Board of Education* (1899), the Court ruled that communities could establish schools for whites only, even if there were no comparable schools for blacks.

Even before these dubious decisions, white southerners were working to separate the races to the greatest extent possible, and were particularly determined to strip African Americans of the right to vote. In some states, disenfranchisement had begun almost as soon as Reconstruction ended. But in other areas, black voting continued for some time

THE MINSTREL SHOW

The minstrel show was one of the most popular forms of entertainment in America in the second half of the nineteenth century. It was also a testament to the high awareness of race (and the high level of racism) in American society both before and after the Civil War. Minstrel performers were mostly white, usually disguised as black. But African American performers also formed their own minstrel shows and transformed them into vehicles for training black entertainers and developing new forms of music and dance.

Before and during the Civil War, when minstrel shows consisted almost entirely of white performers, performers blackened their faces with cork and presented grotesque stereotypes of the slave culture of the American South. Among the most popular of the stumbling, ridiculously ignorant characters invented for these shows were such figures as "Zip Coon" and "Jim Crow" (whose name later resurfaced as a label for late-nineteenth-century segregation laws). A typical minstrel show presented a group of seventeen or more

(Source: Library of Congress, Prints and Photographs Division [LC-USZ62-2659])

MINSTRELSY AT HIGH TIDE The Primrose & West minstrel troupe—a lavish and expensive entertainment that drew large crowds in the 1800s—was one of many companies to offer this brand of entertainment to eager audiences all over the country. Although minstrelsy began with white musicians performing in blackface, the popularity of real African American minstrels encouraged the impresarios of the troupe to include groups of white and black performers alike.

men seated in a semicircle facing the audience. The man in the center ran the show, played the straight man for the jokes of others, and led the music—lively dances and sentimental ballads played on banjos, castanets, and other instruments and sung by soloists or the entire group.

After the Civil War, white minstrels began to expand their repertoire. Drawing from the famous and successful freak shows of P. T. Barnum and other entertainment entrepreneurs, some began to include Siamese twins, bearded ladies, and even a supposedly eight-foot two-inch "Chinese giant" in their shows. They also incorporated sex, both by including women in some shows and, even more popularly, by recruiting female impersonators. One of the most successful minstrel performers of the 1870s was Francis Leon, who delighted crowds with his female portrayal of a flamboyant "prima donna."

One reason white minstrels began to move in these new directions was that they were now facing competition from black performers, who could provide more-authentic versions of black music, dance, and humor. They usually brought more talent to the task than white performers. The Georgia Minstrels, organized in 1865, was one of the first all-black minstrel troupes, and it had great success in attracting white audiences in the Northeast for several years. By the 1870s, touring African American minstrel groups were numerous. The black minstrels used many of the conventions of the white shows. There were dances, music, comic routines, and sentimental recitations. Some black performers even chalked their faces to make themselves look as dark as the white blackface performers with whom they were competing. Black minstrels sometimes denounced slavery (at least indirectly) and did not often speak demeaningly of the capacities of their race. But they could not entirely escape caricaturing African American life as they struggled to meet the expectations of their white audiences.

The black minstrel shows had few openly political aims. They did help develop some important forms of African American entertainment and transform them into a part of the national culture. Black minstrels introduced new forms of dance, derived from the informal traditions of slavery and black community life. They showed the "buck and wing," the "stop time," and the "Virginia essence," which established the foundations for the tap and jazz dancing of the early twentieth century. They also improvised musically and began experimenting with forms that over time contributed to the growth of ragtime, jazz, and rhythm and blues.

Eventually, black minstrelsy—like its white counterpart—evolved into other forms of theater, including the beginnings of serious black drama. At Ambrose Park in Brooklyn in the 1890s, for example, the celebrated black comedian Sam Lucas (a veteran of the minstrel circuit) starred in the play *Darkest America*, which one black newspaper later described as a "delineation of Negro life, carrying the race through all their historical phases from the plantation, into reconstruction days and finally painting our people as they are today, cultured and accomplished in the social graces, [holding] the mirror faithfully up to nature."

But interest in the minstrel show did not die altogether. In 1927, Hollywood released *The Jazz Singer,* the first feature film with sound. It was about the career of a white minstrel performer, and its star was one of the most popular singers of the twentieth century: Al Jolson, whose career had begun on the blackface minstrel circuit years before.   •

UNDERSTAND, ANALYZE, & EVALUATE

1. How did minstrel shows performed by white minstrels reinforce prevailing attitudes toward African Americans?
2. Minstrel shows performed by black minstrels often conformed to existing stereotypes of African Americans. Why?
3. Can you think of any popular entertainments today that carry remnants of the minstrel shows of the nineteenth century?

after Reconstruction—largely because conservative whites believed they could control the black electorate and use it to beat back the attempts of poor white farmers to take control of the Democratic Party.

In the 1890s, however, franchise restrictions became much more rigid. During those years, some small white farmers began to demand complete black disenfranchisement—because they objected to the black vote being used against them by the Bourbons. At the same time, many members of the conservative elite began to doubt their ability to influence black voters and fear that poor whites might unite politically with poor blacks to challenge them.

In devising laws to disenfranchise black males, the southern states had to find ways to evade the Fifteenth Amendment, which prohibited states from denying anyone the right to vote because of race. Two devices emerged before 1900 to accomplish this goal: the poll tax, or some form of property qualification (few blacks were prosperous enough to meet such requirements); and the "literacy" or "understanding" test, which required voters to demonstrate an ability to read and to interpret the Constitution. Even those African Americans who could read had a hard time passing the difficult test white officials gave them, which often required them to interpret an arcane part of the Constitution to the satisfaction of a white elected official. (The laws affected poor white voters as well as blacks.) By the late 1890s, the black vote had decreased by 62 percent, the white vote by 26 percent.

Laws restricting the franchise and segregating schools were only part of a network of state and local statutes—collectively known as the **Jim Crow laws**—that by the first years of the twentieth century had institutionalized an elaborate system of racial hierarchy reaching into almost every area of southern life. Blacks and whites could not ride together in the same railroad cars, sit in the same waiting rooms, use the same washrooms, eat in the same restaurants, or sit in the same theaters. Blacks had no access to many public parks, beaches, or picnic areas; they could not be patients in many hospitals. Much of the new legal structure did no more than confirm what had already been widespread social practice in the South. But the Jim Crow laws also stripped blacks of many of the modest social, economic, and political gains they had made in the late nineteenth century.

More than legal efforts were involved in this process. The 1890s witnessed a dramatic increase in white violence against blacks, which, along with the Jim Crow laws, served to inhibit black agitation for equal rights. The worst such violence—lynching of blacks by white mobs—reached appalling levels. In the nation as a whole in the 1890s, there was an average of 187 lynchings each year, more than 80 percent of them in the South. The vast majority of victims were black men accused of crimes they did not commit and who rarely enjoyed due process or a fair trial. Those who participated in lynchings often saw their actions as a legitimate form of law enforcement, but also as a way to deliver a powerful message about the power of white supremacy—namely, that they could use intimidation as means of controlling the black population.

The rise of lynchings shocked the conscience of many white Americans in a way that other forms of racial injustice did not. In 1892, **Ida B. Wells**, a committed black journalist, published a series of impassioned articles after the lynching of three of her hometown friends in Memphis, Tennessee; her articles launched what became an international anti-lynching movement. The movement gradually attracted substantial support from whites in the North and even the South, particularly from women. Its goal was a federal antilynching law, which would allow the national government to do what state and local governments in the South were generally unwilling to do: punish those responsible for lynchings. Although such a law was introduced to Congress in 1918 and reintroduced in the 1920s, 1930s, and 1940s, it never made it past southern senators.

(Source: Library of Congress, Prints and Photographs Division [LC-USZ62-29285])

LYNCHING OF HENRY SMITH, PARIS, TEXAS, 1893 A large, almost festive crowd numbering about 10,000 gathers to watch the lynching of a Henry Smith. Accused of murdering a four-year-old white girl who was the daughter of a law enforcement officer, Smith was mutilated and burned on this scaffold. Over 4000 lynchings occurred between the end of slavery and the late 1930s, mostly in the South. They reached their peak in the 1890s and the first years of the twentieth century. Lynchings such as this one—publicized well in advance and attracting whole families who traveled great distances to see them—were relatively infrequent. Most lynchings were the work of smaller groups, operating with less visibility.

Opposition to lynching, however, paled in contrast to the overwhelming support among most southern whites for actions that kept African Americans subordinate to them and without the power to effect change. As in the antebellum period, poor whites generally aligned themselves politically with wealthy whites out of a shared feeling of racial superiority, despite having economic concerns in common with African Americans.

CONCLUSION

Reconstruction was a profoundly important moment in American history. Despite the bitter political battles in Washington and throughout the South, culminating in the unsuccessful effort to remove President Andrew Johnson from office, the most important result of the effort to reunite the nation after its long and bloody war was a reshaping of the lives of ordinary people in all regions.

In the North, Reconstruction solidified the power of the Republican Party. The rapid expansion of the northern economy accelerated, drawing more and more of its residents into a burgeoning commercial world.

In the South, Reconstruction fundamentally rearranged the relationship between white and black citizens. African Americans initially participated actively and effectively in southern politics. After a few years of widespread black voting and significant black officeholding, however, the forces of white supremacy shoved most African Americans to the margins of the southern political world, where they would mostly remain until the 1960s.

In other ways, however, the lives of southern blacks changed dramatically and permanently. Overwhelmingly, they left the plantations. Some sought work in towns and cities. Others left the region altogether. But the great majority began farming on small farms of their own—not as landowners, except in rare cases, but as tenants and sharecroppers on land owned by whites. The result was a form of economic bondage, driven by debt, only scarcely less oppressive than the legal bondage of slavery. Within this system, however, African Americans managed to carve out a much larger sphere of social and cultural activity than they had ever been able to create under slavery. Black churches proliferated in great numbers. African American schools and printing presses emerged in some communities, and black colleges began to operate in the region. Some former slaves owned businesses and flourished.

Strenuous efforts by "New South" advocates to advance industry and commerce in the region produced impressive results in a few areas. But the South on the whole remained what it had always been: a largely rural society with a sharply defined class structure. It also maintained a deep commitment among its white citizens to the subordination of African Americans—a commitment solidified in the 1890s and the early twentieth century when white southerners erected an elaborate legal system of segregation (the Jim Crow laws). Tragically, the promise of the great Reconstruction amendments to the Constitution—the Fourteenth and Fifteenth—remained largely unfulfilled in the South as the century drew to its close.

KEY TERMS/PEOPLE/PLACES/EVENTS

Andrew Johnson 359
Atlanta Compromise 375
Black Codes 359
Booker T. Washington 375
carpetbagger 363
Charles Sumner 355
Compromise of 1877 371
crop-lien system 366
Enforcement Acts 370
Fifteenth Amendment 362

Fourteenth
 Amendment 361
Freedmen's Bureau 355
Ida B. Wells 378
impeachment 363
Jim Crow laws 378
Ku Klux Klan 369
minstrel show 375
New South 373
Plessy v. Ferguson 375

Radical Republicans 355
Reconstruction 355
Redeemers 372
scalawag 363
sharecropping 365
Thaddeus
 Stevens 355
Ulysses S. Grant 367
Wade-Davis Bill 357
William H. Seward 358

RECALL AND REFLECT

1. What were the principal questions facing the nation at the end of the Civil War?
2. What were the achievements of Reconstruction? Where did it fail and why?
3. What new problems arose in the South as the North's interest in Reconstruction waned?
4. What was the Compromise of 1877, and how did it affect Reconstruction?
5. How did the "New" South differ from the South before the Civil War?

16 | THE CONQUEST OF THE FAR WEST

THE SOCIETIES OF THE FAR WEST
THE ROMANCE OF THE WEST
THE CHANGING WESTERN ECONOMY
THE DISPERSAL OF THE TRIBES
THE RISE AND DECLINE OF THE WESTERN FARMER

LOOKING AHEAD

1. What various ethnic and racial groups populated the American West, and how did they interact?
2. How did the arrival and settlement of substantial numbers of Anglo-Americans transform the society and economy of the West?
3. What role did the federal government play in shaping the development of the West?

BY THE MID-1840S, WHITE AMERICAN MIGRANTS, along with many others, from the eastern regions of the nation had settled in the West in substantial numbers. Farmers, ranchers, and miners all found opportunity in the western lands. By the end of the Civil War, the West had become legendary in the eastern states. No longer the Great American Desert, it was now widely viewed as the "frontier": an empty land awaiting settlement and civilization; a place of wealth, adventure, opportunity, and untrammeled individualism.

In fact, the real West of the mid-nineteenth century bore little resemblance to its popular image. It was a diverse land, with many different regions, climates, and stores of natural resources. And it was extensively populated. The English-speaking migrants of the late nineteenth century did not find an empty, desolate land. They found Indians, Mexicans, African Americans, French and British Canadians, Asians, and others, some of whose families had been living in the West for generations.

1862
Homestead Act

1865–1867
Sioux Wars

1869
Transcontinental
railroad completed

1873
Barbed wire invented

1874
Black Hills gold rush

1876
Battle of the Little
Bighorn

1877
Desert Land Act

1882
Chinese Exclusion Act

1885
Twain's *Huckleberry Finn*

1887
Dawes Act

1889
Oklahoma opened to
white settlement

1890
Battle of Wounded Knee

1893
Turner thesis

THE SOCIETIES OF THE FAR WEST

The Far West was in fact a composite of many lands. It contained both the most arid regions and some of the wettest and lushest areas of the United States. It contained the flattest plains and the highest mountains. It also contained many peoples.

THE WESTERN TRIBES

The Indian tribes made up the largest and most important western population group before the great white migration. Some were members of eastern tribes who had been forcibly resettled west of the Mississippi. But most were members of indigenous tribes whose roots stretched back generations.

More than 300,000 Indians (among them the Serrano, Chumash, Pomo, Maidu, Yurok, and Chinook) had lived on the Pacific Coast before the arrival of Spanish settlers. They supported themselves through a combination of fishing, foraging, and simple agriculture. The Pueblos of the Southwest had long lived largely as farmers and had established permanent settlements there.

The most widespread Indian groups in the West were the Plains Indians. They were, in fact, made up of many different tribal and language groups. Some lived more or less sedentary lives as farmers, but many subsisted largely through hunting buffalo. Riding small but powerful horses, the tribes moved through the grasslands following the herds, constructing tepees as temporary dwellings. The buffalo, or bison, provided the economic basis for the Plains Indians' way of life. The flesh of the large animal was their principal source of food, and its skin supplied materials for clothing, shoes, tepees, blankets, robes, and utensils. "Buffalo chips"—dried manure—provided fuel; buffalo bones became knives and arrow tips; buffalo tendons formed the strings of bows.

The Plains warriors proved to be the most formidable foes that white settlers would encounter. But the tribes were usually unable to unite against white aggression. At times, tribal warriors even faced white forces who were being assisted by guides and even fighters from rival tribes. Some tribes, however, were able to overcome their divisions and cooperate effectively. By the mid-nineteenth century, for example, the Sioux, Arapaho, and Cheyenne had forged a powerful alliance that dominated the northern plains. That proved no protection, however, against the greatest danger to the tribes: ecological and economic decline. Indians were highly vulnerable to eastern infectious diseases, such as the smallpox epidemics that decimated the Pawnee in Nebraska in the 1840s. And the tribes were, of course, at a considerable disadvantage in any long-term battle against an enemy with a deadlier and more plentiful weaponry, especially repeating rifles guns and cannons.

Hispanic New Mexico

For centuries, much of the Far West had been part of the Spanish Empire and, later, the Mexican Republic. When the United States acquired its new lands there in the 1840s, it also acquired many Mexican residents.

In New Mexico, the centers of Spanish-speaking society were farming and trading communities established in the seventeenth century. Descendants of the original Spanish settlers (and more recent migrants from Mexico) engaged primarily in cattle and sheep ranching. When the United States acquired title to New Mexico in the aftermath of the Mexican War, General Stephen Kearny—who had commanded the American troops in the region—tried to establish a territorial government out of the approximately 1,000 Anglo-Americans in the region, ignoring the more than 50,000 Hispanics. There were widespread fears among Hispanics and Indians that the new American rulers would confiscate their lands. In 1847, before the new government had established itself, Taos Indians rebelled, killing the new governor and other Anglo-American officials before being subdued by U.S Army forces. New Mexico remained under military rule for three years, until the United States finally organized a territorial government there in 1850. The U.S. Army finally broke the power of the Navajo, Apache, and other tribes in the region.

The Anglo-American presence in the Southwest grew rapidly once the railroads heavily penetrated the region in the 1880s and early 1890s. With the railroads came extensive new ranching, farming, and mining. This expansion of economic activity attracted a new wave of Mexican immigrants, who moved across the border in search of work. The English-speaking proprietors of the new enterprises, however, commonly restricted most Mexicans to the lowest-paying and least stable jobs.

Hispanic California and Texas

In California, Spanish settlement began in the eighteenth century with a string of Catholic missions along the Pacific Coast. The missionaries and the soldiers who accompanied them gathered most of the coastal Indians into their communities, some forcibly and others by persuasion. In the 1830s, after the new Mexican government began reducing the power of the church, the mission society largely collapsed. In its place emerged a secular Mexican aristocracy, which controlled a chain of large estates in the fertile lands west of the Sierra mountains. For them, the acquisition of California by the United States was disastrous. So vast were the numbers of English-speaking immigrants that the *Californios* (as the Hispanic residents of the region were known) had struggled to resist the onslaught. English-speaking prospectors organized to exclude them, sometimes violently, from the mines during the gold rush. Many *Californios* also lost their lands—either through corrupt business deals or through outright seizure.

Increasingly, Mexicans and Mexican Americans became part of the lower end of the state's working class, clustered in *barrios* in Los Angeles or elsewhere or laboring as migrant farmworkers. Even small Hispanic landowners who managed to hang on to their farms found themselves unable to raise livestock, as once-communal grazing lands fell under the control of powerful Anglo ranchers.

A similar pattern occurred in Texas after it joined the United States. Many Mexican landowners lost their land—some as a result of fraud and coercion, others because even the most substantial Mexican ranchers could not compete with the emerging Anglo-American ranching kingdoms. In 1859, angry Mexicans, led by the rancher Juan Cortina, raided the jail in Brownsville and freed all the Mexican prisoners inside. But such resistance had little long-term effect. As in California, Mexicans in southern Texas became an increasingly impoverished working class, relegated largely to unskilled farm or industrial labor.

THE CHINESE MIGRATION

At the same time that ambitious or impoverished Europeans were crossing the Atlantic in search of opportunities in the New World, many Chinese were crossing the Pacific in hopes of better lives. Not all came to the United States. Many Chinese—some as "**coolies**" (a nineteenth-century term meaning indentured servants whose conditions were close to slavery)—moved to Hawaii, Australia, Latin America, South Africa, and even the Caribbean.

A few Chinese traveled to the American West even before the gold rush, but after 1848 the flow increased dramatically. By 1880, more than 200,000 Chinese had settled in the United States. Almost all came as free laborers. For a time, white Americans welcomed the Chinese as a conscientious, hardworking people. Very quickly, however, white opinion turned hostile—in part because the Chinese were so industrious and successful that some white Americans began considering them rivals.

In the early 1850s, large numbers of Chinese immigrants joined the hunt for gold. Many of them were well-organized, hardworking prospectors, and for a time some enjoyed considerable success. But opportunities for the Chinese to prosper in the mines were fleeting. In 1852, the California legislature began trying to exclude the Chinese from gold mining by enacting a "foreign miners" tax. Gradually, the effect of the discriminatory laws, the hostility of white miners, and the declining profitability of the surface mines drove most Chinese out of prospecting.

As mining declined as a source of wealth and jobs for the Chinese, railroad employment grew. Beginning in 1865, over 12,000 Chinese found work building the transcontinental railroad, forming 90 percent of the labor force of the Central Pacific. The company preferred them to white laborers because they worked hard, made few demands, and accepted relatively low wages.

Work on the Central Pacific was arduous and often dangerous. In the winter, many Chinese tunneled into snowbanks at night to create warm sleeping areas for themselves, even though such tunnels frequently collapsed, suffocating those inside. In the spring of 1866, 5,000 Chinese railroad workers rebelled against the terrible conditions and went on strike to demand higher wages and a shorter workday. The company isolated them, surrounded them with strikebreakers, and starved them into submission.

In 1869, the transcontinental railroad was completed, and thousands of Chinese lost their jobs. Some moved into agricultural work usually in menial positions. Increasingly, however, the Chinese flocked to cities. By far the largest single Chinese community was in San Francisco. Much of community life there, and in other "Chinatowns" throughout the West, revolved around organizations, somewhat like benevolent societies, that filled many of the roles that

(Source: National Archives and Records Administration)

A CHINESE FAMILY IN SAN FRANCISCO   This portrait of Chun Duck Chin and his seven-year-old son Chun Jan Yut was taken in a studio in San Francisco in the 1870s. Both father and son appear to have dressed up for the occasion, in traditional Chinese garb, and the studio—which likely took many such portraits of Chinese families—provided a formal Chinese backdrop. The son is holding what appears to be a chicken, perhaps to impress relatives in China with his family's prosperity.

political machines often served in immigrant communities in eastern cities. Often led by prominent merchants (in San Francisco, they were known as the "Six Companies"), these organizations became, in effect, employment brokers, unions, arbitrators of disputes, defenders against outside persecution, and dispensers of social services. They also organized elaborate festivals and celebrations that were a conspicuous and important part of life in Chinatowns.

Other Chinese organizations were secret societies known as "tongs." Some of the tongs were violent criminal organizations, involved in the opium trade and prostitution. Few people outside the Chinese communities were aware of their existence, except when rival tongs engaged in violent conflict (or "tong wars").

In San Francisco and other western cities, the Chinese usually occupied the lower rungs of the employment ladder. Many worked as common laborers, servants, and unskilled factory hands. Some established their own small businesses, especially laundries. There were few commercial laundries in China, but they could be started in America with very little capital and required only limited command of English. By the 1890s, Chinese constituted over two-thirds of all the laundry workers in California.

During the earliest Chinese migrations to California, virtually all the relatively small number of women who made the journey did so because they had been sold into prostitution. As late as 1880, nearly half the Chinese women in California were prostitutes. Gradually, however, the overall number of Chinese women increased, and Chinese men in America became more likely to seek companionship in families.

Anti-Chinese Sentiments

As Chinese communities grew larger, more visible, and more powerful, anti-Chinese sentiment among white residents intensified. Anti-Chinese activities, some of them bloody, reflected the resentment of many white workers toward Chinese laborers for accepting lower wages. As the political value of attacking the Chinese grew in California, the Democratic Party took up the call. So did the Workingmen's Party of California—founded in 1878 by Denis Kearney, an Irish immigrant—which gained significant power in the state largely because of its hostility to the Chinese. By the mid-1880s, anti-Chinese agitation and violence had spread up and down the Pacific Coast and into other areas of the West.

In 1882, Congress responded to the political pressure and the growing racial violence by passing the **Chinese Exclusion Act**, which banned Chinese immigration into the United States for ten years and barred Chinese already in the country from becoming naturalized citizens. Congress renewed the law for another ten years in 1892 and made it permanent in 1902. It had a dramatic effect on the Chinese population, which declined by more than 40 percent in the forty years after the act's passage.

Migration from the East

The scale of post–Civil War white migration to the American West dwarfed everything that had preceded it. In previous decades, the settlers had come in thousands. Now they came in millions. Most of the new settlers were from the established Anglo-American societies of the eastern United States, but substantial numbers—over 2 million between 1870 and 1900—were foreign-born immigrants from Europe: Scandinavians, Germans, Irish, Russians, Czechs, and others.

They came to the West for many reasons. Settlers were attracted by gold and silver deposits, by the short-grass pasture for cattle and sheep, and ultimately by the rich sod of the plains and the meadowlands of the mountains. The completion of the great transcontinental railroad line in 1869, and the construction of the many subsidiary lines that spidered out from it, encouraged rapid settlement. So did the land policies of the federal government. The **Homestead Act** of 1862 permitted settlers to buy plots of 160 acres for a small fee if they occupied the land they purchased for five years and improved it.

Supporters of the Homestead Act believed it would create new markets and new outposts of commercial agriculture for the nation's growing economy. But a unit of 160 acres, while ample in much of the East, was too small for the grazing and grain farming of the Great Plains. Eventually, the federal government provided some relief. The Timber Culture Act (1873) permitted homesteaders to receive grants of 160 additional acres if they planted 40 acres of trees on them. The Desert Land Act (1877) allowed claimants to buy 640 acres at $1.25 an acre, provided they irrigated part of their holdings within three years. These and other laws ultimately made it possible for individuals to acquire as much as 1,280 acres of land at little cost.

Political organization followed on the hard heels of settlement. By the mid-1860s, territorial governments were in operation in the new provinces of Nevada, Colorado, Dakota, Arizona, Idaho, Montana, and Wyoming. Statehood rapidly followed. Nevada became a state in 1864, Nebraska in 1867, and Colorado in 1876. In 1889, North and South Dakota,

Montana, and Washington won admission; Wyoming and Idaho entered the next year. Congress denied Utah statehood until its Mormon leaders convinced the government in 1896 that polygamy (the practice of men taking several wives) had been abandoned. At the turn of the century, only Arizona, New Mexico, and Oklahoma remained outside the Union.

THE ROMANCE OF THE WEST

The rapidly developing West occupied a special place in the Anglo-American imagination. Many white Americans continued to consider it a romantic place, a wilderness where individuals could experience true freedom. But such thinking was more fiction than fact.

THE WESTERN LANDSCAPE AND THE COWBOY

Part of the attraction of the West was its spectacular natural landscape. Painters of the new "**Rocky Mountain school**"—of whom the best known were Albert Bierstadt and Thomas Moran—celebrated the new West in grandiose canvases, some of which toured the eastern and midwestern states and attracted enormous crowds eager for a vision of the Great West.

Gradually, paintings and photographs inspired a growing wave of tourism among people eager to see the natural wonders of the region. In the 1880s and 1890s, resort hotels began to spring up near some of the region's most spectacular landscapes.

Even more appealing was the rugged, free-spirited lifestyle that many Americans associated with the West. Many nineteenth-century Americans came especially to idealize the figure of the cowboy. Western novels such as Owen Wister's *The Virginian* (1902) romanticized the cowboy's supposed freedom from traditional social constraints, his affinity with nature, even his supposed propensity for violence. Wister's character—one of the most enduring in popular American literature—was a semi-educated man whose natural decency, courage, and compassion made him a powerful symbol of the supposed virtues of the "frontier." But *The Virginian* was only the most famous example of a type of literature that soon swept throughout the United States. Novels and stories glorified the West and the lives of cowboys in particular, in boys' magazines, pulp novels, theater, and serious literature.

Among the reasons for the widespread admiration of the cowboy were the remarkably popular Wild West shows that traveled throughout the United States and Europe. Most successful were the shows of Buffalo Bill Cody, a former Pony Express rider, Indian fighter, and hero of popular dime novels for children. Cody's Wild West show, which spawned dozens of imitators, exploited his own fame and romanticized the life of the cowboy through reenactments of Indian battles and displays of horsemanship and riflery (many of them by the famous sharpshooter Annie Oakley). Buffalo Bill and his imitators confirmed the popular image of the West as a place of romance and glamour and helped keep that image alive for later generations.

THE IDEA OF THE FRONTIER

It was not simply the particular character of the new West that resonated in the nation's imagination. It was also that many Americans considered it the last natural frontier. Since the earliest moments of European settlement in America, the image of uncharted territory to the west had always comforted and inspired those who dreamed of starting life anew.

THE FRONTIER AND THE WEST

The emergence of the history of the American West as an important field of scholarship can be traced to a paper Frederick Jackson Turner delivered to the American Historical Association in 1893: "The Significance of the Frontier in American History." Turner stated his thesis simply. The settlement of the West by white Americans—"the existence of an area of free land, its continuous recession, and the advance of American settlement westward"—was the central story of the nation's history. The process of westward expansion had transformed a desolate and savage land into modern civilization and had continually renewed American ideas of democracy and individualism.

In the first half of the twentieth century, virtually everyone who wrote about the West echoed at least part of Turner's argument. Ray Allen Billington's *Westward Expansion* (1949) was almost wholly consistent with the Turnerian model. In *The Great Plains* (1931) and *The Great Frontier* (1952), Walter Prescott Webb similarly emphasized the bravery and ingenuity of white settlers in the Southwest.

Serious efforts to displace the Turner thesis as the explanation of western American history began after World War II. In *Virgin Land* (1950), Henry Nash Smith examined many of the same heroic images of the West that Turner and his disciples had presented; but he treated those images less as descriptions of reality than as myths. Earl Pomeroy challenged Turner's notion of the West as a place of individualism, innovation, and democratic renewal. "Conservatism, inheritance, and continuity bulked at least as large," he claimed. Howard Lamar, in *Dakota Territory, 1861–1889* (1956) and *The Far Southwest* (1966), emphasized the highly diverse character of the West.

The western historians who emerged since the late 1970s launched an even more emphatic attack on the Turner thesis and the idea of the "frontier." "New western historians" such as Richard White, Patricia Nelson Limerick, William Cronon, Donald Worster, Peggy Pascoe, and many others challenged the Turnerians on a number of points.

Turner saw the nineteenth-century West as "free land" awaiting the expansion of Anglo-American settlement and American democracy. The more recent western historians reject the concept of an empty "frontier," emphasizing instead the elaborate and highly developed civilizations that already existed in the region. White, English-speaking Americans, they have argued, did not so much "settle" the West as conquer it. And they continued to share the region not only with the Indians and Hispanics who preceded them there, but also with African Americans, Asians, Latin Americans, and others who flowed into the West at the same time they did.

The Turnerian West was a place of heroism, triumph, and above all progress, dominated by the feats of brave white men. The West that the new western historians describe was a less triumphant (and less masculine) place in which bravery and success coexisted with oppression, greed, and failure; in which decaying ghost towns, bleak Indian reservations, impoverished barrios, and ecologically devastated landscapes have been as characteristic of western development as great ranches, rich farms, and prosperous cities.

To Turner and his disciples, the nineteenth-century West was a place where rugged individualism flourished and replenished American democracy. The newer scholars point out that the region was inextricably tied to a national and international capitalist economy. Westerners depended on government-subsidized railroads for access to markets, federal troops for protection from Indians, and (later) government-funded dams and canals for irrigating their fields and sustaining their towns.

And while Turner defined the West as a process—a process of settlement that came to an end with the "closing of the frontier" in the late nineteenth century the newer historians see the West as a region. Its distinctive history did not end in 1890 but continues into our own time. •

UNDERSTAND, ANALYZE, & EVALUATE

1. How and why did the portrayal of the West by the newer western historians differ from the West that Turner described?
2. Why did the newer western historians challenge Turner's views, and why has their depiction of the West, in turn, provoked such controversy?

Mark Twain gave voice to this romantic vision of the frontier in a series of novels and memoirs. In *The Adventures of Tom Sawyer* (1876) and *The Adventures of Huckleberry Finn* (1885), he produced characters who repudiated the constraints of organized society and attempted to escape into a more natural world. (For Huck Finn, the vehicle of escape was a small raft on the Mississippi.) This yearning for freedom reflected a larger vision of the West as the last refuge from the constraints of civilization.

One of the most beloved and successful artists of the nineteenth century was Frederic Remington, a painter and sculptor whose works came to represent the romance of the

(Source: Library of Congress, Prints and Photographs Division [LC-DIG-ppmsca-09855])

AMERICAN PROGRESS, 1872 The Brooklyn artist John Gast painted this image of hardy settlers marching toward the frontier for western travel guides. The goddess of progress, holding a schoolbook and telegraph line, leads the way. Native Americans, buffalo, and a bear are pushed off to the margins by the pioneers' approach.

West. He portrayed the cowboy as a natural aristocrat, much like Wister's *The Virginian,* living in a natural world in which all the normal supporting structures of "civilization" were missing.

Theodore Roosevelt also contributed to the romanticizing of the West. He traveled to the Dakota badlands in the mid-1880s to recover from the sudden death of his young wife. In the 1890s, he published a four-volume history, *The Winning of the West,* with a heroic account of the spread of white civilization into the frontier.

Perhaps the most influential statement of the romantic vision of the frontier came from the young historian Frederick Jackson Turner, in a memorable paper he delivered as a thirty-two-year-old in Chicago in 1893 titled "The Significance of the Frontier in American History." In it he boldly claimed that the experience of western expansion had stimulated individualism, nationalism, and democracy; kept opportunities for advancement alive; and made Americans the distinctive people that they were. "Now," Turner concluded portentously, "the frontier has gone and with its going has closed the first period of American history." The **Turner thesis** was widely accepted by his contemporaries, but later historians have challenged it. (See "Debating the Past: The Frontier and the West.")

In accepting the idea of the "passing of the frontier," many Americans were acknowledging the end of one of their most cherished myths. As long as it had been possible for them to see the West as an empty, open land, it was possible to believe that there were constantly revitalizing opportunities in American life. But by the end of the nineteenth century, there was a vague and ominous sense of opportunities foreclosed.

THE CHANGING WESTERN ECONOMY

Turner accurately captured the popular view of the West as a place of unrivaled opportunity for growth and wealth that was a key motivation for the millions who migrated in the decades after the Civil War. This great wave of Anglo-American and European settlement transformed the economy of the Far West and tied the region firmly to the growing industrial economy of the East.

LABOR IN THE WEST

As commercial activity increased, many farmers, ranchers, and miners found it necessary to recruit a paid labor force—not an easy task given the small labor pool compared to that found in established cities. This labor shortage led to higher wages for some workers than were typical in the East. But working conditions were often treacherous, and job security was almost nonexistent. Once a railroad was built, a crop harvested, a herd sent to market or a mine played out, hundreds and even thousands of workers could find themselves suddenly unemployed.

The western working class was highly multiracial. English-speaking whites worked alongside African Americans and immigrants from southern and eastern Europe, as they did in the East. Even more, they worked with Chinese, Filipinos, Mexicans, and Indians. But the workforce was highly stratified along racial lines. In almost every area of the western economy, white workers (whatever their ethnicity) occupied the upper tiers of employment: management and skilled labor. The lower tiers—unskilled work in the mines, on the railroads, or in agriculture—were filled overwhelmingly by nonwhites.

The western economy was, however, no more a single entity than the economy of the East. In the late nineteenth century, the region produced three major industries, each with distinctive history and characteristics: mining, ranching, and commercial farming.

THE ARRIVAL OF THE MINERS

The first economic boom in the Far West was the result of mining. The mining boom began around 1860 and flourished until the 1890s. Then it abruptly declined.

At first it was news of a gold or silver strike that would start a stampede. The California gold rush of 1849 was the first and most famous gold rush. But it was followed by others. Individual prospectors would pan for gold, extracting the first shallow deposits of ore largely by hand, a method known as placer mining. After these surface deposits dwindled, corporations moved in to engage in lode or quartz mining, which dug deeper beneath the surface. Then, as those deposits dwindled, commercial mining declined, and ultimately ranchers and farmers moved in and established a longer-lasting agricultural economy.

The first great mineral strikes (other than the California gold rush) occurred just before the Civil War. In 1858, gold was discovered in the Pike's Peak district of what would soon be the territory of Colorado; the following year, 50,000 prospectors stormed in. Denver and other mining camps blossomed into "cities" overnight. Almost as rapidly as they had developed, the booms ended. Later, the discovery of silver near Leadville supplied a new source of mineral wealth.

While the Colorado rush of 1859 was still in progress, news of another strike drew miners to Nevada. Gold had been found in the Washoe district. Even more plentiful and more valuable was the silver found in the great Comstock Lode (first discovered in 1858 by Henry Comstock) and other Washoe veins. The first prospectors to reach the Washoe fields came from California, and from the beginning, Californians dominated the settlement and development of Nevada. A remote desert without railroad transportation, the territory produced no supplies of its own, and everything had to be shipped from California to Virginia City, Carson City, and other roaring camp towns. When the first placer (or surface) deposits ran out, Californian and eastern capitalists bought the claims of the pioneer prospectors and began to use the more difficult process of quartz mining, which enabled them to retrieve silver from deeper veins. For a few years, these outside owners reaped tremendous profits: from 1860 to 1880, the Nevada lodes yielded bullion worth $306 million. After that, the mines quickly played out.

The next important mineral discoveries came in 1874, when gold was found in the Black Hills of southwestern Dakota Territory. Prospectors swarmed into the remote area. Like the others, the boom flared for a time, until surface resources faded and corporations took over—above all, the enormous Homestake Mining Company—and came to dominate the fields. The Dakotas, like other boom areas of the mineral empire, ultimately developed a largely agricultural economy.

The gold and silver discoveries generated the most popular excitement. But less glamorous natural resources proved more important to western development. The great Anaconda copper mine, launched by William Clark in 1881, marked the beginning of an industry that would remain important to Montana for many decades. In other areas, mining operations had significant success with lead, tin, quartz, and zinc.

Men greatly outnumbered women in the mining towns, and younger men in particular had difficulty finding female companions of comparable age. Those women who did gravitate to the new communities often came with their husbands. Single women, or women whose husbands were earning no money, did work for wages at times, as cooks, laundresses, and tavernkeepers. And in the sexually imbalanced mining communities, there was always a ready market for prostitutes.

The thousands of people who flocked to the mining towns in search of quick wealth and failed to find it often remained as wage laborers in corporate mines after the boom period, working in almost uniformly terrible conditions. In the 1870s, one worker in every thirty was disabled in the mines, and one in every eighty was killed. That rate fell later in the nineteenth century, but mining remained one of the most dangerous and arduous working environments in the United States.

THE CATTLE KINGDOM

A second important element of the changing economy of the Far West was cattle ranching. The open range—the vast grasslands of the public domain—provided a huge area on the Great Plains where cattle raisers could graze their herds.

The western cattle industry was born slowly and through the pioneering work of Mexicans, Texans, white settlers, and free and enslaved blacks. Long before citizens of the United States entered the Southwest, Mexican ranchers had developed the techniques and equipment that the cattlemen and cowboys of the Great Plains later employed: branding, roundups, roping, and the gear of the herders—their lariats, saddles, leather chaps, and spurs. Americans in Texas, with the largest herds of cattle in the country, adopted these methods and carried them to the northernmost ranges of the cattle kingdom. From Texas, too, came the small, muscular horses (broncos and mustangs) that enabled cowboys to control the herds.

At the end of the Civil War, an estimated 5 million cattle roamed the Texas ranges. Eastern markets offered good prices for steers. The challenge facing the cattle industry lay in getting the animals from the range to towns on major rail lines. Early in 1866, some Texas cattle ranchers began driving their combined herds, up to 260,000 steers, north to Sedalia, Missouri, on the Missouri Pacific Railroad. The caravan suffered heavy losses but established a new and important feature of their business: namely, that cattle could be driven to distant markets and pastured along the trail. This earliest of the **long drives** established the first, tentative link between the isolated cattle breeders of west Texas and the booming urban markets of the East.

Market facilities soon grew up at Abilene, Kansas, on the Kansas Pacific Railroad, and for years the town reigned as the railhead of the cattle kingdom. But by the mid-1870s, agricultural development in western Kansas had eaten away at the open-range land. Cattlemen had to develop other trails and other market outlets. As the railroads reached farther west, other locations began to rival Abilene as major centers of stock herding: Dodge City and Wichita in Kansas, Ogallala and Sidney in Nebraska, Cheyenne and Laramie in Wyoming, and Miles City and Glendive in Montana.

There had always been an element of risk and speculation in the open-range cattle business. Rustlers and Indians frequently seized large numbers of animals. But as the settlement of the plains increased, new forms of competition arose. Sheep breeders from California and Oregon brought their flocks onto the range to compete for grass. Farmers ("nesters") from the East threw fences around their claims, blocking trails and breaking up the open range. A series of **"range wars"**—between sheepmen and cattlemen, ranchers, and farmers—erupted out of the tensions among these competing groups.

Accounts of the lofty profits to be made in the cattle business tempted eastern, English, and Scottish capital to the plains. Increasingly, the structure of the cattle economy became

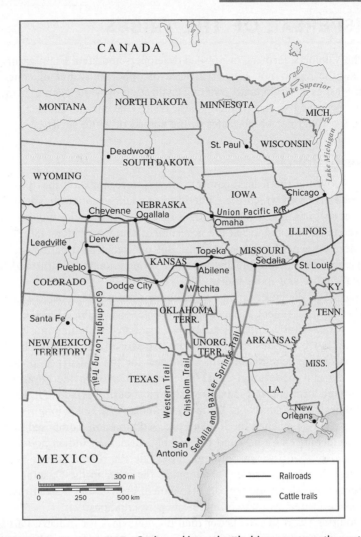

THE CATTLE KINGDOM, CA. 1866–1887 Cattle ranching and cattle drives are among the most romanticized features of the nineteenth-century West. But they were also hardheaded businesses, made possible by the growing eastern market for beef and the availability of reasonably inexpensive transportation—thanks to the dense network of trails and railroads—to take cattle to the urban markets. • *Why was the open range necessary for the great cattle drives, and what eventually ended the cattle trails?*

corporate; in one year, twenty corporations with a combined capital of $12 million were chartered in Wyoming. The result of this frenzied, speculative expansion was that the ranges, already shrunk by the railroads and the farmers, became overstocked. There was not enough grass to support the crowding herds or sustain the long drives. Two severe winters, in 1885–1886 and 1886–1887, and a searing summer between them scorched the plains. Streams and grass dried up. Hundreds of thousands of cattle died. Princely ranches and costly investments disappeared in a season.

The open-range industry never recovered, and the long drive finally disappeared for good. Railroads displaced the trail as the route to market for livestock. But some established cattle ranches survived, grew, and prospered, eventually producing more beef than ever.

THE DISPERSAL OF THE TRIBES

Be they ranchers, miners, farmers, or railroad developers and laborers, migrants to the West tended to view the region not only as a place of opportunity but of conquest. Having imagined the West as a "virgin land" awaiting civilization by white people, many Americans tried to force the region to match their image of it. That meant, above all, ensuring that the Indian tribes would not be obstacles to the spread of white society.

WHITE TRIBAL POLICIES

The traditional policy of the federal government was to regard the tribes simultaneously as independent nations (with which the United States could negotiate treaties) and as wards of the president (who would exercise paternalistic authority over the Indians). The concept of Indian sovereignty had supported the government's attempt before 1860 to erect a permanent frontier between whites and Indians. But the belief in tribal sovereignty and the treaties or agreements with the Indians were not strong enough to withstand the desire of white settlers for more and more Indian lands.

By the early 1850s, the government adopted a new approach known as the **concentration policy**. In 1851, the government assigned each tribe its own defined reservation, confirmed by individual treaties—treaties often illegitimately negotiated with unauthorized Indian "representatives" chosen by whites, people known sarcastically as "treaty chiefs." The new arrangement had many benefits for whites and few for the Indians. It divided the tribes from one another and made them easier to control. It allowed the government to force tribes into scattered locations and to take over the most desirable lands for white settlement. But concentration did not survive as the basis of Indian policy for long.

In 1867, Congress established the Indian Peace Commission, composed of both soldiers and civilians, to recommend a new and presumably permanent Indian policy. The commission recommended that the government move all the Plains tribes into two large reservations—one in Indian Territory (Oklahoma), the other in the Dakotas. At a series of meetings with the tribes, government agents cajoled, bribed, and tricked their representatives into agreeing to treaties establishing the new reservations.

But this "solution" worked little better than previous ones for Indians. Part of the problem were the corrupt or incompetent agents of the Bureau of Indian Affairs who administered the reservations. The problem was also exacerbated by the relentless slaughter of buffalo herds by whites that destroyed the tribes' way of life. After the Civil War, professional and amateur hunters—even casual visitors shooting from passing trains—swarmed over the plains, slaughtering the huge animals. Some Indian tribes (notably the Blackfeet) also began killing large numbers of buffalo to sell in the booming new market for their hides and meat. In 1865, there had been at least 15 million buffalo; two decades later, fewer than 1,000 of the great beasts survived. By destroying the buffalo herds, whites were destroying the Indians' source of food and supplies and their ability to resist white advance.

THE INDIAN WARS

Whites and Indians fought incessantly from the 1850s to the 1880s, as Indians struggled against the growing threats to their civilizations. Indian warriors attacked wagon trains, stagecoaches, and isolated ranches, often in retaliation for earlier attacks on them by whites. As the U.S. Army became more deeply involved in the fighting, the tribes began to focus more of their attacks on white soldiers.

(Source: NPS photo by JR Douglas)

BUFFALO HIDE MANIA A boom in the popularity of Buffalo hides after the Civil War led to the widespread and indiscriminate slaughter of Buffalo, rendering the species nearly extinct by the late 1800s.

At times, this small-scale fighting escalated. During the Civil War, the eastern Sioux in Minnesota, cramped on a small reservation and exploited by corrupt white agents, suddenly rebelled. Led by Little Crow, they killed more than 700 whites before being subdued. Thirty-eight of the Indians were hanged, and the tribe was exiled to the Dakotas.

At the same time, fighting flared up in eastern Colorado, where the Arapaho and Cheyenne were coming into conflict with white miners settling in the region. Bands of Indians attacked stagecoach lines and settlements in an effort to regain territory they had lost. In response to these incidents, whites called up a large territorial militia. The governor urged all friendly Indians to congregate at army posts for protection before the army began its campaign. One Arapaho and Cheyenne band under Black Kettle, apparently in response to the invitation, camped near Fort Lyon on Sand Creek in November 1864. Some members of the party were warriors, but Black Kettle believed he was under official protection and exhibited no hostile intention. Nevertheless, Colonel J. M. Chivington led a volunteer militia force—largely consisting of unemployed miners, many of whom were apparently drunk—to the unsuspecting camp and massacred 133 people, 105 of them women and children. Black Kettle himself escaped the Sand Creek massacre. But four years later, in 1868, he and Cheyenne soldiers went to war with the whites. The Indians were caught on the Washita River, near the Texas border, by Colonel George A. Custer. White troops killed the chief and his people.

At the end of the Civil War, white troops stepped up their wars against the western Indians on several fronts. The most serious and sustained conflict was in Montana, where the army was attempting to build a road, the Bozeman Trail, to connect Fort Laramie, Wyoming, to the new mining centers. The western Sioux resented this intrusion into the heart of their buffalo range. Led by one of their great chiefs, Red Cloud, they so harried the soldiers and the construction party that the road could not be used.

But it was not only the U.S. military that harassed the tribes. White vigilantes engaged in what became known as "Indian hunting" or unofficial campaigns of violence. Sometimes the killing was in response to Indian raids on white communities. But considerable numbers of whites were committed to the goal of literal "elimination" of the tribes whatever their behavior, a goal that rested on the belief in the essential inhumanity of Indians and the impossibility of white coexistence with them. In California, civilians killed close to 5,000 Indians between 1850 and 1880—one of many factors (disease and poverty being the more important) that steadily reduced the Indian population of the state from 150,000 before the Civil War to 30,000 in 1870.

The treaties negotiated in 1867 brought a temporary lull to many of the conflicts. But new forces soon shattered the peace again. In the early 1870s, more waves of white settlers, mostly miners, began to penetrate the lands in Dakota Territory supposedly guaranteed to the tribes in 1867. Indian resistance flared anew. In the northern plains, the Sioux rose up in 1875 and left their reservation. When white officials ordered them to return, bands of warriors gathered in Montana and united under two great leaders: Crazy Horse and Sitting Bull. Three U.S. Army columns set out to round them up and force them back onto the reservation. With the expedition, as colonel of the famous Seventh Cavalry, was the colorful and controversial George A. Custer. At the Battle of the **Little Bighorn** in southern Montana in 1876, an unprecedentedly large army, perhaps 2,500 tribal warriors, surprised Custer and part of his regiment, surrounded them, and killed every soldier.

But the Indians did not have the political organization or the supplies to keep their troops united. Soon the warriors drifted off in bands to elude pursuit or search for food, and the army ran them down and returned them to Dakota. The power of the Sioux quickly collapsed. They accepted defeat and life on reservations.

One of the most dramatic episodes in Indian history occurred in Idaho in 1877. The Nez Percé were a small and relatively peaceful tribe, some of whose members had managed to live unmolested in Oregon into the 1870s without ever signing a treaty with the United States. But under pressure from white settlers, the U.S. government forced them to move onto a reservation. With no realistic prospect of resisting, the Indians began the journey to the reservation; but on the way, several younger Indians, drunk and angry, killed four white settlers.

The leader of the band, **Chief Joseph**, persuaded his followers to flee from the inevitable retribution. American troops pursued and attacked them, only to be driven off in a battle at White Bird Canyon. After that, the Nez Percé scattered in several directions and became part of a remarkable chase. Joseph moved with 200 warriors and 350 women, children, and old people in an effort to reach Canada. Pursued by four columns of American soldiers, the Indians covered 1,321 miles in seventy-five days, repelling or evading the army time and again. They were finally caught just short of the Canadian boundary. Some escaped and slipped across the border; but Joseph and most of his followers, weary and discouraged, finally gave up. "Hear me, my chiefs," Joseph said after meeting with the American general Nelson Miles, "I am tired. My heart is sick and sad. From where the sun now stands, I will fight no more forever."

The last Indians to maintain organized resistance against the whites were the Chiricahua Apache. The two ablest chiefs of this tribe were Mangas Colorados and Cochise. Mangas was murdered during the Civil War by white soldiers who tricked him into surrendering. In 1872 Cochise agreed to peace in exchange for a reservation that included some of the tribe's traditional land. But Cochise died in 1874, and his successor, **Geronimo**, fought on for more than a decade longer, establishing bases in the mountains of Arizona and Mexico and leading warriors in intermittent raids against white outposts. With each raid, however, the number of warring Apache dwindled, as some warriors died and others drifted away to the reservation. By 1886, Geronimo's band consisted of only about 30 people, including women and children, while his white pursuers numbered perhaps 10,000. Geronimo recognized the odds and surrendered.

The Apache Wars, the most violent of all the Indian conflicts, produced brutality on both sides. But it was the whites who committed the most flagrant atrocities. That did not end with the conclusion of the Apache Wars. Another tragic encounter occurred in 1890 as a result of a religious revival among the Sioux—a revival that itself symbolized the catastrophic effects of the white assaults on Indian civilization. As other tribes had done in trying times in the past, many of these Indians turned to a prophet who led them in a religious revival.

This time the prophet was Wovoka, a Paiute who inspired a fervent spiritual awakening that began in Nevada and spread quickly to the plains. Wovoka predicted the imminent coming of a messiah. The new revival's most conspicuous feature was a mass, emotional "Ghost Dance," which inspired ecstatic, mystical visions—including images of the retreat of white people from the plains and a restoration of the great buffalo herds. White agents on the Sioux reservation, bewildered and fearful, warned the army that dances might be the prelude to hostilities.

On December 29, 1890, the Seventh Cavalry tried to round up a group of about 350 cold and starving Sioux at **Wounded Knee**, South Dakota. Fighting broke out in which about 40 white soldiers and up to 200 Indians died. An Indian may have fired the first shot, but the battle soon turned into a one-sided massacre, as the white soldiers turned their new machine guns on the Indians and mowed them down in the snow.

THE DAWES ACT

Even before the Ghost Dance and the Wounded Knee tragedies, the federal government had moved to destroy forever the tribal structure that was the cornerstone of Indian culture. Reversing its policy of nearly fifty years, Congress abolished the practice by which tribes owned reservation lands communally. The new policy required Indians to become landowners and farmers, to abandon their collective society and culture and become part of white civilization. Some supporters of the new policy believed they were acting for the good of the Indians, whom they considered a "vanishing race" in need of rescue by and assimilation into white society.

The **Dawes Severalty Act** of 1887 provided for the gradual elimination of most tribal ownership of land and the allotment of tracts to individual owners: 160 acres to the head of a family, 80 acres to a single adult or orphan, 40 acres to each dependent child. Adult owners were given U.S. citizenship, but unlike other citizens, they could not gain full title to their property for twenty-five years (supposedly to prevent them from selling the land to speculators).

In applying the Dawes Act, the Bureau of Indian Affairs relentlessly promoted the idea of assimilation that lay behind it. Not only did agents of the bureau try to move Indian families onto their own plots of land, they also took many Indian children away from their families and sent them to boarding schools run by whites. They moved as well to stop Indian religious rituals and encouraged the spread of Christianity and the creation of Christian churches on the reservations.

CARLISLE INDIAN SCHOOL. This 1904 photo captures young Native American men at work in a metal shop at The Carlisle School in Carlisle, Pennsylvania. The Carlisle School was a federally-funded boarding school dedicated to "remaking" Indian children and adolescents into hard-working citizens capable of participating in white society. Students were expected to leave behind their tribal culture and clothing and adopt the behavior, values, and fashion of white America. Thousands of Indians from dozens of tribes attended Carlisle during its existence from 1879 to 1918. It was one of twenty-six such schools operated by the Bureau of Indian Affairs at the turn of the twentieth century.

Few Indians were prepared for this wrenching change. In any case, white administration of the Dawes Act was so corrupt and inept that ultimately the government simply abandoned most efforts to enforce it. Much of the reservation land, therefore, was never distributed to individual owners.

THE RISE AND DECLINE
OF THE WESTERN FARMER

The arrival of the miners, the empire building of the cattle ranchers, the dispersal of the Indian tribes—all served as a prelude to the decisive phase of white settlement of the Far West. Even before the Civil War, farmers had begun moving into the plains region, challenging the dominance of the ranchers and the Indians. By the 1870s, what was once a trickle had become a deluge. Western journalists and visitors alike told tall tales of money to be had for the taking: the region's healthy climate, pure water, fertile soil, and nutrient-rich grasses, they crowed, made industries like cattle ranching into can't-miss investment opportunities. (See "Consider the Source: Walter Baron Von Richthofen, *Cattle Raising on the Plains in North America*.") And they came. Farmers poured into the plains and beyond, enclosed land that had once been hunting territory for Indians and open range for cattle, and established a new agricultural region.

For a time in the late 1870s and early 1880s, the new western farmers flourished, enjoying the fruits of an agricultural economic boom. Beginning in the mid-1880s, however, the boom turned to bust, and the western agricultural economy began a long, steady decline.

FARMING ON THE PLAINS

Many factors combined to produce the surge of post–Civil War western agricultural settlement, but the most important was the railroads. Before the war, the Great Plains had been accessible only through a difficult journey by wagon. But beginning in the 1860s, a great new network of railroad lines made huge areas of settlement accessible for the first time.

(Source: Library of Congress, American Memory Collection [rbpe.13401300])

RAILROAD LAND ADVERTISEMENT.   Like many railroad companies in the late 1800s, the Burlington & Missouri sponsored migration to the West by offering favorable terms of credit for land purchase to interested parties.

WALTER BARON VON RICHTHOFEN, *CATTLE RAISING ON THE PLAINS IN NORTH AMERICA* (1885)

Boosters of the West's lucrative economy were plentiful. Walter Baron Von Richthofen, an immigrant and scion of an aristocratic German Austrian family, lauded cattle ranching as a western industry that begged for investors eager to make easy money.

The immense profits which have been universally realized in the Western cattle business for the past, and which will be increased in the future, owing to the more economical methods pursued, so long as ranges can be purchased at present prices, may seem incredible to many of my readers, who, no doubt, have considered the stories of the fortunes realized as myths. Yet it is true that many men who started only a few years ago with comparatively few cattle, are now wealthy, and, in some cases, millionaires. They certainly did not find the gold upon the prairies, nor did they have any source of revenue beyond the increase of their cattle. The agencies producing this immense wealth are very natural and apparent.

The climate of the West is the healthiest on the earth; the pure, high mountain air and dry atmosphere are the natural remedies, or rather preventives, against sickness among cattle in general, and against all epidemic diseases in particular; for "nowhere in the Western states do we find any traces of pleuro-pneumonia, foot or mouth, and such like contagious diseases."

The pure, clear water of the mountain rivers affords to cattle another health preserver, and the fine nutritious and bountiful grasses, and in winter the naturally cured hay, furnish to them the healthiest natural food.

Formerly these pastures cost nothing, and at present only a trifle . . . so that the interest on the investment in purchasing land is of little importance in the estimate of the cost of keeping a herd. In fact, ownership of land is now indispensable for a herd-owner. This land in less than ten years will be a considerable factor in the profits of the cattle business, as the value of pastures will constantly-increase.

The principal cost of raising cattle is only the herding and watching the cattle by herders, without any cost for sheltering or feeding. In time even these expenses will be reduced, as now already herds are kept in large fenced ranges, and many of the herders are dispensed with.

The losses of cattle, as shown by statistics, are larger among Eastern and European herds, which are sheltered in stables and fed the whole year round, than among the shelterless herds of the West. The losses in the West . . . are practically reduced by long experience to a certain percentage, which enables the stockmen to calculate infallibly the profits and losses of their business.

This annual loss is found to average 2 to 3 per cent. We may safely put the loss in the extreme Northern states at about 3 per cent, and in the more Southern and temperate districts at 2 or less per cent. The annual cost of herding the cattle . . . is about $.70 per head; adding the other expenses, such as taxes, loss of interest on the purchase-money of land, etc., we find that the entire annual expense is less than $1.50 per head.

Now let me illustrate the profits realized from one Texas cow, worth $30.00. In ten years she will have eight calves, which, if they are all steers, will have produced at the end of fourteen years $320, or a profit of $272.00. The cow herself still remains, and is worth about her original cost for the butcher. These figures are made without reference to any increase in the value of cattle or beef, and without reference to any improvement of the stock by crossing it with better blood. . . .

Ten years ago an Irish servant-girl wanted money due her, amounting to $150, from a cattle-raiser who lived in Montana. Cattle had been dull, and he could not dispose of any of his herd, but agreed to her to brand fifteen cows in her name, give her the increase, and carry them with his herd, free of cost, until she was ready to sell, he to have the first privilege of purchase. She accepted, held on to her purchase, and last May sold out her master for $25,000.

Source: Von Richthofen, Walter Baron, *Cattle Raising on the Plains of North America,* 1885; repr., Norman, OK: University of Oklahoma Press, 1964, 70–73, 80; located in Marilynn S. Johnson (ed.), *Violence in the West: The Johnson County Range War and the Ludlow Massacre: A Brief History with Documents,* Boston, MA: Bedford St. Martin's, 2009, 37–39.

UNDERSTAND, ANALYZE, & EVALUATE

1. How did Von Richthofen describe the land and natural resources for cattle ranching in the North American plains? Why did Von Richthofen stress the importance of landownership?

2. Does Von Richthofen strike you as a cautious businessman? What might explain the confidence he showed in his projections?

3. Why do you think the author concluded with the example of the Irish servant girl?

The building of the transcontinental train line—completed in 1869 when the two lines met at Promontory Point, Utah—was a dramatic and monumental achievement. But the construction of subsidiary lines in the following years proved of greater importance to the West. State governments, imitating Washington, subsidized railroad development by offering direct financial aid, favorable loans, and more than 50 million acres of land (on top of the 130 million acres the federal government had already provided). Although built and operated by private corporations, the railroads were in many respects public projects.

The railroad companies actively promoted settlement to create new markets. New communities would consume and generate the goods their lines would transport, and the railroads could profit by selling the land they had gained for free, or for very little money, from local and federal government.

Contributing further to the great surge of white agricultural expansion was a pronounced but temporary change in the climate of the Great Plains. For several years in succession, beginning in the 1870s, rainfall in the plains states was well above average. White Americans now rejected the old idea that the region was the "Great American Desert."

But even under the most favorable conditions, farming on the plains presented special problems. First was the problem of fencing. Farmers had to enclose their land, but materials for traditional wood or stone fences were unavailable. In the mid-1870s, however, two Illinois farmers, Joseph H. Glidden and I. L. Ellwood, solved this problem by developing and marketing barbed wire, which became standard equipment on the plains and revolutionized fencing practices all over the world.

The second problem was water. Water was scarce even when rainfall was above average. After 1887, a series of dry seasons began, and lands that had been fertile now returned to semidesert. Some farmers dealt with the problem by using deep wells pumped by steel windmills, by turning to "dryland farming" (a system of tillage designed to conserve moisture in the soil by covering it with a dust blanket), or by planting drought-resistant crops. In many areas of the plains, however, only large-scale irrigation could save the endangered farms. But irrigation projects of the necessary magnitude required government assistance, and neither the federal nor the state governments were prepared to fund the projects.

Most of the people who moved into the region had previously been farmers in the Midwest, the East, or Europe. In the booming years of the early 1880s, with land values rising, the new farmers had no problem obtaining extensive and easy credit. But the arid years of the late 1880s—during which crop prices fell while production became more expensive—changed the farmers' prospects. Tens of thousands of farmers could not pay their debts and were forced to abandon their farms. There was, in effect, a reverse migration: white settlers moving back east, sometimes turning once-flourishing western communities into desolate ghost towns. Those who remained continued to suffer from falling prices (for example, wheat, which had sold for $1.60 a bushel at the end of the Civil War, dropped to 49 cents in the 1890s) and persistent indebtedness.

COMMERCIAL AGRICULTURE

By the late nineteenth century, the sturdy, independent farmer of popular myth was being replaced by the commercial farmer—attempting to do in the agricultural economy what industrialists were doing in the manufacturing economy. Commercial farmers specialized in cash crops that were sold in national or world markets. They did not often make their own household supplies or grow their own food but bought them from merchants. This kind of farming, when it was successful, raised farmers' living standards. But it also made them dependent on bankers and interest rates, railroads and freight rates, national and European markets, world supply and demand. And unlike the capitalists of the industrial order, they could not regulate their production or influence the prices of what they sold.

Between 1865 and 1900, farm output increased dramatically, not only in the United States but in Brazil, Argentina, Canada, Australia, New Zealand, Russia, and elsewhere. Beginning in the 1880s, worldwide overproduction led to a drop in prices for most agricultural goods and hence to great economic distress for many of the more than 6 million American farm families. By the 1890s, 27 percent of the farms in the country were mortgaged; by 1910, 33 percent. In 1880, 25 percent of all farms had been operated by tenants; by 1910, the proportion had grown to 37 percent. Commercial farming made some people fabulously wealthy. But the farm economy as a whole was suffering a significant decline relative to the rest of the nation.

THE FARMERS' GRIEVANCES

American farmers were painfully aware that something was wrong. But few people yet understood the implications of national and world overproduction. Instead, they concentrated their attention and anger on more immediate, more comprehensible—and no less real—problems: inequitable freight rates, high interest charges, and an inadequate currency.

The farmers' first and most burning grievance was against the railroads. In many cases, the railroads charged higher rates for farm goods than for other goods, and for transport in the South and West than in the Northeast. Railroads also controlled elevator and warehouse facilities in buying centers and charged arbitrary storage rates.

Farmers also resented the institutions controlling credit—banks, loan companies, insurance corporations. Since sources of credit in the West and South were few, farmers had to take loans on whatever terms they could get, often at very high interest rates ranging from 10 to 25 percent. Many farmers had to pay back these loans in years when crop prices were dropping and, after 1873, when the supply of money in circulation contracted because the federal government eliminated the minting of silver coins. During times when the money supply tightened, banks and creditors assessed borrowers like farmers much higher fees and interest rates. As a result, expansion of the currency became an increasingly important issue to farmers.

A third grievance concerned prices. A farmer could plant a large crop at a moment when its price was high and find that by the time of the harvest the price had declined. Farmers' fortunes rose and fell in response to unpredictable forces. But many farmers became convinced (often with some reason) that "intermediaries"–speculators, bankers, regional and local agents–were conspiring with one another to fix prices so as to benefit themselves at the growers' expense. Many farmers also came to believe (again, not entirely without reason) that manufacturers in the East were colluding to keep the prices of farm goods low and the prices of industrial goods high. Although farmers sold their crops in a competitive world market, they bought manufactured goods in a domestic market protected by tariffs and dominated by trusts and corporations.

THE AGRARIAN MALAISE

These economic difficulties helped produce social and cultural resentments. Among them was the isolation of farm life. Farm families in some parts of the country were virtually cut off from the outside world. During the winter months, the loneliness and boredom could become nearly unbearable. Many farmers lacked access to adequate education for their children. They had few or no proper medical facilities. There were few organized recreational or cultural activities. Older farmers felt the sting of watching their children leave the farm for the city. They felt the humiliation of being ridiculed as "hayseeds" by the new urban culture that was coming to dominate American life.

This sense of isolation and obsolescence led to a growing malaise among many farmers, a discontent that helped create a great national political movement in the 1890s. It found reflection, too, in some of the literature that emerged from rural America. Writers in the late nineteenth century might romanticize the rugged life of the cowboy and the western miner. For the farmers, however, the image of the agricultural world was different. Hamlin Garland, for example, reflected the growing disillusionment in a series of novels and short stories. In the introduction to his novel *Jason Edwards* (1891), he wrote that in the past, the agrarian frontier had seemed to be "the Golden West, the land of wealth and freedom and happiness." Now, however, the bright promise had faded. The trials of rural life were crushing the human spirit. "So this is the reality of the dream!" a character in *Jason Edwards* exclaims, "A shanty on a barren plain, hot and lone as a desert. My God!" Once, sturdy yeoman farmers had viewed themselves as the backbone of American life. Now they were becoming painfully aware that their position was declining in relation to the rising urban-industrial society to the east.

CONCLUSION

To many Americans in the late nineteenth century, the West seemed an untamed "frontier" in which hardy pioneers were creating a new society. The reality of the West in these years, however, was very different from this enduring image. White Americans moved into the vast regions west of the Mississippi at a remarkable rate in the years after the Civil War, and many of them indeed settled in lands far from any civilization they had ever known. But the West was not an empty place. It contained a large population of Indians, with whom the white settlers sometimes lived uneasily and with whom they sometimes battled; but almost always in the end, the Indians were pushed aside and (with help from the federal government) relocated onto lands whites did not want. There were significant numbers of Mexicans in some areas, small populations of Asians in others, and African Americans moving in from the South in search of land and freedom. The West was no barren frontier but a place of many cultures.

The West was also closely and increasingly tied to the emerging capitalist-industrial economy of the East. The miners who flooded into California, Colorado, Nevada, the Dakotas, and elsewhere were responding to the demand in the East for gold and silver, but even more for iron ore, copper, lead, zinc, and quartz. Cattle and sheep ranchers produced meat, wool, and leather for eastern consumers and manufacturers. Farmers grew crops for sale in national and international commodities markets. The West certainly looked different from the East. But the growth of the West was very much a part of the growth of the rest of the nation. And the culture of the West, despite the romantic images of pioneering individuals embraced by easterners and westerners alike, was at its heart as much a culture of economic growth and capitalist ambition as was that of the rest of the nation.

KEY TERMS/PEOPLE/PLACES/EVENTS

Californios 383	Dawes Severalty Act 397	Mark Twain 389
Chief Joseph 396	Geronimo 396	range wars 392
Chinese Exclusion Act 386	Homestead Act 386	Rocky Mountain school 387
concentration policy 394	Little Bighorn 396	Turner thesis 390
coolies 384	long drive 392	Wounded Knee 397

RECALL AND REFLECT

1. How did ethnic, racial, and cultural prejudice affect western society?
2. What were the three major industries involved in the development of the West, and how did these industries transform the western economy?
3. What was the romantic image of the West, and how was this image expressed in art, literature, and popular culture?
4. How did actions and policies of the federal government affect the fate of Indians in the West?

17 INDUSTRIAL SUPREMACY

SOURCES OF INDUSTRIAL GROWTH
CAPITALISM AND ITS CRITICS
THE ORDEAL OF THE WORKER

LOOKING AHEAD

1. What factors drove America's industrial expansion in the late nineteenth and early twentieth centuries?
2. Who were the critics of America's new industrial economy, what were their criticisms, and what solutions did they propose?
3. How did the conditions and characteristics of the workforce change during this period of rapid industrialization?

"TWENTY-FIVE YEARS AFTER THE DEATH of Lincoln, America had become, in the quantity and value of her products, the leading manufacturing nation of the world. What England had accomplished in a hundred years, the United States had achieved in half the time." So boasted the historians Charles and Mary Beard in the 1920s, expressing the amazement many Americans felt when they considered the remarkable expansion of their industrial economy in the late nineteenth century.

In fact, America's rise to industrial supremacy was not as sudden as such observers suggested. The nation had been building a manufacturing economy since early in the nineteenth century. But Americans were clearly correct in observing that the accomplishments of the last three decades of the nineteenth century overshadowed all the earlier progress.

The remarkable growth did much to increase the wealth and improve the lives of many Americans. But such benefits were unequally shared. While industrial titans and a growing middle class were enjoying a prosperity without precedent in the nation's history, workers, farmers, and others were experiencing an often painful ordeal that slowly edged the United States toward a great economic and political crisis.

TIME LINE

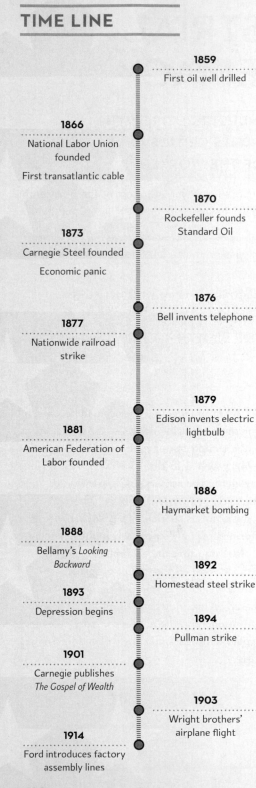

1859
First oil well drilled

1866
National Labor Union founded

First transatlantic cable

1870
Rockefeller founds Standard Oil

1873
Carnegie Steel founded

Economic panic

1876
Bell invents telephone

1877
Nationwide railroad strike

1879
Edison invents electric lightbulb

1881
American Federation of Labor founded

1886
Haymarket bombing

1888
Bellamy's *Looking Backward*

1892
Homestead steel strike

1893
Depression begins

1894
Pullman strike

1901
Carnegie publishes *The Gospel of Wealth*

1903
Wright brothers' airplane flight

1914
Ford introduces factory assembly lines

SOURCES OF INDUSTRIAL GROWTH

Many factors contributed to the growth of American industry: abundant raw materials, a large and growing labor supply, a surge in technological innovation, the emergence of a talented and often ruthless group of entrepreneurs, a federal government eager to assist the growth of business, and an expanding domestic market for the products of manufacturing.

INDUSTRIAL TECHNOLOGIES

The rapid emergence of new technologies, together with the discovery of new materials and productive processes, were among the principal sources of late-nineteenth-century industrial growth. Some of the most important innovations were in communications. In 1866, Cyrus W. Field laid a transatlantic telegraph cable to Europe. During the next decade, Alexander Graham Bell developed the first telephone with commercial capacity. By 1900, there were 1.35 million telephones, and by 1920, 13.3 million. And the Italian inventor Guglielmo Marconi was taking the first steps toward the development of radio in the 1890s; the technology he pioneered quickly found its way to the United States. Other inventions that speeded the pace of business organization were the typewriter (by Christopher L. Sholes in 1868), the cash register (by James Ritty in 1879), and the calculating, or adding, machine (by William S. Burroughs in 1891).

Among the most revolutionary innovations was the introduction in the 1870s of electricity as a source of light and power. The pioneers of electric lighting included Charles F. Brush, who devised the arc lamp for street illumination, and Thomas A. Edison, who invented the incandescent lamp (or lightbulb). Edison and others designed improved generators and built large power plants to furnish electricity to whole cities. By the turn of the century, electric power was becoming commonplace in street railway systems, in the elevators of urban skyscrapers, in factories, and increasingly in offices and homes.

Particularly important to trade and industry was the development of new high-efficiency steam engines capable of powering larger ships at faster speeds than ever before. The new high-speed freighters, for example, made it cheaper for Britain to buy wheat grown in Canada and the United States than to grow it at home. The introduction of refrigerated ships in the 1870s made it possible to transport meat from North America, and even Australia and Asia, to Europe.

The Technology of Iron and Steel Production

Iron production had developed slowly in the United States through most of the nineteenth century, mostly driven by the demand for iron rails; steel production had developed hardly at all by the end of the Civil War. In the 1870s and 1880s, however, iron production soared as railroads added 40,000 new miles of track, and steel production made great strides toward its eventual dominance in the metals industry.

An Englishman, Henry Bessemer, and an American, William Kelly, developed, almost simultaneously, a process for converting iron into the much more durable and versatile steel. (The process, which took Bessemer's name, consisted of blowing air through molten iron to burn out the impurities and create a much stronger metal.) The Bessemer process also relied on the discovery by the British metallurgist Robert Mushet that ingredients could be added during the conversion process to give steel additional strength. In 1868, the New Jersey ironmaster Abram S. Hewitt introduced from Europe another method of making steel—the open-hearth process. These techniques made possible the production of steel in great quantities and large dimensions, for use in the manufacture of locomotives, rails, and girders for the construction of tall buildings.

The steel industry emerged first in western Pennsylvania and eastern Ohio, partly because iron ore could be found there in abundance. It was also because the new forms of steel production created a demand for new kinds of fuel—and particularly for the anthracite (or hard) coal that was plentiful in Pennsylvania. Later, new techniques made it possible to use bituminous (or soft) coal, also easily mined in western Pennsylvania. As a result, Pittsburgh quickly became the center of the steel world. New sources of ore soon emerged. The upper peninsula of Michigan, the Mesabi Range in Minnesota, and central Alabama became important ore-producing locales and new centers of steel production grew up near them: Cleveland, Detroit, Chicago, and Birmingham, among others.

Until the Civil War, iron and steel furnaces were mostly made of stone and usually built against the side of a hill to reduce construction demands. By the 1870s, however, furnaces were redesigned as cylindrical iron shells lined with brick. These massive new furnaces were 75 feet tall and higher and could produce over 500 tons a week.

As the steel industry spread, new transportation systems emerged to serve it. Steel production in the Great Lakes region produced steam freighters that could carry ore on the lakes. Shippers used new steam engines to speed the unloading of ore. The demand for vessels capable of transporting oil and the development of new and more powerful steam engines led to the design of larger and heavier freighters.

There was an even closer relationship between the emerging steel companies and the railroads. Steel manufacturers provided rails and parts for cars; railroads were both markets for and transporters of manufactured steel. But the relationship soon became more intimate than that. The Pennsylvania Railroad, for example, actually created the Pennsylvania Steel Company.

(Source: Library of Congress, Prints and Photographs Division [LC-USZ62-63520])

PIONEER OIL RUN, 1865 The American oil industry emerged first in western Pennsylvania, where speculators built makeshift facilities almost overnight. An oil field on the other side of the hill depicted here had been producing 600 barrels a day, and the wells quickly spilled over the hill and down the slope shown in the photograph.

The steel industry's need for lubrication for its machines helped create another important new industry in the late nineteenth century—oil. (Not until later did oil become important primarily for its potential as a fuel.) The existence of petroleum reserves in western Pennsylvania had been common knowledge for some time. The Pennsylvania businessman George Bissell showed that the substance could be burned in lamps and that it could also yield such products as paraffin, naphtha, and lubricating oil. Bissell raised money to begin drilling; and in 1859, Edwin L. Drake, one of Bissell's employees, established the first oil well near Titusville, Pennsylvania, which soon produced 500 barrels of oil a month. Demand for petroleum grew quickly, and promoters soon developed other oil fields in Pennsylvania, Ohio, and West Virginia.

THE AUTOMOBILE AND THE AIRPLANE

Among the most important technological innovations was the invention of the automobile. Two technologies led to its development: gasoline and the self-contained engine. Gasoline (or petrol) was the product of an extraction process developed in the late nineteenth century in the United States by which lubricating oil and fuel oil were removed separately from crude oil. As early as the 1870s, designers in France, Germany, and Austria had begun to develop an "internal combustion engine," which used the expanding power of burning gas to drive pistons. A German, Nicolaus August Otto, created a gas-powered "four-stroke" engine in the mid-1860s, which was a precursor to automobile engines. But he did not develop a way to untether it from gas lines to be used portably in machines. One of Otto's former employees, Gottfried Daimler, later perfected an engine that could be used in automobiles. Today's automotive giant Daimler-Benz, maker of Mercedes-Benz vehicles, bears his name.

The American automobile industry developed rapidly in the aftermath of these European breakthroughs. Charles and Frank Duryea built the first gasoline-driven motor vehicle in America in 1893. Three years later, **Henry Ford** produced the first of the famous cars that would bear his name. In 1895, there were only four automobiles on the American highways. By 1917, there were nearly 5 million.

The search for a means of human flight, as old as civilization, had been almost entirely futile until the late nineteenth century, when engineers, scientists, and tinkerers in both the United States and Europe began to experiment with a wide range of aeronautic devices. Balloonists began to consider ways to make dirigibles useful vehicles of transportation. Others experimented with kites and gliders.

Two brothers in Ohio, **Wilbur and Orville Wright**, began to construct a glider in 1899 that could be propelled through the air by an internal combustion engine. Four years later, Orville made a celebrated test flight near Kitty Hawk, North Carolina, in which an airplane took off by itself and traveled 120 feet in twelve seconds under its own power before settling back to earth. By the fall of 1904, the Wright brothers had improved the plane to the point where they were able to fly over twenty-three miles, and in the following year they began to take a few passengers on their flights with them.

Although the first working airplane was built in the United States, aviation technology was slow to gain a foothold in America. Most of the early progress in airplane design occurred in France, where there was substantial government funding for research and development. The U.S. government created the National Advisory Committee on Aeronautics in 1915, twelve years after the Wright brothers' flight, and American airplanes became a significant presence in Europe during World War I. But the prospects for commercial flight seemed dim until the 1920s, when Charles Lindbergh's famous solo flight from New York to Paris electrified the nation and the world.

RESEARCH AND DEVELOPMENT

New industrial technologies persuaded many businesses to build their own research operations. The corporate research-and-development (R&D) laboratories coincided with a decline in government support for research, helping corporations attract skilled researchers. It also decentralized the sources of research funding and ensured that inquiry would move in many directions, and not just along paths determined by the government.

A rift began to emerge between scientists and engineers. Engineers—both inside and outside of universities—became increasingly tied up with the R&D agendas of corporations. Many scientists continued to scorn this "commercialization" of knowledge and preferred to stick to basic research that had no immediate practical applications. But many American scientists were more closely connected to practical challenges than were their European counterparts, and some joined engineers in corporate R&D laboratories, which over time began to sponsor both practical and basic research.

MAKING PRODUCTION MORE EFFICIENT

Central to the growth of the automobile and other industries were changes in the techniques of production. By the turn of the century, many industrialists embraced the new principles of "scientific management," dubbed "**Taylorism**" after its leading theoretician, Frederick Winslow Taylor. Taylor aimed to make human labor compatible with the demands of the machine age. He urged employers to reorganize the production process by subdividing tasks into small simple steps that did not require enormous skill or training to complete. The goal

(©Everett Collection Historical/Alamy)

WOMEN ON THE ASSEMBLY LINE This photograph, from 1902, shows women at work on the lock and drill department assembly line at the National Cash Register Company in Dayton, Ohio.

was to minimize worker errors, speed up the production process, and make workers more interchangeable and therefore easier to replace. Scientific management, Taylor claimed, would create a more efficient and less costly workplace.

The most important change in industrial technology was the emergence of mass production and, along with it, the moving assembly line, which Henry Ford introduced in his automobile plants in 1914. The assembly line was a particular place—a factory through which automobiles moved as they were assembled by workers who specialized in particular tasks. It was also a concept. The concept stressed the complete interchangeability of parts. General Motors adopted the same philosophy. Automobile production relied on other technologies, too, in particular the intensive use of electricity—to drive the assembly line, to light the factories, and to run the critical ventilating systems that kept dust from interfering with the machines. The revolutionary assembly-line technique enabled Ford to raise wages and reduce hours while cutting the base price of his Model T from $950 in 1914 to $290 in 1929. It became a standard for many other industries.

RAILROAD EXPANSION AND THE CORPORATION

The principal agent of industrial development in the late nineteenth century was still the expansion of the railroads. Railroads gave industrialists access to distant markets and remote sources of raw materials. Their expansion across the country created thousands of jobs and fueled the growth of hundreds of new and established communities. Their steady demand for track and train boosted the fortunes of steel plants and coal mines, while their sale of excess land stimulated westward migration.

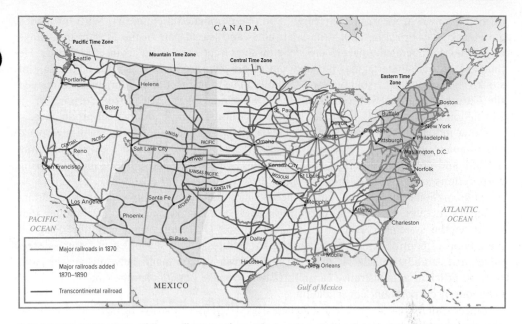

RAILROADS, 1870–1890   This map illustrates the rapid expansion of railroads in the late nineteenth century. In 1870, there was already a dense network of rail lines in the Northeast and Midwest, illustrated here by the green lines. The red lines show the further expansion of rail coverage between 1870 and 1890, much of it in the South and the areas west of the Mississippi River. • *Why were railroads so essential to the nation's economic growth in these years?*

Total railroad trackage increased from 30,000 miles in 1860 to 193,000 in 1900. Vital to this progress was the help of local, state, and federal governments, who provided loans and subsidies. Equally important was the emergence of great railroad "combinations" or mergers that facilitated the development of the industry by concentrating power and resources in the hands of a few powerful men. The achievements and excesses of these tycoons—Cornelius Vanderbilt, James J. Hill, Collis P. Huntington, and others—became symbols to much of the nation of concentrated economic power. But railroad development was less significant for the individual barons it created than for its contribution to the growth of a new institution: the modern corporation.

There had been various forms of corporations in America since colonial times, but the modern corporation emerged as a major force only after the Civil War. By then, railroad magnates and other industrialists realized that their great ventures could not be financed by any single person.

Under the laws of incorporation passed in many states in the 1830s and 1840s, business organizations could raise money by selling stock to members of the public; after the Civil War, one industry after another began doing so. What made these stocks appealing was that investors now had only "limited liability"—they risked only the amount of their investments and were not liable for any debts the corporation might accumulate beyond that point. The ability to sell stock to a broad public made it possible for entrepreneurs to gather vast sums of capital and undertake great projects with manageable financial risk.

The Pennsylvania and other railroads were among the first to adopt the new corporate form of organization. But incorporation quickly spread beyond the railroad industry. **Andrew Carnegie**, a Scottish immigrant, worked his way up from modest beginnings and, in 1873,

opened his own steelworks in Pittsburgh. Soon he dominated the industry. With his associate Henry Clay Frick, he bought up coal mines and leased part of the Mesabi iron range
in Minnesota, operated a fleet of ore ships on the Great Lakes, and acquired railroads. He
financed his vast undertakings not only out of his own profits but also out of the sale of
stock. Then, in 1901, he sold out for $450 million to the banker **J. P. Morgan**, who merged
the Carnegie interests with others to create the giant United States Steel Corporation—a
$14 billion enterprise that controlled almost two-thirds of the nation's steel production.

Other industries developed similarly. Gustavus Swift forged a relatively small meatpacking company into a great national corporation. Isaac Singer patented a sewing machine
in 1851 and created I. M. Singer and Company—one of the first modern manufacturing
corporations.

Large, national business enterprises needed methodical and highly standardized administrative structures. As a result, corporate leaders introduced managerial techniques that
relied on the systematic division of responsibilities. Companies built carefully designed
hierarchies of control, strict cost-accounting procedures, and a new breed of business executives: the "middle managers," who formed a layer of command between workers and
owners. Efficient administrative capabilities helped make possible another major feature of
the modern corporation: consolidation.

Businessmen created large consolidated organizations primarily through two methods.
Horizontal integration combined a number of firms engaged in the same enterprise into a
single corporation such as the consolidation of many different railroad lines into one company. Through **vertical integration**, a company took over all the different businesses on
which it relied for its primary function, for example, Carnegie Steel, which came to control
not only steel mills but also mines, railroads, and other enterprises. In both cases of integration, the result was similar: a new form of business organization that largely eliminated
or severely minimized competition from rivals.

The most celebrated corporate empire of the late nineteenth century was Standard Oil,
owned by **John D. Rockefeller**. Shortly after the Civil War, Rockefeller launched a refining
company in Cleveland and immediately began trying to eliminate his competition. Allying
himself with other wealthy capitalists, he formed the Standard Oil Company of Ohio in
1870, which in a few years had acquired twenty of the twenty-five refineries in Cleveland,
as well as plants in Pittsburgh, Philadelphia, New York, and Baltimore.

So far, Rockefeller had expanded only horizontally—buying many refineries. But soon he
began expanding vertically as well. He built his own barrel factories, terminal warehouses,
and pipelines. Standard Oil owned its own freight cars and developed its own marketing
organization. By the 1880s, Rockefeller had established such dominance within the petroleum industry that to much of the nation he served as a leading symbol of monopoly.

Rockefeller and other industrialists saw consolidation as a way to cope with what they
believed was the greatest curse of the modern economy: "cutthroat competition." Most
businessmen claimed to believe in free enterprise and a competitive marketplace, but in
fact they feared that substantial competition could spell instability and ruin for all.

As the movement toward consolidation accelerated, new vehicles emerged to facilitate
it. The railroads began with so-called pool arrangements—informal agreements among various companies to stabilize rates and divide markets (arrangements that would, in later
years, be known as cartels). But the pool arrangements were too weak and could not ensure
cost stability.

The failure of the pools led to new techniques of consolidation. The next effort to stabilize prices was the creation of the "trust"—pioneered by Standard Oil in the early 1880s

and the banker J. P. Morgan. Under a trust agreement, stockholders in individual corporations transferred their stocks to a small group of trustees in exchange for shares in the trust itself. Owners of trust certificates often had no direct control over the decisions of the trustees; they simply received a share of the profits of the combination. The trustees themselves, on the other hand, might literally own only a few companies but could exercise effective control over many.

In 1889, the state of New Jersey helped produce a third form of consolidation by changing its laws of incorporation to permit companies to buy up rivals. Other states soon followed. Once actual corporate mergers were permitted, the original trusts became unnecessary. Rockefeller, for example, quickly relocated Standard Oil to New Jersey and created what became known as a "holding company"—a central corporate body that would buy up the stock of various members of the Standard Oil trust and establish direct, formal ownership of them.

By the end of the nineteenth century, 1 percent of the corporations in America were able to control more than 33 percent of the manufacturing. A system of economic organization was emerging that lodged enormous power in the hands of very few men—the great bankers of New York such as Morgan, industrial titans such as Rockefeller (who himself gained control of a major bank), and others.

The industrial giants of the era clearly contributed to substantial economic growth. They were also creating the basis for one of the greatest public controversies of their era: a raging debate over concentrated economic and political power that continued well into the twentieth century.

CAPITALISM AND ITS CRITICS

The inequality of the roaring capitalism of the late nineteenth century was not without its critics. Farmers, workers, middle-class businessmen, and many others considered the new capitalism to be a threat to their own destinies. But the industrial titans built a powerful defense for the new corporate economy.

SURVIVAL OF THE FITTEST

The new rationale for capitalism was based on the belief of individualism—an ideology that would remain at the heart of American conservatism for many decades. Wealthy capitalists defended their wealth by saying that they had earned their wealth and power through their own hard work and their acquisitiveness and thrift. Those who failed had only themselves to blame—a result of ignorance, stupidity, or laziness.

Conservative social theories helped support the belief that through "survival of the fittest" wealthy capitalists deserved their success. Among them was the theory of **Social Darwinism.** Darwin's theories argued that the fittest forms of life survived over thousands of years because of their biological fitness. Social Darwinism argued that individuals rose or fell in society because of their innate "fitness." (Darwin himself, along with most scientists, debunked Social Darwinism, but many Americans embraced it nevertheless.) The English philosopher and biologist Herbert Spencer introduced the theory of Social Darwinism in his book *Principles of Biology* (1864). Society, he argued, benefited from the elimination of the unfit and the survival of the strong and talented. William Graham Sumner, a sociologist at Yale, borrowed from Spencer's theory and created a theory of his own in his famous 1906 book *Folkways.* Those who failed, he argued in a 1913 essay, were unfit for success: "Before the tribunal of nature a man has no more right to life than a rattlesnake; he has no more right to liberty than any wild beast; his right to pursuit of happiness is nothing but a license to maintain the struggle for existence." Wealthy corporate leaders were attracted to the ideas of Spencer and Sumner. Their success confirmed their own virtues and "fitness."

Capitalists argued that they earned their wealth through the honest, all-American virtues of competition and the free market. But critics of the industrial and financial titans claimed that they earned their wealth not because of the innate fitness of those who succeeded, but because they replaced the natural workings of the marketplace by building great monopolies that would protect them from competition.

The Gospel of Wealth

Some businessmen attempted to temper the harsh philosophy of Social Darwinism with a gentler, if in some ways equally self-serving, idea: the "**gospel of wealth**." People of great wealth, they argued, had not only great power but also a great responsibility to use their riches to advance social progress. Elaborating on this creed in his 1889 article "The Gospel of Wealth," and elaborated on in the 1901 book of the same title, Andrew Carnegie wrote that people of wealth should consider all revenues in excess of their own needs to be "trust funds" used for the good of the community. (See "Consider the Source: Andrew Carnegie Explains 'The Gospel of Wealth.'") Carnegie was only one of many industrialists who devoted large parts of their fortunes to philanthropic works.

The idea of private wealth as a public blessing existed alongside another popular concept: the notion of great wealth as something available to all. Russell H. Conwell, a Baptist minister, became one of the most prominent spokesmen for the idea by delivering one lecture, "Acres of Diamonds," more than 6,000 times between 1880 and 1900. Conwell told a series of stories, which he claimed were true, of individuals who had found opportunities for extraordinary wealth in their own backyards. (One such story involved a modest farmer who discovered a vast diamond mine in his own fields.) Most of the millionaires in the country, Conwell claimed (inaccurately), had begun on the lowest rung of the economic ladder and had worked their way to success.

But the most famous promoter of the success story was **Horatio Alger**. He was originally a minister in a small town in Massachusetts but was driven from his pulpit as a result of sexual scandals. He moved to New York, where he wrote over a hundred celebrated novels—all of them tributes to social mobility and the ability of Americans to rise from "rags to riches." (See "Patterns of Popular Culture: The Novels of Horatio Alger.")

If Alger's rags-to-riches tales captured the aspiration of many men, **Louisa May Alcott**'s enormously popular novels helped give voice to the often unstated ambitions of many women. Alcott was the daughter of a noted New England reformer, but her family nevertheless experienced considerable hardship. After serving as a nurse in the Civil War and writing a series of popular adventure novels (under a pen name, A. M. Barnard, that disguised her gender), she became a major literary figure with the publication of *Little Women* in 1869 and two sequels over the next twenty years. The main character in these novels, Jo March, struggles to build a life for herself that is not defined by conventional women's roles and ambitions. She spurns a traditional marriage and eventually weds a professor who appears to support her literary ambitions. "Girls write to ask who the little women marry, as if that was the only end and aim of a woman's life," Alcott wrote a friend. "I won't marry Jo to Laurie [the attractive, wealthy neighbor who proposes to her] to please any one." Alcott's female characters, in some ways like Alger's male ones, are remarkable for their independence and drive. Jo March is willful, rebellious, stubborn, ambitious, and often selfish—far from the posed, romantic, submissive women in most popular sentimental novels of Alcott's time aimed at female audiences.

Alternative Visions

Alongside the celebrations of competition and the justifications for great wealth stood a group of alternative philosophies, challenging the corporate ethos and, at times, capitalism itself.

One such philosophy came from the sociologist Lester Frank Ward. In *Dynamic Sociology* (1883) and other books, he argued that civilization was not governed by natural selection but by human intelligence, which could shape society as it wished. In contrast to Sumner, who believed that state intervention to remodel the environment was futile, Ward thought that an active government engaged in positive planning was society's best hope.

Other Americans adopted more-radical approaches to reform. Some dissenters found a home in the Socialist Labor Party, founded in the 1870s and led for many years by Daniel De Leon, an immigrant from the West Indies. Although De Leon attracted a following in the industrial cities, the party never became a major political force and never polled more than 82,000 votes. A dissident faction of De Leon's party, eager to forge stronger ties with organized labor, broke away and in 1901 formed the more enduring **American Socialist Party**.

Other radicals gained a wider following. Among them was the California writer and activist **Henry George**. His angrily eloquent *Progress and Poverty,* published in 1879, became one of the best-selling nonfiction works in American publishing history. George blamed social problems on the ability of a few monopolists to grow wealthy as a result of rising land values. An increase in the value of land, he claimed, was not a result of any effort by the owner, but an "unearned increment," produced by the growth of society around the land. Such profits were rightfully the property of the community. And so George proposed a "single tax" on land, to replace all other taxes, which would return the increment to the people. The tax, he argued, would destroy monopolies, distribute wealth more equally, and eliminate poverty.

Rivaling George in popularity was **Edward Bellamy**, whose utopian novel *Looking Backward,* published in 1888, sold more than 1 million copies. It described the experiences of a young Bostonian who went into a hypnotic sleep in 1887 and awoke in the year 2000 to find a new social order in which want, politics, and vice were unknown. The new society had emerged through a peaceful, evolutionary process: the large trusts of the late nineteenth century had continued to grow in size and to combine with one another until ultimately they formed a single, great trust, controlled by the government, which distributed the abundance of the industrial economy equally among all the people. "Fraternal cooperation" had replaced competition. Class divisions had disappeared. Bellamy labeled the philosophy behind this vision "nationalism."

The Problems of Monopoly

Relatively few Americans shared the views of those who questioned capitalism itself. But as time went on, a growing number of people were becoming deeply concerned about the growth of **monopoly.**

By the end of the century, a wide range of groups had begun to assail monopoly and economic concentration. In the absence of competition, they argued, monopolistic industries

ANDREW CARNEGIE EXPLAINS "THE GOSPEL OF WEALTH" (1889)

Writing for a general audience in the literary and culture magazine the *North American Review*, billionaire Andrew Carnegie made one of the industrial age's most famous arguments about the inherent justness of the unequal distribution of economic power and wealth.

The problem of our age is the proper administration of wealth, that the ties of brotherhood may still bind together the rich and poor in harmonious relationship. The conditions of human life have not only been changed, but revolutionized, within the past few hundred years. In former days there was little difference between the dwelling, dress, food, and environment of the chief and those of his retainers. The Indians are today where civilized man then was. . . . The contrast between the palace of the millionaire and the cottage of the laborer with us to-day measures the change which has come with civilization. This change, however, is not to be deplored, but welcomed as highly beneficial. It is well, nay, essential, for the progress of the race that the houses of some should be homes for all that is highest and best in literature and the arts,—and for all the refinements of civilization, rather than that none should be so. Much better this great irregularity than universal squalor. . . . The "good old times" were not good old times. Neither master nor servant was as well situated then as to-day. A relapse to old conditions would be disastrous to both—not the least so to him who serves—and would sweep away civilization with it. But whether the change be for good or ill, it is upon us, beyond our power to alter, and, therefore, to be accepted and made the best of. It is a waste of time to criticize the inevitable.

It is easy to see how the change has come. . . . In the manufacture of products we have the whole story. . . . To-day the world obtains commodities of excellent quality at prices which even the preceding generation would have deemed incredible. The poor enjoy what the rich could not before afford. What were the luxuries have become the necessaries of life. The laborer has now more comforts than the farmer had a few generations ago. The farmer has more luxuries than the landlord had, and is more richly clad and better housed. The landlord has books and pictures rarer and appointments more artistic than the king could then obtain.

The price we pay for this salutary change is, no doubt, great. . . . Under the law of competition, the employer of thousands is forced into the strictest economies, among which the rates paid to labor figure prominently, and often there is friction between the employer and the employed, between capital and labor, between rich and poor. Human society loses homogeneity.

The price which society pays for the law of competition, like the price it pays for cheap comforts and luxuries, is also great; but the advantages of this law are also greater still than its cost—for it is to this law that we owe our wonderful material development, which brings improved conditions in its train. But, whether the law be benign or not, we must say of it, as we say of the change in the conditions of men to which we have referred: It is here; we cannot evade it; no substitutes for it have been found; and while the law may be sometimes hard for the individual, it is best for the race, because it insures the survival of the fittest in every department.

What is the proper mode of administering wealth after the laws upon which civilization is founded have thrown it into the hands of the few? . . .

There remains . . . only one mode of using great fortunes; in this we have the true antidote for the temporary unequal distribution of wealth, the reconciliation of the rich and the poor—a reign of harmony. . . . It is founded upon the present most intense Individualism, and the race is prepared to put it in practice by degrees whenever it pleases. Under its sway we shall have an ideal State, in which the surplus wealth of the few will become, in the best sense, the property of the many, because administered for the common good; and this wealth, passing through the hands of the few, can be made a much more potent force for the elevation of our race than if distributed in small sums to the people themselves. Even the poorest can be made to see this, and to agree that great sums gathered by some of their fellow-citizens and spent for public purposes, from which the masses reap the principal benefit, are more valuable to them than if scattered among themselves in trifling amounts through the course of many years. . . .

Poor and restricted are our opportunities in this life, narrow our horizon, our best work most imperfect; but rich men should be thankful for one inestimable boon. They have it in their power during their lives to busy themselves in organizing benefactions from which the masses of their fellows will derive lasting advantage, and thus dignify their own lives. The highest life is probably to be reached, not by such imitation of the life of Christ as Count Tolstoi gives us, but, while animated by Christ's spirit, by recognizing the changed conditions of this age, and adopting modes of expressing this spirit suitable to the changed conditions under which we live, still laboring for the good of our fellows, which was the essence of his life and teaching, but laboring in a different manner.

This, then, is held to be the duty of the man of wealth: To set an example of modest, unostentatious living, shunning display or extravagance; to provide moderately for the legitimate wants of those dependent upon him; and, after doing so, to consider all surplus revenues which come to him simply as trust funds, which he is called upon to administer, and strictly bound as a matter of duty to administer in the manner which, in his judgment, is best calculated to produce the most beneficial results for the community—the man of wealth thus becoming the mere trustee and agent for his poorer brethren, bringing to their service his superior wisdom, experience, and ability to administer, doing for them better than they would or could do for themselves. . . .

[T]he best means of benefiting the community is to place within its reach the ladders upon which the aspiring can rise—free libraries, parks, and means of recreation, by which men are helped in body and mind; works of art, certain to give pleasure and improve the public taste; and public institutions of various kinds, which will improve the general condition of the people; in this manner returning their surplus wealth to the mass of their fellows in the forms best calculated to do them lasting good.

Thus is the problem of rich and poor to be solved. The laws of accumulation will be left free, the laws of distribution free. Individualism will continue, but the millionaire will be but a trustee for the poor, intrusted for a season with a great part of the increased wealth of the community, but administering it for the community far better than it could or would have done for itself. . . .

Such, in my opinion, is the true gospel concerning wealth, obedience to which is destined some day to solve the problem of the rich and the poor, and to bring "Peace on earth, among men good will."

UNDERSTAND, ANALYZE, & EVALUATE

1. What did Carnegie think of the inequality of wealth in industrial America? What were the wealthy supposed to do in this inequality of wealth, and what role did Andrew Carnegie envision for the poor?
2. What was the price of this new inequality?

Source: Carnegie, Andrew, "Wealth," *North American Review,* 1889, located in: Michael P. Johnson, *Reading the American Past: Selected Historical Documents,* vol. 2: From 1865, 5th ed., Boston, MA: Bedford St. Martin's, 2012, 52–55.

THE NOVELS OF HORATIO ALGER

A young boy, perhaps an orphan, makes his way through life on the rough streets of the city by selling newspapers or peddling matches. One day, his energy and determination catch the eye of a wealthy man, who gives him a chance to improve himself. Through honesty, charm, hard work, and aggressiveness, the boy rises in the world to become a successful man.

That, in a nutshell, is the story that Horatio Alger presented to his vast public in novel after novel—over a hundred of them in all—for over forty years. During his lifetime, Americans bought millions of copies of his novels. After his death in 1899, his books (and others written in his name) continued to sell at an astonishing rate. Even today, when the books themselves are largely forgotten, the name Horatio Alger has come to represent the idea of individual advancement through (in a phrase Alger coined) "pluck and luck."

Alger was born in 1832 into a middle-class New England family, attended Harvard, and spent a short time as a Unitarian minister. In the mid-1850s, he turned to writing stories and books, and he continued to do so for the rest of his life. His most famous novel, *Ragged Dick*, was published in 1868. Almost all of his books were fables of a young man's rise "from rags to riches." The purpose of his writing, he claimed, was twofold. He wanted to "exert a salutary influence upon the class of whom [he] was writing, by setting before them inspiring examples of what energy, ambition, and an honest purpose may achieve." He also wanted to show his largely middle-class readers "the life and experiences of the friendless and vagrant children to be found in all our cities."

Most Americans of the late nineteenth and early twentieth centuries were attracted to Alger's stories because the stories helped them believe in one of the most cherished national myths: that with willpower and hard work, individuals could rise in the world. That belief was all the more important in the late nineteenth century when large-scale corporate industrialization was making it increasingly difficult for individuals to control their own fates.

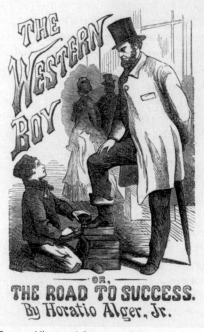

(Source: Library of Congress, Prints and Photographs Division [LC-USZ62-61588])

A NEWSBOY'S STORY Alger's novels were even more popular after his death in 1899 than they had been in his lifetime. This reprint of one of his many rags-to-riches stories—about a New York newsboy's rise to wealth and success—was typical of his work.

Alger placed great emphasis on the moral qualities of his heroes; their success was a reward for their virtue. But many of his readers ignored the moral message and clung simply to the image of sudden and dramatic success. After the author's death, his publishers abridged many of Alger's works, eliminating the parts of his stories where the heroes do good deeds and focusing solely on the success of Alger's heroes in rising in the world.

Alger himself had very mixed feelings about the new industrial order he described. His books were meant to reveal not just the opportunities for advancement it sometimes created, but also its cruelty. That was one reason that in almost all his books, his heroes triumphed not just because of their own virtues or efforts, but because of some amazing stroke of luck. To Alger, at least, the modern age did not guarantee success through hard work alone; there had to be some providential assistance as well. Over time, however, Alger's admirers ignored his own misgivings about industrialism and portrayed his books purely as celebrations of (and justifications for) laissez-faire capitalism and the accumulation of wealth.

An example of the transformation of Alger into a symbol of individual achievement is the Horatio Alger Award, established in 1947 by the American Schools and Colleges Association to honor "living individuals who by their own efforts [have] pulled themselves up by their bootstraps in the American tradition." Among its recipients have been Presidents Dwight D. Eisenhower and Ronald Reagan, evangelist Billy Graham, and Supreme Court Justice Clarence Thomas. ●

UNDERSTAND, ANALYZE, & EVALUATE

1. How do Alger's novels both defend industrial capitalism and criticize it?
2. According to the essay, Alger placed great emphasis on the moral qualities of his heroes, but his publishers later eliminated that aspect of the novels. Why?

could charge whatever prices they wished. Railroads, in particular, charged very high rates along some routes because they knew their customers had no choice but to pay them. Beginning in 1873, the economy fluctuated erratically, producing severe recessions every five or six years, each worse than the last.

(Source: Library of Congress, Prints and Photographs Division [LC-USZC4-435])

A MONSTROUS VISION OF VERTICAL INTEGRATION This 1905 image from *Puck* magazine captures the growing popular fear that businesses like Standard Oil had too much power. See that the Standard Oil octopus controls all in its reach—its tentacles encoil copper, oil, and steel industries as well as a State House and the U.S. Capitol.

THE ORDEAL OF THE WORKER

Most workers in the late nineteenth century experienced a real rise in their standard of living. But they did so at the cost of arduous and often dangerous working conditions, diminishing control over their own work, and a growing sense of powerlessness.

THE IMMIGRANT WORKFORCE

The industrial workforce expanded dramatically in the late nineteenth century as a result of massive migration into industrial cities. Rural Americans continued to flow into factory towns and cities—people disillusioned with or bankrupted by life on the farm. There was also a great wave of immigration from abroad in the decades following the Civil War, primarily from Europe, but also from China, Canada, and Mexico. The 25 million immigrants who arrived in the United States between 1865 and 1915 were more than four times the number who had arrived in the previous fifty years.

In the 1870s and 1880s, most of the immigrants came from England, Ireland, and northern Europe. By the end of the century, however, the major sources of immigrants had shifted, with large numbers of southern and eastern Europeans (Italians, Poles, Russians, Greeks, Slavs, and others) moving into the country and into the industrial workforce.

The new immigrants came to America in part to escape poverty and oppression in their homelands. But they were also attracted by expectations of new opportunities. Railroads lured immigrants into their western landholdings by distributing misleading advertisements overseas. Industrial employers actively recruited immigrant workers under the Labor Contract Law, which—until its repeal in 1885—permitted them to pay for the passage of workers in advance and deduct the amount later from their wages. Even after the repeal of the law, employers continued to encourage the immigration of unskilled laborers, often with the assistance of foreign-born labor brokers, such as the Greek and Italian *padrones,* who recruited work gangs of their fellow nationals.

The arrival of these new groups heightened ethnic tensions within the working class. Low-paid Poles, Greeks, and French Canadians began to displace higher-paid British and Irish workers in the textile factories of New England. Italians, Slavs, and Poles emerged as a major source of labor for the mining industry. Chinese and Mexicans competed with Anglo-Americans and African Americans in mining, farmwork, and factory labor in California, Colorado, and Texas.

WAGES AND WORKING CONDITIONS

At the turn of the century, the average income of the American worker was $400 to $500 a year—below the $600 figure that many believed was required to maintain a reasonable level of comfort. Nor did workers have much job security. All were vulnerable to the boom-and-bust cycle of the industrial economy and the instability caused by technological advances. Even those who kept their jobs could find their wages suddenly and substantially cut in hard times. Few workers, in other words, were ever very far from poverty.

Many first-generation workers, accustomed to the patterns of agrarian life, had trouble adjusting to the nature of modern industrial labor: routine, repetitive tasks on a strict and monotonous schedule. Skilled artisans, whose once-valued tasks were now performed by machines, found the new system impersonal and demeaning. Most factory laborers worked ten hours a day, six days a week; in the steel industry they worked twelve hours a day. Industrial accidents were frequent.

(Source: Library of Congress, Prints and Photographs Division [LC-DIG-nclc-01581])

SPINDLE BOYS   Young boys, some of them barefoot, clamber among the great textile machines in a Georgia cotton mill, mending broken threads and replacing empty bobbins. Many of them were the children or siblings of women who worked in the plant. The photograph is by Lewis Hine, who traveled around the country documenting abuses for the National Child Labor Committee.

The decreasing need for skilled work in factories induced many employers to increase the use of women and children, whom they could hire for lower wages than adult males. By 1900, 20 percent of all manufacturing workers were women. Women labored in all areas of industry, even in some of the most arduous jobs. Most women, however, worked in a few industries where unskilled and semiskilled machine labor (as opposed to heavy manual labor) prevailed. The textile industry remained the largest single industrial employer of women. Domestic service, though, remained the most common female occupation overall. Women worked for wages well below the minimum necessary for survival and well below the wages paid to men working the same jobs.

At least 1.7 million children under sixteen years of age were employed in factories and fields; 10 percent of all girls aged ten to fifteen, and 20 percent of all boys, held jobs. Under public pressure, thirty-eight states passed child labor laws in the late nineteenth century. But 60 percent of child workers were employed in agriculture, which was typically exempt from the laws. For children employed in factories, the laws merely set a minimum age of twelve years and a maximum workday of ten hours, standards that employers often ignored in any case.

EMERGING UNIONIZATION

Laborers attempted to fight back against such conditions by creating national unions. By the end of the century, however, their efforts had met with little success.

There had been craft unions in America, representing small groups of skilled workers, since well before the Civil War. But most unions could not hope to exert significant power in the economy. And during the turbulent recession years of the 1870s, unions faced the additional problem of widespread public hostility. When labor disputes with employers turned bitter and violent, as they occasionally did, much of the public instinctively blamed the workers for the trouble, rarely the employers. Particularly alarming to middle-class Americans was the emergence of the "**Molly Maguires**," an Irish secret society, in the anthracite coal region of western Pennsylvania. This militant labor organization sometimes used violence and even murder in its battle with coal operators.

Excitement over the Molly Maguires paled beside the near hysteria that gripped the country during the railroad strike of 1877, which began when the eastern railroads announced a 10 percent wage cut and soon expanded into something approaching a class war. Strikers disrupted rail service from Baltimore to St. Louis, destroyed equipment, and rioted in the streets of Pittsburgh and other cities. State militias were called out, and in July President Hayes ordered federal troops to suppress the disorders. In Baltimore, eleven demonstrators died and forty were wounded in a conflict between workers and militiamen. In Philadelphia, the state militia killed twenty people when the troops opened fire on thousands of workers and their families who were attempting to block the railroad crossings. In all, over one hundred people died before the strike finally collapsed several weeks after it had begun. The Great Railroad Strike was America's first major national labor conflict.

THE KNIGHTS OF LABOR

In the first major effort to create a genuinely national labor organization, the Noble Order of the **Knights of Labor** was founded in 1869 under the leadership of Uriah S. Stephens. Membership was open to all who "toiled" a definition that included all workers, most business and professional people, and virtually all women—whether they worked in factories, as domestic servants, or in their own homes. Only lawyers, bankers, liquor dealers, and professional gamblers were excluded. The Knights of Labor championed an eight-hour workday and the abolition of child labor, but they were more interested in long-range reform of the economy. The Knights hoped to replace the "wage system" with a new "cooperative system," in which workers would themselves control their workplaces.

For several years, the Knights remained a secret fraternal organization. But in the late 1870s under the leadership of Terence V. Powderly, the order moved into the open and entered a period of spectacular expansion. By 1886, it claimed a total membership of over 700,000. Local unions or assemblies associated with the Knights launched a series of railroad and other strikes in the 1880s in defiance of Powderly's wishes. Their failures to win any meaningful concessions helped discredit the organization. By 1890, membership of the Knights had shrunk to 100,000. A few years later, the organization disappeared altogether.

THE AMERICAN FEDERATION OF LABOR

Even before the Knights began to decline, a rival association appeared. In 1881, representatives of a number of craft unions formed the Federation of Organized Trade and Labor Unions of the United States and Canada. Five years later, this body took the name it has borne ever since, the **American Federation of Labor (AFL)**.

Rejecting the Knights' idea of one big union for everybody, the federation was an association of essentially autonomous craft unions that represented mainly skilled workers. **Samuel Gompers**, the powerful leader of the AFL, concentrated on labor's immediate objectives: wages, hours, and working conditions. As one of its first objectives, the AFL demanded a national eight-hour workday and called for a general strike if the goal was not achieved by May 1, 1886. On that day, strikes and demonstrations for a shorter workday took place all over the country.

In Chicago, a center of labor and radical strength, a strike was already in progress at the McCormick Harvester Company. City police had been harassing the strikers, and labor and radical leaders called a protest meeting at Haymarket Square on May 1. When the police ordered the crowd to disperse, someone threw a bomb that killed seven policemen and injured sixty-seven others. The police, who had killed four strikers the day before, fired into the crowd and killed four more people. Conservative, property-conscious Americans—frightened and outraged—blamed the protesters and demanded retribution. Chicago officials finally rounded up eight anarchists and charged them with murder, on the grounds that their statements had incited whoever had hurled the bomb. All eight scapegoats were found guilty after a remarkably injudicious trial. Seven were sentenced to death. One of them committed suicide, four were executed, and two had their sentences commuted to life imprisonment.

To most middle-class Americans, the **Haymarket bombing** was an alarming symbol of social chaos and radicalism. "Anarchism" now became in the public mind a code word for terrorism and violence, even though most anarchists were relatively peaceful. For the next thirty years, the specter of anarchism remained one of the most frightening concepts in the American imagination. Business owners exploited it to smear labor leaders and disrupt their activities. It became a constant obstacle to the goals of the AFL and other labor organizations, and it did particular damage to the Knights of Labor. However much they tried to distance themselves from radicals, labor leaders were always vulnerable to accusations of anarchism, as the violent strikes of the 1890s occasionally illustrated.

THE HOMESTEAD STRIKE

The Amalgamated Association of Iron and Steel Workers was the most powerful trade union in the country in the late 1800s. Its members were skilled workers, in great demand by employers, and they had long been able to exercise significant power in the workplace. In the mid-1880s, however, demand for skilled workers declined as new production methods changed the steelmaking process. In the streamlined Carnegie system, which was coming to dominate the steel industry, the union was able to maintain a foothold in only one of the corporation's three major factories—the Homestead plant near Pittsburgh.

By 1890, Carnegie and his chief lieutenant, Henry Clay Frick, had decided that the Amalgamated "had to go." Over the next two years, they repeatedly cut wages at Homestead. At first, the union begrudgingly acquiesced, aware that it was not strong enough to wage a successful strike. But in 1892, when the company stopped even discussing its financial decisions with the union and gave it two days to accept another wage cut, the Amalgamated called for a strike.

Frick abruptly shut down the plant and called in 300 guards from the Pinkerton Detective Agency, well known as strikebreakers, to enable the company to hire nonunion workers. They approached the plant by river, on barges, on July 6, 1892. The strikers poured gasoline on the water, set it on fire, and then met the Pinkertons at the docks with guns and dynamite. After several hours of fighting, which killed 3 guards and ten strikers and injured many others, the Pinkertons surrendered and were escorted roughly out of town.

But the workers' victory in the **Homestead strike** was temporary. The governor of Pennsylvania, at the company's request, sent the state's entire National Guard contingent, some 8,000 men, to Homestead. Production resumed, with strikebreakers now protected by troops. And public opinion turned against the strikers when a radical made an attempt to assassinate Frick. Slowly, workers drifted back to their jobs, and finally—four months after the strike began—the Amalgamated surrendered. By 1900, every major steel plant in the Northeast had broken with the Amalgamated. Its membership shrank from a high of 24,000 in 1891 (two-thirds of all eligible steelworkers) to fewer than 7,000 a decade later.

THE PULLMAN STRIKE

A dispute of greater magnitude, if less violence, was the **Pullman strike** in 1894. The Pullman Palace Car Company manufactured railroad sleeping and parlor cars at a plant near Chicago. There the company constructed a 600-acre town, Pullman, and rented its trim, orderly houses to the employees. George M. Pullman, owner of the company, saw the town as a model—a solution to the problems of industrial workers. But many residents chafed at the regimentation (and the high rents). In the winter of 1893–1894, the Pullman Company slashed wages by about 25 percent, citing its own declining revenues in the depression, without reducing the rent it charged its employees. Workers went on strike and persuaded the militant American Railway Union, led by **Eugene V. Debs**, to support them by refusing to handle Pullman cars and equipment. Within a few days, thousands of railroad workers in twenty-seven states and territories were on strike, and transportation from Chicago to the Pacific Coast shut down.

Unlike most elected politicians, the governor of Illinois, John Peter Altgeld, was a man with demonstrated sympathies for workers and their grievances. He refused to call out the militia to protect employers. Infuriated, railroad operators bypassed Altgeld and asked the federal government to send regular army troops to Illinois, using the pretext that the strike was preventing the movement of mail on the trains. In July 1894, President Grover Cleveland ordered 2,000 troops to the Chicago area. A federal court issued an injunction forbidding the union to continue the strike. When Debs and his associates defied it, they were arrested and imprisoned. With federal troops protecting the hiring of new workers and with the union leaders in a federal jail, the strike quickly collapsed.

SOURCES OF LABOR WEAKNESS

In the last decades of the nineteenth century, labor made few real gains despite militant organizing efforts. Industrial wages rose hardly at all. To be sure, labor leaders won a few legislative victories—the abolition of the Contract Labor Law, the establishment of an eight-hour day for government employees, compensation for some workers injured on the job, and others. But many such laws were not enforced, and most business leaders laughed at them. Widespread strikes and protests, and many other working-class forms of resistance, large and small, led to scant enduring gains. The end of the century found most workers with less political power and less control of the workplace than they had had forty years before.

Workers failed to make greater gains for many reasons. The principal labor organizations represented only a small percentage of the industrial workforce; the AFL, the most important, blatantly excluded unskilled workers and most women, blacks, and recent immigrants. Divisions within the workforce, such as tensions among different ethnic and racial groups, contributed further to union weakness.

Another source of labor weakness was the shifting nature of the workforce. Many immigrant workers came to America intending to earn some money and then return home. The assumption that they had no long-range future in the country tamed their enthusiasm to organize. Other workers were in constant motion, moving from one job to another, one town to another, seldom in a single place long enough to establish any institutional ties or exert any real power.

Above all, perhaps, workers made few gains in the late nineteenth century because they faced corporate organizations of vast wealth and power, which were generally determined to crush any efforts by workers to challenge their prerogatives. And as the Homestead and Pullman strikes suggest, the corporations usually had the support of local, state, and federal authorities, who were willing to send in troops to "preserve order" and crush labor uprisings on demand.

Despite the creation of new labor unions and a wave of strikes and protests, workers in the late nineteenth century failed on the whole to create successful organizations or to protect their interests. In the battle for power within the emerging industrial economy, almost all the advantages seemed to lie with capital.

CONCLUSION

In the four decades after the Civil War, the United States propelled itself into the forefront of the industrializing nations of the world. Large areas of the nation remained overwhelmingly rural, to be sure. But even so, America's economy, and along with it the nation's society and culture, was being profoundly transformed.

New technologies, new forms of corporate management, and new supplies of labor helped make possible the rapid growth of the nation's industries and the construction of its railroads. The factory system contributed to the growth of the nation's cities. Immigration provided a steady supply of new workers for the growing industrial economy. The result was a steady increase in national wealth, rising living standards for much of the population, and the creation of great new fortunes.

But industrialization did not spread its fruits evenly. Large areas of the country, most notably the South, and large groups in the population, most notably minorities, women, and recent immigrants, profited relatively little from economic growth. Industrial workers experienced arduous conditions of labor. Small merchants and manufacturers found themselves overmatched by great new combinations.

Industrialists strove to create a rationale for their power and to persuade the public that everyone had something to gain from it. But many Americans remained skeptical of modern capitalism, and some—workers struggling to form unions, reformers denouncing trusts, socialists envisioning a new world, and many others—created broad and powerful critiques of the new economic order. Industrialization brought both progress and pain to late-nineteenth-century America. Controversies over its effects defined the era and would continue to define the first decades of the twentieth century.

KEY TERMS/PEOPLE/PLACES/EVENTS

American Federation of
  Labor (AFL) 422
American Socialist
  Party 415
Andrew Carnegie 411
Edward Bellamy 415
Eugene V. Debs 424
gospel of wealth 414
Haymarket bombing 423

Henry Ford 409
Henry George 415
Homestead strike 423
Horatio Alger 414
horizontal integration 412
John D. Rockefeller 412
J. P. Morgan 412
Knights of Labor 422
Louisa May Alcott 414

Molly Maguires 422
monopoly 415
Pullman strike 424
Samuel Gompers 422
Social Darwinism 413
Taylorism 409
vertical integration 412
Wilbur and Orville
  Wright 409

RECALL AND REFLECT

1. Who were some of the business and industrial titans of the late nineteenth century, and what did they contribute to America's industrial growth?
2. What changes took place in corporate organization in the late nineteenth century, and how did these changes affect the nation's economy?
3. What was the gospel of wealth?
4. How did Social Darwinism attempt to justify the social consequences of industrial capitalism?
5. How did workers respond to the expansion of industrialization and the new industrial economy?

18 | THE AGE OF THE CITY

THE NEW URBAN GROWTH

THE URBAN LANDSCAPE

STRAINS OF URBAN LIFE

THE RISE OF MASS CONSUMPTION

LEISURE IN THE CONSUMER SOCIETY

HIGH CULTURE IN THE URBAN AGE

LOOKING AHEAD

1. What were some of the problems that resulted from rapid urbanization, and how did urban governments respond to these problems?

2. How did the sources of immigration to America shift in the late nineteenth century, and what was the native response to the change?

3. How did the rise of mass consumption affect leisure and entertainment?

THE INDUSTRIALIZATION AND COMMERCIALIZATION of America changed the face of society in countless ways. Nowhere were those changes more profound than in the growth of cities and the creation of an urban society and culture. From its roots as a primarily agrarian republic, the United States in the late nineteenth century was becoming an urban nation.

Cities grew so rapidly that their facilities and institutions could not keep pace. Housing, transportation, sewer systems, social services, governments—all lagged far behind the enormous demands urban populations placed on them. And to observers at the time, crime, poverty, and conflict between groups living in densely packed environments were portents of looming urban chaos.

But despite their problems, people flocked to cities to take advantage of economic, educational, and cultural opportunities. As centers of wealth, cities in the United States and around the world became the sites of great civic projects that came to define the urban experience. These included public parks, museums, theaters, opera houses, railroad stations, libraries, and commercial boulevards. The city of the late nineteenth and early twentieth centuries thus showcased the achievements of modern society as well as the tensions that urbanization generated.

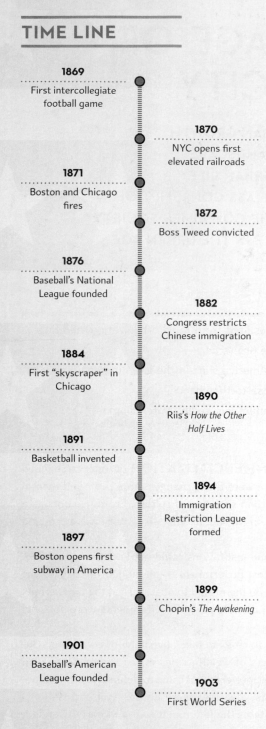

TIME LINE

1869
First intercollegiate
football game

1870
NYC opens first
elevated railroads

1871
Boston and Chicago
fires

1872
Boss Tweed convicted

1876
Baseball's National
League founded

1882
Congress restricts
Chinese immigration

1884
First "skyscraper" in
Chicago

1890
Riis's *How the Other
Half Lives*

1891
Basketball invented

1894
Immigration
Restriction League
formed

1897
Boston opens first
subway in America

1899
Chopin's *The Awakening*

1901
Baseball's American
League founded

1903
First World Series

THE NEW URBAN GROWTH

The urban population in America increased sevenfold in the half century after the Civil War. In 1920, the census revealed that for the first time, a majority of the American people lived in "urban" areas—defined as communities of 2,500 people or more. Natural increase accounted for only a small part of urban growth. Families in cities experienced a high rate of infant mortality, a declining fertility rate, and a high death rate from disease. It was immigration, rather, that expanded the urban population so dramatically.

THE MIGRATIONS

In the late nineteenth century, Americans left the declining agricultural regions of the East at a dramatic rate. Some moved to the newly developing farmlands of the West. But almost as many moved to the growing cities of the East and the Midwest.

Among those leaving rural America for industrial cities in the 1880s were black men and women trying to escape the poverty, debt, violence, and oppression they faced in the rural South. They were also seeking new opportunities in cities. Factory jobs for African Americans were rare and professional opportunities almost nonexistent. Urban black people tended to work in service occupations as cooks, janitors, domestic servants, and so on. Because many such jobs were considered women's work, black women often outnumbered black men in the cities.

The most important source of urban population growth, however, was the great number of new immigrants from abroad, part of a larger pattern of mobility around the world. (See "America in the World: Global Migrations.") Some came from Canada, Latin America, and—particularly on the West Coast—China and Japan. But

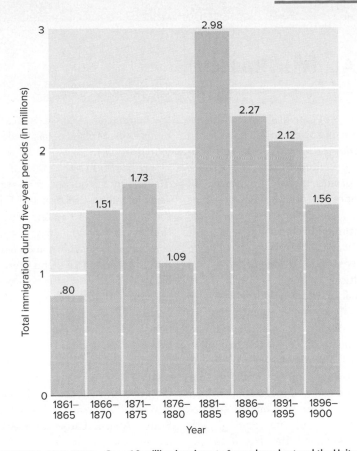

TOTAL IMMIGRATION, 1861–1900 Over 10 million immigrants from abroad entered the United States in the last forty years of the nineteenth century, with particularly high numbers arriving in the 1880s and 1890s. This chart shows the pattern of immigration in five-year intervals. • *What external events might help explain some of the rises and falls in the rates of immigration in these years?*

the greatest number came from Europe. After 1880, the flow of new arrivals began to include large numbers of people from southern and eastern Europe. By the 1890s, more than half of all immigrants came from these regions.

In earlier years, most new immigrants from Europe (particularly Germans and Scandinavians) had arrived with at least some money and education. Most of them arrived at one of the major port cities on the Atlantic Coast, the greatest number landing at New York's immigrant depot at Castle Garden, and then headed west. But the new immigrants of the late nineteenth century, many coming through Ellis Island after 1892, generally lacked the capital to buy farmland and lacked the education to establish themselves in professions. So, like similarly poor Irish immigrants before the Civil War, they settled overwhelmingly in industrial cities, where they worked largely in unskilled jobs.

THE ETHNIC CITY

By 1890, most of the population of the major cities consisted of immigrants: 87 percent of the population in Chicago, 80 percent in New York, 84 percent in Milwaukee and

GLOBAL MIGRATIONS

The great waves of immigration that transformed American society in the nineteenth and early twentieth centuries were not unique to the United States. They were part of a great, global movement of peoples—unprecedented in history—that affected every continent in the world and that has continued to this day. These great migrations were the product of two related forces: population growth and industrialization.

The population of Europe grew faster in the second half of the nineteenth century than ever before and ever since—almost doubling between 1850 and the beginning of World War I. The population growth was a result of growing economies able to support more people and of more efficient and productive agriculture that helped end debilitating famines. But the rapid growth nevertheless strained the resources of many parts of Europe and affected, in particular, rural people, who were now too numerous to live off the available land. Many decided to move to other parts of the world where land was more plentiful.

At the same time, industrialization drew millions of people out of the countryside and into cities—sometimes into cities in their own countries but often to industrial cities in other nations. Historians of migration speak of "push" factors (pressures on people to leave their homes) and "pull" factors (the lure of new lands) in explaining population movements. The "push" for many nineteenth-century migrants was poverty and inadequate land at home; for others it was political and religious oppression. The "pull" was the availability of land or industrial jobs in other regions—and, for some, the prospect of greater freedom abroad. Faster, cheaper, and easier

transportation—railroads, steamships, and much later, airplanes—also aided large-scale immigration.

From 1800 to the start of World War I, 50 million Europeans migrated overseas. They left almost all areas of Europe, but in the later years of the century, when migration reached its peak, most came from poor rural areas in southern and eastern Europe. Italy, Russia, and Poland were among the biggest sources of late-nineteenth-century migrants. Almost two-thirds of these immigrants came to the United States. But nearly 20 million Europeans migrated to other lands. Migrants from England and Ireland (among others) moved in large numbers to those areas of the British Empire with vast, seemingly open territory: Canada, Australia, New Zealand, and South Africa. Large numbers of Italians moved to Argentina and other parts of South America. Many migrants moved to open land in these countries and established themselves as farmers, using the new mechanical farming devices made possible by industrialization. In many places— Australia, New Zealand, Argentina, South Africa, and the United States—immigrants evicted native residents and created societies

(Source: Library of Congress, Prints and Photographs Division [LC-DIG-ggbain-01561])

of their own. Many others settled in the industrial cities that were growing up in all these regions and formed distinctive ethnic and national communities within them.

But it was not only Europeans who were transplanting themselves in these years. Tremendous numbers of poor people left Asia, Africa, and the Pacific Islands in search of better lives. Most of them could not afford the journey abroad on their own. They moved instead as indentured servants, in much the same way many European migrants moved to America in the seventeenth century, agreeing to a term of servitude in their new land in exchange for food, shelter, and transportation. Recruiters of indentured servants fanned out across China, Japan, areas of Africa and the Pacific Islands, and above all, India. French and British recruiters brought hundreds of thousands of Indian migrants to work in plantations in their own Asian and African colonies. Chinese laborers were recruited to work on plantations in Cuba and Hawaii; mines in British Malaya, Peru, South Africa, and Australia; and railroad projects in Canada, Peru, and the United States. African indentured servants moved in large numbers to the Caribbean, and Pacific Islanders tended to move to other islands or to Australia.

The immigration of European peoples was largely voluntary and brought most migrants to the United States, where indentured servitude was illegal, although sometimes imposed on workers through labor contracts. But the migration of non-European peoples often involved an important element of coercion and brought relatively small numbers of people to the United States. This non-European migration was a function of the growth of European empires, and it was made possible by the imperial system—by its labor recruiters, by its naval resources, by its law, and by its economic needs. Together, these various forms of migration produced one of the greatest population movements in the history of the world and transformed not just the United States but much of the globe. •

UNDERSTAND, ANALYZE, & EVALUATE

1. What were some of the "push" and "pull" factors that motivated the migration of both Europeans and non-Europeans?
2. Why did more Europeans than non-Europeans migrate to the United States?

Detroit. Equally striking was the diversity of new immigrant populations. In other countries experiencing heavy immigration in this period, most of the new arrivals were coming from one or two sources. But in the United States, no single national group dominated.

Most of the new arrivals were rural people, and for many of them the adjustment to city life was painful. To help ease the transition, some immigrant groups formed close-knit ethnic communities within the cities, in neighborhoods often called immigrant "ghettoes." Ethnic neighborhoods offered newcomers much that was familiar, including newspapers and theater in their native languages, stores selling their native foods, and church and fraternal organizations that provided links to their national pasts. Many immigrants also maintained close ties with their native countries. They stayed in touch with relatives who had remained behind, and perhaps as many as a third in the early years returned to their homelands after a relatively short time. Others helped bring the rest of their families to America. The cultural cohesiveness of ethnic communities clearly eased the pain of separation from the immigrants' native lands.

But immigrants who aroused strong racial prejudice among native-born whites found it very difficult to advance, whatever their talents. Those white immigrants who arrived with a valuable skill or with some capital did better than those who did not. And over time,

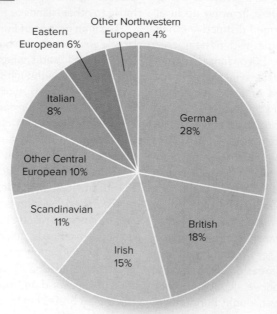

SOURCES OF IMMIGRATION FROM EUROPE, 1860–1900 This pie chart shows the sources of European immigration in the late nineteenth century. The largest number of immigrants continued to come from Britain, Ireland, Germany, and Scandinavia, but the beginnings of what in the early twentieth century would become a major influx of immigrants from new sources—southern and eastern Europe in particular—are already visible here. There was also some immigration from other sources—Mexico, South and Central America, and Asia. • *Why would these newer sources of European and other kinds of immigration create controversy among older-stock Americans?*

those who lived in cities where people of their own nationality came to predominate—for example, the Irish in New York and Boston or the Germans in Milwaukee—gained an advantage as they learned to exert their political power.

ASSIMILATION AND EXCLUSION

Despite the many differences among the various immigrant communities, virtually all groups had certain things in common. Most immigrants shared the experience of settling in cities. Most were young; the majority of newcomers were between fifteen and forty-five years old. And in most communities of the foreign-born, ethnic ties had to compete against the desire for assimilation.

Many of the new arrivals had come with romantic visions of the New World. However disillusioning they might have found their first contact with the United States, they usually retained the dream of becoming true "Americans." Second-generation immigrants were especially likely to attempt to break with old ways. Young women, in particular, sometimes rebelled against parents who tried to arrange or prevent marriages or who opposed women entering the workplace.

Old-stock Americans encouraged or demanded assimilation in countless ways. Public schools taught children in English, and employers often insisted that workers speak English on the job. Most non-ethnic stores sold mainly American products, forcing immigrants to adapt their diets, clothing, and lifestyles to American norms. Church leaders were often native-born Americans or more assimilated immigrants who encouraged their parishioners to adopt American ways. Some even embraced reforms to make their religion more compatible with the norms of the new country. Reform Judaism, imported from Germany in the late nineteenth century, was an effort by American Jewish leaders (as it had been by German ones) to make their faith less "foreign" to the dominant culture.

The vast numbers of new immigrants and their distinctive communities provoked fear and resentment among some native-born Americans just as earlier arrivals had done. In 1887, Henry Bowers, a self educated lawyer, founded the American Protective Association, a group committed to stopping immigration. By 1894, membership in the organization reportedly reached 500,000, with chapters throughout the Northeast and Midwest. That same year, five Harvard alumni in Boston founded the Immigration Restriction League, which proposed screening immigrants through literacy tests and other standards to separate the "desirable" from the "undesirable."

The government responded to popular concern about immigration even earlier. In 1882, Congress excluded the Chinese, denied entry to "undesirables"—convicts, paupers, those with mental illness—and placed a tax of 50 cents on each person admitted. Later legislation of the 1890s enlarged the list of those barred from immigrating.

But these laws kept out only a small number of aliens, and more ambitious restriction proposals made little progress in Congress, for immigration provided a cheap and plentiful labor supply to the rapidly growing economy. Many argued that America's industrial as well as agricultural development would be impossible without it.

THE URBAN LANDSCAPE

The city was a place of remarkable contrasts. It had homes of almost unimaginable size and grandeur and hovels of indescribable squalor. It had conveniences unknown to earlier generations and problems that seemed beyond the capacity of society to solve.

THE CREATION OF PUBLIC SPACE

There wer   w early American cities that were planned from the beginning, Philadelphia and Washington most prominently. By the mid-nineteenth century, reformers, planners, architects, and others began to call for more ordered visions of many other cities.

Among the most important urban innovations of the mid-nineteenth century were great city parks, which reflected the desire of urban leaders to provide an antidote to the congestion of the city landscape. Parks, they argued, would allow city residents a healthy, restorative escape from the strains of urban life by reacquainting them with the natural world. This notion of the park as refuge was most effectively promoted by the landscape designers Frederick Law Olmsted and Calvert Vaux, who together in the late 1850s designed New York's Central Park. They deliberately created a public space that would look as little like the city as possible. Instead of the ordered, formal spaces common in some European cities, they created a space that seemed entirely natural. Central Park was from the start one of the most popular and admired public spaces in the world.

At the same time that cities were creating great parks, they were also creating great public buildings: libraries, art galleries, natural history museums, theaters, and concert and opera halls. New York's Metropolitan Museum of Art was the largest and best known of many great museums taking shape in the late nineteenth century, but giant museums grew up quickly in Boston, Philadelphia, Chicago, and other places. In one city after another, new and lavish public libraries appeared, as if to confirm the city's role as a center of learning and knowledge.

Wealthy residents were the principal force behind the creation of the great art museums, concert halls, opera houses, and, at times, even parks. As their own material and social aspirations grew, they wanted the public life of the city to provide them with amenities to match their expectations. Becoming an important patron of a major cultural institution was an especially effective route to social distinction.

As both the size and aspirations of great cities increased, urban leaders launched monumental projects to remake them. Some cities began to clear away older neighborhoods and streets and create grand, monumental avenues lined with new and more impressive buildings. A particularly important event in inspiring such efforts was the 1893 Columbian Exposition in Chicago, a world's fair constructed to honor the 400th anniversary of Columbus's first voyage to America. At the center of the wildly popular exposition was a cluster of neoclassical buildings—the "Great White City"—arranged symmetrically around a formal lagoon. It became the inspiration for the **city beautiful movement**, led by the architect of the Great White City, Daniel Burnham. The movement strove to impose a similar order and symmetry on the disordered life of cities around the country. Only rarely, however, were planners able to overcome the obstacles of private landowners and complicated urban politics to realize more than a small portion of their dreams.

The effort to remake the city did not focus only on redesigning existing landscapes. It occasionally led to the creation of entirely new ones. In one of the largest public works projects ever undertaken in America to that point, the city of Boston gradually filled in a large area of marshy tidal land in the late 1880s to create the neighborhood known as "Back Bay." Chicago claimed large areas from Lake Michigan and at one point raised the street level for the entire city to help avoid the problems the marshy land created. In New York and other cities, the response to limited space was not so much to create new land as to annex adjacent territory. A great wave of annexations expanded the boundaries of many American cities in the 1890s and beyond, most notably New York City's 1898 annexation of Brooklyn, which had itself been a large and important city.

THE SEARCH FOR HOUSING

One of the greatest urban problems was to provide housing for the thousands of new residents pouring into the cities every day. For the prosperous, housing was seldom a worry. The availability of cheap labor reduced the cost of building and permitted anyone with even a moderate income to afford a house. Some of the richest urban residents lived in palatial mansions located in exclusive neighborhoods in the heart of the city—Fifth Avenue in New York, Back Bay and Beacon Hill in Boston, Society Hill in Philadelphia, Lake Shore Drive in Chicago, Nob Hill in San Francisco, and many others.

Many of the moderately well-to-do city dwellers took advantage of less expensive land on the edges of cities and settled in new suburbs, linked to the downtowns by trains or streetcars. Chicago in the 1870s, for example, connected nearly a hundred residential suburbs to the downtown by railroad. Real estate developers worked to create suburban communities that would appeal to many city dwellers' nostalgia for the countryside, promoting them with lawns, trees, and houses designed to look manorial.

Most urban residents, however, could not afford either to own a house in the city or to move to the suburbs. Instead, they stayed in the city centers and rented. Landlords tried to

(©Bettmann/Corbis)

A TENEMENT LAUNDRY This woman, shown here with some of her children, was typical of many working-class mothers who found income-producing activities they could pursue in the home (in this case, laundry).

squeeze as many rent-paying residents as possible into the smallest available space. In Manhattan, for example, the average population density in 1894 was 143 people per acre, a rate far higher than that of any other American or European city then or since. In the cities of the South—Charleston, New Orleans, Richmond—poor African Americans lived in crumbling former slave quarters. In Boston, immigrants moved into cheap three-story wooden houses ("triple-deckers"). In Baltimore and Philadelphia, the new arrivals crowded into narrow brick row houses. And in New York and many other cities, they lived in **tenements**.

The word *tenement* had originally referred simply to a multiple-family rental building, but by the late nineteenth century it had become a term for slum dwellings only. The first tenements, built in 1850, had been hailed as a great improvement in housing for the poor. But most were, in fact, miserable places, with many windowless rooms and little or no plumbing or heating. **Jacob Riis**, a Danish immigrant and New York newspaper photographer, shocked many middle-class Americans with his sensational descriptions and pictures of tenement life in his 1890 book *How the Other Half Lives*. But the solution reformers often adopted was simply to raze slum dwellings without building any new housing to replace them.

URBAN TECHNOLOGIES: TRANSPORTATION AND CONSTRUCTION

Urban growth posed monumental transportation challenges. Sheer numbers of people mandated the development of mass transportation. Streetcars drawn on tracks by horses had been introduced into some cities even before the Civil War. But the horsecars were not fast enough, so many communities developed new forms of mass transit. In 1870, New York opened its first elevated railway, whose noisy, steam-powered trains moved rapidly above the city streets on massive iron structures. New York, Chicago, San Francisco, Boston, and other cities also experimented with cable cars, towed by continuously moving underground cables. Richmond, Virginia, introduced the first electric trolley line in 1888, and in 1897, Boston opened the first American subway. At the same time, cities were developing new techniques of road and bridge building. One of the great technological marvels of the 1880s was the completion of the Brooklyn Bridge in New York—a dramatic steel-cable suspension span designed by John A. Roebling.

Cities grew upward as well as outward. In Chicago, the 1884 construction of the first modern "skyscraper"—a ten-story building—launched a new era in urban architecture. Critical to the creation of the skyscraper was a new technology of construction, which emerged as a result of several related developments. New kinds of steel girders could support much greater tension than the metals of the past. The invention and development of the passenger elevator made much taller buildings possible. And the search for ways to protect cities from the ravages of great fires, which caused such terrible destruction in wood-frame cities of the late nineteenth century, led to steel-frame construction that, among other things, made cities more fireproof. Once the technology existed to permit the construction of tall buildings, there were few obstacles to building taller and taller structures. The early Chicago skyscrapers paved the way for some of the great construction achievements later in the twentieth century: the Chrysler Building and the Empire State Building in New York, the LaSalle Building in Chicago, and ultimately the vast numbers of steel and glass skyscrapers of post-1945 cities around the world.

STRAINS OF URBAN LIFE

Increasing urban congestion and the absence of adequate public services produced serious hazards. Crime, fire, disease, and indigence all placed strains on the capacities of metropolitan institutions, and both governments and private agencies were for a time poorly equipped to respond.

HEALTH AND SAFETY IN THE BUILT ENVIRONMENT

Chicago and Boston suffered great fires in 1871, and other cities experienced similar disasters. The terrible experience of the fires encouraged the construction of fireproof buildings and the development of professional fire departments. They also forced cities to rebuild at a time when new technological and architectural innovations were available. Some of the high-rise downtowns of American cities arose out of the rubble of great fires.

An even greater hazard than fire was disease, especially in poor neighborhoods with inadequate sanitation facilities. An epidemic that began in a poor neighborhood could and often did spread easily into other neighborhoods as well. Few municipal officials recognized the relationship of improper sewage disposal and water contamination to such epidemic diseases as typhoid fever and cholera. Many cities lacked adequate systems for disposing of human waste until well into the twentieth century. Flush toilets and sewer systems began to appear in the 1870s, but they could not solve the problem as long as sewage continued to flow into open ditches or streams, polluting cities' water supplies. Contributing to the same problem was the urban presence of domestic animals, including horses, cows, and pigs.

Air quality in many cities was poor as well. Few Americans had the severe problems that London experienced in the late nineteenth century with its seemingly perpetual "fogs" created by the burning of soft coal. But air pollution from factories and from stoves and furnaces in offices, homes, and other buildings was constant and at times severe. The incidence of respiratory infection and related diseases was much higher in cities than it was in rural areas, and it accelerated rapidly in the late nineteenth century.

Modern notions of environmental science were unknown to most Americans in these years. But the environmental degradation of many American cities was a visible and disturbing fact of life. The frequency of great fires, the dangers of disease, the crowding of working-class neighborhoods—all exemplified the environmental costs of industrialization and rapid urbanization.

Yet by the early twentieth century, reformers crusading to improve the environmental conditions of cities were beginning to achieve some notable successes. By 1910, most large American cities had constructed sewage disposal systems, often at great cost, to protect the drinking water of their inhabitants and prevent the great bacterial plagues that impure water had helped create in the past, such as the yellow fever epidemic in Memphis that killed 5,000 people.

In 1912, the federal government created the **Public Health Service**, which was charged with preventing such occupational diseases as tuberculosis, anemia, and carbon dioxide poisoning, which were common in the garment industry and other trades. It attempted to create common health standards for all factories; but since the agency had few powers of enforcement, it had limited impact. The creation of the Occupational Safety and Health Administration in 1970, which gave government the authority to require employers to create safe and healthy workplaces, was a legacy of the Public Health Service's early work.

Urban Poverty, Crime, and Violence

Urban expansion spawned widespread and often desperate poverty. Public agencies and private philanthropic organizations offered some relief, but they were generally poorly funded and also dominated by middle-class people who believed that too much assistance would breed dependency. Most tried to restrict aid to the "deserving" poor, those who truly could not help themselves. Charitable organizations conducted elaborate investigations to separate the "deserving" from the "undeserving." Other charitable societies—for example, the Salvation Army, which began operating in America in 1879—concentrated more on religious revivalism than on relief of the homeless and hungry. Middle-class people grew particularly alarmed over the rising number of poor children in the cities, some of them orphans or runaways. They attracted greater attention from reformers than any other group, although that attention produced no lasting solutions to their problems.

Poverty and crowding bred crime and violence. The American murder rate rose rapidly in the late nineteenth century, from twenty-five murders for every million people in 1880 to over a hundred by the end of the century. That reflected in part a very high level of violence in some nonurban areas: the American South, where lynching and homicide were particularly high, and the West, where the rootlessness and instability of new communities (cow towns, mining camps, and the like) created much violence. But the big cities contributed their share to the increase as well. Native-born Americans liked to believe that crime was a result of the violent proclivities of immigrant groups, and they cited the rise of gangs and criminal organizations in various ethnic communities. But native-born Americans in the cities were as likely to commit crimes as immigrants. The rising crime rates encouraged many cities to develop larger and more professional police forces. But police forces themselves could spawn corruption and brutality.

Some members of the middle class, fearful of urban insurrections, felt the need for even more substantial forms of protection. Urban National Guard groups built imposing armories on the outskirts of affluent neighborhoods and stored large supplies of weapons and ammunition in preparation for uprisings that, in fact, virtually never occurred.

The city was a place of strong allure and great excitement. Yet it was also a place of alienating impersonality and, to some, of degradation and exploitation. The novel *Sister Carrie* (1900), written by **Theodore Dreiser**, exposed one troubling aspect of urban life: the plight of single women like Dreiser's heroine, Carrie, who found themselves without any means of support. Carrie first took an exhausting and ill-paying job in a Chicago shoe factory, then drifted into a life of "sin," exploited by predatory men.

(Source: Library of Congress, Prints and Photographs Division [LC-USZC4-7884])

PUCK MAGAZINE *Puck* (1871–1918) was the first successful humor magazine published in the United States. It offered political cartoons, caricatures, and satire on the issues of the day. This cover shows a beer and wine seller shuttering his store by order of the government. The Tammany man indicates that the merchant will be able to operate without penalty in exchange for his support.

The Machine and the Boss

For newly arrived immigrants and other inner-city residents struggling to adjust to urban life, the principal source of assistance was the political "machine." The urban machine owed its existence to the power vacuum that the chaotic growth of cities had created and to the potential voting power of large immigrant communities. Out of that combination emerged urban "bosses." The principal function of the political boss was simple: to win votes for his organization. That meant winning the loyalty of his constituents. To do so, a boss might provide them with occasional relief—a basket of groceries or a bag of coal. He might step in to save those arrested for petty crimes from jail. When he could, he found work for the unemployed. Above all, he rewarded many of his followers with patronage: with jobs in city government or in the police, which the machine's elected officials often controlled; with jobs building or operating the new transit systems; and with opportunities to rise in the political organization itself.

Machines were also vehicles for making money. Politicians enriched themselves and their allies through various forms of graft and corruption. A politician might discover in advance where a new road or streetcar line was to be built, buy land near it, and sell it at a profit when property values rose as a result of the construction. There was also covert graft. Officials received kickbacks from contractors in exchange for contracts to build public projects, and they sold franchises for the operation of public utilities. The most famously corrupt city boss was **William M. Tweed**, head of New York City's **Tammany Hall** in the 1860s and 1870s, whose extravagant use of public funds and kickbacks landed him in jail in 1872.

The urban machine was not without competition. Reform groups frequently mobilized public outrage at the corruption of the bosses and often succeeded in driving machine politicians from office. But the reform organizations typically lacked the permanence of the machine.

THE RISE OF MASS CONSUMPTION

In the last decades of the nineteenth century, developments in urban America began shaping a broader ethos of mass consumption. Much of this phenomenon was driven by middle-class tastes, but more and more Americans participated in the new consumer culture and thereby connected themselves to national trends, styles, and products.

Patterns of Income and Consumption

Incomes rose for almost everyone in the industrial era, although highly unevenly. One result of the new economy was the creation of vast fortunes, but perhaps the most important result for society as a whole was the growth and increasing prosperity of the middle class. Clerks, accountants, middle managers, and other "white-collar" workers saw their salaries rise by an average of a third between 1890 and 1910. Doctors, lawyers, and other professionals experienced a particularly dramatic increase in both the prestige and the profitability of their professions. Working-class incomes rose in those years as well, although from a much lower base and more slowly. The iron and steel industries saw workers' hourly wages increase by a third between 1890 and 1910; but industries with large female workforces—shoes, textiles, and paper—saw more modest increases, as did almost all industries in the South. Wages for African Americans, Mexicans, and Asians also rose more slowly than those for white workers.

JOHN WANAMAKER, THE FOUR CARDINAL POINTS OF THE DEPARTMENT STORE (1874)

The Philadelphia merchant John Wanamaker was one of the most successful and innovative businessmen of his day. A pioneer of the department store, Wanamaker ran this advertisement explaining the policies and benefits for consumers of his new commercial venue.

FOUR CARDINAL POINTS

By which we will hereafter steer our craft

FULL GUARANTEE   CASH PAYMENT

ONE PRICE   CASH RETURNED

Explanation and Elaboration of the New Plan

FIRST POINT—"CASH"—Houses doing a credit business must provide for losses on bad debts, interest on long-standing accounts, capital locked up, etc. To bear such losses themselves would drive them out of business. Therefore a per cent is added to the price of each article sold to cover this leakage, and cash buyers, whether they know it or not, really pay the bad debts and the interest on the long credits of the other customers. Under the cash payment system one pays only for what he gets, and contributes nothing to a "Sinking Fund."

By this radical change we shall lose some of our customers, no doubt, but we will gain ten where we lose one, the advantages being so great to all who can avail themselves of them. So we say CASH THROUGHOUT. Bring money for Clothing and we will supply it at prices possible under no other plan.

SECOND POINT—"ONE PRICE"—The fairness of this feature of our plan all will praise. It is simply treating all alike— exacting nothing from indisposition to bargain or ignorance, and, at the same time, conceding all that shrewdness on the shrewdest customer's part could possibly

extort, because the "One Price" which we mark on our goods shall invariably be Not the "First" Price, but the Last and Lowest Price.

Not the "Top" Price, but the Very Bottom Price.

THIRD POINT—"FULL GUARANTEE"— A printed guarantee, bearing the signature of our firm will accompany each garment as a warrantee. This binds us in every sense, and will be honored as quickly as a good draft of the Government of the United States. This is a sample of the full guarantee, and tells its own story—Guarantee.

WE HEREBY GUARANTEE

First—That the prices of our goods shall be as low as the same quality of material and manufacture are sold anywhere in the United States.

Second—That prices are precisely the same to everybody for same quality, on same day of purchase.

Third—That the quality of goods is as represented on printed labels.

Fourth—That the full amount of cash paid will be refunded, if customers find the articles unsatisfactory, and return them unworn and uninjured within ten days of date of purchase.

FOURTH POINT—"CASH RETURNED"— This is simply a concession on our part to our customers, to secure them full confidence in dealing for goods they know very little about, and we thus prevent any occasion for dissatisfaction from any and every cause whatsoever. If the garment is not exactly what you thought, if your taste changes, if the "home folks" prefer another color or another shape, if you find you can buy the same material and style elsewhere for less money, if you conclude you don't need it after you get home, if the season changes suddenly and you wish you had not bought it, bring it back unworn and uninjured, and the full amount of money you paid will be returned on the spot. What more can we do for our customers than this, when we make our clothing so that they can draw the money value with it equally as well as with a check on the banks?

The ADVANTAGES incident to a system having for its cardinal points these which we have now explained, are simply innumerable. Saving of time and temper, perfect security, absence of all huckstering, etc., etc.

But above all this . . .

All of these "By-ways" lead direct to CHEAPNESS; and this without lowering the quality or style of our celebrated make of MEN'S AND BOY'S CLOTHING.

UNDERSTAND, ANALYZE, & EVALUATE

1. What were the benefits of Wanamaker's four cardinal points for consumers? What were the benefits for Wanamaker? Judging by Wanamaker's new way of doing business, what must business practices and customer service have looked like before?

2. Why might these assurances have been particularly important for a large department store? Why might they have been essential for the urban consumer market?

Source: *Golden Book of the Wanamaker Stores, Jubilee Year, 1861–1911*, Philadelphia, PA: John Wanamaker, 1911, 152–154. This advertisement was originally published in 1874. Located in Regina Lee Blaszczyk and Philip B. Scranton (eds.), *Major Problems in American Business History*, Boston, MA: Houghton Mifflin Company, 2006, 298–299.

Rising incomes created new markets for consumer goods, which were now available to a mass market for the first time, as a result of technological innovations and new merchandising techniques. An example of such changes was the emergence of ready-made clothing. In the early nineteenth century, most Americans had made their own clothing. The invention of the sewing machine and the Civil War demand for uniforms spurred the manufacture of clothing and helped create an enormous industry devoted to producing ready-made garments. By the end of the century, almost all Americans bought their clothing from stores. Partly as a result, much larger numbers of people became concerned with personal style. Interest in women's fashion, for example, had once been a luxury reserved for the relatively affluent. Now middle-class and even working-class women could strive to emulate distinctive styles of dress.

Buying and preparing food also became a critical part of the new **consumerism**. The development and mass production of tin cans in the 1880s created a large new industry devoted to packaging and selling canned food and condensed milk. Refrigerated railroad cars made it possible for perishable foods to be transported over long distances without spoiling. Artificially frozen ice enabled many households to afford iceboxes. The changes brought improved diets and better health. Life expectancy rose six years in the first two decades of the twentieth century.

CHAIN STORES, MAIL-ORDER HOUSES, AND DEPARTMENT STORES

Changes in marketing also altered the way Americans bought goods. New "chain stores" could usually offer a wider array of goods at lower prices than the small local stores with which they competed. The Atlantic and Pacific Tea Company (A&P) began a national network of grocery stores in the 1870s. F. W. Woolworth built a chain of dry goods stores. Sears and Roebuck established a large market for its mail-order merchandise by distributing an enormous catalog each year.

In larger cities, the emergence of great department stores helped make shopping more alluring and glamorous. Marshall Field in Chicago created one of the first American

(©Corbis)

DEPARTMENT STORES   Department stores often created "events" to help promote sales of their many wares. Here, Strawbridge and Clothier department store creates a stir on Market Street in Philadelphia in 1907.

department stores, a place deliberately designed to produce a sense of wonder and excitement. Similar stores emerged in New York, Brooklyn, Boston, Philadelphia, and other cities. (For the philosophy of one of the leading department store innovators, see "Consider the Source: John Wanamaker, the Four Cardinal Points of the Department Store.")

WOMEN AS CONSUMERS

The rise of mass consumption had particularly dramatic effects on American women. Women's clothing styles changed much more rapidly than men's, which encouraged more frequent purchases. Women generally bought and prepared food for their families, so the availability of new food products changed not only how people ate but also how women shopped and cooked.

The consumer economy produced new employment opportunities for women as salesclerks and waitresses. And it spawned the creation of a new movement in which women played a vital role: the consumer protection movement. The **National Consumers League (NCL)**, formed in the 1890s under the leadership of Florence Kelley, attempted to mobilize the power of women as consumers to force retailers and manufacturers to improve wages and working conditions. The NCL encouraged women to buy only products with the League's "white label," which indicated that the product was made under fair working conditions.

LEISURE IN THE CONSUMER SOCIETY

Closely related to the rise of consumption was a growing interest in leisure time. Members of the urban middle and professional classes had large blocks of time during which they were not at work—evenings, weekends, even paid vacations. Working hours in many factories declined, from an average of nearly seventy hours a week in 1860 to under sixty in 1900. Even farmers found that the mechanization of agriculture gave them more free time. As many people's lives became more compartmentalized, with clear distinctions between work and leisure, many Americans began to search for new forms of recreation and entertainment.

Redefining Leisure

In earlier eras, relatively few Americans had considered leisure a valuable thing. Many equated it with laziness. In the late nineteenth century, however, the beginnings of a redefinition of leisure appeared. The economist Simon Patten articulated this new view of leisure in *The Theory of Prosperity* (1902), *The New Basis of Civilization* (1910), and other works. He challenged the centuries-old assumption that the normal condition of civilization was a scarcity of goods. In earlier times, Patten argued, fear of scarcity had caused people to place a high value on thrift, self-denial, and restraint. But in modern industrial societies, new economies could create enough wealth to satisfy not just the needs but also the desires of all.

As Americans became more accustomed to leisure as a normal part of life, they began to look for new experiences and entertainments. Mass entertainment occasionally bridged differences of class, race, and gender. But it could also be sharply divided. Saloons and some sporting events tended to be male preserves. Shopping and going to tea rooms and luncheonettes were more popular among women. Theaters, pubs, and clubs were often specific to particular ethnic communities or particular work groups. When the classes did meet in public spaces—as they did, for example, in city parks—there was often considerable conflict over what constituted appropriate public behavior. Elites in New York City, for example, tried to prohibit anything but quiet activities in Central Park, while working-class people wanted to use the public spaces for sports and entertainment.

Spectator Sports

Among the most important responses to the search for entertainment was the rise of organized spectator sports, especially baseball. A game much like baseball, known as "rounders" and derived from cricket, had enjoyed limited popularity in Great Britain in the early nineteenth century. Versions of the game began to appear in America in the early 1830s. By the end of the Civil War, interest in the game had grown rapidly. More than 200 amateur or semiprofessional teams and clubs existed, many of which joined a national association and proclaimed a set of standard rules. As the game grew in popularity, it offered opportunities for profit. The first salaried team, the Cincinnati Red Stockings, was formed in 1869. Other cities fielded professional teams, and in 1876 the teams banded together in the National League. A rival league, the American Association, appeared and collapsed, but in 1901 the American League emerged to replace it. And in 1903, the first modern World Series was played, in which the American League's Boston Red Sox beat the National League's Pittsburgh Pirates. By then, baseball had become an important business and a national preoccupation.

Baseball had great appeal to working-class males. The second most popular game, football, appealed at first to a more elite segment of the male population, in part because it originated in colleges and universities. The first intercollegiate football game in America occurred between Princeton and Rutgers in 1869. Early intercollegiate football bore only an indirect relation to the modern game; it was more similar to present-day rugby. By the

(©Transcendental Graphics/Getty Images)

THE AMERICAN NATIONAL GAME   Long before the modern major leagues began, local baseball clubs were active throughout much of the United States, establishing the game as the "national pastime." This print of a "grand match for the championship" depicts an 1866 game at Elysian Fields, a popular park just across the river from New York City in Hoboken, New Jersey.

late 1870s, however, the game was becoming standardized and was taking on the outlines of its modern form.

Basketball was invented in 1891 in Springfield, Massachusetts, by Dr. James A. Naismith, a Canadian working as an athletic director for a local college. Boxing, which had long been a disreputable activity concentrated primarily among the urban lower classes, became by the 1880s a more popular and, in some places, more reputable sport.

Participation in the major sports was almost exclusively the province of men, but several sports emerged in which women became involved. Golf and tennis both attracted more and more relatively wealthy men and women. Bicycling and croquet also enjoyed widespread popularity in the 1890s among women as well as men. Women's colleges introduced their students to more strenuous sports as well—track, crew, swimming, and (beginning in the late 1890s) basketball.

MUSIC, THEATER, AND MOVIES

Other forms of popular entertainment also developed in the cities. Many ethnic communities maintained their own theaters, which presented plays in the native languages. Urban theaters in the heart of cities attracted a much broader audience. They introduced new entertainment forms: the musical comedy, which evolved gradually from the comic operettas of Europe; and **vaudeville**, a form of theater adapted from French models, which remained the most popular urban entertainment into the first decades of the twentieth century. Vaudeville consisted of a variety of acts (musicians, comedians, magicians, jugglers, and others) and was, at least in the beginning, inexpensive to produce. As the economic potential of vaudeville grew, some promoters, most prominently Florenz Ziegfeld of New York, staged more elaborate spectacles.

Vaudeville was also one of the few entertainment media open to black performers, who brought to it elements of the minstrel shows they had earlier developed for black audiences in the late nineteenth century. Some minstrel singers (including the most famous, Al Jolson) were white performers wearing heavy makeup (or "blackface"), but most were black. Entertainers of both races performed music based on the gospel and folk tunes of the plantation and on the jazz and ragtime of black urban communities. White and black performers also tailored their acts to prevailing prejudices, ridiculing African Americans by acting out demeaning stereotypes.

American popular entertainment was transformed with the emergence of motion picture shows. Thomas Edison and others had created the technology underpinning the motion picture in the 1880s. Soon after that, short films became available to individual viewers watching peepshows in pool halls, penny arcades, and amusement parks. Soon, larger projectors made it possible to display the images on big screens, which permitted substantial audiences to see films in theaters. By 1900, Americans were becoming attracted in large numbers to these early movies, usually plotless films of trains or waterfalls or other spectacles. The director D. W. Griffith carried the motion picture into a new era with his silent epics—*The Birth of a Nation* (1915), *Intolerance* (1916), and others—which introduced serious if notoriously racist plots and elaborate productions to filmmaking.

PATTERNS OF PUBLIC AND PRIVATE LEISURE

Particularly striking about popular entertainment in the late nineteenth and early twentieth centuries was its public quality. Many Americans spent their leisure time in places where they would find not only entertainment but also other people. Thousands of working-class New Yorkers spent evenings in dance halls, vaudeville houses, and concert halls. More affluent New Yorkers enjoyed afternoons in Central Park, where a principal attraction was seeing other people and being seen by them. Moviegoers were attracted not just by the movies themselves but also by the energy of the audiences at lavish new movie palaces, just as sports fans were drawn by the crowds as well as by the games.

Perhaps the most striking example of popular public entertainment in the early twentieth century was **Coney Island**, the famous amusement park and resort on a popular beach in Brooklyn. Luna Park, the greatest of the Coney Island attractions, opened in 1903 and provided rides, stunts, and lavish reproductions of exotic places and spectacular adventures: Japanese gardens, Venetian canals with gondoliers, a Chinese theater, a simulated trip to the moon, and reenactments of such disasters as burning buildings and earthquakes. A year later, a competing company opened Dreamland, which tried to outdo even Luna Park with a 375-foot tower, a three-ring circus, chariot races, and a Lilliputian village from *Gulliver's Travels*. The popularity of Coney Island in these years was phenomenal. Thousands of people flocked to the large resort hotels that lined the beaches. Many thousands more made day trips out from the city by train and, after 1920, subway. In 1904, the average daily attendance at Luna Park alone was 90,000 people.

Most people found Coney Island appealing in part because it provided an escape from the genteel standards that governed so much of American life at the time. In the amusement parks of Coney Island, decorum was often forgotten, and people delighted in finding themselves in situations that in any other setting would have seemed embarrassing or improper: women's skirts blown above their heads with hot air; people pummeled with water and rubber paddles by clowns; hints of sexual freedom as strangers were forced to come into physical contact with one another on rides and amusements.

Not all popular entertainment, however, involved public events. Many Americans amused themselves privately by reading novels and poetry. The so-called dime novels, cheaply bound and widely circulated, became popular after the Civil War, with detective stories, tales of the Wild West, sagas of scientific adventure, and novels of "moral uplift." Publishers also distributed sentimental novels of romance, which developed a large audience among women, as did books about animals and about young children growing up. Louisa May Alcott's *Little Women,* most of whose readers were female, sold more than 2 million copies.

THE TECHNOLOGIES OF MASS COMMUNICATION

American journalism experienced dramatic change in the decades following the Civil War. Between 1870 and 1910, the circulation of daily newspapers increased nearly ninefold, from under 3 million to more than 24 million, a rate three times as great as the rate of population increase. And while standards varied widely from one paper to another, American journalism was developing the beginnings of a professional identity. Salaries of reporters increased; many newspapers began separating the reporting of news from the expression of opinion; and newspapers themselves became important businesses.

This transformation was to a large degree a result of new technologies of communication. The emergence of national press services, for example, was a product of the telegraph, which made it possible to supply papers with news and features from around the nation and the world. By the turn of the century, important newspaper chains had emerged as well, linked together by their own internal wire services. The most powerful was owned by **William Randolph Hearst**, who by 1914 controlled nine newspapers and two magazines. New printing technologies were making possible more elaborate layouts, the publication of color pictures, and, by the end of the century, the printing of photographs. These advances not only helped publishers make their own stories more vivid, they also made it possible for them to attract more advertisers.

THE TELEPHONE

The most important new technology of communication in the late nineteenth century was the telephone, which Alexander Graham Bell had first demonstrated in 1876. In its first years, the telephone was a relatively impractical tool. Those who subscribed to telephone service had to have direct wire links to everyone else they wished to call. In 1878, the first "switchboard" opened in New Haven, Connecticut, paving the way for more practical uses of the telephone. Once there was a switchboard, a telephone subscriber needed only a line to the central telephone office from which connections could be made to any other subscriber. A new occupation—the telephone "operator"—was born. The Bell System, which controlled all American telephone service, hired young white women to work as operators, hoping that a pleasant female voice would make the experience of using the telephone, and the inconvenience of the frequent technological problems that accompanied it, less irritating to customers. Telephone signals were very weak at first, and callers could seldom reach anyone more than a few miles away. In an effort to increase the range of telephones, engineers created the "repeater," which periodically strengthened the signal as it moved over distances. By 1914, the repeaters had improved to the point that it was now practical to envision a transcontinental line.

In its early years, the telephone was an almost entirely commercial instrument. Of the nearly 7,400 telephone customers in the New York–New Jersey area in 1891, 6,000 were businesses and organizations. Even the residential telephones tended to belong to doctors or business managers.

The growing reach of the telephone in the early years of the twentieth century made the Bell System (formally named American Telephone and Telegraph, or AT&T) one of the most powerful corporations in America and a genuine monopoly. Central to its success was an early decision by executives that the company would exclusively build and own all telephone instruments and then lease them to subscribers. That made it possible for AT&T to control both the equipment and the telephone service itself, and to exclude any competitors in either field. It also gave AT&T effective control over the local telephone companies allied with it and made the nation's telephone system into an effective cartel.

HIGH CULTURE IN THE URBAN AGE

In addition to the important changes in popular culture that accompanied the rise of cities and industry, there were profound changes in the realm of "high culture." The distinction between "highbrow" and "lowbrow" culture was largely new to the industrial era. In the early nineteenth century, most cultural activities had targeted people of all classes. By the late nineteenth century, however, elites were developing a cultural and intellectual life quite separate from the popular amusements of the urban masses.

LITERATURE AND ART IN URBAN AMERICA

One of the strongest impulses in American literature was the effort to recreate urban social reality. This trend toward realism found an early voice in Stephen Crane, who—although perhaps best known for his novel of the Civil War, *The Red Badge of Courage* (1895)—created a sensation in 1893 when he published *Maggie: A Girl of the Streets,* a grim picture of urban poverty and slum life. Theodore Dreiser, Frank Norris, and Upton Sinclair were similarly drawn to social issues as themes. **Kate Chopin**, a southern writer who explored the oppressive features of traditional marriage, encountered widespread public abuse after the publication of her shocking 1899 novel, *The Awakening,* which described a young wife and mother who abandoned her family in search of personal fulfillment. William Dean Howells, in *The Rise of Silas Lapham* and other works, described what he considered the shallowness and corruption of ordinary American lifestyles.

American art through most of the nineteenth century had been overshadowed by that of Europe. By 1900, however, a number of American artists broke from Old World traditions and experimented with new styles. Winslow Homer brought a distinctive approach to his paintings of New England maritime life and other American subjects. James McNeil Whistler was one of the first Western artists to introduce Asian themes into American and European art.

By the first years of the new century, some American artists were turning decisively away from the traditional academic style, perhaps most identified in America by the portraitist John Singer Sargent. Members of the so-called **Ashcan school** produced work startling in its naturalism and stark in its portrayal of the social realities of the era. John Sloan portrayed the dreariness of American urban slums, George Bellows caught the vigor and violence of his time in paintings and drawings of prizefights, Edward Hopper explored

(Source: National Gallery of Art, Washington)

DEMPSEY THROUGH THE ROPES   The artist George Bellows began painting fight scenes in the first years of the twentieth century, when boxing appealed primarily to working-class audiences. By 1924, when he created a lithograph of this moment from a famous prizefight, boxing had become one of the most popular sports in America.

the starkness and loneliness of the modern city. The Ashcan artists were also among the first Americans to appreciate expressionism and abstraction; and they showed their interest in new forms in 1913 when they helped stage the famous **Armory Show** in New York City, which displayed works of the French postimpressionists and of some American moderns.

THE IMPACT OF DARWINISM

One of the most profound intellectual developments in the late nineteenth century was the widespread acceptance of the theory of evolution, associated most prominently with the English naturalist Charles Darwin. Darwin argued that the human species had evolved from earlier forms of life through a process of "natural selection." History, Darwin suggested, was not the working out of a divine plan. It was a natural process dominated by the fiercest or luckiest competitors.

The theory of evolution met widespread resistance at first from educators, theologians, and even many scientists. By the end of the century, however, the evolutionists had converted most members of the urban professional and educated classes. Even many middle-class Protestant religious leaders had accepted the doctrine, making significant alterations in theology to accommodate it. The rise of **Darwinism**, however, contributed to something unseen by most urban Americans at the time: a deep schism between the new, cosmopolitan culture of the city and the more traditional, provincial culture of some rural areas. Thus the late nineteenth century saw not only the rise of a liberal Protestantism in tune with new scientific discoveries but also the beginning of an organized Protestant fundamentalism.

Darwinism helped spawn other new intellectual currents. There was the Social Darwinism of William Graham Sumner and others, which industrialists used so enthusiastically to justify their favored position in American life. But there were also more sophisticated philosophies, among them a doctrine that became known as "pragmatism." **William James**, a Harvard psychologist, was the most prominent publicist of the new theory, although earlier intellectuals such as Charles S. Peirce and later ones such as John Dewey were also important to its development and dissemination. According to the pragmatists, modern society should rely for guidance not on inherited ideals and moral principles but on the test of scientific inquiry. No idea or institution, not even religious faith, was valid, they claimed, unless it "worked," unless it stood the test of experience.

A similar concern for scientific inquiry was influencing the social sciences. Sociologists such as Edward A. Ross and Lester Frank Ward urged applying the scientific method to the solution of social and political problems. Historians such as Frederick Jackson Turner and Charles Beard argued that economic factors more than spiritual ideals had been the governing force in historical development. John Dewey proposed a new approach to education that placed less emphasis on the rote learning of traditional knowledge and more on flexible, democratic schooling.

The implications of Darwinism also promoted the growth of anthropology and encouraged some scholars to begin examining other cultures in new ways. Some white Americans began to look at Indian society, for example, as a coherent culture with its own norms and values that were worthy of respect and preservation, even though they were different from those of white society.

Toward Universal Schooling

The growing demand for specialized skills and scientific knowledge created a growing, and changing, demand for education. The late nineteenth century, therefore, was a time of rapid expansion and reform of American schools and universities.

Free public primary and secondary education spread rapidly. By 1900, compulsory school attendance laws existed in thirty-one states and territories. Education was still far from universal. Rural areas lagged far behind urban-industrial ones in funding public education. In the South, many African Americans had no access to schools at all. But for many white men and women, educational opportunities were expanding.

Educational reformers tried to extend educational opportunities to the Indian tribes as well, in an effort to "civilize" them into white society. In the 1870s, reformers recruited small groups of Native Americans to attend Hampton Institute, a primarily black college. In 1879, they organized the Carlisle Indian Industrial School in Pennsylvania. Like many black colleges, Carlisle emphasized practical "industrial" education. Ultimately, however, these reform efforts failed, in part because they were unpopular with their intended beneficiaries.

Universities and the Growth of Science and Technology

Colleges and universities also proliferated rapidly in the late nineteenth century. The Morrill Land Grant Act of 1862, by which the federal government had donated public land to states for the establishment of colleges, led to the creation of sixty-nine "land-grant" institutions in the last decades of the century—among them the state university systems of California, Illinois, Minnesota, and Wisconsin. Other universities, including Chicago, Columbia, Harvard, Northwestern, Princeton, Syracuse, and Yale, benefited from millions of dollars contributed by business and financial titans such as Rockefeller and Carnegie. Other philanthropists founded new universities or reorganized older ones to perpetuate their family names—Vanderbilt, Johns Hopkins, Cornell, Duke, Tulane, Stanford, and others.

Universities played a vital role in the economic development of the United States in the late nineteenth century and beyond. The land-grant institutions were specifically mandated to advance knowledge in "agriculture and mechanics." From the beginning, therefore, they were committed not just to abstract knowledge but to making discoveries that would be of practical use to farmers and manufacturers. As they evolved into great state universities, they retained that tradition and became the source of many of the discoveries that helped American industry and commerce advance. Private universities emerged that served many of the same purposes: the Massachusetts Institute of Technology, founded in 1865, soon became the nation's premier engineering school; Johns Hopkins University in Baltimore, founded in 1876, did much to advance medical scholarship, as did the Rockefeller Institute for Medical Research in New York (later Rockefeller University) and the Carnegie Institution. By the early twentieth century, older and more traditional universities were beginning to form relationships with the private sector and the government, doing research that did not just advance knowledge for its own sake but that was directly applicable to practical problems of the time.

MEDICAL SCIENCE

Both the culture of and the scientific basis for medical care were changing rapidly in the early twentieth century. Most doctors were beginning to accept the new medical assumption that there were underlying causes to particular symptoms, that a symptom was not itself a disease. They were also beginning to make use of new or improved technologies—the X-ray, improved microscopes, and other diagnostic devices—that made it possible to classify, and distinguish among, different diseases. Laboratory tests could now identify infections such as typhoid and dysentery. These technologies were a critical first step toward the effective treatment of diseases.

At about the same time, pharmaceutical research began to produce some important new medicines. Aspirin was first synthesized in 1899. Other researchers experimented with chemicals that might destroy diseases in the blood, an effort that eventually led to the various forms of chemotherapy that are still widely used in treating cancer. In 1906, an American surgeon, G. W. Crile, became the first physician to use blood transfusion in treatment, which revolutionized surgery. In the past, patients often lost so much blood during operations that extensive surgery could be fatal for that reason alone. With transfusions, it became possible to conduct much longer and more elaborate operations.

The widespread acceptance by the end of the nineteenth century of the germ theory of disease had important implications. Physicians quickly discovered that exposure to germs did not by itself necessarily cause disease, and they began looking for the other factors that determined who got sick and who did not. Among the factors they eventually discovered were general health, previous medical history, diet and nutrition, and eventually genetic predisposition. The awareness of the importance of infection in spreading disease also encouraged doctors to sterilize their instruments, use surgical gloves, and otherwise purify the medical environment.

By the early twentieth century, American physicians and surgeons were generally recognized as among the best in the world, and American medical education was beginning to attract students from many other countries. These improvements in medical knowledge and training, along with improvements in sanitation and public health, did much to reduce infection and mortality in most American communities.

EDUCATION FOR WOMEN

The post–Civil War era saw an important expansion of educational opportunities for women, although such opportunities continued to lag far behind those available to men and were almost entirely denied to women of color.

Most public high schools accepted women readily, but opportunities for higher education were fewer. At the end of the Civil War, only three American colleges were coeducational. After the war, many of the land-grant colleges and universities in the Midwest and such private universities as Cornell and Wesleyan began to admit women along with men. But coeducation was less crucial to women's education in this period than was the creation of a network of women's colleges. Mount Holyoke in central Massachusetts had begun its life in 1836 as a "seminary" for women. It became a full-fledged college in the 1880s, at about the same time that entirely new female institutions were emerging: Vassar, Wellesley, Smith, Bryn Mawr, Wells, and Goucher. A few of the larger private universities created separate colleges for women on their campuses, including Barnard at Columbia and Radcliffe at Harvard.

The female college was part of an important phenomenon in the history of modern American women: the emergence of distinctive women's communities outside the family. Most faculty members and many administrators were women. And college life produced a spirit of collective identity and commitment among educated women that had important effects in later years. Most female college graduates ultimately married, but they married at a more advanced age than their non-college counterparts. A significant minority, perhaps over 25 percent, did not marry at all, but devoted themselves to careers. The growth of female higher education clearly became for some women a liberating experience, persuading them that they had roles other than those of wives and mothers to perform in their rapidly changing urban-industrial society.

CONCLUSION

The extraordinary growth of American cities in the last decades of the nineteenth century led to both great achievements and enormous problems. Cities became centers of learning, art, and commerce and produced great advances in technology, transportation, architecture, and communications. They provided their residents—and their many visitors—with varied and dazzling experiences, so much so that people increasingly left the countryside to move to the city.

But cities were also places of congestion, filth, disease, and corruption. With populations expanding too rapidly for services to keep up, most American cities in this era struggled with makeshift techniques to solve the basic problems of providing water, disposing of sewage, building roads, running public transportation, fighting fire, stopping crime, and preventing or curing disease. City governments, many of them dominated by political machines and ruled by party bosses, were often models of inefficiency and corruption, although in their informal way they also provided substantial services to the working-class and immigrant constituencies who needed them most. Yet they also managed to oversee great public projects: the building of parks, museums, opera houses, and theaters, usually in partnership with private developers.

The city brought together races, ethnic groups, and classes of extraordinary variety, from the families of great wealth that the new industrial age was creating to the vast working class, much of it consisting of immigrants, who crowded into densely packed neighborhoods divided by nationality. The city also spawned temples of consumerism: shops, boutiques, and, above all, the great department stores. And it created forums for public recreation and entertainment, including green spaces, theaters, athletic fields, amusement parks, and, later, movie palaces.

Urban life created anxiety among those who lived within the cities and among those who observed them from afar. But in fact, American cities adapted reasonably successfully over time to the great demands their growth made of them and learned to govern themselves, if not entirely honestly and efficiently, at least enough to allow them to survive and grow.

KEY TERMS/PEOPLE/PLACES/EVENTS

Armory Show 448
Ashcan school 447
city beautiful movement 434
Coney Island 445
consumerism 441
Darwinism 448

Jacob Riis 435
Kate Chopin 447
National Consumers League (NCL) 442
Public Health Service 437
Tammany Hall 439
tenements 435

Theodore Dreiser 438
vaudeville 444
William James 449
William M. Tweed 439
William Randolph Hearst 446

RECALL AND REFLECT

1. What groups of people were most likely to move to the cities of late-nineteenth-century America, and why?
2. What was the relationship between immigration and urbanization in the late nineteenth century?
3. How did the new consumer economy affect roles and expectations for women?
4. What was Darwinism, and what was its impact on American intellectual life?

19 FROM CRISIS TO EMPIRE

THE POLITICS OF EQUILIBRIUM

THE AGRARIAN REVOLT

THE CRISIS OF THE 1890s

STIRRINGS OF IMPERIALISM

WAR WITH SPAIN

THE REPUBLIC AS EMPIRE

LOOKING AHEAD

1. What were the major social and economic problems that beset the United States in the late nineteenth century, and how did the two major political parties respond to these problems?

2. What was Populism, what were its goals, and to what degree were these goals achieved?

3. How did the United States become an imperial power?

THE UNITED STATES APPROACHED the end of the nineteenth century as a fundamentally different nation from what it had been at the beginning of the Civil War. With rapid change came cascading social and political problems—ones the weak and conservative governments of the time showed little inclination or ability to address.

A catastrophic depression that began in 1893 devastated millions of Americans. Farmers responded to this and earlier economic downturns by creating an agrarian political movement known as Populism. American workers, facing massive unemployment, staged large and occasionally violent strikes. Not since the Civil War had American politics been so polarized and impassioned. The election of 1896, which pitted the agrarian hero William Jennings Bryan against the conservative William McKinley, was dramatic but anticlimactic. Supported by the mighty Republican Party and many eastern groups who looked with suspicion and unease at the agricultural demands coming from the West, McKinley easily triumphed.

McKinley did little in his first term in office to resolve the grievances of his time, but the economy revived nevertheless. Having largely ignored the depression, McKinley focused on another national cause: the plight of Cuba in its war with Spain. In the spring of 1898, the United States declared war on Spain and entered the conflict in Cuba, a brief but bloody war that ended with an American victory four months later. The conflict had begun in part as a way to support Cuban independence from the Spanish, but a group of fervent and influential

TIME LINE

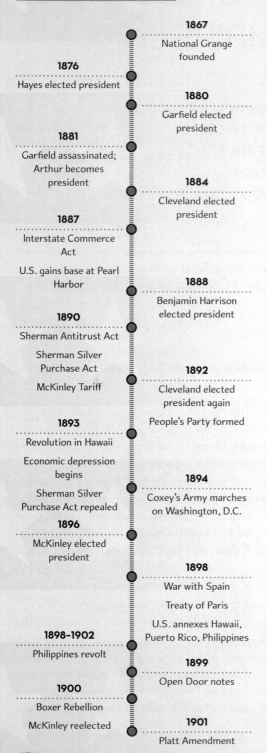

1867
National Grange founded

1876
Hayes elected president

1880
Garfield elected president

1881
Garfield assassinated; Arthur becomes president

1884
Cleveland elected president

1887
Interstate Commerce Act

U.S. gains base at Pearl Harbor

1888
Benjamin Harrison elected president

1890
Sherman Antitrust Act

Sherman Silver Purchase Act

McKinley Tariff

1892
Cleveland elected president again

People's Party formed

1893
Revolution in Hawaii

Economic depression begins

Sherman Silver Purchase Act repealed

1894
Coxey's Army marches on Washington, D.C.

1896
McKinley elected president

1898
War with Spain

Treaty of Paris

U.S. annexes Hawaii, Puerto Rico, Philippines

1898–1902
Philippines revolt

1899
Open Door notes

1900
Boxer Rebellion

McKinley reelected

1901
Platt Amendment

---

imperialists worked to convert the war into an occasion for acquiring overseas possessions. Despite a powerful anti-imperialist movement, the acquisition of the former Spanish colonies proceeded, only to draw Americans into yet another imperial war, this one in the Philippines, where the Americans, not the Spanish, were the targets of local enmity.

THE POLITICS OF EQUILIBRIUM

The enormous social and economic changes of the late nineteenth century strained not only the nation's traditional social arrangements but its political institutions as well. Searching for stability and social justice, Americans looked to the government for leadership. Yet that government during much of this period was ill equipped to confront these new challenges. As a result, problems festered and grew.

THE PARTY SYSTEM

The most striking feature of late-nineteenth-century politics was the stability of the party system. From the end of Reconstruction until the late 1890s, the electorate was divided almost evenly between the Republicans and the Democrats. Sixteen states were solidly and consistently Republican, and fourteen states (most in the South) were solidly and consistently Democratic. Only a handful of states were usually in doubt, and they generally decided the results of national elections, often on the basis of voter turnout. The Republican Party captured the presidency in all but two of the elections of the era, but in the five presidential elections beginning in 1876, the average popular-vote margin separating the Democratic and Republican candidates was 1.5 percent. The congressional balance was similarly stable, with the Republicans generally controlling the Senate and the Democrats generally controlling the House.

Despite the relatively modest differences, most eligible Americans had strong loyalties to their chosen party. Voter turnout in presidential elections between 1860 and 1900 averaged over 78 percent of all eligible voters. Large groups of potential voters were disenfranchised in these years: women in most states and, particularly toward the end of the century, almost all blacks and some poor whites in the South. But for many adult white males, there were few restrictions on voting.

What explains this extraordinary loyalty to the two political parties? It was not that the parties took distinct positions on important public issues; their positions were similar, with a few exceptions. Party loyalties reflected other factors. Region was perhaps the most important. To white southerners, loyalty to the Democratic Party, the vehicle by which they had seceded from the Union and then triumphed over Reconstruction and preserved white supremacy, was a matter of unquestioned faith. Republican loyalties were equally intense in the North. To many, the party of Lincoln remained a bulwark against slavery and treason.

Religious and ethnic differences also shaped party loyalties. The Democratic Party attracted many Catholic voters, recent immigrants, and poorer workers in cities where Democratic political machines held power. The Republican Party appealed to northern Protestants, citizens of old stock, much of the middle class, and industrial elites. The few substantive issues on which the parties took different stands reflected their different constituencies. Republicans tended to support immigration restriction and to favor temperance legislation, which many believed would help discipline foreign-born communities. Catholics and immigrants viewed such proposals as assaults on them and their cultures, and the Democratic Party followed their lead.

Party identification, then, was usually more a reflection of cultural inclinations than a calculation of economic interest. Individuals might affiliate with a party because their parents had done so or because it was the party of their region, their church, or their ethnic group. Both parties, by twentieth- and twenty-first century standards, believed in very limited government.

The National Government

One reason the parties avoided most substantive issues was that the federal government did relatively little. Washington was responsible for delivering the mail, maintaining a military, conducting foreign policy, and collecting tariffs and taxes. It had few other responsibilities and few institutions capable of undertaking additional responsibilities even if it chose to do so.

There was one significant exception. From the end of the Civil War to the early twentieth century, the federal government administered a system of annual pensions for Union Civil War veterans and their widows, and state governments in the South acted similarly on behalf of Confederate ex-soldiers. At its peak, this pension system was making payments to a majority of the male citizens of the North and to many women as well, though African American veterans rarely applied and usually met rejection when they did. Some reformers hoped to make the system permanent and universal, others found it corrupt and expensive; by 1915, it had exceeded the cost of fighting the war. When the Civil War generation died out, the pension system died with it.

In most other respects, the United States in the late nineteenth century was a society without a modern national government. The most powerful institutions were the two political parties, the bosses and machines that dominated them, and the federal courts.

PRESIDENTS AND PATRONAGE

Presidents in the late nineteenth century had great symbolic importance, but they were unable to do very much except distribute government appointments. A new president and his tiny staff had to make almost 100,000 appointments.

It sometimes proved impossible for a president to avoid factional conflict, as the presidency of **Rutherford B. Hayes** demonstrated. By the end of his term, two groups—the **Stalwarts**, led by Roscoe Conkling of New York, and the **Half-Breeds**, captained by James G. Blaine of Maine—were competing for control of the Republican Party. Rhetorically, the Stalwarts favored traditional, professional machine politics, while the Half-Breeds favored reform. In fact, both groups were mainly interested in a larger share of patronage. Hayes tried to satisfy both and ended up satisfying neither.

The battle over patronage overshadowed all else during Hayes's unhappy presidency. His one important, substantive initiative—an effort to create a civil service system—attracted no support from either party. And his early announcement that he would not seek reelection only weakened him further.

The Republicans managed to retain the presidency in 1880 in part because they agreed on a ticket that included a Stalwart and a Half-Breed. They nominated **James A. Garfield**, a veteran congressman from Ohio and a Half-Breed, for president and Chester A. Arthur of New York, a Stalwart, for vice president. The Democrats nominated General Winfield

GETTING HOT ENOUGH FOR HIM.

(Source: Library of Congress, Prints and Photographs Division [LC-DIG-ppmsca-28490])

PRESIDENT CHESTER A. ARTHUR Although originally a Stalwart, Arthur attempted to reform the spoils system. In this *Puck* cartoon, he is catching heat from a variety of Republican factions, including the Stalwarts and Half-Breeds.

Scott Hancock, a minor Civil War commander with no national following. Benefiting from the end of the recession of 1879, Garfield won a decisive electoral victory, although his popular-vote margin was thin.

Garfield began his presidency by defying the Stalwarts and supporting civil service reform. He soon found himself embroiled in an ugly public quarrel with Conkling and the Stalwarts. The dispute was never resolved. On July 2, 1881, only four months after his inauguration, Garfield was shot twice while standing in the Washington railroad station by an apparently deranged gunman, and unsuccessful office seeker, who shouted, "I am a Stalwart and Arthur is president now!" Garfield lingered for nearly three months before dying.

Garfield's successor, **Chester A. Arthur**, had spent his political lifetime as a devoted, skilled, and open spoilsman and a close ally of New York political boss Roscoe Conkling. But on becoming president, he tried, like Hayes and Garfield before him, to follow an independent course and even promote reform. To the dismay of the Stalwarts, Arthur kept most of Garfield's appointees in office and supported civil service reform. In 1883, Congress passed the first national civil service measure, the **Pendleton Act**, which required that some federal jobs be filled by competitive written examinations rather than patronage. Relatively few offices fell under civil service at first, but its reach steadily widened.

Cleveland, Harrison, and the Tariff

In the unsavory election of 1884, the Republican candidate for president was Senator James G. Blaine of Maine, known to his admirers as the "Plumed Knight" but to many others as a symbol of seamy party politics. Rather than support Blaine, a group of disgruntled "liberal Republicans," known to their critics as the "mugwumps," announced they would bolt the party and support an honest Democrat. Rising to the bait, the Democrats nominated **Grover Cleveland**, the reform governor of New York.

In a campaign filled with personal invective, what may have decided the race was the last-minute introduction of a religious controversy. Shortly before the election, a delegation of Protestant ministers called on Blaine in New York City; their spokesman, Dr. Samuel Burchard, referred to the Democrats as the party of "rum, Romanism, and rebellion." Blaine was slow to repudiate Burchard's indiscretion, and Democrats quickly spread the news that Blaine had tolerated a slander on the Catholic Church. Cleveland's narrow victory probably resulted from an unusually heavy Catholic vote for the Democrats in New York.

Grover Cleveland was respected, if not often liked, for his stern and righteous opposition to politicians, grafters, pressure groups, and Tammany Hall. He embodied an era in which few Americans believed the federal government could or should do much. Cleveland had always doubted the wisdom of protective tariffs, taxes on imported goods designed to protect domestic producers. The existing high rates, he believed, were responsible for the annual surplus in federal revenues, which was tempting Congress to pass extravagant legislation, which he frequently vetoed. In December 1887, therefore, he asked Congress to reduce the tariff rates. Democrats in the House approved a tariff reduction, but Senate Republicans defiantly passed a bill of their own, actually raising the rates as part of their broader protective impulse toward American corporations. The resulting deadlock made the tariff an issue in the election of 1888.

The Democrats renominated Cleveland and supported tariff reductions. Endorsing protection, Republicans settled on former senator **Benjamin Harrison** of Indiana, who was obscure but respectable, and the grandson of President William Henry Harrison. Cleveland won the popular vote by 100,000, but Harrison won an Electoral College majority of 233 to 168.

New Public Issues

Benjamin Harrison's record as president was little more substantial than that of his grandfather, who had died a month after taking office. Harrison harbored few visible convictions and made no effort to influence Congress. And yet during Harrison's passive administration, public opinion was beginning to force the government to confront some of the pressing social and economic issues of the day, most notably the power of trusts.

By the mid-1880s, fifteen western and southern states had adopted laws prohibiting combinations that restrained competition. But corporations found it easy to escape limitations by incorporating in states, such as New Jersey and Delaware, that offered them special privileges. If antitrust legislation was to be effective, its supporters believed, it would have to come from the national government. In July 1890, both houses of Congress passed the **Sherman Antitrust Act** almost without dissent. For over a decade after its passage, the law was unevenly enforced and steadily weakened by the courts. As of 1901, the Justice Department had instituted many antitrust suits against unions, but only fourteen against business combinations.

The Republicans were more interested in the issue they believed had won them the 1888 election: the tariff. Representative **William McKinley** of Ohio and Senator Nelson W. Aldrich of Rhode Island drafted the highest protective measure ever proposed to Congress. Known as the McKinley Tariff, it became law in October 1890. But Republican leaders apparently misinterpreted public sentiment. Many voters saw the high tariff as a way to enrich producers and starve consumers. The party suffered a stunning reversal in the 1890 congressional election. The Republicans' substantial Senate majority was slashed to 8; in the House, the party retained only 86 of the 332 seats, losing its majority in that chamber.

Nor were the Republicans able to recover over the next two years. In the presidential election of 1892, Benjamin Harrison once again supported protection. Grover Cleveland, renominated by the Democrats, once again opposed it. A new third party, the People's (or Populist) Party, with James B. Weaver as its candidate, advocated substantial economic reform. Cleveland won 277 electoral votes to Harrison's 145 and had a popular margin of 380,000. Weaver ran far behind.

The policies of Cleveland's second term were much like those of his first. Again, he supported a tariff reduction, which the House approved but the Senate weakened. Cleveland denounced the result but allowed it to become law as the Wilson-Gorman Tariff.

Public pressure had been growing since the 1880s for other reforms, among them regulation of the railroads. Farm organizations in the Midwest had persuaded several state legislatures to pass regulatory legislation in the early 1870s. But in 1886, the Supreme Court—in *Wabash, St. Louis, and Pacific Railway Co. v. Illinois,* known as the *Wabash* case—ruled one of the regulatory laws in Illinois unconstitutional. According to the Court, the law was an attempt to control interstate commerce and thus infringed on the exclusive power of Congress. Later, the courts limited the powers of the states to regulate commerce even within their own boundaries.

Effective railroad regulation, it was now clear, could come only from the federal government. Congress responded to public pressure in 1887 with the **Interstate Commerce Act**, which banned discrimination in rates between long and short hauls, required that railroads publish their rate schedules and file them with the government, and declared that all inter-state rail rates must be "reasonable and just." A five-person agency, the Interstate Commerce Commission (ICC) was to administer the act. But the commissioners, like advocates of the law in Congress once it passed through their chambers, had little power on their own, relying instead on the courts to enforce their rulings. For almost twenty years after its passage, the Interstate Commerce Act, haphazardly enforced and narrowly interpreted by the courts rather like the Sherman Act, had little practical effect.

THE AGRARIAN REVOLT

No group watched the performance of the federal government in the 1880s with greater dismay than American farmers. They helped produce the Populist upheaval—one of the most powerful movements of political protest in American history.

THE GRANGERS

Farmers had been making efforts to organize politically for several decades before the 1880s. The first major farm organization was the National Grange of the Patrons of Husbandry, or **Grangers**, founded in 1867. From it emerged a network of local organizations that tried to teach new scientific agricultural techniques to its members. When the depression of 1873 caused a sharp decline in farm prices, membership rapidly increased and the direction of the organization changed. Granges in the Midwest began to organize marketing cooperatives and to promote political action to curb monopolistic practices by railroads and warehouses. At their peak, Grange supporters controlled the legislatures in most of the midwestern states. The result was the Granger Laws of the early 1870s, by which many states imposed strict regulations on railroad rates and practices. But the destruction of the new regulations by the courts, combined with the political inexperience of many Grange leaders and the return of prosperity in the late 1870s, produced a dramatic decline in the power of the association.

THE FARMERS' ALLIANCES

As early as 1875, farmers in parts of the South were banding together in **Farmers' Alliances** just as the Granges were weakening. By the 1880s, the Southern and Northwestern Alliances had more than 4 million members between them in the South, Midwest, and Great Plains, while a separate Colored Farmers' National Alliance contributed more than a million people to the movement.

Like the Granges, the Alliances formed cooperatives and other marketing mechanisms. They established stores, banks, processing plants, and other facilities to free their members from dependence on the hated furnishing merchants who kept so many farmers in debt. Some Alliance leaders, however, saw the movement in larger terms: as an effort to build a society in which economic competition might give way to cooperation. Alliance lecturers traveled throughout rural areas, lambasting the concentrated power of great corporations, railroads, and financial institutions.

Although the Alliances quickly became far more widespread than the Granges had ever been, they suffered from similar problems. Their cooperatives did not always work well, partly because of mismanagement and partly because of the strength of opposing market forces.

(©Corbis)

MARY E. LEASE The fiery Populist orator Mary E. Lease was a fixture on the Alliance lecture circuit in the 1890s. She made some 160 speeches in 1890 alone. Her critics called her the "Kansas Pythoness," but she was popular among farmers with her denunciations of banks, railroads, and intermediaries, and her famous advice to "raise less corn and more hell."

These economic frustrations helped push the movement into a new phase at the end of the 1880s: the creation of a national political organization.

In 1889, the Southern and Northwestern Alliances agreed to a loose merger. The next year the Alliances held a national convention at Ocala, Florida, and issued the so-called Ocala Demands, which were, in effect, a party platform. In the 1890 off-year elections, candidates supported by the Alliances won partial or complete control of the legislatures in twelve states. They also won six governorships, three seats in the U.S. Senate, and approximately fifty in the U.S. House of Representatives. Many of the successful Alliance candidates were Democrats who had benefited, often passively, from Alliance endorsements. But dissident farmers drew enough encouragement from the results to contemplate further political action.

Alliance leaders discussed plans for a third party at meetings in Cincinnati in May 1891 and St. Louis in February 1892. Then, in July 1892, 1,300 exultant delegates poured into

Omaha, Nebraska, to proclaim the creation of the new party, approve an official set of principles, and nominate candidates for the presidency and vice presidency. The new organization's official name was the People's Party, but the movement was more commonly referred to as **Populism**.

The election of 1892 demonstrated the potential power of the new movement. The Populist presidential candidate—James B. Weaver of Iowa, a former Greenbacker—polled more than 1 million votes. Nearly 1,500 Populist candidates won election to seats in state legislatures. The party elected three governors, five senators, and ten congressmen. It could also claim the support of many Republicans and Democrats in Congress who had been elected by appealing to Populist sentiment.

THE POPULIST CONSTITUENCY

Already, however, there were signs of the limits of Populist strength. Populism had great appeal to farmers, particularly to small farmers with little long-range economic security. But Populism failed to move much beyond that group. Its leaders made energetic efforts to include labor within the coalition by courting the Knights of Labor and adding a labor plank to its platform. But Populism never attracted significant labor support or became a truly cohesive working-class movement, in part because the economic interests of labor and the interests of farmers were often at odds.

In the South, white Populists struggled with the question of whether to accept African Americans into the party. Despite the large and important black component to the Alliance movement, most white Populists accepted the assistance of African Americans only as long as it was clear that whites would remain in control. When southern conservatives began to attack the Populists for undermining white supremacy, party leaders succumbed to such pressures as well their own racial prejudices in marginalizing or excluding black farmers from the movement. Here was a consistent pattern in southern racial politics: white elites, fearful of a biracial coalition of rural or working-class people, used race to drive a wedge between those groups, fomenting white resentment of black economic competition to undermine what might have been shared concerns.

POPULIST IDEAS

The Populists spelled out their program first in the Ocala Demands of 1890 and then, more clearly, in the Omaha platform of 1892. They proposed a system of "subtreasuries," a network of government-owned warehouses where farmers could deposit their crops, to allow them to borrow money from the government at low rates of interest until the price of their goods went up. In addition, the Populists called for the abolition of national banks (which they believed were dangerous institutions of concentrated power), the end of absentee ownership of land, the direct election of U.S. senators (which would weaken the power of conservative state legislatures), and other devices to improve the ability of the people to influence the political process. They called as well for regulation and (after 1892) government ownership of railroads, telephones, and telegraphs. And they demanded a system of government-operated postal savings banks, a graduated income tax, the inflation of the currency, and, later, the remonetization of silver.

Some Populists were anti-Semitic, anti-intellectual, anti-eastern, and anti-urban. But bigotry was not the dominant force behind Populism. It was, rather, a serious effort to find solutions to real problems. Populists emphatically rejected the laissez-faire orthodoxies of their time, including the idea that the rights of ownership are absolute, and in fact called on the federal government to promote a dramatic redistribution of wealth and power. In short, the Populists raised one of the most overt, radical, and powerful challenges of the era to the direction in which American industrial capitalism was moving.

THE CRISIS OF THE 1890s

The agrarian protest was only one of many indications of the national political crisis emerging in the 1890s. There was a severe depression, widespread labor unrest and violence, and the continuing failure of either major party to respond to the growing distress. Grover Cleveland, who took office for the second time just as the economy was collapsing, remained convinced that any government action would be a violation of principle.

THE PANIC OF 1893

The **Panic of 1893** launched the most severe depression the nation had ever experienced. It began in March 1893, when the Philadelphia and Reading Railroad, unable to meet payments on loans, declared bankruptcy. Two months later, the National Cordage Company

(©Fotosearch/Getty Images)

COXEY'S ARMY Jacob S. Coxey leads his "army" of unemployed men through the town of Allegheny, Pennsylvania, in 1894, en route to Washington, where he hoped to pressure Congress to approve his plans for a massive public works program to put people back to work.

failed as well. Together, these two corporate failures triggered a stock market collapse. And since many of the major New York banks were heavy investors in the market, a wave of bank failures soon began. That caused a contraction of credit, which meant that many of the new, aggressive, and loan-dependent businesses went bankrupt.

The depression reflected, among other things, the degree to which all parts of the American economy were now interconnected. And it showed how dependent the economy was on the health of the railroads, which remained the nation's most powerful corporate and financial institutions. When the railroads suffered, as they did beginning in 1893, everyone suffered.

Once the panic began, it spread with startling speed. Within six months, more than 8,000 businesses, 156 railroads, and 400 banks failed. Already low agricultural prices tumbled further. Up to 1 million workers, 20 percent of the labor force, lost their jobs. The depression was unprecedented not only in its severity but also in its persistence. Although conditions improved slightly beginning in 1895, prosperity did not fully return until 1901.

The depression produced widespread social unrest, especially among the enormous numbers of unemployed workers. In 1894, Jacob S. Coxey, an Ohio businessman and Populist, began advocating a massive public works program to create jobs for the unemployed. When it became clear that Congress was ignoring his proposals, Coxey organized a march of the unemployed (known as "**Coxey's Army**") to Washington, D.C., to present his demands to the government. Congress continued to ignore them.

To many middle-class Americans, the labor turmoil of the time—the Homestead and Pullman strikes, for example (see Chapter 17)—was a sign of a dangerous instability, perhaps even revolution. Labor radicalism, some of it real, more of it imagined by the frightened middle class, heightened the general sense of crisis among the public.

THE SILVER QUESTION

The financial panic weakened the government's monetary system. President Cleveland believed that the instability of the currency was the primary cause of the depression. The "money question," therefore, became one of the burning issues of the era.

The debate centered on what would form the basis of the dollar, what would lie behind it and give it value. Today, the value of the dollar rests on little more than public confidence in the government. But in the nineteenth century, many people believed that currency was worthless if there was not something concrete behind it—precious metal (specie), which holders of paper money could collect if they presented their currency to a bank or to the Treasury.

During most of its existence as a nation, the United States had recognized two metals—gold and silver—as a basis for the dollar, a system known as "bimetallism." In the 1870s, however, that had changed. The official ratio of the value of silver to the value of gold for purposes of creating currency (the "mint ratio") was 16 to 1: sixteen ounces of silver equaled one ounce of gold. But the actual commercial value of silver (the "market ratio") was much higher than that. Owners of silver could get more by selling it for manufacture into jewelry and other objects than they could by taking it to the mint for conversion into coins. So they stopped taking it to the mint, and the mint stopped coining silver.

In 1873, Congress passed a law that seemed simply to recognize the existing situation by officially discontinuing silver coinage. Few objected at the time. But later in the 1870s, the market value of silver fell well below the official mint ratio of 16 to 1. Silver was suddenly available for coinage again, and it soon became clear that Congress had foreclosed a potential method of expanding the currency. Before long, many Americans concluded that a conspiracy of big bankers had been responsible for the "demonetization" of silver and referred to the law as the "Crime of '73."

Two groups of Americans were especially determined to undo that crime. One consisted of the silver-mine owners, now understandably eager to have the government take their surplus silver and pay them much more than the market price. The other group was discontented farmers, who wanted an increase in the quantity of money—an inflation of the currency—as a means of raising the prices of farm products and easing payment of the farmers' debts. The inflationists, or advocates of **free silver**, demanded that the government return at once to the "free and unlimited coinage of silver" at the old ratio of 16 to 1. Congress responded weakly to these demands with the Sherman Silver Purchase Act of 1890, which required the government to purchase silver and pay for it in gold. But the government allowed only existing silver coinage. It did not allow any newly minted silver money. Whatever the economic intricacies of the issue, it boiled down to another battle between conservative supporters of corporations or the "monied interests," who preferred gold, and advocates of farmers, workers, and the "little guy," who argued for silver.

At the same time, the nation's gold reserves were steadily dropping. President Cleveland believed that the chief cause of the weakening gold reserves was the Sherman Silver Purchase Act. Early in his second administration, therefore, Congress responded to his request and repealed the Sherman Act—although only after a bitter and divisive battle that helped create a split in the Democratic Party.

"A CROSS OF GOLD"

Republicans, watching the failure of the Democrats to deal effectively with the depression, were confident of success in 1896. Party leaders, led by the Ohio boss Marcus A. Hanna, settled on former congressman William McKinley, author of the 1890 tariff act and now governor of Ohio, as the party's presidential candidate. The tariff, they believed, should be the key issue in the campaign. But they also opposed the free coinage of silver, except by agreement with the leading commercial nations, which everyone realized was unlikely. Thirty-four delegates from the mountain and plains states walked out of the convention in protest and joined the Democratic Party.

The Democratic Convention of 1896 was unusually tumultuous. Southern and western delegates, eager for a way to compete with the Populists, were determined to seize control of the party from conservative easterners, incorporate some Populist demands into the Democratic platform—among them free silver—and nominate a pro-silver candidate.

Defenders of the gold standard seemed to dominate the debate, until **William Jennings Bryan**, a thirty-six-year-old congressman from Nebraska, mounted the podium to address the convention. His great voice echoed through the hall as he delivered what became one of the most famous political speeches in American history. The closing passage sent his audience into something close to a frenzy: "Having behind us the producing masses of this nation and the world, supported by the commercial interests, the laboring interests and the toilers everywhere, we will answer their demand for a gold standard by saying to them: 'You shall not press down upon the brow of labor this crown of thorns; you shall not crucify mankind upon a cross of gold.'" It became known as the "Cross of Gold" speech.

In the glow of Bryan's speech, the convention voted to adopt a pro-silver platform. And the following day, Bryan, as he had hoped, was nominated for president on the fifth ballot.

(Source: Library of Congress, Prints and Photographs Division [LC-USZC2-6263])

THE 1896 DEMOCRATIC TICKET   This political broadside from the 1896 election followed the nomination of William Jennings Bryan and Arthur Sewall at the Democratic National Convention in Chicago. It reflects Bryan's famous "Cross of Gold" speech and reveals how powerfully the promise of bimetallism, with its implications for the distribution of wealth and power, shaped the Democrats' message.

The choice of Bryan and the Democratic platform created a quandary for the Populists. They had expected both major parties to adopt conservative programs and nominate conservative candidates, leaving the Populists to represent the growing forces of protest. But now the Democrats had stolen much of their thunder. The Populists faced the choice of naming their own candidate and splitting the protest vote or endorsing Bryan and losing their identity as a party. Many Populists argued that "fusion" with the Democrats would destroy their party. But the majority concluded that there was no viable alternative. Amid considerable acrimony, the convention voted to nominate Bryan as the Populist candidate, although with a different running mate than the one Democrats had selected.

THE CONSERVATIVE VICTORY

The campaign of 1896 produced panic among conservatives. The business and financial community, frightened at the prospect of a Bryan victory, contributed lavishly to the Republican campaign. From his home in Canton, Ohio, McKinley conducted a traditional front-porch campaign by receiving pilgrimages of the Republican faithful, organized and paid for by Hanna.

Bryan showed no such restraint. He became the first presidential candidate in American history to stump every section of the country systematically. He traveled 18,000 miles and addressed an estimated 5 million people.

On election day, McKinley polled 271 electoral votes to Bryan's 176 and received 51.1 percent of the popular vote to Bryan's 47.7. Bryan carried the areas of the South and West where miners or struggling staple farmers predominated, but he couldn't attract workers in industrial states. The Democratic program, like that of the Populists, had been too narrow to galvanize working people and to win a national election. The Republicans also persuaded many factory workers that their program of high tariffs protected not only corporate profits but also, by extension, laborers' wages.

For the Populists and their allies, the election results were a disaster. They had gambled everything on their fusion with the Democratic Party and lost. Within months of the election, the People's Party began to dissolve.

McKinley and Recovery

The administration of William McKinley saw a return to relative calm. One reason was the exhaustion of frustrated dissenters. Another reason was the shrewd character of the McKinley administration itself, committed as it was to reassuring stability. Most important, however, was the gradual easing of the economic crisis, a development that undercut many of those who were agitating for change.

McKinley and his allies committed themselves fully to only one issue: the need for higher tariff rates. Within weeks of his inauguration, the administration won approval of the Dingley Tariff, raising duties to the highest point in American history. The administration dealt more gingerly with the explosive silver question, an issue that McKinley himself had never considered very important. He sent a commission to Europe to explore the possibility of a silver agreement with Great Britain and France. As he and everyone else anticipated, the effort produced nothing. The Republicans then enacted the Currency, or Gold Standard, Act of 1900, which confirmed the nation's commitment to gold.

And so the "battle of the standards" ended in victory for the forces of conservatism. Economic developments at the time seemed to vindicate the Republicans. Prosperity began

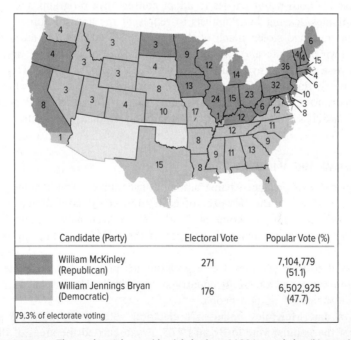

Candidate (Party)	Electoral Vote	Popular Vote (%)
William McKinley (Republican)	271	7,104,779 (51.1)
William Jennings Bryan (Democratic)	176	6,502,925 (47.7)

79.3% of electorate voting

THE ELECTION OF 1896 The results of the presidential election of 1896 revealed striking regional differentiation. William McKinley won the election by a comfortable if not enormous margin, but his victory was not broadbased. He carried all the states of the Northeast and the industrial Midwest, along with California and Oregon, but virtually nothing else. Bryan carried the entire South and almost all of the agrarian West. • *What campaign issues in 1896 helped account for the regional character of the results?*

to return in 1898. Foreign crop failures drove farm prices upward, and American business entered another cycle of expansion. Prosperity and the gold standard, it seemed, were closely allied.

But while the free-silver movement had failed, it had raised an important question for the American economy. In the quarter century before 1900, the countries of the Western world had experienced spectacular growth in productive facilities and population. Yet the supply of money had not kept pace with economic progress. Had it not been for a dramatic increase in the gold supply in the late 1890s, a result of new techniques for extracting gold from low-content ores and the discovery of huge new gold deposits in Alaska, South Africa, and Australia, Populist predictions of financial disaster might in fact have proved correct. In 1898, two and a half times as much gold was produced as in 1890, and the currency supply was soon inflated far beyond anything Bryan and the free-silver forces had anticipated.

By then, however, Bryan—like many other Americans—was becoming engaged with another major issue: the nation's growing involvement in world affairs and its increasing flirtation with **imperialism**.

STIRRINGS OF IMPERIALISM

As the nineteenth century drew to a close, many Americans hoped to translate the era's great industrial feats into global economic, political, and military power. The depression of 1893 further pushed observers to call for greater overseas trade to stimulate the economy. These expansionists—some called them "**jingoes**"—hoped to resume the course of Manifest Destiny.

THE NEW MANIFEST DESTINY

In addition to their economic and political motivations, jingoes believed that domestic tensions in the country might be resolved by a more robust foreign policy and stronger American nationalistic spirit—or even by war. It had been a generation since the Civil War, and some jingoes felt the nation's masculinity had withered in the meantime. Mass industrial wage labor, the same line of reasoning went, had turned American workers from independent producers into faceless cogs in a machine. Some critics of the woman suffrage movement thought it threatened to feminize and weaken the traditional male preserve of politics. Waves of immigration and wars of labor had divided the country. A more stout assertion of power abroad, jingoes hoped, might restore American vitality and unity.

Expansionists were also driven by competitive impulses. Americans were well aware of the imperialist fever that was raging through Europe, leading the major powers to divide much of Africa among themselves and turn eager eyes to the Far East and the Chinese Empire. (See "America in the World: Imperialism.") Some Americans feared their nation would be left out of these potential markets. Scholars and others found a philosophic justification for expansionism in Charles Darwin's theories. They contended that nations or "races," like biological species, struggled constantly for existence and that only the fittest could survive. For strong nations to dominate weak ones was, therefore, in accordance with the laws of nature.

IMPERIALISM

Empires were not, of course, new to the nineteenth century, when the United States acquired its first overseas colonies. They had existed since the early moments of recorded history, and they have continued into our own time.

But in the second half of the nineteenth century, the construction of empires took on a new form, and the word *imperialism* emerged for the first time to describe it. In many places, European powers now created colonies not by sending large numbers of migrants to settle and populate new lands, but instead by creating military, political, and business structures that allowed them to dominate and profit from the existing populations. This new imperialism changed the character of the colonizing nations, enriching them greatly and producing new classes of people whose lives were shaped by the demands of imperial business and administration. It changed the character of colonized societies even more, drawing them into the vast nexus of global industrial capitalism and introducing Western customs, institutions, and technologies to the subject peoples.

As the lure of empire grew in the West, efforts to justify it grew as well. Champions of imperialism argued that the acquisition of colonies was essential for the health, even the survival, of their own industrializing nations. Colonies were sources of raw materials vital to industrial production; they were markets for manufactured goods; and they were suppliers of cheap labor. Defenders of empire also argued that imperialism was good for the colonized people. Many saw colonization as an opportunity to export Christianity to "heathen" lands, and new missionary movements emerged in Europe and America in response. More secular apologists argued that imperialism helped bring colonized people into the modern world.

The invention of steamships, railroads, telegraphs, and other modern vehicles of transportation and communication; the construction of canals (particularly the Suez Canal, completed in 1869, and the Panama Canal, completed in 1914); the creation of new military technologies (repeating rifles, machine guns, and modern artillery)—all contributed to the ability of Western nations to reach, conquer, and control distant lands.

The greatest imperial power of the nineteenth century was Great Britain. By 1800, despite its recent loss of the colonies that became the United States, it already possessed vast territory in North America, the Caribbean, and the Pacific. In the second half of the nineteenth century, Britain greatly expanded its empire. Its most important acquisition was India, one of the largest and most populous countries in the world and a nation in which Great Britain had long exerted informal authority. In 1857, when Indians revolted against British influence, British forces brutally crushed the rebellion and established formal colonial control over India. British officials, backed by substantial military power, now governed India through a large civil service staffed mostly by people from England and Scotland but with some Indians serving in minor positions. The British invested heavily in railroads, telegraphs, canals, harbors, and agricultural improvements to enhance the economic opportunities available to them. They created schools for Indian children in an effort to draw them into British culture and make them supporters of the imperial system.

The British also extended their empire into Africa and other parts of Asia. The great

(©Time Life Pictures/Mansell/Getty Images)

THE BRITISH RAJ   The Drum Corps of the Royal Fusiliers in India poses here for a formal portrait, taken in 1877. Although the drummers are British, an Indian associate is included at top left. This blending of the dominant British with subordinate Indians was characteristic of the administration of the British Empire in India—a government known as the "raj," from the Indian word for "rule."

imperial champion Cecil Rhodes expanded a small existing British colony at Capetown into a substantial colony that included much of what is now South Africa. In 1895, he added new British territories to the north, which he named Rhodesia (and which today are Zimbabwe and Zambia). Others spread British authority into Kenya, Uganda, Nigeria, and much of Egypt. British imperialists also extended the empire into East Asia, with the acquisition of Singapore, Hong Kong, Burma, and Malaya; and they built a substantial presence—although not formal colonial rule—in China.

Other European states, watching the vast expansion of the British Empire, quickly jumped into the race for colonies. France built colonies in Indochina (Vietnam and Laos), Algeria, west Africa, and Madagascar. Belgium moved into the Congo in west Africa. Germany established footholds in the Cameroons, Tanganyika, and other parts of Africa, and in the Pacific islands north of Australia. Dutch, Italian, Portuguese, Spanish, Russian, and Japanese imperialists created colonies as well in Africa, Asia, and the

Pacific—driven both by a calculation of their own commercial interests and by the frenzied competition that had developed among rival imperial powers. In 1898, the United States was drawn into the imperial race, in part inadvertently as an unanticipated result of the Spanish-American War. But the drive to acquire colonies resulted as well from the deliberate efforts of home-grown proponents of empire (among them Theodore Roosevelt), who believed that in the modern industrial-imperial world, a nation without colonies would have difficulty remaining, or becoming, a true great power.   •

UNDERSTAND, ANALYZE, & EVALUATE

1. What motivated the European nations' drive for empire in the late nineteenth century?
2. Why was Great Britain so successful in acquiring its vast empire?
3. How do the imperial efforts and ambitions of the United States at the end of the nineteenth century compare with those of European powers?

The most effective apostle of imperialism was Alfred Thayer Mahan, a captain and, later, admiral in the U.S. Navy. Mahan's thesis, presented in *The Influence of Sea Power upon History* (1890) and other works, was simple: countries with sea power were the great nations of history. Effective sea power required, among other things, colonies. Mahan believed that the United States should, at the least, acquire defensive bases in the Caribbean and the Pacific and take possession of Hawaii and other Pacific islands. He feared that the United States did not have a large enough navy to play the great role he envisioned. But during the 1870s and 1880s, the government launched a shipbuilding program that by 1898 had moved the United States to fifth place among the world's naval powers, and by 1900 to third place.

HAWAII AND SAMOA

The islands of Hawaii in the mid-Pacific had been an important way station for American ships in the China trade since the early nineteenth century. By the 1880s, officers of the expanding U.S. Navy were looking covetously at Pearl Harbor on the island of Oahu as a possible permanent base for American ships. The growing number of Americans who had taken up residence on the islands also pressed for an increased American presence in Hawaii.

Settled by Polynesian people beginning in about 1500 B.C., Hawaii had developed an agricultural and fishing society in which different islands, and different communities on the same islands, each with its own chieftain, lived more or less self-sufficiently. When the first Americans arrived in Hawaii in the 1790s on merchant ships from New England, there were perhaps half a million people living there. Battles among rival communities were frequent, as chieftains tried to consolidate power over their neighbors. In 1810, after a series of such battles, King Kamehameha I established his dominance, welcomed American traders, and helped them develop a thriving trade between Hawaii and China. But Americans soon wanted more than trade. Missionaries began settling there in the early nineteenth century; and in the 1830s, William Hooper, a Boston trader, became the first of many Americans to buy land and establish a sugar plantation on the islands.

The arrival of these merchants, missionaries, and planters was devastating to traditional Hawaiian society. The newcomers inadvertently brought infectious diseases to which the Hawaiians, like the American Indians before them, were vulnerable. By the mid-nineteenth century, more than half the native population had died. The Americans brought other incursions as well. Missionaries worked to replace native religion with Christianity. Other white settlers introduced liquor, firearms, and a commercial economy, all of which eroded the traditional character of Hawaiian society. By the 1840s, American planters had spread throughout the islands, and an American settler, G. P. Judd, had become prime minister of Hawaii under King Kamehameha III, who had agreed to establish a constitutional monarchy. Judd governed Hawaii for over a decade.

In 1887, the United States negotiated a treaty with Hawaii that permitted it to open a naval base at Pearl Harbor. By then, growing sugar for export to America had become the basis of the Hawaiian economy—as a result of an 1875 agreement allowing Hawaiian sugar to enter the United States duty-free. The American-dominated sugar plantation system displaced native Hawaiians from their lands and relied heavily on Asian immigrants, whom the Americans considered more reliable and more docile than the natives.

Native Hawaiians did not accept their subordination without protest. In 1891, they elevated a powerful nationalist to the throne: **Queen Liliuokalani**, who set out to challenge the growing American control of the islands. But she remained in power only two years. In 1890, the United States had eliminated the exemption from American tariffs in Hawaiian sugar trade. The result was devastating to the economy of the islands, and American planters concluded that the only way for them to recover was to become part of the United States, and, hence, exempt from its tariffs. In 1893, they staged a revolution and called on the United States for protection. After the American minister ordered marines from a warship in Honolulu harbor to go ashore to aid the American rebels, the queen yielded her authority.

A provisional government, dominated by Americans, immediately sent a delegation to Washington to negotiate a treaty of annexation. Debate over the treaty continued until 1898, when Congress finally approved the agreement.

Three thousand miles south of Hawaii, the Samoan islands had also long served as a stopover for American ships in the Pacific trade. As American commerce with Asia increased, business groups in the United States regarded Samoa with new interest, and the American navy began eyeing the Samoan harbor at Pago Pago. In 1878, the Hayes administration extracted a treaty from Samoan leaders for an American naval station at Pago Pago.

Great Britain and Germany were also interested in the islands, and they, too, secured treaty rights from the native princes. For the next ten years, the three powers jockeyed for dominance in Samoa, finally agreeing to create a tripartite protectorate over Samoa, with the native chiefs exercising only nominal authority. The three-way arrangement failed to halt the rivalries of its members, and in 1899, the United States and Germany divided the islands between them, compensating Britain with territories elsewhere in the Pacific. The United States retained the harbor at Pago Pago.

WAR WITH SPAIN

Imperial ambitions had thus begun to stir within the United States well before the late 1890s. But a war with Spain in 1898 turned those stirrings into overt expansionism.

CONTROVERSY OVER CUBA

Spain's once-formidable empire had grown rickety but still included two prized island possessions: Cuba, ninety miles off the shores of Florida, and the Philippines, in Asia. As in many imperial holdings, the native peoples in these regions objected to the presence of European colonizers and occasionally waged insurrections. One rebellion in Cuba had ended in 1878 with Spanish rule intact. Nominal Cuban control over the economy followed, but the depression of the 1890s led Spain to withdraw even that privilege. In 1895, Cuban revolutionaries mounted a new insurrection, led by the revolutionary poet José Martí and military heroes of the earlier wars of liberation.

The rebellion soon attracted the sympathies of people in the United States. Popular newspapers reported horrific atrocities committed by the Spanish against Cuban rebels and civilians. The Spanish governor since 1896, General Valeriano Weyler, was rounding up Cubans in detention camps to isolate rebels in the countryside and then destroying agriculture to starve them out. These policies of "the Butcher" led to the deaths of tens of thousands of Cuban civilians. The conflict also imperiled the American-owned sugar plantations in Cuba and regional commerce more broadly. And ever since the articulation

YELLOW JOURNALISM

Joseph Pulitzer was a successful newspaper publisher in St. Louis, Missouri, when he traveled to New York City in 1883 to buy a struggling paper, the *New York World*. "There is room in this great and growing city," he wrote in one of his first editorials, "for a journal that is not only cheap, but bright, not only bright but large, not only large but truly democratic . . . that will serve and battle for the people with earnest sincerity." Within a year, the *World*'s daily circulation had soared from 10,000 to over 60,000. By 1886, it had reached 250,000 and was making enormous profits.

The success of Pulitzer's *World* marked the birth of what came to be known as "yellow journalism," a phrase that reportedly derived from a character in one of the *World*'s comic strips: "the Yellow Kid." Color printing in newspapers was relatively new, and yellow was the most difficult color to print. So in the beginning, the term *yellow journalism* was a comment on the new technological possibilities that Pulitzer was so eagerly embracing. Eventually, however, it came to refer to a sensationalist style of reporting and writing that spread quickly through urban America and changed the character of newspapers.

Sensationalism was not new to journalism in the late nineteenth century, of course. Political scandal sheets had been publishing lurid stories since before the American Revolution. But the yellow journalism of the 1880s and 1890s took the search for a mass audience to new levels. The *World* created one of the first Sunday editions, with lavishly colored special sections, comics, and illustrated features. It expanded coverage of sports, fashion, literature, and theater.

It pioneered large, glaring, overheated headlines that captured the eyes of people who were passing newsstands. It published exposés of political corruption. It made considerable efforts to bring drama and energy to its coverage of crime. It tried to involve readers directly in its stories (as when a *World* campaign helped raise $300,000 to build a base for the Statue of Liberty, with much of the money coming in donations of 5 or 10 cents from working-class readers). And it introduced a self-consciously populist style of writing that appealed to working-class readers. "The American people want something terse, forcible, picturesque, striking," Pulitzer said. His reporters wrote short, forceful sentences. They did not shy away from expressing sympathy or outrage. And they were not always constrained by the truth.

Pulitzer very quickly produced imitators, the most important of them the California publisher William Randolph Hearst, who in 1895 bought the *New York Journal,* cut its price to 1 cent (Pulitzer quickly followed suit), copied many of the *World*'s techniques, and within a year raised its circulation to 400,000. Hearst soon made the *Journal* the largest-circulation paper in the country, selling more than a million copies a day. Pulitzer, whose own circulation was not far behind, accused him of "pandering to the worst tastes of the prurient and the horror-loving" and "dealing in bogus news." But the *World* wasted no time before imitating the *Journal*. The competition between these two yellow journals soon drove both to new levels of sensationalism. Their success drove newspapers in other cities around the nation to copy their techniques.

The civil war in Cuba in the 1890s gave both papers their best opportunities yet for combining sensational reporting with shameless appeals to patriotism and moral outrage. They avidly published exaggerated reports of Spanish atrocities toward the Cuban rebels, fanning popular anger toward Spain. When the American battleship *Maine* mysteriously exploded in Havana harbor in 1898, both papers without evidence blamed Spanish authorities. The *Journal* offered a $50,000 reward for information leading to the conviction of those responsible for the explosion, and it crowded all other stories off its front page ("There is no other news," Hearst told his editors) to make room for such screaming headlines as THE WHOLE COUNTRY THRILLS WITH WAR FEVER and HAVANA POPULACE INSULTS THE MEMORY OF THE *MAINE* VICTIMS. In the three days following the *Maine* explosion, the *Journal* sold more than 3 million copies, a new world's record for newspaper circulation.

In the aftermath of the *Maine* episode, the more conservative press launched a spirited attack on yellow journalism. It responded in part to Hearst's boast that the conflict in Cuba was "the *Journal*'s war." He sent a cable to one of his reporters in Cuba saying: "You furnish the pictures, and I'll furnish the war." Growing numbers of critics tried to discourage yellow journalism, which "respectable" editors both deplored and feared. Some schools, libraries, and clubs began to banish the papers from their premises. But the techniques the yellow press pioneered in the 1890s helped map the way for a tradition of colorful, popular journalism, later embodied in "tabloids," some elements of which eventually found their way into television news and the Internet. •

UNDERSTAND, ANALYZE, & EVALUATE

1. Did Pulitzer's *World,* Hearst's *Journal,* and their imitators report the news or manufacture it?
2. How did the yellow press influence the public's perception of the Spanish-American War?
3. How does television news continue the tradition of yellow journalism? In what other mass media do you see the style and techniques pioneered by the yellow press?

of the Monroe Doctrine in 1823, Americans had dreamed of ridding North and South America of European colonizers. Some hoped to replace the Spanish with a heavy American presence in the region, while others, including William Jennings Bryan and other prominent Democrats and members of Congress, wished only to liberate Cuba and leave it to the Cubans.

The conflict in Cuba came at a particularly opportune moment for the newspaper publishers Joseph Pulitzer of the *New York World* and William Randolph Hearst of the *New York Journal.* In the 1890s, Hearst and Pulitzer were engaged in a ruthless circulation war, and they both sent batteries of reporters and illustrators to Cuba with orders to provide accounts of Spanish atrocities. This sort of sensationalist reporting was known as **yellow journalism**. (See "Patterns of Popular Culture: Yellow Journalism.")

Although President Cleveland worried about the potential disruptions of American trade, he did not intervene. Nor, at first, did his successor, William McKinley. Both men shared commercial and humanitarian concerns, but sought to avoid war with a European power. An irritated Theodore Roosevelt, assistant secretary of the navy, excoriated President McKinley for his un-masculine weakness, charging that he had "no more backbone than a chocolate éclair."

The situation changed in early 1898. In January, pro-Spanish Cubans rioted in Havana against the idea of a free Cuba, or *Cuba libre*, which the two American political parties had at least rhetorically supported even as successive U.S. administrations remained neutral. Thus the riots carried anti-American undertones, and President McKinley, under pressure from the popular media after unfulfilled promises from Spain, sent the **U.S.S. *Maine*** to Havana harbor to protect American citizens. On February 15, 1898, the ship exploded, killing 266 Americans. Although later investigations revealed it likely an accident, most Americans, egged on by the jingoistic press, blamed the Spanish.

For all the earlier arguments about humanity, commerce, and geopolitical strategy, the destruction of the *Maine* challenged American resolve. A Democrat in the House voted for war "to defend the honor and maintain the dignity of this republic"; a Republican sought "peace with honor." On April 25, Congress passed a resolution declaring war against the Spanish. It included the **Teller Amendment**, named for Democratic senator Henry T. Teller from Colorado, which swore off any intentions to occupy, possess, or control Cuba after a future victory against the Spanish.

"A SPLENDID LITTLE WAR"

The American ambassador to England, John Hay, called the ensuing conflict "a splendid little war," an opinion that most Americans, except for many of the enlisted men who fought it, seemed to share. Declared in April, the **Spanish-American War** was over in August, in part because Cuban rebels had already greatly weakened the Spanish resistance, making the American intervention in many respects little more than a mopping-up exercise. Four hundred and sixty Americans were killed in battle or died of wounds, although some 5,200 others perished of malaria, dysentery, typhoid, and other diseases. Casualties among Cuban insurgents, who continued to bear the brunt of the fighting, were much higher.

American soldiers faced serious supply problems: a shortage of modern rifles and ammunition, uniforms too heavy for the warm Caribbean weather, inadequate medical services, and skimpy, almost indigestible food. The regular army numbered only 28,000 troops and officers, most of whom had experience fighting Indians but none in larger-scale warfare. That meant that, as in the Civil War, the United States had to rely heavily on National Guard units, organized by local communities and commanded for the most part by local leaders without military experience.

A significant proportion of the American invasion force consisted of black soldiers. Some were volunteer troops put together by African American communities. Others were members of the four black regiments in the regular army, who had been stationed on the frontier to protect white settlements and were now transferred east to fight in Cuba. As the black soldiers traveled through the South toward the training camps, some resisted the rigid segregation to which they were subjected. African American soldiers in Georgia deliberately made use of a "whites only" park; in Florida, they beat a soda-fountain operator for refusing to serve them; in Tampa, white provocations and black retaliation led to a nightlong riot that left thirty wounded.

Racial tensions continued in Cuba. African Americans played crucial roles in some of the important battles of the war, including the famous charge at San Juan Hill, and won many medals. Nearly half the Cuban insurgents fighting with the Americans were themselves black, including one of the leading insurgent generals, Antonio Maceo. The sight of black Cuban soldiers fighting alongside whites as equals gave African Americans a stronger sense of the injustice of their own situation.

(Source: Library of Congress, Prints and Photographs Division [LC-USZ62-57107])

AFRICAN AMERICAN CAVALRY   Substantial numbers of African Americans fought in the U.S. Army during the Spanish-American War. Although confined to all-black units, they engaged in combat alongside white units and fought bravely and effectively. This photograph shows a troop of African American cavalry in formation in Cuba. It is meant to be viewed through a stereoscope, which would create a single three-dimensional image.

Seizing the Philippines

The assistant secretary of the navy during the Cuban revolution was Theodore Roosevelt, an ardent Anglophile eager to see the United States join the British and other nations as imperial powers. In late February, in the wake of the *Maine* disaster and without the knowledge of his superiors, Roosevelt had sent a message to Commodore George Dewey in Hong Kong. The telegram authorized Dewey's Asiatic Squadron to engage the Spanish fleet in the Philippines should hostilities come. Once war was declared, the Navy ordered Dewey on May 1, 1898, to lead the squadron into Manila harbor, where he quickly destroyed the aging Spanish fleet. Once army reinforcements arrived, Dewey forced the colonial government to surrender Manila with hardly a shot fired. At home, Dewey was lauded as a hero despite the relatively easy time his forces had had subduing the Spanish.

The Battle for Cuba

Cuba remained the principal focus of American military efforts. At first, the commanding general of the Army, Nelson A. Miles, planned a long period of training before actually sending troops into combat. But when a Spanish fleet under Admiral Pascual Cervera slipped past the American navy into Santiago harbor on the southern coast of Cuba, plans changed quickly. As the American Atlantic fleet bottled Cervera up in the harbor, the War Department ordered Major General William R. Shafter to assemble forces in Tampa in June and proceed to Santiago. After a chaotic and delayed mobilization, an American force of 17,000 left on June 14 on dilapidated craft. More than two weeks of sweltering heat and overcrowding stood between the men and Cuba's southern shoreline.

Once on land, Shafter was ordered to advance toward Santiago, which he planned to surround and capture. On the way, his cavalry division, now under the command of the former Confederate Major General Joseph Wheeler, met and defeated Spanish forces at Las Guásimas. Meanwhile problems of disease and supply hampered the American undertaking.

A week later, on July 1, Shafter's forces attacked El Caney and the San Juan Heights, which included San Juan Hill and Kettle Hill. El Caney took twelve hours to subdue, which meant the attack on the Heights had to proceed without expected help from those forces. Among the troops assigned to take the hills were the Rough Riders, headed by Theodore Roosevelt, who had resigned from the Navy Department to get into the war, and the all-black Ninth and Tenth Cavalry Regiments. Roosevelt's passion to join the war undoubtedly reflected the decision of his beloved father, Theodore Roosevelt Sr., not to fight in the Civil War, a source of private shame within the family that his son sought to erase.

The July 1 battles were bloody and miserable engagements, filled with logistical nightmares, hot weather, little water, and fierce Spanish resistance. Into withering fire the Rough Riders advanced up Kettle Hill. Roosevelt himself emerged unscathed, but nearly a hundred soldiers were killed or wounded. "We have won so far at a heavy cost," Roosevelt wrote at the time. "We *must* have help." The African American units in particular put themselves at great risk to cover the Rough Riders' bold, if reckless, charges. Though more than two hundred Americans lay dead by nightfall, the forces took the Heights as the Spanish retreated to Santiago. Blustery headlines back home, and later romanticization of the day's events, made a hero of Roosevelt, who with the benefit of hindsight called July "the great day of my life."

Although Shafter was now in position to assault Santiago, his army was so weakened by sickness that he feared he might have to abandon his position. But unknown to the Americans, the Spanish government had decided Santiago was lost and ordered Cervera to evacuate. On July 3, Cervera tried to escape the harbor. The waiting American squadron destroyed his entire fleet. On July 16, the commander of Spanish ground forces in Santiago ceased fighting. In a sign of things to come, the Cubans so central to the weakening of Spanish forces were not invited to participate in the ceremonies of capitulation. At about the same time, an American army under General Miles landed in Puerto Rico and occupied it against virtually no opposition. On August 12, an armistice ended the war. Under its terms, Spain recognized the independence of Cuba, ceded Puerto Rico and the Pacific island of Guam to the United States, and accepted continued American occupation of Manila pending the final disposition of the Philippines.

Puerto Rico and the United States

The island of **Puerto Rico** had been a part of the Spanish Empire since 1508. By the early seventeenth century, the native people of the island, the Arawaks, had largely disappeared as a result of infectious diseases, Spanish brutality, and poverty. Puerto Rican society developed, therefore, with a Spanish ruling class and a large African workforce for the coffee and sugar plantations that came to dominate its economy.

Puerto Rican resistance to Spanish rule began to emerge in the nineteenth century. The resistance prompted some reforms: the abolition of slavery in 1873, representation in the Spanish parliament, and other changes. Demands for independence continued to grow, and in 1898, Spain granted the island a degree of independence. But before the changes had any chance to take effect, control of Puerto Rico shifted to the United States. American military forces occupied the island during the Spanish-American War and remained in control until 1900, when the Foraker Act ended military rule and established a formal colonial government. Agitation for independence continued, and in 1917, Congress passed the Jones Act, which declared Puerto Rico to be a U.S. territory and made all Puerto Ricans American citizens.

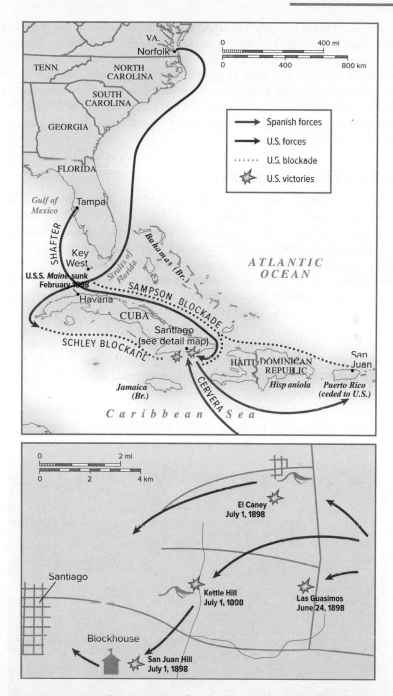

THE SPANISH-AMERICAN WAR IN CUBA, 1898 The military conflict between the United States and Spain in Cuba was a brief affair. The Cuban rebels and an American naval blockade had already brought the Spanish to the brink of defeat. The arrival of American troops was the final blow. In the space of about a week, U.S. troops won four decisive battles in the area around Santiago in southeast Cuba. This map shows the extent of the American naval blockade, the path of American troops from Florida to Cuba, and the location of the actual fighting. • *What were the implications of the war in Cuba for Puerto Rico?*

The Puerto Rican sugar industry flourished as it took advantage of the American market that was now open to it without tariffs. As in Hawaii, Americans from the mainland began establishing large sugar plantations on the island and hiring natives to work them. The growing emphasis on sugar as a cash crop, and the transformation of many Puerto Rican farmers into paid laborers, led to a reduction in the growing of food for the island and greater reliance on imported goods. When international sugar prices were high, Puerto Rico did well. When they dropped, the island's economy sagged, pushing many plantation workers, already poor, into destitution.

The Debate over the Philippines

Although the annexation of Puerto Rico produced relatively little controversy, the seizure of the Philippines created an impassioned debate. Controlling a nearby Caribbean island fit reasonably comfortably into the United States' sense of itself as the dominant power in the Western Hemisphere. But to many Americans, controlling a large and densely populated territory thousands of miles away seemed ominously different.

McKinley claimed to be reluctant to support annexation. But, according to his own accounts, he came to believe there were no acceptable alternatives. Returning the Philippines to Spain would be "cowardly and dishonorable," he claimed. Turning them over to another imperialist power (France, Germany, or Britain) would be "bad business and discreditable." Granting them independence would be irresponsible because the Filipinos were "unfit for self government." The only solution was "to take them all and to educate the Filipinos, and uplift and Christianize them, and by God's grace do the very best we could by them."

The Treaty of Paris, signed in December 1898, confirmed the terms of the armistice and brought a formal end to the war. American negotiators had startled the Spanish by

(Source: Library of Congress, Prints and Photographs Division [LC-DIG-ppmsca-25453])

MEASURING UNCLE SAM FOR A NEW SUIT In this *Puck* cartoon, President McKinley is depicted as a tailor, meaning his client for a suit is large enough to accommodate the new possessions the United States obtained in the aftermath of the Spanish-American War. The stripes on Uncle Sam's pants bear the names of earlier, less controversial acquisitions, such as the Louisiana Purchase.

demanding they also cede the Philippines to the United States, but an American offer of $20 million for the islands softened their resistance. They accepted all the American terms.

In the U.S. Senate, however, resistance was fierce. During debate over ratification of the treaty, a powerful anti-imperialist movement arose to oppose acquisition of the Philippines. The anti-imperialists included some of the nation's wealthiest and most powerful figures: Andrew Carnegie, Mark Twain, Samuel Gompers, Senator John Sherman, and others. Some anti-imperialists believed that imperialism was immoral, a repudiation of America's commitment to human freedom, or a hypocritical turn for a nation that owed its own existence to liberation from distant colonial rule. Others feared "polluting" the American population by introducing Asian races into it. Industrial workers feared being undercut by a flood of cheap laborers from the new colonies. Conservatives worried about the large standing army and entangling foreign alliances they believed imperialism would require and they feared would threaten American liberties. Sugar growers and other anti-imperialists feared unwelcome competition from the new territories. The Anti-Imperialist League, established late in 1898 by upper-class Bostonians, New Yorkers, and others to fight annexation, waged a vigorous campaign against ratification of the Paris treaty. (See "Consider the Source: Platform of the Anti-Imperialist League.")

But favoring ratification was an equally varied group. There were the exuberant imperialists such as Theodore Roosevelt, who saw the acquisition of empire as a way to reinvigorate the nation. Some businessmen saw opportunities to dominate the Asian trade, and more broadly, inject capital into an economic system prone to periodic depressions and panics. Most Republicans saw partisan advantage in acquiring valuable new territories through a war fought and won by a Republican administration. Perhaps the strongest argument in favor of annexation, however, was that the United States already possessed the islands.

When anti-imperialists warned of the danger of acquiring heavily populated territories whose people might have to become citizens, the jingoes had a ready answer. The nation's long-standing policies toward Indians—treating them as dependents rather than citizens—had created a precedent for annexing land without absorbing people.

The fate of the treaty remained in doubt for weeks, until it received the unexpected support of William Jennings Bryan, a fervent anti-imperialist. He backed ratification because he hoped to move the issue out of the Senate and make it the subject of a national referendum in 1900, when he expected to be the Democratic presidential candidate again. Bryan persuaded a number of anti-imperialist Democrats to support the treaty to set up the 1900 debate. The Senate ratified it on February 6, 1899.

But Bryan miscalculated. If the election of 1900 was in fact a referendum on the Philippines, as Bryan expected, it proved beyond a doubt that the nation had decided in favor of imperialism. Once again Bryan ran against McKinley; and once again McKinley won, even more decisively than in 1896. It was not only the issue of the colonies, however, that ensured McKinley's victory. The Republicans benefited from growing prosperity—and also from the colorful personality of their vice presidential candidate, the Rough Rider Theodore Roosevelt.

THE REPUBLIC AS EMPIRE

The new American empire was small by the standards of the great imperial powers of Europe. But it embroiled the United States in the politics of both Europe and the Far East in ways the nation had tried to avoid in the past. It also drew Americans into a brutal war in the Philippines.

CONSIDER THE SOURCE

PLATFORM OF THE AMERICAN ANTI-IMPERIALIST LEAGUE (1899)

As part of their campaign against the annexation of the Philippines by the United States, members of the Anti-Imperialist League circulated this party platform. Here they argue that American political ideals are not compatible with imperialist actions.

We hold that the policy known as imperialism is hostile to liberty and tends toward militarism, an evil from which it has been our glory to be free. We regret that it has become necessary in the land of Washington and Lincoln to reaffirm that all men, of whatever race or color, are entitled to life, liberty, and the pursuit of happiness. We maintain that governments derive their just powers from the consent of the governed. We insist that the subjugation of any people is "criminal aggression" and open disloyalty to the distinctive principles of our Government.

We earnestly condemn the policy of the present National Administration in the Philippines. It seeks to extinguish the spirit of 1776 in those islands. We deplore the sacrifice of our soldiers and sailors, whose bravery deserves admiration even in an unjust war. We denounce the slaughter of the Filipinos as a needless horror. We protest against the extension of American sovereignty by Spanish methods.

We demand the immediate cessation of the war against liberty, begun by Spain and continued by us. We urge that Congress be promptly convened to announce to the Filipinos our purpose to concede to them the independence for which they have so long fought and which of right is theirs.

The United States have always protested against the doctrine of international law which permits the subjugation of the weak by the strong. A self-governing state cannot accept sovereignty over an unwilling people.

The United States cannot act upon the ancient heresy that might makes right.

Imperialists assume that with the destruction of self-government in the Philippines by American hands, all opposition here will cease. This is a grievous error. Much as we abhor the war of "criminal aggression" in the Philippines, greatly as we regret that the blood of the Filipinos is on American hands, we more deeply resent the betrayal of American institutions at home. The real firing line is not in the suburbs of Manila. The foe is of our own household. The attempt of 1861 was to divide the country. That of 1899 is to destroy its fundamental principles and noblest ideals.

Whether the ruthless slaughter of the Filipinos shall end next month or next year is but an incident in a contest that must go on until the Declaration of Independence and the Constitution of the United States are rescued from the hands of their betrayers. Those who dispute about standards of value while the Republic is undermined will be listened to as little as those who would wrangle about the small economies of the household while the house is on fire. The training of a great people for a century, the aspiration for liberty of a vast immigration are forces that will hurl aside those who in the delirium of conquest seek to destroy the character of our institutions.

We deny that the obligation of all citizens to support their Government in times of grave national peril applies to the present situation. If an Administration may with impunity ignore the issues upon which it was chosen, deliberately create a condition of war anywhere on the face of the globe, debauch the civil service for spoils to promote the adventure, organize a truth-suppressing censorship and demand of all citizens a suspension of judgment and their unanimous support while it chooses to continue the fighting, representative government itself is imperiled.

We propose to contribute to the defeat of any person or party that stands for the forcible subjugation of any people. We shall oppose for reelection all who in the White House or in Congress betray American liberty in pursuit of un-American gains. We still hope that both of our great political parties will support and defend the Declaration of Independence in the closing campaign of the century.

Source: Bancroft, Frederick (ed.), "Platform of the American Anti-Imperialist League," in *Speeches, Correspondence, ard Political Papers of Carl Schurz, vol. 6.* New York, NY: G.P. Putnam's Sons, 1913, 77, note 1.

UNDERSTAND, ANALYZE, & EVALUATE

1. On what grounds did the Anti-Imperialist League oppose U.S. expansion, and where were these principles ratified?
2. What were the costs of imperial expansion for the United States and what losses were Filipinos to incur?
3. How did the prospect of an American empire affect the nation's democratic principles?

GOVERNING THE COLONIES

Three American dependencies—Hawaii, Alaska, and Puerto Rico—presented relatively few problems. They received territorial status, and their residents American citizenship, relatively quickly: Hawaii in 1900, Alaska in 1912, and Puerto Rico in 1917. The Navy took control of the Pacific islands of Guam and Tutuila, while it left alone some of the smallest, least populated Pacific islands now under its control. Cuba was a thornier problem. American military forces, commanded by General Leonard Wood, remained there until 1902, theoretically to prepare the island for independence. Americans built roads, schools, and hospitals; reorganized the legal, financial, and administrative systems; and introduced medical and sanitation reforms. But the United States also laid the basis for years of American economic domination of the island.

When Cuba drew up a constitution that made no reference to the United States, Congress responded by passing the Platt Amendment in 1901 and pressuring Cuba into incorporating its terms into its constitution. The Platt Amendment barred Cuba from making treaties with other nations; gave the United States the right to intervene in Cuba to preserve independence, life, and property; and required Cuba to permit American naval stations on its territory. The amendment left Cuba with only nominal political independence.

American capital made the island an American economic appendage as well. American investors poured into Cuba, buying up plantations, factories, railroads, and refineries. Resistance to "Yankee imperialism" produced intermittent revolts against the Cuban government, which at times prompted U.S. military intervention. American troops occupied the island from 1906 to 1909 after one such rebellion; they returned again in 1912 to suppress a revolt by black plantation workers. As in Puerto Rico and Hawaii, sugar production—spurred by access to the American market—increasingly dominated the island's economy and subjected it to the same cycle of booms and busts that plagued other sugar-producing participants in the U.S. economy.

THE PHILIPPINE WAR

Like other imperial powers, the United States soon discovered that local people in colonies resent their subjugation. The American experience in the Philippines began with a long and bloody war.

The conflict in the Philippines is a largely forgotten American war. It was also one of the longest, lasting from 1898 to 1902, and one of the most vicious. It involved 125,000 American troops and resulted in 4,300 American deaths. The number of Filipinos killed in the conflict has long been a matter of dispute, but it seems likely that at least 50,000 natives and perhaps hundreds of thousands died of disease, starvation, or violence. The American occupiers faced a guerrilla war in the Philippines, and soon resorted to the same brutal practices that had outraged so many Americans when Weyler had used them in the Caribbean.

The Filipinos had rebelled against Spanish rule before 1898, and as soon as they realized the Americans had come to stay, rebelled against them as well. Ably led by Emilio Aguinaldo, who claimed to head the legitimate government of the nation, Filipinos harried the American army of occupation from island to island for more than three years. At first, American commanders believed the rebels had only a small popular following. But by early 1900, General Arthur MacArthur, an American commander in the islands (and father of General Douglas MacArthur), was writing, "I have been reluctantly compelled to believe that the Filipino masses are loyal to Aguinaldo and the government which he heads."

To MacArthur and others, that realization was not a reason to abandon the colonial project, moderate American tactics, or conciliate the rebels, but rather to adopt more severe measures. Gradually, the American military effort became more systematically vicious. Captured Filipino guerrillas were treated not as prisoners of war but murderers, many

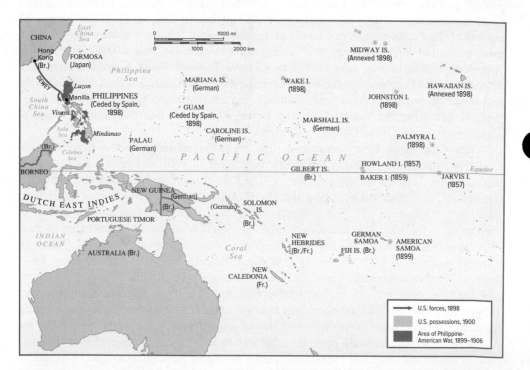

THE AMERICAN SOUTH PACIFIC EMPIRE, 1900   Except for Puerto Rico, all of the colonial acquisitions of the United States in the wake of the Spanish-American War occurred in the Pacific. The new attraction of imperialism persuaded the United States to annex Hawaii in 1898. The war itself gave America control of the Philippines, Guam, and other, smaller Spanish possessions in the Pacific. When added to the small, scattered islands that the United States had acquired as naval bases earlier in the nineteenth century, these new possessions gave the nation a far-flung Pacific empire, even if one whose total territory and population remained small by the standards of the other great empires of the age. • *What was the reaction in the United States to the acquisition of this new empire?*

summarily executed. On some islands, entire communities were evacuated, the residents forced into concentration camps while American troops destroyed their villages. A spirit of savagery grew among some American soldiers, who came to view the Filipinos as subhuman and, at times, seemed to take pleasure in arbitrarily killing them.

The racial undertones of the war—American soldiers called the Filipinos "niggers"—were particularly grating for African American troops serving in segregated units. They were hardly unaware that at home, southern states and lynch mobs were in the process of disfranchising and terrorizing black people. Some noticed a resemblance between the attitude of the American military and government toward the Filipino natives and popular attitudes toward African Americans and Native Americans.

By 1902, reports of brutality and American casualties had soured the American public on the war. But by then, the rebellion had largely exhausted itself and the occupiers had established control over most of the islands. The key to their victory was the March 1901 capture of Aguinaldo, who later signed a document urging his followers to stop fighting and declared his own allegiance to the United States in exchange for a pension. Fighting continued intermittently until as late as 1906, but American possession of the Philippines was now secure. In the summer of 1901, the military transferred authority over the islands to William Howard Taft, who became their first civilian governor and gave the Filipinos broad local autonomy. The Americans also built roads, schools, bridges, and sewers; instituted major administrative and financial reforms; and established a public health system. Filipino self-rule gradually increased, but it was not until July 4, 1946, that the islands finally gained their independence.

THE OPEN DOOR

The American acquisition of the Philippines increased the already strong U.S. interest in Asia. Americans were particularly concerned about the future of China, which provided a tempting target for exploitation by other countries. By 1900, England, France, Germany, Russia, and Japan were beginning to carve up China among themselves, pressuring the Chinese government for concessions that gave them effective control over regions of China. In some cases, they simply seized Chinese territory and claimed it as their own. Many Americans feared the process would soon cut them out of the China trade altogether.

Eager for a way to advance American interests in China without risking war, McKinley issued a statement in September 1898 saying the United States wanted access to China but no special advantages there: "Asking only the open door for ourselves, we are ready to accord the open door to others." The next year, Secretary of State John Hay translated those words into policy when he addressed identical messages—which became known as the "Open Door notes"—to England, Germany, Russia, France, Japan, and Italy. He asked that each nation with influence in China allow other nations to trade freely and equally in its sphere. The principles Hay outlined would allow the United States to do business in China without fear of interference.

Europe and Japan received the Open Door proposals coolly. Russia openly rejected them; the other powers claimed to accept them in principle but to be unable to act unless all the other powers agreed. Hay refused to consider this a rebuff. He boldly announced that all the powers had accepted the principles of the Open Door in "final and definitive" form and that the United States expected them to observe those principles.

No sooner had the diplomatic maneuvering over the Open Door ended than the Boxers, a nationalist Chinese martial-arts society, launched a revolt against foreigners in China.

The **Boxer Rebellion** spread widely across eastern China, targeting Westerners wherever the attackers could find them, including many Christian missionaries. But the climax of the revolt was a siege of the entire Western foreign diplomatic corps, which took refuge in the British embassy in Peking. The imperial powers, including the United States, sent an international expeditionary force into China to rescue the diplomats. In August 1900, it fought its way into the city and broke the siege.

The Boxer Rebellion became an important event for the role of the United States in China. McKinley and Hay had agreed to American participation in quelling the Boxer Rebellion in order to secure a voice in the settlement of the uprising and prevent the partition of China by the European powers. Hay now won support for his Open Door approach from England and Germany and induced the other participating powers to accept compensation from the Chinese for the damages the Boxer Rebellion had caused. Chinese territorial integrity survived at least in name, but the United States retained access to its lucrative China trade.

A MODERN MILITARY SYSTEM

The war with Spain had revealed glaring deficiencies in the American military system. Had the United States been fighting a more powerful foe, disaster might have resulted. After the war, McKinley appointed Elihu Root, an able corporate lawyer in New York, as secretary of war to supervise a major overhaul of the armed forces.

Root's reforms enlarged the regular army from 25,000 to a maximum of 100,000. They established federal military standards for the National Guard, ensuring that never again would the nation fight a war with volunteer regiments trained and equipped differently than those in the regular army. They sparked the creation of a system of officer training schools, including the Army Staff College (later the Command and General Staff School) at Fort Leavenworth, Kansas, and the Army War College in Washington. And in 1903, at Root's urging, a group called the Joint Chiefs of Staff was established to act as military advisers to the secretary of war. As a result of the new reforms, the United States entered the twentieth century with something resembling a modern military system.

CONCLUSION

For nearly three decades after the end of Reconstruction, American politics remained locked in a rigid stalemate. The electorate was almost evenly divided, and the two major parties differed on only a few issues. A series of unimposing presidents presided over this political system as symbols of its stability and passivity.

Beneath the calm surface of national politics, however, social issues were creating deep tensions: battles between employers and workers, growing resentment among American farmers facing declining prosperity, outrage at what many voters considered corruption in government and excessive power in the hands of corporate titans. When a serious depression began in 1893, these social tensions erupted into a heated debate over fundamental questions of power, wealth, and governance in the United States.

The most visible sign of the challenge to the political stalemate was the Populist movement, an uprising of American farmers demanding far-reaching changes in politics and the economy. In 1892, they created their own political party, the People's Party, which for a few years showed impressive strength. But in the climactic election of 1896, in which the

Populist hero William Jennings Bryan became the presidential nominee of both the Democratic Party and the People's Party, the Republicans won a substantial victory—and, in the process, helped create a great electoral realignment that left the Republicans with a clear majority for the next three decades.

The crises of the 1890s helped spur the United States' growing involvement in the world. In 1898, the United States intervened in a colonial war between Spain and Cuba, won a quick military victory, and signed a treaty with Spain that ceded significant territory to the Americans. A vigorous anticolonial movement failed to stop the imperial drive. But taking the overseas possessions proved easier than holding them. In the Philippines, American forces became bogged down in a brutal four-year war with Filipino rebels. The conflict soured much of the American public. The territorial expansion of 1898 proved to be short-lived, but it marked the beginning of an American global interventionism that persisted long past the lifetimes of those who initiated it.

KEY TERMS/PEOPLE/PLACES/EVENTS

Benjamin Harrison 457
Boxer Rebellion 484
Chester A. Arthur 457
Coxey's Army 463
Farmers' Alliances 459
Free silver 464
Grangers 459
Grover Cleveland 457
Half-Breeds 456
imperialism 467

Interstate Commerce Act 458
James A. Garfield 456
jingoes 467
Open Door 483
Panic of 1893 462
Pendleton Act 457
Populism 461
Puerto Rico 476
Queen Liliuokalani 470

Rutherford B. Hayes 456
Sherman Antitrust Act 458
Spanish-American War 474
Stalwarts 456
Teller Amendment 474
William Jennings Bryan 464
William McKinley 458
U.S.S. *Maine* 474
yellow journalism 473

RECALL AND REFLECT

1. How and why did the federal government attempt to regulate interstate commerce in the late nineteenth century?
2. What efforts did farmers undertake to deal with the economic problems they faced in the late nineteenth century?
3. What was the "silver question"? Why was it so important to so many Americans? How did the major political parties deal with this question?
4. How did the Spanish-American War change America's relationship with the rest of the world?
5. What were the main arguments of those who supported U.S. imperialism and those who opposed the nation's imperial efforts?

Design elements: Scale: ©Graphic.mooi/Shutterstock; Phonograph: ©puruan/Shutterstock; Map, Stars and Stripes: ©McGraw-Hill Education.

20 | THE PROGRESSIVES

THE PROGRESSIVE IMPULSE
WOMEN AND REFORM
THE ASSAULT ON THE PARTIES
SOURCES OF PROGRESSIVE REFORM
CRUSADES FOR SOCIAL ORDER AND REFORM
THEODORE ROOSEVELT AND THE MODERN
    PRESIDENCY
THE TROUBLED SUCCESSION
WOODROW WILSON AND THE NEW FREEDOM

LOOKING AHEAD

1. What role did women and women's organizations play in the reforms of the progressive era? How did progressive era reforms affect women?
2. What changes to politics and government did progressive reformers advocate at the local, state, and federal levels? How did government change as a result of their reform efforts?
3. How did Woodrow Wilson's progressivism differ from that of Theodore Roosevelt? In what ways was it similar to Roosevelt's?

WELL BEFORE THE END OF THE NINETEENTH CENTURY, many Americans had become convinced that rapid industrialization and urbanization had created a growing crisis. The nation's most pressing need, they claimed, was to impose order and justice on a society that seemed to be approaching chaos. By the early years of the twentieth century, this outlook had acquired a name: **progressivism**.

Not even those who called themselves progressives could agree on what the term meant, for it was a phenomenon of great scope and diversity. But despite or perhaps because of its broad character, the progressive movement generated a remarkable wave of political and social innovation. From the late nineteenth century until at least the end of World War I, progressive reformers brought into public debate such issues as the role of women in society, racial equality, the rights of labor, and the impact of immigration and cultural diversity.

Progressivism began as a series of local movements and encompassed many different efforts to improve the working of society. Slowly but steadily, these efforts became national efforts.

Ultimately it was the presidency, not the Congress, that became the most important vehicle of national reform—first under the dynamic leadership of Theodore Roosevelt and then under the disciplined, moralistic guidance of Woodrow Wilson. By the time America entered World War I in 1917, the federal government—which had exercised limited powers prior to the twentieth century—had greatly expanded its role in American life.

THE PROGRESSIVE IMPULSE

Progressives believed, as their name implies, in the idea of progress. They were optimistic that society was capable of improvement and that continued advancement was the nation's destiny. But progressives believed, too, that growth must not continue to occur recklessly, as it had in the late nineteenth century. The "natural laws" of the marketplace, and the doctrines of laissez-faire and Social Darwinism that dominated those laws, were not sufficient. Direct, purposeful human intervention was essential to ordering and bettering society. These ideas percolated in the United States as well as many other industrializing parts of the world. (See "America in the World: Social Democracy.")

Progressives did not always agree on the form their interventions should take, and the result was a variety of reform impulses. One powerful impulse was the spirit of "antimonopoly," the fear of concentrated power and the urge to limit and disperse authority and wealth. Another progressive impulse was a belief in the importance of social cohesion: the belief that individuals are part of a great web of social relationships, that each person's welfare is dependent on the welfare of society as a whole. Still another impulse was a deep faith in knowledge—in the possibilities of applying

TIME LINE

1873
Women's Christian Temperance Union (WCTU) founded

1889
Jane Addams opens Hull House in Chicago

1893
Anti-Saloon League founded

1900
Galveston, Texas, establishes commission government

1901
McKinley assassinated; Theodore Roosevelt becomes president

1902
Northern Securities antitrust case

1906
Hepburn Railroad Regulation Act

Meat Inspection Act

1907
Financial panic and recession

1908
Taft elected president

1909
NAACP formed

Pinchot-Ballinger dispute

1911
Triangle Shirtwaist Company fire

1912
Roosevelt forms Progressive Party

Woodrow Wilson elected president

1913
Sixteenth Amendment (income tax)

Seventeenth Amendment (direct popular election of U.S. senators)

1914
Federal Trade Commission Act

Clayton Antitrust Act

Federal Reserve Act

1919
Eighteenth Amendment (prohibition)

1920
Nineteenth Amendment (woman suffrage)

SOCIAL DEMOCRACY

Enormous energy, enthusiasm, and organization drove the reform efforts in America in the late nineteenth and early twentieth centuries, much of it a result of social crises and political movements in the United States. But the "age of reform," as some have called it, was not an American phenomenon alone. It was part of a wave of social experimentation that was occurring throughout much of the industrial world. "Progressivism" in other countries influenced the social movements in the United States. American reform, in turn, had significant influence elsewhere.

Several industrializing nations adopted the term *progressivism* for their efforts—not only the United States, but also England, Germany, and France. But the term that most broadly defined the new reform energies was *social democracy*. Social democrats in many countries shared a belief in the betterment of society through the accumulation of knowledge. They favored improving the social condition of all people through reforms of the economy and government programs of social protection. And they believed that these goals could be achieved through peaceful political change, rather than through radicalism or revolution. Political parties committed to these goals emerged in several countries: the Labour Party in Britain, social democratic parties in various European nations, and the short-lived Progressive Party in the United States. Intellectuals, academics, and government officials across the world shared the knowledge they were accumulating and observed one another's social programs. American reformers at the turn of the century spent much time visiting Germany, France, Britain, Belgium, and the Netherlands, observing the

reforms in progress there; and Europeans, in turn, visited the United States. Reformers from both America and Europe were also fascinated by the advanced social experiments in Australia and, especially, New Zealand, which the American reformer Henry Demarest Lloyd once called "the political brain of the modern world." But New Zealand's dramatic experiments in factory regulation, woman suffrage, old-age pensions, progressive taxation, and labor arbitration gradually found counterparts in many other nations as well. William Allen White, a progressive journalist from Kansas, said of this time: "We were parts of one another, in the United States and Europe. Something was welding us into one social and economic whole with local political variations . . . [all] fighting a common cause."

Social democracy—or, as it was sometimes called in the United States and

(Source: Library of Congress, Prints and Photographs Division [LC-USZ62-94920])

THE PARIS EXPO, A PROGRESSIVE SYMBOL
The Paris Expositions of 1889 and 1900, symbolized by the Eiffel Tower and enormous globe, drew progressive experts as well as tourists with the vision of progress through industrial innovation. During the Expos, an international group of progressives held meetings to share ideas for bettering society.

elsewhere, social justice or the social gospel—was responsible for many public programs. Germany began a system of social insurance for its citizens in the 1880s while simultaneously undertaking a massive study of society that produced over 140 volumes of "social investigation" of the nation's life. French reformers pressed in the 1890s for factory regulation, assistance to elderly people, and progressive taxation. Britain pioneered the settlement houses in working-class areas of London—a movement that soon spread to the United States—and, like America, witnessed growing challenges to the power of monopolies at both the local and national levels.

In many countries, social democrats felt pressure from the rising worldwide labor movement and from the rise of socialist parties in many industrial countries as well. Strikes, sometimes violent, were common in France, Germany, Britain, and the United States in the late nineteenth century. The more militant workers became, the more unions seemed to grow.

Social democrats did not always welcome the rise of militant labor movements, but they took them seriously and used them to support their own efforts at reform.

The politics of social democracy represented a great shift in the character of public life all over the industrial world. Instead of battles over the privileges of aristocrats or the power of monarchs, reformers now focused on the social problems of ordinary people and attempted to improve their lot. "The politics of the future are social politics," the British reformer Joseph Chamberlain said in the 1880s, referring to efforts to deal with the problems of ordinary citizens. That belief was fueling progressive efforts across the world in the years that Americans have come to call the "progressive era."   •

UNDERSTAND, ANALYZE, & EVALUATE

1. What is social democracy?
2. What progressive era reforms in American social and political life can be seen in other nations as well?

to society the principles of natural and social sciences. Most progressives believed, too, that a modern government must play an important role in the process of improving and stabilizing society.

THE MUCKRAKERS AND THE SOCIAL GOSPEL

Among the first people to articulate the new spirit of national reform were crusading journalists who began to direct public attention toward social, economic, and political injustices. Known as the **muckrakers**, after Theodore Roosevelt accused them of raking up muck through their writings, they were committed to exposing scandal, corruption, and injustice.

Their first major targets were the trusts and, particularly, the railroads, which the muckrakers considered powerful and corrupt. Exposés of the great corporate organizations began to appear as early as the 1860s, when Charles Francis Adams Jr. and others uncovered corruption among the railroad barons. Decades later, journalist Ida Tarbell produced a scorching study of the Standard Oil trust. By the turn of the century, many muckrakers were turning their attention to government and particularly to the urban political machines. Among the most influential was Lincoln Steffens, a reporter for *McClure's* magazine. His portraits of "machine government" and "boss rule" in cities, written in a tone of studied moral outrage, helped arouse sentiment for urban political reform.

THE BOSSES OF THE SENATE (1889), BY JOSEPH KEPPLER Keppler was a popular political cartoonist of the late nineteenth century who shared the growing concern about the power of trusts—portrayed here as bloated, almost reptilian figures standing menacingly over the members of the U.S. Senate, to whose chamber the "people's entrance" is "closed."

(Source: Library of Congress, Prints and Photographs Division [LC-USZC4-494])

By presenting social problems to the public with indignation and moral fervor, they helped inspire other Americans to take action.

Growing outrage at social and economic injustice committed many reformers to the pursuit of **social justice**. That impulse helped create the rise of what became known as the "**Social Gospel**," the effort to make faith into a tool of social reform. The Social Gospel movement was chiefly concerned with redeeming the nation's cities. The Salvation Army, which began in England but soon spread to the United States, was a Christian social welfare organization with a vaguely military structure. It had recruited 3,000 "officers" and 20,000 "privates" by 1900 and was offering both material aid and spiritual service to the urban poor. In addition, many ministers, priests, and rabbis left traditional parish work to serve in troubled cities. Charles Sheldon's book *In His Steps* (1898), the story of a young minister who abandoned a comfortable post to work among those in need, sold more than 15 million copies. The Social Gospel was never the dominant element in the movement for urban reform. But the engagement of religion with reform helped bring to progressivism a powerful moral commitment to redeem the lives of even the least-favored citizens.

The Settlement House Movement

An element of much progressive thought was the belief in the influence of the environment on individual development. Nothing produced greater distress, many urban reformers believed, than crowded immigrant neighborhoods. One response to the problems of such communities, borrowed from England, was the "settlement house." The most famous was **Hull House**, which opened in 1889 in Chicago as a result of the efforts of the social worker **Jane Addams**. It became a model for more than 400 similar institutions throughout the nation. Staffed by members of the educated middle class, settlement houses sought to help immigrant families adapt to the language and customs of their new country.

Young, mostly unmarried college women were important participants in the settlement house movement. Working in a settlement house, a protected site that served mainly women, was consistent with the widespread assumption that they needed to be sheltered from difficult environments. The clean and well-tended settlement houses were not only a model for immigrant women, but an appropriate site of social engagement for elite women as well.

The settlement houses also helped create another important institution of reform: the profession of social work. A growing number of programs for the professional training of social workers began to appear in the nation's leading universities, partly in response to the activities of the settlement houses.

THE ALLURE OF EXPERTISE

As the emergence of the social work profession suggests, progressives involved in humanitarian efforts placed a high value on knowledge and expertise. Even nonscientific problems, they believed, could be analyzed and solved scientifically. Many reformers came to believe that only enlightened experts and well-designed bureaucracies could create the stability and order America needed.

Some even spoke of the creation of a new civilization, in which the expertise of scientists and engineers could be brought to bear on the problems of the economy and society. The social scientist Thorstein Veblen, for example, proposed a new economic system in which power would reside in the hands of highly trained engineers. Only they, he argued, could fully understand the "machine process" by which modern society must be governed.

THE PROFESSIONS

The late nineteenth century saw a dramatic expansion in the number of Americans engaged in administrative and professional tasks. Industries needed managers, technicians, and accountants as well as workers. Cities required commercial, medical, legal, and educational services. New technology required scientists and engineers, who, in turn, required institutions and instructors to train them. By the turn of the century, those performing these services had come to constitute a distinct social group—what some historians have called a "new middle class."

By the early twentieth century, millions within this middle class were building organizations and establishing standards to secure their position in society. Most of all, they created the modern, organized professions. The idea of professionalism had been a frail one in America even as late as 1880, but as the demand for professional services increased, so did the pressures for reform.

Among the first to respond was the medical profession. In 1901, doctors who considered themselves trained professionals reorganized the American Medical Association (AMA) into a national professional society. By 1920, nearly two-thirds of all American doctors were members. The AMA called for strict, scientific standards for admission to the practice of medicine. State governments responded by passing laws requiring the licensing of all physicians. By 1900, medical education at a few medical schools—notably Johns Hopkins in Baltimore (founded in 1893)—compared favorably with those in the leading institutions of Europe.

By 1916, lawyers in all forty-eight states had established professional bar associations. The nation's law schools expanded greatly. Businessmen supported the creation of schools of business administration and set up their own national organizations: the National Association of Manufacturers in 1895 and the United States Chamber of Commerce in 1912. Farmers responded to the new order by forming, through the National Farm Bureau Federation, a network of agricultural organizations designed to spread scientific farming methods.

The ethos of professionalization aimed to remove the untrained and incompetent. But the admission requirements also protected those already in the professions from excessive competition and lent them prestige and status. Some professions used their entrance requirements to exclude African Americans, women, immigrants, and other "undesirables" from their ranks. Others used them simply to keep numbers down, ensuring demand for their services would remain high.

WOMEN AND THE PROFESSIONS

American women found themselves excluded from most of the emerging professions. But a substantial number of middle-class women, particularly those emerging from the new women's colleges and coeducational state universities, entered professional careers nevertheless.

A few women managed to establish themselves as physicians, lawyers, engineers, scientists, and corporate managers. Most, however, turned by necessity to those professional outlets that society considered suitable for women: settlement houses, social work, and, most important, teaching. Indeed, in the late nineteenth century, perhaps 90 percent of all professional women were teachers. For educated black women, in particular, the existence of segregated schools in the South created a substantial market for African American teachers.

Women also dominated other professional activities. Nursing had become primarily a women's field during and after the Civil War. By the early twentieth century, it was adopting professional standards. And some women entered academia, often earning advanced degrees at such predominantly male institutions as the University of Chicago, MIT, or Columbia, and then finding professional opportunities in the new and expanding women's colleges.

WOMEN AND REFORM

The prominence of women in reform movements is one of the most striking features of progressivism. In many states in the early twentieth century, women could not vote. They almost never held public office. They had footholds in only a few, usually primarily female professions and lived in a culture in which most people believed women were not suited for the public world. What, then, explains the prominent role so many women played in the reform activities of the period?

THE "NEW WOMAN"

The phenomenon of the "new woman" was a product of social and economic changes in both the private and public spheres. By the end of the nineteenth century, almost all income-producing activity had moved out of the home and into the factory or the office. At the same time, many women were having fewer children, and their children were beginning school at earlier ages and spending more time there. For wives and mothers who did not work for wages, the home was less of an all-consuming place. Hence, more and more women began looking for activities outside the domestic sphere.

Some educated women shunned marriage entirely, believing that only by remaining single could they play the roles they envisioned in the public world. Single women were among the most prominent reformers of the time. Some of these women lived alone. Others lived with other women, often in long-term relationships—some of them secretly romantic—that were known at the time as "Boston marriages." The divorce rate also rose rapidly in the late nineteenth century, from one divorce for every twenty-one marriages in 1880 to one in nine by 1916. Women initiated the majority of divorces.

THE CLUBWOMEN

Among the most visible signs of the increasing public roles of women in the late nineteenth and early twentieth centuries were women's clubs, which proliferated rapidly beginning in the 1880s and 1890s and became the vanguard of many important reforms.

The women's clubs began largely as cultural organizations to provide middle- and upper-class women with an outlet for their intellectual energies. In 1892, when women formed the General Federation of Women's Clubs, there were more than 100,000 members in nearly 500 clubs. By 1917, there were over 1 million members.

Much of what the clubs did was uncontroversial: planting trees; supporting schools, libraries, and settlement houses; building hospitals and parks. But clubwomen were also an important force in winning passage of state and ultimately federal laws that regulated the conditions of woman and child labor. They pushed government to inspect workplaces, regulate the food and drug industries, reform policies toward the Indian tribes, apply new standards to urban housing, and, perhaps most notably, outlaw the manufacture and sale of alcohol. Women's clubs were instrumental in pressuring state legislatures in most states to provide pensions to widowed or abandoned mothers with small children, a system that ultimately became absorbed into the Social Security system. In 1912, they convinced Congress to establish the Children's Bureau in the Labor Department, an agency directed to develop policies to protect children.

In many of these efforts, the clubwomen formed alliances with other women's groups, such as the Women's Trade Union League (WTUL), founded in 1903 by female union members and upper-class reformers and committed to persuading women to join unions. In addition to working on behalf of protective legislation for women, WTUL members held public meetings on behalf of female workers, raised money to support strikes, marched on picket lines, and bailed striking women out of jail.

Black women occasionally joined clubs dominated by whites. But most clubs excluded blacks, and so African Americans formed clubs of their own. Some of them affiliated with the General Federation, but most became part of the independent National Association of Colored Women. Some black clubs also took positions on issues of particular concern to African Americans, such as lynching and segregation.

WOMAN SUFFRAGE

Perhaps the largest single reform movement of the progressive era, indeed one of the largest in American history, was the fight for woman suffrage.

Throughout the late nineteenth century, many suffrage advocates argued that "natural rights" entitled them to the same rights as men—including, first and foremost, the right to vote. Elizabeth Cady Stanton, for example, wrote in 1892 of woman as "the arbiter of her own destiny . . . if we are to consider her as a citizen, as a member of a great nation, she must have the same rights as all other members." This argument challenged the views of many men and women who believed society required a distinctive female sphere, in which women would serve first and foremost as wives and mothers. A powerful antisuffrage movement emerged, dominated by men but with the active support of many women. To these critics, woman suffrage seemed a radical demand.

In the first years of the twentieth century, suffragists were becoming better organized and more politically sophisticated than their opponents. Under the leadership of Anna Howard Shaw, a Boston social worker, and Carrie Chapman Catt, a journalist from Iowa, membership in the National American Woman Suffrage Association (NAWSA) grew from about 13,000 in 1893 to over 2 million in 1917. The movement gained strength because many of its most prominent leaders began to justify suffrage in "safer," less threatening ways. Suffrage, some supporters began to argue, would not challenge the "separate sphere" in which women resided. Instead, they claimed that because women occupied a distinct

(Source: Library of Congress, Prints and Photographs Division [LC-USZ62-70382])

SUFFRAGE PAGEANT On March 3, 1913—the day before Woodrow Wilson's presidential inauguration—more than 5,000 supporters of woman suffrage staged a parade in Washington, D.C., that overshadowed Wilson's arrival in the capital. Crowds estimated at over half a million watched the parade; some of the onlookers attacked the marchers. In this photograph from the event, suffragist Florence Noyce poses as Liberty in front of the U.S. Treasury building.

sphere—because as mothers and wives and homemakers they had special experiences and special sensitivities to bring to public life—woman suffrage would bring those sensitivities to the nation's politics and thereby bolster, not weaken, domestic spaces.

In particular, many suffragists argued that enfranchising women would help the temperance movement by giving its largest group of supporters a political voice. Some suffrage advocates claimed that once women had the vote, war would become a thing of the past, since women would, by their calming, maternal influence, help curb the belligerence of men.

The principal triumphs of the suffrage movement resumed in 1910, when Washington became the first state in fourteen years to extend suffrage to women. California followed a year later, and four other western states in 1912. In 1913, Illinois became the first state east of the Mississippi to embrace woman suffrage. And in 1917 and 1918, New York and Michigan—two of the most populous states in the Union—gave women the vote. By 1919, thirty-nine states had granted women the right to vote in at least some elections, fifteen had allowed full participation. In 1920, finally, suffragists won ratification of the **Nineteenth Amendment**, which guaranteed voting rights to women throughout the nation.

To some feminists, however, the victory seemed less than complete. **Alice Paul**, head of the National Woman's Party (founded in 1916), never accepted the relatively conservative "separate sphere" justification for suffrage. She argued that the Nineteenth Amendment alone would not be sufficient to protect women's rights. Women needed more: a constitutional amendment that would provide full, legal protection for their rights and would prohibit all discrimination on the basis of gender. But Alice Paul's argument found limited favor even among many of the most important leaders of the recently triumphant suffrage crusade.

THE ASSAULT ON THE PARTIES

Most progressive goals required the involvement of the state. Only government, reformers agreed, could effectively counter the many powerful private interests that threatened the nation. But American government at the dawn of the new century was poorly adapted to meet progressive demands. Before progressives could reform society effectively, they would have to reform government itself. Many reformers believed the first step must be an assault on the dominant role political parties played in the life of the state.

EARLY ATTACKS

Attacks on party dominance had been frequent in the late nineteenth century. Greenbackism and Populism, for example, had been efforts to break the hammerlock with which the Republicans and Democrats controlled public life. The Independent Republicans (or mugwumps) had attempted to challenge the grip of partisanship.

The early assaults enjoyed some success. In the 1880s and 1890s, for example, most states adopted the secret ballot. Prior to that, the political parties themselves had printed ballots (or "tickets"), with the names of the party's candidates, and no others. They distributed the tickets to their supporters, who then simply went to the polls to deposit them in the ballot boxes. The old system had made it possible for bosses to monitor the voting behavior of their constituents. The new secret ballot, printed by the government and distributed at the polls to be filled out and deposited in secret, helped chip away at the power of the parties over the voters.

MUNICIPAL REFORM

Many progressives believed the impact of party rule was most damaging in the cities. Municipal government therefore became the first target of those working for political reform. The muckrakers were especially successful in arousing public outrage at corruption and incompetence in city politics. They struck a responsive chord among a powerful group of urban middle-class progressives, who set out to destroy the power of city bosses and their entrenched political organizations.

One of the first major successes in municipal reform came in Galveston, Texas, where the old city government proved completely unable to deal with the effects of a destructive hurricane in 1900. Capitalizing on public dismay, reformers won approval of a new city charter that replaced the mayor and council with an elected, nonpartisan commission. In 1907, Des Moines, Iowa, adopted its own version of the commission plan, and other cities soon followed.

Another approach to municipal reform was the city manager plan, by which elected officials hired an outside expert—often a professionally trained business manager or engineer—to take charge of the government. The city manager would presumably remain untainted by the corrupting influence of politics. By the end of the progressive era, almost 400 cities were operating under commissions, and another 45 employed city managers.

In most urban areas, reformers had to settle for lesser victories. Some cities made the election of mayors nonpartisan, so the parties could not choose the candidates. Or they moved them to years when no presidential or congressional races were in progress, to reduce the influence of the large turnouts that party organizations produced. Reformers tried to make city councilors run at large, to limit the influence of ward leaders and district bosses.

They tried to strengthen the power of the mayor at the expense of the city council, on the assumption that reformers were more likely to succeed in getting a sympathetic mayor elected than they were to win control of the entire council.

STATEHOUSE PROGRESSIVISM

Other progressives turned to state government as an agent for reform. They looked with particular scorn on state legislatures, whose ill-paid, relatively undistinguished members, they believed, were generally incompetent, often corrupt, and totally controlled by party bosses. Reformers began looking for ways to circumvent the boss-controlled legislatures by increasing the power of the electorate. A big victory came in 1913, when the states ratified a constitutional amendment—the seventeenth—that transferred the right to elect U.S. senators from the state legislatures to ordinary voters.

Two other important changes were proposed by Populists in the 1890s: the initiative and the referendum. The initiative allowed reformers to bypass state legislatures by submitting new legislation directly to the voters in general elections. The referendum provided a method by which actions of the legislature could be put to the electorate for approval. By 1918, more than twenty states had enacted one or both of these reforms.

The direct primary and the recall were other efforts to limit the power of parties and improve the quality of elected officials. The primary election was an attempt to remove the selection of candidates from the bosses and give it to the people. Yet in the South, it was also an effort to limit black voting, since primary voting, many white southerners believed, would be easier to control than general elections. The recall gave voters the right to remove a public official from office with a special election, which could be called after a sufficient number of citizens had signed a petition. By 1915, every state in the nation had instituted primary elections for at least some offices. The recall encountered more strenuous opposition, but a few states (such as California) adopted it as well.

The most celebrated state-level reformer was **Robert M. La Follette** of Wisconsin. Elected governor in 1900, he helped turn his state into what reformers across the nation described as a laboratory of progressivism. Under his leadership, Wisconsin progressives won approval of direct primaries, initiatives, and referendums. They regulated railroads and utilities, addressing abuses of power such as rate-fixing and collusion among railway companies. They passed laws to providing compensation for laborers injured on the job. They instituted graduated taxes on inherited fortunes, and they nearly doubled state levies on railroads and other corporate interests.

PARTIES AND INTEREST GROUPS

The reformers did not, of course, eliminate parties from American political life. But they did contribute to a decline in party influence. Evidence of their impact came, among other things, from the decline in voter turnout. In the late nineteenth century, up to 81 percent of eligible voters routinely turned out for national elections. In the early twentieth century, the figure declined markedly. In the presidential election of 1900, 73 percent of the electorate voted. By 1912, turnout had declined to about 59 percent. Never again has voter turnout reached as high as 70 percent.

Why did voter turnout decline in these years? The secret ballot was one reason. Party bosses had less ability to get voters to the polls. Illiterate voters had trouble reading the new ballots. Party bosses lost much of their authority and were unable to mobilize voters as successfully as they had in the past. The popular, highly partisan politics of the nine-teenth century gave way over time to more bureaucratic government and parties and a less inclusive politics; recall the wave of disfranchisement, too, that limited the ballot for blacks and poor whites. But perhaps the most important reason for the decline of party rule and voter turnout was that other power centers were beginning to replace them. They have become known as "interest groups." Beginning late in the nineteenth century and acceler-ating rapidly in the twentieth century, new organizations emerged outside the party system: professional organizations, trade associations representing businesses and industries, labor organizations, farm lobbies, and many others. Social workers, the settlement house move-ments, women's clubs, and others learned to operate as interest groups to advance their demands without relying on parties.

SOURCES OF PROGRESSIVE REFORM

Middle-class reformers, most of them from the East, dominated the public image and much of the substance of progressivism in the late nineteenth and early twentieth centuries. But they were not alone in seeking to improve social conditions. Working-class Americans, African Americans, westerners, and even party bosses played crucial roles in advancing some of the important reforms of the era. (For historians' changing views on who the progressives were and what motivated them, see "Debating the Past: Progressivism.")

LABOR, THE MACHINE, AND REFORM

Although the American Federation of Labor, and its leader Samuel Gompers, remained largely aloof from many of the reform efforts of the time, some unions played important roles in them. Between 1911 and 1913, thanks to political pressure from labor groups such as the newly formed Union Labor Party, California passed a child labor law, a workmen's compensation law, and a limitation on working hours for women. Union pressures contrib-uted to the passage of similar laws in many other states as well.

Party bosses sometimes allowed their machines to become vehicles of social reform. One example was New York's Tammany Hall, the nation's oldest and most notorious city machine. Its astute leader, Charles Francis Murphy, began in the early years of the twenti-eth century to fuse the techniques of boss rule with some of the concerns of social reform-ers. Tammany at times used its political power on behalf of legislation to improve working conditions, protect child laborers, and eliminate the worst abuses of the industrial economy.

In 1911, a terrible fire swept through the factory of the **Triangle Shirtwaist Company** in New York; 146 workers, most of them women, died. Many of them had been trapped inside the burning building because management had locked the emergency exits to prevent malin-gering. For the next three years, a state commission studied the disaster and the conditions of factories generally. In 1914, it issued a series of reports calling for major reforms in the conditions of modern labor. The report itself was a classic progressive document, based on the testimony of experts and filled with statistics and technical data. When its recommen-dations reached the New York legislature, its most effective supporters were two Tammany Democrats from working-class backgrounds: Senator Robert F. Wagner and Assemblyman Alfred E. Smith. With the support of Murphy and the backing of other Tammany legisla-tors, they helped pass a series of pioneering labor laws that imposed strict regulations on factory owners and established effective mechanisms for enforcement.

PROGRESSIVISM

Until the early 1950s, most historians seemed to agree on the central characteristics of early-twentieth-century progressivism. It was just what many progressives themselves had said it was: a movement by the people to curb the power of special interests. More specifically, it was a protest by an aroused citizenry against the excessive power of urban bosses, corporate moguls, and corrupt elected officials.

In 1951, the historian George Mowry began challenging these assumptions by examining progressives in California and describing them as a small, privileged elite of business and professional figures: people who considered themselves the natural leaders of society and who were trying to recover their fading influence from the new capitalist institutions that had displaced them. Progressivism was not, in other words, a popular democratic movement but the effort of a displaced elite to restore its authority. Richard Hofstadter expanded on this idea in *The Age of Reform* (1955) by describing reformers as people afflicted by "status anxiety"—fading elites suffering not from economic but from psychological discontent.

The Mowry-Hofstadter argument soon encountered a range of challenges. Gabriel Kolko, in *The Triumph of Conservatism* (1963), rejected both the older "democratic" view of progressivism and the newer status-anxiety view. Progressive reform, he argued, was not an effort to protect the people from the corporations; it was, rather, a vehicle through which corporate leaders used the government to protect themselves from competition.

A more moderate reinterpretation came from historians embracing what would later be called the "organizational" approach to twentieth-century American history. Samuel Hays, in *The Response to Industrialism* (1957), and Robert Wiebe, in *The Search for Order* (1967), portrayed progressivism as a broad effort by businessmen, professionals, and other middle-class people to bring order and efficiency to political and economic life. In the new industrial society, economic power was increasingly concentrated in large national organizations, while social and political life remained centered primarily in local communities. Progressivism, Wiebe argued, was the effort of a "new middle class"—a class tied to the emerging national economy—to stabilize and enhance its position in society by bringing those two worlds together.

In the 1970s and 1980s, much of the scholarship on progressivism focused on discovering new groups among whom progressive ideas and efforts flourished. Historians found evidence of progressivism in the rising movement by consumers to define their interests; in the growth of reform movements among African Americans; in the changing nature of urban political machines; and in the political activism of working people and labor organizations. Some historians, in turn, found the "movement" becoming so diverse in the scholarship that they ceased to think of it as a movement at all.

Other scholars attempted to identify progressivism with broad changes in the structure and culture of politics. Richard McCormick, writing in 1981, argued that the crucial change in the progressive era was the decline of political parties and the corresponding rise of interest groups working for particular social and economic goals.

At the same time, many historians have focused on the role of women and the vast network of voluntary associations they created in shaping and promoting progressive reform. Some progressive battles, historians such as Kathryn Sklar, Ruth Rosen, Elaine Tyler May, and Linda Gordon have argued, were part of an effort by women to protect their interests within the domestic sphere in the face of jarring challenges from the new industrial world. This protective urge drew women reformers to such issues as temperance, divorce, prostitution, and the regulation of female and child labor. Other women worked to expand their own roles in the public world, particularly through their support of suffrage. The gendered interests of women reformers are, many historians insist, critical to an understanding of progressivism.

More recently, a number of historians have sought to place progressivism in a broader context. Daniel Rodgers's *Atlantic Crossings* (1998) is an important study of how European reformers shaped the goals of many American progressives. Both Michael McGerr, in *A Fierce Discontent* (2003), and Alan Dawley, in *Changing the World* (2003), see progressivism as a fundamentally moral project—McGerr, as an effort by the middle class to create order and stability, and Dawley, as an effort by groups on the left to attack social injustice. Progressivism, they argue, was not just a political movement but also an effort to remake society and reshape social relations. •

UNDERSTAND, ANALYZE, & EVALUATE

1. What is the gendered view of progressive reform advanced by historians?
2. Was progressivism a "people's" movement?

WESTERN PROGRESSIVES

The American West produced some of the most notable progressive leaders of the time: Hiram Johnson of California, George Norris of Nebraska, William Borah of Idaho, and others, almost all of whom spent at least some of their political careers in the U.S. Senate. For western states, the most important vehicle of reform was the federal government, which exercised a kind of authority in the West that it never possessed in the East. Disputes over

(Source: Library of Congress, Prints and Photographs Division [LC-USZ62-29333])

PARADE FOR VICTIMS OF THE TRIANGLE SHIRTWAIST FIRE On a rainy day in the spring of 1911, people and horses in mourning dress walked in commemoration of victims of the fire in the Triangle Shirtwaist Company. This tragedy galvanized New York legislators into passing laws to protect workers.

water, for example, almost always involved rivers and streams that crossed state lines. More significant, perhaps, the federal government exercised enormous power over the lands and resources of the western states and provided substantial subsidies to the region in the form of land grants and support for railroad and water projects. Huge areas of the West remained and still remain public lands, controlled by Washington. Much of the growth of the West was a result of federally funded dams, water projects, and other infrastructure undertakings.

AFRICAN AMERICANS AND REFORM

Most white progressives paid little attention to race or even supported segregation, although they usually rationalized it as a measure to protect imperiled groups including black people and Native Americans. But among African Americans themselves, the progressive era produced significant challenges to existing racial norms.

African Americans faced greater obstacles than any other group in seeking reform. So it was not surprising, perhaps, that so many African Americans embraced the message of Booker T. Washington in the late nineteenth century. Washington encouraged black men and women to work for immediate self-improvement rather than long-range social change. By the beginning of the twentieth century, however, a powerful challenge to the philosophy of Washington was emerging. The chief spokesperson for this new approach was **W. E. B. Du Bois**, a sociologist and historian and one of the first African Americans to receive a degree from Harvard.

In *The Souls of Black Folk* (1903), Du Bois launched an open attack on the philosophy of Washington, accusing him of encouraging white efforts to sustain segregation and of limiting the aspirations of his race. Rather than content themselves with education at trade and agricultural schools, Du Bois encouraged talented blacks to accept nothing less than a full university education and aspire to the professions. They should, above all, fight for their civil rights, not simply wait for them to be granted as a reward for patience. In 1905, Du Bois and a group of his supporters met at Niagara Falls—on the Canadian side of the

(©George Rinhart/Getty Images)

THE CRISIS   W. E. B. Du Bois founded *The Crisis*, the magazine of the NAACP, in 1910. Its object was to "show the danger of race prejudice, particularly as manifested today toward colored people." This photograph shows the magazine's office.

border because no hotel on the American side would have them—and launched what became known as the Niagara Movement. Four years later, they joined with sympathetic white progressives to form the **National Association for the Advancement of Colored People (NAACP)**. In the years that followed, the new organization worked for equal rights.

Among the many issues that engaged the NAACP and other African American organizations was lynching in the South. Among the most determined opponents of lynching were southern women, and the most effective crusader was a black woman, Ida B. Wells-Barnett, who worked both on her own, at great personal risk, and with such organizations as the National Association of Colored Women and the Women's Convention of the National Baptist Church to try to expose lynching and challenge segregation.

CRUSADES FOR SOCIAL ORDER AND REFORM

Many reformers crusaded on behalf of what they considered moral issues—working to eliminate alcohol, curb prostitution, limit divorce, and restrict immigration.

THE TEMPERANCE CRUSADE

Many progressives considered the elimination of alcohol from American life a necessary step in restoring order to society. Scarce wages vanished as male workers spent hours in saloons. Drunkenness spawned violence, and occasionally murder, within urban families. Many working-class wives and mothers hoped through temperance to reform male behavior and thus improve women's lives. Employers, too, regarded alcohol as an impediment to industrial efficiency. Workers often missed time on the job or worked ineffectively because of drunkenness. Critics of economic privilege denounced the liquor industry as one of the nation's most sinister trusts. And political reformers, who correctly looked on the saloon as one of the central institutions of the urban machine, saw an attack on drinking as part of an attack on the bosses. Out of such sentiments emerged the temperance movement.

There had been a major temperance movement before the Civil War, mobilizing large numbers of people in a crusade with strong evangelical overtones. In 1873, the movement developed new strength. Temperance advocates formed the **Women's Christian Temperance Union (WCTU)**, which was led after 1879 by Frances Willard. By 1911, it had 245,000 members and had become the single largest women's organization in American history to that point. In 1893, the Anti-Saloon League joined the movement and, along with the WCTU, began to press for the legal abolition of saloons as a step toward eradicating drinking altogether. Gradually, that demand grew to include the complete prohibition of the sale and manufacture of alcoholic beverages.

Pressure for **prohibition** grew steadily through the first decades of the new century. By 1916, nineteen states had passed prohibition laws. America's entry into World War I, which made the use of grain for alcohol seem wasteful and unnecessary, provided the last push to the advocates of prohibition. In 1917, with the support of rural fundamentalists who opposed alcohol on moral and religious grounds, progressive advocates of prohibition steered through Congress a constitutional amendment. Two years later, after ratification by every state in the nation except Connecticut and Rhode Island (with large populations of Catholic immigrants opposed to prohibition), the Eighteenth Amendment became law, to take effect in January 1920.

IMMIGRATION RESTRICTION

Virtually all reformers agreed that the growing immigrant population had created social problems, but there was wide disagreement on how best to respond. Some progressives believed the proper approach was to help new residents adapt to American society. Others argued the only solution was to limit the flow of new arrivals.

In the first decades of the century, pressure grew to close the nation's gates. New scholarly theories argued that the introduction of immigrants into American society was polluting the nation's racial stock. One of these theories, **eugenics**, began as the science of altering the reproductive processes of plants and animals to produce new hybrids or breeds. But in the late nineteenth century, eugenicists spread the spurious belief that human inequalities were hereditary and that immigration was contributing to the multiplication of the unfit. A special federal commission of "experts," chaired by Senator William P. Dillingham of Vermont, issued a study filled with statistics and scholarly testimony. It argued that the newer immigrant groups, largely southern and eastern Europeans, had proved themselves less assimilable than earlier immigrants. Immigration, the report implied, should be restricted by nationality. Even many people who rejected these racial arguments supported limiting immigration as a way to solve such urban problems as overcrowding, unemployment, strained social services, and social unrest.

The combination of these concerns gradually won the support of some of the nation's leading progressives for limiting immigration, including former president Theodore Roosevelt. Powerful opponents—employers who saw immigration as a source of cheap labor, immigrants themselves, and their political representatives—managed to block the restriction movement for a time. But by the beginning of World War I, which itself effectively blocked immigration temporarily, the nativist tide was gaining strength.

THE DREAM OF SOCIALISM

Although never a force to rival or even seriously threaten the two major parties, **socialism** gained considerable strength during the early years of the twentieth century. In the election of 1900, the Socialist Party of America attracted the support of fewer than 100,000 voters. In 1912, its durable leader and perennial presidential candidate, Eugene V. Debs, received nearly 1 million ballots. Strongest in urban immigrant communities, particularly among Germans and Jews, it also attracted the loyalties of a substantial number of Protestant farmers in the South and the Midwest.

Virtually all socialists agreed on the need for basic structural changes in the economy, but they differed widely on the extent of those changes and the tactics necessary to achieve them. Some socialists endorsed the radical goals of European Marxists (a complete end to capitalism and private property); others envisioned more moderate reform that would allow small-scale private enterprise to survive but would nationalize major industries. Some believed in working for reform through electoral politics; others favored militant direct action. Among the militants was the radical labor union the **Industrial Workers of the World (IWW)**, known to opponents as the "Wobblies." Under the leadership of William "Big Bill" Haywood, the IWW advocated a single union for all workers and was one of the few labor organizations to champion the cause of unskilled workers. Many people believed the Wobblies had been responsible for dynamiting railroad lines and power stations and committing other acts of terror in the first years of the twentieth century.

Moderate socialists who advocated peaceful change through political struggle dominated the Socialist Party. They emphasized a gradual education of the public to the need for change and patient efforts within the system to enact it. But the party refused to support the nation's war effort in World War I. The growing wave of antiradicalism during the war subjected the social-ists to enormous harassment and persecution, contributing to socialism's decline.

DECENTRALIZATION AND REGULATION

Most progressives retained faith in the possibilities of reform within a capitalist system. Rather than nationalize basic industries, many reformers hoped to restore the economy to a more human scale. They argued that the federal government should work to break up the largest combinations and enforce a balance between the need for size and the need for competition. This viewpoint came to be identified particularly closely with **Louis D. Brandeis**, a lawyer and later justice of the Supreme Court, who wrote in his 1913 book *Other People's Money* about the "curse of bigness." Brandeis insisted that government must regulate competition in such a way as to ensure that large combinations did not emerge.

Other progressives were less enthusiastic about the virtues of competition. More impor-tant to them was efficiency. Government, they argued, should not fight corporate growth but rather should guard against abuses of power by large institutions. It should distinguish between good trusts and bad trusts. Since economic consolidation was destined to remain a permanent feature of American society, said many progressives, a strong, modernized government should play a more active role in regulating and planning economic life. One of those who came to endorse that position (although not fully until after 1910) was **Theodore Roosevelt**, who once said: "We should enter upon a course of supervision, control, and regulation of those great corporations." Roosevelt became, for a time, the most power-ful symbol of the reform impulse at the national level.

THEODORE ROOSEVELT AND THE MODERN PRESIDENCY

To a generation of progressive reformers, Theodore Roosevelt was more than an admired pub-lic figure; he was an idol. No president before, and few since, attracted such attention and devotion. Yet for all his popularity among reformers, Roosevelt was in many respects decidedly conservative. He earned his extraordinary popularity less because of the extent of reforms he championed than because he brought to his office a broad conception of its powers. He boosted the presidency into something like its modern position as the center of national political life.

THE ACCIDENTAL PRESIDENT

President William McKinley was in Buffalo, New York, in September 1901 to visit the Pan-American Exposition. He was greeting members of the public when a man named Leon Czolgosz approached McKinley with a pistol concealed in a handkerchief and shot him in the stomach. After appearing on the path to recovery, the president died of an infection about a week later. It turned out the assassin, executed the next month, was an unemployed anarchist who blamed growing federal power for the plight of working people. News of Czolgosz's politics inflamed existing vilification of anarchism and other philosophies of the left, and soon it became illegal for avowed anarchists to enter the country. Secret Service also began shadowing presidents from that time forward.

Roosevelt, at forty-two years old, became the youngest man ever to assume the presi-dency. "I told William McKinley that it was a mistake to nominate that wild man at Philadelphia," party boss Mark Hanna was reported to have exclaimed. "Now look, that damned cowboy is President of the United States!" Yet as president, Roosevelt rarely openly

(Source: Library of Congress, Prints and Photographs Division [LC-DIG-nclc-01130])

BOYS IN THE MINES These young boys, covered in grime and no more than twelve years old, pose for Lewis Hine outside the coal mine in Pennsylvania where they worked as "breaker boys," crawling into newly blasted areas and breaking up the loose coal. The rugged conditions in the mines were one cause of the great strike of 1902, in which Theodore Roosevelt intervened.

rebelled against the leaders of his party. He became, rather, a champion of cautious, moderate change. Reform, he believed, was a vehicle less for remaking American society than for protecting it against more radical challenges.

Roosevelt allied himself with those progressives who urged regulation (but not destruction) of the trusts, wishing to give the government the power to investigate corporations and publicize the results. Yet although Roosevelt was not a trustbuster at heart, he made a few highly publicized efforts to break up combinations. In 1902, he ordered the Justice Department to invoke the Sherman Antitrust Act against a great new railroad monopoly in the Northwest, the Northern Securities Company, a $400 million enterprise pieced together by J. P. Morgan and others. Roosevelt filed more than forty additional antitrust suits during the remainder of his presidency, but he made no serious commitment to reverse the prevailing trend toward economic concentration.

When a bitter 1902 strike by the United Mine Workers endangered coal supplies for the coming winter, Roosevelt asked both the operators and the miners to accept impartial federal arbitration. When the mine owners balked, Roosevelt threatened to send federal troops to seize the mines. The operators finally relented. Arbitrators awarded the strikers a 10 percent wage increase and a nine-hour day, although no recognition of their union—less than the miners had wanted but more than they would likely have won without Roosevelt's intervention.

THE "SQUARE DEAL"

During the 1904 campaign for the presidency, Roosevelt boasted that he had worked in the anthracite coal strike to provide everyone with a "square deal." One of his first targets after winning the election was the powerful railroad industry. The Interstate Commerce Act of 1887, establishing the Interstate Commerce Commission (ICC), had represented an early effort to regulate the industry, but over the years, the courts had sharply limited its influence. The Hepburn Railroad Regulation Act of 1906 sought to restore some regulatory authority to the government by giving the ICC power to oversee railroad rates.

Roosevelt also pressured Congress to enact the Pure Food and Drug Act, which restricted the sale of dangerous or ineffective medicines. *The Jungle*, a powerful novel published by Upton Sinclair in 1906, included appalling descriptions of conditions in the meatpacking industry. Roosevelt pushed for passage of the Meat Inspection Act, which helped eliminate many diseases once transmitted in impure meat. Starting in 1907, he proposed even more stringent reforms: an eight-hour day for workers, broader compensation for victims of industrial accidents, inheritance and income taxes, and regulation of the stock market. Conservative opposition blocked much of his agenda, widening the gulf between the president and the conservative wing of his party.

ROOSEVELT AND THE ENVIRONMENT

Roosevelt's aggressive policies on behalf of conservation contributed to that gulf. Using executive powers, he restricted private development on millions of acres of undeveloped government land, most of it in the West, by adding them to the previously modest national

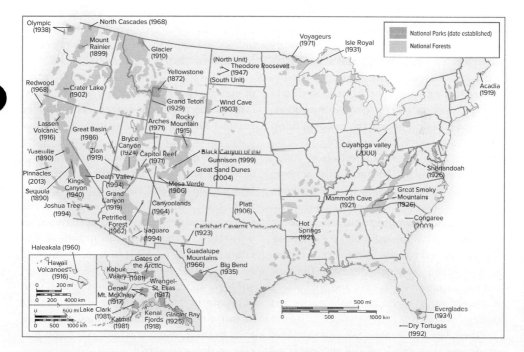

ESTABLISHMENT OF NATIONAL PARKS AND FORESTS This map illustrates the steady growth through the late nineteenth, twentieth, and twenty-first centuries of the systems of national parks and national forests in the United States. Although Theodore Roosevelt is widely and correctly remembered as a great champion of national parks and forests, the greatest expansions of these systems occurred after his presidency. • *How many new areas were added in the 1920s? Where are the most recently designated parks and forests?*

JOHN MUIR ON THE VALUE OF WILD PLACES (1901)

John Muir is often called the "father of the national parks" for his role as advocate on behalf of legislation to designate certain wilderness areas as off-limits for commercial development. In this excerpt from his book *Our National Parks,* **he argues for the restorative benefits of visiting unspoiled nature.**

The tendency nowadays to wander in wildernesses is delightful to see. Thousands of tired, nerve-shaken, over-civilized people are beginning to find out that going to the mountains is going home; that wildness is a necessity; and that mountain parks and reservations are useful not only as fountains of timber and irrigating rivers, but as fountains of life. Awakening from the stupefying effects of the vice of over-industry and the deadly apathy of luxury, they are trying as best they can to mix and enrich their own little ongoings with those of Nature, and to get rid of rust and disease. Briskly venturing and roaming, some are washing off sins and cobweb cares of the devil's spinning in all-day storms on mountains; sauntering in rosiny pinewoods or in gentian meadows, brushing through chaparral, bending down and parting sweet, flowery sprays; tracing rivers to their sources, getting in touch with the nerves of Mother Earth; jumping from rock to rock, feeling the life of them, learning the songs of them, panting in whole-souled exercise, and rejoicing in deep, long-drawn breaths of pure wildness. This is fine and natural and full of promise. So also is the growing interest in the care and preservation of forests and wild places in general, and in the half wild parks and gardens of towns. . . .

When, like a merchant taking a list of his goods, we take stock of our wildness, we are glad to see how much of even the most destructible kind is still unspoiled. Looking at our continent as scenery when it was all wild, lying between beautiful seas, the starry sky above it, the starry rocks beneath it, to compare its sides, the East and the West, would be like comparing the sides of a rainbow. But it is no longer equally beautiful. . . . [T]he continent's outer beauty is fast passing away, especially the plant part of it, the most destructible and most universally charming of all.

Only thirty years ago, the great Central Valley of California, five hundred miles long and fifty miles wide, was one bed of golden and purple flowers. Now it is ploughed and pastured out of existence, gone forever,—scarce a memory of it left in fence corners and along the bluffs of the streams. . . . The same fate, sooner or later, is awaiting them all, unless awakening public opinion comes forward to stop it. . . .

The Grand Cañon Reserve of Arizona, of nearly two million acres, or the most interesting part of it, as well as the Rainier region, should be made into a national park, on account of their supreme grandeur and beauty. . . . No matter how far you have wandered hitherto, or how many famous gorges and valleys you have seen, this one, the Grand Cañon of the Colorado, will seem as novel to you, as unearthly in the color and grandeur and quantity of its architecture, as if you had found it after death, on some other star; so incomparably lovely and grand and supreme is it above all the other cañons in our fire-moulded, earthquake-shaken, rain-washed, wave-washed, river and glacier sculptured world.

1. What benefits does Muir describe as a result of spending time in the "wilderness"? What maladies does Muir believe the "wilderness" will correct? How do his arguments reflect the economic and social history of his time?

2. What is Muir's purpose? Is he attempting primarily to instruct or to persuade? How does that purpose affect the tone of the writing?

Source: Library of Congress, Materials from the General Collection and Rare Book and Special Collections Division of the Library of Congress.

forest system. When conservatives in Congress restricted his authority over public lands in 1907, Roosevelt and his chief forester, Gifford Pinchot, seized all the forests and many of the water power sites still in the public domain before the bill became law.

Roosevelt was the first president to take an active interest in the new and struggling American conservation movement. In the early twentieth century, many people who considered themselves **conservationists**—including Pinchot, the first director of the U.S. Forest Service (which he helped create)—promoted policies to protect land for carefully managed development.

Roosevelt also supported public reclamation and irrigation projects. In 1902, the president backed the National Reclamation Act, which used funds raised by the sale of public lands in the West for the construction of dams, reservoirs, and canals, projects that would "reclaim" arid lands for cultivation and later provide cheap electric power.

Despite his sympathy with Pinchot's vision of conservation, Roosevelt also shared some of the concerns of the naturalists—those committed to protecting the natural beauty of the land and the health of its wildlife from human intrusion. Early in his presidency, Roosevelt spent four days camping in the Sierras with **John Muir**, the nation's leading **preservationist** and the founder of the Sierra Club. Roosevelt also added significantly to the still-young National Park System, whose purpose was to protect public land from exploitation or development. (For Muir's views on the system, see "Consider the Source: John Muir on the Value of Wild Places.")

The contending views of the early conservation movement came to a head beginning in 1906 in a controversy over the **Hetch Hetchy** Valley in Yosemite National Park—a spectacular high-walled valley popular with naturalists. But many residents of San Francisco worried about finding enough water to serve their growing population. They saw Hetch Hetchy as an ideal place for a dam, which would create a large reservoir for the city.

In 1906, San Francisco suffered a devastating earthquake and fire. Widespread sympathy for the city strengthened the case for the dam, and Roosevelt turned the decision over to Pinchot, who approved its construction.

For over a decade, a battle raged between naturalists and the advocates of the dam, a battle that consumed the energies of John Muir for the rest of his life and that eventually, many believed, led him to an early death. To Pinchot, the needs of the city were more important than the claims of preservation. Muir helped place a referendum question on the ballot in 1908, certain that the residents of the city would oppose the project. Instead, San Franciscans approved the dam by a huge margin. Construction of the dam finally began after World War I.

This setback for the naturalists was not, however, a total defeat. The fight against Hetch Hetchy helped mobilize a new coalition of people committed to preservation of wilderness.

Panic and Retirement

Despite the flurry of reforms Roosevelt was able to enact, the government still had relatively little control over the industrial economy. That became clear in 1907, when a serious panic and recession began. Conservatives blamed Roosevelt's "mad" economic policies for the disaster. And while the president naturally disagreed, he nevertheless acted quickly to reassure business leaders that he would not interfere with their recovery efforts.

The financier J. P. Morgan helped construct a pool of the assets of several important New York banks to prop up shaky financial institutions. The key to the arrangement, Morgan told the president, was a purchase by U.S. Steel of the shares of the Tennessee Coal and Iron Company, currently held by a threatened New York bank. Morgan insisted that he needed assurances that the purchase would not prompt antitrust action. Roosevelt tacitly agreed, and the Morgan plan proceeded. Whether or not as a result, the panic soon subsided.

Roosevelt loved being president, and many people assumed that he would run for reelection in 1908, despite the long-standing tradition of presidents serving no more than two terms. But the Panic of 1907 and Roosevelt's reform efforts so alienated conservatives in his own party that he might have had difficulty winning the Republican nomination. In 1904, moreover, he had made a public promise to step down four years later. And so in 1909, Roosevelt, fifty years old, retired from public life—briefly.

THE TROUBLED SUCCESSION

William Howard Taft, who assumed the presidency in 1909, had been Theodore Roosevelt's most trusted lieutenant and his handpicked successor; progressive reformers believed him to be one of their own. But Taft was also a restrained and moderate jurist, a man with a punctilious regard for legal process. Conservatives expected him to abandon Roosevelt's aggressive use of presidential powers. By seeming acceptable to almost everyone, Taft easily won election to the White House in 1908 over William Jennings Bryan, running for the Democrats for the third time.

Four years later, however, Taft would leave office the most decisively defeated president of the twentieth century, his party deeply divided and the government in the hands of a Democratic administration for the first time in twenty years.

Taft and the Progressives

Taft's first problem arose in the opening months of the new administration, when he called Congress into special session to lower protective tariff rates, an old progressive demand. But the president made no effort to overcome the opposition of congressional Old Guard conservatives like House Speaker Joseph Cannon (R-IL), arguing that to do so would violate the constitutional doctrine of separation of powers. The result was the feeble Payne-Aldrich Tariff, which reduced tariff rates scarcely at all. Yet although he tended to refrain from railing against big business in public, Taft filed almost a hundred antitrust suits against corporations during his administration.

Then a sensational controversy breaking out late in 1909 helped destroy Taft's popularity with reformers. Many progressives had been unhappy when Taft replaced Roosevelt's secretary of the interior, James R. Garfield, an aggressive conservationist, with Richard A. Ballinger, a conservative corporate lawyer. Suspicion of Ballinger grew when he attempted to invalidate Roosevelt's removal of nearly 1 million acres of forests and mineral reserves from private development.

In the midst of this mounting concern, Louis Glavis, an Interior Department investigator, charged Ballinger with having once connived to turn over valuable public coal lands in Alaska to a private syndicate for personal profit. Glavis took the evidence to Gifford Pinchot, still director of the U.S. Forest Service and a critic of Ballinger's policies. Pinchot took the charges to the president. Taft investigated them and decided they were groundless. Unsatisfied, Pinchot leaked the story to the press and asked Congress to investigate the scandal. The president discharged Pinchot for insubordination, and the congressional committee appointed to study the controversy, dominated by Old Guard Republicans, exonerated Ballinger. But progressives throughout the country supported Pinchot. The controversy aroused as much public passion as any dispute of its time. By the time it was over, Taft had alienated the supporters of Roosevelt completely, despite his trust-busting record. Taft's shifting devotion to both the conservative and progressive impulses of the Republican Party left him popular with almost no one. To Roosevelt, he had become a tool of big business.

The Return of Roosevelt

During most of these controversies, Theodore Roosevelt was out of the country on a long hunting safari in Africa and an extended tour of Europe. To the American public, however, Roosevelt remained a formidable presence. His return to New York in the spring of 1910

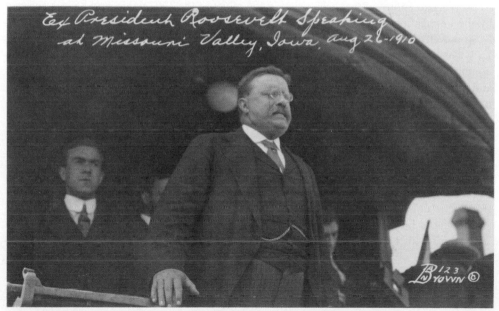

(Source: Library of Congress, Prints and Photographs Division [LC-DIG-ppmsca-36445])

ROOSEVELT AT MISSOURI VALLEY Roosevelt's 1910 speech in Iowa was part of a swing through the Great Plains and Midwest that saw the ex-president mark his break with the Taft administration and the Republican leadership. In Kansas that summer, Roosevelt told his largely conservative audience, "The essence of any struggle for liberty has always been, and must always be to take from some one man or class of men the right to enjoy power, or wealth, or position or immunity, which has not been earned by service to his or their fellows."

was a major public event. Roosevelt insisted that he had no plans to reenter politics, but within a month he announced that he would embark on a national speaking tour before the end of the summer. Furious with Taft, he was becoming convinced that he alone was capable of reuniting the Republican Party.

The real signal of Roosevelt's decision to assume leadership of Republican reformers came in a speech he gave on September 1, 1910, in Osawatomie, Kansas. In it he outlined a set of principles, which he labeled the "**New Nationalism**," that made clear he had moved away from the cautious conservatism of his presidential years. He argued that social justice was possible only through a strong federal government whose executive acted as the "steward of the public welfare." He supported graduated income and inheritance taxes, workers' compensation for industrial accidents, regulation of the labor of women and children, tariff revision, and firmer regulation of corporations.

Spreading Insurgency

The congressional elections of 1910 provided further evidence of how far the progressive revolt had spread. In primary elections, conservative Republicans suffered defeat after defeat, while almost all the progressive incumbents were reelected. In the general election, the Democrats won control of the House of Representatives for the first time in sixteen years and gained strength in the Senate. But Roosevelt still denied any presidential ambitions and claimed his real purpose was to pressure Taft to return to progressive policies. Two events, however, changed his mind. The first, on October 27, 1911, was the announcement by the administration of a suit against U.S. Steel, which charged, among other things, that the 1907 acquisition of the Tennessee Coal and Iron Company had been illegal. Roosevelt had approved that acquisition in the midst of the 1907 panic, and he was enraged by the implication that he had acted improperly.

Roosevelt was still reluctant to become a candidate for president because Senator Robert La Follette, the Wisconsin progressive, had been working since 1911 to secure the presidential nomination for himself. But La Follette's candidacy stumbled in February 1912 when, exhausted and distraught over the illness of a daughter, he appeared to suffer a nervous breakdown during a speech in Philadelphia. Roosevelt announced his candidacy on February 22.

Roosevelt versus Taft

For all practical purposes, the campaign for the Republican nomination had now become a battle between Roosevelt and Taft. Roosevelt scored overwhelming victories in all thirteen presidential primaries. Taft, however, remained the choice of most party leaders, who controlled the nominating process.

The battle for the nomination at the Chicago convention revolved around an unusually large number of contested delegates: 254 in all. Roosevelt needed fewer than half the disputed seats to clinch the nomination. But on the eve of the convention, the Republican National Committee, controlled by the Old Guard, awarded all but 19 of them to Taft. At a rally the night before the convention opened, Roosevelt addressed 5,000 cheering supporters. "We stand at Armageddon," he told the roaring crowd, "and we battle for the Lord." The next day, he led his supporters out of the convention, and out of the party. The convention then quietly nominated Taft on the first ballot.

Roosevelt summoned his supporters back to Chicago in August for another convention, this one to launch the new Progressive Party and to nominate himself as its presidential candidate. Roosevelt approached the battle feeling, as he put it, "fit as a bull moose," thus giving his new party an enduring nickname, the **Bull Moose Party**. But Roosevelt was also aware that his cause was almost hopeless, partly because many of the insurgents who had supported him during the primaries refused to follow him out of the Republican Party. It was also because of the man the Democrats had nominated for president.

WOODROW WILSON AND THE NEW FREEDOM

The 1912 presidential contest was not simply one between conservatives and reformers. It was also one between two brands of progressivism. And it matched the two most important national leaders of the early twentieth century in an unequal contest.

WOODROW WILSON

Reform sentiment had been gaining strength within the Democratic Party as well as the Republican Party in the first years of the century. At the June 1912 Democratic Convention in Baltimore, Champ Clark, the conservative Speaker of the House, was unable to assemble the two-thirds majority necessary for nomination because of progressive opposition. Finally, on the forty-sixth ballot, **Woodrow Wilson**, the governor of New Jersey and the only genuinely progressive candidate in the race, emerged as the party's nominee.

Wilson had been a professor of political science at Princeton until 1902, when he was named president of the university. Elected governor of New Jersey in 1910, he quickly earned a national reputation for winning passage of progressive legislation. As a presidential candidate in 1912, Wilson presented a progressive program that came to be called the **New Freedom**. Roosevelt's New Nationalism supported economic concentration and using government to regulate and control it. Wilson seemed to side with those who (like Louis Brandeis) believed that bigness was both unjust and inefficient, and the proper response to monopoly was not to regulate but destroy it.

The 1912 presidential campaign was an anticlimax. Taft, resigned to defeat, barely campaigned. Roosevelt campaigned energetically, until a gunshot wound from a would-be assassin forced him to the sidelines during the last weeks before the election, but he failed to draw any significant number of Democratic progressives away from Wilson. In November, Roosevelt and Taft split the Republican vote, while Wilson held on to most Democrats and won. He received only 42 percent of the popular vote, compared with 27 percent for Roosevelt, 23 percent for Taft, and 6 percent for the socialist Eugene Debs. But in the electoral college, Wilson won 435 of the 531 votes.

THE SCHOLAR AS PRESIDENT

Wilson was a bold and forceful president. He exerted firm control over his cabinet, and he delegated real authority only to those who were loyal to him. His most powerful adviser, Colonel Edward M. House, was an ambitious Texan who held no office and whose only claim to authority was his personal intimacy with the president.

In legislative matters, Wilson skillfully welded together a coalition that would support his goals. Democratic majorities in both houses of Congress made his task easier. Wilson's first triumph as president was the fulfillment of an old Democratic (and progressive) goal: a substantial lowering of the protective tariff. The Underwood-Simmons

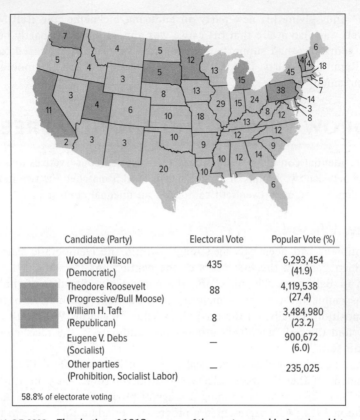

Candidate (Party)	Electoral Vote	Popular Vote (%)
Woodrow Wilson (Democratic)	435	6,293,454 (41.9)
Theodore Roosevelt (Progressive/Bull Moose)	88	4,119,538 (27.4)
William H. Taft (Republican)	8	3,484,980 (23.2)
Eugene V. Debs (Socialist)	—	900,672 (6.0)
Other parties (Prohibition, Socialist Labor)	—	235,025

58.8% of electorate voting

THE ELECTION OF 1912   The election of 1912 was one of the most unusual in American history because of the dramatic schism within the Republican Party. Two Republican presidents—William Howard Taft, the incumbent, and Theodore Roosevelt, his predecessor—ran against each other, opening the way for a victory by the Democratic candidate, Woodrow Wilson, who won with only 42 percent of the popular vote. A fourth candidate, the socialist Eugene V. Debs, received a significant 6 percent of the vote. • *What events caused the schism between Taft and Roosevelt?*

Tariff provided cuts significant enough, progressives believed, to introduce real competition into American markets and thus to help break the power of trusts. To make up for the loss of revenue under the new tariff, Congress approved a graduated income tax, which the recently adopted Sixteenth Amendment to the Constitution now permitted. This first modern federal income tax imposed a 1 percent tax on individuals and corporations earning more than $4,000 a year, with rates ranging up to 6 percent on incomes over $500,000 annually.

Wilson held Congress in session through the summer to work on a major reform of the American banking system: the Federal Reserve Act, which Congress passed and the president signed on December 23, 1913. It created twelve regional banks, each to be owned and controlled by the individual banks of its district. The regional Federal Reserve banks would hold a certain percentage of the assets of their member banks in reserve; they would use those reserves to support loans to private banks at a discounted interest rate that the Federal Reserve system would set; they would issue new, standardized paper bills called Federal Reserve notes that would become the nation's basic

(Source: Library of Congress, Prints and Photographs Division [LC-USZ62-20570])

WOODROW WILSON Woodrow Wilson, the twenty-eighth president of the United States, was a Virginian, the first southerner to be elected president since before the Civil War, a professor of political science and later president of Princeton University, governor of New Jersey, and a progressive. His election to the presidency brought the first Democrat to the White House since 1896.

medium of trade and would be backed by the government (to this day American bills read "Federal Reserve Note" at the top). Most important, they would be able to shift funds quickly to troubled areas to meet increased demands for credit or to protect imperiled banks. Supervising and regulating the entire system was a national Federal Reserve Board, whose members were appointed by the president.

In 1914, turning to the central issue of his 1912 campaign, Wilson proposed two measures to deal with the problem of monopoly, which took shape as the Federal Trade Commission Act and the Clayton Antitrust Act. The Federal Trade Commission Act created a regulatory agency that would help businesses determine in advance whether their actions would be acceptable to the government. The agency would also have authority to launch prosecutions against "unfair trade practices," and it would have wide power to investigate corporate behavior. Wilson signed the Federal Trade Commission Bill happily, but he seemed to lose interest in the Clayton Antitrust Bill, which proposed stronger measures to break up trusts. Wilson did little to protect it from conservative assaults, which greatly weakened it.

RETREAT AND ADVANCE

By the fall of 1914, Wilson believed that the New Freedom program was essentially complete and that agitation for reform would now subside. He refused to support the movement for national woman suffrage. Deferring to southern Democrats, he condoned the reimposition of segregation in the agencies of the federal government, in contrast to Roosevelt, who had ordered the elimination of many such barriers. When congressional progressives attempted to enlist his support for new reform legislation, Wilson dismissed their proposals as unconstitutional or unnecessary.

The congressional elections of 1914, however, shattered the president's complacency. Democrats suffered major losses in Congress, and voters who in 1912 had supported the Progressive Party began returning to the Republicans. Wilson realized he would not be able to rely on a divided opposition when he ran for reelection in 1916. By the end of 1915, therefore, Wilson had begun to support a second flurry of reforms. In January 1916, he appointed Louis Brandeis to the Supreme Court, making him not only the first Jew but also the most advanced progressive to serve there. Later, Wilson supported a measure to make it easier for farmers to receive credit, and another measure creating a system of workers' compensation for federal employees.

In 1916, Wilson supported the Keating-Owen Act, which prohibited the shipment of goods produced by underage children across state lines, thus giving an expanded importance to the constitutional clause assigning Congress the task of regulating interstate commerce. The president similarly supported measures that used federal taxing authority as a vehicle for legislating social change. After the Court struck down Keating-Owen, a new law attempted to achieve the same goal by imposing a heavy tax on the products of child labor. (The Court later struck down that law too.) The Smith-Lever Act of 1914 offered matching federal grants to support agricultural extension education. Over time, these innovative uses of government overcame most of the constitutional objections and became the foundation of a long-term growth in federal power over the economy.

CONCLUSION

The powerful surge of reform efforts in the last years of the nineteenth century and the first years of the twentieth century caused many Americans to identify themselves as "progressives." That label meant many different things to many different people, but at its core was a belief that human effort and government action could improve society. By the early twentieth century, progressivism had become a powerful, transformative force in American life.

This great surge of reform eventually reached the federal government and national politics, as progressives came to believe that success required the engagement of the federal government. Two national leaders, Theodore Roosevelt and Woodrow Wilson, contributed to a period of national reform that made the government in Washington a great center of power for the first time since the Civil War, a position it has never relinquished. Progressivism did not solve the nation's problems, but it gave movements, organizations, and governments new tools to deal with them.

KEY TERMS/PEOPLE/PLACES/EVENTS

Alice Paul 494
Bull Moose Party 511
conservationists 507
eugenics 502
Hetch Hetchy 507
Hull House 490
Industrial Workers of the
  World (IWW) 502
Jane Addams 490
John Muir 507
Louis D. Brandeis 503
muckrakers 489

National Association for the
  Advancement of Colored
  People (NAACP) 501
New Freedom 511
New Nationalism 510
Nineteenth Amendment
  494
progressivism 486
prohibition 501
preservationists 507
Robert M. La Follette 496
Social Gospel 490

socialism 502
social justice 490
Theodore Roosevelt 503
Triangle Shirtwaist
  Company fire 497
W. E. B. Du Bois 500
William Howard Taft 508
Women's Christian
  Temperance Union
  (WCTU) 501
Woodrow Wilson 511

RECALL AND REFLECT

1. What "moral" crusades did progressives undertake in their efforts to reform the social order?
2. How did W. E. B. Du Bois's philosophy on race relations differ from that of Booker T. Washington?
3. What were some of the approaches progressives used to challenge the power and influence of corporate America?
4. What was the difference between Theodore Roosevelt's "New Nationalism" and Woodrow Wilson's "New Freedom"?

21 | AMERICA AND THE GREAT WAR ●

THE "BIG STICK": AMERICA AND THE
WORLD, 1901–1917

THE ROAD TO WAR

"OVER THERE"

THE SEARCH FOR A NEW WORLD ORDER

A SOCIETY IN TURMOIL

LOOKING AHEAD

1. What were the most important events that led up to the United States declaring war on Germany?

2. How did U.S. participation in the Great War affect the nation's economy and society, both during the war and after the conflict ended?

3. Why did the Great War fail to become the "war to end all wars"?

THE "GREAT WAR," AS IT was known to a generation unaware that a greater war would soon follow, began in August 1914 when Austria-Hungary invaded the tiny Balkan nation of Serbia. Within weeks, however, the conflict had grown into a conflagration engaging the armies of most of the major nations of Europe.

Americans looked on with horror as the war became what many people claimed was the most savage in history. It dragged on, brutally and inconclusively, for over four years. Most Americans also believed at first that the conflict had little to do with them. They were wrong. The United States had been deeply involved in world affairs since at least the Spanish-American War, taking on increasing international commitments in the early years of the twentieth century. After nearly three years of attempting to affect the outcome of the conflict without becoming embroiled in it, then, it should not be surprising that the United States entered the war in April 1917.

For America, the war as a military struggle was brief but costly. It killed 116,000 Americans, about half succumbing to influenza and other diseases and half dying by armed violence, though these statistics didn't remotely approach losses among the other major belligerents. Viewed in the long term, the war left a mixed legacy. Economically, it stimulated a great industrial boom that would propel the country into the prosperous era that followed, yet the wartime gains for labor proved temporary. It fostered victories for progressive causes such as prohibition and woman suffrage but also accelerated immigration restriction.

Ethnic and racial minorities served in mass numbers amid the first major conscription in American history, though African Americans in particular endured second-class status in the military and found no postwar extension of political rights awaiting them upon return. Finally, although the conflict propelled the United States into the international arena, it failed to either end war or deliver a democratic world order as President Woodrow Wilson had hoped. Instead, the Great War's resolution led to two decades of global instability and ultimately an even bigger conflict.

THE "BIG STICK": AMERICA AND THE WORLD, 1901–1917

To most of the American public, foreign affairs remained largely remote in the early twentieth century. But to Theodore Roosevelt and later presidents, that remoteness made foreign affairs appealing. Overseas, the president could act with less regard for Congress and the courts.

ROOSEVELT AND "CIVILIZATION"

Theodore Roosevelt believed in using American power in the world, once citing the proverb, "Speak softly, and carry a big stick." But he had two different standards for using that power.

Roosevelt believed an important distinction existed between the "civilized" and "uncivilized" nations of the world. "Civilized" nations, as he defined them, were predominantly white and Anglo-Saxon or Teutonic; "uncivilized" nations were generally nonwhite, Latin, or Slavic. Civilized nations were also, by Roosevelt's definition, producers of industrial goods. Uncivilized nations were suppliers of raw materials and markets for industrial products. Roosevelt

TIME LINE

1914
World War I begins
Panama Canal opened

1915
U.S. troops in Haiti
Lusitania torpedoed
Wilson supports preparedness

1916
Wilson reelected
U.S. troops in Mexico

1917
German unrestricted submarine warfare
U.S. enters World War I
Selective Service Act
War Industries Board created

1918
Sedition Act
Wilson's Fourteen Points
Armistice ends war
Paris Peace Conference

1919
Senate rejects Treaty of Versailles
Race riots in Chicago and other cities
Steel strike and other labor actions

1920
Palmer raids and Red Scare
Harding elected president

1927
Sacco and Vanzetti executed

believed that a civilized society had the right and duty to intervene in the affairs of "backward nations" to preserve order and stability—for the sake of both nations. That belief, the obligation of a "civilized" nation to police the world, was one important reason for Roosevelt's early support of the development of American sea power. By 1906, the American navy had attained a size and strength surpassed only by that of Great Britain.

PROTECTING THE "OPEN DOOR" IN ASIA

In 1904, the Japanese staged a surprise attack on the Russian fleet at Port Arthur in southern Manchuria, a province of China that both Russia and Japan hoped to control. Roosevelt, hoping to prevent either nation from becoming dominant there, agreed to mediate an end to the conflict. Russia, faring badly in the war, had no choice but to agree. At a peace conference in Portsmouth, New Hampshire, in 1905, Roosevelt pressured the embattled Russians to accept Japan's territorial gains. The Japanese agreed to cease the fighting and expand no farther. At the same time, Roosevelt negotiated a secret agreement with the Japanese to ensure that the United States could continue to trade freely in the region. Roosevelt received the Nobel Peace Prize in 1906 for his mediation of what became the Treaty of Portsmouth.

In the years that followed, relations between the United States and Japan steadily deteriorated. Japan, by then the preeminent naval power in the Pacific, began to exclude American trade from many of the territories it controlled. Roosevelt took no direct action against Japan, but to be sure the Japanese government recognized the power of the United States, he sent sixteen battleships of the new American navy (known as the "Great White Fleet" because the ships were temporarily painted white for the voyage) on an unprecedented journey around the world that included a call on Japan.

THE WORLD CONSTABLE.

(Source: Library of Congress, Prints and Photographs Division [LC-DIG-ds-05213])

THE NEW DIPLOMACY This 1904 drawing by the famous *Puck* cartoonist Louis Dalrymple conveys the new image of America as a great power that Theodore Roosevelt hoped to convey. Roosevelt polices the world by dealing with "less civilized" people on the left using the "big stick" and with "civilized" nations on the right by using diplomacy.

THE IRON-FISTED NEIGHBOR

Roosevelt took a particular interest in Latin America. Embarking on a series of ventures in the Caribbean and South America, he established a pattern of American intervention in the region that would outlive his presidency.

In 1902, the government of Venezuela began to renege on debts to European bankers. Naval forces of Britain, Italy, and Germany blockaded the Venezuelan coast in response. Then German ships began to bombard a Venezuelan port. Amid rumors that Germany planned to establish a permanent base in the region, Roosevelt used the threat of American naval power to pressure the German navy to withdraw.

The incident helped persuade Roosevelt that European intrusions into Latin America could result not only from aggression but also from instability or irresponsibility (such as defaulting on debts) within the Latin American nations themselves. As a result, in 1904 he announced what came to be known as the **Roosevelt Corollary** to the Monroe Doctrine. The United States, he claimed, had the right not only to oppose European intervention in the Western Hemisphere but also to intervene in the domestic affairs of its neighbors if those neighbors proved unable to maintain order and national sovereignty on their own.

The immediate motivation for the Roosevelt Corollary, and the first opportunity for using it, was a crisis in the Dominican Republic. A revolution had toppled its corrupt and bankrupt government in 1903, but the new regime proved no better able than the old to make good on the country's $22 million in debts to European nations. Using the rationale provided by the Roosevelt Corollary, Roosevelt established, in effect, an American receivership, assuming control of Dominican customs and distributing 45 percent of the revenues to the Dominicans and the rest to foreign creditors. This arrangement lasted, in one form or another, for more than three decades.

THE PANAMA CANAL

The most celebrated foreign policy accomplishment of Roosevelt's presidency was the construction of the **Panama Canal**, which linked the Atlantic and the Pacific by creating a channel through Central America. At first, Roosevelt and many others favored a route across Nicaragua, which would permit a sea-level canal requiring no locks. But they soon turned instead to the narrow Isthmus of Panama (then part of Colombia), the site of an earlier failed effort by a French company to construct a channel. Although the Panama route was not at sea level, it was shorter than the one in Nicaragua, and construction was already about 40 percent complete. The French then lowered the price for its holdings, and the United States opted for the Panama route through Colombia.

Roosevelt dispatched John Hay, his secretary of state, to negotiate an agreement with Colombian diplomats that would allow construction to begin without delay. Under heavy American pressure, the Colombian chargé d'affaires, Tomás Herrán, signed an agreement giving the United States perpetual rights to a six-mile-wide "Canal Zone" across Colombia; in return, the United States would pay Colombia $10 million and an annual rent of $250,000. The outraged Colombian senate refused to ratify the treaty. Colombia then sent a new representative to Washington with instructions to demand at least $20 million from the Americans plus a share of the payment to the French.

Roosevelt was furious and began to look for ways to circumvent the Colombian government. Philippe Bunau-Varilla, chief engineer of the French canal project, was a ready ally.

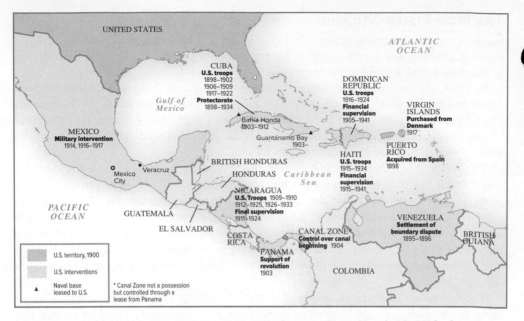

THE UNITED STATES AND LATIN AMERICA, 1895–1941 Except for Puerto Rico, the Virgin Islands, and the Canal Zone, the United States had no formal possessions in Latin America and the Caribbean in the late nineteenth century and the first half of the twentieth. But as this map reveals, the United States exercised considerable influence—both political and economic, augmented at times by military intervention—in these regions throughout this period. Note the particularly intrusive presence of the United States in the affairs of Cuba, Haiti, and the Dominican Republic—as well as the canal-related interventions in Colombia and Panama. • *What were the reasons for American intervention in Latin America?*

In 1903, with the support of the United States, he helped organize and finance a revolution in Panama. Roosevelt landed troops from the U.S.S. *Nashville* there to "maintain order." Their presence prevented Colombian forces from suppressing the rebellion, and three days later Roosevelt recognized Panama as an independent nation. The new Panamanian government quickly agreed to the terms the Colombian senate had rejected. Work on the canal proceeded rapidly, and it opened in 1914.

TAFT AND "DOLLAR DIPLOMACY"

Like his predecessor, William Howard Taft worked to advance the nation's economic interests in Latin America. But he showed little interest in Roosevelt's larger vision of world stability. Instead, Taft's secretary of state, Philander C. Knox, worked aggressively to extend American investments into less-developed regions. Critics called his policies **Dollar Diplomacy**.

The policy was particularly visible in the Caribbean. When a revolution broke out in Nicaragua in 1909, the administration quickly sided with the insurgents and sent American troops into the country to seize the customs houses. As soon as peace was restored, Knox encouraged American bankers to offer substantial loans to the new government, thus increasing Washington's financial leverage over the country. When the new pro-American government faced an insurrection less than two years later, Taft again landed American troops in Nicaragua, this time to protect the existing regime. The troops remained there for more than a decade.

DIPLOMACY AND MORALITY

Woodrow Wilson entered the presidency with relatively little interest or experience in international affairs. Yet he faced international challenges of a scope and gravity unmatched by those of any president before him. In many respects, he continued—and even strengthened—the Roosevelt–Taft approach to foreign policy.

Having already seized control of the finances of the Dominican Republic in 1905, the United States established a military government there in 1916. The military occupation lasted eight years. In Haiti, Wilson landed marines in 1915 to quell a revolution during which a mob had murdered an unpopular president. American military forces remained in the country until 1934, and American officers drafted the new Haitian constitution adopted in 1918. When Wilson began to fear that the Danish West Indies might be about to fall into the hands of Germany, he bought the colony from Denmark and renamed it the Virgin Islands. Concerned about the possibility of European influence in Nicaragua, he signed a treaty with that country's government allowing for intervention to protect American interests.

Closer to the American border, the dictator Porfirio Díaz had long permitted American businessmen to establish an enormous economic presence in Mexico. In 1911, however, Díaz was overthrown by the popular leader Francisco Madero, who promised democratic reform and seemed hostile to American businesses in Mexico. The United States quietly encouraged a reactionary general, Victoriano Huerta, to depose Madero early in 1913. But when the new government under Huerta murdered Madero, Woodrow Wilson announced that he would never recognize Huerta's "government of butchers."

Wilson hoped that by refusing to recognize Huerta he could help topple the regime and bring to power the constitutionalists, now led by Venustiano Carranza. But Huerta, with the support of American business interests, established a full military dictatorship in October 1913; a few months later, one of his army officers briefly arrested several American sailors from the U.S.S. *Dolphin* who had gone ashore in Tampico. The men were immediately released, but the American admiral demanded a twenty-one-gun salute as a public display of penance. Huerta refused. Wilson used the slight as a pretext for seizing the Mexican port of Vera Cruz.

Wilson had envisioned a bloodless action, but in a clash with Mexican troops, the Americans killed 126 of the defenders and suffered 19 casualties. His show of force, however, had helped strengthen the position of the Carranza faction, which captured Mexico City in August 1914 and forced Huerta to flee the country. At last, it seemed, the crisis might be over.

But Wilson reacted angrily when Carranza, whom he had previously supported, refused to accept American guidelines for the creation of a new government, and he briefly considered throwing his support to still another aspirant to leadership: Carranza's erstwhile lieutenant **Pancho Villa**, now staking his own claim to power. When Villa's military position deteriorated, however, Wilson abandoned him and granted preliminary recognition to Carranza. Villa, angry at what he considered an American betrayal, retaliated in early 1916 by shooting sixteen American mining engineers in northern Mexico and seventeen more Americans across the border in Columbus, New Mexico.

Wilson ordered General **John J. Pershing** to lead an American expeditionary force across the Mexican border to capture Villa, who managed to elude them. Carranza's new government acquiesced to but also resented the U.S. military intrusion on Mexican soil, and on June 21, 1916, Carranza's army attacked one of Pershing's units, killing twenty-two Americans. But before a fuller war could erupt, Wilson quietly withdrew American troops from Mexico and, in March 1917, finally granted formal recognition to the Carranza regime. By now, however, Wilson's attention was turning to a far greater international crisis.

THE ROAD TO WAR

By 1914, the European nations had created an unusually precarious international system. It careened into war very quickly on the basis of what seemed to be a minor series of provocations.

THE COLLAPSE OF THE EUROPEAN PEACE

The major powers of Europe were organized by 1914 in two great, competing alliances. The "Triple Entente" linked Britain, France, and Russia. The "Triple Alliance" united Germany, the Austro-Hungarian Empire, and Italy.

The conflict emerged most directly out of a controversy involving nationalist movements within the Austro-Hungarian Empire. On June 28, 1914, Archduke Franz Ferdinand, heir to the throne of the tottering empire, was assassinated while paying a state visit to Sarajevo, the capital of Bosnia, then a province of Austria-Hungary. Slavic nationalists wished to annex Bosnia to neighboring Serbia. The killer of the archduke and his wife Sophie was a Serbian nationalist.

Austria immediately blamed Serbia for the murders and issued impossible ultimatums. Russia, Serbia's Slavic ally and a seeker of greater influence in the Balkans, mobilized its armies along the border with Austria-Hungary. The Germans, faced with that provocation against their ally and concerned about a two-front war against Russia and France, declared war against both. Germany's subsequent invasion of neutral Belgium prompted Britain to declare war on Germany. By August, Austria-Hungary and Germany were fighting Russia, and Germany had charged through Belgium into France.

The coalitions soon changed in name and membership. On one side were the **Central Powers**: Germany and Austria-Hungary, joined in the fall by the Ottoman Empire. On the other side were the **Allies**, made up of Britain, France, and Russia. Hoping to seize territory from the Central Powers, Italy and Japan soon threw in their lot with the Allies.

As these changes suggest, the alliance system did not necessarily *bind* nations to act as they did. Leaders made the decision for war based on their own interests and ambitions, on the assumption that national self-defense required it, and on the erroneous belief that their objectives could be met quickly. What the alliance system did was provide a framework within which the choices for war were made. As tragic as those choices seem in retrospect, no one expected or wanted the ghastly world war that followed.

WILSON'S NEUTRALITY

Wilson called on his fellow citizens in 1914 to remain "impartial in thought as well as deed." But that was impossible. Most Americans sympathized with Britain. Lurid reports of German atrocities in Belgium and France, sometimes (but not always) exaggerated by British propagandists, strengthened American hostility toward Germany.

Economic realities also made it impossible for the United States to deal with the belligerents on equal terms. The British had imposed a naval blockade on Germany to prevent munitions and supplies from reaching the enemy. As a neutral, the United States had the right, in theory, to trade with Germany, but the British blockade made that impossible. A truly neutral response to the blockade would have been to stop trading with Britain as well. But while the United States could survive an interruption of its relatively modest trade with the Central Powers, a potential break in its much more extensive trade with the Allies posed a serious threat to American commerce. So America tacitly accepted the blockade of Germany and continued trading with Britain. By 1915, the United States had gradually transformed itself from a neutral power into the arsenal of the Allies.

The Germans, in the meantime, were resorting to a new and, in American eyes, barbaric tactic: submarine warfare. Unable to challenge British domination on the ocean's surface, the Germans announced early in 1915 that they would sink enemy vessels on sight. Months later, on May 7, a German submarine (or U-boat, from the German *Unterseeboot*) sank the British passenger liner ***Lusitania*** without warning, causing the deaths of 1,198 people, 128 of them Americans. The ship was carrying both passengers and munitions, but most Americans considered the attack an unprovoked act on civilians.

Wilson angrily demanded that Germany promise not to repeat such outrages, and the Germans reluctantly agreed. But early in 1916, in response to an announcement that the Allies were now arming merchant ships to sink submarines, Germany proclaimed that it would fire on such vessels without warning. A few weeks later, it attacked the unarmed French steamer *Sussex,* injuring several American passengers. Again, Wilson demanded that Germany abandon its "unlawful" tactics; again, the German government relented.

Preparedness versus Pacifism

Despite the president's increasing bellicosity in 1916, he was still far from ready to commit the United States to war. One obstacle was American domestic politics.

The question of whether America should make military and economic preparations for war sparked a heated debate between pacifists and interventionists. Wilson at first denounced the idea of an American military buildup as needless and provocative. In the fall of 1915, however, he endorsed an ambitious proposal by American military leaders for a large and rapid increase in the nation's armed forces.

Still, the peace faction wielded considerable political strength, as became clear at the Democratic National Convention in the summer of 1916. The convention became especially enthusiastic when the keynote speaker punctuated his list of the president's diplomatic achievements with the chant, "What did we do? What did we do? . . . We didn't go to war! We didn't go to war!" That speech helped produce one of the most prominent slogans of Wilson's reelection campaign: "He kept us out of war." During the campaign, Wilson did nothing to discourage those who argued that the Republican candidate, the progressive New York governor Charles Evans Hughes, was more likely than he to lead the nation into war. Wilson ultimately won reelection by fewer than 600,000 popular votes and only 23 electoral votes. But he was uncomfortable about a slogan that had aided his victory. "Any little German lieutenant," he said of the U-boat situation, "can put us into the war at any time by some calculated outrage."

Intervention

Wilson was right—but it was the German leadership that provoked him. In January 1917 Germany made a desperate gamble, declaring unrestricted submarine warfare against all maritime traffic in the hopes of defeating the Allies before Wilson could mobilize an army. Meanwhile, the German foreign secretary Arthur Zimmermann sent a telegram to the German ambassador in Mexico instructing him to offer the Mexicans a deal: if they would join a military alliance, Germany would help Mexico take back territory in the present states of Texas, New Mexico, and Arizona. By March, when Wilson released the intercepted and decoded **Zimmermann Telegram**—and after three United States ships were torpedoed by U-boats—war with Germany seemed imminent.

Although German crimes on the seas, the offer to Mexico, and threats to American commerce provided the immediate causes for war, Wilson had broader purposes in mind

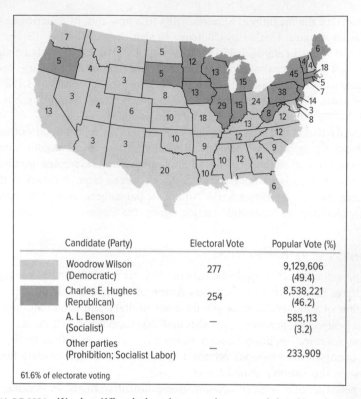

Candidate (Party)	Electoral Vote	Popular Vote (%)
Woodrow Wilson (Democratic)	277	9,129,606 (49.4)
Charles E. Hughes (Republican)	254	8,538,221 (46.2)
A. L. Benson (Socialist)	—	585,113 (3.2)
Other parties (Prohibition; Socialist Labor)	—	233,909

61.6% of electorate voting

THE ELECTION OF 1916 Woodrow Wilson had good reason to be concerned about his reelection prospects in 1916. He had won only about 42 percent of the vote in 1912, and the Republican Party—which had been divided four years earlier—was now reunited around the popular Charles Evans Hughes. In the end, Wilson won a narrow victory over Hughes with just under 50 percent of the vote and a similarly narrow margin in the electoral college. Note the striking regional character of his victory. • *How did Wilson use the war in Europe to bolster his election prospects?*

as well. The president hoped that American intervention, by earning him a seat at the postwar negotiating table, would usher in a new era. In the place of militarism, secret alliances, violence, and autocracy would come democracy, freedom of travel and commerce, open diplomacy, and self-determination.

President Wilson articulated this vision on the rainy evening of April 2, 1917, when he asked Congress for a declaration of war. German U-boat warfare had claimed American lives and treasure. The country's honor could not tolerate such affronts. But aware of divisions in public opinion, Wilson sought to invest the moment with higher meaning. The war would make the world "safe for democracy" and safeguard "the rights of mankind." America would not fight for material gain or territory, the president said, but to guarantee a future of free trade, self-governance, peace, and justice. Opposition to the war would not be tolerated. "If there should be disloyalty," he warned, "it will be dealt with with a firm hand of repression."

Wilson's view carried the session, but dissenters spoke up. Some midwesterners and southerners saw corporate profits, not honor, at stake in the Atlantic. A few pacifists, including the first woman elected to Congress, Jeannette Rankin, a Republican from Montana, argued that no war was worth the costs. Still others argued the United States should stay out of Europe's affairs. When the declaration of war finally passed on April 6, six senators and fifty representatives voted against it.

"OVER THERE"

European armies on both sides of the conflict were decimated and exhausted by the time of Woodrow Wilson's declaration of war. The Allies looked desperately to the United States for help in breaking the stalemate.

MOBILIZING THE MILITARY

By the spring of 1917, Great Britain was suffering such vast losses from German submarines that its ability to receive vital supplies from across the Atlantic was in jeopardy. Within weeks of joining the war, the United States had begun to alter the balance. A fleet of American destroyers aided the British navy in attacking the U-boats and planting antisubmarine mines in the North Sea. The results were dramatic. Losses among Allied ships dropped from nearly 900,000 tons in the month of April 1917 to 350,000 by December 1917 and 112,000 by October 1918.

Many Americans had hoped that providing naval assistance alone would be enough to end the war, but it quickly became clear that a major commitment of American ground forces would be necessary as well. Britain and France had few remaining reserves. After the Bolshevik Revolution in November 1917, a new communist government, led by V. I. Lenin, negotiated a hasty and costly peace between Russia and the Central Powers. That freed German troops to fight on the western front.

The United States did not have a large enough standing army to provide the necessary ground forces in 1917. Even amid recruitment efforts (see "Consider the Source: Race, Gender, and World War I Posters"), enlistments proved inadequate. Only a national draft could provide the needed men. Despite protests, Wilson won passage of the **Selective Service Act** in mid-May. From a prewar total of 121,000 enlisted soldiers, the army grew to more than 4 million, 2 million of whom went to France. Draftees comprised 72 percent of all American soldiers in the war—a far higher percentage than on either side of the Civil War.

The typical American soldier (or "doughboy," a term dating to the mid-nineteenth century but of mysterious origins) in the Great War was a white, single, poorly educated draftee in his early twenties. Women were barred from regular military service, but could sign up for things like nursing, clerical work, and telephone operation. As many as 400,000 African Americans joined the military, the vast majority conscripted. But this was a strict Jim Crow army. Units were segregated, white officers were in charge, and blacks generally performed menial labor. Yet two combat divisions, the Ninety-Second and Ninety-Third, were composed entirely of African American soldiers.

In training camps around the country, selectees learned how to be soldiers. They marched and drilled and practiced maneuvers. In case they weren't sure what they were fighting for, every backpack contained a copy of Wilson's war message. For the huge number of foreign-born soldiers—approaching 20 percent of the wartime army, speaking forty-six different languages—military service acted as a tool of assimilation, to the delight of nativists. Another target of assimilative energies, Native Americans, sent about twelve thousand men into the military. Meanwhile the draftees received moral instruction as well. Progressives in the government, as well as thousands of American parents, worried about the sexual purity of the soldier. One social hygiene poster implored the soldier to "Remember— the folks at home. Go back to them physically fit and morally clean. Don't allow a whore to smirch your record."

CONSIDER THE SOURCE

RACE, GENDER, AND WORLD WAR I POSTERS

Much can be learned about a society's values from how it handles the mobilization of the home front during wartime. Nations typically clarify the terms of citizenship and service—asking some people to fight, some to stay home and support the effort in other ways. As part of the broad national campaign to mobilize public opinion and service during World War I, American officials disseminated the two posters reproduced here. One urged enlistment, the other the purchase of war bonds.

UNDERSTAND, ANALYZE, & EVALUATE

1. How do the posters use images of women or the home to encourage either enlistment or financial support for the war?

2. What do these posters say about contemporary understandings of gender roles? What did the state and society expect from men? What did they expect from women?

3. Like almost all recruiting posters of World War I, these two depict white people—despite the fact that many African Americans and ethnic minorities served as well. What does that say about mainstream attitudes toward race and ethnicity during World War I?

(Source: Library of Congress, Prints and Photographs Division [LC-USZC4-1124])

(Source: Library of Congress, Prints and Photographs Division [LC-USZC4-9884])

The Yanks Are Coming

The United States had sent the first units of the American Expeditionary Forces (AEF) to France in June 1917 under the leadership of General John J. Pershing, but American soldiers weren't heavily implicated in the fighting until the next year. In March 1918, the Germans launched nimble thrusts into the Allied defenses. Under the French commander of Allied forces, Ferdinand Foch, Pershing's troops halted the German offensive at Cantigny and Château-Thierry. Then the American Second Division, including a brigade of marines, lost 9,800 casualties in a savage but successful fight to drive the Germans from Belleau Wood, a place that would live on in Marine Corps lore. In July the Germans attacked again, and at the Second Battle of the Marne, the Allies fought together to repulse them. Over the course of that summer, the influx of American divisions helped the Allies push the German army back roughly to its original position.

By September, with American troops plentiful and the Germans depleted, the Allies prepared to advance toward Germany. Pershing withdrew many of his divisions to the Americans' own sector on the southern edge of the front. From that position, the doughboys took the Saint-Mihiel salient, a bulge into Allied lines that the Germans had held for years. Foch then ordered Pershing's divisions to their place in the war's final Allied push, the Meuse-Argonne offensive. Beginning on September 26, more than a million American doughboys—the great majority of them seeing combat for the first time—advanced against the Germans, while to the northwest the British and French undertook coordinated campaigns. The Germans sagged but held, and something like **trench warfare** set in for a brief time.

Meanwhile Choctaw code talkers relayed messages in their native tongue to thwart German attempts to tap into American telephone lines and decipher battle orders. And black combat units, some fighting under French command, acquitted themselves honorably in the war's late battles, though white military leadership magnified their isolated failures. The Ninety-Second Division in particular suffered charges of poor martial performance as well as unwarranted rumors of rape, and authorities ultimately curtailed the mingling of black doughboys and white Frenchwomen. But the Ninety-Third's 369th Infantry or "Harlem Hell Fighters," fighting with the French, earned 170 Croix de Guerre awards for valor for their part in the war's final offensives.

In October, the push was rolling again, but those weeks of the Meuse-Argonne offensive were terrible for the Americans, with 27,000 men killed. "Those of us who still lived," wrote one doughboy, "who were able to move, in body if not in spirit, wanted to drop to our knees and implore God to stop this horrible slaughter of mankind." Slow transportation, communication glitches, the hasty training of soldiers, logistical bottlenecks, friendly fire accidents, and more generally, the growing pains of a mass American army operating overseas, all combined to generate casualties and low morale among the doughboy rank-and-file and hamper the fighting ability of the AEF. Yet by November the push had driven the Germans back, their civilian population suffering from an effective blockade, their soldiers captured by the hundreds of thousands, their U-boats more or less neutralized by a convoy system, and their rear harassed by airplane bombardment. Facing invasion, the Germans sought an armistice. Early on the morning of November 11, 1918, while men along the front were still dying, representatives of the warring parties signed an armistice in a railway car in the French forest. The four-year "war to end all wars" shuddered to a close.

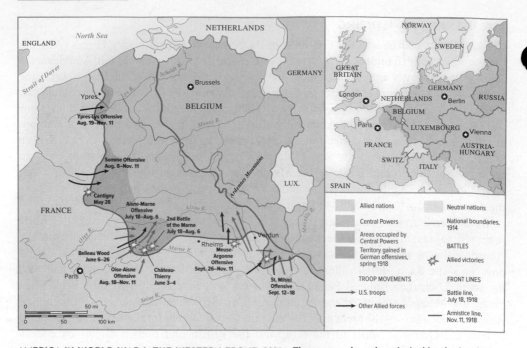

AMERICA IN WORLD WAR I: THE WESTERN FRONT, 1918   These maps show the principal battles in which the United States participated in the last year of World War I. The small map on the upper right helps locate the area of conflict within the larger European landscape. The larger map at left shows the long, snaking red line of the western front in France—stretching from the border between France and southwest Germany all the way to the northeast border between Belgium and France. Along that vast line, the two sides had been engaged in murderous, inconclusive warfare for over three years by the time the Americans arrived. Beginning in the spring and summer of 1918, bolstered by reinforcements from the United States, the Allies began to win a series of important victories that finally enabled them to begin pushing the Germans back. American troops, as this map makes clear, were decisive along the southern part of the front. • *At what point did the Germans begin to consider putting an end to the war?*

THE NEW TECHNOLOGY OF WARFARE

World War I was a proving ground for a range of new military technologies. The trench warfare that characterized the conflict was a result of the enormous destructive power of newly improved machine guns and higher-powered artillery. It was no longer feasible to send troops out into an open field, where new weaponry would slaughter them in an instant. Trenches sheltered troops while allowing limited, and usually inconclusive, fighting. But technology overtook the trenches, too, as mobile weapons—tanks and flamethrowers—proved capable of piercing entrenched positions. Most terrible of all, perhaps, new chemical weapons—poisonous mustard gas, which required troops to carry gas masks at all times—made it possible to attack entrenched soldiers without direct combat.

The new forms of technological warfare required elaborate maintenance. Faster machine guns needed more ammunition. Motorized vehicles required fuel, spare parts, and mechanics capable of servicing them. The logistical difficulties of supply became a major factor in planning tactics and strategy. Late in the war, when the Allied armies were advancing toward Germany, they frequently had to stop for days at a time to wait for their equipment to catch up with them.

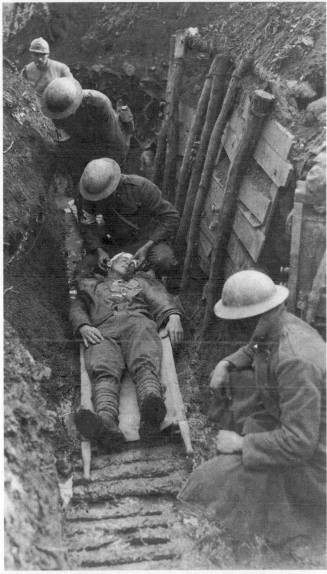

(Source: National Archives and Records Administration)

LIFE IN THE TRENCHES For most British, French, German, and, to a lesser extent, American troops in France, the most debilitating part of World War I was the misery of life in the trenches. Some young men lived in these cold, wet, muddy dugouts for months, even years, surrounded by filth, sharing their space with vermin, eating mostly rotten food. Occasional attacks to try to dislodge the enemy from its trenches usually ended in failure and became the scenes of terrible slaughter.

World War I was the first conflict in which airplanes played a significant role. The planes themselves were relatively simple and not very maneuverable, but antiaircraft technology was not yet highly developed either, so their effectiveness was significant. Planes served various functions: bombing enemy lines, engaging other planes in "dogfights," and performing reconaissance.

The most modern part of the military during World War I was the navy. Battleships emerged that made use of new technologies such as turbine propulsion, hydraulic gun controls, electric light and power, wireless telegraphy, and advanced navigational aids. Submarines, which had made a brief appearance in the American Civil War, now became significant weapons (as the German U-boat campaign in 1915 and 1916 made clear). The new submarines were driven by diesel engines that were more compact than steam engines and used fuel that was less explosive than that of gasoline engines.

The new technologies were responsible for the war's truly stunning statistics of death. Russia lost 1.8 million soldiers; Germany, 2 million; France, 1.4 million; the British Empire, 1 million; Austria-Hungary, 1.5 million; Italy, 460,000. Something like 5 million civilians died under the stress of war—by violence or slower means—though the exact number is hard to know. The United States lost 116,000 soldiers, about half of those in combat, the others to disease. Some perished in the 1918 influenza pandemic that ultimately claimed an estimated 50 to 100 million lives worldwide.

Although only in the war briefly, the Americans had played a significant role in the victory. Their casualty rates in the periods of intense fighting approximated or exceeded those of their allies. The prospect of more doughboys arriving in the future surely affected the German leadership's capitulation in 1918. The British, Russian, and French contributions, of course, dwarfed the American one in sheer numbers. But Wilson's army had acquitted itself well enough to earn him a seat at the negotiating table—one of his ambitions all along.

ORGANIZING THE ECONOMY FOR WAR

By the time the war ended, the federal government had appropriated $32 billion for war expenses—a staggering sum at the time. The entire federal budget had seldom exceeded $1 billion before 1915, and as recently as 1910 the nation's entire gross national product had been only $35 billion. To raise the money, the government relied on two devices. First, it launched a major drive to solicit loans from the American people by selling "Liberty Bonds" to the public. By 1920, the sale of bonds, accompanied by elaborate patriotic appeals, had produced $23 billion. At the same time, new taxes were bringing in an additional sum of nearly $10 billion—some of it coming from levies on the "excess profits" of corporations but much of it coming from new, steeply graduated income and inheritance taxes that ultimately rose as high as 70 percent in some brackets.

An even greater challenge was to organize the economy to meet war needs. In 1916, Wilson established the Council of National Defense, composed of members of his cabinet, and the Civilian Advisory Commission, which set up local defense councils in every state and locality. But this early administrative structure soon proved completely unworkable, and members of the council urged a more centralized approach. The administrative structure that slowly emerged was dominated by a series of "war boards," one to oversee the railroads, one to supervise fuel supplies (largely coal), another to handle food (a board that elevated to prominence the young engineer and business executive Herbert Hoover). The boards generally succeeded in meeting essential war needs without paralyzing the domestic economy.

The **War Industries Board** was created in July 1917 to coordinate government purchases of military supplies. Casually organized at first, it stumbled badly until March 1918, when Wilson restructured it and placed it under the control of Wall Street financier Bernard Baruch. He decided which factories would convert to the production of which war materials and set prices for the goods they produced. When materials were scarce, Baruch decided to whom they should go. When corporations were competing for government contracts, he chose among them.

(©Margaret Bourke-White/The LIFE Picture Collection/Getty Images)

WOMEN INDUSTRIAL WORKERS In World War II, such women were often called "Rosie the Riveter." Their presence in these previously all male work environments was no less startling to Americans during World War I These women are shown working with acetylene torches to bevel armor plate for tanks. The photographer was Margaret Bourke-White, who herself broke gender boundaries as the first female photojournalist for *Life* magazine and the first female war correspondent.

Baruch viewed himself, openly and explicitly, as a partner of business; and within the WIB, businessmen themselves—the so-called dollar-a-year men, who took paid leave from their corporate jobs and worked for the government for a token salary—supervised the affairs of the private economy.

The National War Labor Board, established in April 1918, served as the final mediator of labor disputes. It pressured industry to grant important concessions to workers: an eight-hour day, the maintenance of minimal living standards, equal pay for women doing equal work, recognition of the right of unions to organize and bargain collectively. In return, it insisted that workers forgo strikes and that employers not engage in lockouts.

The Search for Social Unity

Government leaders were painfully aware that public sentiment about the war was sharply divided. The most conspicuous official effort to support the war was a vast propaganda campaign orchestrated by the Committee on Public Information (CPI), under the direction of the progressive journalist George Creel. The CPI supervised the distribution of over 75 million pieces of printed material and controlled much of the information available for newspapers and magazines. Creel encouraged journalists to exercise "self-censorship" when reporting war news, and most complied by covering the war largely as the government wished. By 1918, government-distributed posters and films were offering lurid portrayals of the savagery of the Germans. In this climate, songwriters and other artists produced popular works that heavily favored the war. (See "Patterns of Popular Culture: George M. Cohan, 'Over There,' 1917.")

George M. Cohan, "Over There," 1917

Music was one of the richest forms of American popular culture in the early twentieth century, much of it emanating from New York City companies in a neighborhood known as Tin Pan Alley. Lyricists and composers, eager to peddle their sheet music widely, had long captured popular attitudes toward the issues of their day. In 1915, with men dying in the Great War at a staggering rate, songwriters churned out such antimilitarist numbers as "I Didn't Raise My Boy to Be a Soldier" and "Don't Take My Darling Boy Away!"

In April 1917, however, President Wilson's demand for unanimity changed Tin Pan Alley's tune. Songs now demonized Kaiser Wilhelm II, the emperor of Germany, glorified the American doughboy and sentimentalized the home-front family. Other tunes became anthems of American confidence and strength, none more so than George M. Cohan's "Over There." Even before that hit—which became the best-known song of the war—Cohan was a leading figure in the American entertainment industry, a prolific creator and performer of Broadway productions, and the composer of hundreds of original songs, including classics such as "Yankee Doodle Boy."

Written just after Wilson's war address of April 2, "Over There" offered a jaunty soundtrack for American intervention. It was sung on the home front and in basic training; doughboys in France found it in songbooks issued by various civilian agencies. "Over There" represented a prominent strain in public culture of 1917—deeply patriotic, optimistic, and sentimental—even as many Americans worried quietly about what this new war would mean for them and their families.

Johnnie, get your gun,
Get your gun, get your gun,
Take it on the run,
On the run, on the run.
Hear them calling, you and me,
Every son of liberty.
Hurry right away,
No delay, no delay,
Make your daddy glad
To have had such a lad.
Tell your sweetheart not to pine,
To be proud her boy's in line.

Chorus
Over there, over there
Send the word, send the word over there
That the Yanks are coming,
The Yanks are coming,
The drums rum-tumming
Ev'rywhere.
So prepare, say a pray'r,
Send the word, send the word to beware.
We'll be over, we're coming over,
And we won't come back till it's over
Over there.
Johnnie get your gun,
Get your gun, get your gun,
Johnnie show the Hun
Who's a son of a gun.
Hoist the flag and let her fly,
Yankee Doodle do or die.
Pack your little kit,

Show your grit, do your bit.
Yankee Doodle fill the ranks,
From the towns and the tanks.
Make your mother proud of you,
And the old Red, White and Blue. •

(repeat chorus twice)

Source: Cohan, George M., "Over There" (public domain).

1. How did this song seek to motivate young men to join the army? What image of war did this song convey?
2. What relationship between the United States and Europe did the chorus imply?

The government also suppressed dissent. CPI-financed advertisements in magazines implored citizens to report to the authorities any evidence among their neighbors of disloyalty, pessimism, or yearning for peace. The Espionage Act of 1917 gave the government new tools with which to combat spying, sabotage, or obstruction of the war effort (crimes that were often broadly defined). The Sabotage Act and the Sedition Act, both passed in 1918, expanded the meaning of the Espionage Act to make illegal *any* public expression of opposition to the war; in practice, they allowed officials to prosecute anyone who criticized the president or the government.

The most frequent targets of the new legislation were anticapitalist groups such as the Socialist Party and the Industrial Workers of the World (IWW). Many Americans had favored the repression of socialists and radicals even before the war; the wartime policies now made it possible to move against them with full legal sanction. Eugene V. Debs, the leader of the Socialist Party and an opponent of the war, was sentenced to ten years in prison in 1918. (A pardon by President Warren G. Harding freed him in 1921.) Big Bill Haywood and members of the IWW were energetically prosecuted. Only by fleeing to the Soviet Union did Haywood avoid imprisonment. In all, more than 1,500 people were arrested in 1918 for the crime of criticizing the government or the war.

State and local governments, corporations, universities, and private citizens contributed as well to the climate of repression. A cluster of citizens' groups emerged to mobilize "respectable" members of communities to root out disloyalty. The greatest target of abuse was the German American community. Most German Americans supported the American war effort once it began, but public opinion remained hostile. A campaign to purge society of all things German quickly gathered speed, at times assuming ludicrous forms. Performances of German music were frequently banned. German foods such as sauerkraut and bratwurst were renamed "liberty cabbage" and "liberty sausage." German books were removed from library shelves. Courses in the German language were dropped from school curricula. Germans were routinely fired from jobs in war industries, lest they "sabotage" important tasks.

THE SEARCH FOR A NEW WORLD ORDER

Woodrow Wilson had led the nation into war promising a just and stable peace at its conclusion. Even before the armistice, he was preparing to lead the fight for what he considered a democratic postwar settlement.

THE FOURTEEN POINTS

On January 8, 1918, Wilson appeared before Congress to present the principles for which he believed the nation was fighting. He grouped the war aims under fourteen headings, widely known as the **Fourteen Points**. They fell into three broad categories. First, Wilson's proposals contained a series of eight specific recommendations for adjusting postwar boundaries and establishing new nations to replace the defunct Austro-Hungarian and Ottoman Empires. Second, five general principles would govern international conduct in the future: freedom of the seas, open covenants instead of secret treaties, reductions in armaments, free trade, and impartial mediation of colonial claims. Finally, there was a proposal for a **League of Nations** that would help implement these new principles and territorial adjustments and resolve future controversies.

Wilson's international vision ultimately enchanted not only much of his own generation (in both America and Europe) but also members of generations to come. It reflected his belief that the world was as capable of just and efficient government as were individual nations—that once the international community accepted certain basic principles of conduct and constructed modern institutions to implement them, the world could live in peace.

Despite Wilson's confidence, leaders of the Allied powers were preparing to resist him even before the armistice was signed. Britain and France, in particular, were in no mood for a generous peace. At the same time, Wilson was encountering problems at home. In 1918, with the war almost over, Wilson tied support of his peace plans to the election of Democrats to Congress in November. Days later, the Republicans captured majorities in both houses. Domestic economic troubles, more than international issues, had been the most important factor in the voting; but the results damaged his ability to claim broad popular support for his peace plans. Wilson further antagonized the Republicans when he refused to appoint any important member of their party to the negotiating team attending the peace conference in Paris.

THE PARIS PEACE CONFERENCE

When Wilson entered Paris on December 13, 1918, he was greeted, some claimed, by the largest crowd in the history of France. The peace conference itself, however, proved less satisfying.

The principal figures in the negotiations were the leaders of the victorious Allied nations: President Wilson; David Lloyd George, prime minister of Great Britain; Georges Clemenceau, prime minister of France; and Vittorio Orlando, prime minister of Italy.

From the beginning, Wilson's idealism competed with his counterparts' national self-interest, thirst for revenge, and fears of the unstable situation in eastern Europe and the threat of communism. Russia, whose new Bolshevik government was still fighting anti-Bolshevik counterrevolutionaries, was unrepresented in Paris. But the radical threat it seemed to pose to Western governments was never far from the minds of the delegates.

In this tense and often vindictive atmosphere, Wilson was unable to win approval of many of his broad principles or to prevent the other allies from imposing punitive reparations on Germany. Wilson did manage to win some important victories in Paris in setting boundaries and dealing with former colonies. But his most visible triumph, and the one most important to him, was the creation of a permanent international organization to oversee world affairs and prevent future wars. On January 25, 1919, the Allies voted to accept the "covenant" of the League of Nations.

THE RATIFICATION BATTLE

Wilson presented the Treaty of Versailles, so named for the palace outside Paris where the agreement was signed, to the Senate on July 10, 1919. But members of that chamber had many objections. Some—the so-called irreconcilables—believed that America should remain free of binding foreign entanglements. But many other opponents were principally concerned with constructing a winning issue for the Republicans in 1920. Most notable of these was Senator **Henry Cabot Lodge** of Massachusetts, the powerful chair of the Foreign Relations Committee, who loathed the president and used every possible tactic to obstruct the treaty.

Public sentiment clearly favored ratification, so at first Lodge could do little more than play for time. Gradually, however, his opposition to the treaty crystallized into a series of "reservations"—amendments to the League covenant further limiting American obligations to the organization. Wilson might still have won approval at this point if he had agreed to some relatively minor changes in the language of the treaty. But the president refused to yield.

When he realized the Senate would not budge, Wilson embarked on a grueling, cross-country speaking tour to arouse public support for the treaty. For more than three weeks, he traveled over 8,000 miles by train, speaking as often as four times a day, resting hardly at all. Finally, he reached the end of his strength. After speaking at Pueblo, Colorado, on September 25, 1919, he collapsed with severe headaches.

Canceling the rest of his itinerary, he rushed back to Washington, where, a few days later, he suffered a major stroke. For two weeks, Wilson was close to death; for six weeks more, he was so seriously ill that he was virtually unable to work. His wife and his doctor formed an almost impenetrable barrier around him, shielding the president from any official pressures that might impede his recovery.

Wilson ultimately recovered enough to resume a limited official schedule, but he was essentially an invalid for the remaining eighteen months of his presidency. His condition only intensified his tendency to view public issues in moral terms and resist any attempts at compromise. When the Foreign Relations Committee finally sent the treaty to the Senate, recommending nearly fifty amendments and reservations, Wilson refused to consider any of them. The effort to win ratification failed.

In the aftermath of this defeat, Wilson became convinced that the 1920 national election would serve as a "solemn referendum" on the League of Nations. But the efforts by Lodge and others had defeated American membership in the League for good. What was more, public interest in the peace process had begun to fade as a series of other crises claimed attention.

A SOCIETY IN TURMOIL

Even during the Paris Peace Conference, many Americans were concerned less about international matters than about turbulent events at home. Some of this unease was a legacy of the almost hysterical social atmosphere of the war years, some of it was a response to issues that surfaced after the armistice.

THE UNSTABLE ECONOMY

The war ended sooner than almost anyone had anticipated. Without warning, without planning, the nation lurched into the difficult task of economic reconversion. At first, the boom continued, but accompanied by raging inflation. Through most of 1919 and 1920, prices rose at an average of more than 15 percent a year. Finally, late in 1920, the economic bubble burst as inflation began killing the market for consumer goods. Between 1920 and 1921, the gross national product declined nearly 10 percent; 100,000 businesses went bankrupt; and nearly 5 million Americans lost their jobs.

Well before this severe recession began, labor unrest increased dramatically. The raging inflation of 1919 wiped out the modest wage gains workers had achieved during the war; many laborers were worried about job security as veterans returned to the workforce; arduous working conditions continued to be a source of discontent. Employers aggravated the resentment by using the end of the war to rescind benefits they had been forced to concede to workers in 1917 and 1918—most notably, recognition of unions. The year 1919, therefore, saw an unprecedented strike wave. In January, a walkout by shipyard workers in Seattle, Washington, evolved into a general strike that brought the entire city to a virtual standstill. In September, the Boston police force struck to demand recognition of its union. With its police off the job, Boston erupted in violence and looting. Governor Calvin Coolidge called in the National Guard to restore order and attracted national acclaim by declaring, "There is no right to strike against the public safety."

Coolidge's statement tapped into a broad middle-class hostility to unions and strikes. That hostility played a part in defeating the greatest strike of 1919: a steel strike that began in September, when 350,000 steelworkers in several Midwestern cities demanded an eight-hour day and union recognition. The long and bitter steel strike climaxed in a riot in Gary, Indiana, in which eighteen strikers were killed. Steel executives managed to keep most plants running with nonunion labor, and public opinion was so hostile to the strikers that the American Federation of Labor, at first supportive of the strike, timidly repudiated it. By January, the strike—like most of the others in 1919—had collapsed.

THE DEMANDS OF AFRICAN AMERICANS

Four hundred thousand black World War I veterans came home in 1919 and marched down the main streets of cities. And then in New York and elsewhere they marched again through the streets of black neighborhoods such as Harlem, led by jazz bands and cheered by thousands of African Americans. They hoped the glory of black heroism in the war would make it impossible for white society to continue its mistreatment of African Americans.

As it turned out, the fact that black soldiers had fought in the war had almost no impact on white attitudes. Unfounded stories of black combat cowardice circulated in the popular media, reinforcing what were already entrenched prejudices. But the war profoundly affected black attitudes, accentuated African American bitterness, and increased the determination to fight for civil rights. During the war, nearly half a million blacks had migrated from the rural South to industrial cities, often enticed by northern "labor agents," who offered free transportation, in search of the factory jobs the war was generating. This was the beginning of what became known as the **Great Migration**. Large black communities arose in northern cities, part of the broader twentieth-century transformation of the black population from a generally southern rural one to a northern urban one. African American veterans in these communities helped organize the interwar civil rights movement and set precedents for activism that came later.

By 1919, the racial climate had become tense. In the South, lynchings suddenly increased. More than seventy blacks, some of them war veterans, died at the hands of white mobs in 1919 alone. In the North, black factory workers faced widespread layoffs as returning white veterans displaced them from their jobs. And as whites became convinced that black workers with lower wage demands were hurting them economically, animosity grew.

Wartime riots in East St. Louis and elsewhere were a prelude to a summer of much worse racial violence in 1919. In Chicago, a black teenager swimming in Lake Michigan on a hot July day happened to drift toward a white beach. Whites onshore allegedly stoned

AFRICAN AMERICAN MIGRATION, 1910–1950   Two great waves of migration produced a dramatic redistribution of the African American population in the first half of the twentieth century—one around the time of World War I, the other during and after World War II. The map on the left shows the almost exclusive concentration of African Americans in the South as late as 1910. The map on the right shows both the tremendous increase of black populations in northern states by 1950, and the relative decline of black populations in parts of the South. Note in particular the changes in Mississippi and South Carolina. • *Why did the wars produce such significant migration out of the South?*

him unconscious; he sank and drowned. Angry African Americans gathered in crowds and marched into white neighborhoods to retaliate. Whites formed even larger crowds and roamed into mostly black neighborhoods. For more than a week, Chicago was virtually at war. In the end, 38 people had died—15 whites and 23 blacks—and 537 were injured. Over 1,000 people were left homeless. The Chicago riot was the worst but not the only racial violence during the so-called red summer of 1919. In all, 120 people died in such racial outbreaks in little more than three months.

Racially motivated urban riots were not new. But the 1919 riots were different in one respect: they did not just involve white people attacking blacks, but also blacks fighting back. The NAACP signaled this change by urging blacks not just to demand government protection but also to defend themselves. The poet Claude McKay, one of the major figures of what would soon be known as the Harlem Renaissance, wrote a poem after the Chicago riot called "If We Must Die":

Like men we'll face the murderous cowardly pack.
Pressed to the wall, dying, but fighting back.

At the same time, a black Jamaican, **Marcus Garvey**, began to attract a wide following in the United States with an ideology of black nationalism. Garvey encouraged African Americans to reject assimilation into white society and develop pride in their own race and culture. His Universal Negro Improvement Association (UNIA) launched a chain of black-owned grocery stores and pressed for the creation of other black businesses. Eventually, Garvey began urging his supporters to leave America and return to Africa, where they could create a new society of their own. In the early 1920s, the Garvey movement experienced explosive growth, but it began to decline after Garvey was indicted in 1923 on charges of business fraud. He was deported to Jamaica two years later. But the allure of black nationalism survived in black culture long after Garvey was gone.

THE RED SCARE

Many Americans regarded the industrial warfare and racial violence of 1919 as frightening omens of instability and radicalism. After the Russian Revolution of November 1917, communism was no longer simply a theory, but the basis of an important regime. Concerns about the communist threat grew in 1919 when the Bolshevik government announced the formation of the Communist International (or Comintern), whose purpose was to export revolution around the world.

In America, meanwhile, there was, in addition to the great number of imagined radicals, a modest number of real ones. These small groups of radicals were presumably responsible for a series of bombings in the spring of 1919. In April, the post office intercepted several dozen parcels addressed to leading businessmen and politicians that were triggered to explode when opened. Two months later, eight bombs exploded in eight cities within minutes of one another, suggesting a nationwide conspiracy.

The combination of strikes and the Comintern announcement produced what became known as the **Red Scare**. Nearly thirty states enacted new peacetime sedition laws imposing harsh penalties on promoters of revolution. Spontaneous acts of violence against supposed radicals occurred in some communities, and universities and other institutions tried to expel radicals from their midst. But the greatest agent of the Red Scare was the federal government. In January 1920, Attorney General A. Mitchell Palmer and his ambitious young assistant, J. Edgar Hoover, orchestrated the biggest of the **Palmer Raids**. This particular police action against alleged radical centers resulted in the arrest of more than 6,000 people, and authorities made many of the searches and arrests in 1919 and 1920 without proper warrants. Most of those arrested were ultimately released, but about 500 who were not American citizens were deported. Later in 1920, a bomb exploded on Wall Street, killing thirty-eight people. No one was ever convicted of this bombing.

The ferocity of the Red Scare gradually abated, but its effects lingered well into the 1920s. In May 1920, two Italian immigrants, **Nicola Sacco and Bartolomeo Vanzetti**, were charged with the murder of a paymaster in South Braintree, Massachusetts. The case against them was weak and suffused with nativist prejudices and fears, but because both men were confessed anarchists, they faced widespread public presumption of guilt. They were convicted and eventually sentenced to death. Over the next several years, public support for Sacco and Vanzetti grew to formidable proportions. But on August 23, 1927, amid protests in the United States and around the world, Sacco and Vanzetti, still proclaiming their innocence, died in the electric chair.

REFUTING THE RED SCARE

One result of postwar turmoil was the emergence of a vigorous defense of civil liberties that helped give new force to the Bill of Rights. The heavy-handed and often illegal actions of the federal government after the war created a powerful backlash. It destroyed the career of A. Mitchell Palmer. It almost nipped in the bud the ascent of J. Edgar Hoover. It damaged the Democratic Party. And it led to an organization committed to protecting civil liberties: the National Civil Liberties Bureau, launched in 1917, which in 1920 was renamed the American Civil Liberties Union (ACLU) and which remains a prominent institution today. At the same time, members of the Supreme Court—most notably Justices Oliver Wendell Holmes and Louis Brandeis—gradually moved to defend unpopular speech. The clash of "fighting faiths," Holmes wrote in a dissent in 1920, was best resolved "by free trade in ideas—that the best test of truth is . . . the competition of the market." This and other dissents eventually became law as other justices committed themselves to a robust defense of speech, however unpopular.

The Retreat from Idealism

On August 26, 1920, the Nineteenth Amendment, guaranteeing women the right to vote, became part of the Constitution. To the suffrage movement, this was the culmination of nearly a century of struggle. To many progressives, it seemed to promise new support for reform. Yet the Nineteenth Amendment marked not the beginning of a new era of progressive reform but the end of an earlier one.

Economic problems, labor unrest, racial tensions, and the intensity of the antiradicalism they helped create—all combined in the years immediately following the war to produce a general sense of disillusionment. That became particularly apparent in the election of 1920. Woodrow Wilson hoped the campaign would be a referendum on the League of Nations, and the Democratic candidates, Governor James M. Cox of Ohio and Assistant Secretary of the Navy Franklin D. Roosevelt, dutifully tried to keep Wilson's ideals alive. The Republican presidential nominee, Warren Gamaliel Harding, an obscure Ohio senator, offered a different vision. He embraced no soaring ideals, only a vague promise of a return, as he later phrased it, to "normalcy." Harding won in a landslide, with 61 percent of the popular vote and victories in every state outside the South. The party made major gains in Congress as well. To many Americans it seemed that, for better or worse, a new age had begun.

CONCLUSION

Presidents Roosevelt, Taft, and Wilson contributed to a continuation, and indeed an expansion, of America's active role in international affairs, in part as an effort to abet the growth of American capitalism and in part as an attempt to impose American ideas of morality and democracy on other parts of the world. Similar mixtures of ideals and self-interest soon guided the United States into a great world war.

For a time after the outbreak of war in Europe in 1914, most Americans—President Wilson among them—wanted nothing so much as to stay out of the conflict. But as the war dragged on and the tactics of Britain and Germany began to impinge on American trade and access to the seas, the United States found itself drawn into the conflict. In April 1917, Congress agreed to the president's request that the United States enter the war as an ally of Britain, France, and Russia.

Within a few months of the arrival of American troops in Europe, Germany agreed to an armistice and the war ended. American casualties, although not inconsiderable, were negligible compared to the millions suffered by the European combatants.

Wilson's bold and idealistic dream of a peace based on international cooperation suffered a painful death. The Treaty of Versailles, which he helped draft, contained a provision for a League of Nations, which Wilson believed could transform the international order. But the League quickly became controversial in the United States, and despite strenuous efforts by the president—which hastened his own physical collapse—the treaty was defeated in the Senate. In the aftermath of that traumatic battle, the American people turned away from Wilson and his ideals and faced a very different era.

The social experience of the war in the United States was, on the whole, dismaying to reformers. Although the war enhanced some reform efforts—most notably prohibition and woman suffrage—it also introduced an atmosphere of intolerance and repression into American life. The aftermath of the war was even more disheartening to progressives, because of both a brief but highly destabilizing recession and a wave of repression directed against labor, radicals, African Americans, and immigrants.

KEY TERMS/PEOPLE/PLACES/EVENTS

Allies 522
Central Powers 522
Dollar Diplomacy 520
Fourteen Points 534
Great Migration 536
Henry Cabot Lodge 535
John J. Pershing 521

League of Nations 534
Lusitania 523
Marcus Garvey 537
Nicola Sacco and
   Bartolomeo Vanzetti 538
Palmer Raids 538
Panama Canal 519

Pancho Villa 521
Red Scare 538
Roosevelt Corollary 519
Selective Service Act 525
trench warfare 527
War Industries Board 530
Zimmermann Telegram 524

RECALL AND REFLECT

1. Who opposed U.S. involvement in World War I and why?
2. How did the Wilson administration mobilize the nation for war?
3. What effect did the war have on race relations in the United States?
4. What were some of the ways that U.S. participation in the Great War changed American society?
5. Why did the battle over ratification of the Treaty of Versailles come to an impasse? Why did the Senate ultimately reject the treaty? What was the significance of that rejection?

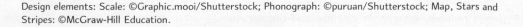
Design elements: Scale: ©Graphic.mooi/Shutterstock; Phonograph: ©puruan/Shutterstock; Map, Stars and Stripes: ©McGraw-Hill Education.

22 | THE NEW ERA

THE NEW ECONOMY
THE NEW CULTURE
A CONFLICT OF CULTURES
REPUBLICAN GOVERNMENT

LOOKING AHEAD

1. How did the technological innovations of the early twentieth century affect industry and American social life of the 1920s?
2. What were some of the cultural conflicts of the 1920s, and what caused them?
3. Is the term the *New Era* a fitting description of the 1920s?

IN POPULAR CULTURE, THE 1920s are often remembered as an era of affluence, conservatism, and cultural frivolity. In reality, the decade was a time of significant, even dramatic, social, economic, and political change. The American economy not only enjoyed spectacular growth but also developed new forms of organization. Many Americans reshaped themselves to reflect the increasingly urban, industrial, consumer-oriented society of the United States. And American government experimented with new approaches to public policy. That was why contemporaries liked to refer to the 1920s as the "New Era"—an age in which America was becoming a modern nation.

At the same time, however, the decade saw the rise of a series of spirited, and at times effective, rebellions against the transformations in American life. The intense cultural conflicts that characterized the 1920s showed that much of American society remained unreconciled to the modernizing currents of the New Era.

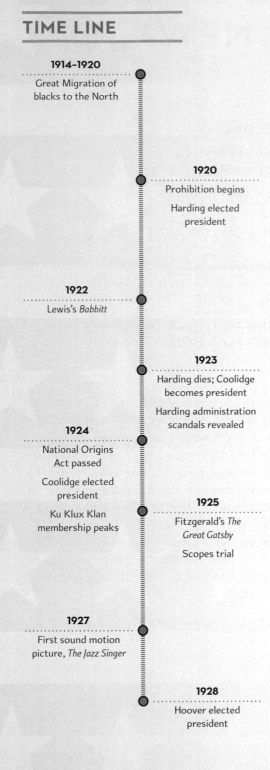

1920

Prohibition begins

Harding elected
president

1922

Lewis's *Babbitt*

1923

Harding dies; Coolidge
becomes president

Harding administration
scandals revealed

1924

National Origins
Act passed

Coolidge elected
president

Ku Klux Klan
membership peaks

1925

Fitzgerald's *The
Great Gatsby*

Scopes trial

1927

First sound motion
picture, *The Jazz Singer*

1928

Hoover elected
president

THE NEW ECONOMY

After the recession of 1921–1922, the United States began a period of almost uninterrupted prosperity and economic expansion. Less visible at the time, but equally significant, was the survival and even growth of inequalities and imbalances.

TECHNOLOGY, ORGANIZATION, AND ECONOMIC GROWTH

No one could deny the remarkable feats of the American economy in the 1920s. The nation's manufacturing output rose by more than 60 percent. Per capita income grew by a third. Inflation was negligible. A mild recession in 1923 briefly interrupted the pattern of growth, but when it subsided early in 1924 the economy expanded with even greater vigor.

The economic boom was a result of many things, but one of the most important was technology. As a result of the development of the assembly line and other innovations, automobiles now became one of the most important industries in the nation, stimulating growth in such related industries as steel, rubber, and glass, tool companies, oil corporations, and road construction. The increased mobility that the automobile made possible increased the demand for suburban housing, fueling a boom in the construction industry.

Radio contributed as well to the economic growth. Early radio had been able to broadcast little besides pulses, which meant that radio communication could occur only through the Morse code. But with the discovery of the theory of modulation, pioneered by the Canadian scientist Reginald Fessenden, it became possible to transmit speech and music. Many people built their own radio sets at home for very little money, benefiting from the discovery that inexpensive crystals could receive signals over long distances. These "shortwave" radios, which allowed individual owners to establish contact with one another, marked the beginning of what later became known as ham radio. Once commercial broadcasting began, families flocked to buy more conventional radio sets powered by reliable vacuum tubes and capable of receiving high-quality signals over short and medium distances. By 1925, there were 2 million sets in American homes, and by the end of the 1920s, almost every family had one.

Commercial aviation developed slowly in the 1920s, beginning with the use of planes to deliver mail. On the whole, airplanes remained curiosities and sources of entertainment. But technological advances—the development of the radial engine and the creation of pressurized cabins—laid the groundwork for the great increase in commercial travel in the 1930s and beyond. Electronics, home appliances, plastics and synthetic fibers (such as nylon), aluminum, magnesium, oil, electric power, and other industries fueled by technological advances— all grew dramatically. Telephones continued to proliferate. By the late 1930s, there were approximately 25 million telephones in the United States, roughly one for every six people.

The seeds of future technological breakthroughs were also visible. In both England and America, scientists and engineers were working to transform primitive calculating machines into devices capable of performing more complicated tasks. By the early 1930s, researchers at MIT, led by Vannevar Bush, had created an instrument capable of performing a variety of complicated tasks—the first analog computer. A few years later, Howard Aiken, with financial assistance from Harvard and MIT, built a much more complex computer with memory, capable of multiplying eleven-digit numbers in three seconds.

Genetic research had begun in Austria in the mid-nineteenth century through the work of Gregor Mendel, a Catholic monk who performed experiments on the hybridization of vegetables in his monastery garden. His findings attracted little attention during his lifetime, but in the early twentieth century several investigators used them to help shape modern genetic research. Among the American pioneers was Thomas Hunt Morgan of Columbia University and, later, Cal Tech, whose experiments with fruit flies revealed how several genes could be transmitted together. He also revealed the way in which genes were arranged along the chromosome. His work helped open the path to understanding how genes could recombine—a critical discovery that led to more advanced experiments in hybridization and genetics.

Large sectors of American business accelerated their drive toward national organization and consolidation. Certain industries—notably those dependent on large-scale mass production, such as steel and automobiles—moved toward concentrating production in a few large firms. Other industries, less dependent on technology and less susceptible to great economies of scale, proved more resistant to consolidation.

The strenuous efforts by industrialists throughout the economy to find ways to curb competition reflected a strong fear of overcapacity. Even in the booming 1920s, industrialists remembered how rapid expansion and overproduction had helped produce recessions in 1893, 1907, and 1920. The great unrealized dream of the New Era was to find a way to stabilize the economy so that such collapses would never occur again.

Workers in an Age of Capital

Despite the remarkable economic growth, more than two-thirds of the American people in 1929 lived at no better than what one major study described as the "minimum comfort level." Half of those were at or below the level of "subsistence and poverty."

American labor experienced both the successes and the failures of the 1920s. On the one hand, most workers saw their standard of living rise during the decade. Some employers adopted paternalistic techniques that came to be known as **welfare capitalism**. Henry Ford, for example, shortened the workweek, raised wages, and instituted paid vacations. By 1926,

(©ullstein bild/Getty Images)

FORD ASSEMBLY LINE This image from the 1920s shows workers arrayed along the assembly, each of them responsible for a particular piece of the process. These were the laborers whom management tried to appease by the cultivation of welfare capitalism.

nearly 3 million industrial workers were eligible for at least modest pensions upon retirement. When labor grievances surfaced despite these efforts, workers could voice them through the so-called company unions that emerged in many industries—workers' councils and shop committees, organized by the corporations themselves. But welfare capitalism, in the end, gave workers no real control over their own fates. Company unions were feeble vehicles. And welfare capitalism survived only as long as industry prospered. After 1929, with the economy in crisis, the entire system collapsed.

Welfare capitalism affected only a relatively small number of firms in any case. Most laborers worked for employers who were interested primarily in keeping their labor costs low. Workers as a whole, therefore, received wage increases that were proportionately far below the growth of the economy. At the end of the decade, the average annual income of a worker remained below $1,500, when $1,800 was considered necessary to maintain a minimally decent standard of living. Only by relying on the combined earnings of several family members could many working-class families make ends meet.

The New Era was a bleak time for labor organization, in part because many unions themselves were relatively conservative and failed to adapt to the realities of the modern economy. The American Federation of Labor (AFL), led after Samuel Gompers's death by William Green, sought peaceful cooperation with employers and remained wedded to the concept of the craft union. In the meantime, the rapidly rising number of unskilled industrial workers received little attention from the craft unions.

But whatever the unions' weaknesses, the strength of the corporations was the principal reason for the absence of effective labor organization in the 1920s. After the turmoil of 1919, corporate leaders worked hard to spread the doctrine that a crucial element of democratic capitalism was the protection of the "open shop," where no worker could be required to join a union. The crusade for the open shop, meaningfully titled the **American Plan**, became a pretext for a harsh campaign of union-busting. As a result, union membership fell from more than 5 million in 1920 to under 3 million in 1929.

WOMEN AND MINORITIES IN THE WORKFORCE

A growing proportion of the workforce consisted of women, who were concentrated in what have since become known as "pink-collar" jobs—low-paying service occupations. Large numbers of women worked as secretaries, salesclerks, and telephone operators and in other nonmanual service capacities. Because technically such positions were not industrial jobs, the AFL and other labor organizations were uninterested in organizing these workers. Similarly, the half-million African Americans who had migrated from the rural South into the cities during the Great Migration after 1914 had few opportunities for union representation. The skilled crafts represented in the AFL usually excluded black workers. Partly as a result of that exclusion, most blacks worked in jobs in which the AFL took no interest at all—as janitors, dishwashers, garbage collectors, and domestics and in other service capacities. **A. Philip Randolph**'s **Brotherhood of Sleeping Car Porters** was one of the few important unions dominated and led by African Americans.

(©John Vachon/Anthony Potter Collection/Getty Images)

AFRICAN AMERICAN WORKER PROTESTING   The frail union movement among African Americans in the 1920s, led by A. Philip Randolph and others, slowly built up a constituency within the black working class. Here, an aspiring dairy worker draws attention to the unjust treatment of African American men who had demonstrated their patriotism during the war.

In the West and the Southwest, the ranks of the unskilled included considerable numbers of Asians and Hispanics. In the wake of the Chinese Exclusion Acts, Japanese immigrants increasingly replaced the Chinese in menial jobs in California. They worked on railroads, construction sites, farms, and in many other low-paying workplaces. Some Japanese

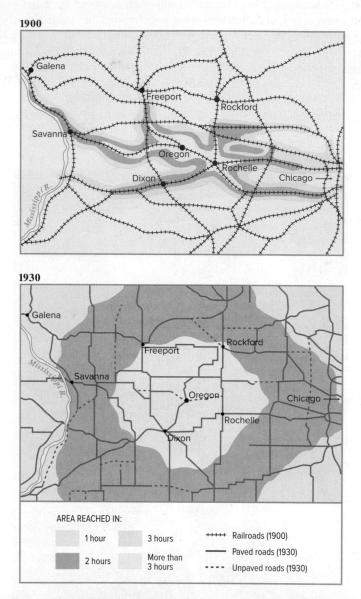

AREA REACHED IN:

▨ 1 hour	▨ 3 hours	┼┼┼ Railroads (1900)
▨ 2 hours	▨ More than 3 hours	— Paved roads (1930)
		- - - Unpaved roads (1930)

BREAKING DOWN RURAL ISOLATION: THE EXPANSION OF TRAVEL HORIZONS IN OREGON, ILLINOIS This map uses the small town of Oregon, Illinois—west of Chicago—to illustrate the way in which first railroads and then automobiles reduced the isolation of rural areas in the early decades of the twentieth century. The gold and purple areas of the two maps show the territory that residents of Oregon could reach within two hours. Note how small that area was in 1900 and how much larger it was in 1930, by which time an area of over 100 square miles had become easily accessible to the town. Note, too, the significant network of paved roads in the region by 1930, few of which had existed in 1900. • *Why did automobiles do so much more than railroads to expand the travel horizons of small towns?*

managed to escape the ranks of the unskilled by forming their own small businesses or setting themselves up as truck farmers. Many of the **Issei** (Japanese immigrants) and **Nisei** (their American-born children) enjoyed significant economic success, so much so that California passed laws in 1913 and 1920 to make it more difficult for them to buy land. Other Asians, most notably Filipinos, also swelled the unskilled workforce and generated considerable hostility. Anti-Filipino riots in California beginning in 1929 helped produce legislation in 1934 virtually eliminating immigration from the Philippines.

Mexican immigrants formed a major part of the unskilled workforce throughout the Southwest and California. Nearly half a million Mexicans entered the United States in the 1920s. Most lived in California, Texas, Arizona, and New Mexico, and by 1930, most lived in cities. Large Mexican barrios grew up in Los Angeles, El Paso, San Antonio, Denver, and many other urban centers. Some of the residents found work locally in factories and shops; others traveled to mines or did migratory labor on farms but returned to the cities between jobs. Mexican workers, too, faced hostility and discrimination from the Anglo population, but there were few efforts actually to exclude them. Employers in the relatively underpopulated West needed this ready pool of low-paid and unorganized workers.

AGRICULTURAL TECHNOLOGY AND THE PLIGHT OF THE FARMER

Like industry, American agriculture in the 1920s embraced new technologies. The number of tractors on American farms quadrupled during the decade, especially after they began to be powered by internal combustion engines, like automobiles, rather than by the cumbersome steam engines of the past. They helped open 35 million new acres to cultivation. Increasingly sophisticated combines and harvesters proliferated, making it possible to produce more crops with fewer workers.

Agricultural researchers worked on other innovations: the invention of hybrid corn, made possible by advances in genetic research, which became available to farmers in 1921 but was not grown in great quantities for a decade or more; and the creation of chemical fertilizers and pesticides, which also had limited use in the 1920s but proliferated quickly in the 1930s and 1940s.

The new technologies greatly increased agricultural productivity, and in fact outpaced the demand for agricultural goods. As a result, the 1920s saw substantial surpluses, a disastrous decline in food prices, and a severe drop in farmers' incomes. More than 3 million people left agriculture altogether in the course of the decade. Of those who remained, many lost ownership of their lands and had to rent instead from banks or other landlords.

In response, some farmers began to demand relief in the form of government price supports. One price-raising scheme in particular came to dominate agrarian demands: the idea of **parity**. Parity was a complicated formula for setting an adequate price for farm goods and ensuring that farmers would earn back at least their production costs no matter how the national or world agricultural market might fluctuate. Champions of parity urged high tariffs against foreign agricultural goods and a government commitment to buy surplus domestic crops at parity and sell them abroad.

The demand for parity found legislative expression in the McNary-Haugen Bill, which required the government to support prices at parity for grain, cotton, tobacco, and rice. It was introduced repeatedly. In 1926 and again in 1928, Congress approved the bill, but President Calvin Coolidge vetoed it both times.

THE NEW CULTURE

The urban and consumer-oriented culture of the 1920s helped Americans in all regions live their lives and perceive their world in increasingly similar ways. That same culture exposed them to new values. But different segments of American society experienced the new culture in different ways.

CONSUMERISM AND COMMUNICATIONS

The United States of the 1920s was a consumer society. More people than ever before could buy items not just because of need but also for convenience and pleasure. Middle-class families purchased electric refrigerators, washing machines, and vacuum cleaners. People wore wristwatches and smoked cigarettes. Women purchased cosmetics and mass-produced fashions. Above all, Americans bought automobiles. By the end of the decade, there were more than 30 million cars on American roads.

No group was more attuned to the emergence of consumerism, or more responsible for creating it, than the advertising industry. In the 1920s, partly as a result of techniques pioneered by wartime propaganda, advertising came of age. Publicists no longer simply conveyed information; they sought to identify products with a particular lifestyle. They also encouraged the public to absorb the values of promotion and salesmanship and to admire those who were effective boosters. One of the most successful books of the 1920s was *The Man Nobody Knows*, by the advertising executive Bruce Barton. It portrayed Jesus as not only a religious prophet but also a "super salesman." Barton's message, one sensitive to the new spirit of the consumer culture, was that Jesus had been concerned with living a full and rewarding life in this world and that twentieth-century men and women should do the same.

The advertising industry made good use of new vehicles of communication. Newspapers were absorbed into national chains. Mass-circulation magazines attracted broad national audiences. Movies in the 1920s became an ever more popular and powerful form of mass communication. Over 100 million people saw films in 1930, as compared to 40 million in 1922. The addition of sound to motion pictures—beginning in 1927 with the first feature-length "talkie," *The Jazz Singer* starring Al Jolson—greatly enhanced film's appeal. A series of scandals in the early 1920s led to the creation of the new Motion Picture Association, which imposed much tighter controls over the content of films. The result was safer, more conventionally acceptable films, which may in fact have broadened the appeal of movies generally. (See "America in the World: The Cinema.")

Meanwhile, the first commercial radio station in America, KDKA in Pittsburgh, began broadcasting in 1920, and the first national radio network, the National Broadcasting Company, was formed in 1927. That same year, Congress passed the Radio Act, which created a Federal Radio Commission to regulate the public airwaves used by private companies. (In 1935, it became the Federal Communications Commission, or FCC, which survives today.)

WOMEN IN THE NEW ERA

College-educated women were no longer pioneers in the 1920s. There were now two and even three generations of graduates of women's or coeducational colleges and universities, and some were making their presence felt in professional areas that in the past women had rarely penetrated. The "new professional woman" was a vivid and widely publicized figure in the 1920s.

In reality, however, most employed women were still nonprofessional, lower-class workers. Middle-class women, in the meantime, remained largely in the home, though advertising brought marketing strategies concerning gender roles and identity into the home. (See "Consider the Source: American Print Advertisements.")

The 1920s constituted a new era for middle-class women nonetheless. In particular, the decade saw a redefinition of motherhood. Shortly after World War I, John B. Watson and other behavioralists began to challenge the long-held assumption that women had an instinctive capacity for motherhood. Maternal affection was not, they claimed, sufficient preparation for child rearing. Instead, mothers should rely on the advice and assistance of experts and professionals: doctors, nurses, and trained educators.

For many middle-class women, these changes devalued what had been an important and consuming activity. Many attempted to compensate through what are often called "companionate marriages," which elevated the importance of compatibility and love between partners. Some women now openly considered their sexual relationships with their husbands not simply as a means of procreation, as earlier generations had been taught, but as important and pleasurable experiences in their own right, the culmination of romantic love.

One result of the new era for women was growing interest in birth control. The pioneer of the American birth-control movement, **Margaret Sanger**, began her career as a promoter of the diaphragm and other birth-control devices out of a concern for working-class women. She believed large families contributed to poverty and distress in poor communities. By the 1920s, she was becoming more effective in persuading middle-class women to see the benefits of birth control. Nevertheless, some birth-control devices remained illegal in many states, and abortion remained illegal nearly everywhere.

To the consternation of many longtime women reformers and progressive suffragists, some women concluded that in the New Era it was no longer necessary to maintain a rigid, Victorian female respectability. They could smoke, drink, dance, wear seductive clothes and makeup, and attend lively parties. Those assumptions were reflected in the emergence of

(©Bettmann/Corbis)

THE FLAPPER By the mid-1920s, the flapper—the young woman who challenged traditional expectations—had become not only a social type but a movement in fashion as well. Here, Catherine Dear is shown posing in a "beach costume," a fashion a long way from the rigid "respectability" of Victorian-age styles.

THE CINEMA

There is probably no cultural or commercial product more closely identified with the United States than motion pictures—or, as they are known in much of the world, the cinema. Although the technology of cinema emerged from the work of inventors in England and France as well as the United States, the production and distribution of films has been dominated by Americans almost from the start. The United States was the first nation to create a film "industry," and it did so at a scale vaster than that of any other country. With 700 feature films a year in the 1920s, Hollywood produced ten times as many movies as any other nation; and even then, its films were dominating not only the huge American market but much of the world's market as well. Seventy percent of the films seen in France, 80 percent of those seen in Latin America, and 95 percent of the movies viewed in Canada and Great Britain were produced in the United States in the 1920s. As early as the 1930s, the penetration of other nations by American movies was already troubling many governments. The Soviet Union responded to the popularity of Walt Disney's Mickey Mouse cartoons by inventing a cartoon hero of its own—a porcupine, designed to entertain in a way consistent with socialist values and not the capitalist ones they believed Hollywood conveyed. During World War II, American films were banned in occupied France, prompting some antifascist dissidents to screen such American films as Frank Capra's *Mr. Smith Goes to Washington* in protest.

American dominance was a result in part of World War I and its aftermath, which debilitated European filmmaking just as movie production was growing in the United States. By 1915, the United States had gained complete control of its own vast market and had so saturated it with movie theaters that by the end of World War I, half the world's theaters were in America. Two decades later, after an expansion of movie houses in other nations, the United States continued to have over 40 percent of the world's cinemas. And while the spread of theaters through other areas of the world helped launch film industries in many other countries, it also increased the market (and the appetite) for American films and strengthened American supremacy in their production. "The sun, it now appears," the *Saturday Evening Post* commented in the mid-1920s, "never sets on the British Empire and the American motion picture." Movies were then, and perhaps remain still, America's most influential cultural export. Even American popular music, which has enormous global reach, faces more significant local competition than American movies do in most parts of the world.

Despite this American dominance, however, filmmaking has flourished—and continues to flourish—in many countries around the world. India's fabled Bollywood, for example, produces an enormous number of movies for its domestic market—almost as many as the American industry creates—although few of them are widely exported. This global cinema has had a significant impact on American filmmaking. The small British film industry had a strong early influence on American movies, partly because of the quality and originality of British films and partly because of the emigration of talented actors, directors, and screenwriters to the United States. The great Alfred Hitchcock, for example, made his first films in London before moving to Hollywood, where he spent the rest of his

(©Hulton Deutsch/Corbis Historical/Getty Images)

VALENTINO The popularity of the film star Rudolph Valentino among American women was one of the most striking cultural phenomena of the 1920s. Valentino was slight and delicate, not at all like the conventional image of "manliness." But he developed an enormous following among women, in part—as this poster is obviously intended to suggest—by baring his body onscreen. Valentino was Italian, which made him seem somehow strange and foreign to many old-stock Americans, and he was almost always cast in exotic roles, never as an American. His sudden death in 1926 (at the age of 31) created enormous outpourings of grief among many American women.

long career. After World War II, French "new wave" cinema helped spawn a new generation of highly individualistic directors in the United States. Filmmakers from Germany, Italy, Sweden, the Netherlands, Japan, Spain, Australia, India, and Hong Kong had enormous influence on Hollywood, and over time perhaps even greater influence on the large and growing "independent film" movement in the United States.

In recent decades, as new technologies and new styles have transformed films around the world, the American movie industry has continued to dominate global cinema. But national boundaries no longer adequately describe moviemaking in the twenty-first century. It is becoming as truly global as other commercial ventures. "American" films today are often produced abroad, often have non-American directors and actors, and are often paid for with international financing. Hollywood still dominates worldwide filmmaking, but Hollywood itself is now an increasingly global community. •

UNDERSTAND, ANALYZE, & EVALUATE

1. Did American movies, as the Soviet Union claimed in the 1930s, promote capitalism?
2. Why has the American movie industry continued to dominate global cinema?

flappers modern women whose liberated lifestyle found expression in dress, hairstyle, speech, and behavior. The flapper lifestyle had a particular impact on urban lower-middle-class and working-class single women, who were filling new jobs in industry and the service sector. At night, such women flocked to clubs and dance halls in search of excitement and companionship. Many more affluent women soon began to copy the flapper style.

Despite all the changes, most women remained highly dependent on men and relatively powerless when men exploited that dependence. The National Woman's Party, under the leadership of Alice Paul, attempted to fight that powerlessness through its campaign for the Equal Rights Amendment, although it found little support in Congress. Responding to the suffrage victory, women organized the League of Women Voters and the women's auxiliaries of both the Democratic and Republican Parties. Female-dominated consumer groups grew rapidly and increased the range and energy of their efforts.

AMERICAN PRINT ADVERTISEMENTS

Companies advertised their products before millions of Americans in the expanding consumer marketplace of the 1920s. Radio and magazines were key venues for reaching the masses, and advertisers began focusing as much on the persuasive power of identity and lifestyle as the quality of the products themselves. This Procter & Gamble ad, appearing in 1928, peddled Ivory Soap to American women.

Your hands *can* keep their good looks *even though they work in the kitchen*

She is a heroine who does all her own housework; but she seems a genius whose hands never show it.

The question women ask every day is, "Can I do dishes, wash clothes and clean house, and still have hands that do not confess it?"

Millions of women answer "Yes."

You can surprise these women in the midst of any one of a dozen soap-and-water tasks and their hands seem by some miracle to have kept their fine, smooth whiteness through it all.

But it is not really a miracle—it is just Ivory Soap.

Here is what some of these women have written:

"The neighbors thought my mother extravagant for buying what they called 'toilet soap' for dish-washing and laundering purposes, but she suffered a great deal with soreness of her hands, and Ivory was the only soap that did not cause suffering. She was not able to hire the washing done so she did the next best thing—used the soap that caused no irritation."
—Mrs. E. H., Elkton, Md.

"Nothing to injure delicate skin"

"I have been using your Ivory Soap for 40 years. There is no other like it—I have tried many of the floating imitations but Ivory is the only soap with great cleansing quality and at the same time nothing to injure delicate skin. I use it exclusively for dish-washing."
—Mrs. I. W. R., Easton, Md.

"There are many other soaps cheaper and very cleansing, but, oh, so hard on the hands, while a daily use of Ivory leaves the hands soft and white. This is of great importance to mothers with young babies, who find it necessary to do the daily washings and tend the baby too. Their hands must be soft to rub the tender skin."
—Mrs. E. R. L., Emeryville, Cal.

You have probably used Ivory for toilet purposes, so you know it is pure and safe. You have used it for fine laundry and found that it harms nothing that can stand the touch of water. Now we suggest that you use it for dishes and general laundry and cleaning, because it cleanses thoroughly while it saves your hands.

Whatever the soap, remember it is the *suds* that do the work. And Ivory of course is famous for its suds, as women who do all their work with it enthusiastically testify.

Use Ivory for all your soap-and-water tasks —try your very next washing with Ivory —see if your hands do not keep their beauty all through the day.

Baby's underclothes need this special attention

If baby's diapers, bands and shirts are tough, or if they are not thoroughly cleansed, or if unrinsed

soap is left in them, skin irritation is almost certain to result.

If you will make sure that all of baby's garments are washed with Ivory (cake or flakes), the likelihood of irritation will be greatly lessened. In the first place Ivory is pure—this is extremely important. Second, Ivory, mild as it is, cleanses thoroughly and rinses out completely, leaving the tiny garments in a perfectly sanitary condition and so soft that chafing becomes practically impossible.

Because of its convenient form, the use of Ivory Flakes for baby clothes saves both time and labor. A brief soaking in warm Ivory suds before the final washing quickens the cleansing and purifying process.

Ivory Flakes *for a very special need— a sample—FREE*

If you have a particularly precious garment that requires the most careful treatment, and you have made certain that it will stand the touch of pure water, let us send you a sample of Ivory Flakes for this particular purpose. With the sample will come also a beautifully illustrated booklet, "The Care of Lovely Garments," which is a veritable encyclopædia of laundering information. Address a postcard or letter to Section 12-JF, Department of Home Economics, Procter & Gamble, Cincinnati, O.

PROCTER & GAMBLE

IVORY SOAP

FLAKES   CAKES

99 44/100 % PURE
IT FLOATS

UNDERSTAND, ANALYZE, & EVALUATE

1. What sort of lifestyle does the image suggest might come with using Ivory Soap?
2. What do the main heading and smaller print indicate would be proper or common roles for women?
3. Does the combination of image and text send a progressive message or a conservative one? Does it trade in the flapper aesthetic or something more traditional?
4. To what groups of women does the advertisement seem aimed? Who are the judges of "good looks" suggested by the text?

Source: Duke University Libraries Hartman Center.

Women activists won a brief triumph in 1921 when they helped secure passage of the Sheppard-Towner Act, which provided federal funds to states to establish prenatal and child health-care programs. From the start, however, the act produced controversy. Alice Paul and her supporters opposed the measure, complaining that it classified all women as mothers. More important, the American Medical Association fought Sheppard-Towner, warning that it would introduce untrained outsiders into the health-care field. In 1929, no longer worried about women voting as a bloc, Congress terminated the program.

THE DISENCHANTED

The generation that lived through (and in many cases fought in) the Great War quickly came to see the conflict as a useless waste of lives lost for no purpose. For some young people in the 1920s, disenchantment with the war contributed to a growing disenchantment with the United States. The newly prosperous and consumer-driven era they encountered seemed meaningless and vulgar to many artists and intellectuals in particular. As a result, they came to view their own culture with contempt. Rather than trying to influence and reform their society, they isolated themselves from it and embarked on a restless search for personal fulfillment. The American writer Gertrude Stein once referred to the young Americans emerging from World War I as a **Lost Generation**, though they faced a consistent counternarrative, pushed by veterans' groups and others, that emphasized the war's ennobling and even glorious character.

Among the artists and intellectuals of the 1920s who experienced disenchantment with modern America was the Baltimore journalist H. L. Mencken, who delighted in ridiculing religion, politics, the arts, even democracy itself. Sinclair Lewis published a series of novels—*Main Street* (1920), *Babbitt* (1922), *Arrowsmith* (1925), and others—in which he lashed out at one aspect of modern bourgeois society after another. Intellectuals of the 1920s claimed to reject the "success ethic" they believed dominated American life. The novelist F. Scott Fitzgerald, for example, attacked the American obsession with material success in *The Great Gatsby* (1925). The roster of important American writers active in the 1920s may have no equal in any other period. It included Fitzgerald, Lewis, Ernest Hemingway, Thomas Wolfe, John Dos Passos, Ezra Pound, T. S. Eliot, Gertrude Stein, Edna Ferber, William Faulkner, Eugene O'Neill, and a remarkable group of African American artists. In New York City, a new generation of black intellectuals created a flourishing artistic life widely described as the **Harlem Renaissance**. The Harlem poets, novelists, and artists drew heavily from their African roots in an effort to prove the richness of their own racial heritage and assert resistance against white racism and stereotyping. The ethos was captured in a single sentence by the author **Langston Hughes**: "I am a Negro—and beautiful."

Other black writers in Harlem and elsewhere—James Weldon Johnson, Countee Cullen, Zora Neale Hurston, Claude McKay, Alain Locke—as well as black artists and musicians helped establish a thriving and at times highly politicized culture.

A CONFLICT OF CULTURES

The modern, secular culture of the 1920s did not go unchallenged. It grew up alongside an older, more traditional culture, with which it continually and often bitterly competed.

PROHIBITION

When the prohibition of the sale and manufacture of alcohol went into effect in January 1920, it had the support of most members of the middle class and most of those who considered themselves progressives. Within a year, however, it had become clear that the "noble experiment," as its defenders called it, was not working well. At first, prohibition did substantially reduce drinking in most parts of the country. But it also produced conspicuous and growing violations. Before long, it was almost as easy to acquire illegal alcohol in many parts of the country as it had once been to acquire legal alcohol. And since an enormous, lucrative industry was now barred to legitimate businessmen, organized crime took it over.

Many middle-class progressives who had originally supported prohibition soon soured on the experiment. But a constituency of largely rural Protestant Americans continued vehemently to defend it. To them, prohibition represented the effort of an older America to protect traditional notions of morality. Drinking, which they associated with the modern city and Catholic immigrants, became a symbol of the new culture they believed was displacing them.

As the decade proceeded, opponents of prohibition (or "wets") gained steadily in influence. Not until 1933, however, when the Great Depression added weight to their appeals, were they finally able to challenge the "drys" effectively and win repeal of the Eighteenth Amendment.

NATIVISM AND THE KLAN

Agitation for a curb on foreign immigration had begun in the nineteenth century and, as with prohibition, had gathered strength in the years before the war largely because of the support of middle-class progressives. In the years immediately following the war, as immigration's association with radicalism intensified and migration from Europe resumed, popular sentiment on behalf of restriction grew rapidly.

In 1921, Congress passed an emergency immigration act, establishing a quota system by which annual immigration from any country could not exceed 3 percent of the number of persons of that nationality who had been in the United States in 1910. The new law cut immigration from 800,000 to 300,000 in any single year, but the nativists remained unsatisfied. The **National Origins Act of 1924** banned immigration from East Asia entirely and reduced the quota for Europeans from 3 to 2 percent. The quota would be based, moreover, not on the 1910 statistics but on the census of 1890, a year in which there had been far fewer southern and eastern Europeans in the country. What new immigration there was, in other words, would heavily favor northwestern Europeans. Five years later, a further restriction set a rigid limit of 150,000 immigrants a year. In the years that followed, immigration officials seldom permitted even half that number actually to enter the country.

To defenders of an older, more provincial America, the growth of large communities of foreign peoples, alien in speech, habits, and values, came to seem a direct threat to their own embattled way of life. Among other things, this nativism helped revitalize the **Ku Klux Klan** as a major force in American society. The first Klan, founded during Reconstruction, had died in the 1870s. But in 1915, a new group of white southerners met on Stone Mountain near Atlanta and established a modern version of the society. Nativist passions had swelled in Georgia and elsewhere in response to the case of Leo Frank, a Jewish factory manager in Atlanta convicted in 1914 on flimsy evidence of murdering a female employee; a mob stormed Frank's jail and lynched him. The premiere, also in Atlanta, of D. W. Griffith's film *The Birth of a Nation*, which glorified the early Klan, also helped inspire white southerners to form a new one.

At first the new Klan, like the old, was largely concerned with intimidating blacks. After World War I, however, concern about blacks gradually became secondary to concern about Catholics, Jews, and foreigners. At that point, membership in the Klan expanded rapidly and dramatically, not just in the small towns and rural areas of the South but in industrial cities in the North and Midwest as well. By 1924, there were reportedly 4 million members, including many women, organized in separate, parallel units. The largest state Klan was not in the South but in Indiana. Beginning in 1925, a series of scandals involving the organization's leaders precipitated a slow but steady decline in the Klan's influence.

Most Klan units (or "klaverns") tried to present their members as patriots and defenders of morality, and some did nothing more menacing than stage occasional parades and rallies. Often, however, the Klan also operated as a brutal, even violent, opponent of "alien" groups. Klansmen systematically terrorized blacks, Jews, Catholics, and foreigners. At times, they engaged in public whipping, tarring and feathering, arson, and lynching. What the Klan feared, however, was not simply "foreign" or "racially impure" groups, but anyone who posed a challenge to traditional values.

Religious Fundamentalism

Another cultural controversy of the 1920s involved the place of religion in contemporary society. By 1921, American Protestantism was already divided into two warring camps. On one side stood the modernists: mostly urban, middle-class people who were attempting to adapt religion to the teachings of modern science and the secularizing forces of their society. On the other side stood the fundamentalists: largely though not exclusively rural men and women fighting to preserve traditional faith and to maintain the centrality of religion in American life. The fundamentalists insisted the Bible was to be interpreted literally. Above all, they opposed the teachings of Charles Darwin, whose theory of evolution had openly challenged the biblical story of Creation. Evangelical fundamentalists sought to spread their doctrine widely through revival meetings. The leading evangelist of the age, Billy Sunday, attracted huge crowds across the country with his fiery delivery, moral certitude, and plain exhortations to follow the Bible or face eternal damnation.

By the mid-1920s, to the great alarm of modernists, fundamentalist demands to forbid the teaching of evolution in public schools were gaining political strength in some states. In Tennessee in March 1925, the legislature adopted a measure making it illegal for any public school teacher "to teach any theory that denies the story of the divine creation of man as taught in the Bible."

The Tennessee law caught the attention of the fledgling American Civil Liberties Union (ACLU), founded in 1917 to defend pacifists, radicals, and conscientious objectors during World War I. The ACLU offered free counsel to any Tennessee educator willing to defy the law and become the defendant in a test case. A twenty-four-year-old biology teacher in the town of Dayton, John T. Scopes, agreed to have himself arrested. When the ACLU decided to send the famous attorney Clarence Darrow to defend Scopes, the aging William Jennings Bryan, now an important fundamentalist spokesman, announced he would travel to Dayton to assist the prosecution. Journalists from across the country flocked to Tennessee. Scopes had, of course, deliberately violated the law, and a verdict of guilty was a foregone conclusion, especially when the judge refused to permit "expert" testimony by evolution scholars. Scopes was fined $100, but the case was ultimately dismissed in a higher court because of a technicality. Nevertheless, Darrow scored an important victory for the modernists by calling Bryan himself to the stand to testify as an "expert on the Bible." In the course of the cross-examination, which was broadcast by radio to much of the nation, Darrow made Bryan's defense of biblical truths appear stubborn and finally maneuvered him into admitting the possibility that religious dogma was open to interpretation.

The **Scopes trial** put fundamentalists on the defensive. It discouraged many of them from participating openly in politics. But it did not resolve the conflict between fundamentalists and modernists, which continued to smolder.

THE DEMOCRATS' ORDEAL

The anguish of provincial Americans attempting to defend an embattled way of life proved particularly troubling to the Democratic Party during the 1920s. The Democrats consisted of a diverse coalition of interest groups, including prohibitionists, Klansmen, fundamentalists, and most white southerners on one side, and Catholics, urban workers, and immigrants on the other.

At the 1924 Democratic National Convention in New York City, a bitter conflict broke out over the platform when the party's urban wing attempted to win approval of planks calling for the repeal of prohibition and a denunciation of the Klan. Both planks narrowly failed. Even more damaging to the party was a deadlock in the balloting for a presidential candidate. Urban Democrats supported Alfred E. Smith, the Irish Catholic governor of New York; rural Democrats backed William McAdoo, Woodrow Wilson's Treasury secretary, who had skillfully positioned himself to win the support of southern and western delegates suspicious of modern urban life but whose reputation had been tarnished by a series of scandals resulting from his work as an attorney for an unsavory oil tycoon. For 103 ballots, the convention dragged on, with Smith supporters chanting "No oil on Al," until finally both Smith and McAdoo withdrew. The party settled on a compromise: the corporate lawyer John W. Davis, who lost decisively to Calvin Coolidge.

A similar schism plagued the Democrats again in 1928, when Al Smith finally secured his party's nomination for president. He was not, however, able to unite his divided party, in part because of widespread anti-Catholic sentiment especially in the South. He was the first Democrat since the Civil War not to carry the entire South. Elsewhere, he carried no states at all except Massachusetts and Rhode Island. Smith's opponent, and the victor in the presidential election, was a man who personified the modern, prosperous, middle-class society of the New Era: Herbert Hoover.

REPUBLICAN GOVERNMENT

For twelve years, beginning in 1921, both the presidency and the Congress rested in the hands of the Republican Party. For most of those years, the federal government enjoyed a warm and supportive relationship with the American business community. Yet the government of the New Era was less passive than critics often described. It attempted to serve in many respects as an agent of economic change.

The Republican administrations also played an active role in world affairs. Far from the "isolationists" their critics later called them, the governments of the 1920s did not sit idly by as the terms of one world war continued to reverberate and the specter of a second one loomed.

THE HARDING ADMINISTRATION

Warren G. Harding was elected to the presidency in 1920. An undistinguished senator from Ohio, he had received the Republican presidential nomination as a result of an agreement among leaders of his party, who considered him, as one noted, a "good second-rater." Harding appointed distinguished men to some important cabinet offices and attempted to stabilize the nation's troubled foreign policy. But he seemed baffled by his responsibilities, as if he recognized his unfitness. "I am a man of limited talents from a small town," he reportedly told friends on one occasion. "I don't seem to grasp that I am President." Harding's intellectual limits were compounded by his penchant for gambling, illegal alcohol, and attractive women.

By the time the Harding administration took office in 1921, American membership in the League of Nations was no longer a realistic possibility. But Secretary of State Charles Evans Hughes wanted to find a replacement for the League as a guarantor of world peace and stability.

The most important effort was the Washington Conference of 1921—an attempt to prevent a destabilizing naval armaments race among the United States, Britain, and Japan. Hughes proposed a plan for dramatic reductions in the fleets of all three nations and a ten-year moratorium on the construction of large warships. To the surprise of almost everyone, the conference ultimately agreed to accept most of Hughes's terms. The Five-Power Pact of February 1922 established limits for total naval tonnage and a ratio of armaments among the signatories. For every 5 tons of American and British warships, Japan would maintain 3 and France and Italy 1.75 each.

When the French foreign minister, Aristide Briand, asked the United States in 1927 to join an alliance against Germany, Secretary of State Frank Kellogg (who had replaced Hughes in 1925) proposed instead a multilateral treaty outlawing war as an instrument of national policy. Fourteen nations signed the agreement in Paris on August 27, 1928, amid wide international acclaim. Forty-eight other nations later joined the Kellogg-Briand Pact. It contained no instruments of enforcement.

Back at home, Harding lacked the strength to abandon the party hacks who had helped give him power. One of them, Ohio party boss Harry Daugherty, he appointed attorney general. Another, New Mexico senator Albert B. Fall, he made secretary of the interior. Members of the so-called Ohio Gang filled important offices throughout the administration. Unknown to the public, Daugherty, Fall, and others were engaged in fraud and corruption. The most spectacular scandal involved the rich naval oil reserves at **Teapot Dome**, Wyoming, and Elk Hills, California. At the urging of Fall, Harding transferred control of those reserves from the Navy Department to the Interior Department. Fall then secretly leased them to two wealthy businessmen and received in return nearly half a million dollars in "loans" to ease his private financial troubles. Fall was ultimately convicted of bribery and sentenced to a year in prison. Harry Daugherty barely avoided a similar fate for his part in another scandal.

In the summer of 1923, only months before Senate investigations and press revelations brought the scandals to light, a tired and depressed Harding left Washington for a speaking tour in the West. In Seattle late in July, he complained of severe pain, which his doctors wrongly diagnosed as food poisoning. A few days later, in San Francisco, he died. He had suffered two major heart attacks.

THE COOLIDGE ADMINISTRATION

Calvin Coolidge succeeded Harding in the presidency. Where Harding was genial, garrulous, and debauched, Coolidge was dour, silent, even puritanical. Elected governor of Massachusetts in 1919, Coolidge had won national attention with his tough response to the Boston police strike that year. That was enough to make him his party's vice presidential nominee in 1920. Three years later, after Harding's death, he took the oath of office from his father, a justice of the peace, by the light of a kerosene lamp.

If anything, Coolidge was even less active as president than Harding, partly as a result of his conviction that government should interfere as little as possible in the life of the nation. In 1924, he received his party's presidential nomination virtually unopposed. Running against John W. Davis, he won a comfortable victory: 54 percent of the popular vote and 382 of the 531 electoral votes. Coolidge probably could have won renomination and reelection in 1928. Instead, in characteristically understated fashion, he walked into a press room one day and handed each reporter a slip of paper containing a single sentence: "I do not choose to run for president in 1928."

In between, Coolidge governed amid the lingering economic fallout of the Great War. The first responsibility of diplomacy, Hughes, Kellogg, and others agreed, was to ensure that American overseas trade faced no obstacles. The Allied powers of Europe were struggling to repay $11 billion in loans they had contracted with the United States during and shortly after the war. At the same time, Germany was attempting to pay the reparations levied by the Allies. The United States stepped in with a solution.

Charles G. Dawes, an American banker who became vice president under Coolidge in 1925, negotiated an agreement in 1924 among France, Britain, Germany, and the United States. Under the **Dawes Plan**, American banks would provide enormous loans to Germany, which would use that money to pay reparations to France and Britain; Britain and France would agree to reduce the amount of those payments and, in turn, use those funds (as well as the large loans they themselves were receiving from American banks) to repay war debts to the United States. One historian said of this circular plan, "It would have made equal sense for the U.S. to have taken the money out of one drawer in the Treasury and put it into another." None of this activity led to economic recovery in Europe. Rather, the flow of funds was able to continue only by virtue of the growing debts the European nations were acquiring to American banks and corporations. The American economic involvement in Europe continued to expand until the worldwide depression shattered the system in 1931.

During the 1920s, American military forces maintained a presence in Nicaragua, Panama, and several other countries in the region, while U.S. investments in Latin America more than doubled. American banks offered large loans to Latin American governments, just as in Europe; and as with the Europeans, the Latin Americans had difficulty earning the money to repay them in the face of the formidable U.S. tariff barrier.

GOVERNMENT AND BUSINESS

However passive the New Era presidents may have been, much of the federal government worked effectively and efficiently during the 1920s to adapt public policy to the widely accepted goal of the time: helping business and industry to operate with maximum efficiency and productivity. The close relationship between the private sector and the federal government forged during World War I continued. Secretary of the Treasury Andrew Mellon, a wealthy steel and aluminum tycoon, worked to achieve substantial reductions in taxes on corporate profits, personal incomes, and inheritances. Largely because of his efforts, Congress cut them all by more than half. Mellon also worked closely with President Coolidge after 1924 on a series of measures to trim dramatically the already modest federal budget, even managing to retire half the nation's World War I debt.

The most prominent member of the cabinet was Commerce Secretary **Herbert Hoover**. During his eight years in the Commerce Department, Hoover constantly encouraged voluntary cooperation in the private sector as the best avenue to stability. But the idea of voluntarism did not require that the government remain passive; on the contrary, public institutions, Hoover believed, had a duty to play an active role in creating the new, cooperative order. Above all, Hoover became the champion of the concept of business "associationalism"—a concept that envisioned the creation of national organizations of businessmen in particular industries. Through these trade associations, private entrepreneurs could, Hoover believed, study and stabilize their industries and promote efficiency in production and marketing.

Many progressives derived encouragement from the election of Herbert Hoover to the presidency in 1928. Hoover easily defeated Al Smith, the Democratic candidate. And he entered office promising bold new efforts to solve the nation's remaining economic problems. But Hoover had few opportunities to prove himself. Less than a year after his inauguration, the nation plunged into the severest and most prolonged economic crisis in its history—a crisis that brought many of the optimistic assumptions of the New Era crashing down and launched the nation into a period of unprecedented social innovation and reform.

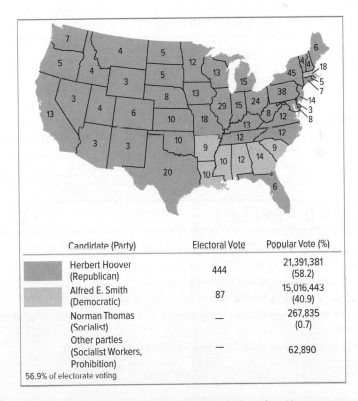

Candidate (Party)	Electoral Vote	Popular Vote (%)
Herbert Hoover (Republican)	444	21,391,381 (58.2)
Alfred E. Smith (Democratic)	87	15,016,443 (40.9)
Norman Thomas (Socialist)	—	267,835 (0.7)
Other parties (Socialist Workers, Prohibition)	—	62,890

56.9% of electorate voting

THE ELECTION OF 1928 The election of 1928 was highly one-sided. Herbert Hoover won over 58 percent of the popular vote to Alfred Smith's 41 percent. Smith carried only Massachusetts, Rhode Island, and some traditionally Democratic states in the South. • *Why did Smith do so poorly even in some parts of the South?*

CONCLUSION

The remarkable prosperity of the 1920s shaped much of what exuberant contemporaries liked to call the "New Era." In the years after World War I, America built a vibrant and extensive national culture. Its middle class moved increasingly into the embrace of the growing consumer culture. Politics were reorganized around the needs of a booming, interdependent industrial economy, undermining many of the reform crusades of the previous generation but also creating new institutions to help promote economic growth and stability.

Beneath the glittering surface of the New Era, however, were great controversies and injustices. Although the prosperity of the 1920s spread more widely than at any time in the nation's industrial history, more than half the population failed to achieve any real benefits from the growth. A new, optimistic, secular culture attracted millions of urban middle-class people, even as many other Americans looked at it with alarm and fought it with great fervor. The unprepossessing conservative presidents of the era suggested a time of stability, but in fact few eras in modern American history have seen so much political and cultural conflict.

The 1920s ended in a catastrophic economic crash that has colored the image of those years ever since. The crises of the 1930s should not obscure the real achievements of the New Era economy. Neither, however, should the prosperity of the 1920s obscure the inequity and instability in those years that helped produce the difficult years to come.

KEY TERMS/PEOPLE/PLACES/EVENTS

A. Philip Randolph 545
American Plan 544
Brotherhood of Sleeping
  Car Porters 545
Calvin Coolidge 558
Dawes Plan 558
flappers 551
Harlem Renaissance 553

Herbert Hoover 559
Issei 547
Ku Klux Klan 555
Langston Hughes 553
Lost Generation 553
Margaret Sanger 549
National Origins Act
  of 1924 554

Nisei 547
parity 547
Scopes trial 556
Teapot Dome 557
The Jazz Singer 548
Warren G. Harding 557
welfare capitalism 543

RECALL AND REFLECT

1. What was the impact of the automobile on American life?
2. How did labor fare during the 1920s? What particular problems did female, black, immigrant, and unskilled laborers face?
3. How did religion respond to the consumer culture of the 1920s?
4. What was the myth and what was the reality of the new professional woman of the 1920s?
5. What was the nature and extent of the nativism of the 1920s?

•23 | THE GREAT DEPRESSION

THE COMING OF THE DEPRESSION
THE AMERICAN PEOPLE IN HARD TIMES
THE DEPRESSION AND AMERICAN CULTURE
THE ORDEAL OF HERBERT HOOVER

LOOKING AHEAD

1. What were some of the causes of the Great Depression? What made it so severe, and why did it last so long?
2. What was the impact of the Depression on farmers, minorities, and women?
3. How did President Hoover and his administration try to deal with the Depression? What was the result of those efforts?

"WE IN AMERICA TODAY," presidential candidate Herbert Hoover proclaimed in August 1928, "are nearer to the final triumph over poverty than ever before in the history of any land. The poorhouse is vanishing from among us." Only fifteen months later, those words would return to haunt him, as the nation plunged into the severest and most prolonged economic depression in its history—a depression that continued in one form or another for a full decade, not only in the United States but throughout much of the world.

The Depression reached into every area of economic and social life. It destroyed the bull market of the 1920s, drove stock prices into a long decline, halted the investment in industrial plants and infrastructure that had helped fuel economic growth, and jeopardized the national banking system. Worst of all, from the perspective of many citizens, it created massive unemployment, which at times approached a full quarter of the workforce.

In the midst of this crisis, President Hoover used the tools of the federal government to address economic problems more aggressively than any president before him. But even these measures were overwhelmed by the Depression. And Hoover refused to consider steps that he believed betrayed basic principles of American life, particularly the rights and responsibilities of individuals. Faith in individualism had been strong throughout American history, but the scale of the Depression called it into question, undermined Hoover's reputation, and eventually led to major shifts in American political and economic life.

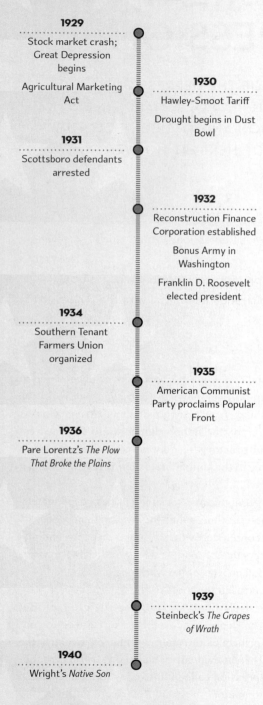

1929

Stock market crash;
Great Depression
begins

Agricultural Marketing
Act

1930

Hawley-Smoot Tariff

Drought begins in Dust
Bowl

1931

Scottsboro defendants
arrested

1932

Reconstruction Finance
Corporation established

Bonus Army in
Washington

Franklin D. Roosevelt
elected president

1934

Southern Tenant
Farmers Union
organized

1935

American Communist
Party proclaims Popular
Front

1936

Pare Lorentz's *The Plow
That Broke the Plains*

1939

Steinbeck's *The Grapes
of Wrath*

1940

Wright's *Native Son*

THE COMING OF THE DEPRESSION

The sudden financial collapse in 1929 came as an especially severe shock because it followed so closely an era of remarkable stock market performance. In February 1928, stock prices began a steady ascent that continued, with only a few temporary lapses, for a year and a half. Between May 1928 and September 1929, the average price of stocks rose over 40 percent. Trading mushroomed from 2 or 3 million shares a day to over 5 million, and at times to as many as 10 or 12 million. In short, a widespread speculative fever grew steadily more intense, particularly once brokerage firms began encouraging the mania by offering easy credit to those buying stocks.

THE GREAT CRASH

In the autumn of 1929, the market began to fall apart. On October 29, "Black Tuesday," after a week of growing instability, all efforts to save the market failed. Sixteen million shares of stock were traded; the industrial index dropped 43 points (or nearly 10 percent), wiping out all the gains of the previous year; stocks in many companies became virtually worthless. Within a month, stocks had lost half their September value, and despite occasional, short-lived rallies, they continued to decline for several years after that.

Popular folklore has established the stock market crash as the beginning, and even the cause, of the **Great Depression**. Although October 1929 might have been the most visible early sign of the crisis, the Depression had earlier beginnings and other causes.

CAUSES OF THE DEPRESSION

Economists and historians have argued for decades about the causes of the Great Depression. But most agree that what was remarkable about the crisis is not that it occurred but that it was so severe and lasted so long. If they agree on little else, most observers attribute that severity and length to several factors.

One was a lack of diversification in the American economy in the 1920s. Prosperity had depended excessively on a few basic industries, notably construction and automobiles, which in the late 1920s began to decline. Expenditures on construction fell from $11 billion in 1926 to under $9 billion in 1929. Automobile sales fell by more than a third in the first nine months of 1929. Newer industries were emerging to take up the slack—among them petroleum, chemicals, electronics, and plastics—but none had developed enough strength to compensate for this decline.

A second important factor was the maldistribution of purchasing power and, as a result, a weakness in consumer demand. As industrial and agricultural production increased, the proportion of the profits going to potential consumers was too small to create an adequate market for the goods the economy was producing. Even in 1929, after nearly a decade of economic growth, more than half the families in America lived on the edge of or below the minimum subsistence level.

A third major problem was the credit structure of the economy. Farmers were deeply in debt, and crop prices were too low to allow them to pay off what they owed. Small banks were in constant trouble as their customers defaulted on loans; large banks were in trouble, too. Although most American bankers were very conservative, some of the nation's biggest banks were investing recklessly in the stock market or making unwise loans. When the market crashed and the loans went bad, some banks failed and others made the crisis worse by contracting already scarce credit and calling in loans that borrowers could not pay.

A fourth factor was America's position in international trade. Late in the 1920s, European demand for American goods began to decline, partly because European industry and agriculture were becoming more productive and partly because some European nations were having financial difficulties of their own. But it was also because the European economy was being destabilized by the international debt structure that had emerged in the aftermath of World War I.

This debt structure, therefore, was a fifth factor contributing to the Depression. When the war came to an end in 1918, all the European nations that had been allied with the United States owed large sums of money to American banks, sums much too large to be repaid out of their shattered economies, which is partly why the Allies had insisted on reparation payments from Germany and Austria. Reparations, they believed, would provide them with a way to pay off their own debts. But Germany and Austria were no more able to pay the reparations than the Allies were able to pay their debts.

The American government refused to forgive or reduce the debts. Instead, American banks began making large loans to European governments, which used them to pay off their earlier loans. Thus debts (and reparations) were being paid only by piling up new and greater debts. At the same time, American protective tariffs were making it difficult for Europeans to sell their goods in American markets. Without any source of foreign exchange with which to repay their loans, they began to default. The collapse of the international credit structure was one of the reasons the Depression spread to Europe after 1931. (See "America in the World: The Global Depression.")

THE GLOBAL DEPRESSION

The Great Depression began in the United States. But it did not end there. The American economy was the largest in the world, and its collapse sent shock waves across the globe. By 1931, the American depression had become a world depression, with important implications for the course of global history.

The origins of the worldwide depression lay in the pattern of debts that had emerged during and after World War I, when the United States loaned billions of dollars to European nations. In 1931, with American banks staggering and in many cases collapsing, large banks in New York began desperately calling in their loans from Germany and Austria. That precipitated the collapse of one of Austria's largest banks, which in turn created panic through much of central Europe. The economic collapse in Germany and Austria meant that those nations could not continue paying reparations to Britain and France (required by the Treaty of Versailles of 1919), which meant in turn that Britain and France could not continue paying off their loans to the United States. This spreading financial crisis was accompanied by a dramatic contraction of international trade, precipitated in part by the Hawley-Smoot Tariff in the United States, which established the highest import duties in history and stifled much global commerce. Depressed agricultural prices—a result of worldwide overproduction—also contributed to the downturn. By 1932, worldwide industrial production had declined by more than one-third, and world trade had plummeted by nearly two-thirds. By 1933, 30 million people in industrial nations were unemployed, five times the number of four years before.

But the Depression was not confined to industrial nations. Imperialism and

(©General Photographic Agency/Hulton Archive/ Getty Images)

LOOKING FOR WORK IN LONDON, 1935 An unemployed London man wears a sign that seems designed to convince passersby that he is an educated, respectable person despite his present circumstances.

industrialization had drawn almost all regions of the world into the international industrial economy. Colonies and nations in Africa, Asia, and South America—critically dependent on exporting raw materials and agricultural goods to industrial countries—experienced a collapse in demand for their products and thus rising levels of poverty and unemployment. Some nations, among them the Soviet Union and China, remained relatively unconnected to the global economy and suffered relatively little from the Great Depression. But in most parts of the world, the Depression caused tremendous social and economic hardship.

It also created political turmoil. Among the countries hardest hit by the Depression was Germany, where industrial production declined by 50 percent and unemployment reached 35 percent in the early 1930s. The desperate economic conditions there contributed greatly to the rise of the Nazi Party and its leader, Adolf Hitler, who became chancellor in 1933. Japan suffered as well, dependent as it was on world trade to sustain its growing industrial economy and purchase essential commodities for its needs at home. And in Japan, as in Germany, economic troubles produced political turmoil and aided the rise of a new militaristic regime. In Italy, the fascist government of Benito Mussolini, which had first taken power in the 1920s, also saw militarization and territorial expansion as a way out of economic difficulties.

In other nations, governments sought solutions to the Depression through reform of their domestic economies. Among the most common responses to the Depression around the world was substantial government investment in public works, such as roads, bridges, dams, public buildings, and other large projects. Among the nations that adopted this approach—in addition to the United States—were Britain, France, Germany, Italy, and the Soviet Union. Another response was the expansion of government-funded relief for the unemployed. All the industrial countries of the world experimented with various forms of relief, often borrowing ideas from one another. And the Depression helped create new approaches to economics, in the face of the apparent failure of classical models of economic behavior to explain, or provide solutions to, the crisis. The British economist John Maynard Keynes revolutionized economic thought in much of the world. His 1936 book *The General Theory of Employment, Interest, and Money* created a sensation by arguing that the Depression was a result not of declining production but of inadequate consumer demand. Governments, he said, could stimulate their economies by growing the money supply and creating investment through a combination of lowering interest rates and increasing public spending. Keynesianism, as Keynes's theories became known, began to have an impact in the United States in 1938, and in much of the rest of the world in subsequent years.

The Great Depression was an important turning point not only in American history but also in the history of the twentieth-century world. It transformed ideas of public policy and economics in many nations. It toppled old regimes and created new ones. And perhaps above all, it was a major factor in the coming of World War II. •

UNDERSTAND, ANALYZE, & EVALUATE

1. How did the 1919 Treaty of Versailles and the Hawley-Smoot Tariff contribute to the global depression of the 1930s?
2. How did the governments of European nations respond to the Depression?
3. What effect did the global depression have on economic theory?

PROGRESS OF THE DEPRESSION

The stock market crash of 1929 did not so much cause the Depression, then, as help trigger a chain of events that exposed larger weaknesses in the American economy. During the next three years, the crisis grew.

The most serious problem at first was the collapse of much of the banking system. Between 1930 and 1933, over 9,000 American banks either went bankrupt or closed their doors to avoid bankruptcy. Partly as a result of these banking closures, the nation's money supply shrank by perhaps a third between 1930 and 1933, which caused a decline in purchasing power and thus deflation. Manufacturers and merchants began reducing prices, cutting back on production, and laying off workers. Some economists argue that a severe depression could have been avoided if the Federal Reserve system had acted responsibly. But late in 1931, in a misguided effort to build international confidence in the dollar, it raised interest rates, which contracted the money supply even further.

The American gross national product plummeted from over $104 billion in 1929 to $76.4 billion in 1932, a 25 percent decline in three years. By 1932, according to relatively crude estimates, 25 percent of the American workforce was unemployed. (Some argue the figure was even higher.) For the rest of the decade, unemployment averaged nearly 20 percent, never dropping below 15 percent. Up to another one-third of the workforce was "underemployed"—experiencing major reductions in wages, hours, or both.

THE AMERICAN PEOPLE IN HARD TIMES

Someone asked the economist John Maynard Keynes in the 1930s whether he was aware of any historical era comparable to the Great Depression. "Yes," Keynes replied. "It was called the Dark Ages, and it lasted 400 years." The Depression was far shorter, but it brought unprecedented economic despair to the United States and much of the Western world.

UNEMPLOYMENT AND RELIEF

In the industrial Northeast and Midwest, cities were virtually paralyzed by unemployment. Cleveland, Ohio, for example, had an unemployment rate of 50 percent in 1932; Akron, 60 percent; Toledo, 80 percent. Unemployed workers walked through the streets day after day looking for jobs that did not exist. An increasing number of families turned to state and local public relief systems, just to be able to eat. But those systems, which in the 1920s had served only a small number of indigents, were totally unequipped to handle the heavy new demands. In many cities, therefore, relief simply collapsed. Private charities attempted to supplement the public relief efforts, but the problem was far beyond their capabilities as well.

In rural areas, conditions were often worse. Farm income declined by 60 percent between 1929 and 1932. A third of all American farmers lost their land. In addition, a large area of agricultural settlement in the Great Plains suffered from one of the worst droughts in the history of the nation. Beginning in 1930, the region that came to be known as the "Dust Bowl," which stretched north from Texas into the Dakotas, experienced a steady decline in rainfall and an accompanying increase in heat. The drought continued for a decade, turning what had once been fertile farm regions into virtual deserts. Severe winds blew dust across the eastern United States.

Many farmers, like the urban unemployed, left their homes in search of work. In the South, in particular, many dispossessed farmers, black and white, simply wandered from town to town, hoping to find jobs or handouts. Hundreds of thousands of families from the Dust Bowl (often known collectively as "**Okies**," though not all came from Oklahoma) traveled to California and other states, where they found conditions little better than those they had left. Many worked as agricultural migrants, traveling from farm to farm, picking fruit and other crops at starvation wages.

(©Bettmann/Getty Images)

THE HUNGRY   Hundreds of men wait to be fed outside the Municipal Lodging House in New York City.

African Americans and the Depression

African Americans were among the groups least aided by the prosperity of the 1920s and most devastated by the hardships of the Great Depression. As the crisis began, over half of all black Americans still lived in the South. Most were farmers. The collapse of prices for cotton and other staple crops left some with no income at all. Many left the land altogether, either by choice or because they had been evicted by landlords who no longer found sharecropping profitable. Some migrated to southern cities. But there, unemployed whites believed they had first claim to what work there was, and some now began displacing African Americans as janitors, street cleaners, and domestic servants. By 1932, over half the blacks in the South were unemployed.

Unsurprisingly, therefore, many black southerners—perhaps 400,000 in all—left the South in the 1930s and journeyed to the cities of the North, where conditions were little better. In New York, black unemployment was nearly 50 percent, in other cities, it was higher. Two million African Americans—half the total black population of the country—were on some form of relief by 1932.

Traditional patterns of segregation and disfranchisement in the South survived the Depression largely unchallenged, while a few particularly notorious examples of racism did attract the attention of the nation. The most celebrated was the **Scottsboro case**. In March 1931, nine young black men, all but one teenagers, were taken off a freight train in northern Alabama (in a small town near Scottsboro) and arrested for vagrancy and disorder. Later, two white women who had also been riding the train accused them of rape. In fact, there was overwhelming evidence, medical and otherwise, that the women had not been raped

(©Bettmann/Getty Images)

DUST STORM, SOUTHWEST PLAINS, 1937 The dust storms of the 1930s were a terrifying experience for all who lived through them. Resembling a black wall sweeping in from the western horizon, such a storm engulfed farms and towns alike, blotting out the light of the sun and covering everything with a fine dirt.

at all; they may have made their accusations out of fear of being arrested themselves. Nevertheless, an all-white jury in Alabama (blacks were routinely barred from jury rolls) quickly convicted all nine of the "Scottsboro boys," as they were known to both friends and foes, and sentenced eight of them to death.

The Supreme Court overturned the convictions in 1932, and a series of new trials began. The International Labor Defense, an organization associated with the Communist Party, came to the aid of the accused youths and began to publicize the case. Meanwhile one of the accusers recanted her testimony. Although the juries who sat on the case never acquitted any of the defendants, all of the accused eventually saw their charges dropped or sentences suspended, though the last of the Scottsboro defendants did not leave prison until 1950.

HISPANICS AND ASIANS IN DEPRESSION AMERICA

Similar patterns of discrimination confronted many Mexicans and Mexican Americans. The Hispanic population of the United States had been growing steadily since early in the century, largely in California and other areas of the Southwest. Chicanos (Mexican Americans) filled many of the same menial jobs there that blacks had traditionally filled in other regions. Some farmed small, marginal tracts, others became agricultural migrants. It had always been a precarious existence, and the Depression made things significantly worse. Unemployed whites in the Southwest demanded jobs held by Hispanics, jobs that whites had previously considered beneath them. Thus Mexican unemployment rose quickly to levels far higher than those for whites. Some officials arbitrarily removed Mexicans from relief rolls or simply rounded up and deported them. Perhaps half a million Chicanos left the United States for Mexico in the first years of the Depression.

There were occasional signs of organized resistance by Mexican Americans themselves, most notably in California, where some formed a union of migrant farmworkers. But harsh repression by local growers and public authorities prevented such organizations from having much impact. As a result, many Hispanics began to migrate to cities such as Los Angeles, where they lived in poverty comparable to that of urban blacks in the South and Northeast.

For Asian Americans, too, the Depression reinforced long-standing patterns of discrimination and economic marginalization. In California, with the largest Japanese American and Chinese American populations, educated Asians had always found it difficult, if not impossible, to move into mainstream professions. Japanese American college graduates often found themselves working in family fruit stands. For those who found jobs in the industrial or service economy, employment was precarious. Like blacks and Hispanics, Asians often lost jobs to white Americans desperate for work. Japanese farmworkers suffered from the increasing competition for even these low-paying jobs with white migrants from the Great Plains.

The overwhelming majority of Chinese Americans worked, as they had for many years, in Chinese-owned laundries and restaurants. Those who moved outside the Asian community could rarely find jobs above the entry level. Chinese women, for example, might find work as stock girls in department stores but almost never as salesclerks. Educated Chinese men and women could hope for virtually no professional opportunities outside the world of Chinatowns.

(©Fox Photos/Hulton Archive/Getty Images)

CHINATOWN, NEW YORK CITY A Chinese man carries a signboard through the streets of New York City's Chinatown bearing the latest news of the war between China and Japan, which in 1938 was well under way. Chinese Americans had the dual challenge in the 1930s of dealing both with large-scale unemployment and with continuing news of catastrophe from China, where most still had family members.

CONSIDER THE SOURCE

MR. TARVER REMEMBERS THE GREAT DEPRESSION (1940)

The Federal Writers' Project (FWP) was a New Deal program that employed authors and researchers during the Great Depression. Participants produced tourist guidebooks, ethnographies, oral histories, and many other kinds of documents. In 1940, an FWP writer interviewed a bank employee named Mr. Tarver.

Yes, I really went through the depression. [. . .] "There were thousands who went down during the panic—lost fortunes, homes, business, and in fact everything. Some have survived, and many never will. A great many were too old to begin building up again. In the kind of work I'm in I have been in position to know some of the devastating effects of it, and it certainly gets on your sympathy.

"I guess you would say I am recovering from it. When I say that though, I'm not boasting, but I'm deeply grateful for the good fortunes that have came my way. Then, too, I feel under everlasting obligations to some of my friends who have helped me to get where I am.

"I had not accumulated a great deal at the time of the panic, but I did have some savings and a good job. That was the trouble, my savings and my job went at the same time. Now that was real trouble. Nobody but my wife and I knew just what we did go through. [. . .]

I was making a fine salary, had a growing savings account, and a host of friends, and no serious troubles to worry about. My wife is just the smartest, thriftiest person you have ever seen. To her I owe a lot of my successes. She is fine with her needle and crocheting, and you never saw her idle. She made all her spending money that way. Even now since we have been in Washington she keeps it up. And her fruit cake! People here rave about it. She cooks an enormous

amount of it every Christmas and sells it for a big profit. She can't fill all the orders she gets. She is very resourceful and right now, if I were to die and not leave her a thing, she would manage some way. One of my hobbies was gardening and it proved to be a profitable one too. This place we rented had a fine garden spot, the finest in Dublin, so every one said. I worked in it early every morning and in the afternoon after banking hours. I sold lots of vegetables, and relied a lot on them—especially the early variety that brought a good price." [. . .]

"One morning we three were at the breakfast table when the phone rang. It was one of the fellows who worked at the bank.

"'Tarver, he said, 'have you heard the news?'

"'What news? No, I haven't heard any news,' said I. What's it all about?'

"'Well,' he said, "hurry on down and see.'

"If you will excuse the expression, when he said that, the seat of my britches almost dropped out. I felt like it meant trouble of some kind. I had had a terrible feeling of uneasiness over the bank for some time. Banks had been closing all over the country. There had been a run on our bank some time previous to that, but we tided that over, and since then it had seemed stronger than ever.

"I hurried down and, sure enough, in front of the bank, there stood a crowd of employees, as blank expressions on their faces as I've ever seen. They were too dumbfounded to be excited even.

"The bank was closed and a notice to that effect on the door. We stood there just looking at each other until finally one said, 'Well, boys, guess we had better go on the inside and see if we can find out what it's all about. I guess there goes our jobs.'

[. . .] "Just as I was getting in the dumps about a regular job, I was notified to report at once, to act as assistant receiver for a defunct bank in Florida. They were feeling the depression there even more than we were in Georgia, and banks were closing every day.

[. . .] "Banks were still closing until it was hard to get enough receivers for them. Oh, we did work. Banks in neighboring towns were added to our work until we were liquidating six banks at one time, all in different places. I had to have another car then but was lucky to pick up a good used car almost at my own price. People had lost their cars as well as their homes, so it was no trouble to buy a good used one. Sometimes I would ride to all six of these banks in one day and when night came I would be completely given out. I couldn't stop even then, for there was scarcely a night that we didn't work."

UNDERSTAND, ANALYZE, & EVALUATE

1. Why was Mr. Tarver doubly affected by the banking crisis of the Great Depression? How did Mr. and Mrs. Tarver compensate for their losses in the job market?

2. How might the Great Depression have shaped the outlook of Mr. and Mrs. Tarver on work, leisure, and consumption for years, if not decades, to come?

Source: Mr. W. W. Tarver (White), Finance Officer in U.S. Treasury (Bank Conservator), 5001 Nebraska Ave., N.W., Washington, D.C., interviewed by Bradley. Library of Congress, *American Life Histories: Manuscripts from the Federal Writers' Project, 1936–1940.* http://memory.loc.gov/cgi bin/query/r?ammem/wpa:@field%28DOCID+@lit%28wpa112060215%29%29

WOMEN AND FAMILIES IN THE GREAT DEPRESSION

The economic crisis strengthened the widespread belief that a woman's proper place was in the home. Many men and women believed that with employment so scarce, what work there was should go to men and that no woman whose husband was employed should accept a job. Indeed, from 1932 until 1937, it was illegal for more than one member of a family to hold a federal civil service job.

But the widespread assumption that married women, at least, should not work outside the home did not stop them from doing so. Both single and married women worked in the 1930s because they or their families needed the money. Some women did small jobs at home or sold food or goods to make ends meet. (See "Consider the Source: Mr. Tarver Remembers the Great Depression.") By the end of the Depression, 25 percent more women were working for wages than had been doing so at the beginning, despite considerable obstacles. Professional opportunities for women declined because unemployed men began moving into professions that had previously been considered women's fields. Female industrial workers were more likely to be laid off or to experience wage reductions than their male counterparts. But white women also had certain advantages in the workplace. The nonprofessional jobs that women traditionally held—salesclerks, stenographers, and other service positions—were less likely to disappear than the predominantly male jobs in heavy industry.

Black women suffered massive unemployment, particularly in the South, because of a great reduction of domestic service jobs. As many as half of all black working women lost their jobs in the 1930s. Even so, at the end of the 1930s, 38 percent of black women were employed, as compared with 24 percent of white women, mirroring the broader historical pattern that economic necessity drove married and unmarried black women into the workforce at a higher rate than white women.

The Depression also worked to erode the strength of many family units. There was a decline in the divorce rate, but largely because divorce was expensive. More common was the informal breakup of families, particularly the desertion of families by unemployed men trying to escape the humiliation of being unable to earn a living. The marriage rate and the birthrate both declined for the first time since the early nineteenth century.

THE DEPRESSION AND AMERICAN CULTURE

The Great Depression was a traumatic experience for millions of Americans. Out of the crisis emerged probing criticisms of American life. But the Depression also produced powerful confirmations of more traditional values and reinforced many traditional goals. There was not one Depression culture, but many.

DEPRESSION VALUES

Prosperity and industrial growth had done much to shape American values in the 1920s. Yet even when hard times came, American social values seemed to change relatively little in response to the Depression. Instead, many people responded to hard times by redoubling their commitment to familiar ideas and goals. The Depression did not destroy the success ethic.

The survival of the ideals of work and individual responsibility was evident in many ways, not least in the reactions of those traumatized by unemployment. Some expressed anger and struck out at the economic system. Many, however, seemed to blame themselves. At the same time, millions responded eagerly to reassurances that they could, through their own efforts, restore themselves to prosperity. **Dale Carnegie**'s *How to Win Friends and Influence People* (1936), a self-help manual preaching individual initiative, was one of the best-selling books of the decade.

Yet the most popular cultural products of the 1930s diverted attention away from the Depression. And they came to Americans primarily through the two most powerful instruments of popular culture in the 1930s—radio and the movies. (For another powerful vehicle of escapist culture, see "Patterns of Popular Culture: The Golden Age of Comic Books.")

RADIO

Almost every American family had a radio in the 1930s. Even in remote rural areas without access to electricity, many families purchased radios and hooked them up to car batteries when they wished to listen.

Radio was often a community experience. Young people would place radios on their front porches and invite friends by to listen, talk, or dance. In poor urban neighborhoods, people would gather on a street or in a backyard to hear sporting events or concerts. Within families, the radio often drew parents and children together to listen to favorite programs.

Although radio stations occasionally carried provocative programs, the staple of broadcasting was escapism, including comedies such as *Amos 'n' Andy* (with its demeaning picture of urban blacks) and adventures such as *Superman, Dick Tracy*, and *The Lone Ranger*. Radio brought a new kind of comedy to a wide audience. Jack Benny, George Burns and Gracie Allen, and other masters of elaborately timed repartee began to develop broad followings. Soap operas were enormously popular escapist entertainment in which emotionally charged stories unfolded on a daily or weekly basis. These radio dramas were generally sponsored by soap companies, whose advertising was targeted at women who were alone in the house during the day.

Radio provided Americans with their first direct access to important public events. On-air coverage of news and sports expanded rapidly to meet the demand. Radio carried some of the most dramatic moments of the 1930s: the World Series, the Academy Awards, political conventions. When the German dirigible *Hindenburg* crashed in flames in Lakehurst, New Jersey, in 1937, it produced an enormous national reaction largely because of the live radio account by a broadcaster, overcome with emotion, who cried out, "Oh the humanity! Oh the humanity!" The actor-director Orson Welles created another memorable event on Halloween night, 1938, when he broadcast a radio play about aliens landing in central New Jersey who had set off toward New York armed with terrible weapons. The play took the form of a news broadcast, and it created panic among some people who believed the events were real.

THE MOVIES

In the first years of the Depression, movie attendance dropped significantly. By the mid-1930s, however, most Americans had resumed their moviegoing habits in part because the movies (now with sound and, by the end of the decade, color) were becoming more appealing.

Hollywood continued to exercise tight control over its products in the 1930s through its resilient censor Will Hays, who ensured that most movies carried no sensational or controversial messages. The studio system—through which a few large movie companies exercised iron control over actors, writers, and directors—also worked to ensure that Hollywood films avoided controversy.

Neither the censor nor the studio system, however, could completely prevent films from exploring social questions. There were many serious films that portrayed the problems of the Depression, including King Vidor's *Our Daily Bread* (1932) and John Ford's adaptation of *The Grapes of Wrath* (1940). Gangster movies such as *Little Caesar* (1930) and *The Public Enemy* (1931) portrayed a dark, gritty, violent world with which few Americans were familiar, but their desperate stories were popular with those engaged in their own struggles.

But the most effective presentation of a social message came from the Italian-born director **Frank Capra**. Capra had a deep love for his adopted country, and he translated that love into a vaguely populistic admiration for ordinary people. He contrasted the decency of small-town America and the common man with what he considered the opportunism of the city and the capitalist marketplace. In *Mr. Deeds Goes to Town* (1936), a simple man from a small town inherits a large fortune, moves to the city, and—not liking the greed and dishonesty he finds there—gives the money away and moves back home. In *Mr. Smith Goes to Washington* (1939), a decent man from a western state is elected to the U.S. Senate, refuses to join in the self-interested politics of Washington, and dramatically exposes the corruption and selfishness of his colleagues. Capra's popular films helped audiences in the 1930s find solace in a vision of an imagined American past of warmth, goodness, and honesty.

More often, however, the commercial films of the 1930s, like most radio programs, were deliberately and explicitly escapist: lavish musicals such as *Gold Diggers of 1933*, "screwball" comedies such as Capra's *It Happened One Night*, or the films of the Marx Brothers, pictures designed to divert audiences from their troubles and indulge fantasies about easy wealth.

The 1930s were the first years of Walt Disney's long reign as the champion of animation and children's entertainment. After producing cartoon shorts for theaters in the late 1920s, many of them starring the newly created character Mickey Mouse, Disney began to produce feature-length animated films, starting in 1937 with *Snow White*. Other enormously popular movies of the 1930s were adaptations of popular novels, such as *The Wizard of Oz* and *Gone with the Wind*, both released in 1939.

THE GOLDEN AGE OF COMIC BOOKS

In the troubled years of the Great Depression (and later, World War II), many Americans sought release from their anxieties in fantasy. Movies, plays, books, radio shows, and other diversions drew people out of their own lives and into a safer or more glamorous or more exciting world. Beginning in 1938, one of the most popular forms of escape for many young Americans was the comic book.

In February 1935, Malcolm Wheeler-Nicholson founded the first comics magazine—what we now know as the "comic book"—titled *New Fun*. It was not successful, but Wheeler founded the company Detective Comics. He began in 1937 to design a new magazine called *Action Comics*. Wheeler ran out of money before he could publish anything, but the company continued without him. In 1938, the first issue of *Action Comics* appeared with a startling and controversial cover—a powerful man in a skintight suit lifting a car over his head. His name was Superman, and he became the most popular cartoon character of all time.

Within a year, Superman had a comic book named after him, which was selling over 1.2 million copies each issue. By 1940, there was a popular Superman radio show, introduced by a breathless announcer crying, "It's a bird! It's a plane! It's . . . Superman!" Soon, other publishers began developing new *superheroes* (a term invented by the creators of Superman) to capitalize on this growing popular appetite. In 1939, a second great comic book publisher appeared—Marvel Comics.

By the early 1940s, Superman had been joined by other superheroes: the Human Torch, the Sub-Mariner, Batman, the Flash, and Wonder Woman, a character created in part to signal the importance of women to the war effort.

It is not hard to imagine why superheroes would be so appealing to Americans in the 1930s and 1940s—particularly to the teenage boys who were the largest single purchasers of comic books. Superman and other superheroes were idealized versions of the ideal boy—smart, good, "the perfect Boy Scout," as one fan put it. But they were also all-powerful, capable of righting wrong and preventing catastrophe. As the national economy faltered, comic book heroes modeled patriotic pride, resilience, and optimism. They operated with moral certainty when so much was uncertain. At a time of suffering, superheroes offered escape.

Many of the early comic book writers were young Jewish men, conscious of their outsider status in an American culture not yet wholly open to them. Almost all the characters they created had alter egos, identities they used while living within the normal world. Superman was Clark Kent, a "mild-mannered reporter." Batman was Bruce Wayne, a wealthy heir. All were part of mainstream American society, and they expressed in part the outsider's dream of assimilation. The superheroes themselves were outsiders too, but outsiders endowed with special powers and abilities unavailable to ordinary people.

In the last years of the Depression, the comic superheroes began battling the Axis powers. Marvel's Human Torch and Sub-Mariner joined forces against the German navy. Superman fought spies and

(©Hulton Archive/Getty Images)

SUPERMAN The most popular action figure in the history of comic books was Superman, whose superhuman powers were particularly appealing fantasies to Americans suffering through the Depression and, later, World War II.

saboteurs at home. Captain America, a new character created in March 1941, was a frail young man rejected by the army who, after being given a secret serum by a military doctor, became extraordinarily powerful. The cover of the first issue of *Captain America* showed the title character punching Adolf Hitler in his headquarters in Germany.

The end of the war was also the end of this first golden age of American comic books. New comic books emphasized romance, mild sexuality, and, over time, violence and cruelty. But comic books never surpassed the heights of popularity they attained during the Depression and World War II. •

UNDERSTAND, ANALYZE, & EVALUATE

1. What could comic books offer readers suffering through the crisis of the Great Depression?
2. How and why have comic book superheroes changed over time?

Hollywood did little to challenge the conventions of popular culture on issues of gender and race. Women in movies were portrayed overwhelmingly as wives, mothers, or attractive flirts. Mae West portrayed herself in a series of successful films as an overtly sexual woman manipulating men through her attractiveness. Few films included important African American characters. Most black men and women on the silver screen were portrayed as servants or farmhands or entertainers, or had their history as enslaved peoples romanticized for white audiences.

LITERATURE AND JOURNALISM

Much literature and journalism in the 1930s dealt directly or indirectly with the tremendous disillusionment, and the increasing radicalism, of the time.

Not all literature, of course, was challenging or controversial. The most popular books and magazines of the 1930s, in fact, were as escapist and romantic as many radio shows and movies. Two of the best-selling novels of the decade were romantic sagas set in earlier eras: Margaret Mitchell's *Gone with the Wind* (1936) and Hervey Allen's *Anthony Adverse* (1933). Leading magazines focused more on fashions, stunts, scenery, and the arts than on the social conditions of the nation. The new and enormously popular photographic journal *Life* **magazine**, first published in 1936, had the largest readership of any publication in the United States other than *Reader's Digest*. It devoted some attention to politics and the economic conditions of the Depression, but it was best known for stunning photographs

(©Silver Screen Collection/Moviepix/Getty Images)

THE WIZARD OF OZ Whatever contemporary political messages L. Frank Baum may have embedded in his 1900 novel, *The Wizard of Oz*, the 1939 cinematic version featured memorable characters shot in vivid Technicolor. Dorothy, the Tin Man, the Cowardly Lion, the Scarecrow, and the Wicked Witch of the West, shown here, offered escapist fantasy for mass audiences during the Great Depression.

of sporting and theater events, natural landscapes, and public projects. One of its most popular features was "*Life* Goes to a Party," which took the chatty social columns of daily newspapers and turned them into glossy photographic glimpses of the rich and famous but also ordinary people at lavish parties.

Other Depression writing, however, frankly challenged the dominant values of American popular culture. Some of the most significant literature offered portraits of the harshness and emptiness of American life: **John Dos Passos**'s *U.S.A.* trilogy (1930–1936), which attacked what he considered the materialistic madness of American culture; **Richard Wright**'s *Native Son* (1940), the story of a young African American man broken by racial oppression; Nathanael West's *Miss Lonelyhearts* (1933), the story of an advice columnist overwhelmed by the sadness he encounters in the lives of those who consult him; Jack Conroy's *The Disinherited* (1933), a harsh portrait of the lives of coal miners; and James T. Farrell's *Studs Lonigan* (1932), the tale of a lost, hardened working-class youth. Perhaps the best-known depiction of Depression-era life is **John Steinbeck**'s *The Grapes of Wrath* (1939). The novel's main characters are the Joad family, migrants from the **Dust Bowl** to California who encounter an unending string of calamities and failures. Their story offers a critique of the exploitative features of agrarian life in the West, as well as a tribute to the fortitude of the community the Joads represent.

THE POPULAR FRONT AND THE LEFT

The American Communist Party (CPUSA), a relatively small organization in the early twentieth century, gained credibility during the Great Depression as the capitalist system's flaws were exposed. Meanwhile, in 1935 the Soviet Union called for a **Popular Front** against fascism, which materialized in the United States as a broad coalition of groups on the left. In this environment of cooperation, the Soviet party leader **Josef Stalin** and the CPUSA softened their attitude toward President Franklin Roosevelt (elected in 1932), hoping that he would become an ally against fascism in Germany. The Popular Front formed loose alliances with progressive groups, and it praised even some strong anticommunists such as the labor leader John L. Lewis. The CPUSA flourished under these conditions, adding tens of thousands of members, though not all members of the Popular Front considered themselves communists. But in its heyday, the antifascist movement enhanced the reputation and influence of the Communist Party while also helping collapse some of the divisions on the American left. For a time, communists, civil rights activists, labor leaders, and liberals united around the Popular Front's cause.

One of the key events of the mid-1930s that rallied the American left was the **Spanish Civil War**. The war pitted the forces supporting Francisco Franco, who received aid from the fascists Hitler and Mussolini, against the republican government of Spain. A substantial group of young Americans—more than 3,000 in all—formed the **Abraham Lincoln Brigade** and traveled to Spain to fight an ultimately losing battle against fascism on the side of the republicans. The CPUSA was instrumental in creating the Lincoln Brigade and directed many of its activities.

The American Communist Party was active as well in organizing the unemployed in the early 1930s, and it staged a hunger march in Washington, D.C., in 1931. Party members were among the most effective union organizers in some industries. And the party was virtually alone among political organizations in taking a firm stand in favor of racial justice.

(©Daily Express/Hulton Archive/Getty Images)

THE SPANISH CIVIL WAR Many Americans took up arms to help the republican forces fight against Franco and his army. The novelist Ernest Hemingway joined them in Spain as a reporter and supporter of the republicans. He spent much of his time talking with both American and Spanish troops as well as (in this image) the Dutch filmmaker Joris Ivens. His novel *For Whom the Bell Tolls* was inspired by his experience in the civil war.

Its active defense of the Scottsboro defendants was but one example of its efforts to ally itself with the aspirations of African Americans.

The CPUSA was not, however, the open, patriotic organization it tried to project. It was always under the close and rigid supervision of the Soviet Union. The subordination of the party leadership to the Russians was most clearly demonstrated in 1939, when Stalin signed a nonaggression pact with Nazi Germany. Moscow sent orders to the American Communist Party to abandon the Popular Front and return to its old stance of harsh criticism of American liberals. Communist Party leaders in the United States immediately obeyed, though thousands of disillusioned members left the party as a result.

The Socialist Party of America, under the leadership of Norman Thomas, also cited the economic crisis as evidence of the failure of capitalism and sought vigorously to win public support for its own political program. Among other things, it attempted to mobilize support among the rural poor. The Southern Tenant Farmers Union (STFU), supported by the party and organized by a young socialist, H. L. Mitchell, attempted to create a biracial coalition of sharecroppers, tenant farmers, and others to demand economic reform. Neither the STFU nor the party itself, however, made any real progress toward establishing socialism as a major force in American politics.

(Source: Library of Congress, Prints and Photographs Division [LC-USF34-009872-E])

MIGRANT FAMILY This photograph by the Great Depression photographer Dorothea Lange portrays the son of an Oklahoma family of migrants on a roadside in California. It suggests the plight of hundreds of thousands of families who fled the regions affected by drought in the 1930s—a devastation that became known as the Dust Bowl.

While the left was broadening its appeal in the 1930s, antiradicalism remained a powerful force. Hostility toward the Communist Party, in particular, was intense at many levels of government. Congressional committees chaired by Hamilton Fish of New York and Martin Dies of Texas investigated communist influence wherever they could find or imagine it. White southerners tried to drive communist organizers out of the countryside, just as growers in California and elsewhere tried unsuccessfully to keep communists from organizing Mexican American and other workers.

At few times before in American history, and few since, did being part of the left seem so respectable and even conventional among workers, intellectuals, and others. The 1930s witnessed an impressive, if temporary, widening of the ideological range of mainstream art and politics. The Roosevelt administration's New Deal, for example, sponsored artistic work through the Works Projects Administration that was frankly challenging to the capitalist norms of the 1920s. The filmmaker Pare Lorentz, with funding from New Deal agencies, made two powerful documentaries—*The Plow That Broke the Plains* (1936) and *The River* (1937)—that combined a celebration of New Deal programs with a harsh critique of industrial capitalism's exploitation of people and the environment.

Other New Deal–sponsored artists sought to reveal the harshness of poverty and the human cost of social neglect. Notable among them were numerous documentary photographers, many of them employed by the Farm Security Administration, who traveled through rural areas recording the ravaged nature of agricultural life. They included some of the great photographers of their era—Dorothea Lange, Margaret Bourke-White, Arthur Rothstein, Russell Lee, Walker Evans, Ben Shahn, and others. Writers, too, devoted themselves to exposing social injustice, some of them working through the New Deal's Federal Writers' Project and Federal Art Project.

THE ORDEAL OF HERBERT HOOVER

Herbert Hoover began his presidency in March 1929 believing, like most Americans, that the nation faced a bright and prosperous future. For the first six months of his administration, he attempted to expand the associational policies he had advocated for eight years as secretary of commerce. The economic crisis that began before the year was out forced Hoover to deal with a new set of problems. But he tended to rely on principles that had always governed his public life.

THE HOOVER PROGRAM

Hoover first responded to the Depression by attempting to restore public confidence in the economy. "The fundamental business of this country, that is, production and distribution of commodities," he said in 1930, "is on a sound and prosperous basis." He then summoned leaders of business, labor, and agriculture to the White House and urged them to adopt a program of voluntary cooperation for recovery. He implored businessmen not to cut production or lay off workers; he talked labor leaders into forgoing demands for higher wages or better hours. But by mid-1931, economic conditions had deteriorated so much that the structure of voluntary cooperation had collapsed.

Hoover also attempted to use government spending as a tool for fighting the Depression. The president proposed to Congress a significant increase ($423 million) in federal public works programs, and he encouraged state and local governments to fund public construction.

But the spending was not nearly enough. And when economic conditions worsened, he became less willing to increase spending, worrying instead about keeping the budget balanced.

Even before the stock market crash, Hoover had begun to construct a program to assist the troubled agricultural economy. In April 1929, he proposed the **Agricultural Marketing Act**, which established the first major government program to help farmers maintain prices. A federally sponsored Farm Board would make loans to national marketing cooperatives or establish corporations to buy surpluses and thus raise prices. At the same time, Hoover attempted to protect American farmers from international competition by raising agricultural tariffs. The **Hawley-Smoot Tariff** of 1930 increased protection on seventy-five farm products. But neither the Agricultural Marketing Act nor the Hawley-Smoot Tariff ultimately helped American farmers significantly. Agricultural surpluses, combined with declining consumption, kept the farm economy in crisis.

By the spring of 1931, Herbert Hoover's political position had deteriorated considerably. In the 1930 congressional elections, Democrats won control of the House and made substantial inroads in the Senate. Many Americans blamed the president personally for the crisis and attached the name "**Hoovervilles**" to the shantytowns unemployed people established on the outskirts of cities. Democrats urged the president to support more vigorous programs of relief and public spending. Hoover, instead, seized on a slight improvement in economic conditions early in 1931 as proof that his policies were working. The international financial panic of the spring of 1931 destroyed that illusion.

By the time Congress convened in December 1931, conditions had grown so desperate that Hoover supported a series of measures designed to keep endangered banks afloat and protect homeowners from foreclosure on their mortgages. Most important was a bill passed in January 1932 establishing the **Reconstruction Finance Corporation (RFC)**, a government agency to provide federal loans to troubled banks, railroads, and other businesses. Unlike some earlier Hoover programs, the RFC operated on a large scale. In 1932, it had a budget of $1.5 billion for public works alone.

That was a large sum, but the RFC did not spend all of it. The new agency lent funds only to financial institutions with sufficient collateral, so much of its money went to large banks and corporations. At Hoover's insistence, it helped finance only those public works projects that promised ultimately to pay for themselves—toll bridges, public housing, and others. So although the RFC represented a more energetic attempt by the federal government to stabilize the economy, it failed to have a major impact on the Depression.

POPULAR PROTEST

For the first several years of the Depression, most Americans were either too stunned or too confused to raise much effective protest. By the middle of 1932, however, dissident voices began to be heard.

In the summer of 1932, a group of unhappy farm owners gathered in Des Moines, Iowa, to establish a new organization: the Farmers' Holiday Association, which endorsed the withholding of farm products from the market—in effect a farmers' strike. The strike began in August in western Iowa, spread briefly to a few neighboring areas, and succeeded in blockading several markets. But in the end, it dissolved in failure.

A more celebrated protest movement emerged from American veterans. In 1924, Congress had approved the payment of a $1,000 bonus in 1945 to all those who had served in World War I. By 1932, however, many veterans were demanding that the bonus be paid immediately. Hoover, concerned about balancing the budget, rejected their appeal. In June, more than

20,000 veterans, members of the self-proclaimed Bonus Expeditionary Force, or "**Bonus Army**," marched into Washington, built crude camps around the city, and promised to stay until Congress approved legislation to pay the bonus. Some of the veterans departed in July after Congress had voted down their proposal. Many, however, remained in Washington.

Their continued presence in Washington embarrassed President Hoover. Finally, in mid-July, he ordered police to clear the marchers out of several abandoned federal buildings in which they had been staying. A few marchers threw rocks at the police. Someone opened fire, and two veterans fell dead. Hoover called the incident evidence of uncontrolled violence and radicalism and ordered the U.S. Army to assist the police in clearing out the buildings.

General Douglas MacArthur, the army chief of staff, carried out the mission himself and greatly exceeded the president's orders. He led the Third Cavalry, two infantry regiments, a machine-gun detachment, and six tanks down Pennsylvania Avenue in pursuit of

(©Bettmann/Getty Images)

CLEARING OUT THE BONUS MARCHERS In July 1932, President Hoover ordered the Washington, D.C., police to evict the Bonus Marchers from some of the public buildings and land they had been occupying. After a series of skirmishes between police and the protesters, Hoover ordered the U.S. Army to complete the eviction.

the Bonus Army. The veterans fled in terror. MacArthur followed them across the Anacostia River, where he ordered the soldiers to burn their tent city to the ground. More than 100 marchers were injured.

The incident dealt another blow to Hoover's already battered political standing. The "Great Engineer," the personification of the optimistic 1920s, had become a symbol of the nation's failure to deal effectively with its startling reversal of fortune.

HOOVER AND THE WORLD CRISIS

By 1931, the world financial crisis had produced a rising nationalism in Europe and Japan. It soon toppled some existing political leaders and replaced them with powerful, belligerent governments committed to expansion. Herbert Hoover thus confronted the beginning of a process that would ultimately lead to war.

In Latin America, Hoover tried to repair some of the damage done by earlier American policies. He made a ten-week goodwill tour through Latin America before his inauguration. Once in office, he generally abstained from intervening in the internal affairs of neighboring nations and moved to withdraw American troops from Nicaragua and Haiti. He also announced a new policy: America would grant diplomatic recognition to any sitting government in the region without questioning the means it had used to obtain power. He even repudiated the Theodore Roosevelt Corollary to the Monroe Doctrine by refusing to permit American intervention when several Latin American countries defaulted on debt obligations in October 1931.

In Europe, the administration enjoyed few successes. When Hoover's proposed moratorium on debts failed to produce financial stability, he refused to cancel all war debts to the United States as many economists advised him to do. Several European nations promptly went into default. Efforts to extend the 1921 limits on naval construction fell victim to French and British fears of German and Japanese militarism.

(©Instituto Nazionale Luce/Alinari Archives/Getty Images)

HITLER AND MUSSOLINI IN BERLIN The German and Italian dictators (shown here reviewing Nazi troops in Berlin in the mid-1930s) acted publicly as if they were equals. Privately, Hitler treated Mussolini with contempt, and Mussolini complained constantly of being a junior partner in the relationship.

The ineffectiveness of American diplomacy in Europe was particularly troubling in light of the rise of **fascism**, an ideology that rejected democratic forms of government in favor of concentrated state power under a dictator. **Benito Mussolini**'s Fascist Party had been in control of Italy since the early 1920s and had become increasingly nationalistic and militaristic. Still more ominous was the growing power of the **National Socialist (or Nazi) Party** in Germany. By the late 1920s, the Weimar Republic, the nation's government since the end of World War I, had been largely discredited by, among other things, a ruinous inflation. **Adolf Hitler**, the leader of the Nazis, grew rapidly in popular favor and took power in 1933. He believed in, among other things, the genetic superiority of the Aryan (German) people and in extending German territory to provide *Lebensraum* (living space) for what he called the German "master race." He displayed a pathological anti-Semitism and a passionate militarism.

More immediately alarming to the Hoover administration was a major crisis in Asia—another early step toward World War II. The Japanese, suffering from an economic depression of their own, were concerned about the increasing power of the Soviet Union and about the insistence of the Chinese leader Chiang Kai-shek on expanding his government's power in Manchuria, officially a part of China but over which the Japanese had maintained informal economic control since 1905. In 1931, Japan's military leaders staged what was, in effect, a coup in Tokyo. Shortly after that, a railroad explosion in southern Manchuria, likely set by Japanese soldiers (and known as the "Mukden Incident"), served as a pretext for a Japanese invasion of northern Manchuria. They had conquered the region by the end of the year. Secretary of State Henry Stimson issued stern warnings to the Japanese but to no avail. Early in 1932, Japan moved farther into China, attacking the city of Shanghai and killing thousands of civilians.

THE ELECTION OF 1932

As the 1932 presidential election approached, few people doubted the outcome. The Republican Party dutifully renominated Herbert Hoover for a second term of office, but few delegates believed he could win. The Democrats, in the meantime, gathered in Chicago to nominate the governor of New York, **Franklin Delano Roosevelt**.

Roosevelt had been a well-known figure in the party for many years already. A Hudson Valley aristocrat, a distant cousin of Theodore Roosevelt, and a handsome, charming young man, he progressed rapidly from a seat in the New York State legislature to a position as assistant secretary of the navy during World War I to his party's vice presidential nomination in 1920 with James M. Cox. Less than a year later, he was stricken with polio. Although he never regained use of his legs, and could walk only by using crutches and braces, he built up sufficient physical strength to return to politics in 1928. When Al Smith received the Democratic nomination for president that year, Roosevelt was elected to succeed him as governor. In 1930, he easily won reelection.

Roosevelt worked no miracles in New York, but he did initiate enough government assistance to be able to present himself as a more imaginative leader than Hoover. In national politics, he avoided divisive cultural issues and emphasized the economic grievances that most Democrats shared. As a result, he was able to assemble a broad coalition within the party and win its nomination. In a dramatic break with tradition, he flew to Chicago to address the Democratic National Convention in person and accept the nomination. In the course of his acceptance speech, Roosevelt made a ringing promise: "I pledge you, I pledge myself, to a new deal for the American people." Neither then nor in the subsequent campaign did Roosevelt give much indication of what that program would be. But Herbert Hoover's unpopularity virtually ensured Roosevelt's election.

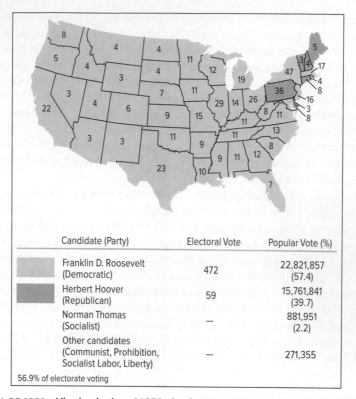

Candidate (Party)	Electoral Vote	Popular Vote (%)
Franklin D. Roosevelt (Democratic)	472	22,821,857 (57.4)
Herbert Hoover (Republican)	59	15,761,841 (39.7)
Norman Thomas (Socialist)	–	881,951 (2.2)
Other candidates (Communist, Prohibition, Socialist Labor, Liberty)	–	271,355

56.9% of electorate voting

THE ELECTION OF 1932 Like the election of 1928, the election of 1932 was exceptionally one-sided. But this time, the landslide favored the Democratic candidate, Franklin Roosevelt, who overwhelmed Herbert Hoover in all regions of the country except New England. Roosevelt obviously benefited from disillusionment with Hoover's response to the Great Depression. • *But what characteristics of Roosevelt himself contributed to his victory?*

Roosevelt won by a landslide, receiving 57.4 percent of the popular vote to Hoover's 39.7, and carried every state except Delaware, Pennsylvania, Connecticut, Vermont, New Hampshire, and Maine. Democrats won large majorities in both houses of Congress. It was a convincing mandate, but it was not yet clear what Roosevelt intended to do with it.

THE "INTERREGNUM"

The period between the election and the inauguration, which in the early 1930s lasted more than four months, was a season of growing economic crisis. Presidents-elect traditionally do not involve themselves directly in government. But in a series of brittle exchanges, Hoover tried to exact a pledge from the incoming Roosevelt to maintain policies of economic orthodoxy. Roosevelt genially refused.

In February, only a month before the inauguration, a new crisis developed when the collapse of the American banking system suddenly and rapidly accelerated. Depositors withdrew their money in panic; and one bank after another closed its doors and declared bankruptcy. Hoover again asked Roosevelt to give prompt public assurances that there would be no tinkering with the currency, no heavy borrowing, no unbalancing of the budget. Roosevelt again refused.

March 4, 1933, was, therefore, a day of both economic crisis and considerable personal bitterness. On that morning, Herbert Hoover rode glumly down Pennsylvania Avenue with a beaming, buoyant Franklin Roosevelt, who would shortly be sworn in as the thirty-second president of the United States.

CONCLUSION

The Great Depression changed many things in American life. It created unemployment unprecedented in the nation's history. It put enormous pressures on families, communities, state and local governments, and Washington. The innovative but ultimately failed presidency of Herbert Hoover was unable to produce policies capable of dealing with the crisis. In the nation's politics and culture, there were strong currents of radicalism and protest, and many middle-class Americans came to fear that a revolution might be approaching.

In reality, while the Great Depression shook much of American society and culture, it actually toppled very little. The capitalist system survived, damaged for a time but never truly threatened. The values of materialism and personal responsibility were shaken but never overturned. The American people in the 1930s were more receptive than they had been in the 1920s to evocations of community, generosity, and the dignity of common people. They were more open to experiments in government and business and even private lives than they had been in earlier years. But for most Americans, belief in the "American way of life" remained strong throughout the long years of economic despair.

KEY TERMS/PEOPLE/PLACES/EVENTS

Abraham Lincoln Brigade 577
Adolf Hitler 583
Agricultural Marketing Act 580
Benito Mussolini 583
Bonus Army 581
Dale Carnegie 572
Dust Bowl 576
fascism 583

Frank Capra 573
Franklin Delano Roosevelt 583
Great Depression 562
Hawley-Smoot Tariff 580
Hindenburg 573
Hoovervilles 580
John Dos Passos 576
John Steinbeck 576
Josef Stalin 577

Life magazine 575
National Socialist (Nazi) Party 583
Okies 566
Popular Front 577
Reconstruction Finance Corporation (RFC) 580
Richard Wright 576
Scottsboro case 567
Spanish Civil War 577

RECALL AND REFLECT

1. Was the 1929 stock market crash the cause of the Depression? Why or why not?
2. How did farmers fare during the Depression? What environmental conditions contributed to their plight?
3. How did popular entertainment and the arts respond to the needs of Depression-era audiences?
4. What popular protests arose in response to the Depression? How successful were these protests?
5. How did Hoover's political beliefs affect his attempt to deal with the economic crisis of the Depression?

24 | THE NEW DEAL ERA

LAUNCHING THE NEW DEAL
THE NEW DEAL IN TRANSITION
THE NEW DEAL IN DISARRAY
ISOLATION AND INTERNATIONALISM
LIMITS AND LEGACIES OF THE NEW DEAL

LOOKING AHEAD

1. What emergency measures did Franklin Delano Roosevelt (FDR) take in his first hundred days as president?
2. Who were the major critics of FDR's New Deal, and how did their criticisms influence FDR's "Second New Deal"?
3. What were the principal achievements of the Second New Deal in 1935?
4. How did the economic crisis of the worldwide Great Depression help create new political orders in many nations?

DURING HIS TWELVE YEARS IN OFFICE, Franklin Roosevelt became more central to the life of the nation than any president had ever been. Simmering tensions around the world exploded into a catastrophic war, one that ultimately enveloped the United States and millions upon millions of its citizens. Meanwhile he faced the worst economic crisis in American history. His administration constructed a series of reforms (the New Deal) that fundamentally altered the federal government and its relationship to society.

Roosevelt never had a single, guiding philosophy for his programs but rather experimented with all manner of reforms to relieve suffering, stabilize the economy, and prevent comparable catastrophes in the future. Nevertheless, the New Deal did change across its two major phases, becoming more anticorporate and more focused on making long-term structural changes to the national economy and people's personal welfare. By the end of the 1930s, the Roosevelt administration had galvanized a powerful coalition within the Democratic Party that would dominate American politics for most of the next thirty years and had generated the beginnings of a new liberal ideology that would drive reform efforts for decades.

Despite its successes, Roosevelt's New Deal did not end the Great Depression. Near the close of Roosevelt's second term in 1940, many of the basic problems of the Depression remained unsolved. The persistence of those problems fueled attacks from dissident groups on the right and the left, some of them of considerable size and strength. These critics mobilized in the business world and outside the conventional party system to promote alternative paths to recovery. Factions with the Democratic Party, mainly conservative southerners, turned against Roosevelt's policies, joined with Republicans, and helped forge a conservative coalition in Congress that thwarted many of his goals. Only the preparations for World War II in 1940 and 1941 succeeded in ending the Great Depression. Although the New Deal ended with the war, some of its initiatives and philosophies, and the criticisms they provoked, would combine to create the broad outlines of the political world we know today.

LAUNCHING THE NEW DEAL

Roosevelt's first task upon taking office was to alleviate the panic that was creating chaos in the financial system. He did so in part by force of personality and in part by rapidly constructing an ambitious and diverse program of legislation. These laws would collectively come to be known by the term Roosevelt had used during the campaign: the **New Deal**.

RESTORING CONFIDENCE

Much of Roosevelt's early success was a result of his ebullient personality. He was the first president to make regular use of the radio. His **fireside chats**, during which he explained in simple terms his programs and plans to the people, helped build confidence in the administration. But Roosevelt could not rely on image alone. On March 6, two days after taking office, he issued a proclamation closing all banks for four days until Congress could meet in special session to consider banking reform legislation. So great was the panic about bank failures that the "bank holiday," as the president euphemistically described it, created a general sense of relief and hope.

TIME LINE

1931
Japan invades Manchuria

1933
"First New Deal" legislation
Prohibition ends
U.S. recognizes Soviet Union
Good Neighbor Policy

1934
American Liberty League founded
Long's Share-Our-Wealth Society established

1935
Supreme Court invalidates NRA
"Second New Deal" legislation, including Social Security and Wagner Acts
Lewis breaks with AFL

1936
Supreme Court invalidates Agricultural Adjustment Act
CIO established
Roosevelt reelected
Sit-down strikes

1937
Roosevelt's "Court-packing" plan
Supreme Court upholds Wagner Act
Severe recession
FDR's "quarantine speech"

1938
Fair Labor Standards Act
Munich Conference

1939
Nazi/USSR pact
Germany invades Poland

Three days later, Roosevelt sent to Congress the Emergency Banking Act, a generally conservative bill designed primarily to protect the larger banks from being dragged down by the weakness of smaller ones. The bill provided for Treasury Department inspection of all banks before they would be allowed to reopen. It also provided federal assistance to some troubled institutions and a thorough reorganization of those banks in the greatest difficulty. Congress passed the bill within a few hours of its introduction. Whatever else the new law accomplished, it helped dispel panic. Three-quarters of the banks in the Federal Reserve system reopened within the next three days, and $1 billion in hoarded currency and gold flowed back into them within a month. The immediate banking crisis was over.

On the morning after passage of the Emergency Banking Act, Roosevelt sent to Congress another measure—the Economy Act—designed to convince the public (and especially the business community) that the federal government was in safe, responsible hands. The act proposed to balance the federal budget by cutting the salaries of government employees and reducing pensions to veterans by as much as 15 percent. Like the banking bill, this one passed through Congress almost instantly, even though the cost cutting reduced the growth of the economy. Roosevelt then signed the Glass-Steagall Act of June 1933, which gave the government authority to curb irresponsible speculation by banks. More important, perhaps, it established the **Federal Deposit Insurance Corporation (FDIC)**, which guaranteed all bank deposits up to $2,500. Even if a bank should fail, small depositors would be able to recover their money.

To restore confidence in the stock market, Congress passed the so-called Truth in Securities Act of 1933, requiring corporations issuing new securities to provide full and accurate information about them to the public. In June 1934, another act established the **Securities and Exchange Commission (SEC)** to police the stock market. Roosevelt also signed a bill to legalize the manufacture and sale of beer with a 3.2 percent alcohol content—an interim measure pending the repeal of prohibition, for which a constitutional amendment (the Twenty-First) was already in process. The amendment was ratified later in 1933.

AGRICULTURAL ADJUSTMENT

These initial actions bought time for more comprehensive programs. The first was the **Agricultural Adjustment Act**, which Congress passed in May 1933. Under the provisions of the act, producers of seven basic commodities (wheat, cotton, corn, hogs, rice, tobacco, and dairy products) would impose production limits on their crops in order to keep the prices they could charge for those crops up. The government, through the Agricultural Adjustment Administration (AAA), would then tell individual farmers how much they should produce and would pay them subsidies for leaving some of their land idle. A tax on food processing (for example, the milling of wheat) would provide the funds for the new payments.

The AAA helped bring about a rise in prices for farm commodities in the years after 1933. Gross farm income increased by half in the first three years of the New Deal, and the agricultural economy as a whole emerged from the 1930s more stable and prosperous than it had been in many years. The AAA did, however, favor larger farmers over smaller ones. By distributing payments to landowners, not those who worked the land, the government allowed planters to reduce their acreage and cultivation output. This could mean evicting tenants and sharecroppers and firing field hands.

In January 1936, the Supreme Court struck down crucial provisions of the AAA, arguing that the government had no constitutional authority to require farmers to limit production. But within a few weeks, the administration had secured passage of new legislation (the Soil Conservation and Domestic Allotment Act), which permitted the government to pay farmers to reduce production to "conserve soil," prevent erosion, and accomplish other secondary goals.

The administration launched several efforts to assist poor farmers as well. The Resettlement Administration, established in 1935, and its successor, the **Farm Security Administration**, created in 1937, provided loans to help farmers cultivating submarginal soil to relocate to better lands. But the programs moved no more than a few thousand farmers. More effective was the Rural Electrification Administration, created in 1935, which worked to make electric power available for the first time to thousands of farmers through utility cooperatives.

Industrial Recovery

Since 1931, leaders of the U.S. Chamber of Commerce and many others had been urging the government to adopt an antideflation program that would permit trade associations to cooperate in stabilizing prices within their industries. Existing antitrust laws clearly forbade such practices, and Herbert Hoover had refused to endorse suspension of the laws. The Roosevelt administration was more receptive. In exchange for relaxing antitrust protections, however, New Dealers insisted on other provisions. Business leaders would have to recognize workers' right to bargain collectively through unions and ensure the incomes of workers would rise along with prices. And to help create jobs and increase consumer buying power, the administration added a major program of public works spending. The result of these and many other impulses was the National Industrial Recovery Act, which Congress passed in June 1933.

At its center was a new federal agency, the **National Recovery Administration (NRA)**, under the direction of Hugh S. Johnson. Johnson called on every business establishment in the nation to accept a temporary "blanket code": a minimum wage of between 30 and 40 cents an hour, a maximum workweek of thirty-five to forty hours, and the abolition of child labor. At the same time, Johnson negotiated another, more specific set of codes with leaders of the nation's major industries. These industrial codes set floors below which no company would lower prices or wages in its search for a competitive advantage, and they included provisions for maintaining employment and production. He quickly won agreements from almost every major industry in the country.

From the beginning, however, the NRA stumbled. The codes themselves were hastily and often poorly written. Large producers consistently dominated the code-writing process and ensured that the new regulations would work to their advantage and to the disadvantage of smaller firms. And the codes at times did more than simply set floors under prices; they actively and artificially raised them, sometimes to levels higher than buyers in the market could afford.

Other NRA goals also worked against recovery. Section 7(a) of the National Industrial Recovery Act promised workers the right to form unions and engage in collective bargaining and encouraged many workers to join unions for the first time. But Section 7(a) contained no enforcement mechanisms. The Public Works Administration (PWA), established to administer the National Industrial Recovery Act's spending programs, only gradually allowed the $3.3 billion in public works funds to trickle out.

Perhaps the clearest evidence of the NRA's failure was that industrial production actually declined in the months after the agency's establishment, despite the rise in prices that the codes

(©MPI/Archive Photos/Getty Images)

THE NRA (1933) This cartoon by Clifford Berryman praised the spirit of cooperation between industry and labor that the National Recovery Administration was supposed to cultivate. It also lent visual expression to the magnified power, reach, confidence, and perhaps benevolence of the federal government in the early days of the New Deal.

had helped create. The NRA failed to increase the buying power for consumers, who were still reeling from unemployment or underemployment, which made the higher prices an obstacle to growth. By the spring of 1934, the NRA was besieged by criticism. That fall, Roosevelt pressured Johnson to resign and established a new board of directors to oversee the NRA.

Then in 1935, the Supreme Court intervened with a case involving alleged NRA code violations by the Schechter brothers, who operated a wholesale poultry business confined to Brooklyn, New York. The Court ruled unanimously that the Schechters were not engaged in interstate commerce (and thus not subject to federal regulation) and, further, that Congress had unconstitutionally delegated legislative power to the president to draft the NRA codes. The justices struck down the legislation establishing the agency. Roosevelt denounced the justices for their "horse-and-buggy" interpretation of the interstate commerce clause. He was rightly concerned, for the reasoning in the Schechter case threatened many other New Deal programs as well.

REGIONAL PLANNING

The AAA and the NRA largely reflected the beliefs of New Dealers who favored economic planning but wanted private interests (farmers or business leaders) to dominate the planning process.

But other reformers believed that the government itself should be the chief planning agent in the economy. Their most conspicuous success was an unprecedented experiment in regional planning: the **Tennessee Valley Authority (TVA)**.

Progressive reformers had agitated for years for public development of the nation's water resources as a source of cheap electric power. In particular, they had urged completion of a great dam at Muscle Shoals on the Tennessee River in Alabama—a dam begun during World War I but left unfinished when the war ended. But opposition from the utilities companies had blocked further progress on the dam.

In 1932, however, the great electricity empire of Samuel Insull collapsed spectacularly amid widely publicized exposés of corruption. Hostility to the utilities soon grew so intense that the companies were no longer able to block the public power movement. The result was legislation, supported by the president and enacted by Congress in May 1933, creating the Tennessee Valley Authority. The TVA was authorized to complete the dam at Muscle Shoals and build other dams in the region, and to generate and sell electricity from them to the public at reasonable rates. It was also intended to encourage the growth of local industries, supervise a substantial program of reforestation, and help farmers improve productivity.

Opposition by conservatives ultimately blocked many of the ambitious social planning projects proposed by the more visionary TVA administrators, but the Authority revitalized the region in numerous ways. By manipulating the flow of water, it made rivers more navigable, virtually eliminated flooding in the region, and provided electricity to thousands who had never before had it. Throughout the country, largely because of the yardstick

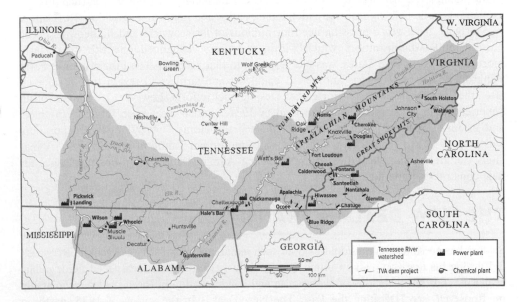

THE TENNESSEE VALLEY AUTHORITY The Tennessee Valley Authority was one of the largest experiments in government-funded public works and regional planning in American history to that point. The federal government had helped fund many projects in its history—canals, turnpikes, railroads, bridges, dams, and others. But never before had it undertaken a project of such great scope, and never before had it maintained such close control and ownership over the public works it helped create. This map illustrates the broad reach of the TVA within the Tennessee Valley region, which spanned seven states. TVA dams throughout the region helped control floods and also provided a source of hydroelectric power, which the government sold to consumers. Note the dam near Muscle Shoals, Alabama, in the bottom left of the map. It was begun during World War I, and efforts to revive it in the 1920s helped create the momentum that produced the TVA. • *Why were progressives so eager to see the government enter the business of hydroelectric power in the 1920s?*

provided by the TVA's cheap production of electricity, private power rates declined. Even so, the Tennessee Valley remained a generally impoverished region despite the TVA's efforts.

THE GROWTH OF FEDERAL RELIEF

The Roosevelt administration did not consider relief to the unemployed its most important task, but it recognized the necessity of doing something to help impoverished Americans survive until the government could revive the economy to the point where relief might not be necessary. Among Roosevelt's first acts as president was the establishment of the Federal Emergency Relief Administration (FERA), which provided cash grants to states to prop up bankrupt relief agencies. To administer the program, he chose the director of the New York State relief agency, Harry Hopkins. Both Hopkins and Roosevelt had misgivings about establishing a government "dole," or handout, but felt more comfortable with work relief. Thus when it became clear that the FERA grants were not enough, the administration established a second program: the Civil Works Administration (CWA), which put more than 4 million people to work on temporary projects between November 1933 and April 1934. Some of the projects were of lasting value, such as the construction of roads, schools, and parks; others were little more than make-work. To Hopkins, however, the important things were pumping money into the economy and providing assistance to people with nowhere else to turn.

Roosevelt's favorite relief project was the **Civilian Conservation Corps (CCC)**. The CCC created camps in national parks and forests and in other rural and wilderness settings. There, young unemployed men from the cities worked in a semimilitary environment on such projects as planting trees, building reservoirs, developing parks, and improving agricultural irrigation.

Mortgage relief was a pressing need for millions of farm owners and homeowners. The Farm Credit Administration, which within two years refinanced one-fifth of all farm mortgages in the United States, was one response to that problem. The Frazier-Lemke Farm Bankruptcy Act of 1933 was another. It enabled some farmers to regain their land even after the foreclosure of their mortgages. Despite such efforts, however, 25 percent of all American farm owners had lost their land by 1934. Homeowners were similarly troubled, and in June 1933 the administration established the Home Owners' Loan Corporation, which by 1936 had refinanced the mortgages of more than 1 million householders. A year later, Congress established the Federal Housing Administration to insure mortgages for new construction and home repairs.

THE NEW DEAL IN TRANSITION

Seldom has an American president enjoyed such remarkable popularity as Franklin Roosevelt did during his first two years in office. But by early 1935, the New Deal faced fierce public criticism. (For reverberations of such praise and condemnation in the historical scholarship on Roosevelt, see "Debating the Past: The New Deal.") In the spring of 1935, partly in response to these growing attacks, Roosevelt launched an ambitious new program of legislation that has often been called the "Second New Deal."

THE CONSERVATIVE CRITICISM OF THE NEW DEAL

Despite his great popularity, Franklin Roosevelt had many conservative critics. Some of them detested him so bitterly that they would refuse to say his name, calling him "that man." Those critics included businessmen, financiers, and wealthy members of society.

Roosevelt himself was among the most aristocratic presidents in American history. But he became the enemy of the very world that he came from. He was an alumnus of Harvard University, but the university president barely spoke to him when he went there to give a speech. He was, as many members of the American elite called him, a "traitor to his class." But even greater hatred came from conservative businessmen and financiers, who correctly accused New Dealers of imposing new regulations on the business and financial worlds. His critics were also infuriated by new taxes imposed by Roosevelt, even though high taxation reached only a few wealthy people.

The hatred of Roosevelt from conservatives took many forms. In 1935, a "whispering campaign" emerged from a New Deal effort to regulate the public utility industry. Stories circulated that the president was a drug addict, that he was insane, and that he was surrounded by psychiatrists. Hamilton Fish Jr., a conservative member of Congress, said on the floor of the House of Representatives that "whom the gods would destroy, they make first mad."

Others leveled ideological critiques. Walter Lippmann, a revered columnist, complained that Roosevelt was moving away from the nation's traditions. "We belong to a generation that has lost its way," he wrote. "Unable to develop the great truths which it inherited from the emancipators, it has returned to the heresies of absolutism, authority, and the domination of men by men." Lippmann and others charged that Roosevelt had become attracted to fascism and communism, with their dangerous investment of power in the government, instead of protecting the freedom of individuals.

Lewis Douglas, Roosevelt's first budget director, resigned in response to the president's determination to spend deficit funds to help provide relief to the unemployed. Al Smith, the former New York governor and twice the Democratic candidate, also turned against the president, partly because he considered the New Deal much too far to the left. However, for the most part, the New Deal lacked a clear ideology and, instead, experimented in many ways, some that conservatives found offensive.

Conservative business leaders were the most committed leaders of the attack on the New Deal. They formed an organization called the **Liberty League**, led by the Du Pont family, owners of the nation's largest chemical company. Its goal was to arouse public opposition to what its members called the "dictatorial" policies of the New Deal and to what they considered its attacks on free enterprise. It was led by John Jacob Raskob, a former head of the Democratic National Committee, former director of General Motors, and a trustee of Du Pont, who had abandoned the Democratic Party and joined the League. The League reached a peak of 125,000 members in 1936. It also recruited college students from 345 institutions, gaining over 10,000 members. Many followers were northeastern industrialists. The League described itself as a "nonpartisan organization founded to defend the Constitution and defend the rights and liberties guaranteed by that Constitution." Its purpose was

> to teach the necessity of respect for the rights of persons and property as fundamental to every form of government . . . to teach the duty of government, to encourage and protect individual and group initiative and enterprise, to foster the right to work, earn, save and acquire property, and to preserve the ownership and lawful use of property when acquired.

The Liberty League attracted considerable attention, but it had relatively little impact on the New Deal. Its leaders tried to remain nonpartisan, even though its members were staunchly anti-Roosevelt. They became a target for the president's 1936 reelection campaign. Soon after Roosevelt's landslide victory, the League dissolved. Hatred of Roosevelt did not disappear, but there was little organized opposition after 1936.

THE NEW DEAL

Contemporaries of Franklin Roosevelt debated the impact of the New Deal with ferocious intensity. Conservatives complained of a menacing tyranny of the state. Liberals celebrated the New Deal's progressive achievements. Some people on the left charged that the reforms of the 1930s were largely cosmetic and ignored the nation's fundamental problems. Although the conservative critique found relatively little scholarly expression until many years after Roosevelt's death, the liberal and left positions continued for decades to shape the way historians described the Roosevelt administration.

The dominant view from the beginning was an approving liberal interpretation, and its most important early voice was that of Arthur M. Schlesinger Jr. He argued in the three volumes of *The Age of Roosevelt* (1957–1960) that the New Deal marked a continuation of the long struggle between public power and private interests, a struggle Roosevelt had moved to a new level. Workers, farmers, consumers, and others now had much more protection than they had enjoyed in the past.

At almost the same time, however, other historians were offering more qualified assessments of the New Deal, although they remained securely within the liberal framework. Richard Hofstadter argued in 1955 that the New Deal gave American liberalism a "social-democratic tinge that had never before been present in American reform movements," but that its highly pragmatic approach lacked a central, guiding philosophy. James MacGregor Burns argued in 1956 that Roosevelt failed to make full use of his potential as a leader.

William Leuchtenburg's *Franklin D. Roosevelt and the New Deal* (1963) was the first systematic "revisionist" interpretation. Leuchtenburg challenged the views of earlier scholars who had proclaimed the New Deal a "revolution" in social policy. Leuchtenburg could muster only enough enthusiasm to call it a "halfway revolution," one that helped some previously disadvantaged groups (most notably farmers and workers) but that did little or nothing for many others (African Americans, sharecroppers, the urban poor).

Harsher criticisms soon emerged. Barton Bernstein in a 1968 essay concluded that the New Deal had saved capitalism, but at the expense of the least powerful. Ronald Radosh, Paul Conkin, and, later, Thomas Ferguson and Colin Gordon expanded on these criticisms. The New Deal, they contended, was part of the twentieth-century tradition of "corporate liberalism"—a tradition in which reform is closely wedded to the needs and interests of capitalism.

Most scholars in the 1980s and 1990s, however, seemed largely to have accepted the revised liberal view: that the New Deal was a significant and valuable chapter in the history of reform, but one that worked within rigid, occasionally crippling limits. Much of that work on the New Deal, therefore, focused on the constraints it faced. Some scholars (notably the sociologist Theda Skocpol) emphasized the issue of "state capacity"—the absence of a government bureaucracy with sufficient strength and expertise to shape or administer many programs. James T. Patterson, Barry Karl, Mark Leff, and others stressed the political constraints the New Deal encountered—the conservative inhibitions about government that remained strong in Congress and among the public. Frank Freidel, Ellis Hawley, Herbert Stein, and many others pointed as well to the ideological constraints affecting Franklin Roosevelt and his supporters—the limits of their own understanding of their time. Alan Brinkley, in *The End of Reform* (1995), described an ideological shift within New Deal liberalism that marginalized older concerns about wealth and monopoly power and replaced them with consumer-oriented Keynesianism. David Kennedy, in *Freedom from Fear* (1999), by contrast argued that the more aggressively anticapitalist measures of the early New Deal actually hampered recovery. Only when Roosevelt embraced the power of the market did prosperity begin to return.

The conservative attacks on the New Deal in the 2000s provided a newly powerful alternative view. A group of conservatives—among them Amity Schlaes and Burton Folsom—attacked the New Deal as a failure that created a vast bureaucracy and caused the Depression to last longer than it had to. Other scholarship has examined such conservative critiques against the New Deal in its own time. Kim Phillips-Fein (2009) wrote about businessmen's "crusade" against Roosevelt's programs, and Kevin Kruse (2015) attributed America's postwar religiosity not to the Cold War but to a concerted and successful effort by those corporate antagonists to mobilize opposition to the New Deal as a threat to "freedom under God."

The phrase "New Deal liberalism" has come in the postwar era to seem synonymous with modern ideas of aggressive federal management of the economy, elaborate welfare systems, a powerful bureaucracy, and large-scale government spending. But many historians of the New Deal would argue that the modern idea of New Deal liberalism bears only a limited relationship to the ideas that New Dealers themselves embraced.   •

UNDERSTAND, ANALYZE, & EVALUATE

1. How has the scholarly understanding of the New Deal changed over time?
2. Did the New Deal save capitalism? If so, how and why?

The Populist Criticism of the New Deal

Roosevelt's policies also generated criticism from the far left. The Communist Party, the Socialist Party, and other radical and semiradical organizations were at times harshly critical of the New Deal. But like the conservatives, they failed to attract genuine mass support.

More menacing to the New Deal than either the far right or the far left was a group of dissident political movements that defied easy ideological classification. Some gained substantial public support within particular states and regions. And three men succeeded in mobilizing genuinely national followings. Dr. Francis E. Townsend, an elderly California physician, rose from obscurity to lead a movement of more than 5 million members with his plan for federal pensions for older adults. According to the **Townsend Plan**, all Americans over the age of sixty would receive monthly government pensions of $200, provided they retired (thus freeing jobs for younger, unemployed Americans) and spent the money in full each month (which would pump needed funds into the economy). By 1935, the Townsend Plan had attracted the support of many older men and women.

Father **Charles E. Coughlin**, a Catholic priest in the Detroit suburb of Royal Oak, Michigan, achieved even greater renown through his weekly national radio sermons. He proposed a series of monetary reforms—remonetization of silver, issuing of greenbacks, and nationalization of the banking system—that he insisted would restore prosperity and ensure economic justice. At first a warm supporter of Roosevelt, Coughlin had become disheartened by late 1934 by what he claimed was the president's failure to deal harshly enough with the "money powers." In the spring of 1935, he established his own political organization, the National Union for Social Justice.

Most alarming to the administration was the growing national popularity of Senator **Huey P. Long** of Louisiana. Long had risen to power in his home state through his strident attacks on the banks, oil companies, and utilities and on the conservative political oligarchy allied with them. Elected governor in 1928, he launched an assault on his opponents so thorough and forceful they were soon left with virtually no political power. But he also maintained the overwhelming support of the Louisiana electorate, in part because of his flamboyant personality and in part because of his solid record of conventional progressive accomplishments: building roads, schools, and hospitals; revising the tax codes; distributing free textbooks; lowering utility rates. Barred by law from succeeding himself as governor, he ran in 1930 for a seat in the U.S. Senate and won easily.

Long, like Coughlin, supported Franklin Roosevelt for president in 1932. But within six months of Roosevelt's inauguration, Long had broken with the president. As an alternative to the New Deal, he advocated a drastic program of wealth redistribution, a program he ultimately named the Share-Our-Wealth Plan. The government, he claimed, could end the

(©Fotosearch/Archive Photos/Getty Images)

HUEY LONG Few public speakers could inflame a crowd more effectively than Huey Long of Louisiana, known to many as "the Kingfish" (a nickname borrowed from a scheming character on the popular radio show *Amos 'n' Andy*). It was Long's effective use of radio, however, that contributed most directly to his spreading national popularity in the early 1930s.

Depression easily by using the tax system to confiscate the surplus riches of the wealthiest men and women in America and distribute these surpluses to the rest of the population. That would, he claimed, allow the government to guarantee every family a minimum "homestead" worth $5,000 and an annual wage of $2,500. In 1934, Long established his own national organization: the Share-Our-Wealth Society, which soon attracted a large following through much of the nation. A poll by the Democratic National Committee in the spring of 1935 disclosed that Long might attract more than 10 percent of the vote if he ran as a third-party candidate, possibly enough to tip a close election to the Republicans.

Members of the Roosevelt administration considered dissident movements—and the broad popular discontent they represented—a genuine threat. An increasing number of advisers were warning Roosevelt that he would have to do something dramatic to counter their strength.

THE "SECOND NEW DEAL"

Roosevelt launched the so-called **Second New Deal** in the spring of 1935 in response both to growing political pressures and to the continuing economic crisis. The new proposals represented a shift in the emphasis of New Deal policy. Perhaps the most conspicuous change was in the administration's attitude toward big business. Symbolically at least, the president was now willing to attack corporate interests openly. In March, for example, he proposed to Congress an act designed to break up the great utility holding companies. The Holding Company Act of 1935 was the result, although furious lobbying by the utilities led to amendments that sharply limited its effects.

Equally alarming to affluent Americans was a series of tax reforms proposed by the president in 1935. Apparently designed to undercut the appeal of Huey Long's Share-Our-Wealth Plan, the Roosevelt proposals called for establishing the highest and most progressive peacetime tax rates in history—although the actual impact of these rates was limited.

The Supreme Court decision in 1935 to strike down the National Industrial Recovery Act also invalidated Section 7(a) of the act, which had guaranteed workers the right to organize and bargain collectively. A group of progressives in Congress, led by Senator Robert E. Wagner of New York, introduced what became the National Labor Relations Act of 1935. The new law, popularly known as the Wagner Act, provided workers with a crucial enforcement mechanism missing from the 1933 law: the **National Labor Relations Board (NLRB)**, which would have power to compel employers to recognize and bargain with legitimate unions. The president was not entirely happy with the bill, but he signed it anyway. That was largely because American workers themselves had by 1935 become so important and vigorous a force that Roosevelt realized his own political future would depend in part on responding to their demands.

LABOR MILITANCY

The emergence of a powerful trade union movement in the 1930s occurred partly in response to government efforts to enhance the power of unions. It was also a result of the increased militancy of American workers after a lull during the 1920s. Business leaders and industrialists lost (at least temporarily) the ability to control government policies. Equally important, new and more powerful labor organizations emerged.

The American Federation of Labor (AFL) remained committed to the idea of the craft union: organizing workers on the basis of their skills. But that concept had little to offer unskilled laborers, who now constituted the bulk of the industrial workforce. During the 1930s, therefore, a newer concept of labor organization challenged the craft union ideal: industrial unionism.

Advocates of this approach argued that all workers in a particular industry should be organized in a single union, regardless of what functions the workers performed. So united, workers would greatly increase their power.

Leaders of the AFL craft unions for the most part opposed the new concept. But industrial unionism found a number of important advocates, most prominent among them **John L. Lewis**, the leader of the United Mine Workers. At first, Lewis and his allies attempted to work within the AFL, but friction between the new industrial organizations Lewis was promoting and the older craft unions grew. At the 1935 AFL convention, Lewis became embroiled in a series of angry confrontations with craft union leaders before finally walking out. A few weeks later, he created the Committee on Industrial Organization. When the AFL expelled the new committee and all the industrial unions it represented, Lewis renamed the committee the **Congress of Industrial Organizations (CIO)** and became its first president.

The CIO expanded the constituency of the labor movement. It was more receptive to women and African Americans than the AFL had been, in part because CIO organizing drives targeted previously unorganized industries (textiles, laundries, tobacco factories, and others) where women and minorities constituted much of the workforce. The CIO was also more militant than the AFL. By the time of the 1936 schism, it was already engaged in major organizing battles in the automobile and steel industries.

ORGANIZING BATTLES

The United Auto Workers (UAW) gradually emerged preeminent in the early and mid-1930s. Although it was gaining recruits, it was making little progress in winning recognition from the corporations. In December 1936, however, autoworkers employed a controversial and effective new technique for challenging corporate opposition: the **sit-down strike**. Employees in several General Motors plants in Detroit simply sat down inside the plants, refusing either to work or to leave, thus preventing the company from using strikebreakers. The tactic spread to other locations, and by February 1937, strikers had occupied seventeen GM plants. The strikers ignored court orders and local police efforts to force them to vacate the buildings. When Michigan's governor refused to call up the National Guard to clear out the strikers, and when the federal government also refused to intervene on behalf of employers, General Motors relented. In February 1937, it became the first major manufacturer to recognize the UAW. Other automobile companies soon did the same.

In the steel industry, the battle for unionization was less easily won. In 1936, the Steel Workers Organizing Committee (SWOC), later the United Steelworkers of America, began a major organizing drive involving thousands of workers and frequent strikes. In March 1937, to the surprise of almost everyone, United States Steel, the giant of the industry, recognized the union rather than risk a costly strike. But the smaller companies, known collectively as "Little Steel," were less accommodating. On Memorial Day 1937, striking workers from Republic Steel gathered with their families for a picnic and demonstration in south Chicago. When they attempted to march peacefully and legally toward the steel plant, police opened fire on them. Ten demonstrators were killed; another ninety were wounded. Despite a public outcry against the "Memorial Day Massacre," the harsh tactics of Little Steel companies succeeded. The 1937 strike failed.

But the victory of Little Steel was among the last gasps of the kind of brutal strikebreaking that had proven effective in the past. In 1937 alone, there were 4,720 strikes, over 80 percent of them settled in favor of the unions. By the end of the year, more than 8 million workers were members of unions recognized as official bargaining units by employers (as compared with

(©Carl Linde/AP Photo)

THE "MEMORIAL DAY MASSACRE" The bitterness of the labor struggles of the 1930s was nowhere more evident than in Chicago in 1937, when striking workers attempting to march on a Republic Steel plant were brutally attacked by Chicago police, who used clubs, tear gas, and guns to turn away the marchers. Ten strikers were killed and many others were injured.

3 million in 1932). By 1941, that number had expanded to 10 million and included the workers of Little Steel, whose employers had finally recognized the SWOC.

SOCIAL SECURITY

From the first moments of the New Deal, important members of the administration had been lobbying for a system of federally sponsored social insurance for elderly people and those who were unemployed—not just for humanitarian reasons, but also to keep those groups active in the nation's economy. In 1935, Roosevelt gave public support to what became the **Social Security Act**, which Congress passed the same year. It established several distinct programs. For older people, there were two types of assistance. Those who were presently destitute could receive up to $15 a month in federal assistance. More important for the future, many Americans presently working were incorporated into a pension system, to which they and their employers would contribute through a payroll tax. These funds would provide them with an income on retirement, though initially these pension payments would provide only $10 to $85 a month to recipients. And at first, payment was not to be distributed until 1942. But public pressure pushed the payment date back to 1937. Broad categories of workers (including domestic servants and agricultural laborers, often women or racial minorities) were excluded from the program. But the act was a crucial first step in building the nation's most important social program for retired Americans.

In addition, the Social Security Act created a system of unemployment insurance that employers alone would finance. It also established a system of federal aid to people with disabilities and a program of aid to dependent children.

The framers of the Social Security Act wanted to create a system of "insurance," not "welfare." And the largest programs (old-age pensions and unemployment insurance) were in many ways similar to private insurance programs. But the act also provided considerable direct assistance based on need—to low-income aging adults, to those with disabilities, to dependent children and their mothers. These groups were widely perceived to be small and genuinely unable to support themselves. But in later generations, the programs for these groups would expand until they assumed dimensions planners of Social Security had not foreseen.

NEW DIRECTIONS IN RELIEF

Social Security was designed primarily to fulfill long-range goals. But millions of unemployed Americans had immediate needs. To help them, the Roosevelt administration established in 1935 the **Works Progress Administration (WPA)**. Like the Civil Works Administration and other earlier efforts, the WPA established a system of work relief for the unemployed. But it was much bigger than the earlier agencies.

Under the direction of **Harry Hopkins**, the WPA was responsible for building or renovating 110,000 public buildings and for constructing almost 600 airports, more than 500,000 miles of roads, and over 100,000 bridges. In the process, the WPA kept an average of 2.1 million workers employed and pumped needed money into the economy.

(©Joseph Schwartz/Corbis Historical/Getty Images)

WPA WORKERS ON THE JOB The Works Progress Administration funded an enormous variety of work projects to provide jobs for unemployed individuals. The majority of WPA employees, however, worked on construction sites.

The WPA also displayed remarkable flexibility and imagination. The Federal Writers' Project of the WPA, for example, gave unemployed writers a chance to do their work and receive a government salary. The Federal Art Project, similarly, helped painters, sculptors, and others continue their careers. The Federal Music Project and the Federal Theatre Project oversaw the production of concerts and plays, creating work for unemployed musicians, actors, and directors. Other relief agencies emerged alongside the WPA. The National Youth Administration (NYA) provided work and scholarship assistance to men and women of high school and college age. The Emergency Housing Division of the Public Works Administration began federal sponsorship of public housing.

The new welfare system dealt with men and women in very different ways. For men, the government concentrated mainly on work relief, including the CCC, the CWA, and the WPA. The principal government aid to women was not work relief but cash assistance—most notably through the Aid to Dependent Children program of Social Security, which was designed largely to assist single mothers. This disparity in treatment reflected a widespread assumption that men should constitute the bulk of the paid workforce. Yet millions of women were already employed by the 1930s.

The 1936 "Referendum"

By the middle of 1936—with the economy visibly reviving—there could be little doubt that Roosevelt would win a second term. The Republican Party nominated the moderate governor of Kansas, Alf M. Landon, who waged a relatively dull campaign. Roosevelt's dissident challengers now appeared powerless. One reason was the assassination of their most effective leader, Huey Long, in Louisiana in September 1935. Another reason was the ill-fated alliance among Father Coughlin, Dr. Townsend, and Gerald L. K. Smith (an intemperate henchman of Huey Long), who joined forces that summer to establish a new political movement—the Union Party, which nominated an undistinguished North Dakota congressman, William Lemke.

The result was the greatest landslide in American history to that point. Roosevelt polled just under 61 percent of the vote to Landon's 36 percent and carried every state except Maine and Vermont. The Democrats increased their already large majorities in both houses of Congress.

The election results demonstrated the party realignment that the New Deal had produced. The Democrats now controlled a broad coalition of western and southern farmers, the urban working classes, the poor and unemployed, and white southerners, as well as traditional progressives and committed new liberals. New Deal aid flowing to black communities in northern cities helped pry that constituency from the Republican column. The resulting coalition constituted a substantial majority of the electorate. It would be decades before the Republican Party could again create a lasting majority coalition of its own.

THE NEW DEAL IN DISARRAY

Roosevelt emerged from the 1936 election at the zenith of his popularity. Within months, however, the New Deal was mired in serious new difficulties.

The Court Fight

The 1936 mandate, Franklin Roosevelt believed, made it possible for him to do something about the Supreme Court. No program of reform, he believed, could long survive the conservative justices, who had already struck down the NRA and the AAA.

In February 1937, Roosevelt sent a surprise message to Capitol Hill proposing an overhaul of the federal court system. Included among the many provisions was one to add up to six new justices to the Supreme Court. The courts were "overworked," the president claimed, and needed additional manpower and younger blood to enable them to cope with their increasing burdens. But Roosevelt's real purpose was to give himself the opportunity to appoint new, liberal justices and change the ideological balance of the Court.

Conservatives were outraged at the "**Court-packing plan**," and even many Roosevelt supporters were disturbed by it. Still, Roosevelt might well have persuaded Congress to approve at least a compromise measure had not the Supreme Court itself intervened. Of the nine justices, three reliably supported the New Deal, and four reliably opposed it. Of the remaining two, Chief Justice Charles Evans Hughes often sided with the progressives, and Associate Justice Owen J. Roberts usually voted with the conservatives. On March 29, 1937, Roberts, Hughes, and the three progressive justices voted together to uphold a state minimum-wage law—in the case of *West Coast Hotel v. Parrish*—thus reversing a 5-to-4 decision of the previous year invalidating a similar law. Two weeks later, again by a 5-to-4 margin, the Court upheld the Wagner Act, and in May it validated the Social Security Act. Whatever the reasons for the decisions, the Court's newly moderate position made the Court-packing bill seem unnecessary. Congress ultimately defeated it.

On one level, Franklin Roosevelt had achieved a victory. The Court was no longer an obstacle to New Deal reforms. But the Court-packing episode politically damaged the administration. From 1937 on, southern Democrats and other conservatives voted against Roosevelt's measures much more often than they had in the past.

RETRENCHMENT AND RECESSION

By the summer of 1937, the national income—which had dropped from $82 billion in 1929 to $40 billion in 1932—had risen to nearly $72 billion. Other economic indices showed similar advances. Roosevelt seized on these improvements as justification for trying to balance the federal budget. Between January and August 1937, he cut the WPA in half, laying off 1.5 million relief workers. A few weeks later, the fragile boom collapsed. An important index of industrial production dropped dramatically from August 1937 to May 1938. Four million additional workers lost their jobs. Economic conditions were soon almost as bad as they had been in the bleak days of 1932–1933.

The recession of 1937, known to the president's critics as the "Roosevelt recession," was a result of many factors. But to many observers at the time, it seemed to be a direct result of the administration's unwise decision to reduce spending. And so in April 1938, the president asked Congress for an emergency appropriation of $5 billion for public works and relief programs, and government funds soon began pouring into the economy once again. Within a few months, another tentative recovery seemed to be under way.

At about the same time, Roosevelt sent a stinging message to Congress, vehemently denouncing what he called an "unjustifiable concentration of economic power" and asking for the creation of a commission to consider major reforms in the antitrust laws. In response, Congress established the Temporary National Economic Committee (TNEC), whose members included representatives of both houses of Congress and officials from several executive agencies. Later in 1938, the administration successfully supported one of its most ambitious pieces of labor legislation, the Fair Labor Standards Act, which for the first time established a national minimum wage and a forty-hour workweek and which also placed strict limits on child labor.

Despite these achievements, however, by the end of 1938 the New Deal had essentially come to an end. Congressional opposition now made it difficult for the president to enact any major new programs. But more important, perhaps, the threat of world crisis hung heavy in the political atmosphere, and Roosevelt was gradually growing more concerned with persuading a reluctant nation to prepare for war than with pursuing new avenues of reform.

ISOLATIONISM AND INTERNATIONALISM

Alongside the deep economic crises Franklin Roosevelt faced, his administration had to deal as well with the effects of a decaying international structure. Those problems owed to continuing fallout from the Great War and confronted Roosevelt from the time he took office.

DEPRESSION DIPLOMACY

When Roosevelt entered office in 1933, the Depression was worldwide. The struggles of American banks had led them to call in loans to the former Central Powers, which spurred the collapse of financial institutions in Germany and Austria and thus their payment of reparations to the Allies. Roosevelt broke with his predecessor on the American role in this system. The Hoover administration had worked to settle the issue of war debts through international agreement. Roosevelt abandoned that effort, signing a bill in April 1934 that prohibited American banks from making loans to any nation in default on its debts. The legislation ended the old, circular system by which debt payments continued only by virtue of increasing American loans. Within months, war-debt payments from every nation except Finland stopped for good.

Roosevelt also parted company with Hoover on the question of the money supply, which pivoted around whether that supply should be backed only by gold. Hoover had firmly argued that reinforcing the gold standard would stabilize the American economy. Roosevelt countered that a fluid money supply would stabilize falling prices and allow the Federal Reserve to more freely provide emergency relief to banks. Though he did not explicitly make the connection, his argument here echoed Populist advocacy of bimetallism in the 1890s as an economic stabilizer. Joining many European countries, he effectively took the United States off the gold standard in April 1933.

Sixteen years after the Bolshevik Revolution of 1917, the American government still had not officially recognized the government of the Soviet Union. But a growing number of influential Americans were urging a change in policy—largely because the Soviet Union appeared to be a possible source of trade. Soviet leader Josef Stalin was hoping for American cooperation in containing Japan. In November 1933, the United States and the Soviet Union agreed to open formal diplomatic exchange. Relations with the Soviet Union, however, soon soured. American trade failed to establish a foothold in Russia, disappointing hopes in the United States. The American government did little to reassure the Soviets that it was interested in stopping Japanese expansion in Asia, dousing expectations in Russia. By the end of 1934, the Soviet Union and the United States were once again viewing each other with considerable mistrust.

The Roosevelt administration was also taking a new approach toward Latin America, an approach that became known as the **Good Neighbor Policy** and that expanded on the changes the Hoover administration had made. At an Inter-American Conference in Montevideo,

Uruguay, in December 1933, Secretary of State Cordell Hull signed a formal convention declaring: "No state has the right to intervene in the internal or external affairs of another."

THE RISE OF ISOLATIONISM

With the international system of the 1920s now beyond repair, the United States faced a choice between more active efforts to stabilize the world or more energetic attempts to isolate itself from it. Many Americans chose isolation. Support for **isolationism** emerged from many quarters. Some Wilsonian internationalists had grown disillusioned with the League of Nations and its inability to stop Japanese aggression in Asia. Other Americans argued that the American role in the Great War was a result of Wall Street and munitions makers; most of the public, according to new polling data, believed intervention in the war had been an error. An investigation by a Senate committee chaired by Senator Gerald Nye of North Dakota claimed to have produced evidence of exorbitant profiteering and tax evasion by many corporations during the war, and it suggested that bankers had pressured Wilson to intervene in the war so as to protect their loans abroad. (Few historians now lend much credence to these charges.)

Roosevelt continued to hope for at least a modest American role in maintaining world peace. In 1935, he proposed to the Senate a treaty to make the United States a member of the World Court—a largely symbolic gesture. Isolationists led by Father Coughlin and William Randolph Hearst aroused popular opposition to the agreement, and the Senate voted it down.

In the summer of 1935, Benito Mussolini's Italy was preparing to invade Ethiopia. Fearing the invasion would provoke a new European war, American legislators tried to prevent the United States from being dragged into the conflict. The Neutrality Act of 1935 established a mandatory arms embargo against both sides in any military conflict and warned American citizens against traveling on the ships of warring nations. Thus, isolationists believed, the "protection of neutral rights" could not again become an excuse for American intervention in war. A 1937 law established the so-called cash-and-carry policy, by which warring nations could purchase only nonmilitary goods from the United States and could do so only by paying cash and shipping their purchases themselves. Collectively these laws were known as the **Neutrality Acts**.

Isolationist sentiment showed its strength again in 1936 in response to the start of the Spanish Civil War. While more than 3,000 Americans had joined the Lincoln Brigade to fight on the side of the republican government's forces, the U.S. government joined with Britain and France in an agreement to offer no assistance to either side. With material support from Hitler and Mussolini, Franco's forces were able to take full control of Spain by 1939.

In the summer of 1937, Japan intensified its six-year-old assault on the northern Chinese region of Manchuria, widening its attack to encompass a large part of southern China, including most of the port cities. China's vulnerability stemmed in part from its own civil war between Chiang Kai-shek's nationalist party and Mao Zedong's Chinese Communist Party, but the two sides settled on an uneasy truce to fight the invaders together. In a speech in Chicago in October 1937, Roosevelt warned that Japanese and other aggressors should be "quarantined" by the international community to prevent the contagion of war from spreading. He was deliberately vague about what such a quarantine would mean. Even so, public response to the speech was hostile, and Roosevelt drew back. On December 12, 1937, Japanese aviators bombed and sank the U.S. gunboat *Panay*, almost certainly deliberately, as it sailed the Yangtze River in China. But so reluctant was the Roosevelt administration to antagonize the isolationists that the United States eagerly seized on Japanese claims that the bombing had been an accident and accepted Japan's apologies.

THE FAILURE OF MUNICH

In 1936, Hitler had moved the revived German army into the Rhineland, rearming an area that had been off-limits to German troops since World War I. In March 1938, German forces marched without opposition into Austria, and Hitler proclaimed a union (or *Anschluss*) between Austria, his native land, and Germany, his adopted one. Neither in America nor in most of Europe was there much more than a murmur of opposition.

Germany had by now occupied territory surrounding three sides of western Czechoslovakia, a region Hitler dreamed of annexing. In September 1938, he demanded that Czechoslovakia cede him the Sudetenland, a part of Czechoslovakia in which many ethnic Germans lived. Although Czechoslovakia was prepared to fight to stop Hitler, it needed assistance from other nations. But most Western governments, including the United States, were willing to pay almost any price to settle the crisis peacefully. On September 29, Hitler met with the leaders of France and Great Britain at Munich in an effort to resolve the crisis. The French and British agreed to accept the German demands in Czechoslovakia in return for Hitler's promise to expand no farther. Americans watched these events nervously.

The Munich agreement, which Roosevelt supported at the time, was the most prominent element of a policy that came to be known as **appeasement** and that came to be identified

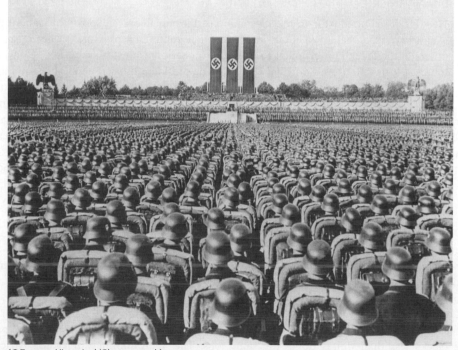

(©Everett Historical/Shutterstock)

1936 NUREMBERG RALLY   The Nazi Party held rallies at Nuremberg in the 1930s to celebrate German military strength, project Adolf Hitler's authority, and deliver political speeches. The gatherings also generated material for propaganda films, including Leni Riefenstahl's *Triumph of the Will*. Here German soldiers assembled for the 1936 event.

(not altogether fairly) with British prime minister Neville Chamberlain. Whoever was to blame, the policy was a failure. In March 1939, Hitler occupied the remaining areas of Czechoslovakia, violating the Munich agreement. And in April, he began issuing threats against Poland.

At that point, both Britain and France assured the Polish government that they would come to its assistance in case of invasion. They even tried, too late, to draw the Soviet Union into a mutual defense agreement. But the Soviet leader **Josef Stalin**, who had not even been invited to the Munich Conference, had decided he could expect no protection from the West. He signed a nonaggression pact with Hitler in August 1939, freeing the Germans (for now) from the danger of a two-front war. Shortly after that, Hitler staged an incident on the Polish border to allow him to claim that Germany had been attacked, and on September 1, 1939, he launched a full-scale invasion of Poland. Britain and France, true to their pledges, declared war on Germany two days later. World War II, already under way in Asia, had begun in Europe.

LIMITS AND LEGACIES OF THE NEW DEAL

While the embers of war began burning in Asia and Europe, the New Deal made major changes in American government, some of them still controversial today. It also left important problems unaddressed.

AFRICAN AMERICANS AND THE NEW DEAL

The New Deal was not hostile to black aspirations. **Eleanor Roosevelt** spoke throughout the 1930s and beyond on behalf of racial justice and put continuing pressure on her husband and others in the federal government to ease discrimination against blacks. (See "Consider the Source: Eleanor Roosevelt on Civil Rights.") The president himself appointed a number of African Americans to significant second-level positions in his administration, creating an informal network of officeholders that became known as the "Black Cabinet." Eleanor Roosevelt, Interior Secretary Harold Ickes, and WPA Director Harry Hopkins all made efforts to ensure that New Deal relief programs did not exclude blacks. By 1935 an estimated 30 percent of all African Americans were receiving some form of government assistance, even amid persistent racial discrimination against people of color by local administrators of aid. One result was a historic change in black electoral behavior. As late as 1932, most black Americans were voting Republican, as they had since the Civil War. By 1936, more than 90 percent were voting Democratic.

African Americans supported Franklin Roosevelt, but they had few illusions that the New Deal represented a major turning point in American race relations. The president was, for example, never willing to risk losing the support of southern Democrats by supporting legislation to make lynching a federal crime or to ban the poll tax, one of the most potent tools keeping blacks from voting.

New Deal relief agencies did not challenge, and indeed reinforced, existing patterns of discrimination. The CCC established separate black camps. The NRA codes tolerated paying blacks less than whites doing the same jobs. The WPA routinely relegated African American and Hispanic workers to the least-skilled and lowest-paying jobs. When funding ebbed, African Americans, like women, were among the first to be dismissed.

The New Deal was not hostile to African Americans, and it made some contributions to their progress. But it never made racial justice a significant part of its agenda.

The New Deal and the "Indian Problem"

New Deal policy toward the Indian tribes marked a significant break from earlier approaches, largely because of the efforts of the commissioner of Indian affairs, **John Collier**. Collier was greatly influenced by the work of twentieth-century anthropologists who advanced the idea of cultural relativism, the theory that every culture should be accepted and respected on its own terms.

Collier wanted to reverse the pressures on Native Americans to assimilate and instead allow them to remain Indians. He effectively promoted the Indian Reorganization Act (1934) that restored to the tribes the right to own land collectively and elect tribal governments. In the thirteen years after passage of the bill, tribal land increased by nearly 4 million acres, and Indian agricultural income increased from under $2 million in 1934 to over $49 million in 1947. Even with the redistribution of lands under the 1934 act, however, Indians continued to possess, for the most part, only territory whites did not want, much of it arid, some of it desert. And as a group, they continued to constitute the poorest segment of the population.

Women and the New Deal

Symbolically at least, the New Deal marked a breakthrough in the role of women in public life. Roosevelt appointed the first female member of the cabinet in the nation's history: Secretary of Labor **Frances Perkins**. He also named more than 100 other women to positions at lower levels of the federal bureaucracy. But the administration was concerned not so much about achieving gender equality as about obtaining special protections for women.

(©George Rinhart/Corbis Historical/Getty Images)

ELEANOR ROOSEVELT   First Lady Eleanor Roosevelt was among the first women to play an important role in politics and government. She oversaw Franklin Roosevelt's political campaigns before he became president as well as developing an important career of her own working on social programs in New York. When she moved to the White House, she championed human rights issues. In this photograph she is on the way to inspect a Washington, D.C., jail that had a reputation for being overcrowded and obsolete.

CONSIDER THE SOURCE

ELEANOR ROOSEVELT ON CIVIL RIGHTS (1942)

Although written in the context of World War II, this article in *The New Republic* captures Eleanor Roosevelt's dedication to the causes of racial and religious equality. Published on May 11, 1942, "Race, Religion, and Prejudice" referred to existing immigration laws and grappled with their place, and the place of stateside racial discrimination, in the evolving political philosophy of twentieth-century liberalism.

We have had a definite policy toward the Chinese and Japanese who wished to enter our country for many years, and I doubt very much if after this war is over we can differentiate between the peoples of Europe, the Near East and the Far East.

Perhaps the simplest way of facing the problem in the future is to say that we are fighting for freedom, and one of the freedoms we must establish is freedom from discrimination among the peoples of the world, either because of race, or of color, or of religion.

The people of the world have suddenly begun to stir and they seem to feel that in the future we should look upon each other as fellow human beings, judged by our acts, by our abilities, by our development, and not by any less fundamental differences.

Here in our own country we have any number of attitudes which have become habits and which constitute our approach to the Jewish people, the Japanese and Chinese people, the Italian people, and above all, to the Negro people in our midst.

Perhaps because the Negroes are our largest minority, our attitude towards them will have to be faced first of all. I keep on repeating that the way to face this situation is by being completely realistic. We cannot force people to accept friends for whom they have no liking, but living in a democracy it is entirely reasonable to demand that every citizen of that democracy enjoy the fundamental rights of a citizen.

Over and over again, I have stressed the rights of every citizen:

Equality before the law.
Equality of education.
Equality to hold a job according to his ability.
Equality of participation through the ballot in the government.

These are inherent rights in a democracy, and I do not see how we can fight this war and deny these rights to any citizen in our own land.

The other relationships will gradually settle themselves once these major things are part of our accepted philosophy.

It seems trite to say to the Negro, you must have patience, when he has had patience so long; you must not expect miracles overnight, when he can look back to the years of slavery and say-how many nights! he has waited for justice. Nevertheless, it is what we must continue to say in the interests of our government as a whole and of the Negro people; but that does not mean that we must sit idle and do nothing. We must keep moving forward steadily, removing restrictions which have no sense, and fighting prejudice. If we are wise we will do this where it is easiest to do it first, and watch it spread gradually to places where the old prejudices are slow to disappear.

There is now a great group of educated Negroes who can become leaders among their people, who can teach them the value of things of the mind and who qualify as the best in any field of endeavor. With these men and women it is impossible to think of any barriers of inferiority, but differences there are and always will be, and that is why on both sides there must be tact and patience and an effort at real understanding. Above everything else, no action must be taken which can cause so much bitterness that the whole liberalizing effort may be set back over a period of many years.

UNDERSTAND, ANALYZE, & EVALUATE

1. What exactly was Eleanor Roosevelt calling for in this piece?

2. What seem to have been her attitudes toward Americans who harbored racial or religious prejudice?

3. How might African American civil rights activists have reacted to the last two paragraphs?

4. What were the dangers, to Roosevelt, of reforming race relations too quickly?

The New Deal generally supported the widespread belief that in hard times women should withdraw from the workplace to open jobs for men. New Deal relief agencies offered relatively little employment for women. The Social Security program excluded domestic servants, waitresses, and other predominantly female occupations.

Repeating its handling of racial justice, the New Deal was not actively hostile to feminist aspirations, but it accepted prevailing cultural norms. There was not yet sufficient political pressure from women themselves to persuade the administration to do otherwise. Indeed, some of the most important supporters of policies that reinforced traditional gender roles (such as Social Security) were themselves women.

THE NEW DEAL AND THE WEST

One part of American society that did receive special attention from the New Deal was the American West. That region received more government funds per capita through relief programs than any other.

Except for the TVA, the largest New Deal public works programs—the great dams and power stations—were mainly in the West, both because the best locations for such facilities were there and because the West had the greatest need for new sources of water and power. The Grand Coulee Dam on the Columbia River was the largest public works project in American history to that point, and it provided cheap electric power for much of the Northwest. Its construction, and that of other, smaller dams and water projects, created a basis for economic development in the region. Without this enormous public investment by the federal government, much of the economic growth that transformed the West after World War II would have been much more difficult.

THE NEW DEAL, THE ECONOMY, AND POLITICS

The most frequent criticisms of the New Deal involve its failure to revive or reform the American economy. New Dealers never fully recognized the value of government spending as a vehicle for recovery. The economic boom sparked by World War II—not the New Deal—finally ended the crisis.

Nevertheless, the New Deal did have a number of important and lasting effects on the American economy. It helped elevate new groups—workers and farmers in particular—to positions from which they could at times challenge the power of the corporations. It increased the regulatory functions of the federal government in ways that helped stabilize previously troubled areas of the economy: the stock market, the banking system, and others. These and other tools for promoting and regulating economic growth would expand in the postwar years.

The New Deal also created the rudiments of the American welfare state through its many relief programs and, above all, through the Social Security system. The conservative inhibitions New Dealers brought to this task ensured that the welfare system did not solve the problem of poverty, would reinforce some traditional patterns of gender and racial discrimination, and would be expensive and cumbersome to administer. But for all its limits, the new system marked a historic break with the federal government's traditional reluctance to offer public assistance to its neediest citizens.

Finally, the New Deal had a dramatic effect on the character of American politics. It took a weak and divided Democratic Party, which had been a minority force in American politics for many decades, and turned it into a mighty coalition that would dominate national party competition for more than thirty years. It turned the attention of many voters away from some of the controversial cultural issues that had preoccupied them in the 1920s and awakened an interest in economic matters of direct importance to the lives of citizens.

CONCLUSION

From the time of Franklin Roosevelt's inauguration in 1933 to the beginning of World War II eight years later, the federal government engaged in a broad and diverse series of experiments designed to relieve the distress of unemployment and poverty; to stabilize the economy; to prevent future crises; and to bring the Great Depression itself to an end. It had only partial success in all those efforts.

Unemployment and poverty remained high throughout the New Deal, although many federal programs provided assistance to millions of people who would otherwise have had none. The structure of the American economy remained essentially the same as it had been in earlier years, but by the end of the New Deal there were some important new regulatory agencies in Washington—and an important new role for organized labor. The New Deal failed to end the Great Depression. However, some of its policies kept the Depression from getting worse; others helped alleviate the suffering of people caught in its grip; and still others pointed the way toward more effective economic policies in the future.

Perhaps the most important legacy of the New Deal was to create a sense of possibilities among many Americans. The New Deal persuaded many citizens that the fortunes of individuals need not be left entirely to chance or to the workings of an unregulated market. Many Americans, Republicans and Democrats alike, emerged from the 1930s convinced that individuals deserved some protections from the unpredictability and instability of the modern economy. Various parts of the Roosevelt reforms persisted amid broad bipartisan support. The New Deal, for all its limitations, had demonstrated the value of enlisting government in the effort to provide for the welfare of the citizenry.

KEY TERMS/PEOPLE/PLACES/EVENTS

Agricultural Adjustment
  Administration (AAA) 588
appeasement 605
Charles E. Coughlin 595
Civilian Conservation
  Corps (CCC) 592
Congress of Industrial
  Organizations (CIO) 598
Court-packing plan 602
Eleanor Roosevelt 606
Farm Security
  Administration 589
Federal Deposit Insurance
  Corporation (FDIC) 588

fireside chats 587
Frances Perkins 607
Good Neighbor Policy 603
Harry Hopkins 600
Huey P. Long 596
isolationism 604
John Collier 607
John L. Lewis 598
Josef Stalin 606
Liberty League 593
National Labor Relations
  Board (NLRB) 597
National Recovery
  Administration (NRA) 589

Neutrality Acts 604
New Deal 587
Second New Deal 597
Securities and Exchange
  Commission (SEC) 588
sit-down strike 598
Social Security Act 599
Tennessee Valley
  Authority (TVA) 591
Townsend Plan 595
Works Progress
  Administration (WPA) 600

RECALL AND REFLECT

1. What New Deal programs were aimed at agricultural and industrial recovery, and what was the effect of the programs in both areas?
2. What criticisms did critics on both the right and the left level at the New Deal? How did FDR and his administration respond to these criticisms?
3. What gains did organized labor make during the 1930s?
4. What was the impact of the New Deal on women?

25 | AMERICA IN A WORLD AT WAR ●

FROM NEUTRALITY TO INTERVENTION

WAR ON TWO FRONTS

THE AMERICAN ECONOMY IN WARTIME

RACE AND ETHNICITY IN WARTIME AMERICA

ANXIETY AND AFFLUENCE IN WARTIME
CULTURE

THE DEFEAT OF THE AXIS

LOOKING AHEAD

1. What was the impact of the war on the U.S. economy?

2. How was the military experience of the United States in World War II different in Europe and the Pacific?

3. How did the war affect life on the home front, especially for women, organized labor, and minorities?

THE ARCHITECTS OF AMERICAN FOREIGN POLICY in the years after 1918 attempted something that ultimately proved impossible. They were determined to be a major power in the world, extend the nation's trade, and influence other nations in ways beneficial to American interests while also staying completely free of alliances and international agreements. The United States would not join the League of Nations or the World Court. It would operate powerfully—and alone.

But forces were at work that would gradually push the United States into greater engagement with other nations. The economic disarray that the Great Depression created around the globe, the rise of totalitarian regimes, the expansionist ambitions of powerful new leaders—all worked to destroy the uneasy stability of the international system. America's own interests, economic and otherwise, were now imperiled. And America's go-it-alone foreign policy seemed powerless to change the course of events.

Franklin Roosevelt tried throughout the later years of the 1930s to nudge the American people into a greater involvement in international affairs. In particular, he tried to cultivate support for taking a more forceful stand against dictatorship and aggression. A powerful isolationist movement helped stymie him for a time, even after war broke out in Europe, Asia, and Africa. Gradually, however, public opinion shifted toward support of one side in that fight. Then, a direct attack on American forces eliminated the last elements of uncertainty and drove the United States into the greatest and most terrible conflict in human history.

FROM NEUTRALITY TO INTERVENTION

"This nation will remain a neutral nation," Roosevelt declared shortly after the hostilities began in Europe, "but I cannot ask that every American remain neutral in thought as well." There was never any question that he and the majority of people favored Britain, France, and the other Allied nations over the Axis (Germany, Italy, and soon, Japan). The question was how much the United States was prepared to do to help.

NEUTRALITY TESTED

At the very least, Roosevelt believed, the United States should make armaments available to the Allied armies to counter the military advantage the large German munitions industry gave Adolf Hitler. In September 1939, he asked Congress to revise the Neutrality Acts and lift the arms embargo against any nation engaged in war. Congress maintained the prohibition on American ships entering war zones, but the 1939 law did permit belligerents to purchase arms on the same cash-and-carry basis that the earlier Neutrality Acts had established for the sale of nonmilitary materials.

After the German armies quickly subdued Poland, the war in Europe settled into a long, quiet lull that lasted through the winter and spring. But in the spring of 1940, Germany launched a massive invasion, known as a "blitzkrieg" (lightning war), to the west. Hitler slashed into Denmark and Norway, then the Netherlands and Belgium, and finally drove deep into the heart of France. On June 10, Mussolini invaded France from

TIME LINE

1940
Tripartite Pact
America First Committee
FDR reelected
Destroyers-for-Bases Deal

1941
Lend-lease
Atlantic Charter
Pearl Harbor
U.S enters WWII

1942
Battle of Midway
Campaign in North Africa
Japanese Americans interned
Manhattan Project begins
CORE founded

1943
Americans capture Guadalcanal
Allied invasion of Italy
Soviet victory at Stalingrad

1944
Allies invade Normandy
Roosevelt reelected
Americans capture Philippines

1945
Roosevelt dies; Truman becomes president
Germany surrenders
U.S. drops atomic bombs on Hiroshima, Nagasaki
Japan surrenders

the south. On June 22, France fell, and Nazi troops marched into Paris. A new French government assembled in Vichy, a regime largely controlled by the German occupiers. In all of Europe, only the shattered remnants of the British and French armies—daringly rescued from the beaches of Dunkirk by a hastily organized armada of English boats, trawlers, and yachts—remained to oppose the Axis forces.

On May 16, in the midst of the offensive, Roosevelt asked Congress for and quickly received an additional $1 billion for defense. That was one day after **Winston Churchill**, the new British prime minister, sent Roosevelt the first of many requests for armaments, without which, he insisted, Britain could not long survive. Some Americans argued that the British plight was already hopeless, that any aid to the English was a wasted effort. But the president was determined to make war materials available to Britain. Roosevelt even circumvented the cash-and-carry provisions of the Neutrality Acts by giving Britain fifty American destroyers, most left over from World War I, in return for the right to build American bases on British territory in the Caribbean. He also facilitated the transfer of new airplanes purchased by the American military for sale to the British.

Roosevelt was able to take such steps in part because of a major shift in American public opinion. By July 1940, polls showed more than 66 percent of the public believing Germany posed a direct threat to the United States. As a result, Congress was more willing to permit expanded assistance to the Allies, and even authorized the first peacetime military draft in American history.

(©Daily Mail/Rex/Alamy)

THE BLITZ, LONDON The German *Luftwaffe* terrorized London and other British cities in 1940–1941 and again late in the war by bombing civilian areas indiscriminately in an effort to break the spirit of the English people. The effort failed, and the fortitude of the British did much to arouse American support for their cause. St. Paul's Cathedral, largely undamaged throughout the raids, looms in the background of this photograph, as other buildings crumble under the force of German bombs.

But a powerful new isolationist lobby—the America First Committee, whose members included such prominent Americans as Charles Lindbergh and Senators Gerald Nye and Burton Wheeler—joined the debate over American policy toward the war. The lobby had at least the indirect support of a large proportion of the Republican Party. Through the summer and fall of 1940, the debate was complicated by a presidential campaign.

The Campaign of 1940

The biggest political question of 1940 was whether Franklin Roosevelt would break tradition and run for an unprecedented third term. The president did not reveal his wishes, but by refusing to withdraw from the contest, he made it impossible for rival Democrats to establish a claim to the nomination. And when, just before the Democratic National Convention in July, he let it be known that he would accept a "draft" from his party, the issue was virtually settled. The Democrats quickly renominated him and even swallowed his choice for vice president: Agriculture Secretary Henry A. Wallace, a man too liberal and controversial for the taste of many party leaders.

The Republicans nominated a politically inexperienced Indiana businessman, Wendell Willkie, who benefited from a powerful grassroots movement as well as strong support from the magazines *Time* and *Life*. The Republicans took positions little different from Roosevelt's: they would keep the country out of war but extend generous assistance to the Allies. Willkie was a vigorous campaigner and managed to evoke more public enthusiasm than any Republican candidate in decades. But Roosevelt still won decisively. He received 55 percent of the popular vote to Willkie's 45 percent, and 449 electoral votes to Willkie's 82.

Neutrality Abandoned

In the last months of 1940, Roosevelt began to make subtle changes to the American role in the war. Great Britain was virtually bankrupt and could no longer meet the cash-and-carry requirements imposed by the Neutrality Acts. The president therefore, proposed a new system for supplying Britain: "**lend-lease**." It would allow the federal government not only to sell but also to lend or lease armaments to any nation deemed "pivotal to the defense of the United States." In other words, America could funnel weapons to the British on the basis of no more than Britain's promise to return them when the war was over. Congress enacted the bill by wide margins in March 1941.

In a repeat of the events leading up to American intervention in World War I, attacks by German submarines had made shipping lanes in the Atlantic extremely dangerous. The British navy was losing vessels more rapidly than it could replace them and finding it difficult to transport materials from America. Roosevelt argued that the western Atlantic was a neutral zone and therefore eligible for patrolling by American ships. By July 1941, the navy was ranging as far east as Iceland.

At first, Germany did little to challenge these American actions. By September 1941, however, the situation had changed. In violation of their nonaggression pact, Nazi forces had invaded the Soviet Union in June of that year. When the Soviets did not surrender as many predicted, Roosevelt persuaded Congress to extend lend-lease privileges to them. Now American industry was providing vital assistance to Hitler's foes on two fronts, and the American navy was protecting the flow of those goods to Europe. In September, Nazi submarines began a concerted torpedo campaign against American vessels. Roosevelt ordered U.S. ships to fire on German submarines "on sight." In October, Hitler's submarines hit two American destroyers and sank one of them, the *Reuben James*, killing many American sailors. Congress quickly voted to allow the United States to arm its merchant vessels and receive escort all the way into belligerent ports. The United States was now in effect engaged in a naval war against Germany. Meanwhile, Roosevelt met with Churchill to issue a statement of shared goals known as the **Atlantic Charter**. In August 1941, the two nations called for a new world order based on self-determination, economic cooperation, and antimilitarism.

THE ROAD TO PEARL HARBOR

Events in the Pacific would draw America directly into the conflict. In September 1940, the Japanese signed the Tripartite Pact, a loose defensive alliance with Germany and Italy, although the European Axis powers never developed a strong relationship with Japan.

Meanwhile the Japanese were still at war with China and expanding into other parts of Asia. After the fall of France, Japan marched into French Indochina and seized the capital of Vietnam in July 1941. The Roosevelt administration responded by making it impossible for the Japanese to buy American oil and by freezing all Japanese assets in the United States, severely limiting Japan's ability to purchase needed American supplies. Japan then eyed the oil-rich Dutch East Indies (present-day Indonesia). Codebreakers in the United States knew of those ambitions and warned Japan against further aggression. Subsequent negotiations to defuse the hostilities went nowhere. Either Tokyo would have to repair relations with the United States to restore the flow of oil and other supplies or find those supplies elsewhere, most notably by seizing British and Dutch possessions in the Pacific. A sense of which direction things were headed came in October, when militants in Tokyo forced the moderate prime minister out of office and replaced him with the leader of the war party, General **Hideki Tojo**.

By late November, the State Department had given up on the possibility of a peaceful settlement. American intelligence had decoded Japanese messages that made clear an attack was imminent, but Washington did not know where. Most officials continued to believe the Japanese would move first against British or Dutch possessions. A combination of confusion, miscalculation, and underestimation of the Japanese military caused the government to overlook indications that Japan intended an assault on American forces.

At 7:55 A.M. on Sunday, December 7, 1941, the first of two waves of Japanese bombers attacked the U.S. naval base in Hawaii at **Pearl Harbor**, part of a coordinated pattern of attacks against American and British holdings in Asia. Within two hours, more than 2,400 soldiers and sailors died, and another 1,000 were injured. The United States lost 8 battleships, 3 cruisers, 4 other vessels, 188 airplanes, and several vital shore installations, although by a fortunate accident, no American aircraft carriers—the heart of the Pacific Fleet—had been at Pearl Harbor. The Japanese suffered only light losses.

American forces were now greatly diminished in the Pacific. Nevertheless, the raid on Hawaii unified the American people behind war. On December 8, after a stirring speech by the president, all but one member of Congress voted to approve a declaration of war against Japan. Three days later, Germany and Italy, Japan's European allies, declared war on the United States. On the same day, December 11, Congress reciprocated without a dissenting vote.

(©GL Archive/Alamy)

PEARL HARBOR, DECEMBER 7, 1941 At least seven aerial torpedoes and two bombs struck the battleship U.S.S. *West Virginia* on that fateful morning. Repair workers discovered 66 bodies of *West Virginia* crewmembers. After it was restored to fighting condition, the ship reentered the war and participated in the Battles of Iwo Jima and Okinawa.

WAR ON TWO FRONTS

Whatever political disagreements and social tensions there may have been among the American people during World War II, there was striking unity of opinion about the conflict itself. But unity and confidence faced severe tests in the first, troubled months of 1942.

CONTAINING THE JAPANESE

Ten hours after the strike at Pearl Harbor, Japanese airplanes attacked American airfields at Manila in the Philippines, destroying much of America's remaining air power in the Pacific. Three days later, Guam, an American possession, fell. Wake Island and Hong Kong followed. The great British fortress of Singapore in Malaya surrendered in February 1942, the Dutch East Indies in March, and Burma in April. In the Philippines, exhausted Filipino and American troops gave up their defense of the islands on May 6. The American commander, General Douglas MacArthur, vowed as he left, "I shall return."

American strategists planned two broad offensives to turn the tide against the Japanese. One, under the command of MacArthur, would move north from Australia, through New Guinea, and eventually to the Philippines. The other, under Admiral Chester Nimitz, would move west from Hawaii toward major Japanese island outposts in the central Pacific. Ultimately, strategists predicted, the two offensives would come together to invade Japan.

The Allies achieved their first important victory in the Battle of the Coral Sea, just northeast of Australia, on May 7–8, 1942, when American forces turned back the previously unstoppable Japanese navy. An even more important turning point occurred a month later northwest of Hawaii, near the small American outpost at Midway Island. There, after an enormous four-day battle (June 3–6, 1942), the American navy, despite terrible losses, regained control of the central Pacific. The United States destroyed four Japanese aircraft carriers without losing one of its own.

The Americans took the offensive several months later in the southern Solomon Islands, to the east of New Guinea. In August 1942, American forces assaulted three of the islands: Gavutu, Tulagi, and Guadalcanal. A struggle of terrible ferocity continued at **Guadalcanal** for six months, inflicting heavy losses on both sides. In the end, however, the Japanese were forced to abandon the island—and with it their last chance of launching an effective offensive to the south. The Americans, with aid from Australians and New Zealanders, now began the slow, arduous process of moving toward the Philippines and Japan itself.

Holding Off the Germans

In the European theater, the United States fought in cooperation with, among others, Britain and the exiled "Free French" forces in the west, and tried also to placate its new ally, the Soviet Union, now fighting Hitler in the east and desperate for the opening of other fronts against Germany. The army chief of staff, General George C. Marshall, supported a plan for a major Allied invasion of France across the English Channel in the spring of 1943, and he placed the little-known General **Dwight D. Eisenhower** in charge of planning the operation. The Soviet Union wanted the Allied invasion to begin at the earliest possible moment. But the British wanted to prioritize a series of Allied offensives around the edges of the Nazi empire in northern Africa and southern Europe before undertaking the invasion of France.

Roosevelt ultimately decided to support the British plan, in part because he was eager to get American forces into combat quickly and knew a cross-channel invasion would take a long time to prepare. At the end of October 1942, the British opened a counteroffensive against General Erwin Rommel and Nazi forces in northern Africa threatening the Suez Canal. In a major battle at El Alamein, they forced the Germans to retreat from Egypt. In early November, British and American troops landed at Oran and Algiers in Algeria and at Casablanca in Morocco—areas under the Nazi-controlled French Vichy government—and began moving east toward Rommel. The Germans threw the full weight of their forces in Africa against the inexperienced Americans and inflicted a serious defeat on them at the Kasserine Pass in Tunisia. General George S. Patton, however, regrouped and began an effective counteroffensive. With the help of Allied air and naval power and of British forces attacking from the east under Field Marshall Bernard Montgomery, victor at El Alamein, the offensive finally drove the Germans from Africa in May 1943.

The North African campaign had tied up a large proportion of Allied resources, postponing the planned May 1943 cross-channel invasion of France amid angry complaints from Soviet leader Josef Stalin. By now, however, the threat of a Soviet collapse seemed much diminished, for during the winter of 1942-1943, the Red Army had successfully held off a major German assault at Stalingrad in southern Russia. Hitler had committed such enormous forces to the battle, and had suffered such appalling losses, that he could not continue his eastern offensive.

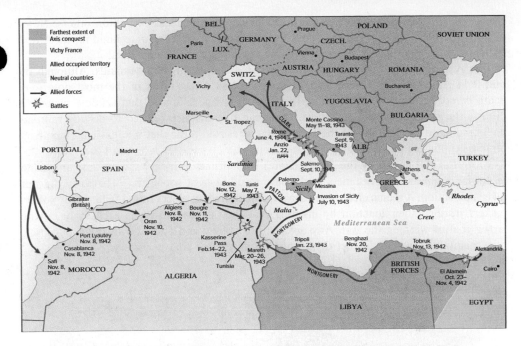

WORLD WAR II IN NORTH AFRICA AND ITALY: THE ALLIED COUNTEROFFENSIVE, 1942-1943
The United States and Great Britain understood from the beginning that an invasion of France across the English Channel would eventually be necessary for a victory in the European war. In the meantime, however, they fought the Axis forces in North Africa, and in the spring of 1943 they began an invasion across the Mediterranean into Italy. This map shows the points along the coast of North Africa where Allied forces landed in 1942, moving east from Morocco and Algeria and west from Egypt. The two armies met in Tunisia and crossed to Italy from there. • *Why were America and Britain reluctant to launch the cross-channel invasion in 1942 or 1943?*

The Soviet successes persuaded Roosevelt to agree, in a January 1943 meeting with Churchill in Casablanca, to a British plan for an Allied invasion of Sicily. Churchill wished to knock Italy out of the war and draw in German divisions that might otherwise be stationed in France. On the night of July 9-10, 1943, American and British armies landed in southeastern Sicily. Thirty-eight days later, they had conquered the island and were moving onto the mainland. Mussolini's government collapsed and the dictator fled north toward Germany, only to be captured later by Italian insurgents and hanged. His successor, Pietro Badoglio, quickly committed Italy to the Allies. Germany nonetheless moved eight divisions into Italy and established a powerful defensive line south of Rome. The Allied offensive, which began on September 3, 1943, got bogged down at that line. Not until May 1944 did the Allies break through the German defenses to resume their northward advance. On June 4, 1944, they captured Rome.

AMERICA AND THE HOLOCAUST

In the midst of this intensive fighting, the leaders of the American government confronted one of history's great tragedies: the Nazi campaign to exterminate the Jews of Europe, which became known as the **Holocaust**. As early as 1942, high officials in Washington had incontrovertible evidence that Hitler's forces were rounding up Jews and others (including Poles, homosexuals, and communists) from all over Europe, transporting them to concentration camps in eastern Germany and Poland, and systematically murdering them.

The death toll would ultimately reach 6 million Jews and at least 4 million others. News of the atrocities soon reached the public as well, and pressure began to build for an Allied effort to end the killing or at least to rescue some of the surviving Jews.

The American government consistently resisted almost all such demands. Although by mid-1944 Allied bombers were flying missions within a few miles of the most notorious death camp, at Auschwitz in Poland, the War Department argued that sending planes to destroy the crematoria was unfeasible. American officials also refused to destroy railroad lines leading to the camp. And the United States resisted pleas that it admit large numbers of Jewish refugees attempting to escape Europe.

More forceful action by the United States, and Britain, which was even less amenable to Jewish requests for assistance, might have saved at least some lives. That they did not take such action, it seems clear in retrospect, constituted an abject moral failure. But policymakers justified their inaction by insisting that they needed to focus exclusively on the larger goal of winning the war. Any diversion of energy and attention to other purposes, they maintained, would distract them from the overriding goal of victory.

(©Bettmann/Getty Images)

THE ST. LOUIS Many people consider the fate of the German liner *St. Louis* to be a powerful symbol of the indifference of the United States and other nations to the fate of European Jews during the Holocaust, even though its forlorn journey preceded both the beginning of World War II and the beginning of systematic extermination of Jews by the Nazi regime. The *St. Louis* carried a group of over 900 Jews fleeing from Germany in 1939, carrying exit visas of dubious legality cynically sold to them by members of Hitler's Gestapo. It became a ship without a port as it sailed from country to country—Mexico, Paraguay, Argentina, Costa Rica, and Cuba—where its passengers were refused entry time and again. Most of the passengers were hoping for a haven in the United States, but the American State Department refused to allow the ship even to dock as it sailed up the American eastern seaboard. Eventually, the *St. Louis* returned to Europe and distributed its passengers among Britain, France, Holland, and Belgium (where this photograph was taken, showing refugees smiling and waving as they prepared to disembark in Antwerp in June 1939). Less than a year later, all those nations except Britain fell under Nazi control.

THE SOLDIER'S EXPERIENCE

The Americans fighting in two theaters represented a cross-section of the country. Conscription helped fill a military force of 16 million that included the vast majority of draft-age men. They came from every ethnic and racial group and all of the communities— Italians, Jews, Russians, Greeks, and many more—largely cut off from new immigration since 1924. Although known later as "the good war," there was nothing good about it to many American GIs. They collectively experienced searing heat, numbing cold, bad food, miserable living conditions, years-long separation from families, and of course the terrors of combat.

Very different war experiences awaited pilots and infantrymen, officers and grunts, generals and nurses. The same was true of white GIs and soldiers of color. During World War II, military leadership consigned African Americans to the most menial assignments, keeping them in segregated training camps and units, and barring them entirely from the Marine Corps and the Army Air Force. In some of the partially integrated army bases— Fort Dix, New Jersey, for example—riots broke out when black soldiers protested mistreatment and segregation. Yet there were signs of change. By the end of the war, the number of black servicemen had increased to almost a million. African Americans were allowed to serve on ships with white sailors, and more black units were sent into combat.

Approximately 25,000 Native Americans served in the military during World War II. Many saw combat, including Ira Hayes, one of the flag-raisers in the famous photograph of Marines on Iwo Jima. Others (mostly Navajo) became military "code talkers," speaking their own language over the radio and the telephones to confound enemy attempts at intelligence-gathering. The war had important effects on the Indians who served in the military. It brought them into intimate contact, often for the first time, with white society, and it awakened among some of them a taste for the material benefits of life in capitalist America. Some never returned to the reservations but chose to remain in the non-Indian world and assimilate to its ways.

A higher proportion of Chinese Americans (22 percent of all adult males) was drafted than that of any other national group, and the entire Chinese community in most cities worked hard and conspicuously for the war effort. And Japanese Americans, eager to prove their patriotism amid vicious prejudice and ultimately internment, fought against the Germans with the 442nd Regiment. Their ranks included future senator Daniel Inouye, who had undergone harrowing experiences as a teenaged medical volunteer at Pearl Harbor on December 7.

The GIs' most faithful chronicler was the beloved war correspondent Ernie Pyle, who spun tales of everyday life, individual personalities, and occasionally tragedy to a stateside audience of millions. Pyle believed no one at home, in part because of censorship, saw the war as he and the soldiers did. After a Japanese sniper killed Pyle in April 1945, GIs found an unfinished column in his pocket. "You didn't see him lying so grotesque and pasty beside the gravel road in France," he wrote of the generic dead soldier. "We saw him, saw him by the multiple thousands. That's the difference."

THE AMERICAN ECONOMY IN WARTIME

Not since the Civil War had the United States been involved in so prolonged and consuming a military experience as World War II. American armed forces engaged in combat around the globe for nearly four years. Stateside changes, in the meantime, reached into every corner of the nation.

PROSPERITY AND THE RIGHTS OF LABOR

World War II had a profound impact on American domestic life by ending the Great Depression. By the middle of 1941, the economic problems of the 1930s—unemployment, deflation, industrial sluggishness—had vanished before the great wave of wartime industrial expansion.

The most important catalyst of the new prosperity was government spending, which after 1939 was pumping more money into the economy each year than had all the New Deal relief agencies combined. In 1939, the federal budget had been $9 billion, the highest in American peacetime history. By 1945, it had risen to $100 billion. Largely as a result, the gross national product soared: from $91 billion in 1939 to $166 billion in 1945. Personal incomes in some regions grew by as much as 100 percent or more.

The West Coast, naturally, became the launching point for the war against Japan, and the government created large manufacturing facilities in California and elsewhere to serve the needs of the military. Altogether, the government made almost $40 billion worth of wartime capital investments (factories, military and transportation facilities, highways, power plants) in the West, more than in any other region. By the end of the war, the Pacific Coast had become the center of a growing American aircraft industry and an important shipbuilding center. Los Angeles, formerly a medium-sized city notable for its film industry, now became a major industrial center as well.

The war created a serious labor shortage. The armed forces took more than 16 million men and women out of the civilian workforce at the same time that the demand for labor was rising rapidly. Nevertheless, the supply of workers increased by almost 20 percent during the war—largely through the employment of many people previously considered inappropriate for the workforce: the young or elderly, minorities, and several million women.

The war gave a substantial boost to union membership, which rose from about 10.5 million in 1941 to over 13 million in 1945. That was in part a result of labor's "maintenance-of-membership" agreement with the government, which ensured that the thousands of new workers pouring into unionized defense plants would be automatically enrolled in the unions. But the government also managed to win two important concessions from union leaders. One was the "no-strike" pledge, by which unions agreed not to stop production in wartime. Another was the so-called Little Steel formula, which set a 15 percent limit on wage increases.

Despite the no-strike pledge, nearly 15,000 work stoppages took place during the war, mostly wildcat strikes (strikes not authorized by the union leadership). When the United Mine Workers defied the government by striking in May 1943, Congress reacted by passing, over Roosevelt's veto, the Smith-Connally Act (the War Labor Disputes Act), which required that unions wait thirty days before striking and which empowered the president to seize a struck war plant. In the meantime, public animosity toward labor rose rapidly, and some states passed laws to limit union power.

STABILIZING THE BOOM AND MOBILIZING PRODUCTION

The fear of deflation, the central concern of the 1930s, gave way during the war to a fear of inflation, particularly after prices rose 25 percent in the two years before Pearl Harbor. Fighting inflation was the task of the **Office of Price Administration (OPA)**, which helped moderate what had been a serious problem during World War I. Even so, the agency was never popular. Black-marketing and overcharging grew in proportions far beyond the OPA's policing capacity.

From 1941 to 1945, the federal government spent a total of $321 billion—twice as much as it had spent in the entire 150 years of its existence as a nation to that point, and ten times as much as the cost of World War I. The national debt rose from $49 billion in 1941 to $259 billion in 1945. The government borrowed about half the revenues it needed by selling $100 billion worth of bonds. Much of the rest it raised by radically increasing income-tax rates, through the Revenue Act of 1942. To simplify collection, Congress enacted a withholding system of payroll deductions in 1943.

In January 1942, to mobilize the wartime economy, the president created the War Production Board (WPB). Throughout its troubled history, the WPB was never able to win complete control over military purchases; the army and navy often circumvented the board. Nor was it able to satisfy the complaints of small business, which griped that most contracts went to large corporations. Gradually, the president transferred much of the WPB's authority to a new office located within the White House: the Office of War Mobilization (OWM). But the OWM was only slightly more successful than the WPB.

Despite the administrative problems, however, the war economy managed to meet almost all of the nation's critical war needs. By the beginning of 1944, American factories were, in fact, producing more than the government needed. Their output doubled that of all the Axis countries combined.

WARTIME SCIENCE AND TECHNOLOGY

More than any previous American war, World War II was a watershed for technological and scientific innovation, partly because the American government poured substantial funds into research and development beginning in 1940. In that year, the government created the National Defense Research Committee (which later became the Office of Scientific Research and Development). By the end of the war, the new agency had spent more than $100 million on research, more than four times the amount spent by the government on military research and development in the previous forty years.

In the first years of the war, all the technological advantages seemed to lie with the Germans and Japanese. Germany had made great advances in tanks and other mechanized armor in the 1930s, particularly during the Spanish Civil War, when it helped arm Franco's forces. German submarine technology surpassed British and American capabilities in 1940. Japan had developed extraordinary naval–air technology, as indicated by the successful raid on Pearl Harbor.

But Britain and America had advantages of their own. American techniques of mass production such as automotive assembly lines were converted efficiently to military production in 1941 and 1942 and soon began producing airplanes, ships, tanks, and other armaments in numbers far beyond what the Germans and Japanese could reach. Allied scientists and engineers moved quickly as well to improve Anglo-American aviation and naval technology, particularly submarines and tanks. By late 1942, Allied weaponry was at least as advanced as, and more plentiful than, that of the enemy. The Allies likewise enjoyed superiority in radar technology and developed effective naval mine detection systems.

Anglo-American antiaircraft technology, on land and on sea, also improved, but never to the point where it could defeat bombing raids altogether. Germany made substantial advances in the development of rocket technology in the early years of the war and managed to launch some rocket-propelled bombs (V1s and V2s) across the English Channel, aimed at London. The psychological effects of the rockets on the British people were considerable. But the Germans were never able to build enough rockets to make a real difference in the balance of military power.

Beginning in 1942, British and American forces seized the advantage in the air war by producing new and powerful four-engine bombing aircraft in great numbers. At higher altitudes and with new navigation systems, they were able to conduct extensive bombing missions over Germany (and, later, Japan) with much less danger of being shot down. The Allies also benefited from a radio device that sent a sonic message to airplanes to tell them when they were within 20 yards of their targets, first introduced in December 1942.

The area in which the Allies had perhaps the greatest advantage was the gathering of intelligence, much of it through Britain's top-secret Ultra project. Some of the benefits the Allies enjoyed came from the capture of German and Japanese intelligence devices. More important, however, were the efforts of cryptologists, or code breakers. Much of Germany's coded communication ran through the so-called Enigma machine, which constantly changed the coding systems it used. In the first months of the war, Polish intelligence had developed an electromechanical computer. It was called the "Bombe," and it could decipher some Enigma messages. After the fall of Poland, British scientists, led by the computer pioneer Alan Turing, took the Bombe and greatly improved it. On April 15, 1940, the new, improved high-speed Bombe deciphered a series of German messages within hours rather than days. A few weeks later, it began decrypting German messages at the rate of 1,000 a day, providing the British (and, later, the Americans) with a constant flow of information about enemy operations throughout the war. British scientists working for the intelligence services, meanwhile, built the first real programmable, digital computer— the Colossus II, which became operational less than a week before the beginning of the Normandy invasion and which could decipher an enormous number of intercepted German messages almost instantly. The United States similarly developed the ability to crack a Japanese coding system.

RACE AND ETHNICITY IN WARTIME AMERICA

The war loosened many traditional barriers that had restricted the lives of minorities and women. There was so much demand for fighting men, so much demand for labor, and so much fluidity and mobility that the social and cultural barriers could not survive intact.

MINORITY GROUPS AND THE WAR EFFORT

In the summer of 1941, A. Philip Randolph, president of the mostly African American Brotherhood of Sleeping Car Porters Union, began to insist that the government require companies receiving defense contracts to integrate their workforces. To mobilize support for the demand, Randolph planned a massive march on Washington. The threat led Roosevelt to promise to establish what became the Fair Employment Practices Commission (FEPC) to investigate discrimination against African Americans in war industries.

The need for labor in war plants greatly increased the migration of African Americans from the rural South into industrial cities. The migration improved the economic conditions of many African Americans. But it also created urban tensions and occasional violence. A terrible race riot in Detroit in 1943 killed thirty-four people, twenty-five of them black.

Despite such tensions, leading black organizations redoubled their efforts to challenge segregation. The **Congress of Racial Equality (CORE)**, organized in 1942, mobilized popular resistance to discrimination in a way that the older, more conservative organizations had never done. Randolph, Bayard Rustin, James Farmer, and other, younger African American leaders helped organize sit-ins and demonstrations in segregated theaters and restaurants. CORE also organized "freedom rides" to desegregate buses and bus terminals. Though often unsuccessful, these efforts strengthened a culture of civil rights activism in the black community.

Leaders called their stateside movement, together with the participation of almost a million black people in the military, the "double-V" campaign—victory at home over racism, abroad over fascism.

The war had important effects, too, on the Native Americans who stayed on the reservations. Little war work reached the tribes. Government subsidies dwindled. Talented young people left the reservations to serve in the military or work in war production, creating workforce shortages in some tribes. The wartime emphasis on national unity undermined support for the revitalization of tribal autonomy that the Indian Reorganization Act of 1934 had launched. New pressures emerged to eliminate the reservation system and to require the tribes to assimilate into white society. The pressures were so severe that John Collier, the energetic director of the Bureau of Indian Affairs who had done so much to promote the reinvigoration of the reservations, resigned in 1945.

Large numbers of Mexican workers entered the United States in response to wartime labor shortages on the Pacific Coast and in the Southwest. The American and Mexican governments agreed in 1942 to a program by which *braceros* (contract laborers) would be admitted to the United States for a limited time. Some worked as migrant farm laborers, but many Mexicans were able for the first time to find factory jobs. They formed the second-largest group of migrants (after African Americans) to U.S. cities in the 1940s. They concentrated mainly in the West but established significant Mexican communities in Chicago, Detroit, and other industrial cities.

The sudden expansion of Mexican American neighborhoods created tensions and occasional conflict. Anglo residents of Los Angeles became alarmed at the activities of Mexican American teenagers, many of whom joined street gangs (*pachucos*). Some wore long, loose jackets with padded shoulders, baggy pants tied at the ankles ("**zoot suits**"), long watch chains, broad-brimmed hats, and greased, ducktail hairstyles. At a time when fabric had been rationed for the war effort, some white people wrongly interpreted the zoot suits to mean Mexican Americans were unsupportive of the war effort— a great number served in the wartime army. But in June 1943, animosity toward the zoot-suiters, driven partly by ethnic prejudice and partly by the apparent disregard of rationing, produced a four-day riot in Los Angeles. Anglo sailors in Long Beach invaded Mexican American communities and attacked zoot-suiters. The police did little to restrain the sailors, who grabbed Hispanic teenagers, tore off and burned their clothes, cut off their ducktails, and beat them. When Mexicans tried to fight back, the police moved in and arrested them. In the aftermath of the "zoot-suit riots," Los Angeles passed a law prohibiting the outfit.

THE INTERNMENT OF JAPANESE AMERICANS

After the attack on Pearl Harbor, government propaganda and popular culture combined to create an image of the Japanese as a devious, malign, and savage people. (See "Consider the Source: The Face of the Enemy.")

This racial animosity soon extended to Americans of Japanese descent. There were not many Japanese Americans in the United States—about 127,000, most of them concentrated in a few areas in California. About one-third were unnaturalized first-generation immigrants (Issei); two-thirds were naturalized or native-born citizens of the United States (Nisei). Because they generally kept to themselves and preserved traditional cultural patterns, it was easy for Anglo Americans to imagine wrongly that the Japanese Americans were engaged in conspiracies on behalf of their ancestral homeland.

THE FACE OF THE ENEMY

During World War II, illustrators used caricature, symbolism, exaggeration, and juxtaposition to mobilize public opinion and behavior. The Japanese were frequent objects of such representation. Early in the war, an artist working under the auspices of the Work Projects Administration (WPA, formerly the Works Progress Administration) produced the poster "Salvage Scrap to Blast the Jap." The second image, Arthur Szyk's cover for *Collier's* magazine in December 1942, depicts the Japanese prime minister Hideki Tojo.

UNDERSTAND, ANALYZE, & EVALUATE

1. The Americans and Japanese are represented by different animals in the WPA poster. What do those choices suggest about how people in the United States viewed the character of the two nations?
2. What event is artist Arthur Szyk depicting in the cartoon on the *Collier's* cover? What evidence can you find in the cartoon to support your choice?

(Source: Library of Congress, Prints and Photographs Division [LC-USZC2-1109])

U.S. NAVY POSTER "SALVAGE SCRAP TO BLAST THE JAP"

(©akg-images/Newscom)

ARTHUR SZYK, *COLLIER'S* COVER, DECEMBER 12, 1942

In February 1942, in response to pressure from military officials and political leaders on the West Coast (including California attorney general Earl Warren) and recommendations from the War Department, the president authorized the army to "intern" the Japanese Americans. The move rested entirely on the assumption that Japanese people harbored characteristics that would make it impossible to tell the guilty from the innocent. So despite the lack of evidence that military necessity required it, and in one of the most extreme cases of racial profiling in American history, more than 100,000 people (Issei and Nisei alike) were rounded up, told to dispose of their property however they could (which often meant abandoning it), and taken to what the government euphemistically called **relocation centers**. In fact, they were facilities little different from prisons, many of them located in the western mountains and desert. A group of innocent people, many of them citizens of the United States, were forced to spend up to three years in grim, debilitating isolation, barred from lucrative employment, provided with only minimal medical care, and deprived of decent schools for their children. The Supreme Court upheld the internment in the 1944 *Korematsu v. U.S.* decision, in part based on evidence from the War Department that later investigation showed had been deliberately stripped of racist language, leaving only the logic of military necessity. Although most of the Japanese Americans were released later that year, they were unable to win any significant compensation for their losses until Congress finally acted in the 1980s. And it was not until June 2018 that the Supreme Court explicitly repudiated the *Korematsu* decision, though that overruling came in the course of upholding President Donald Trump's travel ban on citizens of several predominantly Muslim countries. Critics of the administration quickly pointed out the irony of the Court tossing out *Korematsu* while simultaneously upholding its spirit, in their view, by sanctioning the travel ban.

CHINESE AMERICANS AND THE WAR

At the same time that the war undermined the position of Japanese Americans, the American alliance with China during World War II significantly enhanced both the legal and social status of Chinese Americans. In 1943, partly to improve relations with the government of China, Congress repealed the Chinese Exclusion Act, which had barred almost all Chinese immigration since its renewal in 1892. The new quota for Chinese immigrants was minuscule

(105 a year), but a substantial number of Chinese women managed to gain entry into the country through other provisions covering war brides and fiancées. Over 4,000 Chinese women entered the United States in the first three years after the war. Permanent residents of Chinese descent were finally permitted to become citizens.

Racial animosity toward the Chinese did not disappear, but it did decline—in part because government propaganda and popular culture presented positive images of the Chinese to contrast them with the Japanese and in part because Chinese Americans, like African Americans and other previously marginal groups, began taking jobs in war plants and other areas suffering from labor shortages.

ANXIETY AND AFFLUENCE IN WARTIME CULTURE

The war created considerable anxiety in American lives. Families worried about loved ones at the front, and as the war continued, many mourned relatives who had died in combat. Women struggled to support families in the absence of husbands and fathers. Businesses and communities struggled with shortages of goods and labor.

But the abundance of the war years also created a striking buoyancy in American life. Suddenly people had money to spend again, and despite the many shortages, at least some things to spend it on. In fact, consumerism became, as it had in the 1920s, one of the most powerful forces in American culture.

HOME-FRONT LIFE AND CULTURE

As part of the consumerist resurgence of the war years, Americans spent millions of dollars and hours on entertainment and leisure. Audiences equal to about half the nation's population attended movies each week. Radio ownership increased, and pictorial magazines such as *Life* flourished. Dance halls were packed with young people drawn to the seductive music of bands. Soldiers and sailors home on leave, or awaiting shipment abroad, were special fans of the dances, which became to many of them a symbol of the life they were leaving and fighting to protect. The most popular music was the relatively new jazz form known as swing, which had emerged from the black musical imagination. Bandleaders such as Duke Ellington, who was African American, and Benny Goodman were among the most recognized figures in popular culture, rivaling movie stars.

Much of what Americans read, heard, and saw during the war was managed by the government and military. At the center of the government's propaganda effort was the **Office of War Information (OWI)**. The OWI issued posters, ran magazine advertisements, and produced documentary films. These materials urged ordinary Americans to do their part—buy war bonds, conserve household resources, keep quiet about troop movements.

Government and military officials, meanwhile, censored the reports that journalists filed from the war zone. Correspondents happily refrained from printing anything that might compromise military strategy or effectiveness—they wanted the United States to win too, after all. But Roosevelt and others also believed that gory or depressing war news would sap the public's will, especially in the first two years of the war. It wasn't until September 1943 that officials allowed an image of American dead to appear in print. Federal officials had changed their minds, deciding that slightly more graphic war coverage would awaken a public growing complacent about the sacrifices being made on its behalf.

Hollywood films about the war—and there were hundreds of them—offered a relatively sanitized picture of the conflict. Whether of their own volition or in consultation with military officials, movie producers usually offered a picture of the soldier in line with journalistic reports and government propaganda. In many "platoon films," death came quickly and without blood and guts. Soldiers behaved courageously, missed home, and found maturity (rather than breakdown) through combat. Blacks didn't typically appear in these platoons—true to the reality of a Jim Crow army—but many other white ethnic groups did. In fact, a central point of many wartime pictures, as well as OWI propaganda posters, was that Jews, Polish Americans, Italian Americans, and other groups largely barred by the 1924 immigration restriction had become assimilated contributors to the American military machine. The upshot of all this was a wartime popular culture saturated with combat imagery but which kept some of the worst realities of war obscured, as Ernie Pyle lamented in 1945.

LOVE, FAMILY, AND SEXUALITY IN WARTIME

For men at the front, the image of home both served as a motivational symbol and helped soften the rigors of combat. Letters and mementos from loved ones sustained the morale of millions of service members. They dreamed of music, food, movies, and other material comforts. Many also dreamed of women—wives and girlfriends, but also movie stars and entertainers, who became the source of one of the most popular icons of the front: the pinup. Sailors pasted pinups inside their lockers. Infantrymen carried them (along with pictures of wives, mothers, and girlfriends) in their knapsacks. Fighter pilots gave their planes female names and painted bathing beauties on their nose cones.

For the servicemen who remained in America, and for soldiers and sailors in cities far from home in particular, the company of friendly, "wholesome" women was, the military believed, critical to sustaining morale. The branches of the **United Service Organization (USO)** recruited thousands of young women to serve as hostesses in their clubs. They were expected to dress nicely, dance well, and chat happily with lonely men. Other women joined "dance brigades," traveling by bus to military bases for social evenings with servicemen. The "USO girls" and the members of the dance brigades were forbidden to have any contact with men except at parties at the clubs or during dances. Such regulations were of course often violated. The military took elaborate measures to root out gay men and lesbians from their ranks, vigilantly searching for evidence of homosexuality and unceremoniously dismissing gay people with undesirable discharges. Still, homosexual encounters did occur among and between soldiers. Meanwhile the services quietly tolerated illicit heterosexual activity, which they believed were temporary, natural, and, for many men, necessary.

(Source: Library of Congress, Prints and Photographs Division [LC-USZC4-1047])

WOMEN AT WAR   Many American women enlisted in the army and navy women's corps during World War II, but an equally important contribution to the war effort was their work in factories and offices—often in jobs that would have been considered inappropriate for them in peacetime but that they were now encouraged to assume because of the absence of so many men.

Wartime families also experienced change. The number of women in the workforce increased by nearly 60 percent during the war, as many women replaced male industrial workers serving in the military. These new wage-earning women, on the whole, were older and more likely to be married than most who had entered the workforce in the past.

Many factory owners continued to categorize jobs by gender, reserving the most lucrative positions for men. Female work, like male work, was also categorized by race: black women were usually assigned more menial tasks, and paid at a lower rate, than their white counterparts. But some women began to take on heavy industrial jobs that had long been considered "men's work." The famous wartime image of "**Rosie the Riveter**" symbolized the new importance of the female industrial worker. Women joined unions in substantial numbers and helped erode at least some of the prejudice, including the prejudice against mothers working, that had previously kept many of them from paid employment.

Most women workers during the war, however, were employed not in factories but in service-sector jobs. Above all, they worked for the government, whose bureaucratic needs expanded dramatically alongside its military and industrial needs. Even within the military, which enlisted substantial numbers of women as WAACs (army) and WAVEs (navy), most female work was clerical. But thousands of women, as in Britain, worked for the armed forces cracking enemy codes, though their service was secret and not known about until many decades later.

Many mothers whose husbands were in the military had to combine work with child care. The scarcity of child-care facilities or other community services meant that some working women had no choice but to leave young children at home alone, or locked in cars in factory parking lots, or with relatives or neighbors.

Perhaps in part because of the family dislocations of the war, juvenile crime rose markedly. Young boys were arrested at increasing rates for car theft, burglary, vandalism, and vagrancy. For many children, however, the distinctive experience of the war years was not crime but work. More than a third of all teenagers between the ages of fourteen and eighteen were employed during the last years of the war, causing some reduction in high school enrollments. And lots of children, finally, internalized terrible fears about what might be happening to their fathers or loved ones overseas.

The return of prosperity helped increase the marriage rate and lower the age at which people married, but many marriages were unable to survive the pressures of wartime separation. The divorce rate rose rapidly. Even so, the rise in the birthrate that accompanied the increase in marriages was the first sign of what would become the great postwar "baby boom."

THE GROWTH OF WARTIME CONSERVATISM

Late in 1943, Franklin Roosevelt publicly suggested that "Dr. New Deal," as he called it, had served its purpose and should give way to "Dr. Win-the-War." The statement reflected the president's own genuine shift in concern: victory was now more important than reform. But it reflected, too, the political reality that had emerged during the first two years of war.

The greatest assault on New Deal reforms came from conservatives in Congress, who seized on the war as reason to dismantle many of the achievements of the New Deal. They were assisted by the end of mass unemployment, which decreased the need for such relief programs as the Civilian Conservation Corps and the Works Progress Administration (both of which Congress abolished). They were assisted, too, by their own increasing numbers. In the congressional elections of 1942, Republicans gained 47 seats in the House and 10 in the Senate.

Republicans approached the 1944 election determined to exploit what they believed was resentment of wartime regimentation and Democratic reform. They nominated as their candidate the young and vigorous governor of New York, Thomas E. Dewey. Roosevelt was unopposed within his party, but Democratic leaders pressured him to abandon Vice President Henry Wallace, an advanced New Dealer and hero of the labor movement. Roosevelt agreed to replace him with a more moderate figure, Senator **Harry S. Truman** of Missouri. Truman had won acclaim as chair of the Senate War Investigating Committee, which compiled an impressive record uncovering waste and corruption in wartime production.

The election revolved around domestic economic issues and, indirectly, the president's health. He was in fact gravely ill, suffering from, among other things, advanced arteriosclerosis. But the campaign seemed momentarily to revive him. Roosevelt made strenuous public appearances late in October, which dispelled popular doubts about his health and ensured his reelection. He captured 53.5 percent of the popular vote to Dewey's 46 percent, and 432 electoral votes to Dewey's 99. Democrats lost 1 seat in the Senate, gained 20 in the House, and maintained control of both.

THE DEFEAT OF THE AXIS

By the middle of 1943, America and its allies had succeeded in stopping the Axis advance in both Europe and the Pacific. In the next two years, the Allies themselves seized the offensive and launched a series of powerful drives that led to victory.

THE EUROPEAN OFFENSIVE

By early 1944, American and British bombers were attacking German industrial installations and other targets almost around the clock, drastically cutting production and impeding transportation. A February 1945 incendiary raid on Dresden created a great firestorm that

(©Robert F. Sargent/US Coast Guard/The LIFE Picture Collection/Getty Images)

THE NORMANDY INVASION This photograph, taken from a landing craft, shows American troops wading ashore and onto the Normandy beaches, where one of the decisive battles of World War II was taking shape. The invasion was launched despite threatening weather and rough seas.

destroyed three-fourths of the previously undamaged city and killed approximately 135,000 people, almost all civilians.

An enormous offensive force had been gathering in Britain for two years before the spring of 1944: almost 3 million troops and perhaps the greatest array of naval vessels and armaments ever assembled in one place. On the morning of June 6, 1944 (**D-Day**), this vast invasion force moved into action. The landing came not at the narrowest part of the English Channel, where the Germans had expected and prepared for it, but along sixty miles of the Cotentin Peninsula on the coast of Normandy. While airplanes and battleships offshore bombarded the Nazi defenses, 4,000 vessels landed American, British, Canadian, and other troops and supplies on the beaches. (Three divisions of paratroopers had been dropped behind the German lines the night before.) Fighting was intense along the beach. The superior manpower and equipment of the Allied forces gradually prevailed, though at horrible cost. Within a week, the German forces had been dislodged from virtually the entire Normandy coast.

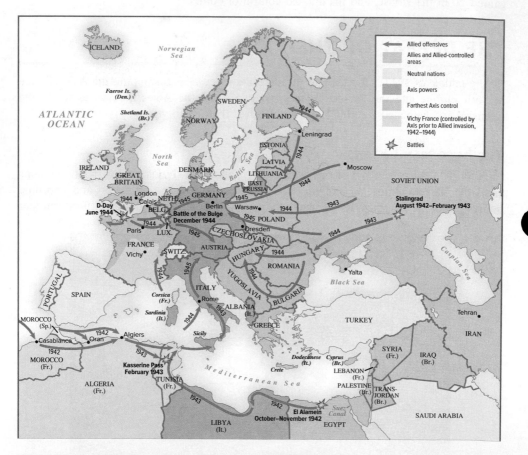

WORLD WAR II IN EUROPE: THE ALLIED COUNTEROFFENSIVE, 1943–1945 This map illustrates the final, climactic movements in the war in Europe—the two great offensives against Germany that began in 1943 and culminated in 1945. The armies of the Soviet Union, having halted the Germans at Stalingrad and Moscow, swept across eastern Europe toward Germany. From the west and the south, American, British, and other Allied forces moved toward Germany through Italy and, after Normandy in June 1944, through France. The two offensives met in Berlin in May 1945. • *Given the history of animosity between the Americans and Soviets, what consequences might have followed from this final positioning of the Allied forces?*

(©Alexander Vorontsov/Keystone/Hulton Archive/Getty Images)

AUSCHWITZ, DECEMBER 1944 This photograph, taken near the end of World War II, shows a group of imprisoned children behind a barbed wire fence in one of the most notorious Nazi concentration camps. A month later, the Soviets reached Auschwitz and liberated the remaining prisoners, though most had been forced to evacuate by the retreating Nazis. Thousands of people met their deaths during those marches.

For the next month, progress remained slow. But in late July, in the Battle of Saint-Lô, General Omar Bradley's First Army smashed through the German lines. George S. Patton's Third Army, spearheaded by heavy tank attacks, then moved through the hole Bradley had created and began a drive into the heart of France. On August 25, Free French forces arrived in Paris and liberated the city from four years of German occupation. By mid-September the Allied armies had driven the Germans almost entirely out of France and Belgium.

The great Allied drive came to a halt, however, at the Rhine River against a firm line of Nazi defenses. In mid-December, German forces struck in desperation along fifty miles of front in the Ardennes Forest. In the **Battle of the Bulge** (named for a large bulge that appeared in the American lines as the Germans pressed forward), they drove fifty-five miles toward Antwerp before they were finally stopped at Bastogne. It was the last major battle on the western front.

While the Allies fought their way through France, Soviet forces swept westward into central Europe and the Balkans. In late January 1945, the Russians launched a great offensive toward the Oder River, inside Germany. By early spring, they were ready to launch a final assault against Berlin. General Omar Bradley, in the meantime, was pushing toward the Rhine from the west. Early in March, Bradley's forces captured the city of Cologne, on the river's west bank. The next day, they discovered and seized an undamaged bridge over the river at Remagen. Allied troops were soon pouring across the Rhine. In the following weeks, the British commander Montgomery, with a million troops, pushed into Germany in the north while Bradley's army, sweeping through central Germany, completed the encirclement of 300,000 German soldiers in the Ruhr region.

The German resistance was now broken on both fronts. American forces were moving eastward faster than they had anticipated and could have beaten the Russians to Berlin and Prague. Instead, the American and British high commands decided to halt the advance along the Elbe River in central Germany to await the Russians. That decision enabled the Soviets to occupy eastern Germany and Czechoslovakia.

On April 30, with Soviet forces on the outskirts of Berlin, Adolf Hitler killed himself in his bunker in the capital. And on May 8, 1945, the remaining German forces surrendered unconditionally. During the drive and in the days and weeks that followed, Allied troops discovered heartbreaking confirmation of earlier reports of Nazi mass murder.

THE PACIFIC OFFENSIVE

In February 1944, American naval forces under Admiral Chester Nimitz won a series of victories in the Marshall Islands and cracked the outer perimeter of the Japanese Empire. Within a month, the navy had destroyed other vital Japanese bastions. American submarines, in the meantime, were decimating Japanese shipping and crippling Japan's domestic economy.

America's principal ally in Asia was China. To assist the Chinese forces, the army sent General Joseph W. Stilwell to help provide critical supplies to China by a land route through India and across the Himalayas. It was a brutal task, but in the fall of 1944, Stilwell's forces succeeded in constructing a road and pipelines across the mountains into China. More dangerously, the Japanese were also threatening the wartime capital of China in Chungking. Chiang Kai-shek, the Chinese premier, was reluctant to use his troops against the Japanese and seemed more concerned with attacking Chinese communists, who were also fighting the Japanese. After Stilwell left China, his successors continued to have trouble prodding Chiang to confront the Japanese.

The decisive battles of the Pacific war occurred not in China but at sea. In mid-June 1944, an enormous American armada struck the heavily fortified Mariana Islands and, after some of the bloodiest operations of the war, captured Tinian, Guam, and Saipan. On October 20, General MacArthur's troops landed on Leyte Island in the Philippines. The Japanese now deployed virtually their entire fleet against the Allied invaders in three

major encounters, which together constituted the decisive Battle of Leyte Gulf, the largest naval engagement in history. American forces held off the Japanese onslaught and
sank four Japanese carriers, all but destroying Japan's capacity to continue a serious
naval war. In February 1945, American marines seized the tiny volcanic island of Iwo
Jima, just 750 miles from Tokyo, but only after the most deadly battle in the history of
the Marine Corps.

The battle for **Okinawa**, an island only 370 miles south of Japan, gave evidence of the
strength of the Japanese resistance in these last desperate days. Week after week, the
Japanese sent kamikaze (suicide) planes against American and British ships, sacrificing

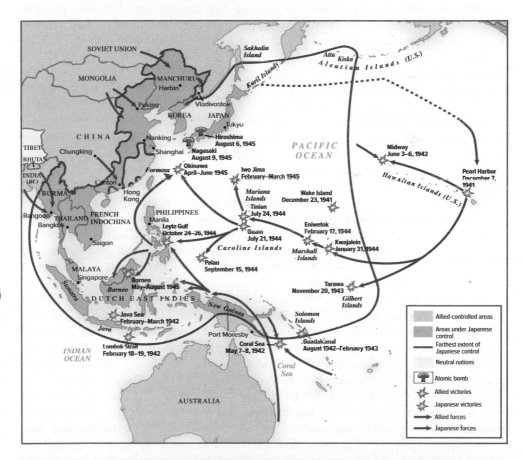

WORLD WAR II IN THE PACIFIC   This map illustrates the changing fortunes of the two combatants
in the Pacific phase of World War II. The long red line stretching from Burma around to Manchuria represents
the eastern boundary of the vast areas of the Pacific that had fallen under Japanese control by the summer
of 1942. The blue lines illustrate the advance of American forces in the Pacific beginning in May 1942
and accelerating in 1943 and after. The American advance was a result of two separate offensives—one
in the central Pacific, under the command of Chester Nimitz, which moved west from Hawaii; and the other,
under the command of Douglas MacArthur, which moved north from Australia. By the summer of 1945,
American forces were approaching the Japanese mainland and bombing Tokyo itself. The dropping of two
American atomic bombs, on Hiroshima and Nagasaki, finally brought the war to an end. • *What might the
Soviet Union have hoped to gain by entering the Pacific war in August 1945, at the very end of the conflict, as shown
in the upper-left corner of the map?*

3,500 of them while inflicting great damage. Japanese troops on shore launched desperate nighttime attacks on the American lines. The United States and its allies suffered nearly 50,000 casualties before finally capturing Okinawa in late June 1945. Over 100,000 Japanese, a huge percentage of the force, died in the siege.

It seemed likely that the same kind of bitter fighting would await the Americans when they invaded Japan. But there were also some signs early in 1945 that such an invasion might not be necessary. The Japanese had almost no ships or planes left with which to fight. The firebombing of Tokyo in March, in which American bombers dropped napalm on the city and created a firestorm in which over 80,000 people died, further weakened the Japanese will to resist. Moderate Japanese leaders, who had long since concluded the war was lost, were looking to end the fighting. But they continued to face powerful opposition from military leaders. Whether the moderates could ultimately have prevailed is a question historians continue to debate. In any case, their efforts became superfluous in August 1945, when the United States made use of a terrible new weapon it had been developing throughout the war.

THE MANHATTAN PROJECT AND ATOMIC WARFARE

Reports had reached the United States in 1939 that Nazi scientists had taken the first step toward the creation of an atomic bomb, a weapon more powerful than any previously devised. The United States and Britain immediately began a race to develop the weapon before the Germans did.

The search for the new weapon emerged from theories developed by atomic physicists, beginning early in the century, and particularly from some of the founding ideas of modern physics developed by Albert Einstein. Einstein's famous theory of relativity had revealed that matter could be converted into tremendous energy. Einstein himself, who by then had left his native Germany and was living in the United States, warned Franklin Roosevelt of German interest in atomic weapons.

By the late 1930s and early 1940s, scientists at American universities were working to catch up with the Germans. Soon after the United States entered the war, the army took over the research and named it the **Manhattan Project**, because it was devised in the Manhattan Engineer District Office of the Army Corps of Engineers. Over the next three years, the government secretly poured nearly $2 billion into a massive scientific and technological effort conducted at hidden laboratories in Oak Ridge, Tennessee; Los Alamos, New Mexico; Hanford, Washington; and other sites. Scientists in Oak Ridge, who were charged with finding a way to create a nuclear chain reaction that could be feasibly replicated within the confined space of a bomb, began experimenting with plutonium—a derivative of uranium first discovered by scientists at the University of California–Berkeley. Plutonium proved capable of providing a practical fuel for the weapon. Scientists in Los Alamos, under the direction of J. Robert Oppenheimer, were charged with the construction of the actual atomic bomb.

By 1944, despite many unforeseen problems, the Manhattan Project scientists pushed ahead much faster than anyone had predicted. Even so, the war in Europe ended before they were ready to test the first weapon. Just before dawn on July 16, 1945, in the desert near Alamogordo, New Mexico, the scientists gathered to witness the first atomic explosion in history: the detonation of a plutonium-fueled bomb that scientists had named Trinity. The explosion—a blinding flash of light, perhaps brighter than any ever before seen on earth, followed by a huge, billowing mushroom cloud—created a vast crater in the barren desert. Watching the test, Oppenheimer was reminded of a passage from Hindu scripture: "I am become death, the destroyer of worlds."

News of the explosion reached President Harry S. Truman, who had taken office in April on the death of Roosevelt, in Potsdam, Germany, where he was attending a conference of Allied leaders. Along with the British, he issued an ultimatum to the Japanese demanding they surrender by August 3 or face utter devastation. When the Japanese failed to meet the deadline, Truman ordered the air force to use the new atomic weapons against Japan.

Controversy has continued for decades over whether Truman's decision to use the bombs was justified and what his motives were. Some have argued that the atomic attack was unnecessary—that had the United States agreed to the survival of the emperor before the bombs were used (which it ultimately did agree to after the bombings), or had it waited only a few more weeks, the Japanese would have surrendered. Others argue that nothing less than the atomic bombs could have persuaded the Japanese to surrender without a costly American invasion. (See "Debating the Past: The Decision to Drop the Atomic Bomb.")

Most of the nation's military and political leaders, however, seemed little concerned about such matters. Truman, who had not even known of the existence of the Manhattan Project until he became president, made what he apparently believed to be a simple military decision. A weapon was available that would end the war quickly; he could see no reason not to use it.

On August 6, 1945, an American B-29, the *Enola Gay*, dropped an atomic weapon on the Japanese industrial center at **Hiroshima**. With a single bomb, the United States completely incinerated a four-square-mile area at the center of the city. More than 80,000 civilians died, according to later American estimates. Many more suffered the crippling effects of radioactive fallout or passed on those effects to their children in the form of birth defects.

The Japanese government, stunned by the attack, was at first unable to agree on a response. Two days later, on August 8, the Soviet Union declared war on Japan. And the following day, another American plane dropped another atomic weapon—this time on the city of Nagasaki—inflicting 100,000 deaths and terrible damage on yet another community. Finally, the emperor intervened to break the stalemate in the cabinet, and on August 14 the government announced it was ready to give up. On September 2, 1945, on board the American battleship *Missouri*, anchored in Tokyo Bay, Japanese officials signed the articles of surrender.

The most destructive war in human history had come to an end, and the United States had emerged from it not only victorious but also in a position of unprecedented power, influence, and prestige. It was a victory, however, that few could greet with unambiguous joy. Fourteen million combatants had died in the struggle. Fifty million or more civilians may have perished, making World War II by far the deadliest war in history. The United States had suffered only light casualties in comparison with some other nations (and particularly in comparison with Russia and Germany), but the cost had still been high: more than 400,000 dead, almost 700,000 injured. And the world continued to face an uncertain future, menaced by the threat of nuclear warfare and by an emerging antagonism between the world's two strongest nations—the United States and the Soviet Union—that would darken the peace for many decades to come.

The Decision to Drop the Atomic Bomb

There has been continuing disagreement since 1945 among historians—and many others—about how to explain and evaluate President Truman's decision to use the atomic bomb against Japan.

Truman himself, both at the time and in his 1955 memoirs, insisted that the decision was a simple and straightforward one. Japan was not ready to surrender in the summer of 1945. The alternative to using atomic weapons, he claimed, was an American invasion of mainland Japan that might have cost hundreds of thousands of American lives. Secretary of War Henry Stimson made the same argument, known as the "orthodox" one, in a 1947 piece in *Harper's Magazine*. That view received considerable support from historians. Herbert Feis argued in *The Atomic Bomb and the End of World War II* (1966) that Truman made his decision on purely military grounds—to ensure a speedy American victory.

(©Bettmann/Getty Images)

NAGASAKI SURVIVORS A Japanese woman and child look grimly at a photographer as they hold pieces of bread in the aftermath of the dropping of the second American atomic bomb—this one on Nagasaki.

Others strongly disagreed. As early as 1948, British physicist P. M. S. Blackett wrote in *Fear, War, and the Bomb* that the destruction of Hiroshima and Nagasaki was "not so much the last military act of the second World War as the first major operation of the cold diplomatic war with Russia." The most important "revisionist" critic of Truman's decision is the historian Gar Alperovitz, the author of two influential books on the subject: *Atomic Diplomacy: Hiroshima and Potsdam* (1965) and *The Decision to Use the Atomic Bomb* (1995). Alperovitz dismissed the argument that the bomb was used to shorten the war and save lives. Japan was likely to have surrendered soon even if the bomb had not been used, he claimed. Instead, he argued, the United States used the bomb less to influence Japan than for what he called "atomic diplomacy"—to intimidate the Soviet Union and "make Russia more manageable in Europe." In *A World Destroyed: The Atomic Bomb and the Grand Alliance* (1975), Martin Sherwin agreed that the bombs carried diplomatic value but also granted the orthodox position that Truman dropped them to end the war quickly.

Other critics of the Truman administration suggested that race played a role in the decision to drop atomic weapons on Japan. These include John Dower's *War Without Mercy: Race and Power in the Pacific War* (1986), Ronald Takaki's *Hiroshima: Why America Dropped the Atomic Bomb* (1995), and Tsuyoshi Hasegawa's *Racing the Enemy: Stalin, Truman, and the Surrender of Japan* (2005). These writers contend that American visions of the Japanese as almost subhuman animated not only Hiroshima and Nagasaki but also the broader character of the war in the Pacific. But there is much disagreement within the revisionist camp. Takaki and Hasegawa agreed with Alperovitz, for instance, that anti-Soviet impulses motivated the deployment of the bomb, but they parted company over other matters including race. Alperovitz wrote that it is "all but impossible to find specific evidence that racism was an important factor in the decision to attack Hiroshima and Nagasaki."

Orthodox scholars, in turn, reasserted their opposition to Alperovitz's idea of "atomic diplomacy" in the 1990s and 2000s with a similar charge: that revisionist scholars misread the evidence or wrote before the release of important new documents. Declassified reports suggested the United States knew in 1945 that Japan was readying itself for an American invasion. Two scholars, Robert H. Ferrell, in *Harry S. Truman: A Life* (1994) and *Harry S. Truman and the Cold War Revisionists* (2006), as well as Alonzo L. Hamby, in *Man of the People* (1995), defended Truman's decision to drop the bomb on military grounds. They cited Japan's unwillingness to surrender and Truman's belief that an invasion would be costly, thus denying the place of atomic diplomacy in the attacks. "One consideration weighed most heavily on Truman," Hamby concluded. "The longer the war lasted, the more Americans killed." In *The Most Controversial Decision: Truman, the Atomic Bombs, and the Defeat of Japan* (2011), Wilson Miscamble likewise called it a "myth" that Japan was ready to give up before Hiroshima and Nagasaki.

The debate over Truman's decision to drop the bomb has generated bitter and even personal exchanges, because at their heart, those exchanges pivot around a wrenching and divisive question: Were Hiroshima and Nagasaki brutal, unnecessary tragedies that killed thousands of innocent people, or terrible but justifiable acts that shortened a war and saved many thousands more? •

UNDERSTAND, ANALYZE, & EVALUATE

1. The United States dropped two atomic bombs on Japan, one on Hiroshima and the other on Nagasaki. Was dropping the bomb on Hiroshima necessary? Was it justifiable? Do the reasons for dropping the bomb on Hiroshima apply equally to the bombing of Nagasaki?
2. How might the war in the Pacific have been different if the United States had decided not to drop the bombs?

CONCLUSION

The United States played a critical role in the war against Germany and Italy. It defeated Imperial Japan in the Pacific largely alone. But America's contributions to and sacrifices in the war paled next to those of its most important allies. Britain, France, and, above all, the Soviet Union, paid a staggering price—in lives, treasure, and social unity—that had no counterpart in the United States. Most American citizens in the United States experienced a booming prosperity and only modest privations during the four years of American involvement in the conflict. There were, of course, jarring social changes during the war that even prosperity could not entirely offset: shortages, restrictions, regulations, family dislocations, and, perhaps most of all, the absence of millions of men and considerable numbers of women who went overseas.

American fighting men and women, of course, had very different experiences from those of the people who remained at home. They endured tremendous hardships, substantial casualties, and much fear and loneliness. They fought effectively and bravely. They helped liberate North Africa and Italy from German occupation. And in June 1944, they joined British, French, and other forces in a successful invasion of France. It led less than a year later to the destruction of the Nazi regime and the end of the European war. In the Pacific, Americans turned back the Japanese offensive through a series of difficult naval and land battles. Ultimately, however, it was not only the American army and navy that brought the war against Japan to a close. It was the unleashing of the most destructive weapon ever created—the atomic bomb—on the people of Japan that finally persuaded the leaders of that nation to surrender.

KEY TERMS/PEOPLE/PLACES/EVENTS

Atlantic Charter 616
Battle of the Bulge 634
braceros 625
Congress of Racial
  Equality (CORE) 624
D-Day 632
Dwight D. Eisenhower 618
Guadalcanal 618
Harry S. Truman 631
Hideki Tojo 616

Hiroshima 637
Holocaust 619
Korematsu v. U.S. 627
lend-lease 615
Manhattan Project 636
Office of Price
  Administration (OPA) 622
Office of War Information
  (OWI) 628
Okinawa 635

Pearl Harbor 616
relocation centers 627
Rosie the Riveter 630
United Service
  Organization (USO) 629
Winston Churchill 614
zoot suits 625

RECALL AND REFLECT

1. List some of the measures that the federal government took to mobilize the nation for the war effort.
2. How did advances in technology affect the course of the military conflict?
3. How did the United States contribute to the Allied victory in Europe? How important were America's allies? Which allies were most important?
4. How did the war affect U.S. society—women, workers, African Americans, Japanese Americans, and immigrants?
5. Why did the United States bomb civilians in Japan and Europe in the last years of the war?

26 | THE COLD WAR

ORIGINS OF THE COLD WAR
THE COLLAPSE OF THE PEACE
AMERICA AFTER THE WAR
THE KOREAN WAR
THE CRUSADE AGAINST SUBVERSION

LOOKING AHEAD

1. What made the growing tension between the United States and the Soviet Union evolve into the Cold War?

2. What is the theory of containment, and how did it drive U.S. foreign policy and foreign interventions in the postwar era?

3. Why did the U.S. government and the American people believe that there was a threat of internal communist subversion?

LONG BEFORE WORLD WAR II ENDED, there were signs of tension between the United States and the Soviet Union. Since 1917, the two states had been suspicious of and opposed to the ideology of the other. Then they were forced into alliance by their mutual antagonism toward the Axis powers, but it infuriated Josef Stalin that the other Allies waited so long to invade mainland Europe. Sensing that hostilities between the two powers might resume after the war, and betting that boots on the ground would translate into influence, both sides sought to occupy as much Nazi territory as possible.

Once the fighting was over, those tensions grew to create what became known as the "**Cold War**"—a long and dangerous rivalry between the two former allies that would cast its shadow over international affairs and American domestic life for more than four decades. The Cold War took shape gradually over a five-year period, during which the relationship between the United States and the Soviet Union deteriorated and the United States crafted a new structure for American foreign policy—known as "containment"—that sought to keep communism from expanding.

Ideological differences between capitalism and communism laced the rivalry with a vocabulary of fear and difference. Yet both sides ultimately fought for something similar, something deeper, and something up for grabs in an era of decolonization—power and credibility around the world and security at home. Sometimes their ideologies led the two sides to pursue such ends very differently. At other times, they behaved similarly. But both sought economic markets, access to resources, military alliances, and above all, to bolster the strength and influence of their states.

ORIGINS OF THE COLD WAR

Few issues in twentieth-century American history have aroused more debate than the origins of the Cold War. Some have claimed that Soviet duplicity and expansionism created the international tensions; others, that American provocations and global ambitions were at least equally to blame. (See "Debating the Past: The Cold War.")

Sources of Soviet–American Tension

For a time, the rivalry between the United States and the Soviet Union rested on a fundamental difference in the ways the great powers envisioned the postwar world. One vision, first openly outlined in the Atlantic Charter in 1941, was a world in which nations abandoned their traditional beliefs in military alliances and spheres of influence and governed their relations with one another through democratic processes, with an international organization serving as the arbiter of disputes and the protector of every nation's right of self-determination. At least in theory, that vision appealed to many Americans, including Franklin Roosevelt.

The other vision was that of the Soviet Union and, to some extent, Great Britain. Both Josef Stalin and Winston Churchill had signed the Atlantic Charter. But Churchill had always been uneasy about the implications of self-determination for Britain's own enormous empire. And the Soviet Union was eager to create a secure sphere for itself in Central and Eastern Europe as protection against possible future aggression from the West. Both Churchill and Stalin, therefore, tended to envision a postwar structure vaguely similar to the traditional European balance of power, in which the great powers would control areas of strategic interest to them.

TIME LINE

1945
Yalta and Potsdam Conferences

United Nations founded

1946
Atomic Energy Commission established

1947
Truman Doctrine

Marshall Plan proposed

National Security Act

Taft-Hartley Act

1948
Berlin blockade

Truman elected president

Hiss case begins

1949
NATO established

Soviet Union explodes A-bomb

Mao victorious in China

1950
NSC-68

Korean War begins

McCarthy's anticommunism campaign begins

1951
Truman fires MacArthur

1952
American occupation of Japan ends

Eisenhower elected president

THE COLD WAR

For more than a decade after the beginning of the Cold War, few historians saw any reason to challenge the official American interpretation of its origins: the breakdown of relations between the United States and the Soviet Union was a direct result of Soviet expansionism and of Stalin's violation of wartime agreements forged at Yalta and Potsdam. The Soviet imposition of communist regimes in Eastern Europe was part of a larger ideological design to spread communism throughout the world. American policy was the logical and necessary response: a firm commitment to oppose Soviet expansionism and to keep American forces in a continual state of readiness.

Disillusionment with official justifications for the Cold War began to find expression even in the late 1950s, when anticommunist sentiment in America remained pervasive. William Appleman Williams's *The Tragedy of American Diplomacy* (1959) insisted that the Cold War was simply the most recent version of a consistent American effort in the twentieth century to preserve an "open door" for American trade in world markets. The confrontation with the Soviet Union, he argued, was less a response to Soviet aggressive designs than an expression of the American belief in capitalist expansion.

As the Vietnam War grew larger and more unpopular in the 1960s, the scholarly critique of the Cold War gained intensity. Walter LaFeber's *America, Russia, and the Cold War*, first published in 1967, maintained that America's supposedly idealistic internationalism at the close of the war was in reality an effort to ensure a postwar order shaped in the American image—with every nation open to American influence and trade. That was why the United States was so apt to misinterpret Soviet policy, much of which reflected a commitment to ensure the security of the Soviet Union itself, as part of a larger aggressive design.

The revisionist interpretations of the Cold War ultimately produced a reaction of their own: what has come to be known as "postrevisionist" scholarship. The most important work in this school attempted to strike a balance between orthodoxy and revisionism and to identify areas of blame and patterns of misconceptions on both sides of the conflict. An important statement of this approach was John Lewis Gaddis's *The United States and the Cold War, 1941–1947* (1972), which argued that "neither side can bear sole responsibility for the onset of the Cold War." Both sides had limited options, given their own political constraints and preconceptions. Other postrevisionist works—by Thomas G. Paterson, Melvyn Leffler, William Taubman, and others—have elaborated on ways in which the United States and the Soviet Union acted in response to genuine, if not necessarily accurate, beliefs about the intentions of the other. "The United States and the Soviet Union were doomed to be antagonists," Ernest May wrote in 1984. "There probably was never any real possibility that the post-1945 relationship could be anything but hostility verging on conflict."

Since the fall of the Soviet Union in 1991, scholars have had access to newly released Russian archives that have enriched the way historians view the Cold War. Those records have shown Soviet ambitions under Stalin in particular to be more tied to strategic and security concerns than to ideological motivations. John Lewis Gaddis, in *We Now Know: Rethinking Cold War History* (1998) and *The Cold War* (2005), portrays a Cold War somewhat more dangerous than his own earlier studies, and those of many other scholars, had portrayed; and he argues that the strong anticommunist positions of Margaret Thatcher, Ronald Reagan, and Pope John Paul II had a larger impact on the weakening of the Soviet Union than was previously understood. Odd Arne Westad, in *The Global Cold War* (2005) and *The Cold War: A World History* (2017), roots the origins of instability in the so-called Third World in the frequent interventions of both the Soviet Union and the United States in the Cold War era. He argues that the conflict reached into every corner of the globe, fueling ideological divides and terrible violence that reverberate to this day. •

UNDERSTAND, ANALYZE, & EVALUATE

1. What are the orthodox, revisionist, and postrevisionist arguments concerning the origins of the Cold War?
2. Was the Cold War inevitable?

But as World War II raged, and even more so as it ended, it became clear that such visions were outdated. The twentieth century had witnessed the diminution or collapse of several major empires—the German, Austro-Hungarian, Ottoman, Italian, Japanese, British, and French. Those upheavals left the Soviets and Americans as the two primary world powers, a situation more dangerous for both parties than one in which strength was spread across various empires that might be played off against one another. As empires shrunk or dissolved, millions of people eventually broke free of the control of distant states. These forces—what historians call decolonization—merged to create an increasingly bipolar world where the United States and the Soviet Union would compete for influence and power, often in places not previously thought to implicate the security of either state. The Cold War ultimately boiled down to that—the search for security and power in a perilous world.

WARTIME DIPLOMACY

Serious strains began to develop in the alliance with the Soviet Union in January 1943, when Roosevelt and Churchill met in Casablanca, Morocco, to discuss Allied strategy. The two leaders could not accept Stalin's most important demand—the immediate opening of a second front in Western Europe to help the Soviet Red Army fight off a German invasion. But they tried to reassure Stalin by announcing that they would accept nothing less than the unconditional surrender of the Axis powers. They would not negotiate a separate peace with Hitler and leave the Soviets to fight alone.

In November 1943, Roosevelt and Churchill traveled to Tehran, Iran, for their first meeting with Stalin. By now, however, Roosevelt's most effective bargaining tool—Stalin's need for American assistance against Germany—had been largely removed. The German advance against Russia had been halted, and Soviet forces were launching their own westward offensive. Nevertheless, the Tehran Conference seemed in most respects a success. Stalin agreed to an American request that the Soviet Union enter the war in the Pacific soon after the end of hostilities in Europe. Roosevelt, in turn, promised that an Anglo-American second front would be established within six months.

On other matters, however, the origins of future disagreements were already visible. Most important was the question of Poland. Roosevelt and Churchill were willing to agree to a movement of the Soviet border westward, allowing Stalin to annex some historically Polish territory. But they differed sharply on the nature of the postwar government in the portion of Poland that would remain independent. Roosevelt and Churchill supported the claims of the Polish government-in-exile that had been functioning in London since 1940. Stalin wished to install another, pro-communist exiled government that had spent the war in Lublin, in the Soviet Union. The three Allied leaders left the Tehran Conference with the issue of the Polish government unresolved.

YALTA

More than a year later, in February 1945, Roosevelt joined Churchill and Stalin again, for a peace conference in the Soviet city of Yalta. In return for Stalin's renewed promise to enter the Pacific war, Roosevelt agreed that the Soviet Union should receive some of the Pacific territory that Russia had lost in the 1904–1905 Russo-Japanese War.

The negotiators also agreed to a plan for a new international organization, one that had been hammered out during the previous summer at a conference in Washington, D.C. The new **United Nations** would contain a General Assembly, in which every member would be represented, and a Security Council, with permanent representatives of the five major powers (the United States, Britain, France, the Soviet Union, and China), each of which would have veto power. The Security Council would also have temporary delegates from several other nations. These agreements became the basis of the UN charter, drafted at a conference of fifty nations beginning April 25, 1945, in San Francisco. In sharp contrast to the American rejection of the League of Nations a generation before, the U.S. Senate ratified the charter in July by a vote of 80 to 2. It was, many internationalists believed, a second chance to create a stable world order.

On other issues, however, the **Yalta Conference** produced no real accord. Basic disagreement remained about the postwar Polish government. Stalin, whose armies now occupied Poland, had already installed a government composed of the pro-communist Lublin Poles. Roosevelt and Churchill insisted that the pro-Western London Poles must be allowed a place in the Warsaw regime. Roosevelt envisioned a government based on free, democratic elections, which both he and Stalin recognized the pro-Western forces would win. Stalin agreed only to a vague compromise by which an unspecified number of pro-Western Poles would be granted a place in the government. He said he would hold "free and unfettered elections" in Poland on an unspecified future date. They did not happen until 1989.

Nor was there agreement about Germany. Roosevelt seemed to want a reconstructed Germany. Stalin wanted to impose heavy reparations on Germany and to ensure a permanent dismemberment of the nation. The final agreement was, like the Polish accord, vague and unstable. The decision on reparations would be referred to a future commission. The United States, Great Britain, France, and the Soviet Union would each control its own "zone of occupation" in Germany—the zones to be determined by the position of troops at the end of the war. Berlin, the German capital, was already well inside the Soviet zone, but because of its symbolic importance, it would itself be divided into four occupied sectors. At an unspecified date, Germany would be reunited. As for the rest of Europe, the conference produced a murky accord on the establishment

(©Bettmann/Getty Images)

YALTA, 1945 Churchill (left) and Stalin (right) were shocked at the physical appearance of Franklin Roosevelt (center) when he arrived for their critical meeting at Yalta. Roosevelt had enough energy to perform capably at the conference, but he was in fact gravely ill. Two months later, not long after he gave Congress what turned out to be an unrealistically optimistic report on the prospects for postwar peace, Roosevelt died.

of governments "broadly representative of all democratic elements" and "responsible to the will of the people."

The Yalta accords, in other words, were less a settlement of postwar issues than a set of loose principles that sidestepped the most difficult questions. Roosevelt, Churchill, and Stalin returned home from the conference, each apparently convinced that he had signed an important agreement. But the Soviet interpretation of the accords differed so sharply from the Anglo–American interpretation that the illusion endured only briefly. In the weeks following the Yalta Conference, Roosevelt watched with growing alarm as the Soviet Union moved systematically to establish pro-communist governments in one Central or Eastern European nation after another and as Stalin refused to make the changes in Poland that the president believed he had promised. Still hoping the differences could be settled, Roosevelt left Washington early in the spring for a vacation at his retreat in Warm Springs, Georgia. There, on April 12, 1945, he suffered a massive stroke and died.

THE COLLAPSE OF THE PEACE

The new president, Harry S. Truman, had almost no familiarity with international issues. Nor did he share Roosevelt's apparent faith in Soviet flexibility. Truman sided with the many people in the government who considered the Soviet Union fundamentally untrustworthy and viewed Stalin himself with suspicion and even hatred.

THE FAILURE OF POTSDAM

Truman had been in office only a few days before he decided to "get tough" with the Soviet Union. On April 23, he met with Soviet foreign minister Molotov and sharply chastised him for violations of the Yalta accords. In fact, Truman had little leverage. Russian forces already occupied Poland and much of the rest of Central and Eastern Europe.

Germany was already divided among the Allies. The United States was still engaged in a war in the Pacific and was neither able nor willing to enter into a renewed conflict in Europe. Truman insisted that the United States should be able to get "85 percent" of what it wanted, but he was ultimately forced to settle for much less.

He conceded first on Poland. When Stalin made a few minor concessions to the pro-Western exiles, Truman recognized the Warsaw government, hoping that noncommunist forces might gradually expand their influence there. (Until the 1980s, they did not.) To settle other questions, Truman met in July at Potsdam, in Russian-occupied Germany, with Stalin and Churchill (who, after elections in Britain in the midst of the talks, was replaced as prime minister by Clement Attlee). Truman reluctantly accepted the adjustments of the Polish–German border that Stalin had long demanded. He refused, however, to permit the Russians to claim any reparations from the American, French, and British zones of Germany. This stance effectively confirmed that Germany would remain divided. The western zones ultimately united into one nation, friendly to the United States, and the Russian zone survived as another nation, with a pro-Soviet, communist government.

The China Problem and Japan

American hopes for an open, peaceful world policed by the great powers required a strong, independent China. But those hopes faced a major obstacle: the Chinese government of Chiang Kai-shek. Chiang was generally friendly to the United States, but his government was corrupt and incompetent, with feeble popular support. Ever since 1927, the nationalist government he headed had been engaged in a bitter rivalry with the communist armies of **Mao Zedong**. By 1945, Mao controlled a quarter of the population.

Some Americans urged the government to try to find a third force as an alternative to Chiang and Mao. Truman, however, decided reluctantly that he had no choice but to continue supporting Chiang. For the next several years, the United States continued to pump money and weapons to Chiang, even as it was becoming clear that the cause was lost. The situation foreshadowed a looming question throughout the Cold War: how far should American leaders go to support anticommunist alternatives around the world, especially when those alternative forces contained their own deep flaws? The Truman administration badly wanted to keep Mao from power in China, but the president was not prepared to intervene militarily to save the nationalist regime.

Instead, the American government began to consider an alternative to China as the strong, pro-Western force in Asia: a revived Japan. Abandoning the strict occupation policies of the first years after the war (when General **Douglas MacArthur** had governed the defeated nation), the United States lifted restrictions on industrial development and encouraged rapid economic growth in Japan. The vision of an open, united world was giving way in Asia, as it was in Europe, to an acceptance of a divided world with a strong pro-American sphere of influence.

The Containment Doctrine

By the end of 1945, a new American foreign policy was slowly emerging. It became known as **containment**. Rather than attempting to create a unified world or destroy communism where it already existed, the United States and its allies would work to prevent Soviet expansion. American leaders almost always assumed the communists sought to spread their ideology in a global revolution and that all communist states were conspiring together to make it happen. Both assumptions, it is clear with hindsight, were problematic. Global revolution and lock-step communist alliances may have been long-term hopes. But Stalin, for his part, put the survival of himself and his regime above all other priorities, and tended to view communist allies more as vehicles for promoting the interests of the Soviet state than as ideological partners. This thirst for security had already led Stalin to murder or exile millions of his own citizens in the purges of the 1930s. Now, fearing capitalist encirclement, he projected that ruthless worldview outward.

But American leaders at the time saw their adversary not as an insecure paranoiac but as an ideologically driven expansionist, and they perceived evidence for that view in Europe and Asia in 1946. In Turkey, Stalin sought control over the vital sea lanes to the Mediterranean, though he harbored no particular hope for communist revolution there. In Greece, communist forces were threatening the pro-Western government, and the British had announced they could no longer provide assistance. And Soviet troops continued to occupy parts of Iran past dates earlier agreed upon. Faced with these challenges, Truman enunciated a firm new policy. In doing so, he drew from the ideas of the American diplomat George F. Kennan, who had warned not long after the war that the only viable American response to Soviet power was "a long-term, patient but firm and vigilant containment of Russian expansive tendencies." On March 12, 1947, Truman appeared before Congress and used Kennan's warnings as the basis of what became known as the **Truman Doctrine**. "I believe," he argued, "that it must be the policy of the United States to support free peoples who are resisting attempted subjugation by armed minorities or by outside pressures." In the same speech, he requested $400 million for aid to Greece and Turkey, which Congress quickly approved.

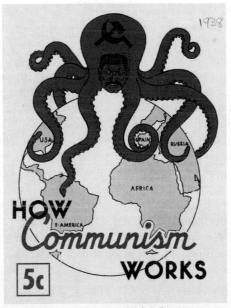

(Source: Rare Book and Special Collections Division, The Library of Congress)

HOW COMMUNISM WORKS   This image and many others like it depicted Stalin as a dangerous expansionist, and communism as an insidious force threatening to take over the world.

The American commitment ultimately helped reduce Soviet pressure on Turkey and helped the Greek government defeat the communist insurgents. In the process, containment became a basis for American policy that survived for more than forty years.

THE CONSERVATIVE OPPOSITION TO CONTAINMENT

The containment doctrine attracted broad, bipartisan support for dealing with the Cold War. But not everyone believed containment was the right way to deal with communism. Some Americans on the left believed that it was an unnecessarily belligerent approach to the Soviet Union and that the United States could have made peace with the Russians. Wider opposition to containment came from conservative Americans, who thought it too weak a response to communism—that, indeed, it was a kind of appeasement.

Among the conservatives who disdained containment were members of an anticommunist organization known as the **John Birch Society**. Its leader was Robert Welch, a man so fearful of communism that he believed that some of the most important leaders of American government were trying to undermine the United States and collaborating with the Soviets. Welch presented his opposition in *The Blue Book of the John Birch Society,* in which he argued that much of the American government was riddled with treason. "For years," he wrote, "we have been taken steadily down the road to Communism by steps supposedly designed . . . as ways of *fighting* Communism." Instead, he argued, it was communist Americans themselves who were undermining the nation. "Both the U.S. and Soviet governments are controlled by the same furtive conspiratorial cabal of internationalists, greedy bankers, and corrupt politicians," Welch wrote. "If left unexposed, the traitors inside the U.S. government would betray the country's sovereignty to the United Nations for a collectivist New World Order, managed by a 'one-world' socialist government." Among the results of treason, Welch claimed, was the creation of the United Nations and other international institutions. Many Americans considered the John Birch Society an extremist organization, but the belief that communism was the greatest danger facing the United States was widely supported.

The opposition to containment reached some of the highest levels of government. John Foster Dulles, who would soon become secretary of state in the Eisenhower administration, wrote the foreign policy plank in the Republican platform in 1952. "We charge that the leaders of the Administration in power lost the peace so dearly earned by World War II," Dulles charged. "They abandoned friendly nations such as Latvia, Lithuania, Estonia, Poland, and Czechoslovakia." Containment, they argued, was a policy of weakness that had allowed the communists to take over much of the world. Instead, those who opposed containment called for what was known as "rollback." Instead of containing communism, the United States should be pushing back the borders of communism, despite the possibility of another war. President Dwight Eisenhower, however, elected in 1952, did not share Dulles's faith in rollback. The government abided by the containment strategy throughout the 1950s and beyond— despite the fevered opposition to what some still considered to be treason.

THE MARSHALL PLAN

An integral part of the containment policy was a proposal to aid in the economic recon-struction of Western Europe. There were many motives: humanitarian concern for the European people; a fear that Europe would remain an economic drain on the United States if not quickly rebuilt; and a desire for a strong European market for American goods.

But above all, American policymakers believed that unless something could be done to strengthen the shaky pro-American governments in Western Europe, those governments might fall under the control of domestic communist parties.

In June 1947, Secretary of State George C. Marshall announced a plan to provide economic assistance to all European nations (including the Soviet Union) that would join in drafting a program for recovery. Although Russia and its Eastern satellites predictably rejected the plan, sixteen Western European nations eagerly participated. Opposition from isolationists in the United States largely vanished after a sudden coup in Czechoslovakia in February 1948 established a Soviet-dominated communist government. In April, Congress approved the creation of the Economic Cooperation Administration, the agency that would administer the **Marshall Plan**, as it became known. Over the next three years, the Marshall Plan channeled $13 billion of American aid into Europe, helping spark a substantial economic revival. By the end of 1950, European industrial production had risen 64 percent, communist strength in the member nations had declined, and opportunities for American trade had revived.

MOBILIZATION AT HOME

In 1948, at the president's request, Congress approved a new military draft and revived the Selective Service System. In the meantime, the United States, having failed to reach agreement with the Soviet Union on international control of nuclear weapons, redoubled its own efforts in atomic research, elevating nuclear weaponry to a central place in its military arsenal. The Atomic Energy Commission, established in 1946, became the supervisory body charged with overseeing all nuclear research, civilian and military alike. And in 1950, the Truman administration approved the development of the new hydrogen bomb, a nuclear weapon far more powerful than those used in 1945.

The National Security Act of 1947 reshaped the nation's military and diplomatic institutions. A new Department of Defense would oversee all branches of the armed services, combining functions previously performed separately by the War and Navy Departments. A National Security Council (NSC), operating out of the White House, would govern foreign and military policy. The **Central Intelligence Agency (CIA)** would replace the wartime Office of Strategic Services and would be responsible for collecting information through open and covert methods. As the Cold War continued, the CIA would also engage in secret political and military operations on behalf of American interests. The National Security Act, in other words, gave the president expanded powers with which to pursue the nation's international goals.

THE ROAD TO NATO

The United States also moved to strengthen the military capabilities of Western Europe. Convinced that a reconstructed Germany was essential to the needs of the West, Truman reached an agreement with Britain and France to merge the three western zones of occupation into a new West German republic (which would include the three non-Soviet sectors of Berlin, even though that city lay within the Soviet zone). Stalin responded quickly. On June 24, 1948, he imposed a tight blockade around the western sectors of Berlin. If Germany was to be officially divided, Stalin was implying, then the country's Western government would have to abandon the capital city in the heart of the Soviet-controlled eastern zone. Truman refused to do so. Unwilling to risk war through a military challenge to the blockade, he ordered a massive airlift to supply the western half of Berlin with food, fuel, and other needed goods. The airlift continued for more than ten months, transporting nearly 2.5 million tons of food and other material, keeping a city of 2 million people alive. In the spring of 1949, Stalin lifted the now ineffective blockade. And in October, the division of Germany into two nations—the Federal Republic in the west (with its new capital in Bonn) and the Democratic Republic in the east (with its capital in East Berlin)—became official.

The crisis in Berlin accelerated the consolidation of what was already in effect an alliance among the United States and the countries of Western Europe. On April 4, 1949, twelve nations signed an agreement establishing the **North Atlantic Treaty Organization (NATO)**,

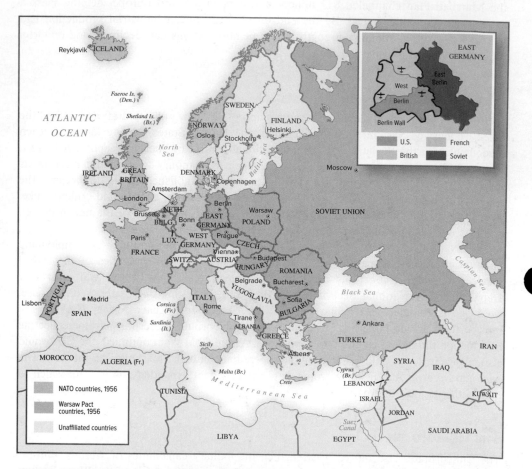

DIVIDED EUROPE AFTER WORLD WAR II This map shows the sharp division that emerged in Europe after World War II between the area under the control of the Soviet Union and the area allied with the United States. In the east, Soviet domination extended into all the nations shaded brown—including the eastern part of Germany. In the west and south, the green-shaded nations were allied with the United States as members of the North Atlantic Treaty Organization (NATO). The countries shaded gold were aligned with neither of the two superpowers. The small map in the upper right shows the division of Berlin among the various occupying powers at the end of the war. Eventually, the American, British, and French sectors were combined to create West Berlin, a city governed by West Germany but entirely surrounded by communist East Germany. The airplane icons represent the airlift of supplies ordered by President Truman into the blockaded zones of West Berlin beginning in June 1948. • *How did the West prevent East Germany from absorbing West Berlin?*

declaring that an armed attack against one member would be considered an attack against all. The NATO countries would, moreover, maintain a standing military force in Europe to defend against what they believed was the threat of a Soviet invasion. The formation of NATO eventually spurred the Soviet Union to create an alliance of its own with the communist governments in Eastern Europe, formalized in 1955 by the **Warsaw Pact**.

REEVALUATING COLD WAR POLICY

In September 1949, the Soviet Union successfully exploded its first atomic weapon. The Russian nuclear capacity came years earlier than predicted, shocking and frightening many Americans. So did the collapse of Chiang Kai-shek's nationalist government in China, which occurred with startling speed in the last months of 1949. Chiang fled with his political allies and the remnants of his army to the offshore island of Formosa (Taiwan), and the entire Chinese mainland came under the control of a communist government led by Mao Zedong that many Americans believed to be an extension of the Soviet Union. The United States refused to recognize the new communist regime.

The fall of China accelerated the fear of communism and persuaded many Americans that the defeat was a result of weakness or even treason. As a result, American friends of China formed what came to be known as the China Lobby. Among its eminent leaders were members of Congress, high-level military figures, and powerful journalists. They believed that the United States had not done enough to prevent the communists from taking over mainland China. The failure persuaded many Americans that the government—particularly members of the State Department—was responsible.

In this atmosphere of escalating crisis, Truman called for a thorough review of American foreign policy. The result, a National Security Council report, issued in 1950 and commonly known as **NSC-68**, outlined a shift in the American position. The first statements of the containment doctrine—the writings of George Kennan, the Truman Doctrine speech—had made distinctions between areas of vital interest to the United States and areas of less importance to the nation's foreign policy. The containment doctrine also called for sharing the military burden of protecting the Western nations. But NSC-68 argued that the United States could no longer rely on other nations to take the initiative in resisting communism. It must move on its own to stop communist expansion virtually anywhere it occurred, regardless of the intrinsic strategic or economic value of the lands in question. To make this happen, the document called for a permanent expansion of American military power, with a defense budget almost four times the previously projected figure.

AMERICA AFTER THE WAR

The crises overseas were not the only frustrations the American people encountered after the war. The nation also faced serious, if short-lived, economic difficulties in adapting to peace. And it suffered from an exceptionally heated political climate that produced a new wave of insecurity and repression.

THE PROBLEMS OF RECONVERSION

Despite widespread predictions that the end of the war would return America to depression conditions, economic growth continued after 1945. Pent-up consumer demand from workers who had accumulated substantial savings during the war helped spur the boom. So did a

$6 billion tax cut. The Servicemen's Readjustment Act of 1944, better known as the **GI Bill** of Rights, provided housing, education, and job-training subsidies to veterans and increased spending even further.

The GI Bill expressed the progressive hopes of many Americans who wanted to see the government do more to assist its citizens. But it also expressed some of the enduring inequalities in American life. Few GI Bill benefits were available to women, even though many women had assisted the war effort in important ways. And while the GI Bill itself did not discriminate against African Americans, its provisions giving local governments jurisdiction allowed southern states, in particular, to deny or limit benefits to black veterans.

The flood of consumer demand contributed to more than two years of inflation, during which prices rose at annual rates of 14 to 15 percent. Compounding the economic difficulties was a sharp rise in labor unrest. By the end of 1945, major strikes had occurred in the automobile, electrical, and steel industries. In April 1946, John L. Lewis led the United Mine Workers out on strike, shutting down the coal fields for forty days. Truman finally forced coal production to resume by ordering government seizure of the mines. But in the process, he pressured mine owners to grant the union most of its demands. Almost simultaneously, the nation's railroads suffered a total shutdown—the first in the nation's history—as two major unions walked out on strike. By threatening to use the army to run the trains, Truman pressured the strikers back to work after only a few days.

Reconversion was particularly difficult for the millions of women and minorities who had entered the workforce during the war. With veterans returning home, employers tended to push women, African Americans, Hispanics, and others out of the plants to make room for white males. Some war workers, particularly women, left the workforce voluntarily, out of a desire to return to their former domestic lives. But a large majority of women workers and virtually all black and Hispanic males wanted to continue working. Postwar inflation, the pressure of a growing high-consumption society, a rising divorce rate that left many women responsible for their own economic well-being—all combined to create a high demand for paid employment among women. As women workers found themselves excluded from industrial jobs, therefore, they moved increasingly into other areas of the economy, above all the service sector.

THE FAIR DEAL REJECTED

Days after the Japanese surrender, Truman submitted to Congress a twenty-one-point domestic program he later named the **Fair Deal**. It called for an expansion of Social Security benefits, the raising of the legal minimum wage from 40 to 65 cents an hour, a program to ensure full employment through aggressive use of federal spending and investment, a permanent Fair Employment Practices Act, public housing and slum clearance, long-range environmental and public works planning, and government promotion of scientific research. Weeks later he added other proposals: federal aid to education, government health insurance and prepaid medical care, funding for the St. Lawrence Seaway, and nationalization of atomic energy.

But most of Truman's programs fell victim to the same public and congressional conservatism that had crippled the last years of the New Deal. Indeed, that conservatism seemed to be intensifying, as the November 1946 congressional elections suggested. Using the simple but devastating slogan "Had Enough?" the Republican Party won control of both houses of Congress, which quickly moved to reduce government spending and chip away at New Deal reforms. Its most notable action was its assault on the Wagner Act of 1935, in the form of the Labor-Management Relations Act of 1947, better known as the

Taft-Hartley Act. It outlawed the closed shop, a workplace in which no one can be hired without first being a member of a union. And although it continued to permit the creation of union shops, in which workers must join a union *after* being hired, it allowed states to pass "right-to-work" laws prohibiting even that. The Taft-Hartley Act also empowered the president to call for a ten-week "cooling-off" period before a strike by issuing an injunction against any work stoppage that endangered national safety or health. Outraged workers and union leaders denounced the measure as a "slave labor bill." Truman vetoed it. But both houses easily overruled him the same day. The Taft-Hartley Act did not destroy the labor movement, but it did damage weaker unions in relatively lightly organized industries such as chemicals and textiles, and it made much more difficult the organizing of workers who had never been union members at all, especially in the South and the West.

THE ELECTION OF 1948

Truman and his advisers believed that the American public was not ready to abandon the achievements of the New Deal, despite the 1946 election results. As they planned their strategy for the 1948 campaign, therefore, they hoped to appeal to enduring Democratic loyalties. Throughout 1948, Truman proposed one reform measure after another (including, on February 2, the first major civil rights bill of the century). To no one's surprise, Congress ignored or defeated them all, but the president was building campaign issues for the fall.

There remained, however, the problems of Truman's personal unpopularity—the assumption among much of the electorate that he lacked stature and that his administration was weak and inept—and the deep divisions within the Democratic Party. At the Democratic National Convention that summer, two factions abandoned the party altogether. Angered by Truman's proposed civil rights bill and by the approval at the convention of a civil rights plank in the platform (engineered by Hubert Humphrey, the reform mayor of Minneapolis), some southern conservatives walked out and formed the States' Rights Democratic (or "Dixiecrat") Party, with Governor Strom Thurmond of South Carolina as its nominee.

At the same time, some members of the party's left wing—contemptuous of what they considered Truman's ineffectual leadership and his excessively confrontational stance toward the Soviet Union—joined the new Progressive Party, whose candidate was Henry A. Wallace.

Many Democratic liberals who were unhappy with Truman were unwilling to leave the party. The Americans for Democratic Action (ADA), a coalition of anticommunist liberals, tried to entice Dwight D. Eisenhower, the popular war hero, to contest the nomination. Only after Eisenhower refused did liberals concede the nomination to Truman. The Republicans, in the meantime, once again nominated Governor Thomas E. Dewey of New York. Austere, dignified, and competent, he seemed to offer an unbeatable alternative to the president.

Only Truman seemed to believe he could win. As the campaign gathered momentum, he became more and more aggressive, turning the fire away from himself and toward Dewey and the "do-nothing, good-for-nothing" Republican Congress, which was, he told voters, responsible for fueling inflation and abandoning workers and common people. To dramatize his point, he called Congress into special session in July to give it a chance, he said, to enact the liberal measures the Republicans had recently written into their platform. Congress met for two weeks and, predictably, managed to pass almost nothing.

On election night, to the surprise of almost everyone, Truman won a narrow but decisive and dramatic victory: 49.5 percent of the popular vote to Dewey's 45.1 percent (with the two splinter parties dividing the small remainder evenly between them), and an electoral margin of 303 to 189. Democrats regained both houses of Congress by substantial margins.

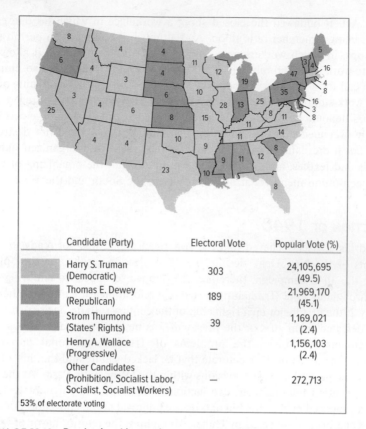

Candidate (Party)	Electoral Vote	Popular Vote (%)
Harry S. Truman (Democratic)	303	24,105,695 (49.5)
Thomas E. Dewey (Republican)	189	21,969,170 (45.1)
Strom Thurmond (States' Rights)	39	1,169,021 (2.4)
Henry A. Wallace (Progressive)	—	1,156,103 (2.4)
Other Candidates (Prohibition, Socialist Labor, Socialist, Socialist Workers)	—	272,713

53% of electorate voting

THE ELECTION OF 1948 Despite the widespread expectation that the Republican candidate, Thomas Dewey, would easily defeat Truman in 1948, the president in fact won a substantial reelection victory that year. This map shows the broad geographic reach of Truman's victory. Dewey swept most of the Northeast, but Truman dominated almost everywhere else. Strom Thurmond, the States' Rights candidate, carried four states in the South. • *What prompted Thurmond to desert the Democratic Party and run for president on his own?*

THE FAIR DEAL REVIVED

With the support of his party in Congress, Truman's Fair Deal reform won some important victories. Congress raised the legal minimum wage from 40 cents to 75 cents an hour. It approved an important expansion of the Social Security system, increasing benefits by 75 percent and extending them to 10 million additional people. And it passed the National Housing Act of 1949, which provided for the construction of 810,000 units of low-income housing accompanied by long-term rent subsidies.

But on other issues—national health insurance and aid to education, among them—Truman made little progress. Nor was he able to persuade Congress to accept the civil rights legislation he proposed in 1949, legislation that would make lynching a federal crime, provide federal protection of black voting rights, abolish the poll tax, and establish a new Fair Employment Practices Commission to curb discrimination in hiring. Southern Democrats filibustered to kill the bill.

Undeterred, Truman proceeded on his own to battle several forms of racial discrimination. He ordered an end to discrimination in the hiring of government employees. He began to dismantle segregation within the armed forces. And he allowed the Justice Department to become actively involved in court battles against discriminatory statutes. The Supreme Court, in the meantime, signaled its own growing awareness of the issue by ruling, in *Shelley v. Kraemer* (1948), that courts could not be used to enforce private "covenants" meant to bar African Americans from residential neighborhoods.

THE NUCLEAR AGE

Looming over the many struggles of the postwar years were images of the terrible mushroom clouds that had risen over Alamogordo in July 1945 and then over the Japanese cities of Hiroshima and Nagasaki. Americans greeted these new instruments of destruction with fear and awe but also expectation. Postwar culture was torn between a dark image of the nuclear war that many Americans feared would result from the rivalry with the Soviet Union, and the bright image of a dazzling technological future that atomic power might help produce.

The fear of nuclear weapons appeared widely in popular culture, but it was often disguised. The late 1940s and early 1950s were the heyday of *film noir*, a kind of filmmaking that originated in France and had been named for the dark lighting characteristic of the genre. American *film noir* portrayed the loneliness of individuals in an impersonal world—a staple of American culture for many decades—but also suggested the menacing character of the age, the looming possibility of vast destruction. Sometimes, popular fears addressed nuclear fear explicitly—for example, the celebrated television show of the 1950s and early 1960s,

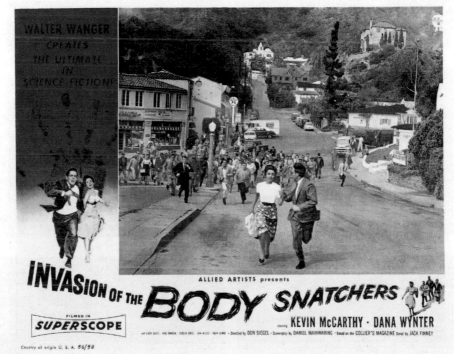

(©Allied Artists/Kobal/REX/Shutterstock)

INVASION OF THE BODY SNATCHERS This 1955 movie was one of many in the decade that imagined dangerous, mysterious invasions or transformations as allegories for the lurking menace of communism. The film told the story of a small town under attack from extraterrestrial, plant-like pods that replicate the townspeople, forming heartless, cold imposters rather like the stereotypical brainwashed communists.

"BERT THE TURTLE (*DUCK AND COVER*)" (1952)

Millions of American schoolchildren watched the 1952 film *Duck and Cover*, issued by the Federal Civil Defense Administration. It featured the animated character Bert the Turtle and a jaunty song whose lyrics are below. The filmmakers used the character to educate children on how to protect themselves during a nuclear attack. Live action sequences showed air-raid sirens and children diving under desks but noted that some attacks might come without warning. Students should "be like Bert! When there is a flash, duck and cover and do it fast!" Desks might seem inadequate protection against an atomic bomb, and indeed, the film has been widely mocked as falsely reassuring Cold War propaganda. But the experiences of survivors in Hiroshima and Nagasaki

(Source: U.S. Office for Emergency Management. Office of Civilian Defense. 5/20/1941-6/30/1945/ NARA (38174))

There was a turtle by the name of Bert
And Bert the Turtle was very alert
When danger threatened him he never got hurt
He knew just what to do
He'd duck and cover, duck and cover

He did what we all must learn to do

You, and you, and you, and you

Duck and cover!

UNDERSTAND, ANALYZE, & EVALUATE

1. What are the main messages of this song?
2. In the context of Cold War America, would "Bert the Turtle" frighten or reassure schoolchildren?
3. How could this song and the film be considered propaganda?

suggested that people outside a certain radius from ground zero could indeed minimize burns and blindness by shielding themselves. In fact, well into the twenty-first century, American officials recommended people take cover and seek shelter in the event of a nuclear terrorist attack.

Source: Federal Civil Defense Administration

The Twilight Zone, which featured dramatic portrayals of the aftermath of nuclear war, or postwar comic books, which depicted powerful superheroes saving the world from destruction. Such images resonated with the public because awareness of nuclear weapons was increasingly built into their daily lives. Schools and office buildings held regular air-raid drills to prepare people for the possibility of nuclear attack. (See "Consider the Source: Bert the Turtle [*Duck and Cover*].") Radio stations regularly tested the Emergency Broadcast System, which stood in readiness for war. Fallout shelters stocked with water and canned goods sprang up in public buildings and private homes. Though few Americans went about their daily lives in a state of panic, anxiety simmered below the surface.

And yet, the United States was also an exuberant nation in these years, dazzled by its own prosperity and excited by the technological innovations transforming the nation, including nuclear power. The same scientific knowledge that could destroy the world, many believed, might also lead it into a glimmering future. The *New York Times*, only days after Hiroshima, expressed its own rosy view of the nuclear future: "This new knowledge . . . can bring to this earth not death but life, not tyranny and cruelty, but a divine freedom."

That kind of optimism soon became widespread. The "secret of the atom," many Americans predicted, would bring "prosperity and a more complete life." A public opinion poll late in 1948 revealed that approximately two-thirds of those questioned believed that, "in the long run," atomic energy would "do more good than harm." Nuclear power plants began to spring up in many areas of the country and were welcomed as the source of cheap and unlimited electricity, their potential dangers scarcely discussed by those who celebrated their creation.

THE KOREAN WAR

Though the Cold War started in Europe, it quickly spread to Asia. On June 24, 1950, the armies of communist North Korea swept across their southern border and invaded the pro-Western half of the Korean peninsula. Within days, they had occupied much of South Korea, including Seoul, its capital. True to the dictates of containment, the United States almost immediately committed itself to the conflict.

THE DIVIDED PENINSULA

When World War II ended, both the United States and the Soviet Union had troops in Korea fighting the Japanese, and neither army was willing to leave. Instead, they divided the nation, supposedly temporarily, along the 38th parallel. The Russians finally departed in 1949, leaving behind a communist government in the north with a strong, Soviet-equipped army. The Americans left a few months later, handing control to the pro-Western government of **Syngman Rhee**. Anticommunist but not reliably democratic, he used his relatively small military primarily to suppress internal opposition.

The relative weakness of South Korea offered a strong temptation to nationalists in the North Korean government who wanted to reunite the country, particularly after the American government implied that it did not consider Korea within its own "defense perimeter." Josef Stalin did, however, view Korea as important to Soviet security, and he approved of North Korean leader Kim Il Sung's decision to launch the invasion. Once again, Stalin's priorities were strategic more than ideological. He held only dim hopes of socialism taking hold on the peninsula but feared that an American-backed South Korean offensive might put a unified pro-Western government at his doorstep. But these distinctions are more apparent in retrospect than they were at the time. To alarmed American leaders, Korea seemed evidence of an ongoing communist crusade to spread itself around the world.

Almost immediately, on June 27, 1950, the president ordered limited American military assistance to South Korea, and on the same day he appealed to the United Nations to intervene. The Soviet Union was boycotting the Security Council at the time (to protest the council's refusal to recognize the new communist government of China) and was thus unable to exercise its veto power. As a result, American delegates were able to win UN agreement to a resolution calling for international assistance to the Rhee government. On June 30, the United States ordered its own ground forces into Korea, and Truman appointed General Douglas MacArthur to command the UN operations there. Several other nations provided assistance and troops, but the "UN" armies were overwhelmingly American.

After a surprise American invasion at Inchon in September had routed the North Korean forces from the south and sent them back across the 38th parallel, Truman gave MacArthur permission to pursue the communists into their own territory. Hoping now to create "a unified, independent and democratic Korea," the president had moved beyond simple containment to an attempted rollback of communist power.

FROM INVASION TO STALEMATE

For several weeks, MacArthur's invasion of North Korea proceeded smoothly. On October 19, the capital, Pyongyang, fell to the UN forces. Victory seemed near, until the Chinese government, alarmed by the movement of American forces toward its border, intervened.

In early November, eight divisions of the Chinese army entered the war. The UN offensive stalled and then collapsed. Through December 1950, outnumbered American forces were forced into a rapid, bitter retreat in numbingly cold temperatures. Within weeks, communist forces had pushed the Americans back below the 38th parallel once again and recaptured the South Korean capital of Seoul. By mid-January 1951 the rout had ceased, and by March the UN armies had regained much of the territory they had recently lost, taking back Seoul and pushing the communists north of the 38th parallel for the second time. With that, the war turned into a protracted stalemate.

From the start, Truman had been determined to avoid a direct conflict with China, which he feared might lead to a new world war. Once China entered the war, he began seeking a negotiated solution to the struggle. But General MacArthur had ideas of his own.

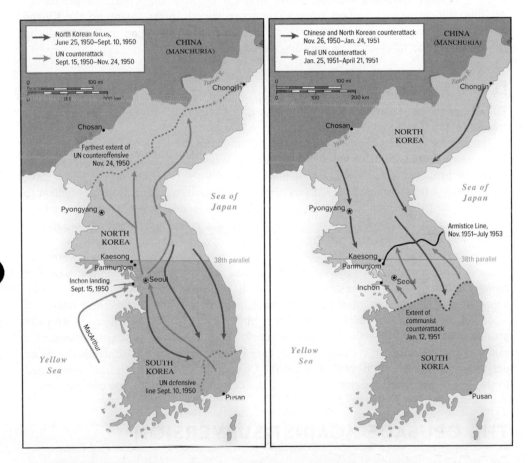

THE KOREAN WAR, 1950–1953 These two maps illustrate the changing fortunes of UN forces during the 1950–1953 Korean War. The map at the left shows the extent of the North Korean invasion of South Korea in 1950. Communist forces for a time controlled all of Korea except a small area around Pusan in the southeast. On September 15, 1950, UN troops under Douglas MacArthur landed in force at Inchon and soon drove the North Koreans back across the border. MacArthur then pursued the North Koreans well into their own territory. The map at right shows the very different circumstances once the Chinese entered the war in November 1950. Chinese forces drove the UN army back below the 38th parallel and, briefly, deep into South Korea, below Seoul. The UN troops fought back to the prewar border between North and South Korea late in 1951, when the war bogged down into a stalemate that continued for a year and a half. • *How did the Korean War reveal the broader character, dangers, and strategies of the Cold War?*

The United States was really fighting the Chinese, MacArthur argued. It should, therefore, attack China itself, if not through an actual invasion, then at least by bombing communist forces massing north of the Chinese border with conventional or even atomic weapons. In March 1951, he indicated his unhappiness with Truman's reluctance to invade China. In a public letter to House Republican Leader Joseph W. Martin, he concluded: "There is no substitute for victory." His position had wide popular support. Yet the release of the Martin letter struck the president as intolerable insubordination. On April 11, 1951, he relieved MacArthur of his command.

Sixty-nine percent of the American people supported MacArthur, a Gallup poll reported. When the general returned to the United States later in 1951, he was greeted with wild enthusiasm. Criticism of Truman finally abated somewhat when a number of prominent military figures, including General Omar Bradley, publicly supported the president's decision. But substantial hostility toward Truman remained. In the meantime, the Korean stalemate continued. Negotiations between the opposing forces began at Panmunjom in July 1951, but the talks—and the war—dragged on until 1953.

LIMITED MOBILIZATION

The war in Korea produced only a limited American military commitment abroad. It also created only a limited economic mobilization at home.

Truman set up the Office of Defense Mobilization to fight inflation by holding down prices and discouraging high union wage demands. When these cautious regulatory efforts failed, the president took more drastic action. Railroad workers walked off the job in 1951, and Truman, who considered the workers' demands inflationary, ordered the government to take control of the railroads. In 1952, during a nationwide steel strike, Truman seized the steel mills, citing his powers as commander in chief. But in a 6-to-3 decision, the Supreme Court ruled that the president had exceeded his authority, and Truman was forced to relent.

The Korean War significantly boosted economic growth by pumping new government funds into the economy. But the war had other, less welcome effects. It came at a time of rising insecurity about America's position in the world and intensified anxiety about communism. As the long stalemate continued, producing 140,000 American dead and wounded, frustration turned to anger. The United States, which had recently won the greatest war in history, seemed unable to conclude what many Americans considered a minor border skirmish in a small country. They began to believe that something must be deeply wrong—not only in Korea but within the United States as well. Such fears contributed to the rise of the second major campaign of the century against domestic communism.

THE CRUSADE AGAINST SUBVERSION

Why did the American people develop a growing fear of internal communist subversion, a fear that by the early 1950s occasionally reached the point of hysteria?

One factor was obvious: communism was not an imagined enemy. It took tangible shape in Josef Stalin and the Soviet Union. Adding to the concern were the Korean stalemate, the "loss" of China, and the Soviet development of an atomic bomb. Searching for someone to blame, many began to believe that there was a communist conspiracy within American borders. But there were other factors as well, rooted in events in American domestic politics.

HUAC and Alger Hiss

Much of the anticommunist furor emerged out of the search by Republicans for an issue with which to attack the Democrats, and out of the efforts of the Democrats to take that issue away from them. Beginning in 1947, the **House Un-American Activities Committee (HUAC)** held widely publicized investigations to prove that, under Democratic rule, the government had tolerated if not actually encouraged communist subversion. The committee turned first to the movie industry, arguing that communists had infiltrated Hollywood and tainted American films with propaganda. Writers and producers, some of them former communists, were called to testify; and when some of them (the "Hollywood Ten") refused to answer questions about their political beliefs and those of their colleagues, they were sent to jail for contempt. Others were barred from employment in the industry when Hollywood, attempting to protect its public image, adopted a "blacklist" of those of "suspicious loyalty."

More alarming to the public was HUAC's investigation into charges of disloyalty leveled against **Alger Hiss**, a former high-ranking member of the State Department. In 1948, Whittaker Chambers, a former communist agent, now a conservative editor at *Time* magazine, told the committee that Hiss had passed classified State Department documents to him in 1937 and 1938. When Hiss sued him for slander, Chambers produced microfilms of the documents (called the "pumpkin papers," because Chambers had kept them hidden in a pumpkin in his vegetable garden). Hiss could not be tried for espionage because of the statute of limitations, which protects individuals from prosecution for most crimes after seven years have passed. But largely because of the relentless efforts of Richard M. Nixon, a first-term congressman from California and a member of HUAC, Hiss was convicted of perjury and served several years in prison. The Hiss case not only discredited a prominent young diplomat, it also cast suspicion on a generation of liberal Democrats. And it transformed Nixon into a national figure and helped him win a Senate seat in 1950.

The Federal Loyalty Program and the Rosenberg Case

Partly to protect itself against Republican attacks and partly to encourage support for the president's foreign policy initiatives, the Truman administration in 1947 initiated a widely publicized program to review the loyalty of federal employees. By 1951, more than 2,000 government employees had resigned under pressure and 212 had been dismissed.

The Federal Employee Loyalty Program helped launch a major assault on subversion throughout the government and beyond. The attorney general established a widely cited list of supposedly subversive organizations. The director of the Federal Bureau of Investigation (FBI), J. Edgar Hoover, investigated and harassed alleged radicals. In 1950, Congress passed the McCarran Internal Security Act, which, among other restrictions on "subversive" activity, required that all communist organizations register with the government and publish their records. Congress easily overrode Truman's veto of the bill.

The successful Soviet detonation of an atomic bomb in 1949 suggested to some that there had been a conspiracy to pass American atomic secrets to the Russians. In 1950, Klaus Fuchs, a young British scientist, seemed to confirm those fears when he testified that he had delivered to the Russians details of the bomb's manufacture. The case ultimately moved to an obscure New York couple, **Julius and Ethel Rosenberg**, members of the Communist Party. The government claimed the Rosenbergs had received secret information from Ethel's brother, a machinist on the Manhattan Project in New Mexico, and had passed it on to the Soviet Union through other agents (including Fuchs). The Rosenbergs were convicted and, on April 5, 1951, sentenced to death. After two years of appeals and public protests, they died in the electric chair on June 19, 1953. Historians now believe that Julius—but not Ethel—was guilty as charged.

All these factors—the HUAC investigations, the Hiss trial, the loyalty investigations, the McCarran Act, the Rosenberg case—combined with other concerns by the early 1950s to create a fear of communist subversion that seemed to grip the country. State and local governments, the judiciary, schools and universities, labor unions—all sought to purge themselves of real or imagined subversives. It was a climate that made possible the rise of an extraordinary public figure.

McCarthyism

Joseph McCarthy was an undistinguished first-term Republican senator from Wisconsin until, in February 1950, in the midst of a speech in Wheeling, West Virginia, he lifted up a sheet of paper and claimed to "hold in my hand" a list of 205 known communists currently working in the American State Department. No person of comparable stature had ever made so bold a charge against the federal government. In the months to come,

(©REX/Shutterstock)

MCCARTHY TESTIFIES IN THE SENATE, MARCH 1950 One of the first consequences of Senator Joseph McCarthy's speech in West Virginia was the creation of a subcommittee of the Senate Foreign Relations Committee to investigate his charges. Although the committee chairman, Democrat Millard Tydings of Maryland, thought McCarthy's infamous list a "hoax," it was from this platform that the senator leveled many of his early accusations of communist State Department infiltration.

as McCarthy repeated and expanded on his accusations, he emerged as the nation's most prominent leader of the crusade against domestic subversion.

Within weeks of his charges against the State Department, McCarthy leveled accusations at other agencies. After 1952, with the Republicans in control of the Senate and McCarthy now the chair of a special subcommittee, he conducted highly publicized investigations of alleged subversion in many areas of the government. McCarthy never produced conclusive evidence that any federal employee was a communist. But a growing constituency adored him nevertheless for his coarse assaults on a government establishment that many considered arrogant, effete, even traitorous. Republicans, in particular, rallied to his claims that the Democrats had been responsible for "twenty years of treason" and that only a change of parties could rid the country of subversion.

McCarthy, in short, provided his followers with an issue into which they could channel a wide range of resentments: fear of communism, animosity toward east coast intellectual foreign policy elites, and frustrated partisan ambitions. Homophobia and racism, too, coursed through the anticommunist crusade. President Truman and many others used phrases like "parlor pinks" to describe communists, suggesting that depraved sexual behaviors accompanied or signaled depraved political philosophies. Opponents of equality for African Americans, as well, increasingly blamed southern civil rights activity on "outside agitators," widely understood to mean communists. Thus McCarthyism and anticommunism more broadly gave their prophets a venue and vocabulary for expressing other frustrations and prejudices.

For a time, McCarthy intimidated all but a few people from opposing him. Even the highly popular Dwight D. Eisenhower, running for president in 1952, did not speak out against him, although he disliked McCarthy's tactics and was outraged at, among other things, McCarthy's attacks on General George Marshall. Eventually his assaults against such respected figures and institutions drove McCarthy from popular favor—but not before "**McCarthyism**" came to define an era of hysterical and often unfounded accusations.

The Republican Revival

Public frustration over the stalemate in Korea and popular fears of internal subversion combined to make 1952 a bad year for the Democratic Party. Truman, now deeply unpopular, withdrew from the presidential contest. The party united instead behind Governor Adlai E. Stevenson of Illinois. Stevenson's dignity, wit, and eloquence made him a beloved figure to many liberals and intellectuals. But those same qualities seemed only to fuel Republican charges that Stevenson lacked the strength or the will to combat communism sufficiently.

Stevenson's greatest problem, however, was the Republican candidate opposing him. Rejecting the efforts of conservatives to nominate Robert Taft or Douglas MacArthur, the Republicans turned to a man who had no previous identification with the party: General Dwight D. Eisenhower—military hero, commander of NATO, president of Columbia University—who won nomination on the first ballot. He chose as his running mate the young California senator who had gained national prominence through his crusade against Alger Hiss: Richard M. Nixon.

In the fall campaign, Eisenhower attracted support through his geniality and his statesmanlike pledges to settle the Korean conflict. Nixon, after surviving early accusations of financial improprieties, which he effectively neutralized in a famous television address, the Checkers speech, exploited the issue of domestic anticommunism by attacking the Democrats for "cowardice" and "appeasement." The response at the polls was overwhelming.

Eisenhower won both a popular and an electoral landslide: 55 percent of the popular vote to Stevenson's 44 percent, 442 electoral votes to Stevenson's 89. Republicans gained control of both houses of Congress for the first time since 1946.

CONCLUSION

Even during World War II, when the United States and the Soviet Union were allies, it was evident to leaders in both nations that America and Russia had quite different visions of what the postwar world should look like. Very quickly after the war ended, the relationship between the world's greatest powers soured. Americans came to believe that the Soviet Union, like Hitler's Germany, harbored dangerous expansionist ambitions. Soviets came to believe that the United States was trying to protect its own dominance in the world by encircling the Soviet Union. The result of these tensions by the end of the 1940s was the Cold War.

In the early years of the rivalry, the United States constructed a series of policies designed to prevent both war and Soviet aggression. It helped rebuild the shattered economies of Western Europe through the Marshall Plan, to stabilize those nations and prevent them from becoming communist. America embraced a new foreign policy—known as containment—that committed it to keeping the Soviet Union from expanding its influence further into the world. The United States and Western Europe formed a strong and enduring alliance, NATO, to defend Europe against possible Soviet advances.

In 1950, the armed forces of communist North Korea launched an invasion of noncommunist South Korea. To many Americans, the conflict seemed a test of American resolve. The Korean War was long, costly, and unpopular, with many military setbacks and frustrations. In the end, however, the United States—working through the United Nations—managed to drive the North Koreans out of South Korea and restore the original division of the peninsula.

The Korean War hardened American foreign policy into a much more rigidly anticommunist form. It undermined the Truman administration, and the Democratic Party, and helped strengthen conservatives and Republicans. It greatly bolstered an already powerful crusade against communists, and those believed to be communists, within the United States—a crusade often known as McCarthyism, because of the notoriety of Senator Joseph McCarthy of Wisconsin, the most celebrated leader of the effort.

America after World War II was indisputably the wealthiest and most powerful nation in the world. But in the harsh climate of the Cold War, neither wealth nor power could dispel deep anxieties and bitter divisions.

KEY TERMS/PEOPLE/PLACES/EVENTS

Alger Hiss 663
Central Intelligence
 Agency (CIA) 651
Cold War 642
containment 648
Douglas MacArthur
 648
Fair Deal 654
GI Bill 654

House Un-American
 Activities Committee
 (HUAC) 663
John Birch Society 650
Julius and Ethel
 Rosenberg 663
Mao Zedong 648
Marshall Plan 651
McCarthyism 665

North Atlantic Treaty
 Organization (NATO) 652
NSC-68 653
Syngman Rhee 660
Taft-Hartley Act 655
Truman Doctrine 649
United Nations 646
Warsaw Pact 653
Yalta Conference 646

RECALL AND REFLECT

1. How did American diplomats plan for the postwar world and settle postwar issues? How did opposing visions of the postwar world order thwart those efforts?
2. How did postwar economic problems affect American politics and society?
3. Why did the United States become involved in the war in Korea? What was the result of U.S. involvement in that war?
4. Why did the fear of communism at home reach such great proportions? What events helped fan that fear?

27 | THE AFFLUENT SOCIETY

THE ECONOMIC "MIRACLE"

THE EXPLOSION OF SCIENCE
  AND TECHNOLOGY

PEOPLE OF PLENTY

THE OTHER AMERICA

THE RISE OF THE CIVIL RIGHTS MOVEMENT

EISENHOWER REPUBLICANISM

EISENHOWER, DULLES, AND THE COLD WAR

LOOKING AHEAD

1. Why did the U.S. economy experience such a boom in the late 1950s and early 1960s? How did this boom affect American society?

2. Who constituted the "other America"—those who failed to share in the economic prosperity and affluence of the postwar era? Why were they left out?

3. What was the response to the Supreme Court decision in *Brown v. Board of Education*? How did the Court's decision affect African Americans and the early civil rights movement? How did it affect white southerners?

4. What policy guided foreign affairs under Eisenhower, and how was that policy implemented around the world?

IF AMERICA EXPERIENCED A GOLDEN age in the 1950s and early 1960s, as many Americans believed at the time and many continue to do so today, it was largely a result of two developments. One was a booming national prosperity, which profoundly altered the social, economic, and even physical landscape of the United States. More Americans had more money than ever before, and this new level of wealth fueled a rise in popular consumption unrivaled in the nation's history.

The other was the continuing struggle against communism, which created considerable anxiety but also encouraged many Americans to look even more approvingly at their own society. As communist powers like the Soviet Union and smaller nations like Cuba staked an increasingly defiant posture against democracy, American leaders responded by building up the nuclear arsenal and fashioning a muscular foreign policy that promised to counter the spread of communism around the globe. These escalating international tensions triggered anxiety at home, however, and prompted lawmakers to search desperately for communists and turncoats that may be living among them. They also motivated everyday citizens to find comfort by celebrating family life and the material abundance that the American way of life supposedly made possible.

But if these powerful forces created a popular sense of national purpose and self-satisfaction, it was far from universal. The poor and the marginalized were largely forgotten while African Americans and other citizens of color were effectively blocked from participating in them. These forces also helped blind many Americans to serious problems brimming at home, such as racism and high rates of poverty among many rural and urban communities, and they helped set the stage for civil rights protests that shook the country in the mid-twentieth century.

THE ECONOMIC "MIRACLE"

Perhaps the most striking feature of American society in the 1950s and early 1960s was the booming economic growth that made even the heady 1920s seem pale by comparison. It was a better-balanced and more widely distributed prosperity than that of thirty years earlier. But it was far from universal.

ECONOMIC GROWTH

By 1949, despite the continuing problems of postwar reconversion, an economic expansion had begun that would continue with only brief interruptions for almost twenty years.

The causes of this growth were varied. Part of it came from Americans throwing off the emotional shackles of the Great Depression. Buoyed by victory in the world war, Americans again began to believe in a brighter future and they invested heavily in it. Politicians led the way by committing

TIME LINE

1947
Levittown construction begins

1953
Korean War ends

1954
Brown v. Board of Education

Army–McCarthy hearings

1955
Montgomery bus boycott

1956
Federal Highway Act

Eisenhower reelected

Suez crisis

1957
Sputnik launched

Kerouac's *On the Road*

Little Rock desegregation crisis

1959
Castro seizes power in Cuba

1960
U-2 incident

Eisenhower's farewell address

1961
First American in space

U.S. severs diplomatic relations with Cuba

1969
Americans land on moon

near-record levels of public money to accelerate the growth of different facets of the economy. As it had during the Great Depression and World War II, government spending stimulated rapid economic progress. Millions of dollars flowed to public schools and housing, veterans' benefits, welfare, interstate highways, and the especially the military.

The results were impressive. Between 1945 and 1960, the gross national product grew by a staggering 250 percent, from $200 billion to over $500 billion. Unemployment remained at about 5 percent or lower throughout the 1950s and early 1960s. Inflation, in the meantime, hovered around 3 percent a year or less. Economic growth actually peaked during the first half of the 1950s, when the government upped its military spending to fight the Korean War. Additionally, trade agreements forged immediately after the war opened new and profitable markets for goods and services like no other time before. Virtually untouched by the destruction of war, U.S. manufacturing and services reaped the initial rewards of international trade.

The rising economy inspired confidence in the future for many Americans. Not surprisingly, the national birthrate jumped, replacing a long pattern of decline with what is now commonly called the **Baby Boom**. It began during World War II and peaked in 1957. The nation's population rose almost 20 percent in this decade, from 150 million in 1950 to 179 million in 1960, which in turn boosted consumer demand and spending and further contributed to the expanding economy.

Many parents sought to raise their growing families in the suburbs, a critical reason for the 47 percent increase in the suburban population during the 1950s. Related sectors of the economy expanded as well. The number of privately owned cars, for example,

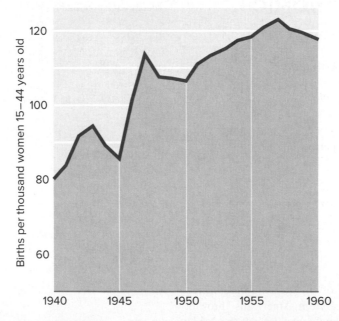

THE AMERICAN BIRTHRATE, 1940–1960   This chart shows how the American birthrate grew rapidly during and after World War II (following a long period of decline in the 1930s) to produce what became known as the "Baby Boom." At the peak of the Baby Boom, during the 1950s, the nation's population grew by 20 percent. • *What impact did the Baby Boom have on the nation's economy?*

more than doubled in a decade. The housing industry boomed. And road construction suddenly jumped.

The combination of post-WWII economic growth, rising rates of government spending, and surging population increase led to a renewed American prosperity. And while not every American—especially black, Hispanic, and Native American—shared equally in that prosperity, the average American in 1960 still had over 20 percent more purchasing power than in 1945 and more than twice as much as during the prosperous 1920s. By 1960, the American people had achieved the highest standard of living of any society in the history of the world.

THE RISE OF THE MODERN WEST

No region experienced more dramatic changes than the American West. Its population expanded dramatically; its cities boomed; its industrial economy flourished. By the 1960s, the West contained some of the most important industrial and cultural centers in the nation.

As during World War II, federal spending and investment powered much of the growth of the West. Funding from Washington made possible the construction of new dams, power stations, highways, and irrigation projects. Massive military contracts continued to flow to factories in California and Texas, as they had during the war. The increasing number of automobiles created new demand for petroleum, which led to the swift expansion in the number oil fields and refineries in Texas and Colorado and the development of Houston, Dallas, Denver, and other key cities.

State legislatures also fueled growth by investing heavily in higher education. The University of Texas and University of California systems, in particular, became among the largest universities in the country and established themselves as national leaders in medical, aerospace, petroleum, and computer research—which helped attract technology-intensive industries to the region.

Climate also contributed to growth in the West. Southern California, Nevada, and Arizona, in particular, attracted many migrants from the East because of their warm, dry climates. Symbolizing the rise of the West in the postwar era was the city of Los Angeles. More than 10 percent of all new businesses in the United States between 1945 and 1950 began in Los Angeles. And its population soared by over 50 percent between 1940 and 1960.

CAPITAL AND LABOR

Booming corporations were reluctant to allow strikes to interfere with their operations; and since the most important labor unions were now so large and entrenched that they could not easily be suppressed or intimidated, leaders of large businesses made important concessions to them. By the mid-1950s, factory wages in most industries had risen substantially, to an average of $80 per week. In December 1955, the American Federation of Labor and the Congress of Industrial Organizations ended their twenty-year rivalry and merged to create the powerful **AFL-CIO**, under the leadership of George Meany.

But labor success also bred stagnation and corruption in some union bureaucracies. In 1957, the powerful Teamsters Union became the subject of a congressional inquiry, and its president, David Beck, was charged with the misappropriation of union funds. Beck ultimately stepped down to be replaced by Jimmy Hoffa, whom government investigators pursued for nearly a decade before finally winning a conviction against him in 1964 for jury tampering. The United Mine Workers, similarly, became tainted by violence and charges of corruption.

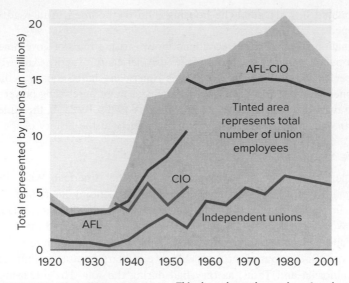

WORKERS REPRESENTED BY UNIONS, 1920–2001   This chart shows the number of workers represented by unions over an eighty-year period. Note the dramatic rise in the unionized workforce during the 1930s and 1940s, the slower but still significant rise in the 1960s and 1970s, and the steady decline that began in the 1980s. The chart, in fact, understates the decline of unionized labor in the postwar era, since it shows union membership in absolute numbers and not as a percentage of the rapidly growing workforce. • *Why did the total number of union members continue to rise in the 1970s, despite a plateau in AFL-CIO membership?*

THE EXPLOSION OF SCIENCE AND TECHNOLOGY

In 1961, *Time* magazine selected as its "man of the year" not a specific person but "the American Scientist." The choice was an indication of the widespread fascination with which Americans in the age of atomic power viewed science and technology.

MEDICAL BREAKTHROUGHS

The twentieth century saw greater progress in the development of medical science than had occurred in all the centuries before it. Much of it was concentrated during and after World War II. Especially important was the development of new antibacterial drugs capable of fighting infections that had once been all but untreatable.

To be sure, the development of antibiotics originated in the discoveries of Louis Pasteur and Jules-Francois Joubert. Working in France in the 1870s, they produced the first conclusive evidence that virulent bacterial infections could be defeated by other, more ordinary bacteria. Using their discoveries, the English physician Joseph Lister revealed the value of antiseptic solutions in preventing infection during surgery several years later.

But the practical use of antibacterial agents to combat disease did not begin until many decades later. In the 1930s, scientists in Germany, France, and England demonstrated the power of so-called sulfa drugs—drugs derived from an antibacterial agent known as sulfanilamide—which could be used effectively to treat streptococcal blood infections. New sulfa drugs were soon being developed at an astonishing rate and continuously improved; they were enormously successful in treating what had once been a major cause of death.

In the meantime, in 1928, Alexander Fleming, an English medical researcher, accidentally discovered the antibacterial properties of an organism that he named penicillin, after the mold (*pencillium notatum*) from which it was attained. There was little progress in using penicillin to treat human illness, however, until a group of researchers at Oxford University, directed by Howard Florey and Ernest Chain, learned how to produce stable, potent penicillin in sizable enough quantities to make it a practical weapon against bacterial disease. The first human trials of the new drug, in 1941, were dramatically successful, but progress toward the mass availability of penicillin was stalled in England because of World War II. American laboratories further developed methods for the mass production and commercial distribution of penicillin, which became widely available to doctors and hospitals around the world by 1948. Since then, a wide range of new antibiotics of highly specific character have been developed so that bacterial infections are now among the most successfully treated of all human illnesses.

Immunization—the development of vaccines that can protect humans from contracting both bacterial and viral diseases—also progressed dramatically. The first great immunological triumph was the development of the smallpox vaccine by the English researcher Edward Jenner in the late eighteenth century. A vaccine effective against typhoid was developed by an English bacteriologist, Almroth Wright, in 1897 and was in wide use by World War I. Vaccination against tetanus became widespread just before and during World War II. Medical scientists also developed a vaccine against another major killer, tuberculosis, in the 1920s; but controversy over its safety stalled its adoption, particularly in the United States, for many years. It was not widely used in America until after World War II, when it largely eliminated tuberculosis until a limited recurrence began in the 1990s.

Viruses are much more difficult to prevent and treat than bacterial infections, and progress toward vaccines against viral infections—except for smallpox—was relatively slow. Not until the 1930s, when scientists discovered how to grow viruses in tissue cultures, could researchers study them with any real effectiveness. Gradually, they discovered how to produce forms of a virus capable of triggering antibodies that would protect vaccinated people from contracting disease. An effective vaccine against yellow fever was developed in the late 1930s, and one against influenza—one of the great killers of the early twentieth century—appeared in 1945.

A major postwar triumph in medicine was the development of a vaccine against polio, which for decades had killed or crippled thousands of children and adults (among them President Franklin Roosevelt). The federal government provided the vaccine, developed by American scientist Jonas Salk, for free beginning in 1955. After 1960, an oral vaccine developed by Albert Sabin—usually administered in a sugar cube—made widespread vaccination even easier. By the early 1960s, these vaccines had virtually eliminated polio from American life and from much of the rest of the world.

These new drugs and vaccines drove down both infant mortality and the death rate among young children in the first twenty-five years after the war. They also helped raise the average life expectancy for that same period by five years, to seventy-one. While these medical advances have saved millions, however, their overuse in the decades that followed created a new round of contemporary problems. Indeed, the overuse of antibacterial agents has slowly led to genetic mutations in once-controlled diseases. New "super bugs" resist traditional treatment, and their defeat represents the next great challenge of the medical field.

Pesticides

Scientists also developed new kinds of chemical pesticides to protect crops from destruction by insects and to protect humans from such insect-carried diseases as typhus and malaria. Perhaps the most famous of the new pesticides was dichlorodiphenyltrichloro-ethane, generally known as DDT, a compound discovered in 1939 by the Swiss chemist Paul Muller. He had discovered that although DDT seemed harmless to human beings and other mammals, it was extremely toxic to insects. American scientists learned of Muller's discovery in 1942, just as the army was grappling with the insect-borne tropical diseases—especially malaria and typhus—that threatened American soldiers.

DDT was first used on a large scale in Italy in 1943–1944 during a typhus outbreak, which it quickly helped end. Soon DDT was being sprayed in mosquito-infested areas of Pacific islands where American troops were fighting the Japanese. The incidence of malaria dropped precipitously. DDT quickly gained a reputation as a miraculous tool for controlling insects, and it undoubtedly saved thousands of lives. Only later did it become evident that DDT had long-term toxic effects on animals and humans.

POSTWAR ELECTRONIC RESEARCH

The 1940s and 1950s saw dramatic new developments in electronic technology. Researchers in the 1940s produced the first commercially viable televisions and created a technology that made it possible to broadcast programming over large areas. In the late 1950s, scientists at Radio Corporation of America, better known as RCA, developed color television, which first became widely available in the early 1960s.

In 1948, Bell Labs, the research arm of AT&T, produced the first transistor, a solid-state device capable of amplifying electrical signals that was much smaller and more efficient than the cumbersome vacuum tubes that had powered most electronic equipment up until that time. Transistors made possible the miniaturization of many devices (radios, televisions, audio equipment, hearing aids) and also led to advances in modern aviation, weaponry, and satellites. They contributed as well to another major breakthrough in electronics: the development of integrated circuitry in the late 1950s.

Integrated circuits combined a number of once-separate electronic elements (transistors, resistors, diodes) and embedded them into a single, microscopically small device. Suddenly the construction of faster and more compact electronic machines—like the computer—became possible.

POSTWAR COMPUTER TECHNOLOGY

Prior to the 1950s, computers had been constructed mainly to perform complicated mathematical tasks, such as breaking military codes. In the 1950s, they began to perform commercial functions for the first time.

The first significant computer of the 1950s was the Universal Automatic Computer (or UNIVAC), which was developed initially for the U.S. Bureau of the Census by the Remington Rand Company. It was able to handle both alphabetical and numerical information easily. It used tape storage and could perform calculations and other functions much faster than its predecessor, the Electronic Numerical Integrator and Computer. Searching for a larger market for its very expensive new device, Remington Rand arranged to use a UNIVAC to predict the results of the 1952 election for CBS television news. Analyzing early voting results, the UNIVAC accurately predicted an enormous landslide victory for Eisenhower over Stevenson. Few Americans had ever heard of a computer before that night, and the UNIVAC's television debut was a breakthrough in public awareness of computer technology.

The UNIVAC and its technology was not much used outside of government circles until the mid-1950s, when the International Business Machines Company (IBM) successfully introduced its first major data-processing computers and marketed them aggressively to businesses in the United States and abroad. Pouring money into research and development of computers made IBM into the worldwide leader in computers for many years, until the emergence of Apple in the late twentieth century.

Bombs, Rockets, and Missiles

In 1952, the United States successfully detonated the first hydrogen bomb. The Soviet Union quickly followed suit and tested one a year later. Unlike the plutonium and uranium bombs developed during World War II, the hydrogen bomb derives its vastly greater power not from fission (the splitting of atoms) but fusion (the joining together of lighter atomic elements with heavier ones).

The hydrogen bomb reignited a stalled scientific project in both the United States and the Soviet Union: the effort to develop unmanned rockets and missiles capable of carrying this new and more deadly weapon to its target. These projectiles were to fly on their own power, unaided by any aircraft. Both nations funneled money and manpower to create them. The United States had a decided advantage in this international competition, benefiting from the emigration during World War II of some of Germany's top rocket scientists.

In the United States, early missile research, conducted almost entirely by the newly formed air force, quickly produced rockets capable of traveling several hundred miles. But American and Soviet scientists struggled to build longer-range missiles that were capable of traveling through space and across oceans and continents to reach distant targets. These were dubbed **intercontinental ballistic missiles (ICBMs)**. American scientists experimented in the 1950s first with the Atlas and then the Titan ICBM. Despite some early limited successes, the difficulty of massing sufficient stable fuel to provide the tremendous power needed to launch and then propel missiles far beyond the atmosphere choked progress. By 1958, however, scientists had created a solid fuel to replace the volatile liquid fuels of the early missiles and a miniaturized guidance systems capable of ensuring that missiles could travel to reasonably precise destinations. Within a few years, a new generation of missile capable of traveling several thousand miles, known as the Minuteman, became the basis of the American atomic weapons arsenal. American scientists also pioneered a nuclear missile capable of being carried and fired by submarines—the Polaris, which is launched from below the surface of the ocean by compressed air and fires its engines only after it surfaces. A Polaris was first successfully fired from underwater in 1960.

The Space Program

The origins of the American space program traces most directly to a dramatic event in 1957, when the Soviet Union announced that it had launched an earth-orbiting satellite—*Sputnik*—into outer space. The United States had yet to perform any similar feat, and the American government (and much of American society) reacted with alarm. Almost overnight, Washington demanded and generously funded efforts to improve scientific education in the schools, to create more research laboratories, and, above all, to speed the development of America's own exploration of outer space. The United States launched its own first satellite, *Explorer I*, in January 1958.

The centerpiece of space exploration, however, soon became the manned space program, established in 1958 along with a new agency, the National Aeronautics and Space Administration (NASA). The first American space pilots, or "astronauts," quickly became national heroes. On May 5, 1961, Alan Shepard became the first American launched into space. But his short

(Source: NASA)

MOON WALK   Edwin ("Buzz") Aldrin is photographed by his fellow astronaut Neil Armstrong in July 1969, when they became the first humans to set foot on the surface of the moon.

suborbital flight came several months after a Soviet "cosmonaut," Yuri Gagarin, had made a flight in which he had actually orbited the earth. On February 2, 1962, John Glenn (later a U.S. senator from Ohio) became the first American to orbit the globe. NASA later introduced the Gemini program, whose spacecraft could carry two astronauts at once.

These early successes led to the creation of the **Apollo program**, whose purpose was to land astronauts on the moon. It suffered catastrophic setbacks, most notably a fire in January 1967 that killed three astronauts during a training session. But on July 20, 1969, Neil Armstrong, Edwin "Buzz" Aldrin, and Michael Collins successfully traveled in a space capsule into orbit around the moon. Armstrong and Aldrin then detached a smaller craft from the capsule, landed on the surface of the moon, and became the first humans to walk on a celestial body other than earth. It sparked a national celebration. Six more lunar missions followed, the last in 1972.

Eventually, the space program became a relatively modest effort to make travel in near-space easier and more practical through the development of the "space shuttle," an airplane-like vehicle launched by a missile but capable of both navigating in space and landing on earth much like a conventional aircraft. The first space shuttle was successfully launched in 1982. One shuttle, *Challenger*, exploded in January 1986 shortly after takeoff, killing all seven astronauts including Ronald McNair, one of America's first black astronauts. The tragedy stalled the program for two years. Missions resumed in the late 1980s, but problems remained, as illustrated by the explosion of the space shuttle *Columbia* during reentry in 2003. The space shuttle was used to launch and repair communications satellites and to insert the Hubble Space Telescope into orbit in 1990 (and to repair its flawed lens on several occasions, including in 2009). The space shuttle program officially ended in 2011.

PEOPLE OF PLENTY

Among the most striking social developments of the postwar era was the rapid extension of a middle-class lifestyle and outlook to an expanding portion of the population. The historian David Potter published an influential examination of "economic abundance and American character" in 1954. He called it *People of Plenty*. For the American middle class in the 1950s, especially among whites, it seemed an appropriate label.

THE CONSUMER CULTURE

At the center of middle-class culture in the 1950s was a growing preoccupation with consumer goods—a result of increased prosperity, suburbanization, greater variety and availability of products, and the skillfulness of advertisers in exciting demand for what they sold. Making many of these purchases possible as well was the modern expansion of consumer credit, which jumped by 800 percent between 1945 and 1957 through the development of credit cards, revolving charge accounts, and easy-payment plans. Americans now snapped up new products such as dishwashers, garbage disposals, television, and stereos. No good was more popular than the automobile and Detroit responded by turning out ever-flashier styling and accessories.

Because consumer goods were so often marketed and advertised nationally, the 1950s were notable for the rapid spread of national consumer crazes. For example, children, adolescents, and even some adults became entranced in the late 1950s with the hula hoop—a large plastic ring kept spinning around the waist. The popularity of the Walt Disney–produced children's television show *The Mickey Mouse Club* created a widespread demand for Mickey Mouse watches and hats and contributed to the stunning success of Disneyland, an amusement park near Los Angeles that re-created many of the characters and events of Disney entertainment programs.

THE SUBURBAN NATION

A third of the nation's population lived in suburbs by 1960—a result not only of increased affluence but of important innovations in home building, which made single-family houses affordable to millions of new people. The most famous of the suburban developers, William Levitt, built low-cost, mass-produced houses in large suburban developments known as "**Levittowns**." These types of relatively inexpensive developments popped up in New York, New Jersey, and Pennsylvania and eventually throughout the country.

Why did so many Americans want to move to the suburbs? One reason was the enormous importance postwar Americans placed on family life after soldiers returned from World War II. Suburbs provided families with larger homes than they could find or afford in the cities and thus made it easier to raise larger numbers of children. The suburbs provided privacy and a sense of security from the noise and supposed dangers of urban living. They offered space for new consumer goods—the appliances, cars, boats, outdoor furniture, and other products that many middle-class Americans craved.

Another factor motivating white Americans in particular to move to the suburbs was race. Most suburbs were essentially restricted to white inhabitants—both because relatively few African Americans could afford to live in them and because formal and informal barriers kept even prosperous blacks out of all but a few. Some suburban communities, for example, carried restrictive convenants that prohibited property owners from renting or selling to blacks. In an era when the black population of most cities was rapidly growing, many white families fled to the suburbs in part to escape the integration of urban neighborhoods and schools.

THE SUBURBAN FAMILY

For professional men who tended to work in the city, at some distance from their homes, suburban life generally meant a rigid division between their working and personal worlds. For many middle-class women, it meant an increased isolation from the workplace. Middle-class husbands often considered it demeaning for their wives to be employed. And many women themselves shied away from the workplace when they could afford to, in part because of prevailing ideas about motherhood popularized by such widely consulted books as Dr. Benjamin Spock's *Baby and Child Care.* First published in 1946, it strongly advised women to devote themselves strictly to child-rearing. "Stay-at-home" mothers presumably raised healthier, more disciplined children. Other factors included the practice of many professional schools—law, medicine, business—to deny admissions to women.

Some women, however, had to balance these domestic pressures against other, contradictory ones. As expectations of material comfort rose, many middle-class families needed a second income to maintain the standard of living they desired. Consequently, the number of married women working outside the home actually increased in the postwar years. By 1960, nearly a third of all married women were part of the paid workforce.

THE BIRTH OF TELEVISION

During the 1950s, television quickly emerged as perhaps the most powerful medium of mass communication in history. Experiments in broadcasting pictures (along with sound) had begun as early as the 1920s, but commercial television began only shortly after World War II. Its growth was phenomenally rapid. In 1946, there were only 17,000 sets in the country; by 1957, there were 40 million—almost as many television sets as there were families. More people had television sets, according to one report, than had refrigerators.

The television industry emerged directly out of the radio industry, and all three of the major networks—the National Broadcasting Company, the Columbia Broadcasting System, and the American Broadcasting Company—had started as radio companies. Advertising drove the television business. The need to attract advertisers determined most programming decisions; and in the early days of television, corporate sponsors often played a direct role in determining the content of programs. Many early television shows bore the names of the corporations that were paying for them: the *General Electric Theater*, the *Chrysler Theatre*, and the *Camel News Caravan*. Some daytime serials (known as "soap operas," because their sponsors were almost always companies making household goods targeted at women) were actually written and produced by Procter & Gamble and other companies.

By the late 1950s, television news had replaced newspapers, magazines, and radios as the nation's most important vehicle of information. Television advertising helped create a vast market for new fashions and products. Televised athletic events made college and professional sports one of the most important sources of entertainment and one of the biggest businesses in America by the 1970s. And television entertainment programming—almost all of it controlled by the three national networks and their corporate sponsors—replaced movies and radio as the principal source of diversion for American families.

Much of the programming of the 1950s and early 1960s created a common image of American life—predominantly white, middle class, and suburban. Most popular were the situation comedies, featuring families in which, as the title of one of the most successful shows put it, *Father Knows Best*, and women were mothers and housewives striving to serve their children and please their husbands. Another top comedy, *I Love Lucy*, featured women in conventional roles but also tried to expand them, often in hilarious ways. *I Love Lucy* both idealized and poked fun at conventional domestic life. (See "Patterns of Popular Culture: Lucy and Desi.")

Yet television also could create conditions that could accentuate social conflict. Even those unable to share in the affluence of the era could, through television, acquire a vivid picture of how the rest of their society lived. While television was celebrating the white middle class, it was also showing glimpses of the alienation and powerlessness of groups who felt excluded from the world it portrayed. And television news conveyed with unprecedented power the social upheavals that gradually spread beginning in the late 1950s.

TRAVEL, OUTDOOR RECREATION, AND ENVIRONMENTALISM

Although the idea of a paid vacation for American workers, and the connection of that idea with travel, had entered American culture beginning in the 1920s, it was not until the postwar years that vacation travel became truly widespread among middle-income Americans. The construction of the interstate highway system contributed dramatically to the growth of travel. So did the increasing affluence of workers. Even in the 1950s, there was a healthy market for vacation vehicles—trailers and small vans. That market grew steadily larger in subsequent decades. But the urge to travel was also an expression of some of the same impulses that produced suburbs: a desire to escape the crowding and stress of densely populated areas and find a place where it was possible to experience the natural world.

Nowhere was this surge in travel and recreation more visible than in national parks, which underwent a surge in attendance in the 1950s. People who traveled to national parks did so for many reasons—some to hike and camp, others to fish and hunt, and still others simply to see the extraordinary landscape. But whatever their motives, most visitors came in search of an experience in the wilderness. The importance of that search became clear in the early 1950s with the fight to preserve **Echo Park**.

Echo Park is a spectacular valley in the Dinosaur National Monument, on the border between Utah and Colorado and near the southern border of Wyoming. In the early 1950s, the federal government's Bureau of Reclamation—which encouraged irrigation, electric power, and water supplies—proposed building a dam across the Green River, which runs through Echo Valley, to create a lake for recreation and a source of hydroelectric power. The American environmental movement had been relatively quiet since its searing defeat early in the century in its effort to stop a similar dam in the Hetch Hetchy Valley at Yosemite National Park. But the Echo Park proposal helped rouse it from its slumber.

In 1950, Bernard DeVoto—a well-known writer and a great champion of the American West—published an essay in the *Saturday Evening Post* titled "Shall We Let Them Ruin Our National Parks?" It had a sensational impact, arousing opposition to the Echo Valley dam from many areas of the country. The Sierra Club, relatively obscure in previous decades, sprang into action. The controversy helped elevate a new and aggressive leader, David Brower, who eventually transformed the club into one of the nation's leading environmental organizations. By the mid-1950s, a large coalition of environmentalists, naturalists, and wilderness vacationers had mobilized in opposition to the dam, and in 1956, Congress—bowing to public

LUCY AND DESI

The most popular show in the early history of network television began as an effort by a young comedian to strengthen her troubled marriage. In 1950, Lucille Ball was performing in a popular weekly CBS radio comedy, *My Favorite Husband*, in which she portrayed a slightly zany housewife who tangled frequently with her banker husband, played by Richard Denning. The network proposed to transfer the show from radio to television. Lucy said she would do so only if she could replace Denning with her real-life husband of

(©CBS-TV/Kobal/REX/Shutterstock)

LUCY AT HOME Although Lucy and Desi at first portrayed a childless, ethnically mixed couple living in a Manhattan apartment, many of the comic situations in the early years of the show were purely domestic. Here, Lucy, wearing an apron, deals with one of her many household predicaments with the extraordinary physical comedy that was part of her great success. Desi, watching skeptically, played a buttoned-down bandleader to Lucy's zaniness.

ten years, Desi Arnaz—a Cuban-born bandleader whose almost constant traveling was putting a strain on their marriage. Network officials tried in vain to talk her out of the idea. Arnaz had no acting experience, they told her. Lucy herself recognized another reason for their reluctance: the radicalism of portraying an ethnically mixed marriage on the air. But she held her ground.

On Monday, October 15, 1951, the first episode of *I Love Lucy* was broadcast over CBS. Desi Arnaz played Ricky Ricardo, a Cuban bandleader and singer who spoke, at times, with a comically exaggerated Latin accent. Lucille Ball was Lucy Ricardo, his stage-struck and slightly dizzy wife. Performing with them were William Frawley and Vivian Vance, who played their neighbors and close friends, Fred and Ethel Mertz. In the premiere episode, "The Girls Want to Go to a Nightclub," Ricky and Fred want to go to a boxing match on the night of Fred and Ethel's anniversary, while the wives are arranging an evening at a nightclub.

The opening episode contained many of the elements that characterized the show throughout its long run and ensured its extraordinary success: the remarkable chemistry among the four principal actors, the unexpected comedic talent of Desi Arnaz, and most of all the brilliance of Lucille Ball. She was a master of physical comedy, and many of her funniest moments involved scenes of absurdly incongruous situations (Lucy working an assembly line, Lucy stomping grapes in Italy). Her characteristic yowl of frustration became one of the most familiar sounds in American culture. She was a beautiful woman, but she never hesitated to make herself look ridiculous. "She was everywoman," her long-time writer Jess Oppenheim once wrote; "her little expressions and inflections stimulated the shock of recognition in the audience."

But it was not just the great talents of its cast that made *I Love Lucy* such a phenomenon. It was the skill of its writers in evoking some of the most common experiences and desires of television viewers in the 1950s. Lucy, in particular, mined the frustrations of domestic life for all they were worth, constantly engaging in zany and hilarious schemes to break into show business or somehow expand her world. The husbands wanted calm and conventional domestic lives—and time to themselves for conspicuously male activities: boxing, fishing, baseball. In the first seasons, the fictional couples lived as neighbors, without children, in a Manhattan apartment building. Later, Lucy had a child and they all moved to the suburbs. (The show used Lucy's real-life pregnancy on the air; and on January 19, 1953—only hours after Lucille Ball gave birth to her real son and second child—CBS aired a previously filmed episode of the fictional Lucy giving birth to a fictional son, "Little Ricky" Ricardo.)

Lucille Ball remained a major television star for nearly twenty years after *I Love Lucy* (and its successor, *The Lucille Ball–Desi Arnaz Comedy Hour*) left the air in 1960. Desi Arnaz, whom Lucy divorced in 1960, remained for a time one of Hollywood's most powerful and successful studio executives as the head of Desilu Productions. And nearly seventy years after the first episode of *I Love Lucy* aired, the series remains extraordinarily popular all over the world—shown so frequently in reruns that in some American cities it is sometimes possible to see six Lucy episodes in a single evening. "People identified with the Ricardos," Lucille Ball once said, "because we had the same problems they had. We just took ordinary situations and exaggerated them." •

UNDERSTAND, ANALYZE, & EVALUATE

1. In what ways did *I Love Lucy* reflect American society and family life of the 1950s?
2. How have television situation comedies since *I Love Lucy* copied the formula for success established by that program? Do you see elements of the *I Love Lucy* pattern in today's situation comedies?
3. Why do you think *I Love Lucy* has continued to be so popular, both in the United States and throughout the world?

pressure—blocked the project and preserved Echo Park in its natural state. The controversy was a major victory for those who wished to preserve the sanctity of the national parks and it was an important spur to the dawning of modern environmental consciousness.

ORGANIZED SOCIETY AND ITS DETRACTORS

Large-scale organizations and bureaucracies increased their influence over American life in the postwar era, as they had been doing for many decades before. White-collar workers came to outnumber blue-collar laborers for the first time, and an increasing proportion of them worked in corporate settings with rigid hierarchical structures. Industrial workers also confronted large bureaucracies both in the workplace and in their own unions.

The debilitating impact of bureaucratic life on the individual became one of the central themes of popular and scholarly debate. William H. Whyte, Jr., produced one of the most widely discussed books of the decade: *The Organization Man* (1956), which attempted to describe the special mentality of the worker in a large bureaucratic setting. Self-reliance, Whyte claimed, was losing place to conformity and the ability to "get along" and "work as a team." The sociologist David Riesman made similar observations in *The Lonely Crowd* (1950), in which he argued that the traditional "inner-directed man," who judged himself on the basis of his own values and the esteem of his family, was giving way to a new "other-directed man," more concerned with winning the approval of his boss and the larger organization or community.

Novelists, too, expressed misgivings about the impersonality of modern society. Saul Bellow produced a series of novels—*The Adventures of Augie March* (1953), *Seize the Day* (1956), *Herzog* (1964), and many others—that chronicled the difficulties of American Jewish men in finding fulfillment in modern urban America. J. D. Salinger wrote in *The Catcher in the Rye* (1951) of a prep-school student, Holden Caulfield, who is unable to find any area of society—school, family, friends, city—in which he can feel secure or committed.

THE BEATS AND THE RESTLESS CULTURE OF YOUTH

The most derisive critics of bureaucracy and middle-class society were a group of young poets, writers, and artists known as the "**Beats**" and often called "beatniks" by disapproving critics. They wrote harsh critiques of what they considered the sterility and conformity of American life, the meaninglessness of American politics, and the banality of popular culture. Jack Kerouac produced the most popular document of the Beat Generation in his novel *On the Road* (1957), an account of a cross-country automobile trip that depicts the rootless, iconoclastic lifestyle of Kerouac and his friends.

The culture of alienation that the Beats so vividly represented had counterparts even in ordinary middle-class behavior: teenage rebelliousness toward parents, youthful fascination with fast cars and motorcycles, and increasing sexual activity, assisted by the greater availability of birth-control devices. The popularity of James Dean, who starred in *Rebel Without a Cause* (1955), *East of Eden* (1955), and *Giant* (1956), was a particularly vivid sign of youth culture in the 1950s. Both in the roles he played (moody, alienated teenagers and young men with a streak of self-destructive violence) and in the way he lived his own life (he died in 1955, at the age of 24, in an automobile accident), Dean became an icon of the unfocused rebelliousness of American youth in his time.

For middle-class adults in the 1950s, Dean was less an icon of cool than a symbol of "juvenile delinquency." In both politics and popular culture, dire warnings surfaced about the growing criminality of American youth. The 1955 film *Blackboard Jungle*, for example, was a frightening depiction of crime and violence in city schools. Scholarly studies, presidential commissions, and journalistic exposés all contributed to the sense of alarm about the spread of delinquency—although in fact, youth crime did not dramatically increase in the 1950s.

Rock 'n' Roll

One of the most important cultural developments of the 1950s was the birth of rock 'n' roll—and the enormous popularity of the greatest early rock star, Elvis Presley. Presley became a symbol of a youthful determination to push at the borders of the conventional and the acceptable. His sultry good looks, his self-conscious effort to dress in the vaguely rebellious style of urban gangs (motorcycle jackets and slicked-back hair, even though Presley himself was a product of the conservative rural South), and, most of all, the open sexuality of his music and his public performances all made him wildly popular among young Americans in the 1950s. His first great hit, "Heartbreak Hotel," established him as a national phenomenon in 1956, and he remained a powerful figure in American popular culture well after his death in 1977.

Presley's music, like that of many early white rock musicians, drew heavily from black rhythm and blues traditions. Sam Phillips, a record promoter who had recorded some of the important black R&B musicians of his time, reportedly said in the early 1950s: "If I could find a white man with a Negro sound, I could make a billion dollars." Soon after that, he found Presley. But there were others as well—among them Buddy Holly and Bill Haley

(©Hulton Archive/Getty Images)

ELVIS This photograph of the musician in performance is from very early in his career.

(whose 1955 song "Rock Around the Clock," used in the film *Blackboard Jungle*, announced the arrival of rock 'n' roll to millions of young people)—who were closely connected to African American musical traditions. Rock drew from other sources, too: from country western music (another strong influence on Presley), from gospel music, even from jazz.

The 1950s also saw African American bands and singers grow in popularity among both black and white audiences. Chuck Berry, Little Richard, B. B. King, Chubby Checker, the Temptations, the Miracles, the Supremes, and others—many of them recorded by the black producer Berry Gordy, the founder and president of Motown Records in Detroit—never rivaled Presley in their popularity among white youths but did develop significant multiracial audiences of their own.

The rapid rise of rock owed a great deal to innovations in radio and television programming. By the 1950s, radio stations no longer felt obliged to present mostly live programming—especially once television took over many of the entertainment functions radio had once performed. Instead, many radio stations devoted themselves almost entirely to playing recorded music. Early in the 1950s, a new breed of radio announcers, known as "disk jockeys" or "djs" for the record disks they played, began to create programming aimed specifically at young fans of rock music; and when their programs became enormously successful, other stations quickly followed suit. *American Bandstand*, which began airing in 1957, was a televised showcase for rock 'n' roll hits in which a live audience danced to recorded music. The program helped spread the popularity of rock—and made its host, Dick Clark, one of the best-known figures among young Americans.

Radio and television were important to the recording industry, of course, because they encouraged the rapidly increasing sale of records in the mid- and late 1950s, especially in the inexpensive and popular 45 rpm format—small disks that contained one song on each side and turned at the rate of 45 revolutions per minute. Also important were jukeboxes, which played individual songs on 45s and became stock items in soda fountains, diners, bars, and other places where young people congregated. Sales of records increased from $182 million to $521 million between 1954 and 1960. So eager were record promoters to get their songs on the air that they routinely made secret payments to station owners and disk jockeys to encourage them to showcase their artists. These payments, which became known as "payola," produced a series of scandals when they were exposed in the late 1950s and early 1960s.

THE OTHER AMERICA

It was relatively easy for white middle-class Americans in the 1950s to believe that the world of economic growth, personal affluence, and cultural homogeneity was universal and that their values and assumptions were ones that other Americans shared. But such beliefs were false. Large groups of Americans remained outside the circle of abundance and shared neither in the affluence of the middle class nor many of its values.

On the Margins of the Affluent Society

In 1962, the socialist writer Michael Harrington published a celebrated book called *The Other America*, which chronicled the continuing existence of poverty in the United States.

The great economic expansion of the postwar years reduced poverty dramatically but did not eliminate it. In 1960, at any given moment, more than a fifth of all American families (over 30 million people) continued to live below what the government defined as the poverty line (down from a third of all families fifteen years before). Many millions more lived just above the official poverty line, but with incomes that gave them little comfort and no security.

Most of the poor—up to 80 percent—experienced poverty intermittently and temporarily. But approximately 20 percent were people for whom poverty was a continuous, often inescapable reality. That included approximately half the nation's elderly population and a significant proportion of African Americans and Hispanics. Native Americans constituted the single poorest group in the country.

This "hard-core" poverty rebuked the popular assumption that "a rising tide lifts all boats." It was a poverty that the growing prosperity of the postwar era seemed to affect hardly at all, a poverty, as Harrington observed, that appeared "impervious to hope."

Rural Poverty

Among those on the margins of the affluent society were many rural Americans. In 1948, farmers had received 8.9 percent of the national income; in 1956, they received only 4.1 percent. In part, this decline reflected the steadily shrinking farm population; in 1956 alone, nearly 10 percent of the rural population moved into or was absorbed by cities. But it also reflected declining farm prices. Because of enormous surpluses in basic staples, prices fell 33 percent in those years, even though national income as a whole rose 50 percent at the same time. The surpluses were the result of higher yields per acre as well as increases in the amount of acreage under production, a function of the widespread use of tractors.

Sharecroppers and tenant farmers (most of them African American) continued to live at or below subsistence levels throughout the rural South—largely because of the mechanization of cotton picking after 1944 and the development of synthetic fibers that reduced demand for cotton. (Two-thirds of the cotton acreage went out of production between 1930 and 1960.) Migrant farmworkers, a group concentrated especially in the West and Southwest and heavily composed of Mexican Americans and Asian Americans, lived in similarly dire circumstances. In rural areas without much commercial agriculture—such as the Appalachian region in the East, where the decline of the coal economy reduced the one significant source of support for the region—whole communities lived in desperate poverty, increasingly cut off from the market economy. All these groups were vulnerable to malnutrition and even starvation.

The Inner Cities

As prospering white families moved from cities to suburbs in vast numbers, more and more inner-city neighborhoods became repositories for the poor—"ghettoes" from which there was no easy escape. The growth of these neighborhoods owed much to a vast migration of African Americans out of the countryside and into industrial cities. Not all these black migrants were poor, and many found in the city routes to economic progress similar to those of whites. But urban African Americans were substantially more likely to live in poverty than most other groups, in part because of the persistent patterns of discrimination that denied them any real opportunities.

More than 3 million black men and women moved from the South to northern cities between 1940 and 1960. Chicago, Detroit, Cleveland, New York, and other eastern and midwestern industrial cities experienced a major expansion of their black populations at the same time many whites were leaving cities.

Similar migrations from Mexico and Puerto Rico expanded Hispanic neighborhoods in many American cities. Between 1940 and 1960, nearly a million Puerto Ricans moved into American cities, especially New York. Mexican workers crossed the borders into Texas and California and swelled the already substantial Latino communities of such cities as San Antonio, Houston, San Diego, and Los Angeles (which by 1960 had the largest Mexican American population of any city, approximately 500,000 people). Many of these Americans also struggled to make it into the middle-class.

Inner cities filled up with poorer minority residents at the same time that the unskilled industrial jobs they sought diminished. Employers were moving factories and mills from old industrial cities to new locations in suburban and rural areas, smaller cities, and even abroad—places where the costs of labor were lower. Even in the factories that remained, automation reduced the number of unskilled jobs. The economic opportunities that had helped earlier immigrant groups to rise up from poverty were simply unavailable to many of the postwar migrants. Racial discrimination in hiring, education, and housing further hampered many members of these communities as they strove to escape poverty.

THE RISE OF THE CIVIL RIGHTS MOVEMENT

Ever since the end of Reconstruction, there was never a time when African Americans were not pushing to preserve their freedoms and defeat those who would snatch them away. The long battle for black liberty in the modern era came to a head in the 1950s and 1960s, forcing white Americans to recast their understanding about the meaning of citizenships and the moral wrong of segregation.

THE *BROWN* DECISION AND "MASSIVE RESISTANCE"

On May 17, 1954, the Supreme Court announced its decision in the case of *Brown v. Board of Education of Topeka*. In considering the legal segregation of a Kansas public school system, the Court rejected its own 1896 *Plessy v. Ferguson* decision, which had ruled that communities could provide African Americans with separate facilities as long as the facilities were equal to those of whites. The *Brown* decision declared that segregating public schools on the basis of race was unconstitutional. The justices argued that school segregation inflicted unacceptable damage on those it affected, regardless of the relative quality of the separate schools. Chief Justice Earl Warren explained the unanimous opinion of his colleagues: "We conclude that in the field of public education the doctrine of 'separate but equal' has no place. Separate educational facilities are inherently unequal." The following year, the Court issued another decision (known as *Brown II*) to provide rules for implementing the 1954 order. It ruled that communities must work to desegregate their schools "with all deliberate speed," but it set no timetable and left specific decisions up to lower courts.

Some communities, such as Washington, D.C., complied relatively quickly and quietly. But they were rare. More than 100 southern members of Congress signed a 1956 "manifesto" denouncing the *Brown* decision and urging their constituents to defy it. Most did, embarking on campaigns of "massive resistance" to obstruct and delay any effort to mix black and white students in public schools. Southern governors, mayors, local school boards, and White Citizens Councils—groups of local whites dedicated to preserving

(©Everett Collection/SuperStock)

LITTLE ROCK, 1957   African American student Elizabeth Eckford passes by jeering whites on her way to Little Rock Central High School, newly integrated by federal court order.

segregation—worked feverishly to block desegregation. By the fall of 1957, only 684 of 3,000 affected school districts in the South had even begun to integrate their schools.

The Eisenhower administration was reluctant to join the battle over desegregation. But in September 1957, it faced a case of direct state defiance of federal authority and felt compelled to act. Federal courts had ordered the desegregation of Central High School in Little Rock, Arkansas. But Governor Orval Faubus disagreed and argued in public that his authority superseded that of the court on matters of local public education. Ignoring pleas for cooperation from Washington, the governor looked the other way when a violent white mob attempted to stop eight black students from entering Central High by surrounding the school and blockading its doors. He then ordered the Arkansas National Guard to turn away the black students. Eisenhower responded swiftly and angrily, federalizing the National Guard and ordering them to enforce the court's decision and sending in battle-hardened troops from the famed 101st Airborne Division to ensure full compliance. Only then did Central High School admit its first black students.

The Expanding Movement

The *Brown* decision sparked a growing number of popular challenges to other forms of segregation in the South. On December 1, 1955, forty-two-year-old **Rosa Parks**, an African American seamstress, was arrested in Montgomery, Alabama, when she refused to give up her seat on a city bus to a white passenger as required by the Jim Crow laws throughout most of the South. Her arrest ignited outrage in the city's African American community and set in motion plans for a boycott.

Almost immediately the Woman's Political Committee jumped into action. Begun after World War II in Montgomery as a benevolent organization for middle-class black women, it sponsored voter registration drives, campaigns to raise awareness of sexual assault against black women, and publicly opposed segregated seating on buses. The night of Parks's arrest, President Joanne Robinson, an English professor at nearby Alabama State University, printed and distributed hundreds of fliers calling for the boycott and instructing blacks how to get to work the next day. Their work drew on earlier efforts of black boycotts in the South, such as the one in Mississippi protesting segregated public restrooms in service stations and in 1953 in Baton Rouge, Louisiana, against segregated buses.

Parks's arrest was no random event. Black leaders for years had schemed about how to upset the laws dictating segregated bus transportation. They had carefully selected Parks, the secretary for the local chapter of NAACP and a pillar of the black community, and coached her how to act. Nor was this the first arrest of a black women from Montgomery refusing to sit in the back of the bus. Others had already broken the law and been fined. Most dramatically, nine months before the Parks incident **Claudette Colvin**, a fifteen-year-old, sat in front, ignored the bus driver's command to move back, and squared off against two police officers. After she refused to leave the bus, they handcuffed her and hauled her off to jail. Colvin would later become a lead plaintiff in *Browder v. Gayle*, the federal case that would overturn bus segregation laws in Montgomery in 1956 and, along with the boycott, compel buses to abandon their discriminatory policies.

Formal organization of the boycott fell to the newly formed Montgomery Improvement Organization and its president, twenty-six-year-old Baptist pastor, **Martin Luther King Jr.** Son of a prominent Atlanta minister, a powerful orator, brilliant intellectual, and talented community leader, King had just accepted a call to serve as pastor of Montgomery's most influential black house of worship, Dexter Avenue Baptist church, in 1954. His prodigious gifts and newcomer status—meaning that local police and white politicians had had little time to threaten and terrorize him—made him the perfect candidate to lead.

King based his approach to civil rights protest on the doctrine of nonviolent resistance to injustice, even in the face of direct attack. Never should he return a punch or an insult but instead seek to love his enemy and peacefully persuade him to change his ways. His approach to racial struggle injected it with a new dimension of moral power that helped him recruit supporters and eventually win over onetime segregationists and capture the moral high ground for his supporters. For the next thirteen years—as leader of the Southern Christian Leadership Conference (SCLC), an interracial group he founded shortly after the boycott—he was the most influential and most widely admired black leader in the country. The popular movement he came to represent soon spread throughout the South and the country.

CAUSES OF THE CIVIL RIGHTS MOVEMENT

Several factors contributed to the rise of African American protest in the postwar years. In addition to the role of pathbreaking legal decisions such as *Brown* and *Browder v. Gayle* and local community activism often sparked by the work of black women, the legacy of World War II was critical. Many black women and men had served directly in the military or worked in industrial plants supporting the war effort. They had joined an effort to end totalitarianism and the suppression of freedom abroad and frequently labored side by side with whites—only to confront blatant discrimination once again when they returned home after the war. Veterans in particular demanded the same liberties and opportunities they had enjoyed in the service and refused to accept living under segregation's grip.

Another factor was the growth of an urban black middle class, which had been developing for decades and began to flourish after the war. Much of the impetus for the civil rights movement came from the leaders of these communities—ministers like Martin Luther King Jr., but also educators and professionals. Much of it came as well from students at black colleges and universities, which had expanded significantly and taught students about the history of discrimination and revolution. These younger African Americans frequently put themselves on the front lines of the struggle.

Television and other forms of popular culture also played a role in the rising consciousness of racism. More than any previous generation, postwar blacks had constant, vivid reminders of how the white majority lived—of the world from which they were effectively excluded. Television also conveyed the activities of demonstrators to a national audience, ensuring that activism in one community would inspire similar protests in others. It gave the movement a national character and momentum.

Other forces mobilized many white Americans to support the movement once it began. The Cold War made racial injustice an embarrassment to Americans trying to present their nation as a model to the world. Political mobilization of northern blacks created a valuable voting bloc within the Democratic Party. Politicians from northern industrial states especially could not ignore their views. Labor unions with powerful black memberships mobilized to help the movement, providing public support and funding.

Still becoming organized and gathering steam in the 1950s, the civil rights movement would shortly emerge as the most powerful social revolution of the twentieth century.

EISENHOWER REPUBLICANISM

Dwight D. Eisenhower was the least experienced politician to serve in the White House in the twentieth century. He was also among the most popular and politically successful presidents of the postwar era. At home, he pursued essentially moderate policies, avoiding most new initiatives but accepting the work of earlier reformers. Abroad, he continued and even intensified American commitments to oppose communism but also brought a measure of restraint that his successors did not always match.

"WHAT WAS GOOD FOR . . . GENERAL MOTORS"

The first Republican administration in twenty years staffed itself with men drawn from the same quarter as those who had staffed Republican administrations in the 1920s: the business community. But by the 1950s, many business leaders had acquired a social and political outlook very different from that of their predecessors. Above all, many had reconciled themselves to at least the broad outlines of the Keynesian welfare state, named after the famed Great Depression economist John Maynard Keynes and launched during the New Deal. Indeed, some corporate leaders had come to see it as something that actually benefited them—by helping maintain social order, by increasing mass purchasing power, and by stabilizing labor relations.

To his cabinet, Eisenhower appointed wealthy corporate lawyers and business executives who were unapologetic about their backgrounds. Charles Wilson, president of General Motors, assured senators considering his nomination for secretary of defense that "what was good for our country was good for General Motors, and vice versa."

Eisenhower encouraged private enterprise. He supported the private rather than public development of natural resources. To the chagrin of farmers, he lowered federal support for farm prices. He also removed the last limited wage and price controls maintained by the Truman administration, opposed the creation of new social service programs such as national health insurance, and strove constantly to reduce federal expenditures (even during the recession of 1958) and balance the budget. He ended 1960, his last full year in office, with a $1 billion budget surplus.

The Survival of the Welfare State

While the president took few new initiatives in domestic policy, he steadily resisted conservative pressure to dismantle the welfare policies of the New Deal. Indeed, during his term he agreed to extend the Social Security system to an additional 10 million people and unemployment compensation to an additional 4 million, and he approved an increase to the minimum hourly wage from 75 cents to one dollar. One of the most significant legislative accomplishments of the Eisenhower administration was the **Federal Highway Act of 1956**, which authorized $25 billion for a ten-year project that built over 40,000 miles of interstate highways—the largest public works project in American history to that point. The program was funded through a highway "trust fund," whose revenues would come from new taxes on the purchase of fuel, automobiles, trucks, and tires.

In 1956, Eisenhower ran for a second term on the Republican ticket, even though he had suffered a serious heart attack the previous year. With Adlai Stevenson opposing him once again, he won by another, even greater, landslide, receiving 57.6 percent of the popular vote and 457 electoral votes to Stevenson's 73. Democrats retained control of both houses of Congress they had won back in 1954. In 1958—even during a serious recession—they increased that control by substantial margins.

The Decline of McCarthyism

The Eisenhower administration did little in its first years in office to discourage the anticommunist furor that had gripped the nation. By 1954, however, what came to be known as McCarthyism began to become increasingly unpopular.

During the first year of the Eisenhower administration, McCarthy continued to operate with impunity. But in January 1954, he attacked Secretary of the Army Robert Stevens and the armed services in general, claiming that communists had intruded into the military. At that point, the administration and influential members of Congress organized a special investigation of the charges, the **Army–McCarthy hearings**, which were among the first congressional hearings to be nationally televised. Watching McCarthy in action—bullying witnesses, hurling groundless and often cruel accusations, evading issues—much of the public turned on him and began to see him as a villain, even a buffoon. In December 1954, the Senate voted 67 to 22 to condemn him for "conduct unbecoming a senator." Three years later, he died—a victim, apparently, of complications arising from alcoholism. The Red Scare did not die with McCarthy, but its intensity began to decline.

EISENHOWER, DULLES, AND THE COLD WAR

The threat of nuclear war created a sense of high anxiety in international relations in the 1950s. But the nuclear threat also encouraged both superpowers to edge away from direct confrontations. Indeed, the attention of both the United States and the Soviet Union began to turn instead to the rapidly growing instability in the Third World.

DULLES AND "MASSIVE RETALIATION"

Secretary of State **John Foster Dulles** was the most important figure in the Eisenhower administration next to the president himself. He was an aristocratic corporate lawyer with a stern moral revulsion to communism. He entered office denouncing the containment policies of the Truman years as excessively passive, arguing that the United States should pursue an active program of "liberation," which would lead to a "rollback" of communist expansion. Once in power, however, he had to defer to the more moderate views of the president himself.

The most prominent of Dulles's innovations was the policy of "massive retaliation," which he announced early in 1954. The United States would, he explained, respond to communist threats to its allies in part by relying on "the deterrent of massive retaliatory power," by which he clearly meant nuclear weapons. In part, the new doctrines reflected Dulles's inclination for tense confrontations, an approach he once defined as **brinksmanship**—pushing the Soviet Union to the brink of war in order to exact concessions. But the real force behind the massive-retaliation policy was economics. With pressure growing both in and out of government for a reduction in American military expenditures, an increasing reliance on atomic weapons seemed to promise, as some advocates put it, "more bang for the buck."

FRANCE, AMERICA, AND VIETNAM

On July 27, 1953, negotiators at Panmunjom finally signed an agreement ending the hostilities in Korea. Each antagonist was to withdraw its troops a mile and a half from the existing battle line, which ran roughly along the 38th parallel, the prewar border between North and South Korea. A conference in Geneva was to consider means by which to reunite the nation peacefully—although in fact that 1954 meeting produced no agreement and left the cease-fire line in place as the apparently permanent border between the two countries into the twenty-first century.

Almost simultaneously, however, the United States was entering into a long, bitter struggle in Southeast Asia. Ever since 1945, France had been attempting to restore its authority over Vietnam, its one-time colony, which it had been forced to abandon to the Japanese during World War II. Opposing the French, however, were the powerful nationalist forces of **Ho Chi Minh**, determined to win independence for their nation. Ho had hoped for American support in 1945, on the basis of the anticolonial rhetoric of the Atlantic Charter and Franklin Roosevelt's speeches, and also because he had received support from American intelligence forces during World War II while fighting the Japanese. But because he was not only a nationalist but also a communist, the Truman administration ignored him and supported the French, one of America's most important Cold War allies. Ho Chi Minh launched a war of national liberation against the French in 1946.

By 1954, Ho was receiving aid from communist China and the Soviet Union. America, in the meantime, had been paying most of the costs of France's ineffective military campaign in Vietnam since 1950. Early in 1954, 12,000 French troops became surrounded in a disastrous siege at the village of Dien Bien Phu. Only American intervention, it was clear, could prevent the total collapse of the French military effort. Yet despite the urgings of Secretary of State Dulles, Vice President Nixon, and others, Eisenhower refused to permit direct American military intervention in Vietnam, claiming that neither Congress nor America's other allies would support such action.

Without American aid, the French defense of Dien Bien Phu finally collapsed on May 7, 1954, and France soon abandoned Vietnam. The French agreed to a settlement of the conflict at the same international conference in Geneva that was considering the Korean settlement. The Geneva accords on Vietnam of July 1954 established a supposedly temporary division of the country along the 17th parallel. The north would be governed by Ho Chi Minh, the south by a pro-Western regime. Democratic elections would reunite the nation in 1956. The agreement marked the end of the French commitment to Vietnam and the beginning of an expanded American presence there. The United States helped establish a pro-American government in the south, headed by Ngo Dinh Diem, a member of his country's Roman Catholic minority. Because he enjoyed the full military backing of the American government, Diem acted ruthlessly, refusing, for example, to permit the 1956 popular elections when he realized he would lose.

COLD WAR CRISES

American foreign policymakers in the 1950s were challenged by both real and imagined crises in far-flung areas of the world. Among them were a series of crises in the Middle East, a region in which the United States had been little involved until after World War II.

On May 14, 1948, after years of Zionist efforts and a decision by the new United Nations, the nation of Israel proclaimed its independence. President Truman recognized the new Jewish homeland the next day. But the creation of Israel, while resolving some conflicts, created others. Palestinian Arabs, unwilling to accept being displaced from what they considered their own country, joined with Israel's Arab neighbors and fought determinedly against the new state in 1948—the first of several Arab–Israeli wars.

Committed as the American government was to Israel, it was also concerned about the stability and friendliness of the Arab regimes in the oil-rich Middle East, where American petroleum companies had major investments. Thus the United States reacted with alarm as it watched Mohammed Mossadegh, the nationalist prime minister of Iran, begin to resist the presence of Western corporations in his nation in the early 1950s. In 1953, the American CIA joined forces with conservative Iranian military leaders to engineer a coup that drove Mossadegh from office. To replace him, the CIA helped elevate the young shah of Iran, Mohammed Reza Pahlevi, from his position as token constitutional monarch to that of virtually absolute ruler. The shah remained closely tied to the United States for the next twenty-five years.

The U.S. State Department was less effective in influencing the nationalist government of Egypt, under the leadership of General Gamal Abdel Nasser. He began to develop a trade relationship with the Soviet Union in the early 1950s. In 1956, to punish Nasser for his friendliness toward the communists, Dulles withdrew American offers to assist in building the Aswan Dam across the Nile. A week later, Nasser retaliated by seizing control of the Suez Canal from the British, saying that he would use the income from it to build the dam himself.

On October 29, 1956, Israeli forces attacked Egypt. The next day the British and French landed troops in the Suez to drive the Egyptians from the canal. Dulles and Eisenhower feared that the Suez crisis would drive the Arab states toward the Soviet Union and precipitate a new world war. By refusing to support the invasion, and by joining in a UN denunciation of it, the United States helped pressure the French and British to withdraw and persuaded Israel to agree to a truce with Egypt.

Cold War concerns affected American relations in Latin America as well. In 1954, the Eisenhower administration ordered the CIA to help topple the new, leftist government of Jacobo Arbenz Guzmán in Guatemala, a regime that Dulles (responding in part to the requests of the United Fruit Company, a major investor in Guatemala) argued was potentially communist.

No nation in the region had been more closely tied to America than Cuba. Its leader, Fulgencio Batista, had ruled as a military dictator since 1952, when American assistance helped him topple a more moderate government. Cuba's relatively prosperous economy had become a virtual colony of American corporations, which controlled almost all the island's natural resources and had cornered over half the vital sugar crop. American organized-crime syndicates controlled much of Havana's lucrative hotel and nightlife business. In 1957, a popular movement of resistance to the Batista regime began to gather strength under the leadership of **Fidel Castro**. On January 1, 1959, as Batista fled to exile in Spain, Castro marched into Havana and established a new government.

Castro soon began implementing policies of land reform and expropriating foreign-owned businesses and resources. He established himself as a dictator by canceling promised elections and jailing or killing political rivals and critics. When Castro began accepting assistance from the Soviet Union in 1960, the United States cut back the "quota" by which Cuba could export sugar to America at a favored price. Early in 1961, as one of its last acts, the Eisenhower administration severed diplomatic relations with Castro. Isolated by the United States, Castro soon cemented an alliance with the Soviet Union.

(©Bettmann/Getty Images)

THE CUBAN REVOLUTION Fidel Castro (standing at center) is shown here in the Cuban jungle in 1957 with a small group of his staff and soldiers. Two years later, Castro's forces toppled the U.S.-backed Batista government and elevated Castro to the nation's leadership, where he remained for almost fifty years.

CONSIDER THE SOURCE

EISENHOWER WARNS OF THE MILITARY–INDUSTRIAL COMPLEX (1961)

In the tradition of outgoing presidents, Eisenhower delivered a "farewell address" that offered a summary of his accomplishments and vision for the future of the country. He warned of a growing "military–industrial complex" that, if left unchecked, would drive the nation's economy and politics.

Good evening, my fellow Americans. [. . .] This evening I come to you with a message of leave-taking and farewell, and to share a few final thoughts with you, my countrymen. Like every other citizen, I wish the new President, and all who will labor with him, Godspeed. I pray that the coming years will be blessed with peace and prosperity for all. [. . .]

America is today the strongest, the most influential, and most productive nation in the world. Understandably proud of this pre-eminence, we yet realize that America's leadership and prestige depend, not merely upon our unmatched material progress, riches and military strength, but on how we use our power in the interests of world peace and human betterment. [. . .]

A vital element in keeping the peace is our military establishment. Our arms must be mighty, ready for instant action, so that no potential aggressor may be tempted to risk his own destruction. Our military organization today bears little relation to that known by any of my predecessors in peacetime, or, indeed, by the fighting men of World War II or Korea. [. . .]

Now this conjunction of an immense military establishment and a large arms industry is new in the American experience. The total influence—economic, political, even spiritual—is felt in every city, every Statehouse, every office of the Federal government. We recognize the imperative need for this development. Yet we must not fail to comprehend its grave implications. Our toil, resources, and livelihood are all involved. So is the very structure of our society.

In the councils of government, we must guard against the acquisition of unwarranted influence, whether sought or unsought, by the military–industrial complex. The potential for the disastrous rise of misplaced power exists and will persist. We must never let the weight of this combination endanger our liberties or democratic processes. We should take nothing for granted. Only an alert and knowledgeable citizenry can compel the proper meshing of the huge industrial and military machinery of defense with our peaceful methods and goals, so that security and liberty may prosper together.

Akin to, and largely responsible for the sweeping changes in our industrial-military posture, has been the technological revolution during recent decades. In this revolution, research has become central, it also becomes more formalized, complex, and costly. A steadily increasing share is conducted for, by, or at the direction of, the Federal government.

Today, the solitary inventor, tinkering in his shop, has been overshadowed by task forces of scientists in laboratories and testing fields. In the same fashion, the free university, historically the fountainhead of free ideas and scientific discovery, has experienced a revolution in the conduct of research. Partly because of the huge costs involved, a government contract becomes virtually a substitute for intellectual curiosity. For every old blackboard there are now hundreds of new electronic computers. The prospect of domination of the nation's scholars by Federal employment, project allocations, and the power of money is ever present—and is gravely to be regarded.

Yet, in holding scientific research and discovery in respect, as we should, we must also be alert to the equal and opposite danger that public policy could itself become the captive of a scientific-technological elite.

It is the task of statesmanship to mold, to balance, and to integrate these and other forces, new and old, within the principles of our democratic system—ever aiming toward the supreme goals of our free society.

. . . As we peer into society's future, we—you and I, and our government—must avoid the impulse to live only for today, plundering for our own ease and convenience the precious resources of tomorrow. We cannot mortgage the material assets of our grandchildren without risking the loss also of their political and spiritual heritage. We want democracy to survive for all generations to come, not to become the insolvent phantom of tomorrow. [. . .]

Disarmament, with mutual honor and confidence, is a continuing imperative. Together we must learn how to compose differences, not with arms, but with intellect and decent purpose. Because this need is so sharp and apparent, I confess that I lay down my official responsibilities in this field with a definite sense of disappointment. As one who has witnessed the horror and the lingering sadness of war, as one who knows that another war could utterly destroy this civilization which has been so slowly and painfully built over thousands of years, I wish I could say tonight that a lasting peace is in sight. [. . .]

You and I, my fellow citizens, need to be strong in our faith that all nations, under God, will reach the goal of peace with justice. May we be ever unswerving in devotion to principle, confident but humble with power, diligent in pursuit of the Nations' great goals. [. . .]

Now, on Friday noon, I am to become a private citizen. I am proud to do so. I look forward to it.

Thank you, and good night.

UNDERSTAND, ANALYZE, & EVALUATE

1. What specifically was the military–industrial complex, and how did it support American postwar prosperity? How did it change the relationship between knowledge, industrial production, and defense?
2. What dangers for American political traditions did Eisenhower foresee? What economic dangers did he envision for future generations of Americans?

Source: Farewell address by President Dwight D. Eisenhower, January 17, 1961; Final TV Talk 1/17/61 (1), Box 38, Speech Series, Papers of Dwight D. Eisenhower as President, 1953–61, Eisenhower Library; National Archives and Records Administration [Public Domain].

The U-2 Crisis

Although the problems of the developing world were moving slowly toward the center of American foreign policy, the direct relationship with the Soviet Union and the effort to resist communist expansion in Europe remained the principal foreign policy concerns of the Eisenhower administration. Relations between the Soviet Union and the West soured further in 1956 in response to the Hungarian Revolution. Hungarian dissidents had launched a popular uprising in November to demand democratic reforms. Before the month was out, Soviet tanks and troops rolled into Budapest to crush the uprising and restore an orthodox, pro-Soviet regime.

In November 1958, Nikita Khrushchev, who had become leader of the Soviet Union upon Josef Stalin's death in 1953, renewed the demands of his predecessors that the NATO powers abandon West Berlin. When the United States and its allies predictably refused,

Khrushchev suggested that he and Eisenhower discuss the issue personally, both in visits to each other's countries and at a summit meeting in Paris in 1960. The United States agreed. Khrushchev's 1959 visit to America produced a cool but polite public response. Plans proceeded for the summit conference and for Eisenhower's visit to Moscow shortly thereafter. Only days before the Paris meeting, however, the Soviet Union announced that it had shot down an American U-2, a high-altitude spy plane, over Russian territory. Its pilot, Francis Gary Powers, was in captivity. Khrushchev lashed out angrily at the American incursion into Soviet airspace, breaking up the Paris summit almost before it could begin and withdrawing his invitation to Eisenhower to visit the Soviet Union. The Soviets convicted Powers of espionage (he was later exchanged for a Soviet spy), and the U-2 **crisis** ratcheted up mistrust on both sides.

After eight years in office, Eisenhower had failed to eliminate, and in some respects had actually increased, the tensions between the United States and the Soviet Union. Yet Eisenhower had also brought to the Cold War his own sense of the limits of American power. He had resisted military intervention in Vietnam, but he could not find a solution to Vietnam's likely slide into communism. And he had placed a measure of restraint on those who urged the creation of an enormous American military establishment. In his farewell address in January 1961, he warned of the "unwarranted influence" of a vast "military–industrial complex." (See "Consider the Source: Eisenhower Warns of the Military–Industrial Complex.") His caution, in both domestic and international affairs, stood in marked contrast to the attitudes of his successors, who argued that the United States must act more boldly and aggressively on behalf of its goals at home and abroad.

CONCLUSION

The booming economic growth of the 1950s—and the anxiety over the Cold War that formed a backdrop to it—shaped the politics and the culture of the decade. For most Americans, the 1950s were years of increasing personal prosperity. Sales of private homes increased dramatically; suburbs grew precipitously; young families had children at an astounding rate—creating what came to be known as the postwar "Baby Boom." After the end of the divisive Korean War, the nation's politics entered a period of relative calm, symbolized by the genial presence in the White House of General Dwight D. Eisenhower, who provided moderate and undemanding leadership through most of the decade.

The nation's culture, too, helped create a broad sense of stability and calm. Television, which emerged in the 1950s as the most powerful medium of mass culture, presented largely uncontroversial programming dominated by middle-class images and traditional values. Movies, theater, popular magazines, and newspapers all contributed to a broad sense of well-being.

But the 1950s were not, in the end, as calm and contented as the politics and popular culture of the time suggested. A powerful youth culture emerged in these years, displaying a considerable level of restiveness and even disillusionment. African Americans and other minorities who did not share in the economic boom equally with whites began to escalate their protests against segregation and inequality. The continuing existence of widespread poverty among large groups of Americans attracted increasing attention as the decade progressed. These pulsing anxieties, combined with frustration over the continuing tensions of the Cold War, eventually produced a growing sense of impatience with the calm, placid public culture of the time. That was a powerful reason for the growing desire for political action and social innovation as the 1960s began.

KEY TERMS/PEOPLE/PLACES/EVENTS

AFL-CIO 671
Apollo program 676
Army–McCarthy
 hearings 690
Baby Boom 670
Beats 682
brinksmanship 691
Browder v. Gayle 688
*Brown v. Board of Education
 of Topeka* 686

Claudette Colvin 688
Echo Park 679
Federal Highway Act
 of 1956 690
Fidel Castro 693
Ho Chi Minh 691
intercontinental ballistic
 missiles (ICBM) 675
John Foster Dulles 691
Levittowns 677

Martin Luther King Jr. 688
Rosa Parks 687
Sputnik 675
The Other America 684
U-2 crisis 696

RECALL AND REFLECT

1. How did the economic boom of the postwar era change American lifestyles?
2. What were some of the significant scientific and technological breakthroughs, especially in medicine, chemistry, electronics, weaponry, and space exploration, of the 1950s and 1960s? How did these developments affect American life?
3. How did the increasing popularity of the automobile change the American landscape and American society?
4. Why did the struggle for black freedom accelerate in the postwar years?

28 | THE TURBULENT SIXTIES

EXPANDING THE LIBERAL STATE
THE BATTLE FOR RACIAL EQUALITY
"FLEXIBLE RESPONSE" AND THE COLD WAR
THE AGONY OF VIETNAM
THE TRAUMAS OF 1968

LOOKING AHEAD

1. What was the domestic reform agenda of Kennedy's New Frontier, and how did Johnson's Great Society programs expand on that agenda?
2. Why did the civil rights movement become increasingly assertive and militant over the course of the 1960s?
3. In what ways did the liberal politics and domestic agenda of the 1960s ignite the rise of the modern conservative movement?

IN THE LATE 1950s, few predicted that sweeping political protests were coming. The economic prosperity of the postwar years had left more Americans better off than ever before. Popular culture, especially television, portrayed a contented, smiling people enjoying the highest standard of living of any generation of Americans. And indeed the 1960s dawned with political leaders confidently attacking social and international problems within a traditional framework of modern liberalism.

Yet just beneath the apparently placid surface of American society in the 1950s smoldered the embers of social revolution. Segregation and sexism, among other social ills, had made a mockery of any notion of a content and unified citizenry during the Truman and Eisenhower administrations. Large-scale public battles would soon erupt over the meaning of citizenship and freedom that would ultimately make the 1960s one of the most turbulent and divisive eras of the twentieth century.

At the heart of some of those battles would be one of the most traumatic foreign policy experiences in the nation's history, the war in Vietnam. Though far less damaging in material and human terms to Americans than to the Vietnamese, the war generated great division and discord. What began as a relatively quiet, small, and popular intervention consonant with established Cold War policy ended up stimulating the mobilization of the biggest antiwar movement in American history, ending a presidency, and putting limits on what subsequent administrations felt they could do abroad for decades.

EXPANDING THE LIBERAL STATE

Those who yearned for a more active government in the late 1950s, and who accused the Eisenhower administration of failing to address racial inequality and other social problems, hoped for vigorous new leadership from the next presidents. The two men who served in the White House through most of the 1960s—**John Kennedy** and **Lyndon Johnson**—promised just that and seemed for a time to embody these hopes.

JOHN KENNEDY

The campaign of 1960 produced two candidates with differing visions of the role of government in society. Eisenhower's vice president, Richard Nixon, easily scooped up the Republican nomination by pledging only moderate governmental action on social reform. The Democrats, in the meantime, emerged from a spirited primary campaign united, although somewhat uneasily, behind John Fitzgerald Kennedy, a senator from Massachusetts who had narrowly missed being the party's vice presidential candidate in 1956. He hinted at making robust changes to society, especially in matters of welfare and civil rights.

John Kennedy came from a family of great wealth and influence. His father, the powerful and highly controversial Joseph P. Kennedy, was a former American ambassador to Britain. Unlike Nixon, Kennedy based his campaign "on the single assumption that the American people are uneasy at the present drift in our national course." But nearly as important as his politics was his carefully managed public image, which helped him win popular support. Handsome, a war hero, and married to socialite Jacqueline Bouvier Kennedy who was pregnant with their second child during the presidential campaign, he was at ease on

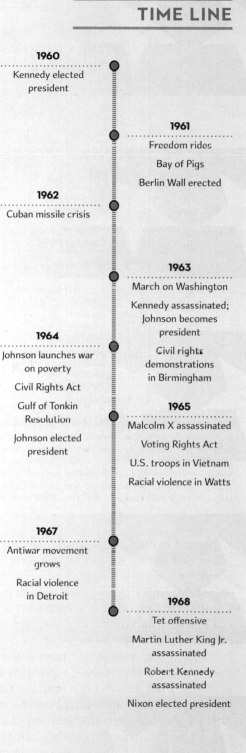

1960
Kennedy elected president

1961
Freedom rides

Bay of Pigs

Berlin Wall erected

1962
Cuban missile crisis

1963
March on Washington

Kennedy assassinated; Johnson becomes president

Civil rights demonstrations in Birmingham

1964
Johnson launches war on poverty

Civil Rights Act

Gulf of Tonkin Resolution

Johnson elected president

1965
Malcolm X assassinated

Voting Rights Act

U.S. troops in Vietnam

Racial violence in Watts

1967
Antiwar movement grows

Racial violence in Detroit

1968
Tet offensive

Martin Luther King Jr. assassinated

Robert Kennedy assassinated

Nixon elected president

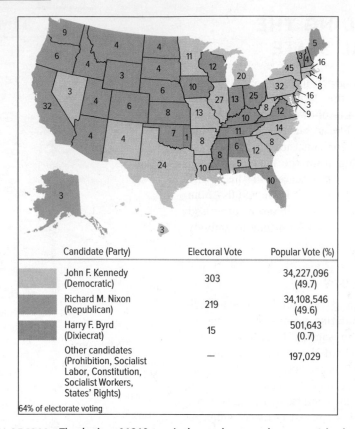

Candidate (Party)	Electoral Vote	Popular Vote (%)
John F. Kennedy (Democratic)	303	34,227,096 (49.7)
Richard M. Nixon (Republican)	219	34,108,546 (49.6)
Harry F. Byrd (Dixiecrat)	15	501,643 (0.7)
Other candidates (Prohibition, Socialist Labor, Constitution, Socialist Workers, States' Rights)	—	197,029

64% of electorate voting

THE ELECTION OF 1960 The election of 1960 was, in the popular vote at least, one of the closest in American history. John Kennedy's margin over Richard Nixon was less than one-third of 1 percent of the total national vote, but greater in the electoral college. Note the distribution of electoral strength of the two candidates. Kennedy was strong in the industrial Northeast and the largest industrial states of the Midwest, and he retained at least a portion of his party's traditional strength in the South and Southwest. But Nixon made significant inroads into the upper South, carried Florida, and swept most of the plains and mountain states. • *What was the significance of this distribution of strength to the future of the two parties?*

stump and in front of the camera. Indeed, he regularly appeared on television talk shows before and during his run for president, and these appearances helped the American people look beyond his perceived weaknesses. He overcame doubts about his youth (he turned forty-three in 1960) and religion (he was only the second Catholic ever to secure a major party presidential nomination) to win with a tiny plurality of the popular vote (49.7 percent to Nixon's 49.6 percent) and only a slightly more comfortable electoral majority (303 to 219).

Kennedy had campaigned promising a set of domestic reforms that he dubbed the **"New Frontier."** He entreated Americans to join him and become "pioneers" dedicated to forging a new America that provided health care to elderly and poor individuals, lower tax rates, economic aid for rural counties mired in poverty, and better funding for education. He also asked that they seek to end segregation. But his razor-thin popular mandate and a Congress dominated by a coalition of Republicans and conservative Democrats frustrated many of his hopes. Indeed, his most ambitious social programs came into being only under his successor.

More than any other president of the century (except perhaps the two Roosevelts and, later, Ronald Reagan), Kennedy made his own personality an integral part of his presidency and a focus of national attention. Nothing illustrated this more clearly than the public's outpouring of grief and sorrow following the tragedy of November 22, 1963. In Texas for a series of political appearances, the president was riding in a motorcade with his wife Jacqueline, Texas governor John Connally, and Connally's wife Nellie when shots rang out. Two bullets struck the president—one in the throat, the other in the head. Secret Service agents sped him to a nearby hospital, where minutes later he was pronounced dead. Lee Harvey Oswald—a young man who had spent time in the Soviet Union and, later, in Cuba—was arrested for the crime. Later that day Oswald was mysteriously murdered by a Dallas nightclub owner, Jack Ruby, as he was being moved from one jail to another. Most Americans at the time accepted the conclusions of a federal commission appointed by President Johnson to investigate the assassination. The commission, chaired by Supreme Court Chief Justice Earl Warren, found that both Oswald and Ruby had acted alone and there was no larger conspiracy. In later years, however, many Americans came to believe that the Warren Commission report had ignored evidence of a wider conspiracy behind the murders. Controversy over the assassination continues still.

LYNDON JOHNSON

The Kennedy assassination was a national trauma—a defining event for almost everyone old enough to be aware of it. At the time, however, much of the country took great comfort in the personality and performance of Kennedy's successor in the White House, Lyndon Baines Johnson. Johnson was a native of the hill country of west Texas and had risen from bitter poverty to become majority leader of the U.S. Senate by dint of extraordinary, even obsessive, effort and ambition. Having failed to win the Democratic nomination for president in 1960, he surprised many who knew him by agreeing to accept the vice presidential nomination on the ticket with Kennedy. The events in Dallas thrust him into the White House.

Johnson's first year in office was, by necessity, dominated by the campaign for reelection. There was little doubt that he would win—particularly after the Republican Party nominated the very conservative Senator Barry Goldwater of Arizona. In the November 1964 election, the president received a larger plurality, over 61 percent, than any candidate before or since. Goldwater, with his hard-line stance against communism and government expansion, managed to carry only his home state of Arizona and five states in the Deep South. Nevertheless, the failed Goldwater campaign mobilized many right-wing activists who would in later years propel the growth of conservative political strength for decades to come.

Johnson's rough-edged, even crude, personality could hardly have been more different from Kennedy's urbane manner. But like Kennedy, Johnson was a man who believed in the active use of power. Between 1963 and 1966, he compiled the most impressive legislative record of any president since Franklin Roosevelt. How did he do it? Following the death of Kennedy, the grieving public embraced many of his New Frontier proposals almost as a form of tribute to their fallen leader. Building on this popular approval for domestic reform, and benefiting from the vocal support of civil rights leaders like Martin Luther King Jr., Johnson introduced a series of social programs far more comprehensive and far-reaching than anything Kennedy had articulated. He called them the "**Great Society**." Record Democratic majorities in both houses of Congress, several

(Source: Lyndon Baines Johnson Library)

THE JOHNSON TREATMENT   Lyndon Johnson was legendary for his powers of persuasion—for a combination of charm and intimidation that often worked on even the most experienced politicians. He is shown here in the Oval Office meeting with his old friend Senator Richard Russell of Georgia and demonstrating one of his most powerful and unsettling techniques: moving so close to the person with whom he was talking as to be almost touching him.

of whose members had been swept on Johnson's coattails, ensured that the president would be able to fulfill many of his legislative goals. And for those members of Congress who stood in the president's way, Johnson employed the same sort of skillful and aggressive lobbying that had previously made him such an effective majority leader in the House of Representatives.

THE ASSAULT ON POVERTY

For the first time since the New Deal, the federal government took steps in the 1960s to create important new social welfare programs. The most significant of these was **Medicare**, which provides federal aid to elderly individuals for medical expenses. Its enactment in 1965 came at the end of a bitter twenty-year debate between those who believed in the concept of national health assistance and those who denounced it as "socialized medicine." But Medicare pacified many critics. For one thing, it avoided the stigma of "welfare" by making Medicare benefits available to all older Americans, regardless of need (just as Social Security had done with pensions). That created a large middle-class constituency for the program. It also defused the opposition of the medical community by allowing doctors serving Medicare patients to practice privately and (at first) to charge their normal fees; Medicare simply shifted responsibility for paying those fees from the patient to the government. In 1966, Johnson steered to passage the **Medicaid** program, which extended federal medical assistance to welfare recipients and other indigent people of all ages.

Medicare and Medicaid were early steps in a much larger assault on poverty—one that Kennedy had been planning in the last months of his life and that Johnson launched only weeks after taking office. The centerpiece of this "war on poverty," as Johnson called it, was the Office of Economic Opportunity (OEO), which created an array of new educational, employment, housing, and health-care programs. Yet the OEO was controversial from the start, in part because of its commitment to the idea of "Community Action."

Community Action was an effort to involve members of poor communities themselves in the planning and administration of the programs designed to help them. The **Community Action programs** provided jobs for many poor people and gave them valuable experience in administrative and political work. But despite its achievements, the Community Action approach proved impossible to sustain. Administrative failures damaged the program. So did the apparent excesses of a few agencies, which damaged the popular image of the Community Action programs and indeed the war on poverty as a whole.

The OEO spent nearly $3 billion during its first two years of existence, and it helped reduce poverty in some areas. But it fell far short of eliminating poverty altogether. That was in part because of the weaknesses of the programs themselves and in part because funding for them, inadequate from the beginning, dwindled as the years passed and a costly war in Southeast Asia became the nation's first priority.

CITIES, SCHOOLS, AND IMMIGRATION

Closely tied to the antipoverty program were federal efforts to revitalize decaying cities and strengthen the nation's schools. The Housing Act of 1961, passed under the Kennedy administration, offered $4.9 billion in federal grants to cities for the preservation of open spaces, the development of mass-transit systems, and the subsidization of middle-income housing. In 1966, Johnson established a new cabinet agency, the Department of Housing and Urban Development (whose first secretary, Robert Weaver, was the first African American ever to serve in the cabinet). Johnson also inaugurated the Model Cities Program, which offered federal subsidies for urban redevelopment pilot programs.

Kennedy had fought for federal aid to public education, but he had failed to overcome two important obstacles. Many Americans feared that aid to education was the first step toward federal control of the schools, and Catholics insisted that federal assistance must extend to parochial as well as public schools. Johnson managed to circumvent both objections with the Elementary and Secondary Education Act of 1965 and a series of subsequent measures. The bills extended aid to all types of schools and based the aid on the economic conditions of the students, not on the needs of the schools themselves.

The Johnson administration also supported the **Immigration Act of 1965**, one of the most important pieces of legislation of the 1960s. For decades since the 1920s, the law maintained a strict limit on the number of newcomers admitted to the country each year (170,000). But the 1965 act eliminated the "national origins" system established in the 1920s, which gave preference to immigrants from northern Europe over those from other parts of the world. It continued to restrict immigration from some parts of Latin America, but it allowed people from all parts of Europe, Asia, and Africa to enter the United States on an equal basis. By the early 1970s, the character of American immigration had changed dramatically. The numbers of immigrants grew significantly, with members of new national groups—and particularly large groups of Asians—entering the United States and transforming the character of the American population.

LEGACIES OF THE GREAT SOCIETY

Taken together, the Great Society reforms significantly increased federal spending. For a time, rising tax revenues from the growing economy nearly compensated for the new expenditures. In 1964, Johnson managed to win passage of the $11.5 billion tax cut that Kennedy had first proposed in 1962. The cut increased the federal deficit, but substantial economic growth over the next several years made up for much of the revenue initially lost. As Great Society programs began to multiply, however—particularly as they began to compete with the escalating costs of America's military ventures—the federal budget rapidly outpaced increases in revenues. In 1961, the federal government had spent $94.4 billion. By 1970, that sum had risen to $196.6 billion.

The high costs of the Great Society, and the failures of some of it, eventually weakened the popularity of the federal efforts to solve social problems. But the Great Society was also responsible for some remarkable achievements. It significantly reduced hunger in America. It made medical care available to millions of elderly and poor people who would otherwise have had great difficulty affording it. It contributed to the greatest reduction in poverty in American history. In 1959, according to the most widely accepted estimates, 21 percent of the American people lived below the officially established poverty line (a level that did not survive for very long). Ten years later, only 12 percent remained below that line. Some of that progress was a result of economic growth, but much of it was a direct result of Great Society programs.

THE BATTLE FOR RACIAL EQUALITY

By the early 1960s, African Americans forced issues of racial justice and equality to the forefront of American politics. While scholars debate the origins and legacies of the modern civil rights movement, none challenge how deeply it influenced the nation's history in the late twentieth century. (See "Debating the Past: The Civil Rights Movement.")

EXPANDING PROTESTS

John Kennedy was sympathetic to the cause of racial justice, but he was far from a committed crusader. Like presidents before him, he feared alienating southern voters and powerful southern Democrats in Congress. His administration, like Eisenhower's, hoped to contain the racial problem by enforcing existing laws and using executive orders—not proposing new legislation. That reluctance would not last very long, however.

The pressure for change was growing uncontainable even before Kennedy took office. Throughout the 1950s, African Americans in southern cities had grown increasingly active in opposing discrimination. They demanded progress in housing, jobs, and education. The Montgomery bus boycott from 1955 to 1956 showcased the resolve and ability of southern blacks to fight against segregation. Protests grew in the early 1960s, mainly centered in the South. In February 1960, black college students in Greensboro, North Carolina, staged a sit-in at a segregated Woolworth's lunch counter; and in the following months, similar demonstrations spread throughout the former states of the Confederacy, forcing many merchants to integrate their facilities. In the fall of 1960, some of those who had participated in the sit-ins formed the Student Nonviolent Coordinating Committee (SNCC)—a student branch of Martin Luther King Jr.'s Southern Christian Leadership Conference dedicated to defeating the color line through campaigns of nonviolent action.

In 1961, an interracial group of students, working with the Congress of Racial Equality (CORE), began what they called "**freedom rides**." Traveling by bus throughout the South, they tried to force the desegregation of bus stations. Their activism infuriated segregationists and functioned like a call to arms for many of them. On Mother's Day in 1961 in Anniston, Alabama, Klansmen stormed the Greyhound Station once word got out that freedom riders were in town. The alert bus driver pulled away before the angry mob could sack the bus, but attackers still managed to slit the tires. Just outside of town the tires blew and the bus came to a complete stop, where infuriated Klansmen tracked it down and renewed their assault. They firebombed the bus and blocked the doors, hoping to burn the passengers alive. But riders pushed their way outside, where the Klansmen began to beat them with bricks, clubs, and iron pipes. Only warning shots fired by a highway patrol officer in plainclothes who was secretly riding with the bus scattered the crowd and saved the riders. Widely covered in the press, the bus bombing actually encouraged new waves of civil rights protesters to become freedom riders. They met similar savagery in Birmingham and Montgomery, prompting Attorney General Robert Kennedy to dispatch federal marshals to help keep the peace and order the integration of all bus and train stations serving interstate travel.

Even more dramatic and bloody events in the Deep South in 1963 propelled the movement to the forefront of the nation's conscience. In April, Martin Luther King Jr. helped launch a series of nonviolent demonstrations in Birmingham, Alabama. Police Commissioner Eugene "Bull" Connor personally supervised a brutal effort to break up the peaceful marches, arresting hundreds of demonstrators and using attack dogs, tear gas, electric cattle prods, and fire hoses—at times even against small children—in full view of television cameras that broadcast images nationally. Two months later, on June 11, Governor George Wallace stood in the doorway of the Foster Auditorium at the University of Alabama, his alma mater, to block the court-ordered enrollment of two black students, Vivian Malone and James Hood. It was a tense standoff, carried live by the television networks. The stakes were high because Wallace was quickly becoming the face of resistance to integration in the South. At his inauguration in Montgomery earlier in January, he had catapulted to national prominence by urging southerners to resist federal encroachment and reject the Kennedy administration's attempts at desegregation. In the most famous line from his speech, Wallace had declared that "In the name of the greatest people that have ever trod this earth, I draw the line in the dust and toss the gauntlet before the feet of tyranny and I say segregation today, segregation tomorrow, segregation forever." But even while he relished the spotlight in Tuscaloosa, the governor knew that he was not going to win this particular battle. Indeed, he quickly stepped aside after President Kennedy federalized the Alabama National Guard to ensure integration.

Later that day, the president addressed the nation on live television and made his most forceful statement to date for his support for civil rights. Kennedy told his viewers, "It ought to be possible for American consumers of any color to receive equal service in places of public accommodation, such as hotels and restaurants and theaters and retail stores, without being forced to resort to demonstrations in the street, and it ought to be possible for American citizens of any color to register and to vote in a free election without interference or fear of reprisal." Tragically, only several hours later the NAACP official and key leader of the movement in Mississippi, Medgar Evers, was gunned down in his driveway by white supremacist Byron De La Beckwith.

A NATIONAL COMMITMENT

The events in Alabama and Mississippi were a warning to the president that he could no longer avoid the issue of race. Days after delivering his civil rights address and the murder of Evers, he introduced new legislative proposals prohibiting segregation in "public accommodations" (stores, restaurants, theaters, hotels), barring discrimination

THE CIVIL RIGHTS MOVEMENT

The civil rights movement was one of the most important events in the modern history of the United States. It helped force the dismantling of legalized segregation and disenfranchisement of African Americans and also served as a model for other groups mobilizing to demand dignity and rights. And like all important events in history, it has produced scholarship that examines the movement in a number of different ways.

The early histories of the civil rights movement remain widely accepted. They rest on a heroic narrative of moral purpose and personal courage by which great men and women inspired ordinary people to rise up and struggle for their rights. This narrative generally begins with the *Brown* decision of 1954 and the Montgomery bus boycott of 1955, continues through the civil rights campaigns of the early 1960s, and culminates in the Civil Rights Acts of 1964 and 1965. Among the central events in this narrative are the March on Washington of 1963, with Martin Luther King Jr.'s famous "I Have a Dream" speech, and the assassination of King in 1968, which has often symbolized the end of the movement and the beginning of a different, more complicated period of the black freedom struggle. The key element of these narratives is the central importance to the movement of a few great leaders, most notably King himself. Among the best examples of this narrative are Taylor Branch's powerful studies of the life and struggles of King, *Parting the Waters* (1988), *Pillar of Fire* (1998), and *At Canaan's Edge* (2006), as well as David Garrow's important study, *Bearing the Cross* (1986).

Few historians would deny the importance of King and other leaders to the successes of the civil rights movement. But a number of scholars have argued that the leader-centered narrative obscures the vital contributions of ordinary people in communities throughout the South, and the nation, to the struggle. John Dittmer's *Local People: The Struggle for Civil Rights in Mississippi* (1994) and Charles Payne's *I've Got the Light of Freedom* (1995) both examine the day-to-day work of the movement's rank and file in the early 1960s and argue that their efforts were at least as important as those of King and other leaders. The national leadership helped bring visibility to these struggles, but King and his circle were usually present only briefly, if at all, for the actual work of communities in challenging segregation. Only by understanding the local origins of the movement, these and other scholars argue, can we understand its true character.

Scholars also disagree about the time frame of the movement. Rather than beginning the story in 1954 or 1955 (as in Robert Weisbrot's 1991 synthesis *Freedom Bound* or in William Chafe's 1981 local study *Civilities and Civil Rights*, which examined the Greensboro sit-ins of 1961), a number of scholars have tried to move the story into both earlier periods and later ones. Robin Kelly's *Race Rebels* (1994) emphasizes the important contributions of working-class African Americans, some of them allied for a time with the Communist Party, to the undermining of racist assumptions starting in the 1930s. These activists organized some of the earliest civil rights demonstrations— sit-ins, marches, and other efforts to challenge segregation—well before the

(©Carl Iwasaki/The LIFE Images Collection/Getty Images)

BROWN V. BOARD OF EDUCATION This photograph, taken for an Atlanta newspaper, illustrated the long and dangerous walk that Linda Brown, one of the plaintiffs in the famous desegregation case that ultimately reached the Supreme Court, had to travel each day on her way to a segregated school in Topeka, Kansas. An all-white school was located close to her home, but to reach the black school she had to attend required a long walk and a long bus ride each day. Not only does the picture illustrate the difficulties segregation created for Linda Brown, it was also part of a broad publicity campaign launched by the supporters of the case.

conventional dates for the beginning of the movement. Gail O'Brien's *The Color of the Law* (1999) examines a 1946 "race riot" in Columbia, Tennessee, arguing for its importance as a signal of the early growth of African American militancy and the movement of that militancy from the streets into the legal system.

Other scholars have looked beyond the 1960s and have incorporated events outside the orbit of the formal "movement" to explain the history of the civil rights struggle. A growing literature on northern, urban, and relatively radical activists has suggested that focusing too much on mainstream leaders and the celebrated efforts in the South in the 1960s diverts our view from the equally important challenges facing northern African Americans and the very different tactics and strategies that

they often chose to pursue their goals. Thomas Sugre makes this point in his *Origins of the Urban Crisis: Race and Poverty in Postwar Detroit* (1988). The enormous attention historians have given to the life and legacy of Malcolm X—among them Alex Haley's influential *Autobiography of Malcolm X* (1965), Michael Eric Dyson's *Making Malcolm* (1996), and Manning Marable's important biography, *Malcolm X: A Life of Reinvention* (2012)— is also an example of the growing focus on ideas of black power, as is the increasing attention scholars like Hassan Jeffries in *Bloody Lowndes: Civil Right and Black Power in Alabama's Black Belt* (2010) have given to black radicalism and such militant groups as the Black Panthers. Other literature has extended the civil rights struggle even further. Carol Anderson, in *Eyes Off the Prize: The United Nations and the African American Struggle for Civil Rights, 1945–1955* (2003) and Mary Dudziak, in *Cold War Civil Rights: Race and the Image of American Democracy* (2011) offer international perspectives on the movement. Others have brought into focus such issues as the highly disproportionate number of African Americans sentenced to death within the criminal justice system. Randall Kennedy's *Race, Crime, and the Law* (1997), Michelle Alexander's *The New Jim Crow: Mass Incarceration in the Age of Color Blindness* (2012), and Bryan Stevenson's *Just Mercy: A Story of Justice and Redemption* (2014) are particularly important studies of this issue.

Even *Brown v. Board of Education* (1954), the great landmark of the legal challenge to segregation, has been subject to reexamination. Richard Kluger's narrative history of the *Brown* decision, *Simple Justice* (1975), is a classic statement of the traditional view of *Brown* as a triumph over injustice. But others have been less certain of the dramatic success of the ruling. James T. Patterson's *Brown v. Board of Education: A Civil Rights Milestone and Its Troubled Legacy* (2001) argues that the *Brown* decision long preceded any national consensus on the need to end segregation and that its impact was far less decisive than earlier scholars have suggested. Michael Klarman's *From Jim Crow to Civil Rights* (2004) examines the role of the Supreme Court in advancing civil rights and suggests, among other things, that the *Brown* decision may actually have retarded racial progress in the South for a time because of the enormous backlash it created. Charles Ogletree's *All Deliberate Speed* (2004) and Derrick Bell's *Silent Covenants* (2004) both argue that the Court's decision did not provide an effective enforcement mechanism for desegregation and in many other ways failed to support measures that would have made school desegregation a reality. Stephen Tuck's *We Ain't What We Ought to Be: The Black Freedom Struggle from Emancipation to Obama* (2011)

concludes his broad narrative about the road to racial equality by focusing on the continued activism of African Americans into the present.

As the literature on the African American freedom struggles of the twentieth century has grown, historians have begun to speak of civil rights *movements*, rather than a single, cohesive movement. •

UNDERSTAND, ANALYZE, & EVALUATE

1. If historians now speak of plural civil rights *movements*, what are these movements?
2. Why are the contributions of local grassroots workers so often overlooked, in studies of the civil rights movement as well as in accounts of other great events in American history?

in employment, and increasing the power of the government to file suits on behalf of school integration. These proposals would eventually become key elements of the Civil Rights Act of 1964.

To generate support for Kennedy's legislation, and to dramatize the power of the growing movement, more than 200,000 demonstrators marched on the Mall in Washington, D.C., in August 1963 and gathered before the Lincoln Memorial for the largest civil rights demonstration in the nation's history to that point. Martin Luther King Jr., in one of the greatest speeches of American politics, "I Have a Dream," set the movement in historical perspective and called upon the nation to fulfill its moral obligations to all of its citizens and usher in a new era of full equality.

Joining King on the dais that day was twenty-three-year-old John Lewis, chair of the Student Nonviolent Coordinating Committee and a key organizer of the march who had grown up the son of sharecroppers in Pike County, Alabama. As a freedom rider in 1961 he had faced angry mobs in Montgomery and been attacked by them. Now looking back to the birth of the country, Lewis begged Americans to join him in "this great revolution that is sweeping this nation. Get in and stay in the streets of every city, every village and hamlet of this nation until true freedom comes, until the revolution of 1776 is complete." No longer would there be any pause in the push for freedom, he continued. "They're talking about slow down and stop. We will not stop. . . . If we do not get meaningful legislation out of this Congress, the time will come when we will not confine our marching to Washington." The protest, however, would always be a public statement of nonviolence and profession of faith in the ability of the nation to progress to a higher state of equality and justice. "But we will march with the spirit of love and with the spirit of dignity that we have shown here today. By the force of our demands, our determination, and our numbers,

(©AP Photo)

MARTIN LUTHER KING JR. IN WASHINGTON Moments after completing his memorable speech during the August 1963 March on Washington, King waves to the vast and enthusiastic crowd that had gathered in front of the Lincoln Memorial to demand "equality and jobs."

we shall splinter the segregated South into a thousand pieces and put them together in the image of God and democracy. We must say: 'Wake up America! Wake up!' For we cannot stop, and we will not and cannot be patient."

The assassination of President Kennedy three months later gave new impetus to civil rights legislation. The ambitious measure that Kennedy had proposed in June 1963 was stalled in the Senate after having passed through the House of Representatives with relative ease. Early in 1964, however, after Lyndon Johnson had applied both public and private pressure, supporters of the measure finally mustered the two-thirds majority necessary to end a filibuster by southern senators, and the Senate passed the most important civil rights bill of the twentieth century.

THE BATTLE FOR VOTING RIGHTS

With the passage of the Civil Rights Act of 1964 and banning of segregation in public spaces, leaders of the movement shifted focus to another area of racial discrimination: voting rights. Beginning in the late nineteenth century, southern legislatures had successfully disfranchised blacks and many poor whites through a variety of means. Some were straightforward: politicians modified state constitutions and passed laws that blocked access to the ballot box. Others were more creative but no less effective: they required literacy tests with intentionally confusing and unanswerable questions, assessed poll taxes, and made it difficult to met residency requirements. These measures produced dramatic results: in 1940, only 3 percent of southern blacks were registered to vote. That number moved up slowly in response to civil rights activism, to 16.8 percent in 1950 and almost 29 percent in 1960. But in some parts of the South, few blacks ever voted.

During the summer of 1964, thousands of civil rights workers, black and white, northern and southern, spread throughout the South but primarily into Mississippi to work on behalf of black voter registration and participation. The state was a logical choice to make a stand for voting rights: it had long been a flashpoint in the struggle for equality, and only 6.7 percent of its eligible black voters were registered in 1962, the lowest percentage in America. The campaign was known as "**Freedom Summer**," and it met with stiff resistance from local whites. Activists faced harassment, beatings, arrest, and jail. Their churches were bombed, their cars shot at. Three of the first freedom workers to arrive in the South—two whites, Andrew Goodman and Michael Schwerner, and one African American, James Chaney—were murdered in June. The men had been arrested in Philadelphia, Mississippi, and the local sheriff released them at night. Local Klansmen overtook their car as they drove away, shot all three, and hid their bodies in a nearby earthen dam where the FBI, called in by an infuriated Attorney General Robert Kennedy, found them six weeks later. During the search, federal officials turned up eight other bodies, all African American, who had apparently been murdered as well.

Freedom Summer also helped birth the Mississippi Freedom Democratic Party (MFDP). It was a natural outgrowth of the voting rights campaign, offering an integrated alternative to the whites-only state Democratic Party organization. Under the leadership of Fannie Lou Hamer and others, the MFDP challenged the regular party's right to its seats at the Democratic National Convention that summer. Hamer, appearing before the Credentials Committee and televised live by NBC News, spoke stirringly about growing up poor and black in Mississippi and enduring brutal sexual assaults as she tried to vote. (See "Consider the Source: Fannie Lou Hamer on the Struggle for Voting Rights.") Her testimony and unrelenting demand for proper representation within her state's delegation caused a stir among the national Democratic Party. President Johnson, with King's help, managed to broker a compromise by which members of the MFDP could be seated as observers, without formal power but with a promise of future party reforms, while the regular party leadership retained its official standing. Many MFDP members rejected the agreement and left the convention embittered.

A year later, on Sunday, March 7, 1965, John Lewis and Rev. Hosea Williams helped organize a major voting rights march in Selma, Alabama. Selma Sheriff Jim Clark led local police, some on horseback, others armed with shotguns, billy clubs, and tear gas canisters, in a vicious attack on the demonstrators as they attempted to cross the Edmund Pettus Bridge and make their way to the state capital of Montgomery. Bloody Sunday, as the day came to be known, sparked national outrage and helped push Lyndon Johnson to win passage of the **Voting Rights Act of 1965**, which provided federal protection to African Americans attempting to exercise their right to the ballot. But important as such gains were, they failed to satisfy the rapidly rising expectations of civil rights activists nationally as the focus of the movement began to move from political to economic issues and to include the North.

THE CHANGING MOVEMENT

By the mid-1960s, the scope of the movement became more national and city-based. Given that in 1966 about 45 percent of all blacks lived outside the South, many in urban neighborhoods, it was hardly surprising. Indeed, the publicity of the civil rights movement in the South intensified civil rights efforts in northern cities, where black leaders had labored for decades to alleviate discriminatory practices. While black northerners typically enjoyed a greater range of freedom in the practice of daily life and were not subject to the same discriminatory state laws that marred the South, they still battled harsh local customs and municipal codes that placed a strict color line around where they could live, work, travel, and play.

A symbol of the movement's new direction, and of the problems it would cause, was a major campaign in the summer of 1966 in Chicago, in which King played a prominent role. Organizers of the Chicago campaign hoped to direct the nation's attention to housing and employment discrimination in northern industrial cities. But the Chicago campaign evoked vicious and at times violent opposition from white residents and failed to attract wide attention or support in the way events in the South had done.

Many African American leaders (and their white supporters), having struggled in relative obscurity in the 1940s and 1950s, now began to move the battle against job discrimination to a new level. They argued that the only way for employers to prove they were not discriminating against African Americans was to demonstrate that they were indeed hiring minorities. If necessary, they should adopt positive measures to recruit minorities. Lyndon Johnson gave his support to this concept of **affirmative action** in 1965. Over the next decade, affirmative action guidelines gradually extended to virtually all institutions doing business with or receiving funds from the federal government (including schools and universities)— and to many others as well. Discrimination based on gender also began to receive federal interest. When "sex" was added at the last minute to Title VII of the 1964 Civil Rights Act, many thought it was an attempt to kill the bill. Regardless, the result added federal authority to begin dismantling the entrenched discrimination of women in the workplace and higher education.

Urban Violence

Well before the Chicago campaign, the problem of urban poverty and violence had flared and captured national prominence. In July 1964 in Harlem, New York City, a police shooting death of a fifteen-year-old black student set off six days of rioting that left 1 dead, 118 injured, and 465 arrested. Yet the most serious race riot since the end of World War II occurred the following summer in the Watts section of Los Angeles. In the midst of a traffic arrest, a white police officer struck a protesting black bystander with his club. The incident triggered a storm of anger and a week of violence. Thirty-four people died during the uprising, which was eventually quelled by the National Guard. In the summer of 1966, forty-three additional outbreaks occurred, the most serious in Chicago and Cleveland. And in the summer of 1967, eight major disorders took place, including the largest of them all—a racial clash in Detroit in which forty-three people died.

Televised images of the violence alarmed millions of Americans and set off a round of soul-searching among politicians and civil rights activists. What was the solution to the violence? A special Commission on Civil Disorders, ordered by President Johnson in response to the riots, issued a celebrated report in the spring of 1968 recommending massive spending to eliminate the abysmal conditions of the ghettoes. To many white Americans, however, the riots exposed the need for stern measures to stop violence and lawlessness. But to some black Americans, the time was ripe for a more aggressive attack on segregation.

FANNIE LOU HAMER ON THE STRUGGLE FOR VOTING RIGHTS (1964)

Fannie Lou Hamer shone a harsh spotlight on racial terror in her native state of Mississippi during her speech before the Credentials Committee of the Democratic National Convention in Atlantic City, New Jersey, in August 1964. With this testimony, Hamer tried—unsuccessfully—to unseat the all-white Mississippi delegation and seat members of the Mississippi Freedom Democratic Party (MFDP). Four years later, the MFDP succeeded in winning seats at the Convention.

Mr. Chairman, and to the Credentials Committee, my name is Mrs. Fannie Lou Hamer, and I live at 626 East Lafayette Street, Ruleville, Mississippi, Sunflower County, the home of Senator James O. Eastland, and Senator Stennis.

It was the 31st of August in 1962 that eighteen of us traveled twenty-six miles to the county courthouse in Indianola to try to register to become first-class citizens.

We was met in Indianola by policemen, Highway Patrolmen, and they only allowed two of us in to take the literacy test at the time. After we had taken this test and started back to Ruleville, we was held up by the City Police and the State Highway Patrolmen and carried back to Indianola where the bus driver was charged that day with driving a bus the wrong color.

After we paid the fine among us, we continued on to Ruleville, and Reverend Jeff Sunny carried me four miles in the rural area where I had worked as a timekeeper and sharecropper for eighteen years. I was met there by my children, who told me that the plantation owner was angry because I had gone down to try to register.

After they told me, my husband came, and said the plantation owner was raising Cain because I had tried to register. Before he quit talking the plantation owner came

and said, "Fannie Lou, do you know—did Pap tell you what I said?"

And I said, "Yes, sir."

He said, "Well I mean that." He said, "If you don't go down and withdraw your registration, you will have to leave." Said, "Then if you go down and withdraw," said, "you still might have to go because we are not ready for that in Mississippi."

And I addressed him and told him and said, "I didn't try to register for you. I tried to register for myself."

I had to leave that same night.

On the 10th of September 1962, sixteen bullets was fired into the home of Mr. and Mrs. Robert Tucker for me. That same night two girls were shot in Ruleville, Mississippi. Also Mr. Joe McDonald's house was shot in.

And June the 9th, 1963, I had attended a voter registration workshop; was returning back to Mississippi. Ten of us was traveling by the Continental Trailway bus. When we got to Winona, Mississippi, which is Montgomery County, four of the people got off to use the washroom, and two of the people—to use the restaurant—two of the people wanted to use the washroom.

The four people that had gone in to use the restaurant was ordered out. During this time I was on the bus. But when I looked through the window and saw they had rushed out I got off of the bus to see what had happened. And one of the ladies said, "It was a State Highway Patrolman and a Chief of Police ordered us out."

I got back on the bus and one of the persons had used the washroom got back on the bus, too.

As soon as I was seated on the bus, I saw when they began to get the five people in a highway patrolman's car. I stepped off of the bus to see what was happening and somebody screamed from the car that the five workers was in and said, "Get that one there." When I went to get in the car, when the man told me I was under arrest, he kicked me.

I was carried to the county jail and put in the booking room. They left some of the people in the booking room and began to place us in cells. I was placed in a cell with a young woman called Miss Ivesta Simpson. After I was placed in the cell I began to hear sounds of licks and screams, I could hear the sounds of licks and horrible screams. And I could hear somebody say, "Can you say, 'yes, sir,' nigger? Can you say 'yes, sir'?"

And they would say other horrible names.

She would say, "Yes, I can say 'yes, sir.'"

"So, well, say it."

She said, "I don't know you well enough."

They beat her, I don't know how long. And after a while she began to pray, and asked God to have mercy on those people.

And it wasn't too long before three white men came to my cell. One of these men was a State Highway Patrolman and he asked me where I was from. I told him Ruleville and he said, "We are going to check this."

They left my cell and it wasn't too long before they came back. He said, "You are from Ruleville all right," and he used a curse word. And he said, "We are going to make you wish you was dead."

I was carried out of that cell into another cell where they had two Negro prisoners. The State Highway Patrolmen ordered the first Negro to take the blackjack.

The first Negro prisoner ordered me, by orders from the State Highway Patrolman, for me to lay down on a bunk bed on my face.

I laid on my face and the first Negro began to beat. I was beat by the first Negro until he was exhausted. I was holding my hands behind me at that time on my left side, because I suffered from polio when I was six years old.

After the first Negro had beat until he was exhausted, the State Highway Patrolman ordered the second Negro to take the blackjack.

The second Negro began to beat and I began to work my feet, and the State Highway Patrolman ordered the first Negro who had beat me to sit on my feet—to keep me from working my feet. I began to scream and one white man got up and began to beat me in my head and tell me to hush.

One white man—my dress had worked up high—he walked over and pulled my dress—I pulled my dress down and he pulled my dress back up.

I was in jail when Medgar Evers was murdered.

All of this is on account of we want to register, to become first-class citizens. And if the Freedom Democratic Party is not seated now, I question America. Is this America, the land of the free and the home of the brave, where we have to sleep with our telephones off the hooks because our lives be threatened daily, because we want to live as decent human beings, in America?

Thank you.

UNDERSTAND, ANALYZE, & EVALUATE

1. What tactics were used to prevent Hamer from registering to vote?
2. Why did the Highway Patrolmen choose black prisoners to beat Hamer?
3. When the television networks broadcast this speech, the level of public support for the Mississippi Freedom Democratic Party rose sharply. What aspects of Hamer's speech were so effective?

Source: Fannie Lou Hamer, "Testimony Before the Credentials Committee," Democratic National Convention, August 22, 1964. Copyright ©1964 by Fannie Lou Hamer. All rights reserved. Used with permission.

BLACK POWER

Disillusioned with the ideal of peaceful change through cooperation with whites, an increasing number of African Americans turned to a new approach to solving racial conflict and promoting civil rights: the philosophy of **black power**. Black power meant many different things. But in all its forms, it suggested a shift away from the goals of assimilation and toward increased awareness of racial distinctiveness and the promotion of black-run institutions.

Perhaps the most enduring impact of the black-power ideology was a social and psychological one: instilling racial pride in African Americans. But black power took political forms as well, and it created a deep schism within the civil rights movement. Traditional black organizations that emphasized cooperation with sympathetic whites—groups such as the NAACP, the Urban League, and King's Southern Christian Leadership Conference—now faced competition from more radical groups. The Student Nonviolent Coordinating Committee and the Congress of Racial Equality had both begun as relatively moderate interracial organizations. By the mid-1960s, however, these and other groups were calling for more radical and occasionally even violent action against white racism and were openly rejecting the approaches of older, more established black leaders.

The most radical expressions of the black-power idea came from such revolutionary organizations as the Black Panthers. Formed in Oakland, California, in the fall of 1966 by Huey Newton and Bobby Seale, the Black Panthers originally aimed to curb what it saw as the problem of police mistreatment of black citizens. Armed Panthers, often uniformed in close-fitting leather jackets and black berets, closely monitored police patrols and promised to intervene in acts of police brutality. Images of Black Panthers marching and shouting "Off the Pigs" stunned many white Americans who associated civil rights protests with nonviolent marches and sit-ins. At the height of its popularity in the early 1970s, the Panthers had chapters in over sixty cities and thousands of members. Importantly, the Panthers spreading popularity was not simply a fact of their militant image. Rather, they also grew because of their efforts to improve local communities—bettering schools, opening health clinics, and providing food for the hungry. Indeed, their Ten-Point program, which functioned as a public declaration of their core principles, included calls for freedom as well as full employment, acceptable housing, clothing, justice and peace. They also actively recruited and promoted women into high-ranking and visible leadership posts, uncommon among most civil rights groups at the time.

Similar to the Black Panthers, the Nation of Islam preached a radical form of black power. It openly denounced whites as "devils" and appealed to African Americans to embrace its version of Islamic faith and work for complete racial separation. The most celebrated of the "Black Muslims," as the media often termed them, was Malcolm Little. Born in Boston in 1925, imprisoned at age twenty for larceny, he discovered the Nation of Islam while behind bars and adopted the name **Malcolm X** —"X" to denote his lost African surname. Upon his release, he rose quickly through the ranks by advocating a fiery brand of black separatism, even encouraging black Americans to move to Africa. He brashly challenged the leadership and legacy of the modern civil rights movement, which he claimed capitulated too quickly to the fears of white Americans and didn't do enough to promote black communities. A captivating speaker who packed auditoriums and halls around the country, he offered a stark alternative to King's vision of nonviolent social reform, urging black Americans to defend themselves when threatened or struck and not shy away from physical violence as a source of protest. His popularity captured a rising frustration among many young blacks about the pace of change in the pursuit of racial equality.

Malcolm X had a change of heart in 1964, however, and left the Nation of Islam and founded the Muslim Mosque, Inc., and the Organization of Afro-American Unity, which he hoped would allow him to work more cooperatively with other civil rights leaders. He soon became a Sunni Muslim and, after a pilgrimage to Mecca, espoused a new hope that racial problems could be overcome through nonviolent means and with the full support of whites. He died in 1965 when gunmen, possibly under orders from rivals within the Nation of Islam, assassinated him. But he remained a major figure in many African American communities long after his death, attaining a stature near comparable to that of Martin Luther King Jr.

"FLEXIBLE RESPONSE" AND THE COLD WAR

In international affairs as much as in domestic reform, the optimistic liberalism of the Kennedy and Johnson administrations dictated a more active and aggressive approach to dealing with the nation's problems than that of the 1950s.

DIVERSIFYING FOREIGN POLICY

The Kennedy administration entered office convinced that the United States needed to be able to counter communist aggression in more flexible ways than the atomic-weapons-oriented defense strategy of the Eisenhower years. In particular, Kennedy was unsatisfied with the nation's ability to meet communist threats in the Third World, areas in which, Kennedy believed, the real struggle against communism would be waged in the future. He gave enthusiastic support to the expansion of the Special Forces (or "Green Berets"), soldiers trained specifically to fight guerrilla conflicts and other limited wars.

Kennedy also favored expanding American influence through peaceful means. To repair badly deteriorating relationships in Latin America, he proposed an "Alliance for Progress," a series of projects for peaceful development and stabilization of the nations of that region. Kennedy also inaugurated the Agency for International Development (AID) to coordinate foreign aid. And he established what became one of his most popular innovations: the Peace Corps, which sent young American volunteers abroad to work in developing areas. But these programs served the broader Cold War strategy of anticommunist containment. By nurturing good will toward the United States, they aimed to maximize American access to natural resources, cultivate commercial markets, expand geopolitical influence, and above all, counter comparable communist efforts in the developing world and deprive the Soviet Union of potential allies.

Yet one of the first foreign policy ventures of the Kennedy administration was a military one, a disastrous assault on the Castro government in Cuba. The Eisenhower administration had started the project, and by the time Kennedy took office, the CIA had been working for months to train a small army of anti-Castro Cuban exiles. On April 17, 1961, with the approval of the new president, 2,000 of the armed exiles landed at the **Bay of Pigs** in Cuba, expecting American air support and then a spontaneous uprising by the Cuban people. They received neither. At the last minute, as it became clear that things were going badly, Kennedy withdrew the air support, fearful of involving the United States too directly in the invasion. Nor did the expected uprising occur. Instead, well-armed Castro forces easily crushed the invaders, and within two days the entire mission had collapsed.

CONFRONTATIONS WITH THE SOVIET UNION

In the grim aftermath of the Bay of Pigs, Kennedy traveled to Vienna in June 1961 for his first meeting with Soviet Premier Nikita Khrushchev. Their frosty exchange of views did little to reduce strains between the two nations—nor did Khrushchev's veiled threat of war unless the United States ceased to support a noncommunist West Berlin in the heart of East Germany.

Khrushchev was particularly unhappy about the mass exodus of residents of East Germany to the West through the easily traversed border in the center of Berlin. But he ultimately found a method short of war to stop it. Just before dawn on August 13, 1961, the East German government, complying with directives from Moscow, constructed a wall between East and West Berlin. Guards fired on those who continued to try to escape. For nearly thirty years, the Berlin Wall served as the most potent physical symbol of the conflict between the communist and noncommunist worlds.

The rising tensions culminated the following October in the most dangerous moment of the Cold War—the **Cuban missile crisis**. During the summer of 1962, American intelligence agencies became aware of the arrival of a new wave of Soviet technicians and equipment in Cuba and of military construction in progress. On October 14, aerial reconnaissance photos produced clear evidence that the Soviets were constructing sites on the island for offensive nuclear weapons. To the Soviets, placing missiles in Cuba probably seemed a reasonable—and relatively inexpensive—way to counter the presence of American missiles in Turkey (and a way to deter any future American invasion of Cuba). But to Kennedy and most other Americans, the missile sites represented an act of naked aggression by the Soviets toward the United States. Almost immediately, the president—working with a special executive committee assembled to deal with the crisis—decided that the weapons must go. On October 22, he ordered a naval and air blockade around Cuba, a "quarantine" against all offensive weapons. Preparations were under way for an American air attack on the missile sites when, late in the evening of October 26, Kennedy received a message from Khrushchev implying that the Soviet Union would remove the missile bases in exchange for an American pledge not to invade Cuba. The president agreed. And, in secret, Kennedy agreed to withdraw the missiles from Turkey in what is now called the Kennedy-Khrushchev Pact. The resolution of the conflict was a political victory for Kennedy, and in an effort to avoid the threat of war again, the two leaders established a Moscow-Washington hotline that created a direct link between the nuclear nations. The improved dialogue between the nuclear superpowers also paved the way for the Nuclear Test Ban Treaty of 1963, which banned atmospheric tests.

JOHNSON AND THE WORLD

Lyndon Johnson entered the presidency with little prior experience in international affairs. He was eager, therefore, not only to continue the flexible response policies of his predecessor but also to prove quickly that he, too, was a strong and forceful leader.

An internal rebellion in the Dominican Republic gave him an opportunity to do so. A 1961 assassination had toppled the dictatorship of General Rafael Trujillo, and for the next four years various factions in the country had struggled for dominance. In the spring of 1965, a conservative regime began to collapse in the face of a revolt by a broad range of groups on behalf of the left-wing nationalist Juan Bosch. Arguing without evidence that Bosch planned to establish a pro-Castro communist regime, Johnson dispatched 30,000 American troops to quell the disorder. Only after a conservative candidate defeated Bosch in a 1966 election were the forces withdrawn.

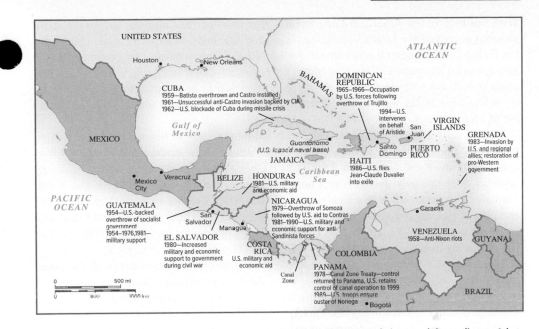

THE UNITED STATES IN LATIN AMERICA, 1954–2006 The Cold War greatly increased the readiness of the United States to intervene in the affairs of its Latin American neighbors. This map presents the many times and ways in which Washington ordered interventions in Central America, the Caribbean, and the northern nations of South America. During much of this period, the interventions were driven by Cold War concerns—by fears that communists might take over nations near the United States as they had taken over Cuba in the early 1960s. • *What other interests motivated the United States to exert influence in Latin America even after the end of the Cold War?*

From Johnson's first moments in office, however, his foreign policy was almost totally dominated by the bitter war in Vietnam and by the expanding involvement of the United States there.

THE AGONY OF VIETNAM

George Kennan, who helped devise the containment doctrine in the name of which America went to war in Vietnam, once called the conflict "the most disastrous of all America's undertakings over the whole 200 years of its history." Yet at first, the conflict in Vietnam seemed simply one more foreign struggle on the periphery of the Cold War.

AMERICA AND DIEM

Having thrown its support to the new leader of South Vietnam, Ngo Dinh Diem, in the aftermath of the 1954 Geneva accords, and having supported Diem in his refusal to hold the elections in 1956 that the accords had required, the United States found itself drawn steadily deeper into the unstable politics of this fractious new nation.

Diem, an aristocratic Catholic from central Vietnam and an outsider in the south, was also a hard-line nationalist uncontaminated by any collaboration with the French and bent on shoring up the authority of his regime. And he was, for a time, apparently successful.

With the help of the American CIA, Diem waged an effective campaign against powerful religious sects and the South Vietnamese organized crime syndicate, which had challenged the authority of the central government. As a result, the United States came to regard Diem as a powerful alternative to Ho Chi Minh, his communist rival in North Vietnam who had come to rule the northern regions of what was supposed to be a temporarily divided country at the close of the war with the French in 1954. America threw military and economic aid at Diem's feet.

Diem's early successes in suppressing sects led him in 1959 to begin a similar campaign to eliminate supporters of Ho Chi Minh in the south. Those southern communists thus created the National Liberation Front (NLF)—whose soldiers became known to many Americans pejoratively as the **Viet Cong**—an organization closely allied with the North Vietnamese government and which shared Ho Chi Minh's desire to unify Vietnam under communist rule. In 1960, under orders from Hanoi, and with both material and manpower support from North Vietnam, the NLF began military operations in the south. This marked the beginning of what Americans know as the Vietnam War.

By 1961, NLF forces had established effective control over many areas of the countryside and were threatening Diem's power. Diem also began losing the support of many other groups in South Vietnam, including his own military, despite increasing assistance under the Kennedy administration in the form of 16,000 military advisers. In 1963, a desperate Diem regime precipitated a major crisis by trying to repress the South Vietnamese Buddhists in an effort to limit political dissent. The Buddhists staged enormous antigovernment demonstrations. One of them saw a monk sit cross-legged in downtown Saigon, douse himself with gasoline, and set himself on fire—in full view of photographers and television cameras. Later, other Buddhists burned themselves in other areas.

Alarmed American officials pressured Diem to reform his now tottering government, but the president made no significant concessions. As a result, in the fall of 1963, Kennedy gave his approval to a plot by a group of South Vietnamese generals to topple Diem. In early November 1963, the generals staged the coup, assassinated Diem along with his brother Ngo Dinh Nhu (killings the United States had not wanted or expected), and established the first of a series of new governments that were, for over three years, even less stable than the one they had overthrown. A few weeks after the coup, John Kennedy was assassinated.

From Aid to Intervention

Lyndon Johnson inherited what was already a substantial American commitment to the survival of an anticommunist South Vietnam. During his first months in office, he expanded the American involvement in Vietnam only slightly, sending an additional 5,000 military advisers there and preparing to send 5,000 more. Then, early in August 1964, the president announced that American destroyers on patrol in international waters in the Gulf of Tonkin had been attacked by North Vietnamese torpedo boats. Later information raised serious doubts as to whether the administration reported the attacks accurately. At the time, however, virtually no one questioned Johnson's portrayal of the incident as a serious act of aggression. By a vote of 416 to 0 in the House and 88 to 2 in the Senate, Congress hurriedly passed the **Gulf of Tonkin Resolution**, which authorized the president to "take all necessary measures" to protect American forces and "prevent further aggression" in Southeast Asia. The resolution became, in Johnson's view at least, an open-ended legal authorization for escalation of the conflict, though at the time the president had little desire to see Vietnam erupt into a larger war.

With the South Vietnamese leadership still in disarray and communist military pressure growing stronger, more and more of the burden of opposition to the Viet Cong fell on the United States. In February 1965, after communist forces attacked an American military base at Pleiku, Johnson ordered American bombings of the north, in an attempt to destroy the depots and transportation lines responsible for the flow of North Vietnamese soldiers and supplies into South Vietnam. The bombing continued intermittently until 1972. A month later, in March 1965, two battalions of American marines landed at Da Nang in South Vietnam, bringing the total American troop strength to over 100,000.

Four months later, the president announced that American soldiers would now begin playing an active role in the conflict. By the end of the year, there were more than 180,000 American combat troops in Vietnam; in 1966, that number doubled; and by the end of 1967, over 500,000 American soldiers fought there. In the meantime, the air war intensified. By the spring of 1966, more than 4,000 Americans and an unknown number of Vietnamese had been killed.

THE QUAGMIRE

Central to the American war effort in Vietnam was a strategy known as "attrition," premised on the belief that the United States could inflict more damage on the enemy than the enemy could absorb. But the attrition strategy failed because the North Vietnamese, believing that they were fighting a war for national independence, were willing to commit many more soldiers and resources to the conflict than the United States had predicted. Increasing numbers of North Vietnamese fighters joined the Viet Cong, making their way through neutral Laos and Cambodia and delivering military supplies via what became known as the Ho Chi Minh trail. The emphasis on attrition, which invited the "body count" of enemy dead as one of the main measures of progress, had tragic consequences for the people of South Vietnam. The Vietnam War featured blurry lines between villages and battlefields, between civilians and soldiers. Most Americans worked diligently to avoid killing noncombatants, but returning fire or calling in airstrikes often led to that result, and commanders were encouraged by the attrition strategy to count all dead as enemy dead. In rare cases, most notoriously during the **My Lai massacre**, American soldiers deliberately murdered civilians believed to have harbored the Viet Cong, who themselves often came from or could blend into the villages of South Vietnam.

The United States also failed in expecting its bombing of the north to eliminate the communists' war-making capacity. North Vietnam was not a modern industrial society, and it had relatively few of the sorts of targets against which bombing is effective. The North Vietnamese also responded to the bombing with great ingenuity. They created a network of underground tunnels, shops, and factories. The North Vietnamese also were provided substantial aid from the Soviet Union and China. They continually moved the Ho Chi Minh Trail to make it elusive to American bombers. Far from breaking the north's resolve, the bombing seemed actually to strengthen popular commitment to the war.

Another important part of the American strategy was the "pacification" program, whose purpose was to push the Viet Cong from particular regions and then "pacify"

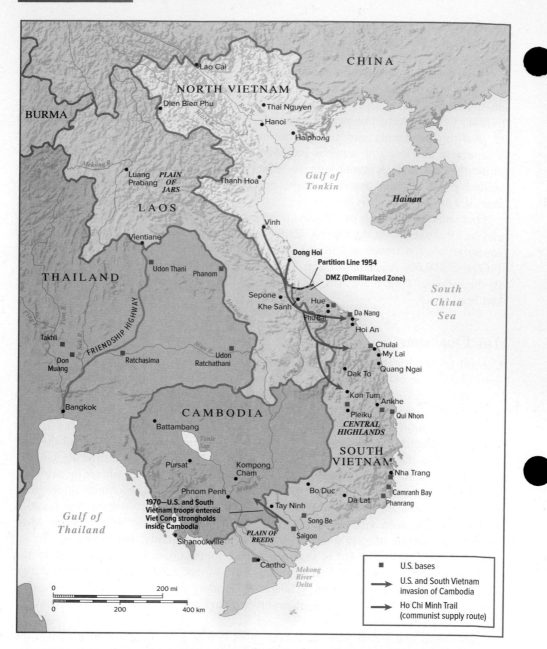

THE WAR IN VIETNAM AND INDOCHINA, 1964–1975 Much of the Vietnam War was fought in small engagements in widely scattered areas and did not conform to traditional notions of combat. But as this map shows, there were traditional battles and invasions and supply routes as well. The red arrows in the middle of the map show the general path of the Ho Chi Minh Trail, the main supply route by which North Vietnam supplied its troops and allies in the south. The blue arrow in southern South Vietnam indicates the point at which American troops invaded Cambodia in 1970. • *What is there in the geography of Indochina, as presented on this map, that helps explain the great difficulty the American military had in securing South Vietnam against communist attacks?*

those regions by winning the "hearts and minds" of the people. Routing the Viet Cong was often possible, but the subsequent pacification was more difficult. Gradually, the pacification program gave way to a more heavy-handed relocation strategy, through which American troops uprooted villagers from their homes, sent them fleeing to refugee camps or into the cities (producing by 1967 more than 3 million refugees), and then destroyed the vacated villages and surrounding countryside. "It became necessary to destroy the village in order to save it," an American military official famously said of one such action, thus revealing the flawed assumptions of the pacification program.

As the war dragged on and victory remained elusive, some American officers and officials urged the president to expand the military efforts. But Johnson resisted—in part because he remembered the Korean War. He feared drawing China directly into the Vietnam War, and he was beginning to encounter obstacles and frustrations at home.

THE WAR AT HOME

Few Americans, and even fewer influential ones, had protested the American involvement in Vietnam as late as the end of 1965. But as the war dragged on inconclusively, political support for it began to erode.

By the end of 1967, American students opposed to the war (and to the military draft) had become a significant political force. Enormous peace marches in New York, Washington, D.C., and other cities drew broad public attention to the antiwar movement. (Music also raised awareness; see "Patterns of Popular Culture: The Folk-Music Revival.") In the meantime, a growing number of journalists, particularly reporters who had spent time in Vietnam, helped sustain the movement with their frank revelations about the brutality and apparent futility of the war. Later, some critics would blame the media for such reporting, but many of them had gone to Vietnam in the early 1960s believing in the American fight there and only wishing to see it conducted more effectively.

Senator J. William Fulbright of Arkansas, chair of the Senate Foreign Relations Committee, also turned against the war and in January 1966 began to stage highly publicized and occasionally televised congressional hearings to air criticisms of it. Other members of Congress joined Fulbright in opposing Johnson's policies—including, in 1967, Robert F. Kennedy, brother of the slain president, now a senator from New York. Even within the administration, the consensus seemed to be crumbling. Robert McNamara, who had done much to help extend the initial American involvement in Vietnam, quietly left the government, disillusioned, in 1968. His successor as secretary of defense, Clark Clifford, became a quiet but powerful voice within the administration on behalf of a cautious scaling down of the commitment.

In the meantime, Johnson's commitment to fighting the war while continuing his Great Society reforms helped cause a rise in inflation, from the 2 percent level it had occupied through most of the early 1960s to 3 percent in 1967, 4 percent in 1968, and 6 percent in 1969. In August 1967, Johnson asked Congress for a tax increase to avoid even more ruinous inflation. In return, congressional conservatives demanded a $6 billion reduction in the funding for Great Society programs. The president accepted the reduction as a way to mollify congressional conservatives unnerved by economic troubles and critical of social welfare programs.

THE FOLK-MUSIC REVIVAL

Two impulses of the 1960s—the renewed interest among young people in the politics of the left, and the search for an "authentic" alternative to what many considered the artificial, consumerist culture of modern America—helped produce the revived popularity of folk music in that turbulent era. Although the harder music of rock 'n' roll was more visible and more popular in the 1960s, folk music more clearly expressed many of the political ideas and aspirations that were welling up in the youth culture of the time.

The folk-music tradition, like most American musical traditions, had many roots. It drew from some of the black musical traditions of the South, and from the white country music of Appalachia. And it drew most immediately from a style of music developed by musicians associated with the Communist Party's Popular Front in the 1930s. Woody Guthrie, Pete Seeger, the Weavers, and others whose music would become popular again in the 1960s began their careers singing in Popular Front and union rallies during the Great Depression. Their music, like the Popular Front itself, set out to seem entirely American, rooted in the nation's folk traditions.

Folk music remained alive in the 1940s and 1950s, but it had only a modest popular following. Pete Seeger and the Weavers continued to perform and to attract attention on college campuses. Harry Belafonte and the Kingston Trio recorded slick, pop versions of folk songs in an effort to bring them to mass audiences. In 1952, Folkway Records released the *Anthology of American Folk Music*, a collection of eighty-four performances recorded in the 1920s and 1930s that became an inspiration and an important source of material to many younger folk musicians. Folk-music festivals—at Berkeley, Newport, and Chicago—began to proliferate beginning in 1959. And an important community of folk musicians lived and performed together in the 1950s and early 1960s in New York City's Greenwich Village.

As the politics of the 1960s became more heated, it was folk music that most directly reflected their new values and concerns. Peter, Paul, and Mary—although only intermittently political—became icons to much of the New Left, beginning with their 1962 recording of "If I Had a Hammer," a song first performed at Communist Party rallies in the 1940s by Pete Seeger and the Weavers. Bob Dylan, whose own politics were never wholly clear to the public, had a large impact on the 1960s left, even inadvertently providing a name to the most radical offshoot of Students for a Democratic Society (SDS), the Weathermen, who named themselves after a line from one of his songs: "You don't need a weatherman to know which way the wind blows."* Joan Baez, whose politics were no secret to anyone, was actively engaged in the antiwar movement and was arrested several times for participating in militant protests.

But it was not just the overt political messages of folk musicians that made them so important to young Americans in the 1960s. In addition, folk was a kind of music that seemed to reflect the "authenticity" the youth culture was attempting to find. In truth, neither the musicians themselves nor the young Americans attracted to them had much real connection with the traditions they were trying to evoke.

(©John Orris/New York Times Co./Getty Images)

COFFEEHOUSE MUSIC The Feejon Coffee House in Manhattan was popular among young writers, poets, and others in the late 1950s, in part because it was a gathering place for folk musicians, two of whom are shown here performing at right.

The audiences for folk music—a product of rural and working-class traditions—were overwhelmingly urban, middle-class people. But the message of folk music—that there was a "real" America rooted in values of sharing and community, hidden beneath the crass commercialism of modern culture—resonated with the yearnings of many people in the 1960s (and beyond) for an alternative to their own troubled world. When young audiences responded to Woody Guthrie's famous ballad "This Land Is Your Land," they were expressing a hope for a different America—more democratic, more honest, and more natural than the land they knew. •

UNDERSTAND, ANALYZE, & EVALUATE

1. What did folk music, with roots in the musical traditions of blacks, rural folk, and working-class people, offer that made it so appealing to and popular with urban, middle-class audiences?

2. What similarities between the 1930s and the 1960s might help explain the popularity of folk music during both those decades?

3. What musical style or form today continues the folk-music tradition of expressing a political message and reflecting the search for "authenticity"?

THE TRAUMAS OF 1968

By the end of 1967, the twin crises of the war in Vietnam and the deteriorating racial situation at home had produced great social and political tensions. In the course of 1968, those tensions burst to the surface and seemed to threaten national chaos. (The year 1968 was turbulent elsewhere in the world as well; see "America in the World: 1968.")

1968

The year 1968 was one of the most turbulent in the postwar history of the United States. Much of what made it so traumatic were specifically American events—the growing controversy over the war in Vietnam, the assassinations of Martin Luther King Jr. and Robert Kennedy, racial unrest across the nation's cities, student protests on campuses throughout America. But the turmoil of 1968 was not confined to the United States. There were tremendous upheavals in many parts of the globe that year.

The most common form of turbulence around the world in 1968 was student unrest. In France, a student uprising in May far exceeded in size and ferocity anything that occurred in the United States. It attracted the support of French workers and briefly paralyzed Paris and other cities. It contributed to the downfall of the government of Charles de Gaulle a year later. In England, Ireland, Germany, Italy, the Netherlands, Mexico, Canada, Japan, and South Korea, students and other young people demonstrated in great numbers, and at times with violence, against governments, universities, and other structures of authority. Elsewhere, there was more widespread protest, as in Czechoslovakia, where hundreds of thousands of citizens took to the streets in support of what became known as "Prague Spring." It caused a demand for greater democracy and a repudiation of many of the oppressive rules and structures imposed on the nation by its Soviet-dominated communist regimes. Russian tanks rolled into the city to crush the uprising.

Many people have tried to explain why so much instability emerged in so many nations at the same time. One factor that contributed to the worldwide turbulence of 1968 was simple numbers. The postwar Baby Boom had created a very large age cohort in many nations, and by the late 1960s it was coming of age. In the industrial West, the sheer size of the new generation produced a tripling of the number of people attending colleges and universities. In fewer than twenty years it also created a heightened sense of the power of youth. The long period of postwar prosperity and relative peace in which this generation had grown up contributed to heightened expectations of what the world should offer them—and a greater level of impatience than previous generations had demonstrated with the obstacles that stood in the way of their hopes. A new global youth culture emerged that was in many ways at odds with the dominant culture of older generations. It valued nonconformity, personal freedom, and even rebellion.

A second force contributing to the widespread turbulence of 1968 was the power of global media. Satellite communication introduced in the early 1960s made it possible to transmit live news across the world. Videotape technology and the creation of lightweight portable television cameras enabled media organizations to respond to events much more quickly and flexibly than in the past. The audience for these televised images was by now global and enormous, particularly in industrial nations but even in the poorest areas of the world. Protests in one country were suddenly capable of inspiring protests in others. Demonstrators in Paris, for example, spoke openly of how campus protests in the United States in 1968—for example, the student uprising at Columbia University in New York the previous month—had helped motivate French students to rise up as well. Just as American students were protesting against what they considered antiquated, paternalistic features of their universities, French students demanded an end to the rigid, autocratic character of their own academic world.

In most parts of the world, the 1968 uprisings came and went without fundamentally altering institutions and systems. But many changes came in the wake of these protests. Universities around the globe undertook significant reforms. Religious observance in mainstream churches and synagogues in the West declined dramatically after 1968. New concepts of personal freedom gained legitimacy, helping to inspire social movements in the years that followed—among them the dramatic growth of feminism in many parts of the world and the emergence of the gay and lesbian rights movement. The events of 1968 did not produce a revolution in the United States or in most of the rest of the world, but it did help launch a period of dramatic social, cultural, and political changes that affected the peoples of many nations. •

UNDERSTAND, ANALYZE, & EVALUATE

1. What factors combined to produce the turbulence that resulted in the uprisings of 1968?
2. Did the demonstrators of 1968 succeed or fail to achieve their objectives? What were the long-term effects of the 1968 uprisings?

THE TET OFFENSIVE

On January 31, 1968, the first day of the Vietnamese New Year (Tet), communist forces launched an enormous, concerted attack on American strongholds throughout South Vietnam. A few cities, most notably Hue, fell temporarily to the communists. But what made the **Tet offensive** so shocking to the American people, who saw vivid reports of it on television, was the sight of communist forces in the heart of Saigon, setting off bombs, shooting down South Vietnamese officials and troops, and holding down fortified areas (including, briefly, the American embassy). The Tet offensive also suggested to the American public something of the brutality of the fighting in Vietnam. In the midst of the fighting, television cameras recorded the sight of a South Vietnamese officer shooting a captured and defenseless young Viet Cong soldier in the head in the streets of Saigon.

American forces soon dislodged the Viet Cong from most of the positions they had seized. And during the battle they had inflicted enormous casualties on the communists and permanently depleted the ranks of the NLF, forcing North Vietnamese troops to take on a much larger share of the subsequent fighting. But such accomplishments registered little with the American people, who felt betrayed by an administration that had sworn the war was nearly over and the enemy was on his heels. Tet may have been a military victory for the United States, but it was a political defeat for the administration.

In the following weeks, opposition to the war grew substantially. Leading newspapers and magazines, television commentators, and mainstream politicians began taking public stands against the conflict. Public opposition to the war almost doubled, and Johnson's personal popularity rating slid to 35 percent, the lowest of any president since Harry Truman.

THE POLITICAL CHALLENGE

Beginning in the summer of 1967, dissident Democrats tried to mobilize support behind an antiwar candidate who would challenge Lyndon Johnson in the 1968 primaries.

When Robert Kennedy turned them down, they recruited Senator Eugene McCarthy of Minnesota. A brilliantly orchestrated campaign by young volunteers in the New Hampshire primary produced a startling showing by McCarthy in March; he nearly defeated the president.

A few days later, Robert Kennedy did an about-face and entered the campaign, embittering many McCarthy supporters but bringing his own substantial strength among minorities, poor people, and workers to the antiwar cause. With Kennedy now in the race, polls showed the president trailing badly in the next scheduled primary, in Wisconsin. And so Johnson adjusted. On March 31, 1968, Johnson went on television to announce a limited halt in the bombing of North Vietnam—his first major concession to the antiwar forces and a major departure from his normally hawkish policies. And then, stunningly, Johnson declared that he was withdrawing from the presidential contest.

In the aftermath of Johnson's withdrawal, Robert Kennedy quickly established himself as the champion of the Democratic primaries, winning one election after another. In the meantime, however, Vice President Hubert Humphrey, with the support of President Johnson, entered the contest and began to attract the support of party leaders and of the many delegations that were selected not by popular primaries but by state party organizations. He soon overtook Kennedy as the front-runner in the race.

Assassinations and Politics

On April 4, Martin Luther King Jr., who had traveled to Memphis, Tennessee, to lend his support to striking black sanitation workers in the city, was shot and killed while standing on the balcony of his motel. The assassin, James Earl Ray, who was captured two months later in London, had no apparent motive. Subsequent evidence suggested that he had been hired by others to do the killing, but he himself never revealed the identity of his alleged employers.

King's murder produced a great outpouring of grief. Among some African Americans, it also produced anger. In the days after the assassination, major riots broke out in more than sixty American cities. Forty-three people died.

Tragedy struck again only two months later. Late in the night of June 6, Robert Kennedy appeared in the ballroom of a Los Angeles hotel to acknowledge his victory in that day's California primary. As he left the ballroom after his speech, Sirhan Sirhan, a young Palestinian apparently enraged by pro-Israeli remarks Kennedy had recently made, emerged from a crowd and shot him in the head. Early the next morning, Kennedy died. The shock of this second death of a national politician in two months—and only five years after the assassination of John Kennedy—cast a pall over the remainder of the presidential campaign.

When the Democrats finally gathered in Chicago in August, for a convention in which Hubert Humphrey was now the only real contender, even the most optimistic observers predicted turbulence. Inside the hall, delegates bitterly debated an antiwar plank in the party platform that both Kennedy and McCarthy supporters favored. Miles away, in a downtown park, thousands of antiwar protesters staged demonstrations. On the third night of the convention, as the delegates began their balloting on the now virtually inevitable nomination of Hubert Humphrey, demonstrators and police clashed in a bloody riot in the streets of Chicago. Hundreds of protesters were injured as police attempted to disperse them with tear gas and billy clubs. Aware that the violence was being televised to the nation, the demonstrators taunted the authorities with the chant, "The whole world is watching!" And Hubert Humphrey, who had spent years dreaming of becoming his party's candidate for president, finally got the nomination but from a badly fractured party that would make it difficult for him to manage his campaign.

THE CONSERVATIVE RESPONSE

The turbulent events of 1968 persuaded some observers that American society was in the throes of revolutionary change leading to the creation of a better society. In fact, however, the response of many Americans to the turmoil was to question the social changes of the prior decade and take a conservative political turn.

The most visible sign of the conservative backlash was the surprising success of the campaign of segregationist George Wallace for the presidency. In 1968, the former Alabama governor became a third-party candidate for president, basing his campaign on a host of conservative grievances. He denounced the forced busing of students to achieve racial integration in public schools, the proliferation of government regulations and social programs, and what he called the permissiveness of authorities toward crime, race riots, and antiwar demonstrations. There was never any serious chance that Wallace

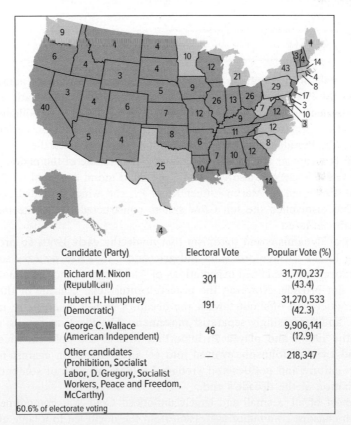

Candidate (Party)	Electoral Vote	Popular Vote (%)
Richard M. Nixon (Republican)	301	31,770,237 (43.4)
Hubert H. Humphrey (Democratic)	191	31,270,533 (42.3)
George C. Wallace (American Independent)	46	9,906,141 (12.9)
Other candidates (Prohibition, Socialist Labor, D. Gregory, Socialist Workers, Peace and Freedom, McCarthy)	—	218,347

60.6% of electorate voting

THE ELECTION OF 1968 The 1968 presidential election, which Richard Nixon won, was almost as close as the election of 1960, which he lost. Nixon might have won a more substantial victory had it not been for the independent candidacy of Governor George C. Wallace, who attracted many of the same conservative voters to whom Nixon appealed. • *How does the distribution of Democratic and Republican strength in this election compare to that in 1960?*

would win the election, but his standing in the polls rose at times to over 20 percent. He also earned the approval of many in his state, who reelected him as governor in 1970 and then for two more terms.

At the same time, a more effective effort to mobilize the conservative middle in favor of order and stability was under way within the Republican Party. **Richard Nixon**, whose political career had seemed dead after his losses in the presidential race of 1960 and a California gubernatorial campaign two years later, reemerged as the spokesperson for what he called the "silent majority." By offering a vision of stability, law and order, government retrenchment, and "peace with honor" in Vietnam, he easily captured the nomination of his party for the presidency. And despite a last-minute surge by Humphrey, he hung on to eke out a victory almost as narrow as his defeat in 1960. In the three-way race for the presidency, Nixon netted 43.4 percent of the popular vote to Humphrey's 42.3 percent (a margin of only about 500,000 votes), and 301 electoral votes to Humphrey's 191. George Wallace, who like most third-party candidates faded in the last weeks of the campaign, still managed to poll 12.9 percent of the popular vote and to carry five southern states with a total of 46 electoral ballots. Nixon had hardly won a decisive political mandate. But the election made clear that a majority of the American electorate was more interested in restoring stability than in promoting social change.

CONCLUSION

Perhaps no decade of the twentieth century created more powerful and enduring images in America than the 1960s. It began with the election—and then the traumatic assassination—of a young president, John Kennedy, who captured the imagination of millions and seemed to symbolize the rising idealism of the time. It produced a dramatic period of political innovation, led by President Lyndon Johnson, who greatly expanded the size and functions of the federal government and its responsibility for the welfare of the nation's citizens. He called it the Great Society. It also included a profound moral and legal revolution in matters of racial justice led by Martin Luther King, Jr., and which included two major civil rights acts that dismantled the Jim Crow system constructed in the late nineteenth and early twentieth centuries.

The spirit of dynamism and optimism that made the early 1960s so productive also helped bring to the surface problems and grievances that had no easy solutions. The civil rights movement awakened expectations of social and economic equality that laws alone could not provide. However, the peaceful, interracial crusade of the early 1960s gradually produced an offshoot toward the decade's end—a much more militant, confrontational, and increasingly separatist movement. The idealism among white youths that began the 1960s, and played an important role in the political success of John Kennedy and Lyndon Johnson, evolved into an angry rebellion against many aspects of American culture and politics and produced a large upsurge of student protest that rocked the nation at the decade's end.

Perhaps most of all, a small and largely unnoticed Cold War commitment to defend South Vietnam against communist aggression from the north led to a large and disastrous war that destroyed the presidency of Lyndon Johnson, sent thousands of young men and women to their deaths, and showed no signs of producing a victory. A decade that began with high hopes and soaring ideals ended with division and deep disillusionment.

KEY TERMS/PEOPLE/PLACES/EVENTS

affirmative action 711
Bay of Pigs 715
black power 714
Community Action
  programs 703
Cuban missile crisis 716
freedom rides 704
Freedom Summer 710
Great Society 701

Gulf of Tonkin
  Resolution 718
Immigration Act
  of 1965 703
John Kennedy 699
Lyndon Johnson 699
Malcolm X 714
Medicaid 702
Medicare 702

My Lai massacre 719
New Frontier 700
Richard Nixon 728
Tet offensive 725
Viet Cong (National
  Liberation Front) 718
Voting Rights Act
  of 1965 710

RECALL AND REFLECT

1. What were the political effects of John Kennedy's assassination?
2. How did increasing radicalism affect the successes and the setbacks of the civil rights movement?
3. What was the military strategy of the United States in Vietnam? What were the U.S. aims in that conflict? Why did the United States ultimately fail in Vietnam?
4. What accounted for growing opposition to the war in Vietnam?
5. What events made 1968 such a turbulent year both in the United States and elsewhere in the world? How did these events affect U.S. politics?

29 | THE CRISIS OF AUTHORITY

THE YOUTH CULTURE

THE MOBILIZATION OF MINORITIES

WOMEN AND SOCIAL CHANGE

ENVIRONMENTALISM IN A TURBULENT
    SOCIETY

NIXON, KISSINGER, AND THE VIETNAM WAR

NIXON, KISSINGER, AND THE WORLD

POLITICS AND ECONOMICS IN THE NIXON
    YEARS

THE WATERGATE CRISIS

LOOKING AHEAD

1. What were some of the characteristics of the social and cultural revolutions of the 1960s and 1970s?

2. How did the U.S. strategy in Vietnam change under Nixon? What was the result of the change in strategy?

3. What was the Watergate scandal and how did it affect the presidency?

THE 1960 AND 1970s SHOOK traditional foundations of stability and order in America. Long-cherished political assumptions about what was "normal" came under sharp attack. The rising death tolls of soldiers fighting in the Vietnam War and the failure of leaders to communicate effectively and truthfully about the progress of the war triggered a crisis of public trust in the military and the federal government. At the same time, the African American freedom movement cracked open the evil edifice of Jim Crow and inspired other Americans to demand the enjoyment and protection of their own civil liberties. Latinos, Indians, prisoners, gays, and women accelerated their own quests for full citizenship and in the process upturned decades-old assumptions about who could and could not enjoy the basic menu of constitutional rights.

Not surprisingly, many Americans who openly questioned the "rights movement" looked for a measure of relief from their candidates for president in 1968. The election of Richard Nixon, then, was the result not only of the unpopularity of Lyndon Johnson and the Vietnam War but also Nixon's perceived commitment to rejecting what many saw as an assault on

American society itself. And indeed Nixon projected an image of stern dedication to traditional values and promised a return to law and order. But nothing was as it seemed. Nixon's presidency would unravel because of lies he and his staff repeatedly told to the American public. Ironically, his time in office and eventual resignation would leave the country with even greater levels of political crisis and popular mistrust in traditional institutions than when he first entered the White House.

THE YOUTH CULTURE

Many conservatives in the 1960s and 1970s were alarmed by what they saw as a pattern of social and cultural anger by younger Americans. The protesters gave vent to two related impulses. One, emerging from the political left, was to create a great new community of "the people," which would rise up to break the traditional power of elites and force the nation to end the war, pursue racial and economic justice, and transform its political life. The other, at least equally powerful impulse was the vision of personal "liberation." It found expression in part through the efforts of many groups—African Americans, Indians, Hispanics, women, gay people, and others—to define and assert themselves and make demands on the larger society. It also found expression through the efforts of individuals to create a new culture—one that would allow them to escape from what some considered the dehumanizing pressures of the modern "technocracy."

THE NEW LEFT

Among the products of the racial crisis and the war in Vietnam was a radicalization of many American students. In the course of the 1960s, they formed what became known as the New Left. In 1962, a group of students (most of them white and many of

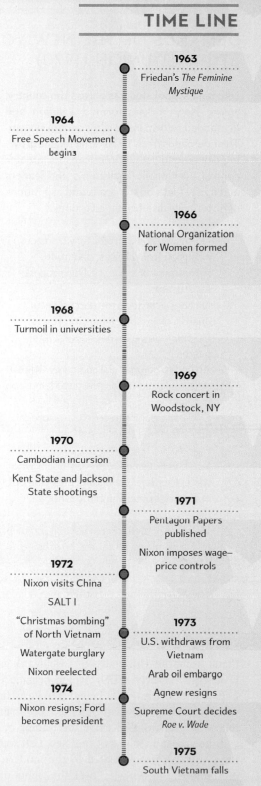

TIME LINE

1963
Friedan's *The Feminine Mystique*

1964
Free Speech Movement begins

1966
National Organization for Women formed

1968
Turmoil in universities

1969
Rock concert in Woodstock, NY

1970
Cambodian incursion

Kent State and Jackson State shootings

1971
Pentagon Papers published

Nixon imposes wage–price controls

1972
Nixon visits China

SALT I

"Christmas bombing" of North Vietnam

Watergate burglary

Nixon reelected

1973
U.S. withdraws from Vietnam

Arab oil embargo

Agnew resigns

1974
Nixon resigns; Ford becomes president

Supreme Court decides *Roe v. Wade*

1975
South Vietnam falls

CONSIDER THE SOURCE

DEMANDS OF THE NEW YORK HIGH SCHOOL STUDENT UNION (1970)

Like high school students across the country, young New Yorkers formed a union and demanded reform in the city's school system. Their demands from 1970 reflected the growing call among young Americans for greater control over public institutions and leaders and a new focus on the needs and aspirations of historically disadvantaged groups.

1—No suspensions, involuntary transfers, exclusion from classes, detention, harassment of students. Due process for students.

2—No cops in schools, no narcos, security guards, plain clothesmen, informers.

3—No program cards, hall checks, ID's, passes.

4—An end to commercial and general diplomas, one diploma for every student upon graduation.

5—Open admissions to colleges, a college education free for everyone who wants one.

6—Jobs and housing for every student who wants them on graduating, dropping out, or leaving home. The army is not a decent job.

7—No military recruiting in schools, no military assemblies, literature, no sending names to draft boards or recruiters. An immediate end to the draft.

8—Black and Latin departments controlled by Black and Latin students.

9—Community control of the schools and every other community facility. Students are part of the community.

10—POWER! Student control of curriculum, publications, assemblies, clubs, student government, dress, etc. The right to organize politically.

11—We support the fifteen points of the Black and Puerto Rican Citywide HS Council.

UNDERSTAND, ANALYZE, & EVALUATE

1. What might have inspired the students' demand for "due process"? What other evidence of an anti-authoritarian sentiment can you detect here?

2. How did the civil rights and the black power movements shape this Student Union? What are some of the rights movements covered in this chapter that were *not* reflected in this statement?

3. What role did the Vietnam War play for these students—what made this a possibly quite personal issue?

Source: *New York High School Free Press (an underground newspaper)*, No. 8, reprinted in John Birmingham, *Our Time Is Now: Notes from the High School Underground*, New York: Praeger, 1970, 178.

them from the University of Michigan) gathered in Michigan to form **Students for a Democratic Society (SDS)**, which became the most prominent organization of the New Left. Their declaration of beliefs, the Port Huron Statement, expressed their disillusionment with the society they had inherited and their determination to build a new politics. In the following years, SDS became the leading organization of student radicalism.

Since most members of the New Left were students, much of their radicalism centered for a time on issues related to the modern university. A 1964 dispute at the University of California at Berkeley over the rights of students to engage in political activities on campus—the Free Speech Movement—was the first major outburst of what was to be nearly a decade of campus turmoil. Berkeley's most prominent Free Speech leader, Mario Savio, seized national attention during a protest in December that landed him and about 800 others in jail. The twenty-two-year-old portrayed the Berkeley administration—and by extension, America's political establishment—as out of touch with student's aspirations and heartlessly treating them as "raw material" for corporate America. The only response was to rebel and break this "machine."

The antiwar movement greatly inflamed and expanded the challenge to the universities, and beginning in 1968, campus demonstrations, riots, and building seizures became almost commonplace. At Columbia University in New York, students seized the offices of the president and others and occupied them for several days until local police forcibly ejected them. Over the next several years, hardly any major university was immune to some level of disruption. Small groups of especially dogmatic radicals—among them the "Weathermen," an offshoot of SDS—were responsible for a few cases of arson and bombing that destroyed campus buildings and claimed several lives. Protests also erupted in high schools, where students voiced similar demands for greater control over the curriculum on the subjects taught to them and over disciplinary policy. (See "Consider the Source: Demands of the New York High School Student Union.")

Not many people accepted the radical political philosophy of the New Left. But many supported the position of SDS and other groups on particular issues, and above all on the Vietnam War. Between 1967 and 1969, student activists organized some of the largest political demonstrations in American history to protest American military involvement in the Southeast Asian conflict.

A related issue that helped fuel the antiwar movement was opposition to the military draft. The gradual abolition of many traditional deferments—for graduate students, teachers, husbands, fathers, and others—swelled the ranks of those faced with conscription (and thus likely to oppose it). Of the almost 2 million drafted, about 7,000 draft-age Americans simply refused induction, accepting what were occasionally long terms in jail as a result. Thousands of others draftees fled to Canada, Sweden, and elsewhere, where they were joined by deserters directly from the armed forces.

THE COUNTERCULTURE

Closely related to the New Left was a new youth culture openly scornful of the values and conventions of middle-class society. The most visible characteristic of the **counterculture**, as it became known, was a change in personal styles. As if to display their contempt for conventional standards, young Americans flaunted long hair, shabby or flamboyant clothing, and a rebellious disdain for traditional speech and decorum. Also important to the counterculture was a new, more permissive view of sex and drugs.

Like the New Left, the counterculture challenged modern American society, attacking what it claimed was its banality, its hollowness, its artificiality, and its isolation from nature. The most committed adherents of the counterculture—the hippies, who came to dominate the Haight-Ashbury neighborhood of San Francisco and other places, and the social dropouts, many of whom retreated to rural communes—rejected modern society altogether and attempted to find refuge in a simpler, more natural existence. But even those whose commitment to the counterculture was less intense shared the idea of personal fulfillment through rejecting the inhibitions and conventions of middle-class culture and giving fuller expression to personal instinct and desire.

The counterculture was only an exaggerated expression of impulses coursing through the larger society. Long hair and outlandish clothing became the badge not only of hippies and radicals but of an entire generation. The widespread use of marijuana, the freer attitudes toward sex, the iconoclastic (and often obscene) language—all spread far beyond the true devotees of the counterculture.

One of the most powerful elements of the new youth society was rock music. Its growing influence in the 1960s was a result in part of the phenomenal popularity of the Beatles, the English group whose first visit to the United States in 1964 created a remarkable sensation. For a time, most rock musicians—like most popular musicians before them—concentrated largely on uncontroversial romantic themes. By the late 1960s, however, rock had begun to reflect many of the new iconoclastic values of its time. The Beatles, for example, abandoned their once simple and seemingly innocent style for a new, experimental, even mystical approach that reflected the growing popular fascination with drugs and Eastern religions. Other groups, such as the Rolling Stones, turned even more openly to themes of anger, frustration, and rebellion. Many popular musicians used their music to express explicit political radicalism as well—especially some of the leading folk singers of the era, such as Bob Dylan and Joan Baez. Rock's driving rhythms, its undisguised sensuality, its often harsh and angry tone—all made it an appropriate vehicle for expressing the themes of the social and political unrest of the late 1960s.

A powerful symbol of the fusion of rock music and the counterculture was the massive music festival at **Woodstock**, New York, in the summer of 1969, where 400,000 people gathered on a farm for nearly a week. Despite heavy rain, mud, inadequate facilities, and impossible crowding, the attendees remained peaceful and harmonious. Champions of the counterculture spoke rhapsodically at the time of how Woodstock represented the birth of a new youth culture, the "Woodstock nation." Four months later, however, another large rock concert—at the

(©Don Hogan Charles/The New York Times Photo Archives/Redux)

WOODSTOCK In the summer of 1969, more than 400,000 people gathered for a music festival on a farm near Woodstock, New York. The gathering became a symbol of the youth movement of the sixties.

Altamont racetrack near San Francisco, featuring the Rolling Stones and attended by 300,000 people—exposed a darker side of the youth culture. Altamont became a brutal and violent event at which four people died, several accidentally or from drug overdoses but one because of injuries inflicted by members of a Hells Angels motorcycle gang, who were ostensibly serving as security guards at the concert and who brutally beat and stabbed a number of people.

THE MOBILIZATION OF MINORITIES

The growth of African American protest encouraged other minorities to assert themselves and demand redress of their grievances. For Indians, Hispanic Americans, gay men and lesbians, and others, the late 1960s and 1970s were a time of growing self-expression and political activism.

Seeds of Native American Militancy

Few minorities had deeper or more justifiable grievances against the prevailing culture than did American Indians—or Native Americans, as they began defiantly to call themselves in the 1960s. Indians were the least prosperous, least healthy, and least stable ethnic group in the nation. And while African Americans attracted the attention (for good or for ill) of many whites, Indians for years had remained largely ignored.

For much of the postwar era, federal tribal policies tried to incorporate Indians into mainstream American society whether Indians wanted to assimilate or not. Two laws passed in 1953 established the basis of this policy, which became known as "termination." Through termination, the federal government withdrew all official recognition of the tribes as legal entities; they were no longer administratively separate from state governments and were subject to the same local jurisdictions as non–Native American residents. At the same time, the government encouraged Indians to assimilate into the white world and worked to funnel Native Americans into cities, where, presumably, they would adapt themselves to the larger society and lose their cultural distinctiveness.

Despite some individual successes, the new policies were a disastrous failure on the whole. Indians themselves fought so bitterly against these policies that in 1958, the Eisenhower administration barred further terminations. In the meantime, the struggle against termination mobilized a new generation of Indian militants and breathed life into the principal Native American organization, the National Congress of American Indians, which had been created in 1944.

The Democratic administrations of the 1960s made no effort to revive termination. Instead, they made modest efforts to restore at least some degree of tribal autonomy such as funneling Office of Economic Opportunity money to tribal organizations through the Community Action programs. In the meantime, the tribes themselves began to fight for greater self-determination. The new militancy benefited from the rapid increase in the Indian population, which was growing much faster than that of the rest of the nation (nearly doubling between 1950 and 1970 to a total of about 800,000).

The Indian Civil Rights Movement

In 1961, more than 400 members from sixty-seven tribes gathered in Chicago and issued the Declaration of Indian Purpose, which stressed the "right to choose our own way of life" and the "responsibility of preserving our precious heritage." Another example of a growing

Indian self-consciousness, the National Indian Youth Council, created in the aftermath of the 1961 Chicago meeting, promoted the idea of Indian nationalism and intertribal unity. In 1968, a group of young, militant Indians established the **American Indian Movement (AIM)**, which drew support from urban areas and reservations alike.

The new activism produced results. In 1968, Congress passed the **Indian Civil Rights Act**. It guaranteed reservation Indians protections by the Bill of Rights, but also recognized the legitimacy of tribal laws within the reservations. In 1968, Indian fishermen, citing old treaty rights, clashed with Washington State officials on the Columbia River and in Puget Sound. The following year, members of several tribes occupied the abandoned federal prison on Alcatraz Island in San Francisco Bay, claiming the site "by right of discovery."

In response, the Nixon administration appointed Louis Bruce, a Mohawk-Sioux, as commissioner of Indian affairs in 1969; and in 1970, the president promised both increased tribal self-determination and an increase in federal aid. But the protests continued. In November 1972, nearly a thousand demonstrators, most of them Lakota Sioux, forcibly occupied the building of the Bureau of Indian Affairs in Washington, D.C., for six days. In February 1973, members of AIM seized the town of Wounded Knee, South Dakota, the site of the 1890 massacre of Sioux by federal troops. For two months, they occupied the town, demanding that the government honor its long-forgotten treaty obligations.

The Indian civil rights movement, like other civil rights movements of the same time, fell far short of winning full equality for Native Americans. But it helped the tribes win a series of new legal rights and protections that, together, gave them a stronger position than they had enjoyed at any previous time in the twentieth century.

(©AP Photo)

THE OCCUPATION OF ALCATRAZ Alcatraz, an island in San Francisco Bay, once housed a large federal prison that by the late 1960s had been abandoned. In 1969, a group of Indian activists occupied the island and claimed it as Indian land—precipitating a long standoff with authorities.

LATINO ACTIVISM

The fastest-growing minority group in the United States in the 1970s was Latinos, or Hispanic Americans. Large numbers of Mexicans had entered the country during World War II in response to the wartime labor shortage, and many had remained in the cities of the Southwest and the Pacific Coast. By 1960, Los Angeles had a bigger Mexican population than any place except Mexico City.

But the greatest expansion in the Latino population of the United States was yet to come. In 1960, the census reported slightly more than 3 million Latinos living in the United States. By 1970, that number had grown to 9 million and by 2000 to 35 million. By 2010, the number passed 50 million. Hispanics constituted more than a third of all legal immigrants to the United States after 1960.

Large numbers of Puerto Ricans (who were entitled to American citizenship by birth) migrated to eastern urban areas, particularly New York City, where they formed one of the poorest communities in the city. South Florida's substantial Cuban population began with a wave of middle-class refugees fleeing the Castro regime in the early 1960s. These first Cuban migrants quickly established themselves as a successful and highly assimilated part of Miami's middle class. In 1980, a second, much poorer wave of Cuban immigrants—the so-called Marielitos, named for the port from which they left Cuba—arrived in Florida when Castro temporarily relaxed exit restrictions. Later in the 1980s, large numbers of immigrants (both legal and illegal) began to arrive from Central and South America—from Guatemala, Nicaragua, El Salvador, Peru, and other countries.

(©Michael Rougier/The LIFE Images Collection/Getty Images)

KENNEDY AND CHÁVEZ César Chávez, leader of the United Farm Workers, endured a hunger strike in 1968 in the spirit of nonviolent protest against the treatment of field workers. Robert F. Kennedy, just beginning his campaign for the presidency, visited the union leader to show his support. At this point, Chávez had been fasting for several weeks.

They intended to be an advocacy group for women of all colors that pressured the government to vigorously enforce the new antidiscrimination laws and expose negligent employers. NOW also intended to promote full equality for women by boosting the number of women in colleges and universities, professional schools, politics, and business. No longer should the majority of working women be found performing domestic labor.

By the late 1960s, younger, white, educated women began to push for new and more radical feminist demands. Many drew inspiration from the New Left and the counterculture and were involved in the civil rights movement or antiwar crusade. Some had found that even within those movements, they faced discrimination and exclusion because of their gender.

In its most radical form, this new feminism rejected the whole notion of marriage, family, and even heterosexual relationships (a vehicle, some women claimed, of male domination). While only a few women embraced such extremes, by the early 1970s large numbers were coming to see themselves as an exploited group united against oppression with a culture of their own. In cities and towns across the country, feminists opened women's bookstores, bars, and coffee shops and founded feminist newspapers and magazines. They also created women's health clinics, centers to assist victims of rape and abuse, day-care centers, and, particularly after 1973, abortion clinics.

EXPANDING ACHIEVEMENTS

In 1971, the government extended its affirmative action guidelines to include women—linking sexism with racism as an officially acknowledged social problem. Women made rapid progress, in the meantime, in their efforts to move into the economic and political mainstream. The nation's all-male educational institutions began to crack open their doors to women. (Princeton and Yale did so in 1969, and many others soon did the same.) In 1972, Congress approved legislation (known as Title IX) requiring universities to support male and female athletic programs at equal levels.

Women were also becoming an important force in business and the professions. Nearly half of all married women held jobs by the mid-1970s, and almost 90 percent of all women with college degrees worked. The two-career family, in which both the husband and the wife maintained active professional lives, slowly became a widely accepted middle-class norm. (It had been common within much of the working class for decades.) There were also important symbolic changes, such as the refusal of many women to adopt their husbands' surnames when they married and the use of the term "Ms." in place of "Mrs." or "Miss" to signal the irrelevance of a woman's marital status in the professional world.

By the mid-1980s, women were serving in both houses of Congress, on the Supreme Court, in numerous federal cabinet positions, as governors of several states, and in many other political positions. In 1981, Ronald Reagan named the first female Supreme Court justice, Sandra Day O'Connor. In 1984, the Democratic Party was the first to choose a woman, Representative Geraldine Ferraro of New York, as its vice presidential candidate. In academia, women were expanding their presence in traditional scholarly fields; they were also creating new fields—women's and gender studies, which in the 1980s and 1990s were among the fastest-growing areas of American scholarship.

In 1972, Congress approved the Equal Rights Amendment (ERA) to the Constitution and sent it to the states. For a while, ratification seemed almost certain. By the late 1970s, however, the momentum behind the amendment had died because of a rising chorus of objections to it from people (including many antifeminist women) who feared that it would disrupt traditional social patterns. In 1982, the ten years allotted for ratification expired.

THE ABORTION ISSUE

A major goal of American feminists since the 1920s has been to win greater control of their own sexual and reproductive lives, and in the 1970s feminists made a number of strides toward that goal. They fostered awareness of and responses to the problems of rape, sexual abuse, and domestic abuse. They countered resistance to contraceptives and helped women gain greater access to birth-control information, pills, and devices. And they lead the "pro-choice" movement on the heated issue of abortion.

Abortion had once been legal in much of the United States, but by the beginning of the twentieth century, it was banned by statute in most of the country and remained so into the 1960s. Nonetheless, many abortions continued to be performed quietly, and often dangerously, out of sight of the law. Responding to pressure from women's rights groups, several states had abandoned restrictions on abortion by the end of the 1960s. The challenge to abortion laws reached the Supreme Court in 1973, with *Roe v. Wade*. The Court's decision, based on an implied but not specified "right to privacy" first protected by the Court only a few years earlier in *Griswold v. Connecticut*, invalidated all laws prohibiting abortion during the "first trimester"—the first three months of pregnancy. But even then, the issue remained far from settled.

ENVIRONMENTALISM IN A TURBULENT SOCIETY

Like feminism, environmentalism entered the 1960s with a long history but relatively little public support. Also like feminism, environmentalism profited from the turbulence of the era and emerged by the 1970s as a powerful force in American life. The rise of this new movement was in part a result of the intensifying level of environmental degradation in advanced industrial societies of the late twentieth century. It was a result, too, of the growth of ecology, a science that provided environmentalists with new and powerful arguments.

THE NEW SCIENCE OF ECOLOGY

Until the mid-twentieth century, most people who considered themselves environmentalists based their commitment on aesthetic or moral grounds. They wanted to preserve nature because it was too beautiful to despoil, because it was a mark of divinity on the world, or because it permitted humans a spiritual experience that would otherwise be unavailable to them. Other groups took their cue from the late President Theodore Roosevelt. These conservationists wanted to protect the environment for use in outdoor activities like camping and hunting. In the course of the twentieth century, however, scientists in much of the world began to create a new rationale for environmentalism. They called it ecology.

Ecology is the science of the interrelatedness of the natural world. It addresses such problems as air and water pollution, the destruction of forests, the extinction of species, and toxic wastes, which are not separate, isolated problems. All elements of the earth's environment are intimately and delicately linked. Damaging any one of those elements, therefore, risks damaging all the others.

Among the early contributions to popular knowledge of ecology was the work of writer and naturalist Aldo Leopold. During a career in forest management, Leopold sought to apply the new scientific findings on ecology to his interactions with the natural world.

And in 1949, he published a classic of environmental literature, *The Sand County Almanac*, in which he argued that humans had a responsibility to understand and maintain the balance of nature, that they should behave in the natural world according to a code that he called the "land ethic." By then, the science of ecology was spreading widely in the scientific community. Among the findings of ecologists were such now-common ideas as the "food chain," the "ecosystem," "biodiversity," and "endangered species." **Rachel Carson's** sensational 1962 book, *Silent Spring*, which revealed the dangers of pesticides, was based solidly on the ideas of ecologists and did at least as much as Leopold's work to introduce those ideas to a larger public.

Environmental Advocacy

Among the major environmental organizations were the Wilderness Society, the Sierra Club, the National Audubon Society, the Nature Conservancy, the National Wildlife Federation, and the National Parks and Conservation Association. All of these organizations predated the rise of modern ecological science, but the growth of environmental threats and scientific efforts to address them kept these organizations engaged like never before. They found allies among such groups as the American Civil Liberties Union, the League of Women Voters, the National Council of Churches, and even the AFL-CIO.

Out of these organizations emerged a new generation of environmental activists able to contribute to the legal and political battles of the movement. Scientists provided the necessary data. Lawyers fought battles with government agencies and in the courts.

Many other forces contributed to what became the environmental movement. Lady Bird Johnson, the first lady, helped raise public awareness of the landscape with her energetic "beautification" campaign in the mid-1960s—a campaign unconnected to any ecological concepts, but one that reflected a growing popular dismay at the despoiling of the landscape by rapid economic growth. Members of the counterculture contributed to environmental awareness with their romanticization of the natural world and their repudiation of the "technocracy."

But perhaps the greatest force behind environmentalism was the condition of the environment itself. By the 1960s, the damage to the natural world from postwar population and economic growth was becoming hard to ignore. Water pollution—which had been a problem in some areas of the country for many decades—was becoming so widespread that almost every major city was dealing with the unpleasant sight and odor, as well as the health risks, of polluted rivers and lakes. In Cleveland, Ohio, for example, the Cuyahoga River actually burst into flame from time to time from the petroleum waste being dumped into it; the city declared the river an official fire hazard.

Perhaps more alarming was the growing awareness that the air itself was becoming unhealthy, that toxic fumes from factories, power plants, and, most of all, automobiles were poisoning the atmosphere. Weather forecasts and official atmospheric information began to refer to "smog" levels—using a relatively new word formed from a combination of "smoke" and "fog," which became an almost perpetual fact of daily life in such cities as Los Angeles and Denver. In 1969, a damaged oil-well platform off Santa Barbara, California, spewed hundreds of thousands of gallons of crude oil into the ocean just off the popular beaches of this affluent city. This oil spill had a tremendous impact on the environmental consciousness of millions of Americans. Another, much larger spill—indeed, the largest in American history—occurred off the coast of Alaska in 1989 when the giant tanker *Exxon Valdez* hit a reef in Prince William Sound. The damage it caused to the nearby shoreline and wildlife also greatly increased environmental consciousness. In April 2010, the Deepwater Horizon oil rig exploded forty-one miles off the Louisiana coast, killing eleven. Over the next three months, chemical dispersants used to control the spill and 5 million gallons of crude oil spread into the Gulf of Mexico, destroying sea life and damaging the coastline. The long-term effects are still unknown.

Environmentalists brought to public attention many long-term dangers and helped create a broad and powerful movement.

EARTH DAY AND BEYOND

On April 22, 1970, people all over the United States participated in the first **Earth Day**. Originally proposed by Wisconsin senator Gaylord Nelson as a series of teach-ins on college campuses, Earth Day gradually took on a much larger life. Carefully managed by people who wanted to avoid associations with the radical left, it had a less threatening quality than antiwar demonstrations and civil rights rallies seemed to have. According to some estimates, over 20 million Americans participated in Earth Day observances, making Earth Day, possibly, the largest single demonstration in the nation's history.

The cautious, centrist character of Earth Day and related efforts to popularize environmentalism helped create a movement that was for a time less divisive than other, more controversial causes. Gradually, environmentalism became more than simply a series of demonstrations and protests. It became part of the consciousness of the vast majority of Americans—absorbed into popular culture, built into primary and secondary education, and endorsed by almost all politicians (even if many of them actually opposed some environmental goals).

It also became part of the fabric of public policy. In 1970, Congress passed and President Nixon signed the National Environmental Protection Act, which created a new agency— the Environmental Protection Agency—to enforce antipollution standards on businesses and consumers. The Clean Air Act, also passed in 1970, and the Clean Water Act, passed in 1972, became additional tools in the government's arsenal of weapons against environmental degradation.

Different administrations displayed varying levels of support for environmental goals, and new environmental problems continued to emerge even as older ones sometimes found solutions. Environmentalism became simultaneously a movement, a set of public policies, and a broad national ideal—and it was the combination of all those aspects that made it a powerful force in American life.

NIXON, KISSINGER, AND THE VIETNAM WAR

Richard Nixon assumed office in 1969 committed not only to restoring stability at home but also to creating a new and stabler order in the world. Central to his hopes for international stability was a resolution of the stalemate in Vietnam. Yet the new president felt no freer than his predecessor to abandon the American commitment there.

VIETNAMIZATION

Despite Nixon's own deep interest in international affairs, he brought with him into government a man who at times seemed to overshadow the president himself in the conduct of diplomacy: Henry Kissinger, a Harvard professor whom Nixon appointed as his special assistant for national security affairs. Kissinger quickly established dominance over

Secretary of State William Rogers and Secretary of Defense Melvin Laird. Together, Nixon and Kissinger set out to find an acceptable solution to the stalemate in Vietnam.

The new Vietnam policy moved along several fronts. One was the move to "Vietnamize" the conflict—that is, train and equip the South Vietnamese military to assume the burden of combat in place of American forces. In the fall of 1969, Nixon announced the withdrawal of 60,000 American ground troops from Vietnam. By the fall of 1972, relatively few American soldiers remained in Indochina. From a peak of more than 540,000 in 1969, the number had dwindled to about 60,000.

Vietnamization produced some immediate short-term benefits. As the number of Americans called up for the draft decreased, opposition to the war quieted for a time. The shift in combat responsibility to the South Vietnamese military, however, did nothing to break the stalemate in the negotiations with the North Vietnamese in Paris. The new administration decided that new military pressures would be necessary to do that.

ESCALATION

By the end of 1969, Nixon and Kissinger had decided that the most effective way to tip the military balance in South Vietnam's favor was to destroy bases in Cambodia and Laos that the U.S. military believed were the launching points for many communist attacks. (Laos, Cambodia, and Vietnam are neighboring states in the peninsula of Indochina.) Very early in his presidency, Nixon secretly ordered the air force to bomb these bases. On April 30, 1970, the president announced that he was sending U.S. ground troops across the border into Cambodia to destroy them.

Literally overnight, the Cambodian invasion restored the dwindling antiwar movement to life. The first days of May saw widespread and vocal antiwar demonstrations. A mood of crisis was already mounting when, on May 4, four college students were killed and nine injured after members of the National Guard opened fire on antiwar demonstrators at Kent State University in Ohio. Ten days later, police killed two African American students at Jackson State University in Mississippi during a demonstration there.

The clamor against the war spread into the government and the press. Congress angrily repealed the Gulf of Tonkin Resolution in December. Then, in June 1971, first the *New York Times* and later other newspapers began publishing excerpts from a secret study of the war prepared by the Defense Department during the Johnson administration. The so-called Pentagon Papers were leaked to the press by former Defense official Daniel Ellsberg. They provided evidence the government had been dishonest, both in reporting the military progress of the war and in explaining its own motives for American involvement. The administration went to court to suppress the documents, but the Supreme Court ruled that the press had the right to publish them.

Morale and discipline among American troops in Vietnam were rapidly deteriorating in the waning years of the war. After the 1968 massacre near My Lai came to light, Lieutenant William Calley was tried and convicted in 1971 of the murder of unarmed South Vietnamese civilians (he was soon pardoned and released). The case attracted wide public attention to the dehumanizing impact of the war on Americans and the far more tragic consequences of that dehumanization for the Vietnamese. Somewhat less publicized though still visible were other, more widespread problems among American troops in Vietnam: desertion, drug addiction, racism, refusal to obey orders, even the killing of unpopular officers by enlisted men.

By 1971, polls indicated that nearly two-thirds of Americans supported withdrawal from Vietnam. President Nixon, however, believed that a defeat in Vietnam would cause unacceptable damage to the nation's credibility. The FBI, the CIA, the White House itself, and other federal agencies increased their efforts to discredit and harass antiwar and radical groups, often through illegal means.

In Indochina, meanwhile, the fighting raged on. American bombing in Vietnam and Cambodia increased. In March 1972, the North Vietnamese mounted their biggest offensive since 1968 (the so-called Easter offensive). American and South Vietnamese forces managed to halt the communist advance, but it was clear that without American support, the South Vietnamese would not have succeeded. At the same time, Nixon ordered American planes to bomb targets near Hanoi, the capital of North Vietnam, and Haiphong, its principal port, and called for the mining of seven North Vietnamese harbors.

THE END OF THE WAR

As the 1972 presidential election approached, the administration stepped up its effort to produce a breakthrough in negotiations with the North Vietnamese. In April, the president dropped his longtime insistence on the removal of North Vietnamese troops from the south before any American withdrawal. Meanwhile, Henry Kissinger met privately in Paris with the North Vietnamese foreign secretary, Le Duc Tho, to work out terms for a cease-fire. On October 26, only days before the presidential election, Kissinger announced that "peace is at hand."

Several weeks later (after the election), negotiations broke down once again. Although both the American and North Vietnamese governments were ready to accept the Kissinger–Tho plan for a cease-fire, President Nguyen Van Thieu of South Vietnam balked, still insisting on a full withdrawal of North Vietnamese forces from the south. Kissinger tried to win additional concessions from the communists to meet Thieu's objections, but on December 16 talks broke off.

The next day, December 17, American B-52s began the heaviest and most destructive air raids of the entire war on Hanoi, Haiphong, and other North Vietnamese targets. Civilian casualties were high, and fifteen American B-52s were shot down by the North Vietnamese. In the entire war to that point, the United States had lost only one of the giant bombers. On December 30, Nixon terminated the "Christmas bombing." The United States and the North Vietnamese returned to the conference table, and on January 27, 1973, they signed the Paris Peace Accord, an "agreement on ending the war and restoring peace in Vietnam." Nixon claimed that the Christmas bombing had forced the North Vietnamese to relent and allowed Americans to secure "peace with honor." At least equally important, however, was the enormous American pressure on Thieu to accept the cease-fire.

The terms of the Paris Peace Accord were little different from those Kissinger and Thieu had accepted in principle a few months before. Nor were they much different from the peace plan Johnson had proposed in 1968. The Paris Accord specified that there would be an immediate cease-fire. The Thieu regime would survive in South Vietnam, but North Vietnamese forces in the south would not have to withdraw. The North Vietnamese would release several hundred American prisoners of war. An undefined committee would work out a permanent settlement.

DEFEAT IN INDOCHINA

American forces were hardly out of Indochina before the Paris accords began to collapse. In March 1975, the North Vietnamese launched a full-scale offensive against the now greatly weakened forces of South Vietnam. Thieu appealed to Washington for assistance. The president (now Gerald Ford) appealed to Congress for additional funding; Congress refused.

(©AP Photo)

THE EVACUATION OF SAIGON A harried U.S. official struggles to keep panicking Vietnamese from boarding an already overpacked helicopter on the roof of the U.S. embassy in Saigon. The hurried evacuation of Americans took place only hours before the arrival of North Vietnamese troops, signaling the final defeat of South Vietnam.

Late in April 1975, communist forces marched into Saigon, shortly after officials of the Thieu regime and the staff of the American embassy had fled the country in humiliating disarray. The communist forces quickly occupied the capital, renamed it Ho Chi Minh City, and began the process of reuniting Vietnam under the government based in Hanoi. At about the same time, the Lon Nol regime in Cambodia fell to the murderous forces of the Khmer Rouge—whose brutal policies led to the death of more than a third of the country's people over the next several years.

Such were the dismal results of three decades of support for an anticommunist South Vietnam and almost ten years of direct American military involvement. More than 1.2 million Vietnamese soldiers had died in combat, along with countless civilians throughout the region. A beautiful land had been ravaged, its agrarian economy left in ruins. Until an economic revival began in the early 1990s, Vietnam remained one of the poorest nations in the world. The United States had paid a heavy price as well. The war had cost the nation almost $150 billion in direct costs and much more indirectly. It had resulted in the deaths of over 58,000 young Americans and the injury of 300,000 more. And the nation had suffered a blow to its confidence and self-esteem from which it did not soon recover.

NIXON, KISSINGER, AND THE WORLD

The continuing war in Vietnam provided an unhappy backdrop to what Nixon considered his larger mission in world affairs: the construction of a new international order. The president had become convinced that the old assumptions of a "bipolar" world—in which the United States and the Soviet Union were the only real great powers—were now obsolete. America must adapt to the new "multipolar" international structure, in which China, Japan, Western Europe, and the Middle East were becoming major, independent forces. Nixon had a considerable advantage over many other politicians in changing the assumptions behind American foreign policy. His long anticommunist record gave him credibility among many conservatives for his effort to transform American relations with communist China and the Soviet Union.

THE CHINA INITIATIVE AND SOVIET–AMERICAN DÉTENTE

For more than twenty years, ever since the fall of Chiang Kai-shek in 1949, the United States had treated China, the most populous nation on earth, as if it did not exist. Instead, America recognized the regime-in-exile on the small island of Taiwan as the legitimate government of China. Nixon and Kissinger wanted to forge a new relationship with the Chinese communists, in large part to strengthen them as a counterbalance to the Soviet Union. The Chinese, for their part, were eager to end China's own isolation from the international arena.

In July 1971, Nixon sent Henry Kissinger on a secret mission to Beijing. When Kissinger returned, the president made the startling announcement that he would visit China himself within the next few months. That fall, with American approval, the United Nations admitted

(©Universal Images Group/Getty Images)

NIXON IN CHINA   President Nixon's 1972 visit to China was an important step in normalizing relations between the United States and the People's Republic of China. Here, Nixon toasts the developing relationship with Prime Minister Zhou Enlai.

THE END OF COLONIALISM

On July 4, 1946, less than a year after the close of World War II, a ceremony in Manila marked what Senator Millard Tydings of Maryland called "one of the most unprecedented, most idealistic, and most far-reaching events in all recorded history." On that day, the United States voluntarily ended nearly five decades of colonial control of the Philippines, which it had acquired as part of the spoils from the 1898 Spanish-American War. Philippine independence was only a small part of a dramatic change in the political structure of the world. The close of World War II marked not only the defeat of fascism in Germany, Italy, and Japan, but also the beginning of the end of the formal system of imperialism that European powers had maintained for centuries. The repudiation of colonialism was driven in part by the heightened belief in democracy and self-determination that the war helped strengthen through much of the world. It was also driven by the weakness of the European powers after World War II and their inability to sustain control over their increasingly restive colonies. Like most great geopolitical changes, the drive for colonial independence was turbulent and often violent.

The United States had been a latecomer to the imperialist system. But even its peaceful divestiture of the Philippines reflected the challenges many imperial powers and postcolonial nations faced in renegotiating colonial relationships. America was not quite as ready to cede military presence and economic influence in the region as it was to give up political responsibility over the islands. Philippine independence came with important caveats: that the United States maintained control

of Fillipino military bases and that required (through the Bell Trade Act, passed by Congress in 1946) that the Philippines not engage in any direct economic competition with the United States and that it revise its constitution to allow American interests free and unfettered access to the nation's natural resources. Many Filipinos argue that their nation did not achieve full independence until 1991, when the Philippine Senate refused to ratify a treaty that would have extended the American lease on the Subic Bay naval base (once the largest U.S. Navy installation in the Pacific). A year later, the United States closed the base and left, marking the first time in 400 years that the Philippines (once a Spanish possession) was not home to a foreign military power.

Britain's imperial holdings were the vastest in the world, and the existence of the British Empire was deeply embedded in the country's economic life and national self-image. But it, too, withdrew from most of its colonies in the decades after World War II—beginning in 1947 with its largest and most important colony, India. The British Raj—as the colonial government was known—withdrew from South Asia in response to a growing independence movement on the subcontinent. As often happened as colonial rule ended, suppressed conflicts in the native population quickly emerged—in the case of India, between Hindus and Muslims. The price of Indian independence, therefore, was the partition of the country into India and Pakistan (and, several decades later, Bangladesh).

A year later, the British gave up their World War I mandate of Palestine (ceding the territory to the United Nations and allowing for the creation of Israel) as well as many of its holdings in Southeast Asia, including Burma and Ceylon. Malaya followed in 1957 and Singapore in 1965. In 1982, Britain passed the Canada Act, effectively severing Canada from the United Kingdom and culminating a move toward full Canadian self-government that had begun several decades earlier. In 1997, England returned one of its last important overseas territories, Hong Kong, to the control of China, bringing nearly to an end the era of the British Empire.

The dissolution of the British Empire did not always proceed smoothly. The Suez Crisis of 1956, in which the combined efforts of Britain, France, and Israel failed to halt Egypt's nationalization of the Suez Canal, dealt a decisive blow to Britain's status as a major power in the Middle East. In 1982, Britain's dispute over the tiny Falkland Islands erupted into war with Argentina, which claimed the islands (just off its coast) as its own. After the deaths of 258 British and 649 Argentine soldiers, Britain maintained its control of the Falklands, although Argentina continues to assert its right to the islands.

Despite these controversies, the dissolution of the British Empire proceeded relatively smoothly compared to the experience of the French, who became engaged in several major conflicts after 1945. In late 1946, Vietnamese nationalists rose up against the French colonial government that had recently reoccupied the region after the defeat of Japan in World War II. France's effort to keep Vietnam culminated in its defeat at Dien Bien Phu in 1954 and its subsequent withdrawal from Indochina. France also became embroiled in, and tried to suppress by force, a number of other violent colonial uprisings—in Madagascar, Cameroon, and, most notably, Algeria. The Algerian War (1954–1962) was a particularly bloody and costly conflict, taking on aspects of a civil war and involving guerrilla warfare, torture, acts of terrorism,

and, eventually, the collapse of the French government in 1958. Algeria ultimately won its independence.

The end of the colonial system had a great impact on Africa. European powers had carved up almost all of sub-Saharan Africa in the nineteenth century. In the decades after World War II, almost all the African colonies won their independence, even if not always easily: Morocco (1956), Ghana (1957), the Congo (1960), Nigeria (1960), Uganda (1962), Kenya (1963), and Gambia (1965). African nationalism was troubled for decades by political instability and, in some countries, extreme poverty. The Caribbean also saw many new independent nations born in the postwar era, including Jamaica (1961), Trinidad and Tobago (1962), Barbados (1966), and Guyana (1966).

The most recent epicenter of independence movements has been in the lands that used to comprise the Soviet Union. A long and costly war in Afghanistan began in the 1970s as the Soviet Union struggled to retain control of the nation in the face of powerful local insurgencies. The war was one of the principal factors in the unraveling of the Soviet Empire that began in 1991. Many of the former Soviet republics—which considered themselves colonies of Russia—soon separated from Russia and became independent nations. These included Estonia, Latvia, and Lithuania, the formerly independent Baltic nations seized by the Soviet Union during World War II. Other former Soviet possessions that became independent nations included Ukraine, Moldova, Armenia, Georgia, Azerbaijan, Kazakhstan, Uzbekistan, Tajikistan, and Turkmenistan. Russia continues to deal with the problems of empire. A vicious conflict with Chechnya, an Islamic area of Russia insisting on independence, created terror and instability for years.

The end of colonialism was one of the most epochal global changes of the last several centuries—a change that brought to an end a system that was based on the assumption of European (and American) superiority over other peoples. Yet although formal colonialism came to an end in the post–World War II era, other aspects of imperialism did not. Many former colonies, which comprise much of the nonindustrialized world, still struggle with the indirect exercise of economic power that wealthy nations continue to exert over them.   •

UNDERSTAND, ANALYZE, & EVALUATE

1. How did the experience of World War II contribute to the end of colonialism?
2. What have been the effects of colonialism—and the end of colonialism—on Africa? Why have the effects been so pronounced on that continent, more so than in other areas of the world?

the communist government of China and expelled the representatives of the Taiwan regime. Finally, in February 1972, Nixon paid a formal visit to China. It erased much of the deep animosity between the United States and the Chinese communists. Nixon did not yet formally recognize the communist regime, but in 1972 the United States and China began low-level diplomatic relations.

The initiatives in China coincided with an effort by the Nixon administration to improve relations with the Soviet Union, an initiative known by the French word **détente**, which favored diplomacy over militarism though with the same end goals of containing communism and ensuring American security. In 1971, American and Soviet diplomats produced the first Strategic Arms Limitation Treaty (SALT I), which froze the arsenals of some nuclear missiles on both sides at present levels. In May of that year, the president traveled to Moscow to sign the agreement. The next year, the Soviet premier, Leonid Brezhnev, visited Washington.

DEALING WITH THE "THIRD WORLD"

The policies of rapprochement with communist China and détente with the Soviet Union reflected Nixon's and Kissinger's belief in the importance of stable relationships among the great powers. But, as America's experience in Vietnam already illustrated, the vast areas of the globe unaligned with either superpower—what became known in the 1950s as the Third World—remained volatile and dangerous sites of international tension. In many cases such tension arose *because* of the Cold War proxy battles carried out in those regions. Since the end of World War I, the United States and the European powers had lost or withdrawn control over former colonies. The result was a number of newly independent but economically fragile and politically unstable nations around the world. (See "America in the World: The End of Colonialism.")

The Nixon–Kissinger policy toward the Third World tried to maintain the status quo without involving the United States too deeply in local disputes. In 1969 and 1970, the president described what became known as the **Nixon Doctrine**, by which the United States would "participate in the defense and development of allies and friends" but would leave the "basic responsibility" for the future of those "friends" to the nations themselves. In practice, the Nixon Doctrine meant a declining American interest in contributing to Third World development. There was also a growing contempt for the United Nations, where underdeveloped nations were gaining influence through their sheer numbers. And there was increasing American support for authoritarian regimes attempting to withstand radical challenges from within.

In 1970, for example, the CIA poured substantial funds into Chile to help support the government against a communist challenge. When the Marxist candidate for president, Salvador Allende, came to power through an open election despite American efforts, the United States began funneling more money to opposition forces in Chile to help destabilize the new government. In 1973, a military junta seized power from Allende, who was subsequently murdered. The United States developed a friendly relationship with the new, repressive military government of General Augusto Pinochet.

In the Middle East, conditions grew more volatile in the aftermath of a 1967 war in which Israel had occupied substantial new territories, dislodging many Palestinian Arabs from their homes. The refugees were a source of considerable instability in Jordan, Lebanon, and the other surrounding countries into which they moved. In October 1973, on the Jewish high holy day of Yom Kippur, Egyptian and Syrian forces attacked Israel. For ten days, the Israelis struggled to recover from the surprise attack. Finally, they launched an effective counteroffensive against Egyptian forces in the Sinai. At that point, the United States intervened, supporting Israel but placing heavy pressure on that country to accept a cease-fire rather than press its advantage.

The Yom Kippur War demonstrated the growing dependence of the United States and its allies on Arab oil. A brief but painful embargo in 1973–1974 by the Arab members of the Organization of the Petroleum Exporting Companies (OPEC) against the United States and other allies that supported Israel provided an ominous warning of the costs of dependence on foreign oil. It also prompted Congress to pass fuel economy standards, requiring automakers to raise average mileage from 13.5 miles per gallon to 27. (The standard has since been raised to 54.5 mpg by 2025.)

POLITICS AND ECONOMICS IN THE NIXON YEARS

Nixon ran for president in 1968, promising a return to more conservative social and economic policies and a restoration of law and order. Once he was in office, however, his domestic policies ironically continued and even expanded some liberal initiatives of the previous two administrations.

DOMESTIC INITIATIVES

Many of Nixon's domestic policies were a response to what he believed to be the demands of his constituency—the "**silent majority**" of conservative, mostly middle-class people who, he believed, wanted to reduce federal interference in local affairs. He tried, unsuccessfully, to persuade Congress to pass legislation prohibiting school desegregation through the use of forced busing. He was, however, able to protect school districts that ignored court orders to integrate by forbidding the Department of Health, Education, and Welfare (now called the Department of Health and Human Services) from cutting their federal funding. At the same time, he began to reduce or dismantle many of the social programs of the Great Society and the New Frontier. In 1973, he abolished the Office of Economic Opportunity—a centerpiece of the antipoverty program of the Johnson years.

Yet Nixon's domestic policies had progressive and creative elements as well. He signed legislation creating the Environmental Protection Agency and establishing the most stringent environmental regulations in the nation's history. He ordered the first affirmative action program for workers on federally funded projects. One of the administration's boldest efforts was an attempt to overhaul the nation's welfare system. Nixon proposed replacing the existing system with what he called the Family Assistance Plan (FAP). It would, in effect, have created a guaranteed annual income for all Americans: $1,600 in federal grants, which could be supplemented by outside earnings up to $4,000. The FAP won approval in the House in 1970, but the bill failed in the Senate. Nixon also became the first president since Truman to propose a plan for national health insurance, which likewise made no progress in Congress.

From the Warren Court to the Nixon Court

Of all the liberal institutions that aroused the enmity of the conservative silent majority in the 1950s and 1960s, none evoked more anger and bitterness than the Supreme Court under Chief Justice Earl Warren. The Warren Court's rulings on racial matters disrupted traditional social patterns in both the North and the South. Its defense of civil liberties directly contributed to the increase in crime, disorder, and moral decay in the eyes of many Americans. In *Roth v. United States* (1957), the Court sharply limited the authority of local governments to curb pornography. In *Engel v. Vitale* (1962), the Court ruled that prayers in public schools were unconstitutional, sparking outrage among religious fundamentalists and others. In a series of other decisions, the Court greatly strengthened the civil rights of criminal defendants and, many Americans believed, greatly weakened the power of law enforcement officials to do their jobs. For example, in *Gideon v. Wainwright* (1963), the Court ruled that every felony defendant was entitled to a lawyer, regardless of his or her ability to pay. In *Escobedo v. Illinois* (1964), it ruled that a defendant must be allowed access to a lawyer before questioning by police. In *Miranda v. Arizona* (1966), the Court confirmed the obligation of authorities to inform a criminal suspect that he or she has the right to remain silent and to be represented by an attorney. By 1968, the Warren Court had become the scorn of Americans who felt the United States had shifted too far toward helping poor, dispossessed, and criminal individuals at the expense of the middle class.

Their complaints caught the ear of the president and he promised to give the Court a more conservative cast. When Chief Justice Earl Warren retired early in 1969, Nixon swiftly replaced him with a federal appeals court judge of conservative leanings, Warren Burger. But after watching the Senate reject his nominees for the next vacancy on the court on the basis of either political extremism or an unimpressive legal career, Nixon carefully selected more moderate candidates with impeccable resumes: Harry Blackmun, an esteemed jurist from Minnesota; Lewis F. Powell Jr., a respected lawyer from Virginia; and William Rehnquist, a member of the Nixon Justice Department.

The new Court, however, fell far short of what the president and many conservatives had expected. Rather than retreating from its commitment to social reform or reversing earlier decisions, the Court continued to expand protections for individual liberties. In *Swann v. Charlotte-Mecklenburg Board of Education* (1971), it ruled in favor of forced busing to achieve racial balance in schools. Despite intense and occasionally violent opposition by local communities as diverse as Boston and Louisville, the judicial commitment to integration was not overturned. In *Furman v. Georgia* (1972), the Court ruled that the death penalty had been imposed in a way that was illegal. It forced states to retool their capital punishment laws to ensure that the death penalty was not imposed arbitrarily and instead was determined in a fair and nondiscriminatory manner. In *Roe v. Wade* (1973), one of the most controversial decisions in the Court's modern history, it struck down laws forbidding abortions in the first three months of pregnancy and ruled that the right to an abortion was constitutionally protected.

In other decisions, however, the Burger Court did demonstrate a more conservative temperament than the Warren Court had shown. Although the justices approved busing as a tool for achieving integration, they rejected, in *Milliken v. Bradley* (1974), a plan to transfer students across municipal lines (in this case, between Detroit and its suburbs) to achieve racial balance. While the Court upheld the principle of affirmative action in its celebrated 1978 decision, *Bakke v. Board of Regents of California*, it established restrictive new guidelines for such programs in the future. In *Stone v. Powell* (1976), the Court agreed to certain limits on the right of a defendant to appeal a state conviction to the federal judiciary.

The 1972 Landslide

Nixon entered the presidential race in 1972 with substantial strength. His energetic reelection committee had collected enormous sums of money. The president himself used the powers of incumbency to strengthen his political standing among conservatives by challenging some civil rights legislation. And Nixon's foreign policy successes, especially his trip to China, increased his stature in the eyes of the nation.

The Republican Nixon was most fortunate in 1972, however, in his Democratic opposition. George Wallace, partly at Nixon's urging, entered the Democratic primaries and helped divide the party. Now renouncing his past support of segregation but voicing opposition to forced busing as a means to desegregate public schools, Wallace began to woo Democratic voters and set up a battle for the nomination against the party's more liberal wing. But after being shot by a would-be assassin during a campaign rally in a Maryland shopping mall, Wallace was left paralyzed from the waist down and withdrew from the campaign. His departure left the conservative leaders of the Democratic Party in disarray and paved the way for the most liberal factions to establish their candidate, Senator George S. McGovern of South Dakota, as the front-runner for the nomination. An outspoken critic of the Vietnam War and a forceful advocate of liberal positions on many social and economic issues, McGovern profited greatly from party reforms (which he himself had helped draft) that gave increased influence to women, minorities, and young people in the selection of the Democratic ticket. In the process, the McGovern campaign came to be tarred with aspects of the turbulent 1960s that many middle-class Americans were eager to reject.

On election day, Nixon won reelection by one of the largest margins in history: 60.7 percent of the popular vote to McGovern's 37.5 percent and an electoral margin of 520 to 17. The Democratic candidate carried only Massachusetts and the District of Columbia. But serious problems, some beyond the president's control and others of his own making, lurked in the wings.

The Troubled Economy

Although it was a political scandal that would ultimately destroy the Nixon presidency, the most important issue of the early 1970s was the beginning of a long-term transformation of the American economy. For three decades, that economy had been the envy of the world.

In fact, however, America's prosperity rested in part on several artificial conditions that were rapidly disappearing by the late 1960s.

The most immediate change was the end of the nation's easy access to cheap raw materials, a change that became a major cause of the serious inflation that plagued the economy through much of the 1970s. For many years, OPEC had operated as an informal bargaining unit for the sale of oil by Third World nations but had seldom managed to exercise any real strength. But in the early 1970s, OPEC began to use its oil both as an economic tool and as a political weapon. In 1973, in the midst of the Yom Kippur War, Arab members of OPEC announced that they would no longer ship petroleum to nations supporting Israel—that is, to the United States and its allies in Western Europe. At about the same time, the OPEC nations agreed to raise their prices 500 percent (from $3 to $15 a barrel). These twin shocks produced momentary economic chaos in the West. The United States suffered its first fuel shortage since World War II. And although the crisis eased a few months later, the price of energy continued to rise.

Another, longer-term change in the American economy was the transformation of the nation's manufacturing sector. Ever since World War II, American industry had enjoyed relatively little competition from the rest of the world. By the end of the 1960s, however, both Western Europe and Japan had recovered from the damage their manufacturing sectors had absorbed during World War II. By the early 1970s, they were providing stiff competition to American firms in the sale of automobiles, steel, and many other products, both in world markets and within the United States. Some American corporations failed. Others restructured themselves to become more competitive again in world markets but in the process closed many older plants and eliminated hundreds of thousands of once-lucrative manufacturing jobs. The high-wage, high-employment industrial economy that had been a central fact of American life since the 1940s was gradually disappearing.

THE NIXON RESPONSE

Nixon's initial answer to these mounting economic problems was a conventional anti-inflationary one. He reduced federal spending and raised taxes, producing a modest budget surplus in 1969. But when those policies proved difficult to sustain, Nixon turned increasingly to control of the currency. Placing conservative economists at the head of the Federal Reserve Board, he ensured sharply higher interest rates and a contraction of the money supply. Even so, the cost of living rose a cumulative 15 percent during Nixon's first two and a half years in office. Economic growth, in the meantime, declined.

In the summer of 1971, Nixon imposed a ninety-day freeze on all wages and prices at their existing levels. Then, in November, he launched the second phase of his economic plan: mandatory guidelines for some wage and price increases, to be administered by a federal agency. Inflation subsided temporarily, but the recession continued. Fearful that the recession would be more damaging than inflation in an election year, the administration reversed itself late in 1971: interest rates were allowed to drop sharply, and government spending increased—producing the largest budget deficit since World War II. The new tactics helped revive the economy in the short term, but inflation rose substantially. In 1973, prices rose 9 percent; in 1974, after the Arab oil embargo and the OPEC price increases, they rose 12 percent—the highest rate since shortly after World War II. The new energy crisis, in the meantime, was quickly becoming a national preoccupation. But while Nixon talked often about the need to achieve "energy independence," he offered few concrete proposals.

THE WATERGATE CRISIS

Although economic problems greatly concerned the American people in the 1970s, another stunning development preoccupied the nation beginning early in 1973: the fall of Richard Nixon. Scholars wrangle over the exact origins and legacies of Nixon's fall from grace, but they widely agree that the president's demise was in part a result of the turbulent climate of the early 1970s. It was also a result of his own reckless personality, disregard for the constitutional limits placed on his power, and overpowering fear that he and the nation faced grave dangers from radicals and dissidents openly challenging his policies.

THE SCANDALS

Early on the morning of June 17, 1972, police arrested five men who had broken into the headquarters of the Democratic National Committee in the **Watergate** office building in Washington, D.C. Two others were seized a short time later and charged with supervising the break-in. When reporters for the *Washington Post* began researching the backgrounds of the culprits, they discovered that among those involved in the burglary were former employees of the Committee for the Re-Election of the President (CRP). One of them had worked in the White House itself. They had, moreover, been paid for the break-in from a secret fund of Nixon's reelection committee—a fund controlled by members of the White House staff, among others.

Public interest in the disclosures grew slowly in the last months of 1972. Early in 1973, however, the Watergate burglars went on trial; and under prodding from federal judge John J. Sirica, one of the defendants, James W. McCord, agreed to cooperate both with the grand jury and with a special Senate investigating committee recently established under Senator Sam J. Ervin of North Carolina. McCord's testimony opened a floodgate of confessions, and for months a parade of White House and campaign officials exposed one illegality after another. Foremost among them was a member of the inner circle of the White House, John Dean, counsel to the president, who had warned Nixon that the Watergate affair was a "cancer on the presidency" and who later leveled allegations against Nixon himself.

Two different sets of scandals emerged from the investigations. One was a general pattern of abuses of power involving both the White House and the Nixon campaign committee, which included, but was not limited to, the Watergate break-in. The other scandal, and the one that became the major focus of public attention for nearly two years, was the way in which the administration tried to manage the investigations of the Watergate break-in and other abuses—a pattern of behavior that became known as the "cover-up." There was never any conclusive evidence that the president had planned or approved the burglary in advance. But there was mounting evidence that he had been involved in illegal efforts to obstruct investigations of the episode. (See "Debating the Past: Watergate.")

Nixon accepted the departure of members of his administration implicated in the scandals. But the president continued to insist on his own innocence. There the matter might have rested had it not been for the disclosure during the Senate hearings of a White House taping system that had recorded virtually every conversation in the president's office during the period in question. All those investigating the scandals sought access to the tapes. Nixon, pleading "executive privilege," refused to release them. A special prosecutor appointed by the president to handle the Watergate cases, Harvard law professor Archibald Cox, took Nixon to court in October 1973 in an effort to force him to relinquish the recordings.

WATERGATE

Forty-two years after Watergate—one of the most famous political scandals in American history—historians and others continue to argue about its causes and significance. Their interpretations tend to fall into several broad categories.

One argument emphasizes the evolution of the institution of the presidency over time and sees Watergate as the result of a much larger pattern of presidential usurpations of power that stretched back at least several decades. Arthur M. Schlesinger Jr. helped develop this line of reasoning in his 1973 book *The Imperial Presidency*, which argues that ever since World War II, Americans have believed that the nation was in a state of permanent crisis—threatened from abroad by the menace of communism and from within by the danger of insufficient will. A succession of presidents believed in the urgency of this crisis, and in their duty to take whatever measures might be necessary to combat it. That led them gradually to usurp more and more power from Congress, from the courts, and from the public. Initially, this expansion of presidential power came in the realm of international affairs. It included covert and at times illegal activities overseas. Gradually, presidents began to look for ways to circumvent constraints in domestic matters as well. Nixon's actions in the Watergate crisis were, in other words, a culmination of this long and steady expansion of covert presidential power. Jonathan Schell, in *The Time of Illusion* (1975), offers a variation of this argument, tying the crisis of the presidency to the pressure that nuclear weapons place

on presidents to protect the nation's—and their own—"credibility." Historians today rarely stake their understanding of Nixon's downfall on this particular view of government and society, preferring instead to treat this notion of a society in an unending crisis as one of many orientations that motivated Nixon to see himself engaged in a battle to preserve American values and empowered him to take strong and illegal measures to win.

Another explanation of Watergate emphasizes the difficult social and political environment of the late 1960s and early 1970s. Nixon entered office, according to this view, facing an unprecedentedly radical opposition that would stop at nothing to discredit the war and destroy his authority. He found himself, therefore, drawn into taking similarly desperate measures of his own to defend himself. Nixon made this argument in his own 1978 memoirs:

> Now that this season of mindless terror has fortunately passed, it is difficult—perhaps impossible—to convey a sense of the pressures that were influencing my actions and reactions during this period, but it was this epidemic of unprecedented domestic terrorism that prompted our efforts to discover the best means by which to deal with this new phenomenon of highly organized and highly skilled revolutionaries dedicated to the violent destruction of our democratic system.*

The historian Herbert Parmet echoes parts of this argument in *Richard Nixon and His America* (1990). Stephen Ambrose offers a more muted version of the same view in *Richard Nixon* (1989). Though this particular form of

---

RN: The Memoirs of Richard Nixon, New York: Grosset & Dunlap, 1978.

analysis has not been popular of late, Evan Thomas in *Being Nixon: A Man Divided* (2016), offers a compelling portrait of how Nixon viewed his presidency as a war between his values and those who would undermine him.

Most of those who have written about Watergate, however, search for the explanation not in institutional or social forces but in the personalities of the people involved and, most notably, in the personality of Richard Nixon. Even many of those who have developed structural explanations (Schlesinger, Schell, and Ambrose, for example) return eventually to Nixon himself as the most important explanation for Watergate. Others begin there, perhaps most notably Stanley I. Kutler, in *The Wars of Watergate* (1990) and, later, *Abuse of Power* (1997), in which he presents extensive excerpts from conversations about Watergate taped in the Nixon White House. Kutler emphasizes Nixon's lifelong resort to vicious political tactics and his long-standing belief that he was a special target of unscrupulous enemies and had to "get" them before they got him. Watergate was rooted, Kutler

argues, "in the personality and history of Nixon himself." A "corrosive hatred," he claims, "decisively shaped Nixon's own behavior, his career, and eventually his historical standing." This focus on Nixon's personality continues to be the subject of excellent studies, now aided by the declassification of presidential documents, including those by Tim Wiener, *One Man Against the World: The Tragedy of Richard Nixon* (2016) and John Farrell, *Richard Nixon: The Life* (2017). •

UNDERSTAND, ANALYZE, & EVALUATE

1. For scholars who cite social and institutional forces as explanations for Watergate, what are these forces? How did they contribute to the Watergate scandal?
2. Most scholars see Nixon himself as the party most responsible for Watergate. How did Nixon's personality contribute to both his rise to power as president and his downfall as a result of Watergate?
3. What have been the lasting effects of Watergate on the public's perception of the presidency and the government?

Nixon summarily fired Cox only to suffer the humiliation of watching both Attorney General Elliot Richardson and his deputy resign in protest. This "Saturday night massacre," as it was called, quickly backfired on Nixon. Public pressure forced him to appoint a new special prosecutor, Texas attorney Leon Jaworski, who proved just as determined as Cox to subpoena the tapes. And an outraged Congress set in motion an investigation by the House of Representatives into the possibility of impeachment.

THE FALL OF RICHARD NIXON

Nixon's situation deteriorated further in the following months. Late in 1973, Vice President Spiro Agnew became embroiled in a scandal of his own when evidence surfaced that he had accepted bribes and kickbacks while serving as governor of Maryland and even as vice president. In return for a Justice Department agreement not to prosecute the case, Agnew pleaded no contest to a lesser charge of income-tax evasion and resigned from the government. With the controversial Agnew no longer in line to succeed to the presidency, the prospect of removing Nixon from the White House became less worrisome to his opponents. The new vice president was House Minority Leader Gerald Ford, an amiable and popular Michigan congressman.

The impeachment investigation quickly gathered momentum. In April 1974, in an effort to head off further subpoenas of the tapes, the president released transcripts of a number of relevant conversations, claiming that they proved his innocence. Investigators and much of the public felt otherwise. Even these edited tapes seemed to suggest Nixon's complicity in the cover-up. In July, the crisis reached a climax. First the Supreme Court ruled unanimously, in *United States v. Richard M. Nixon*, that the president must relinquish the tapes to Special Prosecutor Jaworski. Days later, the House Judiciary Committee voted to recommend three articles of impeachment.

Even without additional evidence, Nixon might well have been impeached by the full House and convicted by the Senate. Early in August, however, he provided at last the "smoking gun"—the concrete proof of his guilt—that his defenders had long contended was missing from the case against him. Among the tapes that the Supreme Court compelled Nixon to relinquish were several that offered apparently incontrovertible evidence of his involvement in the Watergate cover-up. Only three days after the burglary, the recordings disclosed, the president had ordered the FBI to stop investigating the break-in. Impeachment and conviction now seemed inevitable.

Barbara Jordan, a thirty-eight-year-old, second-term congresswoman from Houston, Texas, and the first black women from the state to ever serve in the House of Representatives, boldly set the stage for impeachment. Speaking on July 25 as a member of the House Judiciary Committee, she passionately addressed her colleagues and a rapt national audience watching on television on the severity of Nixon's malfeasance and the pressing need to impeach him. Identifying herself as "an inquisitor," she confessed that she could not "sit here and be an idle spectator to the diminution, the subversion, the destruction, of the Constitution." Impeachment, she intoned, "is designed to 'bridle' the Executive if he engages in excesses." Quoting James Madison from the Federalist Papers, she reminded her audience that impeachment "is designed as a method of national inquest into the conduct of public men" and that

(©Bettmann/Getty Images)

NIXON'S FAREWELL   Only moments before, Nixon had been in tears, saying good-bye to his staff in the East Room of the White House. But as he boarded a helicopter to begin his trip home to California shortly after resigning as president, he flashed his trademark "victory" sign to the crowd on the White House lawn.

"the framers confided in the Congress the power if need be, to remove the President in order to strike a delicate balance between a President swollen with power and grown tyrannical, and preservation of the independence of the Executive." After reviewing the president's crimes, she closed with a flourish. "If the impeachment provision in the Constitution of the United States will not reach the offenses charged here, then perhaps that 18th-century Constitution should be abandoned to a 20th-century paper shredder!"

For several days, Nixon cloistered himself in the White House. Finally, on August 8, 1974, he announced his resignation—the first president in American history ever to do so. At noon the next day, while Nixon and his family flew west to their home in California, **Gerald R. Ford** took the oath of office as president.

Many Americans expressed relief and exhilaration that, as the new president put it, "our long national nightmare is over." But the wave of good feeling could not obscure the deeper and more lasting damage of the Watergate crisis. In a society in which distrust of leaders and institutions of authority was already widespread, the fall of Richard Nixon confirmed for many Americans their most cynical assumptions about the untrustworthy character of American public life.

CONCLUSION

The victory of Richard Nixon in the 1968 presidential election represented a popular repudiation of turbulence and radicalism. It was a call for a restoration of order and stability. But order and stability were not the dominant characteristics of Nixon's troubled years in office. Nixon entered office when the political left and the counterculture were approaching the peak of their influence. American culture and society in the late 1960s and early 1970s were shaped decisively by, and were deeply divided over, the challenges by young people to the prevailing social norms. These were also the years in which a host of new liberation movements joined the drive for racial equality and when, above all, women mobilized effectively to demand changes in the way society treated gender differences.

Nixon had run for office attacking the failure of his predecessor to end the war in Vietnam. But for four years under his presidency, the war—and the protests against it—continued and even in some respects escalated. The division of opinion over the war was as deep as any of the other divisions in national life. It continued to poison the nation's politics and social fabric until the American role in the conflict finally shuddered to a close in 1973.

But much of the controversy and division in the 1970s was a product of the Nixon presidency itself. Nixon was in many ways a dynamic and even visionary leader, who proposed some important domestic reforms and who made important changes in American foreign policy, most notably making overtures to communist China and forging détente with the Soviet Union. He was also, however, a devious, secretive man whose White House became engaged in a series of covert activities that produced the most dramatic political scandal in American history. Watergate, as it was called, preoccupied much of the nation for nearly two years beginning in 1972; and ultimately, in the summer of 1974, the scandal forced Richard Nixon—who had been reelected to office only two years before by one of the largest majorities in modern history—to become the first president in American history to resign. Nixon was elected to lead the nation out of a war it no longer wanted, but his shameful exit from office and the ongoing Vietnam War continued to damage the nation's self-confidence and trust in government.

KEY TERMS/PEOPLE/PLACES/EVENTS

American Indian Movement
  (AIM) 736
Betty Friedan 739
César Chávez 738
counterculture 733
détente 750
Earth Day 743

Gerald R. Ford 759
Indian Civil Rights Act 736
National Organization
  for Women (NOW) 739
Nixon Doctrine 750
Rachel Carson 742
Roe v. Wade 741

silent majority 751
Stonewall Riot 738
Students for a Democratic
  Society (SDS) 732
Vietnamization 744
Watergate 755
Woodstock 734

RECALL AND REFLECT

1. What was the New Left? How was it related to the counterculture?
2. How did ethnic minorities, especially Native Americans and Latinos, challenge the status quo in the 1970s?
3. What were the objectives of the new feminism of the 1970s? What gains did women achieve in this era? What setbacks did the feminist movement experience?
4. What was the "Nixon Doctrine"? How did this doctrine play out in foreign policy?
5. What was the effect of Nixon's policies on the U.S. economy? What was Nixon's response to escalating economic difficulties?

30 | FROM "THE AGE OF LIMITS" TO THE AGE OF REAGAN

POLITICS AND DIPLOMACY AFTER WATERGATE

THE RISE OF THE NEW CONSERVATIVE MOVEMENT

THE "REAGAN REVOLUTION"

THE WANING OF THE COLD WAR

LOOKING AHEAD

1. What economic and energy problems plagued the presidencies of Gerald Ford and Jimmy Carter? How did Ford and Carter attempt to deal with these problems?
2. What was the "New Right," and what effect did its rise have on American politics?
3. What was Reaganomics, and how did this policy affect the national economy?

THE FRUSTRATIONS OF THE EARLY 1970s—the defeat in Vietnam, the Watergate crisis, the decay of the American economy—inflicted damaging blows to the confident, optimistic nationalism that had characterized so much of the postwar era. Nixon's resignation in particular left Americans wondering if they could ever fully trust their government. And Americans battling to overcome generations of segregation were unsure how far the country would go to recognize and protect their freedoms.

Some Americans responded to these problems by announcing the arrival of an "age of limits," in which Americans would have to learn to live with lowered expectations for prosperity and global stature. By the end of the decade, however, another response was gaining strength—one that combined a steady retreat from some of the heady liberal visions of the 1960s with a reinforced commitment to traditional ideas of economic growth, international power, and American virtue.

1974

"Stagflation"

Ford pardons Nixon

1976

Carter elected
president

1977

Panama Canal
treaties signed

1978–1979

Camp David accords

American hostages in
Iran

Apple introduces first
personal computer

1980

Soviet Union invades
Afghanistan

U.S. boycotts Moscow
Olympics

U.S. and China restore
relations

Reagan elected president

Three Mile Island
nuclear accident

1981

American hostages in
Iran released

1982

Severe recession

Reagan wins tax and
budget cuts

1983

U.S. invades Grenada

AIDS first reported in U.S.

1984

Reagan reelected

1985

Reagan and
Gorbachev meet

1986

Iran-Contra scandal
revealed

1988

George H. W. Bush
elected president

1989

Berlin Wall dismantled

1990

Iraq invades Kuwait

Communist regimes
collapse

U.S. troops in Panama

1991

Collapse of Soviet regime

Persian Gulf War

1992

Los Angeles race riots

Clinton elected
president

POLITICS AND DIPLOMACY AFTER WATERGATE

In the aftermath of Richard Nixon's shameful departure from office, many Americans wondered whether faith in the presidency, and in the government as a whole, could ever be restored. The administrations of the two presidents who succeeded Nixon did little to answer those questions.

THE FORD CUSTODIANSHIP

Gerald R. Ford inherited the presidency under difficult circumstances. He desperately tried to rebuild confidence in government in the wake of the Watergate scandals and to restore prosperity in the face of major economic difficulties. Unfortunately, he met with little success on either account.

The new president's effort to establish himself as a symbol of political integrity suffered a setback only a month after he took office, when he granted Richard Nixon "a full, free, and absolute pardon" for any crimes he may have committed during his presidency. It was a gutsy move designed to get Americans past the trauma of Watergate. But the pardon angered Congress and a public eager to see Nixon face criminal charges and caused a sharp decline in Ford's popularity from which he never fully recovered. Indeed, it was a key reason for his failure to win reelection two years later. Nevertheless, most Americans considered Ford a decent man; his honesty and amiability did much to reduce the bitterness and acrimony of the Watergate years. Twenty-five years later, in recognition of the political resolution required by Ford to issue the pardon, the John F. Kennedy Center awarded him its Profile in Courage Award.

The Ford administration enjoyed far less success in its effort to solve the problems of the economy. Central to the economic problems was the continuing energy crisis. In the aftermath of the Arab oil embargo of 1973, the OPEC cartel raised the price of oil—by 400 percent in 1974 alone—and the price of goods and services that were dependent on oil rose in response. To curb inflation, the president called for largely ineffective voluntary efforts. After supporting high interest rates, opposing increased federal spending (through liberal use of his veto power), and resisting pressures for a tax reduction, Ford had to deal with a confounding economic mix of rising unemployment, high inflation, and slowing economic growth in 1974 and 1975 known as **stagflation**. While it occurred only during this two-year period, it was synonymous with most of the economic troubles of the seventies.

Ford retained Henry Kissinger as secretary of state and generally continued the foreign policies of the Nixon years. Late in 1974, Ford met with Leonid Brezhnev, the leader of the Soviet Union, at Vladivostok in Siberia and signed an arms control accord. Meanwhile, in the Middle East, Henry Kissinger helped produce a new accord by which Israel agreed to return large portions of the occupied Sinai to Egypt. The two nations pledged not to resolve future differences by force.

As the 1976 presidential election approached, Ford's policies came under increasing attack from both the right and the left. In the Republican primary campaign, Ford faced a powerful challenge from former California governor Ronald Reagan, leader of the party's

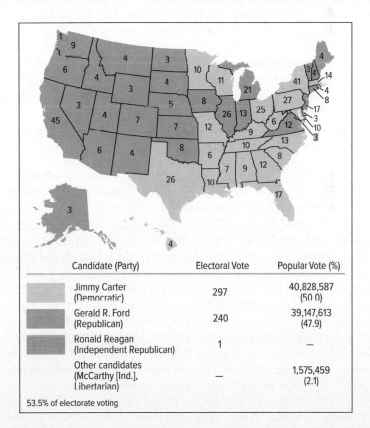

Candidate (Party)	Electoral Vote	Popular Vote (%)
Jimmy Carter (Democratic)	297	40,828,587 (50.0)
Gerald R. Ford (Republican)	240	39,147,613 (47.9)
Ronald Reagan (Independent Republican)	1	—
Other candidates (McCarthy [Ind.], Libertarian)	—	1,575,459 (2.1)

53.5% of electorate voting

THE ELECTION OF 1976 Jimmy Carter, a former governor of Georgia, swept the South in the 1976 election and carried enough of the industrial states of the Northeast and Midwest to win a narrow victory over President Gerald R. Ford. His showing indicated the importance to the Democratic Party of having a candidate capable of attracting support in the South, which was becoming increasingly Republican by the 1970s. • *What drove so many southerners into the Republican Party?*

conservative wing, who spoke for many Americans on the right who opposed any agree-ments with communists. The president barely survived the assault to win his party's nomination. The Democrats, in the meantime, were gradually uniting behind a new and until recently almost entirely unknown candidate: **Jimmy Carter**, a former governor of Georgia who appealed to the general unhappiness with Washington by offering honesty, piety, and an outsider's skepticism of the federal government. Unhappiness with the econ-omy and a general disenchantment with Ford enabled the Democrat to win a narrow victory. Carter received 50 percent of the popular vote to Ford's 47.9 percent and 297 electoral votes to Ford's 240.

THE TRIALS OF JIMMY CARTER

Like Ford, Jimmy Carter assumed the presidency at a moment when the nation faced problems of staggering complexity and difficulty. But Carter seemed at times to make his predicament worse by a style of leadership that many Americans considered self-righteous and inflexible.

Carter devoted much of his time to the problems of energy and the economy. Entering office in the midst of a recession, he moved first to reduce unemployment by raising pub-lic spending and cutting federal taxes. Unemployment declined, but inflation soared—mostly because of the continuing, sharp increases in energy prices by OPEC. During Carter's last two years in office, retail prices rose at over a 10 percent annual rate. Like Nixon and Ford before him, Carter responded with a combination of tight money and calls for voluntary restraint. Determined to stop inflation, he appointed conservative economists to head the Federal Reserve Board, which helped push interest rates to the highest levels in American history; at times, they exceeded 20 percent.

In the summer of 1979, instability in the Middle East produced a second major fuel shortage in the United States. In the midst of the crisis, OPEC announced another major price increase. Faced with increasing pressure to act, Carter went to Camp David, the presidential retreat in the Maryland mountains. Ten days later, he emerged to deliver a remarkable television address. It included a series of proposals for resolving the energy crisis. But it was most notable for Carter's bleak assessment of the national condition and his remarkable claim that there was a "crisis of confidence" that had struck "at the very heart and soul of our national will." The address became known as the "malaise" speech (although Carter himself had never used that word), and it helped fuel charges that the president was trying to blame his own problems on the American people. Carter's sudden firing of several members of his cabinet a few days later only deepened his political dilemma.

While the president struggled to find the right strategy to correct the economy, he championed a steady course on civil rights. Black and Latino voters had helped him win the White House and Carter never forgot it. Building on his longstanding commitment to full equality for all Americans, he zealously defended modern civil rights acts. He built a senior leadership team that included the first black female cabinet member (Patricia Roberts Harris), ambassador to the United Nations (Andrew Young), and head of the Civil Rights Division of the Department of Justice (Drew Days). He appointed more women, Latinos, and blacks as federal judges than all former administrations combined. Carter also expanded funding for historically black colleges and universities and defended federal policies on affirmative action. Although he failed to significantly improve employment, housing, and health-care policies for poor minority Americans, Carter was still a strong advocate for them.

HUMAN RIGHTS AND NATIONAL INTERESTS

Among Jimmy Carter's most frequent campaign promises was a new American foreign policy based partly on the defense of "human rights." Carter spoke out sharply about human rights violations in many countries (including, most prominently, the Soviet Union). But the administration also focused on more traditional concerns. Carter completed negotiations begun several years earlier on a pair of treaties to turn over control of the Panama Canal to the government of Panama. After an acrimonious debate, the Senate ratified the treaties by 68 to 32, only one vote more than the necessary two-thirds majority.

Carter's greatest success was in arranging a peace treaty between Egypt and Israel. Middle East negotiations had seemed hopelessly stalled until Egyptian president Anwar Sadat accepted an invitation in November 1977 from Prime Minister Menachem Begin to visit Israel. In Tel Aviv, he announced that Egypt was now willing to accept the state of Israel as a legitimate political entity.

When talks between Israeli and Egyptian negotiators stalled, Carter invited Sadat and Begin to a summit conference at Camp David in September 1978 and persuaded them to remain there for two weeks. On September 17, Carter escorted the two leaders into the White House to announce an agreement on a "framework" for an Egyptian–Israeli peace treaty, known as the **Camp David accords**. On March 26, 1979, Begin and Sadat returned together to the White House to sign a formal peace treaty between their two nations.

In the meantime, Carter continued trying to improve relations with China and the Soviet Union. He responded eagerly to the overtures of Deng Xiaoping, the new Chinese leader attempting to open his nation to the outside world. On December 15, 1978, Washington and Beijing announced the resumption of formal diplomatic relations. A few months later, Carter traveled to Vienna to meet with the aging and ailing Brezhnev to finish drafting the new Strategic Arms Limitations Treaty II (SALT II) arms control agreement, which set limits on the number of long-range missiles, bombers, and nuclear warheads on each side. Almost immediately, however, SALT II met with fierce conservative opposition in the U.S. Senate. The agreement was never ratified.

THE YEAR OF THE HOSTAGES

Since the early 1950s, the United States had provided political support and, more recently, massive military assistance to the government of the shah of Iran, hoping to make his nation a bulwark against Soviet expansion in the Middle East. By 1979, however, the shah was in deep trouble with his own people. Many Iranians resented the repressive, authoritarian tactics through which the shah had maintained his autocratic rule. At the same time, Islamic clergy (and much of the fiercely religious populace) opposed his efforts to modernize and Westernize Iranian society. The combination of resentments fueled a powerful revolutionary movement, which forced the shah to flee the country in January 1979.

By late 1979, power in Iran resided with a zealous religious leader, the **Ayatollah Ruhollah Khomeini**, who was fiercely anti-Western and anti-American. In late October 1979, the deposed shah arrived in New York to be treated for cancer. Days later, on November 4, an armed crowd stormed the American embassy in Tehran, seized the diplomats and military personnel inside, and demanded the return of the shah to Iran in exchange for their freedom. Fifty-three Americans remained hostages in the embassy for over a year.

Only weeks after the hostage seizure, on December 27, 1979, Soviet troops invaded Afghanistan, the mountainous Islamic nation lying between the Soviet Union and Iran. The Soviet Union had been a power in Afghanistan for years and the dominant force since

April 1978; a rebellion by radical Islamic guerrilla groups threatened the new Soviet-backed government. But while some observers claimed that the Soviet invasion was a Russian attempt to secure the status quo, Carter claimed it was a Russian "stepping stone to their possible control over much of the world's oil supplies" and the "gravest threat to world peace since World War II." Carter angrily imposed a series of economic sanctions on the Russians, canceled American participation in the 1980 summer Olympic Games in Moscow, and announced the withdrawal of SALT II from Senate consideration.

THE RISE OF THE NEW CONSERVATIVE MOVEMENT

The jarring social and economic changes in American life in the 1960s and 1970s provided the political right with its most important opportunity in generations to recapture a dominant position of political authority in American life.

THE SUNBELT AND ITS POLITICS

One of the most widely discussed demographic phenomena of the 1970s was the rise of what became known as the **Sunbelt**—the states of the Southeast and the Southwest. By 1980, the population of the Sunbelt had risen to exceed that of the older industrial regions of the North and the East, which gave the region newfound political power through an increased number of members of the House of Representative. This shift of people and politics directly contributed to the explosive growth of the modern conservative movement.

The strong Populist traditions in the South and the West helped produce opposition to the growth of government and resentment of the proliferating regulations and restrictions. Many of those regulations and restrictions—environmental laws, land-use restrictions, and other laws—affected the West more than any other region.

In the late 1970s, for example, a small movement arose to roll back environmental laws and policies governing and protecting western lands. Nicknamed the **Sagebrush Rebellion** for the shrub common to the mountainous region of the West, its advocates aimed to privatize large swaths of federal land or transfer ownership of them to the states so that they could be opened for commercial development, including mining. While none of the goals of the Sagebrush Rebellion were achieved, it showcased a building popular appetite for local control over politics and land.

The growth of suburbs also fueled a burgeoning spirit of localism and suspicion of federal intervention in the conduct of everyday life. Indeed, beginning in the 1950s but accelerating in the 1960s and 1970s, some of the most conservative communities developed in the suburbs ringing major Sunbelt cities like Dallas, Phoenix, and Los Angeles. The new suburbanites—often but not always white and middle class—hoped to escape rising crime rates and struggling public schools in urban areas. Some also desired to bring up their children in insular communities with others of their own race and class.

RELIGIOUS REVIVALISM

Mainstream denominations within Christianity began to decline or grow very slowly after World War II. The political and social tumult of the 1960s deepened this trend by firing suspicion of traditional authority, both civil and religious. But it also fueled a spiritual revival.

GROWTH OF THE SUNBELT, 1970–1990   One of the most important demographic changes of the last decades of the twentieth century was the shift of population out of traditional population centers in the Northeast and Midwest and toward the states of the so-called Sunbelt—most notably the Southwest and the Pacific Coast. This map gives a dramatic illustration of the changing concentration of population between 1970 and 1990. The orange states are those that lost population, while the purple and blue states are those that made significant gains (30 percent or more). • *What was the impact of this population shift on the politics of the 1980s?*

Seeking to cast off familiar conventions of worship, Americans sought new forms of spiritual experience that promised fresh understandings of the divine and new communities. It led to the rise of alternative movements and unorthodox faiths: the Church of Scientology; the Unification Church of the Reverend Sun Myung Moon; and even the tragic People's Temple, many of whom committed mass suicide in their jungle retreat in Guyana in 1978. But most importantly it inspired the growth of modern evangelical Christianity.

Evangelicals share a belief in being "born again" through direct communication with Jesus. Evangelical Christianity, with its emphasis on personal conversion and salvation, has roots in American religious history extending as far back as the eighteenth century. In its modern form, it became increasingly visible during the early 1950s when evangelicals such as Billy Graham and Pentecostals such as Oral Roberts began to attract huge national and international audiences for their energetic revivals. In the following decades, evangelical Christians became even more visible, printing their own newspapers and founding their own radio stations and television networks. Three modern presidents—Jimmy Carter, Bill Clinton, and George W. Bush—and more than 70 million Americans today openly identify themselves as evangelicals.

Some evangelical Christians, following the path of religious civil rights leaders like Rev. Martin Luther King, worked tirelessly to promote racial and economic justice and world peace. But many others had a different political focus, aimed at preserving the traditional values that they believed were being eroded by the new youth culture and progressive movements. This group became known as the "Christian right."

By the late 1970s, the Christian right had become a powerful political force. Jerry Falwell, a fundamentalist minister in Virginia with a substantial television audience, launched a highly visible movement he called the Moral Majority. He founded Liberty University in Lynchburg, Virginia, to train men and women according to conservative Christian principles. The Pentecostal minister Pat Robertson began a political movement of his own and, in the 1990s, launched an organization known as the **Christian Coalition**. These and other organizations of the Christian right opposed federal interference in local affairs; denounced abortion, divorce, feminism, and homosexuality; defended unrestricted free enterprise; and supported a strong American posture in the world. Some denied the scientific doctrine of evolution and instead urged the teaching in schools of the biblical story of the Creation or—beginning in the early twenty-first century—the idea of "intelligent design." Their goal was a new era in which "Christian values" once again dominated American life.

Evangelicals were not the only Christians to back conservative causes. In the 1970s, the Catholic Church also began to insert itself more directly into politics, making a strong case

(©Mark Meyer/The LIFE Images Collection/Getty Images)

NEW SPIRITUAL LEADERS Rev. Jerry Falwell, a Baptist minister and pioneer in Christian television and radio, founded the Moral Majority in 1979 to inject evangelical values into the political mainstream. It was a key component of the Christian Coalition that helped elected Ronald Reagan to the White House.

for what it called "traditional values" as well. The Church fought most aggressively against abortion, joining evangelicals in the "right to life" movement. Not all Catholics were or are conservatives; indeed, many priests and parishioners took strong liberal positions. But in the political world, Catholics became strong allies of evangelicals on most issues.

Mormons, too, became active members of the Christian right. For many years, Mormons did not publicize their conservatism. But like Catholics, many began to take openly conservative stances in the 1970s on some of the most controversial battles of the time. Some of these Mormons, wealthy and successful businesspeople, became powerful conservative politicians in various parts of the country. In 2012, Republican Mitt Romney was the first Mormon to secure his party's nomination for the presidency.

THE EMERGENCE OF THE NEW RIGHT

Religious issues were only a part—although an important part—of what became known as the **New Right**—a diverse but powerful movement that enjoyed rapid growth in the 1970s and early 1980s. It had begun to take shape after the 1964 election, in which Republican Barry Goldwater had suffered his shattering defeat. Energetic organizers responded to that disaster by building a new and powerful set of right-wing institutions to help conservatives campaign more effectively in the future. Among their innovations was the creation of a direct-mail operation that ultimately reached millions of conservative voters. Beginning in the 1970s, largely because of these organizational advances, conservatives found themselves almost always better funded and organized than their opponents. By the late 1970s, there were right-wing think tanks, consulting firms, lobbyists, foundations, and colleges and universities. Conservatives also succeeded in developing systems to raise money, mobilize activists, and project their ideas to a broad audience. Evangelicals such as Pat Robertson used cable television to reach the conservative faithful. Conservative radio hosts such as Rush Limbaugh created shows that attracted a vast national audience.

Another factor in the revival of the right was the emergence in the late 1960s and early 1970s of **Ronald Reagan**. Once a moderately successful actor, he had moved into politics in the early 1960s and in 1964 delivered a memorable television speech on behalf of Goldwater. After Goldwater's defeat, Reagan worked quickly to seize the leadership of the conservative wing of the party. In 1966, with the support of a group of wealthy conservatives, he won the first of two terms as governor of California.

The presidency of Gerald Ford also played an important role in the rise of conservatism. Ford, probably without realizing it, touched on some of the right's rawest nerves. He appointed as vice president Nelson Rockefeller, the liberal Republican governor of New York and an heir to one of America's great fortunes; many conservatives had been demonizing Rockefeller and his family for more than twenty years. Ford proposed an amnesty program for draft resisters, embraced the hated Nixon–Kissinger policies of détente, presided over the fall of Vietnam, and agreed to cede the Panama Canal to Panama. When Reagan challenged Ford in the 1976 Republican primaries, the president survived, barely, only by dumping Nelson Rockefeller from the ticket and replacing him with Kansas senator Robert Dole, a steadfast conservative. He also agreed to a platform largely written by conservatives.

THE TAX REVOLT

At least equally important to the success of the New Right was a new and potent conservative issue: the tax revolt. It had its public beginnings in 1978, when Howard Jarvis, a conservative activist in California, launched Proposition 13, a referendum question on the state ballot rolling back property tax rates. Because property taxes were the most important source of funding for schools, the passage of Proposition 13 began the slow deterioration of much of the California education system. Similar antitax movements soon began in other states and eventually spread to national politics.

In Proposition 13 and similar initiatives, members of the right succeeded in separating the issue of taxes from the issue of what taxes supported. Instead of attacking popular programs such as Social Security, they attacked taxes themselves and argued that much of the money government raised through taxes was wasted. Virtually no one liked to pay taxes, and as the economy grew weaker and the relative burden of paying taxes grew heavier, that resentment naturally rose.

THE CAMPAIGN OF 1980

By the time of the crises in Iran and Afghanistan, Jimmy Carter was in desperate political trouble—his standing in popularity polls was lower than that of any president in history. Senator Edward Kennedy, younger brother of John and Robert Kennedy, challenged him in the primaries. And while Carter managed to withstand the confrontation and win his party's nomination, his campaign aroused little popular enthusiasm. The stage was set for sweeping political change.

The Republican Party, in the meantime, rallied enthusiastically behind the man who, four years earlier, had nearly stolen the nomination from Gerald Ford. Ronald Reagan was

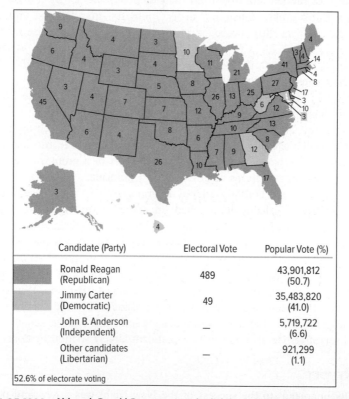

Candidate (Party)	Electoral Vote	Popular Vote (%)
Ronald Reagan (Republican)	489	43,901,812 (50.7)
Jimmy Carter (Democratic)	49	35,483,820 (41.0)
John B. Anderson (Independent)	—	5,719,722 (6.6)
Other candidates (Libertarian)	—	921,299 (1.1)

52.6% of electorate voting

THE ELECTION OF 1980   Although Ronald Reagan won only slightly more than half of the popular vote in the 1980 presidential election, his electoral majority was overwhelming—a reflection to a large degree of the deep unpopularity of President Jimmy Carter in 1980. • *What had made Carter so unpopular?*

a sharp critic of the excesses of the federal government. He linked his campaign to the spreading tax revolt by promising substantial tax cuts. He claimed that he would restore America's standing as the greatest economic and military power in the world, tapping into the public's frustration over a flagging economy and the fact that American citizens remained hostages in Iran.

On election day 1980, the anniversary of the seizure of the hostages in Iran, Reagan swept to victory, winning 51 percent of the vote to 41 percent for Jimmy Carter and 7 percent for John Anderson—a moderate Republican congressman from Illinois who had mounted an independent campaign. The Republican Party won control of the Senate for the first time since 1952; and although the Democrats retained a modest majority in the House, the lower chamber, too, seemed firmly in the hands of conservatives.

On the day of Reagan's inauguration, the American hostages in Iran were released after their 444-day ordeal. The government of Iran, desperate for funds to support its floundering war against neighboring Iraq, had ordered the hostages freed in return for a release of billions in Iranian assets that the Carter administration had frozen in American banks. Americans welcomed the hostages home with demonstrations of joy and patriotism seldom seen since the end of World War II. But while the celebration in 1945 had marked a great American triumph, the euphoria in 1981 marked something quite different—a troubled nation grasping for reassurance. Ronald Reagan set out to provide it.

THE "REAGAN REVOLUTION"

Ronald Reagan assumed the presidency in January 1981, promising a revolution in government more fundamental than any since the New Deal of fifty years before. (See "Consider the Source: Ronald Reagan on the Role of Government.") While his eight years in office produced a significant shift in public policy, they brought nothing so fundamental as many of his supporters had hoped or his opponents had feared. But Reagan succeeded brilliantly in making his own engaging personality the central fact of American politics in the 1980s. He also benefited from the power of the diverse coalition that had united behind him.

THE REAGAN COALITION

The Reagan coalition included a relatively small but highly influential group of wealthy Americans firmly committed to capitalism with little to no interference by the government. Reagan courted these free-market conservatives carefully and effectively, and in the end it was their interests his administration most effectively served. They believed that the "market" offered the best solutions to most problems, and they shared a deep hostility to most (although not all) government interference in markets. Central to this group's agenda in the 1980s was opposition to what it scorned as the "redistributive" economic politics of the government (especially its highly progressive tax structure) and hostility to the rise of what they believed were "antibusiness" government regulations. "Smaller government" was one of their favorite mantras.

A second element of the Reagan coalition consisted of a small but influential group of intellectuals commonly known as **neoconservatives**, who gave to the right something it had not had in many years—a firm base among "opinion leaders," people with access to the most influential public forums of ideas. Many of these people had once been liberals and, before that, socialists. But during the turmoil of the 1960s, they had become alarmed by

RONALD REAGAN ON THE ROLE OF GOVERNMENT (1981)

In this excerpt from his first inaugural address, on January 20, 1981, Ronald Reagan laid out his central vision for the role of government in society. Questioning the ability of government to solve society's social and economic ills, Reagan argued that the key to the nation's future lay in reducing the role of government in everyday life.

The economic ills we suffer have come upon us over several decades. They will not go away in days, weeks, or months, but they will go away. They will go away because we as Americans have the capacity now, as we've had in the past, to do whatever needs to be done to preserve this last and greatest bastion of freedom.

In this present crisis, government is not the solution to our problem; government is the problem. From time to time we've been tempted to believe that society has become too complex to be managed by self-rule, that government by an elite group is superior to government for, by, and of the people. Well, if no one among us is capable of governing himself, then who among us has the capacity to govern someone else? All of us together, in and out of government, must bear the burden. The solutions we seek must be equitable, with no one group singled out to pay a higher price.

We hear much of special interest groups. Well, our concern must be for a special interest group that has been too long neglected. It knows no sectional boundaries or ethnic and racial divisions, and it crosses political party lines. It is made up of men and women who raise our food, patrol our streets, man our mines and factories, teach our children, keep our homes, and heal us when we're sick—professionals, industrialists, shopkeepers, clerks, cabbies, and truck drivers. They are, in short, "We the people," this breed called Americans.

Well, this administration's objective will be a healthy, vigorous, growing economy that provides equal opportunities for all Americans with no barriers born of bigotry or discrimination. Putting America back to work means putting all Americans back to work. Ending inflation means freeing all Americans from the terror of runaway living costs. All must share in the productive work of this "new beginning," and all must share in the bounty of a revived economy. With the idealism and fair play which are the core of our system and our strength, we can have a strong and prosperous America, at peace with itself and the world.

So, as we begin, let us take inventory. We are a nation that has a government—not the other way around. And this makes us special among the nations of the Earth. Our government has no power except that granted it by the people. It is time to check and reverse the growth of government, which shows signs of having grown beyond the consent of the governed.

It is my intention to curb the size and influence of the Federal establishment and to demand recognition of the distinction between the powers granted to the Federal Government and those reserved to the States or to the people. All of us need to be reminded that the Federal Government did not create the States; the States created the Federal Government.

Now, so there will be no misunderstanding, it's not my intention to do away with government. It is rather to make it work—work with us, not over us; to stand by our side, not ride on our back. Government can and must provide opportunity, not smother it; foster productivity, not stifle it.

If we look to the answer as to why for so many years we achieved so much, prospered as no other people on Earth, it was because here in this land we unleashed the energy and individual genius of man to a greater extent than has ever been done before. Freedom and the dignity of the individual have been more available and assured here than in any other place on Earth. The price for this freedom at times has been high, but we have never been unwilling to pay that price.

It is no coincidence that our present troubles parallel and are proportionate to the intervention and intrusion in our lives that result from unnecessary and excessive growth of government. It is time for us to realize that we're too great a nation to limit ourselves to small dreams. We're not, as some would have us believe, doomed to an inevitable decline. I do not believe in a fate that will fall on us no matter what we do. I do believe in a fate that will fall on us if we

do nothing. So, with all the creative energy at our command, let us begin an era of national renewal. Let us renew our determination, our courage, and our strength. And let us renew our faith and our hope.

UNDERSTAND, ANALYZE, & EVALUATE

1. What does Reagan mean when he says, in the opening lines of the second paragraph, that "government is the problem"?
2. Why did Reagan's call for a curb on the government's role in society and the economy strike such a popular chord in the 1980s?
3. According to Reagan, who has been treated unfairly under the previous administration? Whom are the disadvantaged?

Source: The Ronald Reagan Presidential Library, National Archives and Records Administration, www.reagan.utexas.edu/archives/speeches/1981/12081a.htm

what they considered a dangerous and destructive radicalism. Neoconservatives were sympathetic to the complaints and demands of capitalists, but their principal concern was to reassert legitimate authority and reaffirm Western democratic, anticommunist values and commitments. They considered themselves soldiers in a battle to "win back the culture"— from the crass, radical ideas that had polluted it.

Neoconservatives also strongly dissented from the new foreign policy orthodoxies of liberals and the left in the aftermath of the Vietnam War. These self-proclaimed "defense hawks" utterly rejected the idea that America should be a less interventionist nation, that it should work to ease tensions with the Soviet Union, and that it should tolerate radical regimes. Instead, they argued for an escalation of the Cold War as part of an effort to destabilize the Soviet Union. They insisted that the Vietnam War was an appropriate American commitment and that its abandonment was a terrible mistake. They believed that the United States had a special role to play in the world and should be willing to use military intervention to secure its vision. These ideas strongly influenced the foreign policy of the Reagan administration. The same ideas (and some of the same people) resurfaced in the early twenty-first century to help shape the international policies of the George W. Bush administration.

Free-market conservatives and neoconservatives formed an uneasy alliance with the broad grassroots conservative movement to collectively create the New Right. All shared a fundamental distrust of the "eastern establishment" that supposedly ruled Washington: a suspicion of its motives and goals and a sense that it exercised a dangerous, secret power in American life. Grassroots conservatives also feared living in a world where distant, secretive forces controlled society and threatened individual freedom and community autonomy—a point of view that could have turned them against the elite leaders who led the free-market conservatives and the neoconservatives. It was a testament to

Ronald Reagan's political skills and personal charm that he was able to generate enthusiastic support from all of these factions.

REAGAN IN THE WHITE HOUSE

Even many people who disagreed with Reagan's policies found themselves drawn to his attractive and carefully honed public image. He was sixty-nine upon taking office and was the oldest man to serve as president, until the inauguration of the seventy-year-old Donald Trump in 2017. But through most of his presidency, he appeared to be vigorous, resilient, even youthful. When wounded in an assassination attempt in 1981, he joked with doctors on his way into surgery and appeared to bounce back from the ordeal with remarkable speed. Even when things went wrong, as they often did, the blame seldom seemed to attach to Reagan himself (inspiring some Democrats to refer to him as the "Teflon president").

Reagan was not much involved in the day-to-day affairs of running the government; he surrounded himself with tough, energetic administrators who insulated him from many of the pressures of the office and who apparently relied on him largely for general guidance, not specific decisions. At times, the president revealed a startling ignorance about the nature of his own policies or the actions of his subordinates. But Reagan did make active use of his office to generate public support for his administration's programs.

(©Dirck Halstead/The LIFE Images Collection/Getty Images)

RONALD AND NANCY REAGAN   The president and the first lady greet guests at a White House social event. Nancy Reagan was committed to making the White House, and her husband's presidency, seem more glamorous than those of most recent administrations. But she also played an important, if usually quiet, policy role in the administration.

"Supply-Side" Economics

Reagan's 1980 campaign for the presidency had promised to restore the economy to health by a bold experiment that became known as "supply-side"—or, to its critics, "trickle-down"—economics. Eventually, it was called **Reaganomics**. Supply-side economics operated from the assumption that the woes of the American economy were in large part a result of excessive taxation, which left inadequate capital available to investors to stimulate growth. The solution, therefore, was to reduce taxes, with particularly generous benefits to corporations and wealthy individuals, in order to encourage new investments.

In its first months in office, the new administration hastily assembled a legislative program based on the supply-side idea. It proposed $40 billion in budget reductions and managed to win congressional approval of almost all of them. In addition, the president proposed a bold three-year, 30 percent reduction on both individual and corporate tax rates. In the summer of 1981, Congress passed it, too, after lowering the reductions to 25 percent. Reagan owed his legislative success to a disciplined Republican majority in the Senate and a Democratic majority in the House that was weak and riddled with defectors.

Reagan appointees in the executive branch of government aimed to reduce the role of government in American economic life. **Deregulation**, an idea many Democrats had begun to embrace in the Carter years, became almost a religion in the Reagan administration, especially in its environmental policies. Secretary of the Interior James Watt, a major figure in the Sagebrush Rebellion, opened up public lands and water to development and led a charge to reverse older conservationist policies. The administration ultimately permitted coal, gas, and oil corporations to prospect and develop millions of acres of federal land. Anne Gorsuch, director of the Environmental Protection Agency, slashed its budget by about 25 percent and relaxed or eliminated enforcement against polluters. She eventually resigned amid accusations that she mismanaged the $1.6 billion superfund dedicated for the cleanup of toxic waste sites. Despite his deregulation focus, Reagan signed the Montreal Protocol in 1987, an international treaty committing nations to reducing the production of harmful substances shown to deplete the ozone. And during his term of office he designated more than 10 million acres across twenty-seven states as federal wilderness.

By early 1982, the nation had sunk into a severe recession. The Reagan economic program was not directly to blame for the problems, but neither did it offer a quick solution. During 1982, unemployment reached 11 percent, one of the highest levels since the 1930s. But before the recession could do great damage to Reagan, the economy recovered more rapidly and impressively than almost anyone had expected. By late 1983, unemployment had fallen to 8.2 percent, and it declined steadily for several years after that. The gross national product (GNP) grew 3.6 percent in a year, the largest increase since the mid-1970s. Inflation fell below 5 percent. The economy continued to grow, and both inflation and unemployment remained low through most of the decade.

The recovery was a result of many things. Prior years of tight money policies by the Federal Reserve Board had helped lower inflation; perhaps equally important, the Fed had lowered interest rates early in 1983 in response to the recession. A worldwide "energy glut" and the virtual collapse of the OPEC cartel had produced at least a temporary end to the inflationary pressures of spiraling fuel costs. Gas prices now came down. At the same time, the federal government began to pump more money into the economy, especially in research and development for businesses. As a result of this "deficit spending" (when the government spends more money than it takes in and thus incurs a deficit in its budget), business investment and consumer spending increased. The stock market rose up from its doldrums of the 1970s and began a sustained and historic boom. In August 1982, the Dow Jones Industrial Average stood at 777. Five years later it had passed 2,000. Despite a frightening crash in the fall of 1987, the market continued to grow for more than another decade.

The Fiscal Crisis

The economic revival did little at first to reduce the staggering, and to many Americans alarming, federal budget deficits (the gap between revenue and spending in a single year) or to slow the growth in the national debt (the debt the nation accumulates over time to pay its bills). By the mid-1980s, this growing fiscal crisis had become one of the central issues in American politics. Having entered office promising a balanced budget within four years, Reagan presided over record budget deficits and accumulated more debt in his eight years in office than the American government had accumulated in its entire previous history. Before the 1980s, the highest single-year budget deficit in American history had been $66 billion (in 1976). Throughout the 1980s, the annual budget deficit consistently exceeded $100 billion. (The deficit peaked in 1991 at $268 billion.) The national debt rose from $907 billion in 1980 to nearly $3.5 trillion by 1991. Much larger deficits—and debt—were soon to come.

The enormous deficits had many causes. The budget suffered from steep increases in the costs of "entitlement" programs (especially both Social Security and Medicare), a result of the aging of the population and dramatic increases in the cost of health care. The 1981 tax cuts, the largest in American history, also contributed to the deficit. The massive increase in military spending on which the Reagan administration insisted added much more to the federal budget than its cuts in domestic spending removed.

In the face of these deficits, the administration proposed further cuts in "discretionary" domestic spending, which included many programs aimed at the poorest (and politically weakest) Americans. By the end of Reagan's third year in office, funding for domestic programs had been cut nearly as far as Congress (and, apparently, the public) was willing to tolerate, and still no end to the rising deficit was in sight. By the late 1980s, many fiscal conservatives were calling for a constitutional amendment mandating a balanced budget—a provision the president himself claimed to support. But Congress never approved the amendment.

Reagan's policies of reduced government hurt the very poor. In his enthusiasm to minimize the scope and power of the federal government in daily life and trim the budget, he reversed decades of Washington-led efforts to revitalize and improve local communities. During his eight years in the White House, Reagan cut federal assistance to state and municipal governments by about 60 percent. He slashed funds for public transportation, job training, legal services for the poor, and the Community Development Block Grant Program. America's largest cities felt the biggest pinch: federal aid fell from 22 percent of their overall budgets to 6 percent. Housing for the poor was hit especially hard. The president aimed to increase the nation's reliance on the private market to house the indigent. And so he sliced in half the budget for public housing and Section 8 housing, where the government subsidizes private landlords to rent to low-income individuals. He also reduced the budget for the Department of Housing and Urban Development from $32 billion to $7.5 billion. Not surprisingly, rates of homelessness skyrocketed to over 2 million by the time the president left office.

Reagan and the World

Relations with the Soviet Union, which had been steadily deteriorating in the last years of the Carter administration, grew still chillier in the first years of the Reagan presidency. The president spoke harshly of the Soviet regime (which he once called the "evil empire"), accusing it of sponsoring world terrorism and declaring that any armaments negotiations must be linked to negotiations on Soviet behavior in other areas. Although the president had long denounced the SALT II arms control treaty as unfavorable to the United States, he continued to honor its provisions. But the president proposed the most ambitious (and potentially most expensive) new military program in many years: the **Strategic Defense Initiative (SDI)**, widely known as "Star Wars" after the popular movie of that name. Reagan claimed that SDI, through the use of lasers and satellites, could provide an effective shield against incoming missiles and thus make nuclear war obsolete. The Soviet Union claimed that the new program would elevate the arms race to new and more dangerous levels and insisted that any arms control agreement should begin with an American abandonment of SDI.

The escalation of Cold War tensions and the slowing of arms control initiatives helped produce an important popular movement in Europe and the United States calling for a "nuclear freeze," an agreement between the two superpowers not to expand their atomic arsenals. In what many at the time believed was the largest mass demonstration in American history, nearly a million people rallied in New York City's Central Park in 1982 to support the freeze. Perhaps partly in response to this growing pressure, the administration began tentative efforts to revive arms control negotiations in 1983.

The administration created a new policy known as the **Reagan Doctrine**, designed to help resist communism and anti-Americanism in the Third World. The United States sent soldiers and money to aid guerrillas and resistance movements in countries with anti-American governments—among them Grenada, El Salvador, and Nicaragua. But Reagan generally backed away from more serious warfare. In 1982, when the Israeli army invaded Lebanon, American peacekeeping forces entered Beirut to stabilize the nation. But when a terrorist bombing of a U.S. military barracks in Beirut led to the death of 241 marines, Reagan quickly withdrew the American forces.

Reagan approached the campaign of 1984 at the head of a united Republican Party firmly committed to his candidacy. The Democrats nominated Carter's vice president, Walter Mondale. Mondale brought momentary excitement to the Democratic campaign by selecting a woman, Representative Geraldine Ferraro of New York, to be his running mate and the first female candidate ever to appear on a national ticket. But Reagan's triumphant campaign scarcely took note of his opponents and spoke instead of what he claimed was the remarkable revival of American fortunes and spirits under his leadership, or what he sometimes called "Morning in America." He won 59 percent of the vote and carried every state but Mondale's native Minnesota and the District of Columbia.

THE WANING OF THE COLD WAR

Many factors contributed to the collapse of the Soviet Empire. The long, stalemated war in Afghanistan proved at least as disastrous to the Soviet Union as the Vietnam War had been to America. The government in Moscow failed to address a long-term economic decline in the Soviet republics and the Eastern-bloc nations. Restiveness with the heavy-handed policies of communist police states was growing throughout much of the Soviet Empire. But the most visible factor at the time was the emergence of **Mikhail Gorbachev**, who succeeded to the leadership of the Soviet Union in 1985 and, to the surprise of almost everyone (probably including himself), very quickly became the most revolutionary figure in world politics in decades.

THE FALL OF THE SOVIET UNION

Gorbachev transformed Soviet politics with two dramatic new initiatives: *glasnost* (openness), the dismantling of many of the repressive mechanisms that had been conspicuous features of Soviet life for over half a century, and *perestroika* (reform), an effort to restructure the rigid and unproductive Soviet economy by introducing, among other things, such elements of capitalism as private ownership and the profit motive. He also began to transform Soviet foreign policy.

The severe economic problems at home evidently convinced Gorbachev that the Soviet Union could no longer sustain its extended commitments around the world. As early as 1987, he began reducing the Soviet presence in Eastern Europe. And in 1989, in the space of a few months, every communist state in Europe—Poland, Hungary, Czechoslovakia, Bulgaria, Romania, East Germany, Yugoslavia, and Albania—either overthrew its government or forced it to transform itself into an essentially noncommunist (and in some cases, actively anticommunist) regime. Perhaps the most dramatic event of this extraordinary revolution was the tearing down of the infamous Berlin Wall.

Not all international protests against communism were so successful. In May 1989, students in China launched a mass movement calling for greater democratization. But in June, hard-line leaders seized control of the government and sent military forces to crush the uprising. The result was a bloody massacre on June 3, 1989, in **Tiananmen Square** in Beijing, in which an unknown number of demonstrators died. The assault crushed the democracy movement and restored hard-liners to power. It did not, however, stop China's efforts to modernize and even Westernize its economy.

But China was an exception to the widespread movement toward democratization. Early in 1990, the government of South Africa, long an international pariah for its rigid enforcement

(©Sueddeutsche Zeitung Photo/Alamy)

THE FALL OF THE BERLIN WALL The Berlin Wall is widely considered to have "fallen" on November 9, 1989. Starting on that date and in the days and weeks that followed, people used sledgehammers and picks to tear down the wall, often keeping the broken pieces as souvenirs of this symbolic conclusion of the Cold War.

of "apartheid" (a system designed to protect white supremacy, much like the Jim Crow system had done in the American South) legalized the chief black party in the nation, the African National Congress (ANC), which had been banned for decades. The government also released from prison the leader of the ANC, **Nelson Mandela**, who had been in jail for twenty-seven years. Over the next several years, the South African government repealed its apartheid laws. And in 1994, there were national elections in which all South Africans could participate. As a result, Nelson Mandela became the first black president of South Africa.

In 1991, communism began to collapse in the Soviet Union itself. An unsuccessful coup by hard-line Soviet leaders on August 19 precipitated a dramatic unraveling of communist power. Within days, the coup itself collapsed in the face of resistance from the public and crucial elements within the military. By the end of August, many of the republics of the Soviet Union had declared independence; the Soviet government was clearly powerless to stop the fragmentation. Gorbachev himself finally resigned as leader of the now virtually powerless Communist Party and Soviet government, and the Soviet Union itself ceased to exist.

The last years of the Reagan administration coincided with the first years of the Gorbachev regime; and while Reagan was skeptical of Gorbachev at first, he gradually became convinced that the Soviet leader was sincere in his desire for reform. In 1988, the two superpowers signed a treaty eliminating American and Soviet intermediate-range nuclear forces (INF) from Europe—the most significant arms control agreement of the nuclear age. At about the same time, Gorbachev ended the Soviet Union's long and frustrating military involvement in Afghanistan.

THE FADING OF THE REAGAN REVOLUTION

For a time, the dramatic changes around the world and Reagan's personal popularity deflected attention from a series of scandals that might well have destroyed another administration, including revelations of illegal and ethical lapses in the Environmental Protection Agency, the CIA, the Department of Defense, the Department of Labor, the Department of Justice, and the Department of Housing and Urban Development. A more serious scandal emerged within the savings and loan industry, which the Reagan administration had helped deregulate in the early 1980s. By the end of the decade, the industry was in chaos, and the government was forced to step in to prevent a complete collapse. The cost of the debacle to the public eventually ran to more than half a trillion dollars.

But the most politically damaging scandal of the Reagan years came to light in November 1986, when the White House conceded that it had sold weapons to the revolutionary government of Iran as part of a largely unsuccessful effort to secure the release of several Americans being held hostage. Even more damaging was the revelation that some of the money from the arms deal with Iran had been covertly and illegally funneled into a fund to aid the Contras, a loose group of commandos who fought against the anti-American government after the 1979 revolution in Nicaragua.

In the months that followed, aggressive reporting and a series of congressional hearings exposed a widespread pattern of covert activities orchestrated by the White House and dedicated to advancing the administration's foreign policy aims through secret and at times illegal means. Reagan's zeal for eliminating communism lay at the heart of the **Iran–Contra scandal**, as it came to be known. Under the president's directive, the CIA had long trained anticommunist fighters around the globe. But Reagan's hands were tied in Nicaragua after the Democrat-controlled Congress passed the Boland Amendment, which severely restricted the CIA and Department of Defense from operating there and prompted senior staff to devise a way around the restriction. The Iran–Contra scandal did serious damage to the Reagan presidency—even though the investigations never tied the president himself to the most serious violations of the law. Most of the highest-ranking Reagan officials indicted or found guilty were either pardoned by future president George H. W. Bush or released on a legal technicality, some after serving a stint in jail.

THE PRESIDENCY OF GEORGE H. W. BUSH

The fraying of the Reagan administration helped the Democrats regain control of the U.S. Senate in 1986 and fueled hopes in the party for a presidential victory in 1988. Michael Dukakis, a three-term governor of Massachusetts, eventually captured the nomination. Vice President **George H. W. Bush** was the largely unopposed Republican candidate. Neither candidate, however, succeeded in whipping up much public enthusiasm.

Beginning at the Republican National Convention, Bush made his campaign a long, relentless attack on Dukakis, tying him to all the unpopular social and cultural stances Americans had come to identify with "liberals" since the 1960s. Bush won a substantial victory in November: 54 percent of the popular vote to Dukakis's 46 percent, and 426 electoral votes to Dukakis's 112. But Bush carried few Republicans into office with him; the Democrats retained secure majorities in both houses of Congress. His victory over Dukakis reflected his subdued, traditional, unthreatening image and years of decorated military and public service. While in the White House, Americans strongly supported him at first because of beneficial turns of international events during his tenure, including most notably the fall of the Berlin Wall, the signing of significant arms agreements with the Soviet Union, and ultimately the Soviet Union's collapse altogether. Equally important were successful military actions in Panama and the prosecution of the Persian Gulf War (see below).

On domestic issues, the Bush administration was less successful. It inherited a staggering burden of debt and a federal deficit that had been growing dramatically for nearly a decade. Constantly concerned about shoring up support from the right wing of his own party, Bush aggressively opposed current laws governing abortion and affirmative action, but his efforts severely damaged his ability to work with the Democratic Congress.

Despite this political stalemate, Congress and the White House managed on occasion to agree on significant measures. In 1990, the president agreed to a significant tax increase as part of a multiyear "budget package" designed to reduce the deficit—thus violating his own 1988 campaign pledge of "no new taxes." But the most serious domestic problem facing the Bush administration was one for which neither the president nor Congress had any answer: a recession that began late in 1990 and became more serious in 1991 and 1992.

THE GULF WAR

The fall of the Soviet Union left the United States in the unanticipated position of being the only real superpower in the world. It forced the Bush administration to consider what to do with America's formidable political and military power.

The events of 1989–1991 suggested two possible answers. One was that the United States would reduce its military strength dramatically and concentrate its energies and resources on pressing domestic problems. The other was that America would continue to use its power actively, not to fight communism but to defend its regional and economic interests.

The answer came quickly. In 1989, the administration ordered an invasion of Panama, which overthrew the unpopular military leader Manuel Noriega (under indictment in the United States for drug trafficking) and replaced him with an elected, pro-American regime. And in 1990, that same impulse drew the United States into the turbulent politics of the Middle East.

On August 2, 1990, the armed forces of Iraq invaded and quickly overwhelmed the emirate of Kuwait, the small oil-rich neighbor of Iraq. **Saddam Hussein**, the militaristic leader of Iraq, soon announced that he was annexing Kuwait. The Bush administration soon agreed to lead other nations in a campaign to force Iraq out of Kuwait—through the pressure of economic sanctions if possible, through military force if necessary. Within a few weeks, Bush had persuaded virtually every important government in the world, including the Soviet Union and almost all the Arab and Islamic states, to join in a United Nations–sanctioned trade embargo of Iraq.

At the same time, the United States and its allies (including the British, French, Egyptians, and Saudis) began deploying a large military force along the border between Kuwait and Saudi Arabia, a force that ultimately reached 690,000 troops (425,000 of them American). And on January 16, American and allied air forces began a massive bombardment of Iraqi troops in Kuwait and of military and industrial installations in Iraq itself.

The allied bombing continued for six weeks. On February 23, allied (primarily American) forces under the command of General Norman Schwarzkopf began a major ground offensive to the north of the Iraqi forces. The allied armies encountered almost no resistance and suffered only light casualties (141 fatalities). Estimates of Iraqi deaths in the war were 100,000 or more. On February 28, Iraq announced its acceptance of allied terms for a cease-fire, and the brief Persian Gulf War was over.

THE ELECTION OF 1992

President Bush's popularity reached a record high in the immediate aftermath of the Gulf War. But the glow of that victory faded quickly as the recession worsened in late 1991. That gave **Bill Clinton**, the young two-term Democratic governor of Arkansas, an opportunity to emerge as the early front-runner. Clinton survived a bruising primary campaign and a series of damaging personal controversies to win his party's nomination.

Complicating the campaign was the emergence of Ross Perot, a blunt, forthright Texas billionaire who became an independent candidate by tapping popular resentment of the federal bureaucracy and by promising tough, uncompromising leadership to deal with the fiscal crisis. At several moments in the spring, Perot led both Bush and Clinton in public opinion polls. But in July, as he began to face hostile scrutiny from the media, he abruptly withdrew from the race. Early in October, he reentered and soon regained much (although never all) of his early support.

After a campaign in which the economy was the principal issue, Clinton won a clear, but hardly overwhelming, victory over Bush and Perot. He received 43 percent of the vote in the three-way race, to the president's 38 percent and Perot's 19 percent (the best showing for a third-party or independent candidate since Theodore Roosevelt in 1912). Clinton won 370 electoral votes to Bush's 168; Perot won none. Democrats also retained control of both houses of Congress. Republicans would have to wait eight years to reclaim the White House, when Bush's son—George W. Bush–would win the presidency.

Candidate (Party)	Electoral Vote	Popular Vote (%)
Bill Clinton (Democratic)	370	44,909,889 (43.0)
George Bush (Republican)	168	39,104,545 (37.5)
Ross Perot (Independent)	0	19,742,267 (18.9)
Other candidates	—	669,958 (0.6)

55.2% of electorate voting

THE ELECTION OF 1992 In the 1992 election, for the first time since 1976, a Democrat captured the White House. And although the third-party candidacy of Ross Perot deprived Bill Clinton of an absolute majority, he nevertheless defeated George Bush by a decisive margin in both the popular and electoral votes. • *What factors had eroded President Bush's once-broad popularity by 1992? What explained the strong showing of Ross Perot?*

CONCLUSION

America in the late 1970s was, by the standards of its own recent history, an unusually troubled nation—numbed by the Watergate scandals, the fall of Vietnam, and perhaps most of all the nation's increasing economic difficulties. The unhappy presidencies of Gerald Ford and Jimmy Carter provided little relief from these accumulating problems and anxieties. Indeed, in the last year of the Carter presidency, the nation's future seemed particularly bleak in light of severe economic problems, a traumatic seizure of American hostages in Iran, and a Soviet invasion of Afghanistan.

In the midst of these problems, American conservatives slowly and steadily prepared for a political revolution. A coalition of disparate but impassioned groups on the right—including a large movement known as the "New Right," with vaguely Populist impulses—gained strength from the nation's troubles and from their own success in winning support for a broad-ranging revolt against taxes. Their efforts culminated in the election of 1980, when Ronald Reagan became the most conservative man in at least sixty years to be elected president of the United States.

Reagan's first term was a dramatic contrast to the troubled presidencies that had preceded it and signaled a reversal or at least a modification of ruling economic and social policies.

He won substantial victories in Congress (cutting taxes, reducing spending on domestic programs, building up the military). Perhaps equally important, he made his own engaging personality one of the central political forces in national life. Easily reelected in 1984, he seemed to have solidified the conservative grip on national political life. In his second term, however, a series of scandals and misadventures—and the president's own declining energy—limited the administration's effectiveness. Nevertheless, Reagan's personal popularity remained high, and the economy continued to prosper—factors that propelled his vice president, George H. W. Bush, to succeed him in 1989.

Bush's presidency was not as successful as Reagan's had been, and the perception of his disengagement with and inability to solve the nation's growing economic problems contributed to Bush's defeat in 1992. But a colossal historic event overshadowed most domestic concerns during Bush's term in office: the collapse of the Soviet Union and the fall of communist regimes all over Europe. The United States was to some degree a dazzled observer of this process. The end of the Cold War also propelled the United States into the possession of unchallenged global preeminence—and drew it increasingly into the role of international arbiter and peacemaker. The Gulf War of 1991 was the most dramatic example of the new global role the United States would now increasingly assume as the world's only true superpower.

KEY TERMS/PEOPLE/PLACES/EVENTS

Ayatollah Ruhollah
  Khomeini 765
Bill Clinton 781
Camp David accords 765
Christian Coalition 768
deregulation 775
George H. W. Bush 780
Gerald R. Ford 762

Iran–Contra scandal 779
Jimmy Carter 764
Mikhail Gorbachev 777
Nelson Mandela 779
neoconservatives 771
New Right 769
Reagan Doctrine 777
Reaganomics 775

Ronald Reagan 769
Saddam Hussein 781
Sagebrush Rebellion 766
stagflation 763
Strategic Defense Initiative
  (SDI) 777
Sunbelt 766
Tiananmen Square 778

RECALL AND REFLECT

1. Why were the Ford and Carter presidencies unable to repair the damage done to the reputation of the presidency by the Watergate scandal and Nixon's resignation?
2. Why did the American electorate become increasingly conservative during the 1970s and 1980s? What are some examples that testify to this increasing conservatism?
3. What philosophy guided foreign policy under Reagan? How did the rise of Mikhail Gorbachev alter Reagan's foreign policy toward the Soviet Union?

31 | THE AGE OF GLOBALIZATION

●

A RESURGENCE OF PARTISANSHIP

SCIENCE AND TECHNOLOGY
  IN THE NEW ECONOMY

A CHANGING SOCIETY

AMERICA IN THE WORLD

LOOKING AHEAD

1. How did increasing partisanship affect governing during the late 1900s and early 2000s? How does it continue to affect the relationship between the president and Congress?

2. How did the growth of the "new economy" affect how Americans worked and lived?

3. How was the American population changing at the turn of the century? What characterized it, and what key challenges does it pose?

4. How did the terrorist attack of September 11, 2001, affect the United States and begin a new era in American foreign policy?

●

ON AN EARLY TUESDAY MORNING IN 2001, a commercial airliner crashed into the side of one of two tallest buildings in New York, the North Tower of the World Trade Center. Within thirty minutes, another commercial airliner struck the South Tower. Before the steel girders in both towers buckled and collapsed from the tremendous heat of the burning wreckage, Americans learned of even more disasters. A plane flew into the Pentagon in Washington, D.C., and another crashed a few hundred miles away in a field not far from Pittsburgh, after passengers apparently seized the cockpit and prevented the hijackers from reaching their unknown target. In these four, almost simultaneous, catastrophes, nearly 3,000 people died.

The events of September 11 and their aftermath sparked significant changes in American life. And yet there was at least one great continuity between the world of the 1990s and the world that seemed to begin on September 11, 2001. The United States in the last years of the twentieth century and the first decades of the twenty-first, more than at any other time in its history, was becoming more and more deeply entwined in a new age of globalism—an age that combined great promise with great peril.

A RESURGENCE OF PARTISANSHIP

When Bill Clinton took the presidential oath of office in January 1993, little did he realize that partisan politics would become a crippling problem for his administration and the country in general. While partisanship had always been a steady factor of modern American political life, the turn of the twenty-first century showcased new levels of mistrust and bitter splits between the parties that fundamentally affected how the White House and Congress functioned. Clinton and the presidents to follow would find it extraordinarily difficult to engineer change on the significant issues of the day through the legislative process when the opposing party held majorities in Congress. Fewer members of Congress were willing to work out solutions that required bipartisanship, preferring to have no bill at all rather than one that required them to compromise. The inability of politicians to find middle ground between contrasting bills and initiatives gummed up the machinery of the federal government and even brought it to the brink of a shutdown on more than one occasion. At times the impasse occurred within a party, such as conservative Republicans refusing to negotiate with moderate members of their party on matters of higher taxes, raising the national debt ceiling, or supporting national health insurance.

LAUNCHING THE CLINTON PRESIDENCY

Bill Clinton entered office as the first Democratic president since Jimmy Carter and the first self-proclaimed "activist" president, meaning a president seeking to expand the active role of the federal government in solving social problems, since Lyndon Johnson. Indeed, his domestic agenda was more liberal and ambitious than that of any president since the 1960s. But Clinton also

TIME LINE

1992
Bill Clinton elected

1993
NAFTA ratified

1995
Government shutdown

1996
Welfare reform passed

Defense of Marriage Act

Clinton reelected

1998
Lewinsky scandal breaks

Clinton impeached by House

1999
Clinton acquitted by Senate

2000
George W. Bush wins contested election

2001
9/11 attacks

U.S. defeats Taliban regime in Afghanistan

2003
U.S. invades Iraq

2004
Abu Ghraib scandal

Bush reelected

2005
Hurricane Katrina

2007
"Tea Party" fields candidates

Troop "surge" in Iraq

Mortgage crisis

2008
The Great Recession

Obama elected nation's first African American president

2010
Affordable Care Act signed

Deepwater Horizon (BP) oil spill

2012
Obama reelected

Sandy Hook school shooting

2015
Obergefell v. Hodges

2016
Trump elected

had significant political weaknesses. Having won the vote of well under half the electorate, he had no powerful mandate for change.

The new administration began with a series of missteps and misfortunes in its first months. The president's effort to end the longtime ban on gay men and lesbians serving in the military met with ferocious resistance, and he was forced to settle for a compromise known as "Don't Ask, Don't Tell," which forbade recruiters to *ask* recruits about their sexual preferences but also forbade servicemen and servicewomen to *tell* about or reveal them. Several of his early appointments became so controversial he had to withdraw them. Then Vince Foster, a longtime friend of the president who served as a deputy White House counsel and previous legal partner of First Lady **Hillary Rodham Clinton**, committed suicide in the summer of 1993. His death sparked an escalating inquiry into the Clinton's banking and real estate ventures with the Whitewater Development Corporation back in Arkansas the early 1980s. The Office of the Independent Counsel began examining these issues in what became known as the Whitewater affair in 1998 and only cleared the Clintons of wrongdoing in 2000.

Despite its many problems, the Clinton administration scored important achievements in its first year. The president narrowly won approval of a budget that marked a significant turn away from some of the policies of the Reagan–Bush years, especially the focus on reducing personal and corporate taxes. It included a substantial tax increase on the wealthiest Americans, a sizable reduction in many areas of government spending, and a major expansion of tax credits to low-income working people. He also passed the popular Family and Medical Leave Act, which permitted employees to take up to four months of unpaid maternity leave or leave to care for an infant or sick family member.

Clinton was a committed advocate of free trade. After a long and difficult battle against, among others, Ross Perot, the AFL-CIO, and many Democrats in Congress, he secured passage of the North American Free Trade Agreement (NAFTA), which eliminated most trade barriers among the United States, Canada, and Mexico. Later he won approval to sign a global accord that created the World Trade Organization (WTO), an international organization charged with negotiating agreements and settling disputes among its members.

The president's most notable and ambitious initiative was a major reform of the nation's health-care system. Early in 1993, he appointed a task force chaired by the first lady. It proposed a sweeping reform designed to guarantee coverage to every American and hold down the costs of medical care. But substantial opposition from those who believed the reform would transfer too much power to the government ultimately doomed the plan. The foreign policy of the Clinton administration was at first cautious and tentative. Yugoslavia, a nation created after World War I out of a group of small Balkan countries, dissolved again into several different countries in the wake of the 1989 collapse of its communist government. Bosnia was among the new nations, and it quickly became embroiled in a bloody civil war between its two major ethnic groups: one Muslim, the other Serbian and Christian, backed by the neighboring Serbian republic. All efforts by the other European nations and the United States to negotiate an end to the struggle failed until 1995, when the American negotiator Richard Holbrooke finally brought the warring parties together and crafted an agreement to partition Bosnia.

REPUBLICAN WINS AND LOSSES

The trials of the Clinton administration, and the failure of health-care reform in particular, proved damaging to the Democratic Party as it faced the congressional elections of 1994. Many Americans began to grow distrustful of the president and suspicious of his liberal policy goals. They looked for alternatives. For the first time in over forty years, Republicans, promising to counter Clinton and implement a Reagan-style conservative agenda, gained control of both houses of Congress.

Republicans interpreted their resounding victory at the polls as permission to fundamentally change American politics. Throughout 1995, the Republican Congress, under the leadership of House Speaker Newt Gingrich, worked feverishly to build an ambitious legislative program that they dubbed the "Contract with America." The Republicans proposed a series of measures to transfer important powers from the federal government to the states; pushed for dramatic reductions in federal spending, including a major restructuring of the Medicare program, to reduce costs; and attempted to scale back a wide range of federal regulatory functions.

President Clinton responded to the 1994 election results by shifting his own activist agenda conspicuously to the political center—announcing his own plan to cut taxes and balance the budget. But any compromise between the president and Congress was still very difficult. In November 1995 and again in January 1996, the federal government literally shut down for several days because Clinton and Congress could not agree on a budget. Utterly convinced that voters wholeheartedly embraced their aggressive conservative agenda, Republican leaders daringly refused to pass a "continuing resolution" (to allow government operations to continue during negotiations) in hopes of pressuring the president to agree to their terms. That proved to be an epic political blunder. Public opinion turned quickly and powerfully against the Republican leadership and much of its agenda. Newt Gingrich emerged as one of the most unpopular political leaders in the nation, while President Clinton slowly improved his standing in public opinion polls.

By the time the 1996 campaign began in earnest, President Clinton was in a commanding position to win reelection. Unopposed for the Democratic nomination, he faced a Republican opponent—Senator Robert Dole of Kansas—who inspired little enthusiasm even within his own party. Clinton benefited from the disastrous errors by congressional Republicans in 1995 and early 1996. But his greatest strength came from the remarkable success of the American economy and the marked reduction in the federal deficit. Like Reagan in 1984, he could campaign as the champion of peace, prosperity, and national well-being.

In a flurry of activity in the spring and summer of 1996, Congress passed several important bills. The most dramatic was a welfare reform bill that ended the fifty-year federal guarantee of assistance to families with dependent children and turned most of the responsibility for allocating federal welfare funds to the states. Most of all, it shifted the bulk of welfare benefits away from those without jobs and toward low-wage workers.

CLINTON TRIUMPHANT AND EMBATTLED

Clinton handily won reelection, becoming the first Democrat since Franklin Roosevelt to win two terms as president. Congressional Democrats, however, failed to gain a majority in the House and Senate. Clinton worked effectively with the Republican leadership on the shared goal of a balanced budget, which passed with much fanfare late in 1997. By the end of 1998, the federal budget was generating its first surplus in thirty years.

Clinton's renewed popularity was critical to his political survival in the turbulent year that followed, when the most serious crisis of his presidency suddenly erupted. Clinton had been the target of accusations of corruption and scandal since his first weeks in office: the investigation into Whitewater, charges of corruption against members of his cabinet and staff, accusations of illegalities in financing his 1996 campaign, and a civil suit for sexual harassment filed early in his first term by a former Arkansas state employee, Paula Jones.

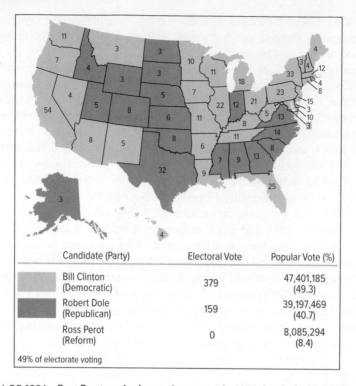

Candidate (Party)	Electoral Vote	Popular Vote (%)
Bill Clinton (Democratic)	379	47,401,185 (49.3)
Robert Dole (Republican)	159	39,197,469 (40.7)
Ross Perot (Reform)	0	8,085,294 (8.4)

49% of electorate voting

THE ELECTION OF 1996 Ross Perot received many fewer votes in 1996 than he had in 1992, and President Clinton came much closer than he had four years earlier to winning a majority of the popular vote. Once again, Clinton defeated his Republican opponent, this time Robert Dole, by a decisive margin in both the popular and electoral votes. • *After the 1994 Republican landslide in the congressional elections, Bill Clinton had seemed permanently weakened. What explains his political revival?*

In early 1998, inquiries associated with the Paula Jones case led to charges that the president had had a sexual relationship with a twenty-two-year-old White House intern, Monica Lewinsky. The most damaging charge was that he had lied about it in a sworn statement given as part of his deposition before Jones's attorneys. Those revelations produced a new investigation by the independent counsel in the Whitewater case, Kenneth Starr, who was a former judge and official in the Reagan Justice Department.

Clinton forcefully denied the charges and a majority of the public strongly backed him. His popularity soared to record levels and remained high throughout the year that followed. In the meantime, a federal judge dismissed the Paula Jones case.

But the scandal revived again with great force in August 1998, when Lewinsky struck a deal with the independent counsel and testified about her relationship with Clinton. Starr then subpoenaed Clinton himself, who—faced with the prospect of speaking to a grand jury—finally admitted that he and Lewinsky had had what he called an "improper relationship." A few weeks later, Starr submitted a lengthy and salacious report to Congress on the results of his investigation, recommending that Congress impeach the president.

IMPEACHMENT, ACQUITTAL, AND RESURGENCE

On December 19, 1998, the House, voting on strictly partisan lines, narrowly approved two counts of impeachment: perjury and obstructing justice. The matter then moved to the Senate, where a trial of the president—the first since the trial of Andrew Johnson in 1868—began in early January. It ended with a decisive acquittal of the president. Neither of the charges attracted even a majority of the votes, let alone the two-thirds necessary for conviction.

Still, the trial dampened public support for the president and stiffened congressional opposition to any of his initiatives. Indeed, the last two years of the Clinton presidency were relatively quiet. The president had no real hope of major domestic achievements in the face of a hostile Republican Congress. Overseas, however, he was more active.

In 1999, the president faced another crisis in the Balkans. This time, the conflict involved a province of Serbian-dominated Yugoslavia—Kosovo—most of whose residents were Albanian Muslims. A savage civil war erupted there in 1998 between Kosovo nationalists and Serbians. In May 1999, NATO forces—dominated and led by the United States—began a major bombing campaign against the Serbians, which after little more than a week led the leader of Yugoslavia, Slobodan Milosevic, to agree to a cease-fire. Serbian troops withdrew from Kosovo entirely, replaced by NATO peacekeeping forces. A precarious peace returned to the region.

Buoyed by his success in Europe and a rising economy, Clinton actually finished his eight years in office with his popularity higher than it had been when he had begun. No president in the years since has experienced the same approval ratings. Indeed, despite politicians' use of new technology and polling data to connect with the public, the relationship between the elected and the voter has steadily deteriorated.

The Election of 2000

The 2000 presidential election was one of the most extraordinary in American history—not because of the campaign that preceded it but because of the sensational controversy over its results, which preoccupied the nation for more than five weeks after the actual voting.

On the ballot in November 2000 were Republican **George W. Bush**, son of the former president and a second-term governor of Texas, and Democrat Al Gore, former Tennessee senator and vice president under Clinton. Both men ran cautious, centrist campaigns. Gore won the national popular vote by the thin margin of about 540,000 votes out of about 100 million cast (a difference of 0.5 percent). But on election night, both candidates remained short of the 270 electoral votes needed for victory because the Florida results were too close to call.

After a mandatory recount over the next two days, Bush led Gore in the state by fewer than 300 votes. That total was in serious question, however, because many of the ballots cast were old-fashioned punch cards that had failed to conclusively register the choice of many voters. Instead, Florida election officials confronted cards whose holes were not cleanly punched through, leaving only a "hanging chad" or incompletely torn corner of paper for them to interpret voter intent. The Gore campaign asked for hand recounts in three critical counties, which the Florida Supreme Court unanimously supported.

The battle over the ballots continued between the candidates in the news and the courts until the U.S. Supreme Court decided *Bush v. Gore* on December 12. Voting 5 to 4 along ideological lines, the conservative majority ruled that the Florida Supreme Court's order for a recount was unconstitutional; they insisted that according to U.S. Code any revised recount order be completed by December 12 (the same day that the ruling was issued and therefore impossible to execute); and they argued that the standards for evaluating punch-card ballots were too arbitrary and unfair to withstand constitutional scrutiny. The hand recount could not proceed, and Bush's victory in Florida—and thus nationally—stood.

As the nomination campaigns were heating up in early 2008, the nation confronted its worst financial crisis since the Great Depression. The problem had several causes. Since the repeal in 1999 of the Glass-Steagall Act that had mandated layers of government oversight designed to catch fraud or risky investment strategies, financial institutions had been experimenting with new and risky credit instruments intended to make borrowing easier and cheaper. One such instrument, called an adjustable rate mortgage (ARM), offered homebuyers mortgages with low interest rates that would "adjust" upward in later years. Another, the "jumbo loan," extended credit that exceeded conforming loan limits to people with uncertain financial means to pay the loans back. These instruments, coupled with lax monitoring of the mortgage industry as a whole, allowed millions of people to take on large and risky mortgages to purchase homes, causing a "housing bubble"—a rapid rise in housing prices fueled by high demand. Banks offset their risks by bundling mortgages into mortgage-backed securities (MBSs), which other banks and financial firms invested heavily in. The housing bubble eventually burst. The price of homes soon leveled off and even dipped. Homeowners with ARMs saw their loans' higher rates grow beyond what they could afford, while their home's market values sunk below the value of the mortgage itself. Unable to pay off their loans, they defaulted and banks took possession of their properties; foreclosures skyrocketed across the country. Compounding the collapse of the housing bubble, the MBSs based on those loans failed as well, causing many of the nation's largest banks to teeter on the brink of collapse. Their creditors and the federal government forced them to merge with or be purchased by other, more solvent banks as a way to protect customers.

This so-called **Great Recession of 2008**, sparked by the loan crisis, pushed down wages and triggered widespread job layoffs. The increased unemployment rate further accelerated the downward economic spiral. Many Americans simply could not meet basic financial obligations such as the repayment of home, car, or school loans or credit card debt. There was also less money available for investing, stalling the potential for economic growth. Blue-collar and trades workers, manufacturers, and the poor were hardest hit by the crisis. Popular anger surfaced in art, literature, and especially contemporary music. Rap, one of the newest and most successful forms of popular music, chronicled lives of despair and called for economic change. (See "Patterns of Popular Culture: Rap.")

By mid-September 2008, the economy seemed to be spinning out of control. Secretary of the Treasury Henry Paulson, supported by other economic leaders, stepped in. He proposed a massive use of federal funds to help the government bail out banks that were failing. Both the Bush administration and eventually the Obama administration won congressional support for $750 billion in the form of the Troubled Asset Relief Program (TARP) to shore up the tottering financial institutions. The bailout kept the economy from collapsing, but it remained very weak for several years, with exceptionally high unemployment rates.

This extraordinary crisis formed the backdrop against which the two presidential candidates fought out the last two months of their campaign. Neither offered clear or convincing solutions to the crisis, but most voters came to believe that Obama would likely be a better steward of the economy than McCain. Obama benefited both from the unpopularity of George W. Bush and from his success at persuading voters that McCain would continue Bush's policies. Obama held on to—and indeed increased—his lead through late September and October, helped by a heavily financed and highly disciplined campaign.

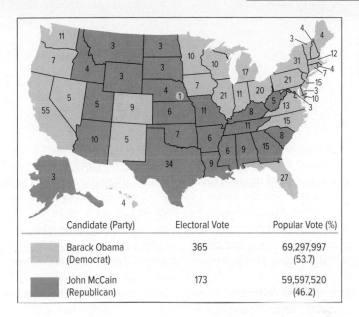

Candidate (Party)	Electoral Vote	Popular Vote (%)
Barack Obama (Democrat)	365	69,297,997 (53.7)
John McCain (Republican)	173	59,597,520 (46.2)

THE ELECTION OF 2008 The election of 2008 produced a decisive victory for Barack Obama. Democrats won majorities in both the House and the Senate, only to see the Republicans win a majority of the House two years later. • *Compare this map to the election of 2000 map. Which states did Bush win that went to Obama in 2008?*

On November 4, 2008, Barack Obama won the popular vote 53 percent to 46 percent and the electoral vote by an even larger margin. Obama became the first Democratic candidate since Lyndon Johnson to score such a decisive victory.

OBAMA AND HIS OPPONENTS

The global exuberance that Obama's election created in 2008 did not linger for long. The first two years of his presidency coincided with the worst period of the economic crisis. But large supportive Democratic majorities in both houses of Congress strengthened Obama's ability to enact broad reforms. During those years, Obama passed a stimulus package of $800 billion to support state and local budgets, public works, and other investments that he hoped would generate economic growth. He and his congressional allies also succeeded in passing significant financial regulations that were designed to avoid another crisis like the one that began in 2008. His signature achievement was the passage of the **Affordable Care Act**, a broad health-care bill aimed to give almost all Americans access to insurance, regardless of their means. Yet Obama's legislation, and especially his health-care initiative, triggered fear among many Republicans about a federal government becoming too powerful and overstepping its limits. Indeed, only one Republican member of Congress supported the health-care bill. For Obama, who had built much of his presidential bid around the idea of bipartisanship and conciliation, the polarization of the two parties was a significant setback. Many Republican states' attorneys sued to stop the health bill. Judges were divided as to whether the bill was constitutional, and only favorable rulings by the Supreme Court in June 2012 and 2015 preserved it.

The 2010 midterm congressional campaigns were dominated by the emergence of the **Tea Party movement**, a vigorous conservative effort to reduce the national debt, lower taxes, and limit the role of government. This broad movement attracted mostly white men and women, largely from the middle class. Tea Party members viewed Obama and his peers as

RAP

The long musical lineage of rap includes elements of the disco and street funk of the 1970s; of the fast-talking jive of black radio DJs in the 1950s; of the onstage patter of Cab Calloway and other African American stars of the first half of the twentieth century. It contains reminders of tap and break dancing—even of the boxing-ring poetry of Muhammad Ali.

Rap's most important element is its words. Rap is as much a form of language as a form of music. It bears a distant resemblance to some traditions of African American pulpit oratory, which also included forms of spoken song. It draws from some of the verbal traditions of urban black street life, including the "dozens"—a ritualized trading of insults particularly popular among young black men.

But rap is also the product of a distinctive place and time: the South Bronx in the 1970s and 1980s and the hip-hop culture that was born there and that soon dominated the appearance and public behavior of many young black males. "Hip hop is how you walk, talk, live, see, act, feel," said one Bronx hip-hopper. Some elements of hip-hop culture faded, and by the 1990s the most popular element of hip-hop culture was rap, which had by then been developing for nearly twenty years.

Beginning in the early 1970s, Bronx DJs began setting up their equipment on neighborhood streets and staging block parties, where they not only played records but also put on shows of their own—performances that featured spoken rhymes, jazzy phrases, and pointed comments about the audience, the neighborhood, and themselves.

Gradually, the DJs began to bring "rappers" into shows—young men who developed the DJ style into a much more elaborate form of performance, usually accompanied by dancing. As rap grew more popular in the inner city, record promoters began signing some of its new stars. In 1979, the Sugarhill Gang's "Rapper's Delight" became the first rap single to be played on mainstream commercial radio and the first to become a major hit. In the early 1980s, Run-DMC became the first national rap superstars. From there, rap moved quickly to become one of the most popular and commercially successful forms of popular music. In the 1990s and early 2000s, rap recordings routinely sold millions of copies.

Rap has taken many forms. There have been white rappers (Eminem, House of Pain), female rappers (Missy Elliott, Queen Latifah), even religious rappers and children's rappers. But it has always been primarily a product of the young male culture of the inner city, and some of the most successful rap has conveyed the frustration and anger that these men have felt about their lives—"a voice for the oppressed people," one rap artist said, "that in many other ways don't have a voice." In 1982, the rap group Grandmaster Flash and the Furious Five released a rap called "The Message," a searing description of the ghetto and the lack of educational and economic opportunities.

In the late 1980s, the Compton and Watts neighborhoods of Los Angeles—two of the most distressed minority communities in the city—produced their own style, known as West Coast rap, with such groups

(left: ©PAN Photo Agency/Shutterstock; right: ©MediaPunch/REX/Shutterstock)

SEAN "P. DIDDY" COMBS Testifying to the continued popularity of rap, Sean "P. Diddy" Combs smashed records for successful artists in 2017. Rapper, songwriter, record producer, film director, entrepreneur, and fashion designer, Combs's net worth totals $820 million. *Forbes* lists him as the most influential rapper of his time.

as Ice Cube, Ice-T, Tupac Shakur, and Snoop Doggy Dog. West Coast rap often had a harsh, angry character, and at its extremes (the so-called gangsta' rap), it could be strikingly violent and highly provocative. Scandals erupted over controversial lyrics—Ice-T's "Cop Killer," which some critics believed advocated murdering police; and the sexually explicit lyrics of 2 Live Crew and other groups, which critics accused of advocating violence against women.

But it was not just the lyrics that caused the furor. Rap artists were almost all products of tough inner-city neighborhoods, and the rough-edged styles many took with them into the public eye made many people uncomfortable. Some rappers got caught up in highly publicized trouble with the law. Several—including two of rap's biggest stars, Tupac Shakur and Notorious B.I.G.—were murdered. The business of rap, particularly the confrontational business style of Death Row Records (founded by Dr. Dre, a veteran of the first major West Coast rap group NWA), was a source of public controversy as well.

But rap is undeniably lucrative. The wealthiest artists are the most creative business minds. Kanye West invested in all aspects of the music industry. So did Sean "P. Diddy" Combs, who also started a popular clothing line bearing his name, a TV network, "Revolt TV," and designer brands of tequila and bottled water. His net worth was estimated at $820 million in 2017, tops among rappers.

Controversies at times unfairly dominated the image of rap as a whole. Some rap is angry and cruel, as are many of the realities of the world from which it comes. But much of it is explicitly positive, some of it deliberately gentle. Chuck D, who founded Public Enemy in the mid-1980s, exhorted young black men to avoid drugs and crime, to take responsibility for their families, to get an education. More recently, St. Louis–based artist and rapper Tef Poe traveled to sites of public protests following the police shooting of unarmed black men to spread a message of peace and social activism. He has penned essays in *Time* magazine and addressed the United Nations on the need for young and old to engage in politics to improve society. And the form, if not the content, of the original rappers has spread widely through American culture. Rap came to dominate the music charts in America, and its styles made their way onto *Sesame Street* and other children's shows, into television commercials, Hollywood films, and the everyday language of millions of people, young and old, black and white. It became another of the arresting, innovative African American musical traditions that have shaped American culture for more than a century. •

UNDERSTAND, ANALYZE, & EVALUATE

1. What other African American musical forms have helped shape American popular culture?
2. If rap is so closely associated with the inner-city culture where it originated,

what accounts for its widespread popularity and commercial success? What other forms or styles of popular music enjoy a popularity that extends far beyond its cultural origins?
3. Do you think rap's popularity will endure? Why or why not?

dangerous enemies to a stronger, more prosperous America. They helped send a large majority of anti-Obama Republicans to the House and reduced the majority of Democrats in the Senate. For the next two years, President Obama struggled to get proposals passed by Congress because nearly every Republican summarily rejected them.

In September 2011, another movement emerged—**Occupy Wall Street (OWS)**. But this movement preached a radically different agenda than the Tea Party movement. Significantly smaller and younger than the Tea Party, OWS argued for stricter financial regulation, progressive taxation, stronger support for unions, more resources to reduce unemployment, assaults on economic inequality, and the end of what it believed were unnecessary and failed wars. Its rallying cry was "We are the 99%," referring to the growing gap of income equality between the richest 1 percent and the rest of Americans. They symbolically demonstrated their grievances by camping in Zuccotti Park in the Wall Street area of lower Manhattan. Soon after, similar demonstrations took place in many other places in the United States and around the world. OWS, never a broad-based popular movement, quickly lost steam and was largely extinguished by 2013. Yet it served as an emblem of popular concern over the unsteady recent history of the economy and the ability of politicians to solve crises in general.

(Source: Official White House Photo by Pete Souza)

FIGHTING TERRORISM President Barack Obama and Vice President Joe Biden, along with members of the national security team, receive an update on the mission against Osama bin Laden in the Situation Room of the White House, May 1, 2011. The next day a team of U.S. Navy Seals killed bin Laden, concluding a near ten-year search for the mastermind of the 9/11 attack on America.

Obama and the Challenge of Governing

The election of 2012—the most expensive campaign in history—pitted President Obama against Mitt Romney, a former governor of Massachusetts. The race was up in the air until the very end, and enormous amounts of campaign money and effort flooded into the few states that were still up for grabs—among them Ohio, Virginia, Florida, Wisconsin, Iowa, and New Hampshire. On election night, it became clear that these states had tilted toward Obama in the last few days. The Democrats also won several new senators, giving the party a majority. The House of Representatives remained Republican, but the majority was now smaller.

The political gridlock of Obama's presidency continued after his reelection. Many of his initiatives faced serious obstacles or simply did not come to pass. A major disappointment for Obama and his supporters involved the failure to enact meaningful gun-control measures despite a series of horrific shootings occurring during his terms in office, including the shooting of twenty children and six adults at the Sandy Hook Elementary School in Newtown, Connecticut, on December 14, 2012. The National Rifle Association and the conservative wing of the Republican Party successfully warded off more than 100 attempts at introducing gun-control measures, and indeed gun sales spiked after each mass shooting.

The gridlock of the House also dashed any hopes President Obama had of gaining a deal on immigration. While he had moved aggressively to deport illegal immigrants with criminal records during his presidency, Obama also defended the essential dignity of all immigrants and highlighted their historical accomplishments in America. He now hoped to pass legislation protecting those who had lived here for long periods even if they originally entered America illegally. On June 27, 2013, the Senate, in a rare show of bipartisanship, passed a comprehensive package of provisions, including a path to U.S. citizenship for illegal immigrants already in the country. But powerful conservative Republican opposition in the House, based largely on the idea that illegal immigrants should not be granted citizenship, doomed the bill and it died in Congress. Obama responded by issuing an executive order that would delay the deportation of some immigrants, much as he had issued an executive order in 2012 protecting "dreamers" or people brought to the country illegally as children. Republicans decried what they saw as presidential overreach, and a federal judge ruled against it.

The fate of the immigration bill embodied the challenge of governing for Obama. He had whipped up popular support for a bill tackling a pressing social issue and rallied the Senate to pass it—only to see it die in the Republican-controlled House. As Clinton and Bush had before him, Obama confronted the painful realities of political leadership in modern America, where fealty to political ideology often trumped the desire to compromise with a member of the opposite party or even with those in the same party.

The Election of 2016 and President Trump

The turmoil of the 2016 presidential election overshadowed much of Obama's last year in office. Hillary Clinton, the formidable and highly experienced Democratic candidate, slugged it out with the surprise Republican nominee, **Donald Trump**. Trump, a real estate tycoon from Manhattan with no formal experience in government, had bested a strong slate of opponents during the primary by promising to "Make America Great Again" and undo or severely restrict many of Obama's policy initiatives. Campaigning to lower personal and corporate taxes, repeal and replace the Affordable Care Act, limit Muslim entry into the country, build a wall along the Mexico–U.S. border to stop illegal immigrants, roll back environmental regulations, and bolster the military, Trump appealed to voters who identified as conservatives as well as a sizable number of moderates, many of whom were dissatisfied with the status quo or viewed Hillary Clinton as untrustworthy. An emerging group of far-right white nationalists dubbed the "alt-right" also contributed to his victory. But his biggest surprise was narrowly beating Clinton, whom pundits had widely projected to become the first woman to occupy the White House. Trump lost the popular vote by nearly 2.9 million but earned 304 electoral votes to Clinton's 227. The Republican Party also retained majorities, though slim, in both the Senate and the House.

Trump's success, however, was not without controversy. Allegations that the Russian government officials had interfered with the election in favor of Trump—hacking into the e-mail accounts of the Democratic National Committee and dumping the politically damaging contents onto WikiLeaks, for example—clouded the results. In early May of his first year in office, Trump abruptly fired the FBI director, James Comey, allegedly because Comey refused to stop probes into the role of the Russians in the election, thereby giving rise to a portrayal of him as an autocratic leader. Later the same month, the Department of Justice appointed a special investigator to analyze the possibility that members of Trump's campaign staff had unsanctioned contacts or ties with representatives of the Russian government.

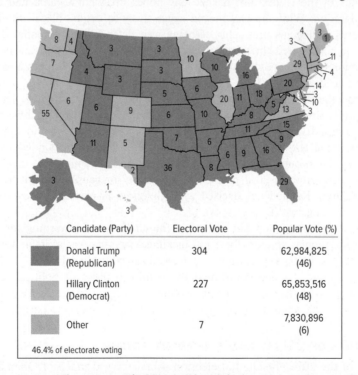

Candidate (Party)	Electoral Vote	Popular Vote (%)
Donald Trump (Republican)	304	62,984,825 (46)
Hillary Clinton (Democrat)	227	65,853,516 (48)
Other	7	7,830,896 (6)

46.4% of electorate voting

THE ELECTION OF 2016   The outcome of the 2016 presidential election was a surprise to pundits and pollsters alike. Hillary Clinton was the constant front-runner throughout much of the last weeks of the campaign. She was predicted to win, though in a close race. But Trump picked up states that traditionally voted for a Democrat in the race for the White House, including Pennsylvania, Florida, and Michigan, and won the electoral college while losing the popular vote. The race revealed a stark pattern of geographic partisanship, where voters in the South and much of the Midwest cast their ballot for Trump while those living on the West Coast and the northern half of the East Coast pledged their loyalty to Clinton. • *Compare this map to that of the election of 2000 earlier in this chapter.*
• *How did the pattern of party support change over the course of the twentieth century?*
• *What does the change—or lack of it—suggest about the state of party politics today?*

Despite the turmoil surrounding the early days of his presidency, Trump has moved aggressively if with limited success to deliver on campaign promises. His budget included tax cuts for all Americans, especially the wealthy and business owners, and a boost for the military. He worked closely with Republicans to replace the Affordable Care Act, though their efforts have failed to date. And he issued a temporary ban on Muslim immigration from countries with proven records of terrorism, only to have it rejected in federal court.

Like his predecessors in the White House, Trump is discovering the perils of governing in an era of intensely partisan politics. He struggles to reach deals with Democrats and even hold the support of members of his own party. Compounding his difficulty is his lack of experience in elected office and propensity to share his antipathies and political opinions via Twitter. His ability to "Make America Great Again" may well depend on reaching across the political divide, compromising on policy goals with political foes, and disciplining his messages to the American public.

SCIENCE AND TECHNOLOGY IN THE NEW ECONOMY

The last three decades have seen remarkable changes in American life—some a result of the end of the Cold War, some the changing character of the American population, and some a product of a rapidly evolving culture. But most of these changes were at least in part a product of the dramatic transformation of American trade and industry. Indeed, this "new economy" represented a profound shift in the nation's financial history. Throughout much of the twentieth century, manufacturing had powered the nation's economy. Making cars, rubber, steel, and airplanes, for example, had provided many workers with steady jobs and decent wages and benefits as well as entry into the middle class. But in the face of the sluggish growth and persistent inflation of the last decades of the 1900s, many American corporations began making drastic changes in the way they ran their businesses. They invested heavily in new technology to make themselves more efficient and productive and, more significantly, slashed their labor costs, which were among the highest in the world and which many economists and business leaders believed had made the United States uncompetitive against the emerging economies that relied on low-wage workers. Businesses now took a much harder line against unions. And nonunion companies became more successful in staving off unionization drives. Some companies actually moved their operations to areas of the country where unions were weak and wages low—the American South and Midwest in particular. Others simply relocated much of their production out of the United States, to such nations as Mexico and China, where there were large pools of unorganized cheap labor.

At the same time, the digital revolution took hold. The rapid development of the personal computer and the Internet profoundly reshaped how companies operated and organized themselves, rewarding in particular college-educated workers skilled in software design and application. It also redefined how people communicated, worked, shopped, and spent their free time.

THE DIGITAL REVOLUTION

The dramatic growth in the use of computers and other digital devices was among the most significant innovations of the late twentieth and early twenty-first centuries. In 1947, Bell Labs invented the transistor, which has continued to develop and is the foundation of almost all electronic devices. The creation of the microprocessor (a specially designed collection of transistors) was first introduced in 1971 by Intel and it represented a notable advance in computational speed, energy use, and size. In 1975, Ed Roberts introduced the Altair 8800, the world's first "minicomputer," and later a personal computer or "PC." The Apple Computer Company followed by producing the Apple I desktop computer shortly thereafter in 1976 for $666, making it the first computer widely available to the public. Several years later, International Business Machines (IBM) launched its first PC, with an operating system designed by Microsoft, then a small outside developer. Over time Microsoft would overshadow IBM, as its operating systems and software became integral to most PCs with the notable exception of Apple's Mac OS (Operating System), which is preferred by professionals in the audio and visual professions. In 2007, Apple transformed personal computing with the introduction of the iPhone, combining the features of a phone, media player, and search engine in a handheld device with a novel touchscreen interface.

THE INTERNET

Out of the computer revolution emerged another dramatic source of information and communication: the Internet—a vast, geographically far-flung network of computers that allows people to communicate with others all over the world. It began in 1963, in the U.S. government's Advanced Research Projects Agency (ARPA), which funneled federal funds into scientific research projects. In the early 1960s, J. C. R. Licklider, the head of ARPA's Information Processing Techniques Office, launched a program to link together computers over large distances and create an electronic network. It was known as ARPANET.

ARPANET developed quickly because of two new technologies. The first was a system for transmitting large quantities of data in "packets." The second was the development of the Transmission Control Protocol/Internet Protocol (TCP/IP), which not only provided a way to assign addresses to machines and networks but also provided protection against lost data packets on the network.

(©Iain Masterton/Alamy)

TWENTY-FOUR-HOUR NEWS CYCLE The digital revolution has contributed to a vast change in the reporting of news events and political commentary. Politicians now have much less control over how their messages are transmitted and received.

In the early 1980s, the Defense Department, an early partner in the development of ARPANET, withdrew from the project for security reasons. The network, soon renamed the Internet, was then free to develop independently. In 1989, Tim Berners-Lee, a British scientist working at a laboratory in Geneva, introduced the World Wide Web, which helped establish an orderly system for both the distribution and retrieval of electronic information over the Internet. The growth in computer usage was remarkable. In 1971, ARPANET had linked twenty-three computers. By 2012, there were well over a billion computers in use in the world (and many more now-obsolete ones). Virtually all of them are connected to the Internet either with a physical connection or wireless (WiFi) connections that became available to the public in 1997.

The development of the Internet, along with the emergence of the computer industry and digital technology, made possible an enormous range of new products and services that quickly became central to economic life: digital music, video, and cameras; iPods, smartphones, and tablets; and Facebook, Instagram, YouTube, and Google. These modern industries employed hundreds of thousands of people (many of them from outside the United States) and created new consumer needs and appetites.

Breakthroughs in Genetics

Computers helped create new scientific breakthroughs in genetics. Early discoveries in genetics by Gregor Mendel, Thomas Hunt Morgan, and others laid the groundwork for more dramatic breakthroughs—the discovery of DNA by the British scientists Oswald Avery, Colin MacLeod, and Maclyn McCarty in 1944; and in 1953, the dramatic discovery by the American biochemist James Watson and the British biophysicist Francis Crick of the double-helix structure of DNA, and thus of the key to identifying genetic codes. From these discoveries emerged the new science—and, ultimately, the new industry—of genetic engineering, through which new medical treatments and new techniques for hybridization of plants and animals have already become possible.

Scientists began to identify specific genes in humans and other living things. But the identification of genes was painfully slow; and in 1989, in an effort to accelerate the process, the federal government appropriated $3 billion to fund the National Center for the Human Genome. The Human Genome Project formally began its mission to identify and classify all of the more than 20,000 genes in 1990 and declared its work complete in 2003.

But genetic research was (and continues to be) a source of great controversy. Many people feared that the new science might alter aspects of human life that previously seemed beyond human control. Some critics opposed genetic research on religious grounds, seeing it as an interference with "God's plan" for human nature. Still others complained that it equipped humans with immoral powers such that, for example, parents could "design" their children and "order" certain desirable traits. And a particularly heated controversy emerged over the ways in which scientists obtained genetic material. One of the most promising sources of genetic research comes from stem cell material from human embryos, but the research deeply offends those who believe that the embryo is an early-aged human life deserving of protection from harm. In 2001, President Bush issued an executive order banning federal funding of research using new sources of human stem cells. President Obama reversed the order in 2009, and in 2016 he signed the 21st Century Cures Act. The Cures Act promotes the acceleration of research on a number of fronts, including stem cell research into cell therapies that could heal damaged tissues and organs.

A CHANGING SOCIETY

The American population changed dramatically in the late twentieth and early twenty-first centuries. It grew larger, older, and more racially and ethnically diverse. It debated the success and scope of earlier landmark events, such as the civil rights movement and the Supreme Court's affirmation of a woman's right to an abortion. At the same time, the nation's citizenry confronted powerful new challenges, such as the spread of AIDS, the debate over gay rights and same-sex marriage, the prospect of dwindling natural resources, and extreme weather events and their relationship to climate change.

A SHIFTING POPULATION

Decreasing birthrates and growing life spans contributed to one of the most important characteristics of the American population in the early twenty-first century: its increasing agedness. The enormous Baby-Boom generation—people born in the first ten years after World War II—drove the median age steadily upward (from thirty-four in 1996 to thirty-eight in 2015 to a projected forty-two by 2065). It had important implications for the workforce. In the last twenty years of the twentieth century, the number of people aged twenty-five to fifty-four (known statistically as the "prime workforce") grew by over 26 million. In the first fifteen years of the twenty-first century, the number of American-born workers in that age group

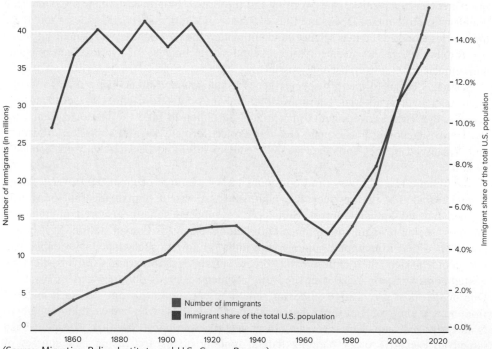

(Source: Migration Policy Institute and U.S. Census Bureau.)

U.S. IMMIGRANT POPULATION AND SHARE OVER TIME, 1850–PRESENT   This chart shows the tremendous increase in immigration to the United States in the decades since the Immigration Reform Act of 1965. • *At what point since 1850 was the immigrant share of the total U.S. population highest? When was the last time that the immigrant share was at its current level?*

grew very little. This combination of fewer Americans working and more of them retired put enormous stress on the Social Security and Medicare systems to continue to fulfill their financial obligations.

The slowing growth of the native-born population, and the workforce shortages it helped create, was one reason for the rapid growth of immigration. In 2015, the number of foreign-born residents of the United States was the highest in American history—more than 43.3 million people or 13.5 percent of the entire population. These immigrants came from a wider variety of backgrounds than ever before, largely the result of the 1965 Immigration Reform Act, which eliminated national origins as a criterion for admission. The growing presence of the foreign-born contributed to a significant drop in the percentage of white residents in the United States—from 90 percent in 1965 to 76.9 percent in 2016. (Relative to overall population, non-Hispanic whites constituted just over 61 percent in 2016.) Latinos and Asians were by far the largest groups of immigrants in these years. But others came in significant numbers from Africa, the Middle East, Russia, and eastern Europe.

African Americans in the Post–Civil Rights Era

The civil rights movement and other liberal efforts of the 1960s had two very different effects on African Americans. On one hand, they increased opportunities for advancement to those in a position to take advantage of them. And they helped make possible the election of the first black American to the White House, an event unthinkable to all but the most optimistic freedom fighter during the King years. On the other hand, as the industrial economy declined and government services dwindled, there was a growing sense of helplessness and despair among large groups of the poor who continued to find themselves barred from upward mobility.

By the early twenty-first century, the black middle class constituted over half of the African American population; its progress was remarkable in the decades after the high point of the civil rights movement. African American families moved into more affluent urban communities and, in many cases, into suburbs—at times as neighbors of whites, more often into predominantly black communities. The percentage of black high school graduates going on to college was virtually the same as that of white high school graduates by the early twenty-first century (although a smaller proportion of blacks than whites completed high school). And African Americans were making rapid strides in many professions. A generation earlier, they had been barred from many jobs because of segregation. Over half of all employed African Americans in the United States had skilled white-collar jobs in 2010. There were few areas of American life from which blacks were entirely excluded.

But the rise of the black middle class also accentuated the increasingly desperate plight of less fortunate African Americans. Economic growth and the activist programs of the 1960s and beyond had never reached them in great numbers. For the school year 2012–2013, only 59 percent of black male youth graduated from high school, compared with 65 percent Latino male and 80 percent white male. In 2015, a quarter of the nation's black population was categorized as still living below the federal poverty rate, more than double that of whites. And since 1970, the percentage of black children living in poverty has rarely dipped below one-third. Black children today are three times more likely to be in poverty than white children. The black family structure changed as well from the dislocations of poverty. There was an increase in the number of single-parent black households. In 1970, 59 percent of all black children under eighteen years old lived with both their parents (already down from 70 percent a decade earlier). In 2016, only 38.7 percent of black children lived in such households, compared to 74.3 percent of white children.

Poorer African Americans were also disadvantaged by many other factors in the changing social and economic climate of the late twentieth and early twenty-first centuries. Among them was Clinton's revision of federal welfare policies and a growing impatience with affirmative action. There was also a steady decline in the number of unskilled jobs in the economy. Not surprisingly, then, many blacks openly questioned the long-term successes of the civil rights movement. A steady rise in the rate of the incarceration of young black men—indeed, perhaps one out of four black men will go to prison in the course of their lifetimes—prompted calls for better schools and intervention programs as well as a review of the justice system as a whole. Signs of popular despair surfaced during moments of racial tension, especially after the use of questionable policing tactics left black men dead, as in the case of Eric Garner in New York City in July 2014, eighteen-year-old Michael Brown in Ferguson, Missouri, in August 2014, Freddie Gray in Baltimore in April 2015, and Alton Sterling in Baton Rouge in July 2016. These highly publicized cases gave rise to the Black Lives Movement, dedicated to drawing attention to the history of questionable treatment of blacks by police and calling for formal inquiries into the killing of black men by law enforcement. It sparked national protests in cities across America, in which thousands of blacks took to the streets, demanding fairer treatment by local police and decrying a lack of racial respect between Americans of different colors.

THE ABORTION DEBATE

Conservatives became more assertive about challenging feminist causes in the late twentieth and early twenty-first centuries. Leaders of the New Right campaigned successfully against the proposed Equal Rights Amendment to the Constitution. And they won a series of legislative and judicial efforts to restrict access to abortion.

For abortion rights or "pro-choice" advocates, the Supreme Court's decision in *Roe v. Wade* (1973) had seemed to settle the question. But at the same time, critics of abortion began to build a powerful grassroots movement. These "pro-life" or "right-to-life" advocates objected to abortion on religious and moral grounds, arguing that human life was sacred from the moment of conception and that abortion itself was murder; Catholics, Mormons, and evangelical Christians passionately supported this position. The opposition of other anti-abortion activists often had less to do with religion than with their commitment to traditional morality and notions of family and gender relations. They viewed abortion as one of several assaults by feminists and their supporters on the conventional roles of women as wives, mothers, and moral guardians of the household.

Although the right-to-life movement was persistent in its demand for a reversal of *Roe v. Wade* or, barring that, a constitutional amendment banning abortion, it also attacked abortion rights in more limited ways and at their most vulnerable points. State legislatures enacted more than 1,000 restrictions in the period between 1973 and 2015, including limits on insurance coverage and on certain procedures and medications as well as imposing waiting periods, state-mandated counseling, parental consent, and tough requirements for abortion facilities. Congress passed several laws that affected abortion services, among them the Hyde Amendment—named for its chief sponsor, Rep. Henry Hyde of Illinois—that prohibited the use of federal funds for abortions except in the case of incest, rape, or threat to the mother's life. It also brought into law the Partial Birth Abortion Ban Act that banned a medical procedure called intact dilation and extraction. Presidents Reagan, Bush, and Trump were able to affect abortion policy not only by signing such laws, but also by appointing judges, health agency directors, and law enforcement officials who acted to promote a pro-life agenda.

The pro-choice movement was in many parts of the country at least as strong as, and in some areas much stronger than, the right-to-life movement. Their legislative victories included the Freedom of Access to Clinic Entrances Act (1993), which responded to the aggressive and sometimes lethal tactics of abortion protestors against abortion providers and their patients while also allowing for peaceful protests. Presidents Clinton and Obama made pro-choice appointments and supported family planning initiatives that their predecessors had curtailed. However, in order to gain support for his health-care initiative, Obama signed an order stating that the Affordable Care Act would maintain current Hyde Amendment restrictions and prohibit the use of federal funds for abortions. With the election of Donald Trump and fears of a rollback in women's reproductive rights, the feminist movement experienced a surge in activism, focusing on issues that include but are not limited to reproductive health. The Women's March on Washington, held the day after the Trump inauguration and encompassing over 650 marches across the country, has been estimated as the largest single-day demonstration in U.S. history. Planned Parenthood and NARAL (National Association for the Repeal of Abortion Laws) Pro-Choice America, among other progressive causes, saw their membership and donations spike in the aftermath of the election.

AIDS AND MODERN AMERICA

Two new and deadly epidemics ravaged many American towns and cities beginning in the 1980s. One was a dramatic increase in drug use, which penetrated nearly every community in the nation. The enormous demand for drugs, and particularly for "crack" cocaine in the late 1980s and early 1990s, spawned what was in effect a multibillion-dollar industry. Drug use declined significantly among middle-class people beginning in the late 1980s, largely because of educational campaigns, but the epidemic declined much more slowly in the poor urban neighborhoods, where it was doing the most severe damage. Yet drug abuse has never gone away. Indeed, death rates from drug overdoses have increased almost every year since 1980. More recently, widespread usage of heroin and other opioids (typically prescription painkillers) has spiked drug overdose deaths to a record high in 2016, to over 59.000. And nearly half of all federal inmates are currently serving time for drug-related offenses.

The drug epidemic facilitated the rapid spread of a new and lethal disease first documented in 1981 and soon named **AIDS** (acquired immune deficiency syndrome). AIDS is the product of the human immunodeficiency virus (HIV), which is transmitted by the exchange of body fluids (blood or semen) as can easily happen when individuals share hypodermic needles during intravenous drug usage or have unprotected sex. The virus gradually destroys the body's immune system and makes its victims highly vulnerable to a number of diseases (particularly to various forms of cancer and pneumonia) to which they would otherwise have a natural resistance.

During the early history of the disease, those infected with the virus (that is, those who identified as "HIV-positive") and became ill were almost certain to die. The first American victims of AIDS (and for many years the group among whom cases remained the most numerous) were gay, usually men. But by the late 1980s, as the gay community began to implement aggressive education and intervention programs, the most rapid increase in the spread of the disease occurred among heterosexuals, many of them intravenous drug users sharing needles.

In the mid-1990s, AIDS researchers, after years of frustration, finally began discovering effective treatments for the disease. By taking a combination of powerful drugs on a rigorous schedule, among them a group known as protease inhibitors, even people with advanced cases of AIDS experienced dramatic improvement—so much so that in many cases there were no measurable quantities of the virus left in their bloodstreams. Currently a diagnosis of AIDS is not the near-certain death sentence it was in the late nineties; rather, new medication regimes permit those living with AIDS to successfully manage the disease and live mostly normal lives. Every president has steadily increased federal funding for AIDS research and education and for the care of individuals living with AIDS, both domestically and abroad. President George W. Bush provided $15 billion to fight AIDS in Africa, where the epidemic was rampant and the poor had little access to drugs. In the budget for 2017, President Obama called for $30.4 billion to combat AIDS.

The Centers for Disease Control and Prevention (CDC) estimates that 1.1 million Americans currently suffer from AIDS, nearly one in seven not even realizing that they are infected. But the United States represents only a tiny proportion of the worldwide total of people afflicted with HIV, an estimated 36.7 million people at the end of 2015 (when the last census was taken). Over two-thirds of those cases are concentrated in Africa.

Gay Americans and Same-Sex Marriage

In the late twentieth century, inspired in part by the success of AIDS activists in winning political support and funding, many gay men and lesbians began to lobby for greater protections under the law, particularly the right to marry. Until the 1990s, the issue of same-sex marriage was not a national political issue. But in 1993, Hawaii's Supreme Court ruled in *Baehr v. Lewin* that the state needed a compelling reason to bar same-sex marriage. In response, Congress easily passed the **Defense of Marriage Act (DOMA)** in 1996 with rare bipartisan support. President Clinton signed it into law. DOMA exempted states from being required to recognize same-sex marriages from other states. It also defined marriage as being between a man and a woman and denied same-sex married couples the ability to be classified as "spouses" for federal purposes, such as the filing of joint tax returns, Social Security survivor benefit claims, adoption papers, and immigration applications. Gay rights activists identified more than 1,000 protections and responsibilities of marriage denied them by DOMA. Thirty states quickly followed suit with similar laws.

Almost immediately, gay men and lesbians and their supporters took to the courts in protest. They typically argued that DOMA and related state laws violated the Equal Protection Clause of the Fourteenth Amendment of the U.S. Constitution. They gained many victories. By 2013, eleven states had passed new legislation making same-sex marriage legal. That year as well the U.S. Supreme Court struck down the section of DOMA defining marriage as being between two people of the opposite sex, so that all married couples living in states where same-sex marriage is legal are classified as spouses by the federal government. The tide against same-sex marriage appeared to be turning.

Driving the radical change in the legal status of same-sex marriage, in addition to the guidance and political savvy of its advocates, was a profound shift in public opinion about the issue. Indeed, broad popular support for same-sex marriage grew steadily since the end of the twentieth century, primarily among younger generations of Americans. Still, there was no national consensus about the legality of same-sex marriage, and many southern and midwestern states had laws on the books preventing same-sex marriage or were engaged in heated legal battles over it. For example, in January 2015 in Alabama, a federal judge ruled in favor of same-sex marriage. (See "Consider the Source: Same-Sex Marriage, 2015.") But less than two months later, Alabama's Supreme Court, by a vote of 7 to 1, forbade county officials from issuing a marriage license to any same-sex couple. Ultimately a decision in June by the U.S. Supreme Court broke the legal stalement and compelled Alabama (and all states with gay marriage bans) to issue the licenses. In *Obergefell v. Hodges*, the Court, in a 5-to-4 decision, ruled that the U.S. Constitution guaranteed same-sex couples the fundamental right to marry. Writing for the majority, Justice Anthony Kennedy proclaimed that "No longer may this liberty be denied."

The issue of sexual orientation and citizenship, however, is far from settled. The rights of gay, transgendered, and bisexual Americans are currently being debated in courtrooms and statehouses across the country. Their ability to live free from discrimination typically depends on where they reside; different states practice different statutes because there are few federal laws binding all states to a uniform standard. Indeed, there is no federal law barring a person from being dismissed or denied employment because of sexual orientation. In July 2017, President Trump, in a reversal of policy under President Obama, announced his intention to ban transgendered men and women from serving in the military, although many were already in uniform and serving with distinction. As with the matter of same-sex marriage, the rights of gay, transgendered, and bisexual Americans will likely be settled by the Supreme Court.

THE CONTEMPORARY ENVIRONMENTAL MOVEMENT

The environmental movement in the United States continued to expand in the decades after the 1980s. It drew inspiration from the older international environmental movement, which organized in the 1960s and steadily grew in political power. (See "America in the World: The Global Environmental Movement.") After the first Earth Day, domestic environmental issues gained increasing attention and support. Although the federal government displayed only intermittent interest in the subject, environmentalists won a series of significant battles, mostly at the local level. They blocked the construction of roads, airports, and other projects that they claimed would be ecologically dangerous, taking advantage of new legislation protecting endangered species and environmentally fragile regions.

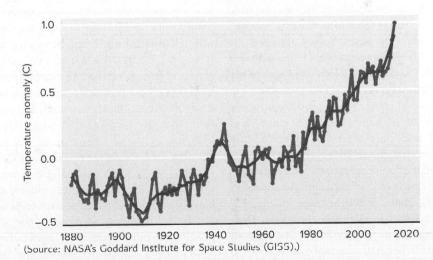

(Source: NASA's Goddard Institute for Space Studies (GISS).)

RISING GLOBAL TEMPERATURES This graph of the Global Land-Ocean Temperature Index from NASA's Goddard Institute for Space Studies illustrates the change in global surface temperature relative to 1951–1980 average temperatures.

SAME-SEX MARRIAGE, 2015

The debate over the right of people of the same sex to marry legally and enjoy the full range of benefits accorded to married couples under federal and state law hit a fever pitch in early January 2015.

Nearly four years earlier, Cari Searcy and Kimberly McKeand, a same-sex couple who were legally married in California under that state's laws, wanted Searcy to be able to adopt McKeand's eight-year-old biological son under a provision of Alabama's adoption code that allows a person to adopt her "spouse's child." But Searcy's petition was denied in December 2011 based on the Alabama Sanctity of Marriage Amendment and the closely related Alabama Marriage Protection Act. Both laws declared that "Marriage is inherently a unique relationship between a man and a woman," that "No marriage license shall be issued in the State of Alabama to parties of the same sex," and that "The State of Alabama shall not recognize as valid any marriage of parties of the same sex that occurred or was alleged to have occurred as a result of the law of any jurisdiction regardless of whether a marriage license was issued." Therefore, because Alabama does not recognize the legality of same-sex plaintiffs' marriage, Searcy failed to qualify as a "spouse" for adoption purposes. Searcy appealed the denial of her adoption petition to the Alabama Court of Civil Appeals, which ruled against her and affirmed the decision of the probate court.

In federal court, Searcy sued the attorney general of Alabama, Luther Strange, and sought to declare these two Alabama state laws unconstitutional on the grounds that they violated the due-process clause and equal protection clause of the Fourteenth Amendment. Callie Granade, a federal judge for the U.S. District Court in Alabama (Southern Division), agreed in January 2015. She ordered the state to begin to issue marriage licenses to same-sex couples immediately, though the order was delayed while Attorney General

Strange appealed to the U.S. Supreme Court for a stay. But once the High Court refused to hear the case, on February 9, Granade's order took effect. Some counties obliged, but others didn't, heeding the encouragement of Alabama's Supreme Court justice, Roy Moore, to ignore the federal ruling. Then, in March 2015, the state's Supreme Court ruled 7 to 1 that all probate justices (county officials charged with the management of marriage licenses) must cease issuing marriage licenses to same-sex couples. In June, the U.S. Supreme Court ruled that gay marriage bans such as Alabama's were unconstitutional.

In the following excerpt from Judge Granade's ruling, she clarifies why she ruled in favor of same-sex marriage.

Defendant contends that Alabama has a legitimate interest in protecting the ties between children and their biological parents and other biological kin. However, the Court finds that the laws in question are not narrowly tailored to fulfill the reported interest. The Attorney General does not explain how allowing or recognizing same-sex marriage between two consenting adults will prevent heterosexual parents or other biological kin from caring for their biological children. He proffers no justification for why it is that the provisions in question single out same-sex couples and prohibit them, and them alone, from marrying in order to meet that goal. Alabama does not exclude from marriage any other couples who are either unwilling or unable to biologically procreate. There is no law prohibiting infertile couples, elderly couples, or couples who do not wish to procreate from marrying. Nor does the state prohibit recognition of marriages between such couples from other states. The attorney general fails to demonstrate any rational, much less compelling, link between its prohibition and non-recognition of same-sex marriage and its goal of having more children raised in the biological family structure the state wishes to promote. There has been no evidence presented that these marriage laws have any effect on the choices of couples to have or raise children, whether they are same-sex couples or opposite-sex couples. In sum, the laws in question are an irrational way of promoting biological relationships in Alabama. . . .

If anything, Alabama's prohibition of same-sex marriage detracts from its goal of promoting optimal environments for children. Those children currently being raised by same-sex parents in Alabama are just as worthy of protection and recognition by the State as are the children being raised by opposite-sex parents. Yet Alabama's Sanctity laws harms the children of same-sex couples for the same reasons that the [U.S.] Supreme Court found that the Defense of Marriage Act harmed the children of same-sex couples. Such a law "humiliates . . . thousands of children now being raised by same-sex couples. The law in question makes it even more difficult for the children to understand the integrity and closeness of their own family and its concord with other families in their community and in their daily lives." [Windsor, 133 S. Ct. at 2694] Alabama's prohibition and non-recognition of same-sex marriage "also brings financial harm to children of same-sex couples," [id at 2695] because it denies the families of these children a panoply of benefits that the State and the federal government offer to families who are legally wed. Additionally, these laws further injures those children of all couples who are themselves gay or lesbian, and who will grow up knowing that Alabama does not believe they are as capable of creating a family as their heterosexual friends.

For all of these reasons, the court finds that Alabama's marriage laws violate the Due Process Clause and Equal Protection Clause of the Fourteenth Amendment to the United States Constitution.

UNDERSTAND, ANALYZE, & EVALUATE

1. How does Judge Granade's ruling reflect—or not reflect—changing popular attitudes toward gay men and lesbians?
2. How is the definition of a "family" being redefined?
3. In what ways do the actions of Judge Roy Moore and the Alabama Supreme Court evoke tensions between the state and civil rights protesters of the 1950s and 1960s? Or are the civil rights of black Americans and gay and lesbian Americans two very different issues?
4. In his dissenting opinion in *Obergefell v. Hodges*, Supreme Court Justice John Roberts said, "The fundamental right to marry does not include a right to make a state change its definition of marriage." What does the decision in *Searcy v. Strange* have to say about the state's definition of marriage?

Source: *Searcy v. Strange*, Civil Action No. 14-0208-CG-N (S.D. Ala. Jan. 25, 2015), https://scholar.google.com/scholar_case?case=14084561318965877067&hl=en&as_sdt=6&as_vis=1&oi=scholarr (accessed March 19, 2015).

In the late 1980s, the environmental movement began to mobilize around a new and ominous challenge—"global warming." Many scientists argued that a steady rise in the earth's temperature and corresponding climate changes could be linked to CO_2 emissions from the burning of fossil fuels (most notably coal and oil). Although these findings were disputed, by the early twenty-first century a growing consensus began to emerge—in part as a result of the leadership of significant public figures, such as former vice president Al Gore, who won a Nobel Peace Prize in 2007 for his efforts to draw attention to the problem.

THE GLOBAL ENVIRONMENTAL MOVEMENT

An international movement for well over a century, environmentalism has grown rapidly throughout the world in the late twentieth and early twenty-first centuries. What began as a series of localized efforts to preserve wilderness sites and to clean up air and water has evolved into a broad effort to deal with concerns that affect, and threaten, the entire globe.

During the 1960s, 1970s, and 1980s, while long-standing American environmental associations such as the Wilderness Society, the Sierra Club, and the National Audubon Society were being rejuvenated, organizations elsewhere in the world sought to create an international environmental movement. The World Wildlife Fund (WWF), created in Switzerland in 1961, eventually attracted more than 5 million supporters in over 150 countries and now claims to be the world's largest independent conservation organization. Greenpeace was founded in Canada in 1971 to oppose U.S. nuclear testing off the coast of Alaska. It, too, has grown into an international organization, with 2.8 million financial supporters worldwide and a presence in forty nations.

Nongovernmental organizations (NGOs) such as Greenpeace and WWF were not the only institutions to recognize environmental concerns. In June 1972, the United Nations (UN) held its first Conference on the Human Environment in Stockholm, Sweden. Representatives of 113 countries attended the conference to discuss issues of global environmental importance—including the role of chlorofluorocarbons (CFCs), a chemical compound used in refrigerants and aerosol sprays, in depleting the ozone layer.

After the conference, the UN created the United Nations Environment Programme (UNEP) to help coordinate international efforts for environmentalism and encourage sustainable development in poorer nations around the world.

The world's first "Green" parties—political parties explicitly devoted to environmental concerns (and often to other issues of social justice)—appeared in 1972, beginning in New Zealand (the Values Party) and Tasmania (the United Tasmania Group). Since then, Green parties have proliferated throughout the world, including in the United States. The most powerful Green party to date has been *Die Grünen* in Germany, founded in 1980. *Die Grünen* allied with the Social Democratic Party in a governing coalition from 1998, and in 2000, this coalition successfully passed the Nuclear Exit Law, which set a timetable of twenty years for Germany's eventual abandonment of nuclear power and a switch to renewable energy.

Large-scale ecological catastrophes have often helped galvanize the global environmental movement. Among the more significant of these events was the Bhopal disaster of 1984, in which a gas leak at a Union Carbide pesticide plant in Bhopal, India, resulted in the deaths of between 3,000 and 15,000 people. Two years later, a nuclear reactor accident in the Soviet city of Chernobyl, in Ukraine, caused fifty-six direct deaths, with predictions of many thousands more deaths to follow as a result of exposure. The area around Chernobyl itself is expected to be partially contaminated for 24,000 years, the radioactive half-life of plutonium-239. A less catastrophic nuclear accident at Three Mile Island, Pennsylvania, in 1979 heightened antinuclear sentiment in the United States. In 1989, the oil tanker *Exxon Valdez* ran aground on Bligh Reef in Prince William Sound, Alaska, and spilled approximately 10.9 million gallons of crude oil. Eventually covering thousands of square miles of ocean water (and 1,300 miles of Alaska shoreline) in oil, the spill killed hundreds of thousands of animals instantly and devastated the fragile ecosystem of the sound. The 2010 explosion of the Deepwater Horizon well about 50 miles southeast of the Mississippi Delta caused the largest marine oil spill in history.

In developed, industrialized nations, environmental advocacy has largely focused on energy policy, conservation, clean technologies, and changing individual and social attitudes about consumption (as in the recycling movement). The growth of environmentalism is often linked to issues of human and democratic rights and freedom from First World exploitation. For example, the Green Belt Movement in Kenya, begun in 1977 by Wangari Maathai, encouraged Kenyan women to plant over 30 million trees across the nation to address the challenges of deforestation, soil erosion, and lack of water. The Green Belt Movement became an important human rights and women's rights organization, focused on reducing poverty and promoting peaceful democratic change through environmental conservation and protection. Maathai won the 2004 Nobel Peace Prize for her achievements.

Over the past two decades, the environmental movement has grown even more global in scope, with multilateral environmental treaties and worldwide summits becoming the principal strategies of advocates. In 1997, an international effort to reduce global warming by mandating the lowering of greenhouse gas emissions culminated in the Kyoto Protocol (which the United States did not join). While the George W. Bush administration rejected most efforts to limit carbon emissions, other leading Americans helped bring the issue of global warming to wide attention both in the United States and around the world. Perhaps most notable has been former vice president Al Gore, whose 2006 film *An Inconvenient Truth* may have done more to raise awareness of the threat of global warming than any other recent event—both in the United States and in many other nations. As a result of his efforts, Gore won the 2007 Nobel Peace Prize—an honor he shared with others, appropriately, given the global character of the movement he has championed. His cowinner was the Inter-governmental Panel on Climate Change, launched in Switzerland in 1988 and affiliated with the United Nations.

In the years since Gore's Nobel Peace Prize, climate change has become a major international issue. Overwhelming evidence that increased levels of atmospheric carbon dioxide produced by the use of fossil fuels has began to alter the world's climate has prompted world leaders to take notice. In particular, oceans have begun to rise slowly, large snow and ice bodies melt, and plants grow earlier in their life cycles. In 2015, 195 countries, including the United States, pledged to combat climate change by signing the Paris Accord. In 2017, however, President Trump removed America from the agreement. •

UNDERSTAND, ANALYZE, & EVALUATE

1. Why are environmental movements in developing nations often linked to issues of human rights and protection from exploitation by developed nations? How do developed nations threaten the environment of developing nations?
2. Why do you think the global environmental movement is growing in strength today?

In 1997, representatives of the major industrial nations met in Kyoto, Japan, and agreed to a broad treaty establishing steps toward reducing carbon emissions and thus slowing or reversing global warming. The Clinton administration formally signed the Kyoto Protocol, but nothing came of it. Indeed, Clinton never even submitted it for ratification because the Senate had earlier passed the Byrd-Hagel Resolution by a vote of 95 to 0 that formally rejected the treaty's key tenets. President George W. Bush, while proclaiming grave concern over climate concern, refused to support the Kyoto Protocol because it excluded developing countries like China and India.

Unlike Bush, President Obama met with some success on climate change issues. He championed and signed legislation raising fuel efficiency in passenger cars and trucks in 2012 and directed the Environmental Protection Agency to regulate coal ash, a major CO_2 emitter primarily used in creating electricity. In 2015, Obama notched one of his biggest and most personally meaningful victories despite continued Republican protest. With 195 other countries, he entered into the Paris Accord to combat global climate change. Under the Accord, the United States promised to cut its own greenhouse gas emissions somewhere between 26 and 28 percent of its 2005 levels by 2025. Obama then pledged up to $3 billion to help for poor countries develop ways to battle climate change.

But U.S. participation was short-lived. Five months after taking office, President Trump sharply reversed the American position. He informed other signees of the Paris Accord that the United States would withdraw from the international climate agreement, arguing that it imposed unjust standards on American businesses and consumers. Even though America's departure promises to limit global effort aimed at slowing or reversing global warming, the other signees to the Paris Accord have vowed to keep their work and press on.

AMERICA IN THE WORLD

The celebration of the beginning of a new millennium on January 1, 2000, was an important moment not just because of the change in the calendar. It was notable above all as a global event—a shared and for the most part joyous experience that united the world in its exuberance. But if the millennium celebrations suggested the bright promise of an interconnected world, other events at the dawn of the new century suggested its dark perils. Indeed, the United States' increasing role as an economic and military superpower triggered fears among many Americans about a foreign policy that was too aggressive and trade initiatives that took advantage of low-wage workers in other countries and unfairly benefited large international businesses. The rise of mass protests over America's global economic policies and terrorism painfully brought home the dangers of living in the twenty-first century.

Opposing the "New World Order"

In the United States and other industrial nations, opposition to globalization—or to what President George H. W. Bush once called the "new world order"—took several forms. To many Americans on both the political left and right, the nation's increasingly interventionist foreign policy was deeply troubling. Critics on the left charged that the United States was using military action to advance its economic interests, arguing that the 1991 Gulf War and the Iraq War that began in 2003 were primarily intended to preserve access to foreign oil.

Critics on the right complained that humanitarian interventions in Somalia in 1993 and the Balkans in the late 1990s were too costly and risky. Others worried that the United States was ceding its sovereignty to international organizations, such as United Nations-led peacekeeping missions.

Labor unions insisted that the rapid expansion of free-trade agreements unfairly led to the export of jobs from advanced nations to less developed ones. They pointed to the trend of American manufacturers relocating plants in foreign countries where labor was cheaper and government regulation less. Civil rights groups argued that the global economy was creating new classes of "slave laborers" working in conditions that few Western nations would tolerate. Environmentalists argued that globalization, in exporting industry to low-wage countries, also exported industrial pollution and toxic waste into nations that had no effective laws to control them, and contributed significantly to global warming. And still others opposed global economic arrangements on the grounds that they enriched and empowered large multinational corporations and threatened the freedom and autonomy of individuals and communities.

Varied opponents of globalization found a common enemy in the multinational institutions that policed and advanced the global economy. Among them were the World Trade Organization, which monitored the enforcement of the General Agreement on Tariffs and Trade (GATT) treaties of the 1990s; the International Monetary Fund (IMF), which controlled international credit and exchange rates; and the World Bank, which made money available for development projects in many countries. In November 1999, when leaders of leading industrial nations gathered for their annual meeting in Seattle, Washington, tens of thousands protested—most of them peacefully. But some of them clashed with police, smashed store windows, and all but paralyzed the city. A few months later, a smaller but still substantial demonstration disrupted meetings of the IMF and the World Bank in Washington, D.C. And in July 2001, at a meeting of the same leaders in Genoa, Italy, an estimated 50,000 demonstrators battled with police in a melee that left one protester dead and several hundred injured. The participants in the meeting responded to the demonstrations by pledging $1.2 billion to fight the AIDS epidemic in developing countries—and by deciding to hold future meetings in remote locations far from major cities.

THE RISE OF TERRORISM

Outside the industrialized West, the impact of globalization sparked other controversies. Many citizens of nonindustrialized nations resented the way the world economy had left them in poverty. In their view, the developed world exploited and oppressed them. In some parts of the nonindustrialized world—particularly in some of the Islamic nations of the Middle East—the increasing reach of globalization created additional grievances, rooted not just in economics but also in religion and culture.

The Iranian Revolution of 1979, in which orthodox Muslims ousted a despotic government, was one of the first large and visible manifestations of a phenomenon that eventually reached across much of the Islamic world. It threatened the stability of the globe. Militants used isolated incidents of violence and mayhem, designed to disrupt societies and governments and to create fear among their peoples. Such tactics are known to the world as terrorism.

Terrorism refers to the use of violence as a form of intimidation against peoples and governments. It is neither a new term nor one confined to contemporary America. Acts of what came to be called terrorism have occurred in many parts of the world. Irish revolutionaries engaged in terrorism regularly against the English through much of the twentieth century. Jews used it in Palestine against the British before the creation of Israel, and Palestinians have used it frequently against Jews in Israel—particularly in the past several decades. Revolutionary groups in Italy, Germany, Japan, and France have engaged in terrorist acts intermittently over the past several decades.

The United States, too, has experienced terrorism for many years, much of it against American targets abroad—including the bombing of the Marine barracks in Beirut in 1983; the explosion that brought down an American airliner over Lockerbie, Scotland, in 1988; the bombing of American embassies in 1998; and the assault on the U.S. naval vessel *Cole* in 2000. Terrorist incidents were relatively rare, but not unknown, within the United States itself prior to September 11, 2001. Militants on the American left performed various acts of terror in the 1960s and early 1970s as part of antiwar and anarchist movements. Timothy McVeigh, part of a militant right-wing movement, executed the largest single terrorist act on American soil before 9/11 when he blew up a federal building in Oklahoma City in 1995, killing 168 people. A year later, serial bomber Eric Robert Rudolph wreaked havoc at the Summer Olympics in Atlanta. And in 1993, foreign Islamic militants launched a successful terrorist attack on American soil, detonating a bomb in the parking garage of the World Trade Center that killed six people, injured a thousand, and caused serious but not irreparable structural damage to the towers.

Most Americans, however, considered terrorism a problem mainly confined to other nations. That changed swiftly on September 11, 2001, when **Al Qaeda** terrorists, in a series of coordinated attacks, hijacked four planes. They drove two into the World Trade towers in New York, collapsing both structures; and another into the Pentagon outside Washington, damaging it heavily. The final plane, on route to Washington, crashed in rural Pennsylvania after passengers fought with the hijackers. Nearly 3,000 Americans

(©Robert J Fisch/Flickr Open/Getty Images)

SEPTEMBER 11, 2001 At 9:03 AM, hijackers crashed United Airlines Flight 175 into floors 75-85 of the New York City's World Trade Center South Tower, killing all on board and hundreds inside the building. Only 16 minutes earlier another group of hijackers had piloted American Airlines Flight 11 into floors 93-99 of the North Tower, seen here burning.

were killed. The **9/11 attacks** jolted Americans out of any sense of complacency and made them confront the dangers of international terrorism. They also initiated a new and aggressive campaign by the federal government and military to combat foreign threats to American security.

THE WAR ON TERROR

In the aftermath of September 11, 2001, the U.S. government launched what President Bush called a "war on terror." The attacks on the World Trade Center and the Pentagon, government intelligence indicated, had been planned and orchestrated by Middle Eastern agents of a powerful terrorist network known as Al Qaeda. Its leader, **Osama bin Laden**—until 2001 little known outside the Arab world—quickly became one of the most notorious figures in the world. The militant Taliban government of Afghanistan had sheltered and supported Al Qaeda previously, and most reports placed bin Laden in its continued care. In 2001, NATO, led by the United States, began a sustained campaign of bombing against the regime and sent in ground troops. Afghanistan's Taliban regime quickly collapsed, and its leaders—along with the Al Qaeda fighters allied with them—fled the capital, Kabul. American and anti-Taliban Afghan troops pursued them into the mountains but failed to capture bin Laden and the other leaders of his organization.

American forces in Afghanistan rounded up several hundred people with suspected connections to the Taliban and Al Qaeda and moved these prisoners (and eventually others) to a facility at the American military base in **Guantánamo**, Cuba. They were among the first suspected terrorists to be handled by the Bush administration in dealing with terrorism after September 11, 2001. They were held for months, and in some cases years, without access to lawyers, without facing formal charges, and were subjected to intensive interrogation and at times even torture. Critics denounced the dangers to basic civil liberties. At the same time, the federal government dramatically increased the approval of secret surveillance warrants against alleged foreign spies living in the United States. Overseeing these warrants is the Foreign Intelligence Surveillance (FISA) Court, established in 1978, whose proceedings are strictly shielded from public view. The covert nature of the court and its controversial rulings caused a long-running debate over the government's tactics to fight terror. Most notably, and as exposed in a cache of leaked documents by one-time CIA contractor Edward Snowden, the court compelled Verizon to turn over a log of customer cell phone records to the National Security Administration in 2013. Still, pointing to Guantánamo Bay and the newly expanded reach of the FISA Court, others argued that these new tactics were sadly necessary to protect Americans. In the matter of how to combat terrorism effectively and constitutionally, there were no easy answers. President Obama, in his first month in the White House, pledged to close the prison at Guantánamo in part because of the unfair treatment of its prisoners. But he soon found that the promise was impossible to keep during the war on terror.

THE IRAQ WAR

In his State of the Union address to Congress in January 2002, President Bush spoke of an "axis of evil," which included the nations of Iraq, Iran, and North Korea—all countries with anti-American regimes that either possessed or assumed to be trying to acquire nuclear weapons. Although Bush did not say so at the time, many people around the world interpreted these words to mean that the United States would soon try to topple the government of Saddam Hussein in Iraq.

For over a year, the Bush administration slowly built a public case for invading Iraq. Much it rested on two claims, neither of which directly implicated Hussein in the 1993 or 2001 deadly attacks on the World Trade Center in New York City. One was that Iraq was supporting terrorist groups that were hostile to the United States. The other, and eventually the more important, was that Iraq either had or was developing what came to be known as "weapons of mass destruction," which included nuclear weapons and agents of chemical and biological warfare. Less central to these arguments, at least in the United States, was the charge that the Hussein government was responsible for major violations of human rights. Except for the last, none of these claims turned out to be accurate.

In March 2003, American troops, with support from Great Britain and several other countries and partial authorization from the United Nations, invaded Iraq and quickly toppled the Hussein regime, beginning the **Iraq War**. Hussein himself went into hiding but was eventually captured in December 2003. He was executed in Iraq on December 30, 2006. In May 2003, shortly after the American capture of Baghdad, President Bush made a dramatic appearance on an aircraft carrier off the coast of California, where he declared victory in the Battle of Iraq, praised the military and allies in the war effort, and warned of the "difficult work to do in Iraq" while standing in front of a large sign reading "Mission Accomplished."

In the following months, however, events in Iraq suggested that the mission had only just begun. Of the more than 4,800 American soldiers killed in Iraq as of 2014, over 4,000 of them died after the "mission accomplished" speech. And despite significant efforts by the United States and its allies to hand over authority to an Iraqi government and to restore order to the country, insurgents continued to disrupt the recovery with persistent attacks and terrorist actions throughout the fragile nation.

Support for the war in the United States steadily declined in the years after the first claim of victory. The failure to find widespread and conclusive evidence of the weapons of mass destruction was a hammer blow to the war's credibility. Another blow came from reports of the torture and humiliation of Iraqi prisoners by American soldiers at the Abu Ghraib prison in Baghdad and other sites in Iraq and around the world.

The invasion of Iraq was the most visible evidence of a basic change in the long-term structure of modern American foreign policy. Ever since the late 1940s, the containment policy had become the cornerstone of America's role in the world. The United States had worked to maintain global stability by containing, but not often directly threatening or attacking, its adversaries. Even after the Cold War ended, the United States strove to practice containment and exercise military constraint despite its unchallenged military preeminence. In the administrations of George H. W. Bush and Bill Clinton, for example, American leaders still worked closely with the United Nations and NATO to achieve U.S. international goals and resisted taking unilateral military action.

There had always been those who criticized these constraints. They believed that America should do more than maintain stability and move actively to topple undemocratic regimes and destroy potential enemies of the United States. In the administration of George W. Bush, these critics took control of American foreign policy and began to reshape it. The legacy of containment was largely repudiated. Instead, the public stance of the American government was that the United States had the right and the responsibility to fight tyranny and spread freedom throughout the world—not just by exhortation and example but also, when necessary, by military force. In Latvia in May 2005, President Bush spoke of the decision at the end of World War II not to challenge Soviet domination of Eastern Europe. That decision had rested on the belief that such a challenge would lead the United States into another war. The controversial agreement negotiated at Yalta in 1945 by Roosevelt,

Churchill, and Stalin, which failed to end the Soviet occupation of Poland and other Eastern European nations, was, the president said, part of an "unjust tradition" by which powerful governments sacrificed the interests of small nations. "This attempt to sacrifice freedom for the sake of stability," the president continued, "left a continent divided and unstable." The lesson, Bush suggested, was that the United States and other great powers should value stability less and freedom more, and should be willing to take greater risks in the world to end tyranny and oppression.

New Challenges in the Middle East

The end of the American combat role in Iraq was already under way in the last year of the Bush administration. Obama brought it to a close in 2010 and withdrew the last combat troops in 2011. At the same time, he committed significant additional soldiers to the war in Afghanistan, where Americans had been fighting since 2001. Obama escalated the **Afghan war** in 2011. For almost ten years, a major goal of American foreign policy was to find Osama bin Laden, the head of Al Qaeda, the organization behind the destruction of 9/11. In May 2011, Navy Seals found and killed bin Laden. Shortly afterward, leaders from countries of the North Atlantic Treaty Organization drafted a plan for the withdrawal of international forces from Afghanistan and facilitated peace talks between the Afghan government and the Taliban. Obama ordered nearly all American troops to leave the country and cease combat operations by the close of 2014, in effect ending American involvement in the conflict.

Despite the end of the Iraq War and the killing of bin Laden, conflict in the Middle East continued to dominate American foreign policy under Obama. The president had appointed Hillary Clinton as his secretary of state and together they tried to create peace between Israel and Palestine—an effort that made little or no progress. Elsewhere they sought to improve relationships damaged by the Iraq War and to build new international trade opportunities. But resurgent turmoil in the Middle East created new challenges. The United States intervened in a civil war in Libya and helped end the regime of the long-standing leader Muammar al-Qaddafi. And in 2012, Obama and Clinton began to pressure Iran from creating nuclear weapons. Three years later, Iran signed an international pact effectively halting its development of any nuclear arms in exchange for lifting economic sanctions originally put in place to check its nuclear ambitions. Yet that deal is currently in danger of crumbling. President Trump openly doubts Iran will ever keep its word while Iran now says it could restart its nuclear program immediately if Trump follows through on his threat to cancel the deal.

On a different front, Syria, a country locked in violent civil war since 2011, experienced a new and terrifying level of bloodshed. Opponents of the Ba'ath government sought the ouster of President Bashar al-Assad and his repressive regime. Assad unleashed the army in response, killing an estimated 120,000 of his own people by September 2013. The displacement of hundreds of thousands of Syrians into neighboring countries threatened to further destabilize the region. Assad's use of chemical weapons triggered a strong condemnation by the United States and its European allies, such as Britain, France, and Germany. Working with Russia, a traditional ally of the Assad regime, the United States and Europe brokered a delicate deal to remove the stockpile of chemical weapons from the country. Obama, aware of his nation's unwillingness to become involved in another ground war, resisted calls for sending troops to dislodge Assad. But four months after Obama left office, in April 2017, Syria thumbed its nose at its earlier anti-chemical weapons pledge and gassed over eighty to death. President Trump swiftly ordered the firing of fifty-nine cruise missiles on the Syrian government air base from which the chemical attacks were launched.

A volatile element in the Syrian conflict—as well as politics in Iraq and throughout the Middle East and Europe—has been the rise of ISIS (the Islamic State of Iraq and Syria). Composed of former Al Qaeda fighters and their supporters, this powerful rebel group seeks not only to topple the Assad regime but more broadly to install itself as a conservative Islamic state that would stamp out any Western cultural and political influence throughout the world. As a result, it violently opposes Western nations like America and its allies, including Islamic countries such as Jordan and Saudi Arabia that support America's position. ISIS has steadily conducted campaigns of terror against Western nations, kidnapping and murdering American and British citizens and posting gruesome videos of beheadings to social media websites around the world. It has used online propaganda to radicalize individuals who have carried out more than 140 terrorist attacks in twenty-nine countries beyond Iraq and Syria, killing at least 2,000 people and injuring many more. In 2018, ISIS serves as a symbol of the persistent instability of the region and a reminder of the continuing threat of terrorism.

DIPLOMACY AND THREATS IN EAST ASIA

Even though Obama focused much of his foreign policy on the Middle East, China's growing military and economic power also grabbed his attention. Recognizing the need to open new doors of cooperation, Obama became the first president to visit China during his first year in office. Secretary of State Clinton followed by announcing a "pivot" of American diplomatic and military focus to Asia as a way to expand and protect American interests there.

(©Kirsty Wigglesworth/AP Photo)

DRONES Unmanned combat air vehicles (UCAVs), also known as drones, have become weapons of choice during many U.S. military engagements throughout the world. Pilots operate these vehicles from remote sites, a practice that was unimaginable when the international laws of war were last drafted in 1949. In calling for an examination of the use of drones, critics have cited the unintended killing of citizens in Pakistan and the targeting of three American citizens by U.S. drones in Yemen.

In particular she intended to facilitate greater access to booming Chinese markets for struggling U.S. manufacturers and to defuse the threat of aggression and nuclear proliferation by China's close ally, North Korea. But Obama and Secretary Clinton were also wary of China's economic ambitions. When China established the Asian Infrastructure Investment Bank in 2016 as a way to bolster its leadership in regional trade, the Obama administration accelerated efforts to forge the Trans-Pacific Partnership with Asian and Pacific allies—a partnership that never came into being before Obama left office and, given President Trump's unfavorable opinion of it, probably never will.

China has become a major focus for the Trump administration during its early days as well, although for a very different reason—to help establish better relations with North Korea. North Korea has publicly bragged of getting close to developing a fully fledged nuclear program and begun to test long-range missiles capable of delivering a nuclear payload to American allies like South Korea and Japan and the American territory of Guam. North Korea's dictator, Kim Jong-un, has also boasted that his scientists are nearing completion of a new intercontinental ballistic missile capable of reaching Hawaii. In response, Trump officials have sought to enlist China in an effort to restrain North Korea's bellicosity and halt the progress of its nuclear program. At the same time, the United States had led a successful effort at the United Nations to impose economic sanctions on North Korea as a way of encouraging it to curb its nuclear ambitions and tamp down its aggressive posture. President Trump himself has sworn to respond militarily to any effort by North Korea to threaten or attach an American ally.

A New Cold War?

Turmoil in the Middle East and the threat of terrorism are not the only focal points of current American foreign policy. In a bold move that reignited memories of the Cold War, Russia, under the leadership of President **Vladimir Putin**, annexed the Ukrainian territory of Crimea in March 2014. Putin inserted military troops to support Russian separatists and quickly established a firm grip over the local government and untrammeled access to the city and Bay of Sevastopal, home to Russia's Black Sea fleet. Ignoring a flurry of international peace initiatives and sanctions imposed by the United States, its allies, and the United Nations, Putin tightened his hold over Crimea and even implemented sanctions of his own: he eliminated most agricultural imports from countries opposing him.

Closer to home, American intelligence services concluded that Russia meddled in the run-up to the 2016 presidential elections. Despite denials from Putin, they claim that Russian hackers penetrated Democratic Party electronic files and e-mails and leaked their contents as part of a concerted effort to benefit the Trump campaign. In summer 2017, the Justice Department appointed Robert S. Mueller, the former director of the Federal Bureau of Investigation, as special counsel to oversee a formal investigation into any links between the Russian government and the Trump presidential campaign. His work is ongoing. And in July 2018, President Trump visited Putin to improve relations between their countries but achieved no clear resolution.

The relationship between Russia and America remains tense, with no resolution satisfactory to both countries over the issue of Crimea or the 2016 presidential election in sight. It reminds us that major conflicts between the United States and countries in central and eastern Europe did not end with the fall of the Berlin Wall or collapse of the Soviet Union, but persist in the form of nations like Russia intent on aggressively expanding its sphere of international influence.

CONCLUSION

The United States in the first years of the twenty-first century battled new challenges and anxieties. U.S. foreign policy after the attacks of September 11, 2001, not only divided the American people but had also deeply alienated much of the world. Crises in the Middle East made it impossible to ignore the persistent threat of terrorism and extremism while conflict with Russia brought back Cold War fears of instability in eastern and central Europe. The American economy was struggling as early as 2007 and, in the fall of 2008, experienced the worst economic crisis since the Great Depression. By 2014 the economy had improved but polls indicated a continuing sense of uncertainty about the future among many Americans. Gridlock continued at the federal level, making it difficult to achieve sweeping reform in several key areas. Political divisions—not only among politicians but also among voters—are as great as they have been in many years.

The United States still remains the wealthiest and most powerful nation in the world, and it continues to cherish great ideals and great hopes. Moving forward into an uncertain future, Americans are burdened with serious problems and great challenges, but they are also armed with extraordinary resilience and energy that has allowed the nation—through its long and turbulent history—to endure, to flourish, and to imagine and strive for a better future.

KEY TERMS/PEOPLE/PLACES/EVENTS

Affordable Care Act 793
Afghan war 817
AIDS 805
Al Qaeda 814
Barack Obama 791
Defense of Marriage Act
  (DOMA) 806

Donald Trump 797
George W. Bush 789
Great Recession
  of 2008 792
Guantánamo 815
Hillary Rodham Clinton 786
Iraq War 816

9/11 attacks 815
Occupy Wall Street
  (OWS) 796
Osama bin Laden 815
Tea Party movement 793
terrorism 813
Vladimir Putin 819

RECALL AND REFLECT

1. How has partisanship affected how presidents governed in the last twenty-five years?
2. How has America's relationship to the rest of the world changed as a result of the war on terror and in particular the Iraq War?
3. How did the digital revolution affect the American economy?
4. What were the key causes of the Great Recession?

APPENDIX

The Declaration of Independence
The Constitution of the United States

THE DECLARATION OF INDEPENDENCE

In Congress, July 4, 1776,

THE UNANIMOUS DECLARATION OF THE THIRTEEN UNITED STATES OF AMERICA

When, in the course of human events, it becomes necessary for one people to dissolve the political bands which have connected them with another, and to assume, among the powers of the earth, the separate and equal station to which the laws of nature and of nature's God entitle them, a decent respect to the opinions of mankind requires that they should declare the causes which impel them to the separation.

We hold these truths to be self-evident, that all men are created equal; that they are endowed by their Creator with certain unalienable rights; that among these, are life, liberty, and the pursuit of happiness. That, to secure these rights, governments are instituted among men, deriving their just powers from the consent of the governed; that, whenever any form of government becomes destructive of these ends, it is the right of the people to alter or to abolish it, and to institute a new government, laying its foundation on such principles, and organizing its powers in such form, as to them shall seem most likely to effect their safety and happiness. Prudence, indeed, will dictate that governments long established, should not be changed for light and transient causes; and, accordingly, all experience hath shown, that mankind are more disposed to suffer, while evils are sufferable, than to right themselves by abolishing the forms to which they are accustomed. But, when a long train of abuses and usurpations, pursuing invariably the same object, evinces a design to reduce them under absolute despotism, it is their right, it is their duty, to throw off such government and to provide new guards for their future security. Such has been the patient sufferance of these colonies, and such is now the necessity which constrains them to alter their former systems of government. The history of the present King of Great Britain is a history of repeated injuries and usurpations, all having, in direct object, the establishment of an absolute tyranny over these States. To prove this, let facts be submitted to a candid world:

He has refused his assent to laws the most wholesome and necessary for the public good.

He has forbidden his governors to pass laws of immediate and pressing importance, unless suspended in their operation till his assent should be obtained; and, when so suspended, he has utterly neglected to attend to them.

He has refused to pass other laws for the accommodation of large districts of people, unless those people would relinquish the right of representation in the legislature; a right inestimable to them, and formidable to tyrants only.

He has called together legislative bodies at places unusual, uncomfortable, and distant from the depository of their public records, for the sole purpose of fatiguing them into compliance with his measures.

He has dissolved representative houses repeatedly for opposing, with manly firmness, his invasions on the rights of the people.

He has refused, for a long time after such dissolutions, to cause others to be elected; whereby the legislative powers, incapable of annihilation, have returned to the people at large for their exercise; the state remaining, in the meantime, exposed to all the danger of invasion from without, and compulsions within.

He has endeavored to prevent the population of these States; for that purpose, obstructing the laws for naturalization of foreigners, refusing to pass others to encourage their migration hither, and raising the conditions of new appropriations of lands.

He has obstructed the administration of justice, by refusing his assent to laws for establishing judiciary powers.

He has made judges dependent on his will alone, for the tenure of their offices, and the amount and payment of their salaries.

He has erected a multitude of new offices, and sent hither swarms of officers to harass our people, and eat out their substance.

He has kept among us, in time of peace, standing armies, without the consent of our legislatures.

He has affected to render the military independent of, and superior to, the civil power.

He has combined, with others, to subject us to a jurisdiction foreign to our Constitution, and unacknowledged by our laws; giving his assent to their acts of pretended legislation:

For quartering large bodies of armed troops among us:

For protecting them by a mock trial, from punishment, for any murders which they should commit on the inhabitants of these States:

For cutting off our trade with all parts of the world:

For imposing taxes on us without our consent:

For depriving us, in many cases, of the benefit of trial by jury:

For transporting us beyond seas to be tried for pretended offences:

For abolishing the free system of English laws in a neighboring province, establishing therein an arbitrary government, and enlarging its boundaries, so as to render it at once an example and fit instrument for introducing the same absolute rule into these colonies:

For taking away our charters, abolishing our most valuable laws, and altering, fundamentally, the powers of our governments:

For suspending our own legislatures, and declaring themselves invested with power to legislate for us in all cases whatsoever.

He has abdicated government here, by declaring us out of his protection, and waging war against us.

He has plundered our seas, ravaged our coasts, burnt our towns, and destroyed the lives of our people.

He is, at this time, transporting large armies of foreign mercenaries to complete the works of death, desolation, and tyranny, already begun, with circumstances of cruelty and perfidy scarcely paralleled in the most barbarous ages, and totally unworthy the head of a civilized nation.

He has constrained our fellow citizens, taken captive on the high seas, to bear arms against their country, to become the executioners of their friends, and brethren, or to fall themselves by their hands.

He has excited domestic insurrections amongst us, and has endeavored to bring on the inhabitants of our frontiers, the merciless Indian savages, whose known rule of warfare is an undistinguished destruction of all ages, sexes, and conditions.

In every stage of these oppressions, we have petitioned for redress, in the most humble terms; our repeated petitions have been answered only by repeated injury. A prince, whose character is thus marked by every act which may define a tyrant, is unfit to be the ruler of a free people.

Nor have we been wanting in attention to our British brethren. We have warned them, from time to time, of attempts made by their legislature to extend an unwarrantable jurisdiction over us. We have reminded them of the circumstances of our emigration and settlement here. We have appealed to their native justice and magnanimity, and we have conjured them, by the ties of our common kindred, to disavow these usurpations, which would inevitably interrupt our connections and correspondence. They, too, have been deaf to the voice of justice and consanguinity. We must, therefore, acquiesce in the necessity which denounces our separation, and hold them as we hold the rest of mankind, enemies in war, in peace, friends.

We, therefore, the representatives of the United States of America, in general Congress assembled, appealing to the Supreme Judge of the world for the rectitude of our intentions, do, in the name, and by the authority of the good people of these colonies, solemnly publish and declare, that these united colonies are, and of right ought to be, free and independent states: that they are absolved from all allegiance to the British Crown, and that all political connection between them and the state of Great Britain is, and ought to be, totally dissolved; and that, as free and independent states, they have full power to levy war, conclude peace, contract alliances, establish commerce, and to do all other acts and things which independent states may of right do. And, for the support of this declaration, with a firm reliance on the protection of Divine Providence, we mutually pledge to each other our lives, our fortunes, and our sacred honor.

The foregoing Declaration was, by order of Congress, engrossed, and signed by the following members:

John Hancock

NEW HAMPSHIRE
Josiah Bartlett
William Whipple
Matthew Thornton

CONNECTICUT
Roger Sherman
Samuel Huntington
William Williams
Oliver Wolcott

NEW YORK
William Floyd
Philip Livingston
Francis Lewis
Lewis Morris

NEW JERSEY
Richard Stockton
John Witherspoon
Francis Hopkinson
John Hart
Abraham Clark

MASSACHUSETTS BAY
Samuel Adams
John Adams
Robert Treat Paine
Elbridge Gerry

PENNSYLVANIA
Robert Morris
Benjamin Rush
Benjamin Franklin
John Morton
George Clymer
James Smith
George Taylor
James Wilson
George Ross

DELAWARE
Caesar Rodney
George Read
Thomas M'Kean

MARYLAND
Samuel Chase
William Paca
Thomas Stone
Charles Carroll, of Carrollton

RHODE ISLAND
Stephen Hopkins
William Ellery

VIRGINIA
George Wythe
Richard Henry Lee
Thomas Jefferson
Benjamin Harrison
Thomas Nelson Jr.
Francis Lightfoot Lee
Carter Braxton

NORTH CAROLINA
William Hooper
Joseph Hewes
John Penn

SOUTH CAROLINA
Edward Rutledge
Thomas Heyward Jr.
Thomas Lynch Jr.
Arthur Middleton

GEORGIA
Button Gwinnett
Lyman Hall
George Walton

Resolved, That copies of the Declaration be sent to the several assemblies, conventions, and committees, or councils of safety, and to the several commanding officers of the continental troops; that it be proclaimed in each of the United States, at the head of the army.

THE CONSTITUTION OF THE UNITED STATES[1]

We the People of the United States, in Order to form a more perfect Union, establish Justice, insure domestic Tranquility, provide for the common defence, promote the general Welfare, and secure the Blessings of Liberty to ourselves and our Posterity, do ordain and establish this CONSTITUTION for the United States of America.

Article I

Section 1.

All legislative Powers herein granted shall be vested in a Congress of the United States, which shall consist of a Senate and House of Representatives.

Section 2.

The House of Representatives shall be composed of Members chosen every second Year by the People of the several States, and the Electors in each State shall have the Qualifications requisite for Electors of the most numerous Branch of the State Legislature.

No Person shall be a Representative who shall not have attained to the Age of twenty-five Years, and been seven Years a Citizen of the United States, and who shall not, when elected, be an Inhabitant of that State in which he shall be chosen.

[Representatives and direct Taxes[2] shall be apportioned among the several States which may be included within this Union, according to their respective Numbers, which shall be determined by adding to the whole Number of free Persons, including those bound to Service for a Term of Years, and excluding Indians not taxed, three fifths of all other Persons.][3] The actual Enumeration shall be made within three Years after the first Meeting of the Congress of the United States, and within every subsequent Term of ten Years, in such Manner as they shall by Law direct. The Number of Representatives shall not exceed one for every thirty Thousand, but each State shall have at Least one Representative; and until such enumeration shall be made, the State of New Hampshire shall be entitled to chuse three, Massachusetts eight, Rhode-Island and Providence Plantations one, Connecticut five, New York six, New Jersey four, Pennsylvania eight, Delaware one, Maryland six, Virginia ten, North Carolina five, South Carolina five, and Georgia three.

When vacancies happen in the Representation from any State, the Executive Authority thereof shall issue Writs of Election to fill such Vacancies.

The House of Representatives shall chuse their Speaker and other Officers; and shall have the sole Power of Impeachment.

Section 3.

The Senate of the United States shall be composed of two Senators from each State, chosen by the Legislature thereof, for six Years; and each Senator shall have one Vote.

Immediately after they shall be assembled in Consequence of the first Election, they shall be divided as equally as may be into three Classes. The Seats of the Senators of the

---

1 This version, which follows the original Constitution in capitalization and spelling, was published by the United States Department of the Interior, Office of Education, in 1935.
2 Altered by the Sixteenth Amendment.
3 Negated by the Fourteenth Amendment.

first Class shall be vacated at the Expiration of the second Year, of the second Class at the Expiration of the fourth Year, and of the third Class at the Expiration of the sixth Year, so that one-third may be chosen every second Year; and if Vacancies happen by Resignation, or otherwise, during the Recess of the Legislature of any State, the Executive thereof may make temporary Appointments until the next Meeting of the Legislature, which shall then fill such Vacancies.

No Person shall be a Senator who shall not have attained to the Age of thirty Years, and been nine Years a Citizen of the United States, and who shall not, when elected, be an Inhabitant of that State for which he shall be chosen.

The Vice President of the United States shall be President of the Senate, but shall have no vote, unless they be equally divided.

The Senate shall chuse their other Officers, and also a President pro tempore, in the absence of the Vice President, or when he shall exercise the Office of President of the United States.

The Senate shall have the sole Power to try all Impeachments. When sitting for that purpose they shall be on Oath or Affirmation. When the President of the United States is tried, the Chief Justice shall preside: And no person shall be convicted without the Concurrence of two thirds of the Members present.

Judgment in Cases of Impeachment shall not extend further than to removal from Office, and disqualification to hold and enjoy any Office of honor, Trust, or Profit under the United States: but the Party convicted shall nevertheless be liable and subject to Indictment, Trial, Judgment, and Punishment, according to Law.

Section 4.
The Times, Places and Manner of holding Elections for Senators and Representatives, shall be prescribed in each State by the Legislature thereof; but the Congress may at any time by Law make or alter such Regulations, except as to the Places of Chusing Senators.

The Congress shall assemble at least once in every Year, and such Meeting shall be on the first Monday in December, unless they shall by Law appoint a different Day.

Section 5.
Each House shall be the Judge of the Elections, Returns and Qualifications of its own Members, and a Majority of each shall constitute a Quorum to do Business; but a smaller number may adjourn from day to day, and may be authorized to compel the Attendance of absent Members, in such Manner, and under such Penalties, as each House may provide.

Each House may determine the Rules of its Proceedings, punish its Members for disorderly Behaviour, and, with the Concurrence of two thirds, expel a Member.

Each House shall keep a Journal of its Proceedings, and from time to time publish the same, excepting such Parts as may in their Judgment require Secrecy; and the Yeas and Nays of the Members of either House on any question shall, at the Desire of one fifth of those Present, be entered on the Journal.

Neither House, during the Session of Congress, shall, without the Consent of the other, adjourn for more than three days, nor to any other Place than that in which the two Houses shall be sitting.

Section 6.
The Senators and Representatives shall receive a Compensation for their Services, to be ascertained by Law, and paid out of the Treasury of the United States. They shall in all

Cases, except Treason, Felony, and Breach of the Peace, be privileged from Arrest during their Attendance at the Session of their respective Houses, and in going to and returning from the same; and for any Speech or Debate in either House, they shall not be questioned in any other Place.

No Senator or Representative shall, during the Time for which he was elected, be appointed to any civil Office under the Authority of the United States, which shall have been created, or the Emoluments whereof shall have been increased, during such time; and no Person holding any Office under the United States shall be a Member of either House during his continuance in Office.

Section 7.

All Bills for raising Revenue shall originate in the House of Representatives; but the Senate may propose or concur with Amendments as on other bills.

Every Bill which shall have passed the House of Representatives and the Senate, shall, before it become a Law, be presented to the President of the United States; If he approve he shall sign it, but if not he shall return it, with his Objections, to that House in which it shall have originated, who shall enter the Objections at large on their Journal, and proceed to reconsider it. If after such Reconsideration two thirds of that House shall agree to pass the bill, it shall be sent, together with the objections, to the other House, by which it shall likewise be reconsidered, and if approved by two thirds of that House, it shall become a Law. But in all such Cases the Votes of both Houses shall be determined by Yeas and Nays, and the Names of the Persons voting for and against the Bill shall be entered on the Journal of each House respectively. If any Bill shall not be returned by the President within ten Days (Sundays excepted) after it shall have been presented to him, the Same shall be a Law, in like Manner as if he had signed it, unless the Congress by their Adjournment prevent its Return, in which Case it shall not be a Law.

Every Order, Resolution, or Vote to which the Concurrence of the Senate and House of Representatives may be necessary (except on a question of Adjournment) shall be presented to the President of the United States; and before the Same shall take Effect, shall be approved by him, or being disapproved by him, shall be repassed by two thirds of the Senate and House of Representatives, according to the Rules and Limitations prescribed in the Case of a Bill.

Section 8.

The Congress shall have Power To lay and collect Taxes, Duties, Imposts and Excises, to pay the Debts and provide for the common Defence and general Welfare of the United States; but all Duties, Imposts and Excises shall be uniform throughout the United States;

To borrow money on the credit of the United States;

To regulate Commerce with foreign Nations, and among the several States, and with the Indian Tribes;

To establish an uniform rule of Naturalization, and uniform Laws on the subject of Bankruptcies throughout the United States;

To coin Money, regulate the Value thereof, and of foreign Coin, and fix the Standard of Weights and Measures;

To provide for the Punishment of counterfeiting the Securities and current Coin of the United States;

To establish Post Offices and post Roads;

To promote the Progress of Science and useful Arts, by securing for limited Times to Authors and Inventors the exclusive Right to their respective Writings and Discoveries;

To constitute Tribunals inferior to the Supreme Court;

To define and punish Piracies and Felonies committed on the high Seas, and Offenses against the Law of Nations;

To declare War, grant Letters of Marque and Reprisal, and make Rules concerning Captures on Land and Water;

To raise and support Armies, but no Appropriation of Money to that Use shall be for a longer Term than two Years;

To provide and maintain a Navy;

To make Rules for the Government and Regulation of the land and naval forces;

To provide for calling forth the Militia to execute the Laws of the Union, suppress Insurrections and repel Invasions;

To provide for organizing, arming, and disciplining the Militia, and for governing such Part of them as may be employed in the Service of the United States, reserving to the States respectively, the Appointment of the Officers, and the Authority of training the Militia according to the discipline prescribed by Congress;

To exercise exclusive Legislation in all Cases whatsoever, over such District (not exceeding ten Miles square) as may, by Cession of particular States, and the acceptance of Congress, become the Seat of the Government of the United States, and to exercise like Authority over all Places purchased by the Consent of the Legislature of the State in which the Same shall be, for the Erection of Forts, Magazines, Arsenals, Dock-yards, and other needful Buildings;—And

To make all Laws which shall be necessary and proper for carrying into Execution the foregoing Powers, and all other Powers vested by this Constitution in the Government of the United States, or in any Department or Officer thereof.

Section 9.

The Migration or Importation of such Persons as any of the States now existing shall think proper to admit, shall not be prohibited by the Congress prior to the Year one thousand eight hundred and eight, but a tax or duty may be imposed on such Importation, not exceeding ten dollars for each Person.

The privilege of the Writ of Habeas Corpus shall not be suspended, unless when in Cases of Rebellion or Invasion the public Safety may require it.

No bill of Attainder or ex post facto Law shall be passed.

No capitation, or other direct, Tax shall be laid unless in Proportion to the Census or Enumeration herein before directed to be taken.

No Tax or Duty shall be laid on Articles exported from any State.

No Preference shall be given by any Regulation of Commerce or Revenue to the Ports of one State over those of another: nor shall Vessels bound to, or from, one State, be obliged to enter, clear, or pay Duties in another.

No Money shall be drawn from the Treasury, but in Consequence of Appropriations made by Law; and a regular Statement and Account of the Receipts and Expenditures of all public Money shall be published from time to time.

No Title of Nobility shall be granted by the United States: And no Person holding any Office of Profit or Trust under them, shall, without the Consent of the Congress, accept of any present, Emolument, Office, or Title, of any kind whatever, from any King, Prince, or foreign State.

Section 10.

No State shall enter into any Treaty, Alliance, or Confederation; grant Letters of Marque and Reprisal; coin Money; emit Bills of Credit; make any Thing but gold and silver Coin a Tender in Payment of Debts; pass any Bill of Attainder, ex post facto Law, or Law impairing the Obligation of Contracts, or grant any Title of Nobility.

No State shall, without the Consent of the Congress, lay any Imposts or Duties on Imports or Exports, except what may be absolutely necessary for executing its inspection Laws; and the net Produce of all Duties and Imposts, laid by any State on Imports or Exports, shall be for the use of the Treasury of the United States; and all such Laws shall be subject to the Revision and Control of the Congress.

No state shall, without the Consent of Congress, lay any duty of Tonnage, keep Troops, or Ships of War in time of Peace, enter into any Agreement or Compact with another State, or with a foreign Power, or engage in War, unless actually invaded, or in such imminent Danger as will not admit of delay.

Article II

Section 1.

The executive Power shall be vested in a President of the United States of America. He shall hold his Office during the Term of four years, and, together with the Vice President, chosen for the same Term, be elected, as follows:

Each State shall appoint, in such Manner as the Legislature thereof may direct, a Number of Electors, equal to the whole Number of Senators and Representatives to which the State may be entitled in the Congress: but no Senator or Representative, or Person holding an Office of Trust or Profit under the United States, shall be appointed an Elector.

[The Electors shall meet in their respective States, and vote by Ballot for two persons, of whom one at least shall not be an Inhabitant of the same State with themselves. And they shall make a List of all the Persons voted for, and of the Number of Votes for each; which List they shall sign and certify, and transmit sealed to the Seat of the Government of the United States, directed to the President of the Senate. The President of the Senate shall, in the Presence of the Senate and House of Representatives, open all the Certificates, and the Votes shall then be counted. The Person having the greatest Number of Votes shall be the President, if such Number be a Majority of the whole Number of Electors appointed; and if there be more than one who have such Majority, and have an equal Number of Votes, then the House of Representatives shall immediately chuse by Ballot one of them for President; and if no Person have a Majority, then from the five highest on the List the said House shall in like Manner chuse the President. But in chusing the President, the Votes shall be taken by States, the Representation from each State having one Vote; a quorum for this Purpose shall consist of a Member or Members from two-thirds of the States, and a Majority of all the States shall be necessary to a Choice. In every Case, after the Choice of the President, the Person having the greatest Number of Votes of the Electors shall be the Vice President. But if there should remain two or more who have equal votes, the Senate shall chuse from them by Ballot the Vice President.][4]

The Congress may determine the Time of chusing the Electors, and the Day on which they shall give their Votes; which Day shall be the same throughout the United States.

No person except a natural-born Citizen, or a Citizen of the United States, at the time of the Adoption of this Constitution, shall be eligible to the Office of President; neither

4 Revised by the Twelfth Amendment.

shall any Person be eligible to that Office who shall not have attained to the Age of thirty-five years, and been fourteen Years a Resident within the United States.

In Case of the Removal of the President from Office, or of his Death, Resignation, or Inability to discharge the Powers and Duties of the said Office, the same shall devolve on the Vice President, and the Congress may by Law provide for the Case of Removal, Death, Resignation, or Inability, both of the President and Vice President, declaring what Officer shall then act as President, and such Officer shall act accordingly, until the disability be removed, or a President shall be elected.

The President shall, at stated Times, receive for his Services a Compensation, which shall neither be increased nor diminished during the Period for which he shall have been elected, and he shall not receive within that Period any other Emolument from the United States, or any of them.

Before he enter on the execution of his Office, he shall take the following Oath or Affirmation:—"I do solemnly swear (or affirm) that I will faithfully execute the Office of President of the United States, and will, to the best of my Ability, preserve, protect, and defend the Constitution of the United States."

Section 2.

The President shall be Commander in Chief of the Army and Navy of the United States, and of the Militia of the several States, when called into the actual Service of the United States; he may require the Opinion, in writing, of the principal Officer in each of the executive Departments, upon any subject relating to the Duties of their respective Offices, and he shall have Power to Grant Reprieves and Pardons for Offenses against the United States, except in Cases of Impeachment.

He shall have Power, by and with the Advice and Consent of the Senate, to make Treaties, provided two-thirds of the Senators present concur; and he shall nominate, and by and with the Advice and Consent of the Senate, shall appoint Ambassadors, other public Ministers and Consuls, Judges of the supreme Court, and all other Officers of the United States, whose Appointments are not herein otherwise provided for, and which shall be established by Law: but the Congress may by Law vest the Appointment of such inferior Officers, as they think proper, in the President alone, in the Courts of Law, or in the Heads of Departments.

The President shall have Power to fill up all Vacancies that may happen during the Recess of the Senate, by granting Commissions which shall expire at the End of their next Session.

Section 3.

He shall from time to time give to the Congress Information of the State of the Union, and recommend to their Consideration such Measures as he shall judge necessary and expedient; he may, on extraordinary occasions, convene both Houses, or either of them, and in Case of Disagreement between them, with respect to the Time of Adjournment, he may adjourn them to such Time as he shall think proper; he shall receive Ambassadors and other public Ministers; he shall take care that the Laws be faithfully executed, and shall Commission all the Officers of the United States.

Section 4.

The President, Vice President and all civil Officers of the United States, shall be removed from Office on Impeachment for, and Conviction of, Treason, Bribery, or other high Crimes and Misdemeanors.

Article III

Section 1.
The judicial Power of the United States, shall be vested in one supreme Court, and in such inferior Courts as the Congress may from time to time ordain and establish. The Judges, both of the supreme and inferior Courts, shall hold their Offices during good Behaviour, and shall, at stated Times, receive for their Services, a Compensation, which shall not be diminished during their Continuance in Office.

Section 2.
The judicial Power shall extend to all Cases, in Law and Equity, arising under this Constitution, the Laws of the United States, and Treaties made, or which shall be made, under their Authority;—to all Cases affecting ambassadors, other public ministers and consuls;—to all cases of admiralty and maritime Jurisdiction;—to Controversies to which the United States shall be a Party;—to Controversies between two or more States;—between a State and Citizens of another State;[5]—between Citizens of different States—between Citizens of the same State claiming Lands under Grants of different States, and between a State, or the Citizens thereof, and foreign States, Citizens, or Subjects.

In all Cases affecting Ambassadors, other public Ministers and Consuls, and those in which a State shall be Party, the supreme Court shall have original Jurisdiction. In all the other Cases before mentioned, the supreme Court shall have appellate Jurisdiction, both as to Law and Fact, with such Exceptions, and under such Regulations as the Congress shall make.

The trial of all Crimes, except in Cases of Impeachment, shall be by Jury; and such Trial shall be held in the State where the said Crimes shall have been committed; but when not committed within any State, the Trial shall be at such Place or Places as the Congress may by Law have directed.

Section 3.
Treason against the United States, shall consist only in levying War against them, or in adhering to their Enemies, giving them Aid and Comfort. No Person shall be convicted of Treason unless on the Testimony of two Witnesses to the same overt Act, or on Confession in open Court.

The Congress shall have power to declare the Punishment of Treason, but no Attainder of Treason shall work Corruption of Blood, or Forfeiture except during the Life of the Person attained.

Article IV

Section 1.
Full Faith and Credit shall be given in each State to the public Acts, Records, and judicial Proceedings of every other State. And the Congress may by general Laws prescribe the Manner in which such Acts, Records and Proceedings shall be proved, and the Effect thereof.

Section 2.
The Citizens of each State shall be entitled to all Privileges and Immunities of Citizens in the several States.

---

5 Qualified by the Eleventh Amendment.

A Person charged in any State with Treason, Felony, or other Crime, who shall flee from Justice, and be found in another State, shall on demand of the executive Authority of the State from which he fled, be delivered up, to be removed to the State having Jurisdiction of the crime.

No Person held to Service or Labour in one State, under the Laws thereof, escaping into another, shall, in Consequence of any Law or Regulation therein, be discharged from such Service or Labour, but shall be delivered up on Claim of the Party to whom such Service or Labour may be due.

Section 3

New States may be admitted by the Congress into this Union; but no new State shall be formed or erected within the Jurisdiction of any other State; nor any State be formed by the Junction of two or more States, or parts of States, without the Consent of the Legislatures of the States concerned as well as of the Congress.

The Congress shall have Power to dispose of and make all needful Rules and Regulations respecting the Territory or other Property belonging to the United States; and nothing in this Constitution shall be so construed as to Prejudice any Claims of the United States, or of any particular State.

Section 4.

The United States shall guarantee to every State in this Union a Republican Form of Government, and shall protect each of them against Invasion; and on Application of the Legislature, or of the Executive (when the Legislature cannot be convened) against domestic Violence.

Article V

The Congress, whenever two-thirds of both Houses shall deem it necessary, shall propose Amendments to this Constitution, or, on the Application of the Legislatures of two-thirds of the several States, shall call a Convention for proposing Amendments, which, in either Case, shall be valid to all Intents and Purposes, as part of this Constitution, when ratified by the Legislatures of three-fourths of the several States, or by Conventions in three-fourths thereof, as the one or the other Mode of Ratification may be proposed by the Congress; Provided that no Amendment which may be made prior to the Year One thousand eight hundred and eight shall in any Manner affect the first and fourth Clauses in the Ninth Section of the first Article; and that no State, without its Consent, shall be deprived of its equal Suffrage in the Senate.

Article VI

All Debts contracted and Engagements entered into, before the Adoption of this Constitution, shall be as valid against the United States under this Constitution, as under the Confederation.

This Constitution, and the Laws of the United States which shall be made in Pursuance thereof; and all Treaties made, or which shall be made, under the Authority of the United States, shall be the supreme Law of the Land; and the Judges in every State shall be bound thereby, any Thing in the Constitution or Laws of any State to the Contrary notwithstanding.

The Senators and Representatives before mentioned, and the Members of the several State Legislatures, and all executive and judicial Officers, both of the United States and of the several States, shall be bound by Oath or Affirmation to support this Constitution; but no religious Tests shall ever be required as a qualification to any Office or public Trust under the United States.

Article VII

The Ratification of the Conventions of nine States shall be sufficient for the Establishment of this Constitution between the States so ratifying the same.

Done in Convention by the Unanimous Consent of the States present the Seventeenth Day of September in the Year of our Lord one thousand seven hundred and Eighty seven, and of the Independence of the United States of America the Twelfth. In Witness whereof We have hereunto subscribed our Names.[6]

George Washington
President and deputy from Virginia

NEW HAMPSHIRE
John Langdon
Nicholas Gilman

MASSACHUSETTS
Nathaniel Gorham
Rufus King

CONNECTICUT
William Samuel Johnson
Roger Sherman

NEW YORK
Alexander Hamilton

NEW JERSEY
William Livingston
David Brearley
William Paterson
Jonathan Dayton

PENNSYLVANIA
Benjamin Franklin
Thomas Mifflin
Robert Morris
George Clymer
Thomas FitzSimons
Jared Ingersoll
James Wilson
Gouverneur Morris

DELAWARE
George Read
Gunning Bedford Jr.
John Dickinson
Richard Bassett
Jacob Broom

MARYLAND
James McHenry
Daniel of St. Thomas Jenifer
Daniel Carroll

VIRGINIA
John Blair
James Madison Jr.

NORTH CAROLINA
William Blount
Richard Dobbs Spaight
Hugh Williamson

SOUTH CAROLINA
John Rutledge
Charles Cotesworth
   Pinckney
Charles Pinckney
Pierce Butler

GEORGIA
William Few
Abraham Baldwin

Articles in Addition to, and Amendment of, the Constitution of the United States of America, Proposed by Congress, and Ratified by the Legislatures of the Several States, Pursuant to the Fifth Article of the Original Constitution.[7]

[Article I]

Congress shall make no law respecting an establishment of religion, or prohibiting the free exercise thereof; or abridging the freedom of speech, or of the press; or the right of the people peaceably to assemble, and to petition the Government for a redress of grievances.

[Article II]

A well regulated Militia, being necessary to the security of a free State, the right of the people to keep and bear Arms shall not be infringed.

6 These are the full names of the signers, which in some cases are not the signatures on the document.
7 This heading appears only in the joint resolution submitting the first ten amendments.

[Article III]

No Soldier shall, in time of peace, be quartered in any house, without the consent of the Owner, nor in time of war, but in a manner to be prescribed by law.

[Article IV]

The right of the people to be secure in their persons, houses, papers, and effects, against unreasonable searches and seizures, shall not be violated, and no Warrants shall issue, but upon probable cause, supported by Oath or affirmation, and particularly describing the place to be searched, and the persons or things to be seized.

[Article V]

No person shall be held to answer for a capital or otherwise infamous crime, unless on a presentment or indictment of a Grand Jury, except in cases arising in the land or naval forces, or in the Militia, when in actual service in time of War or public danger; nor shall any person be subject for the same offence to be twice put in jeopardy of life or limb; nor shall be compelled in any criminal case to be a witness against himself, nor be deprived of life, liberty, or property, without due process of law; nor shall private property be taken for public use, without just compensation.

[Article VI]

In all criminal prosecutions, the accused shall enjoy the right to a speedy and public trial, by an impartial jury of the State and district wherein the crime shall have been committed, which district shall have been previously ascertained by law, and to be informed of the nature and cause of the accusation; to be confronted with the witnesses against him; to have compulsory process for obtaining witnesses in his favour, and to have the Assistance of Counsel for his defense.

[Article VII]

In suits at common law, where the value in controversy shall exceed twenty dollars, the right of trial by jury shall be preserved, and no fact tried by a jury, shall be otherwise reexamined in any Court of the United States, than according to the rules of the common law.

[Article VIII]

Excessive bail shall not be required, nor excessive fines imposed, nor cruel and unusual punishments inflicted.

[Article IX]

The enumeration of the Constitution, of certain rights, shall not be construed to deny or disparage others retained by the people.

[Article X]

The powers not delegated to the United States by the Constitution, nor prohibited by it to the States, are reserved to the States respectively, or to the people.

[Amendments I–X, in force 1791.]

[Article XI]⁸

The Judicial power of the United States shall not be construed to extend to any suit in law or equity, commenced or prosecuted against one of the United States by Citizens of another State, or by Citizens or Subjects of any Foreign State.

[Article XII]⁹

The Electors shall meet in their respective States and vote by ballot for President and Vice-President, one of whom, at least, shall not be an inhabitant of the same State with themselves; they shall name in their ballots the person voted for as President, and in distinct ballots the person voted for as Vice-President, and they shall make distinct lists of all persons voted for as President, and of all persons voted for as Vice-President, and of the number of votes for each, which lists they shall sign and certify, and transmit sealed to the seat of the government of the United States, directed to the President of the Senate;—The President of the Senate shall, in the presence of the Senate and House of Representatives, open all the certificates and the votes shall then be counted;—The person having the greatest number of votes for President, shall be the President, if such number be a majority of the whole number of Electors appointed; and if no person have such majority, then from the persons having the highest numbers not exceeding three on the list of those voted for as President, the House of Representatives shall choose immediately, by ballot, the President. But in choosing the President, the votes shall be taken by states, the representation from each state having one vote; a quorum for this purpose shall consist of a member or members from two-thirds of the states, and a majority of all the states shall be necessary to a choice. And if the House of Representatives shall not choose a President whenever the right of choice shall devolve upon them, before the fourth day of March next following, then the Vice-President shall act as President, as in the case of the death or other constitutional disability of the President.—The person having the greatest number of votes as Vice-President, shall be the Vice-President, if such number be a majority of the whole number of Electors appointed, and if no person have a majority, then from the two highest numbers on the list, the Senate shall choose the Vice-President; a quorum for the purpose shall consist of two-thirds of the whole number of Senators, and a majority of the whole number shall be necessary to a choice. But no person constitutionally ineligible to the office of President shall be eligible to that of Vice-President of the United States.

[Article XIII]¹⁰

Section 1.
Neither slavery nor involuntary servitude, except as a punishment for crime whereof the party shall have been duly convicted, shall exist within the United States, or any place subject to their jurisdiction.

Section 2.
Congress shall have power to enforce this article by appropriate legislation.

8 Adopted in 1798.
9 Adopted in 1804.
10 Adopted in 1865.

[Article XIV][11]

Section 1.

All persons born or naturalized in the United States, and subject to the jurisdiction thereof, are citizens of the United States and of the State wherein they reside. No State shall make or enforce any law which shall abridge the privileges or immunities of citizens of the United States; nor shall any State deprive any person of life, liberty, or property, without due process of law; nor deny to any person within its jurisdiction the equal protection of the laws.

Section 2.

Representatives shall be apportioned among the several States according to their respective numbers, counting the whole number of persons in each State, excluding Indians not taxed. But when the right to vote at any election for the choice of electors for President and Vice-President of the United States, Representatives in Congress, the Executive and Judicial officers of a State, or the members of the Legislature thereof, is denied to any of the male inhabitants of such State, being twenty-one years of age, and citizens of the United States, or in any way abridged, except for participation in rebellion, or other crime, the basis of representation therein shall be reduced in the proportion which the number of such male citizens shall bear to the whole number of male citizens twenty-one years of age in such State.

Section 3.

No person shall be a Senator or Representative in Congress, or elector of President and Vice-President, or hold any office, civil or military, under the United States, or under any State, who, having previously taken an oath, as a member of Congress, or as an officer of the United States, or as a member of any State legislature, or as an executive or judicial officer of any State, to support the Constitution of the United States, shall have engaged in insurrection or rebellion against the same, or given aid or comfort to the enemies thereof. But Congress may by a vote of two-thirds of each House, remove such disability.

Section 4.

The validity of the public debt of the United States, authorized by law, including debts incurred for payment of pensions and bounties for services in suppressing insurrection or rebellion, shall not be questioned. But neither the United States nor any State shall assume or pay any debts or obligation incurred in aid of insurrection or rebellion against the United States, or any claim for the loss or emancipation of any slave; but all such debts, obligations, and claims shall be held illegal and void.

Section 5.

The Congress shall have the power to enforce, by appropriate legislation, the provisions of this article.

[Article XV][12]

Section 1.

The right of citizens of the United States to vote shall not be denied or abridged by the United States or by any State on account of race, color, or previous condition of servitude—

Section 2.

The Congress shall have power to enforce this article by appropriate legislation.

11 Adopted in 1868.
12 Adopted in 1870.

[Article XVI][13]

The Congress shall have power to lay and collect taxes on incomes, from whatever source derived, without apportionment among the several States, and without regard to any census or enumeration.

[Article XVII][14]

The Senate of the United States shall be composed of two Senators from each State, elected by the people thereof, for six years; and each Senator shall have one vote. The electors in each State shall have the qualifications requisite for electors of the most numerous branch of the State legislatures.

When vacancies happen in the representation of any State in the Senate, the executive authority of such State shall issue writs of election to fill such vacancies: *Provided*, That the legislature of any State may empower the executive thereof to make temporary appointments until the people fill the vacancies by election as the legislature may direct.

This amendment shall not be so construed as to affect the election or term of any Senator chosen before it becomes valid as part of the Constitution.

[Article XVIII][15]

Section 1.

After one year from the ratification of this article the manufacture, sale, or transportation of intoxicating liquors within, the importation thereof into, or the exportation thereof from the United States and all territory subject to the jurisdiction thereof for beverage purposes is hereby prohibited.

Section 2.

The Congress and the several States shall have concurrent power to enforce this article by appropriate legislation.

Section 3.

This article shall be inoperative unless it shall have been ratified as an amendment to the Constitution by the legislatures of the several States, as provided in the Constitution, within seven years from the date of the submission hereof to the States by the Congress.

[Article XIX][16]

The right of citizens of the United States to vote shall not be denied or abridged by the United States or by any State on account of sex.

Congress shall have power to enforce this article by appropriate legislation.

[Article XX][17]

Section 1.

The terms of the President and Vice-President shall end at noon on the 20th day of January, and the terms of Senators and Representatives at noon on the 3d day of January,

---

13 Adopted in 1913.
14 Adopted in 1913.
15 Adopted in 1918.
16 Adopted in 1920.
17 Adopted in 1933.

of the years in which such terms would have ended if this article had not been ratified; and the terms of their successors shall then begin.

Section 2.
The Congress shall assemble at least once in every year, and such meeting shall begin at noon on the 3d day of January, unless they shall by law appoint a different day.

Section 3.
If, at the time fixed for the beginning of the term of the President, the President elect shall have died, the Vice-President elect shall become President. If a President shall not have been chosen before the time fixed for the beginning of his term or if the President elect shall have failed to qualify, then the Vice-President elect shall act as President until a President shall have qualified; and the Congress may by law provide for the case wherein neither a President elect nor a Vice-President elect shall have qualified, declaring who shall then act as President, or the manner in which one who is to act shall be selected, and such person shall act accordingly until a President or Vice-President shall have qualified.

Section 4.
The Congress may by law provide for the case of the death of any of the persons from whom the House of Representatives may choose a President whenever the right of choice shall have devolved upon them, and for the case of the death of any of the persons from whom the Senate may choose a Vice-President whenever the right of choice shall have devolved upon them.

Section 5.
Sections 1 and 2 shall take effect on the 15th day of October following the ratification of this article.

Section 6.
This article shall be inoperative unless it shall have been ratified as an amendment to the Constitution by the legislatures of three-fourths of the several States within seven years from the date of its submission.

[Article XXI] [18]

Section 1.
The eighteenth article of amendment to the Constitution of the United States is hereby repealed.

Section 2.
The transportation or importation into any State, Territory, or possession of the United States for delivery or use therein of intoxicating liquors, in violation of the laws thereof, is hereby prohibited.

Section 3.
This article shall be inoperative unless it shall have been ratified as an amendment to the Constitution by conventions in the several States, as provided in the Constitution, within seven years from the date of the submission hereof to the States by the Congress.

18 Adopted in 1933.

[Article XXII][19]

No person shall be elected to the office of the President more than twice, and no person who has held the office of President, or acted as President, for more than two years of a term to which some other person was elected President shall be elected to the office of the President more than once.

But this Article shall not apply to any person holding the office of President when this Article was proposed by the Congress, and shall not prevent any person who may be holding the office of President, or acting as President, during the term within which this Article becomes operative from holding the office of President or acting as President during the remainder of such term.

This article shall be inoperative unless it shall have been ratified as an amendment to the Constitution by the legislatures of three-fourths of the several states within seven years from the date of its submission to the states by the Congress.

[Article XXIII][20]

Section 1.
The District constituting the seat of Government of the United States shall appoint in such manner as the Congress may direct:

A number of electors of President and Vice-President equal to the whole number of Senators and Representatives in Congress to which the District would be entitled if it were a State, but in no event more than the least populous State; they shall be in addition to those appointed by the States, but they shall be considered, for the purposes of the election of President and Vice-President, to be electors appointed by a State; and they shall meet in the District and perform such duties as provided by the twelfth article of amendment.

Section 2.
The Congress shall have power to enforce this article by appropriate legislation.

[Article XXIV][21]

Section 1.
The right of citizens of the United States to vote in any primary or other election for President or Vice President, for electors for President or Vice President, or for Senator or Representative in Congress, shall not be denied or abridged by the United States or any state by reason of failure to pay any poll tax or other tax.

Section 2.
The Congress shall have the power to enforce this article by appropriate legislation.

[Article XXV][22]

Section 1.
In case of the removal of the President from office or of his death or resignation, the Vice President shall become President.

---

19 Adopted in 1951.
20 Adopted in 1961.
21 Adopted in 1964.
22 Adopted in 1967.

Section 2.

Whenever there is a vacancy in the office of the Vice President, the President shall nominate a Vice President who shall take office upon confirmation by a majority vote of both Houses of Congress.

Section 3.

Whenever the President transmits to the President Pro Tempore of the Senate and the Speaker of the House of Representatives his written declaration that he is unable to discharge the powers and duties of his office, and until he transmits to them a written declaration to the contrary, such powers and duties shall be discharged by the Vice President as Acting President.

Section 4.

Whenever the Vice President and a majority of either the principal officers of the executive departments or of such other body as Congress may by law provide, transmit to the President Pro Tempore of the Senate and the Speaker of the House of Representatives their written declaration that the President is unable to discharge the powers and duties of his office, the Vice President shall immediately assume the powers and duties of the office as Acting President.

Thereafter, when the President transmits to the President Pro Tempore of the Senate and the Speaker of the House of Representatives his written declaration that no inability exists, he shall resume the powers and duties of his office unless the Vice President and a majority of either the principal officers of the executive departments or of such other body as Congress may by law provide, transmit within four days to the President Pro Tempore of the Senate and the Speaker of the House of Representatives their written declaration that the President is unable to discharge the powers and duties of his office. Thereupon Congress shall decide the issue, assembling within forty-eight hours for that purpose if not in session. If the Congress, within twenty-one days after receipt of the latter written declaration, or, if Congress is not in session, within twenty-one days after Congress is required to assemble, determines by two-thirds vote of both Houses that the President is unable to discharge the powers and duties of his office, the Vice President shall continue to discharge the same as Acting President; otherwise, the President shall resume the powers and duties of his office.

[Article XXVI][23]

Section 1.

The right of citizens of the United States, who are eighteen years of age or older, to vote shall not be denied or abridged by the United States or by any State on account of age.

Section 2.

The Congress shall have power to enforce this article by appropriate legislation.

[Article XXVII][24]

No law varying the compensation for the services of the Senators and Representatives shall take effect until an election of Representatives shall have intervened.

23 Adopted in 1971.
24 Adopted in 1992.

GLOSSARY

9/11 attacks A series of coordinated attacks on September 11, 2001, in which Al Qaeda operatives hijacked four planes, destroyed the World Trade towers in New York, damaged the Pentagon outside Washington, and caused the death of all aboard United Flight 93, altogether killing 3,000 people.

A. Philip Randolph Leader of the Brotherhood of Sleeping Car Porters and activist in the American labor and civil rights movements.

Aaron Burr Vice president of the United States during Thomas Jefferson's first term, he killed Alexander Hamilton in a duel in 1804 and was rumored to be involved in several plots that could destabilize the United States.

Abigail Adams Supporter of expanding women's rights and protections in the new United States; wife of John Adams.

abolitionist An advocate for the end of a state-approved practice or institution; the term is used most often in connection with the eradication of slavery.

Abraham Lincoln Lawyer and diplomat originally from Kentucky who served as the 16th president of the United States during the Civil War.

Abraham Lincoln Brigade A group of roughly 3,000 young Americans who traveled to Spain to join a fight against the fascists there.

Adams-Onís Treaty Agreement between the United States and Spain in 1819 that gave Florida to the United States in exchange for dropping its claims to Texas.

Adolf Hitler Leader of the German Nazi Party who took power in 1933; fascist whose assumption of dictatorial powers and belief in Aryan racial superiority resulted in the deaths of millions of innocent people including six million Jews in the Holocaust.

affirmative action A policy that grants special consideration in the hiring and promoting of members of groups that historically have faced discrimination.

Affordable Care Act Also known as Obamacare, health-care legislation meant to expand Americans' access to insurance.

Afghan war Post-9/11 military campaign against the Taliban in Afghanistan who were believed to aid Al Qaeda and harbor Osama bin Laden.

AFL-CIO New name of the 1955 merger of the labor groups American Federation of Labor and the Congress of Industrial Organizations.

Agricultural Adjustment Act Act that created a federal agency empowered to achieve parity by controlling the production of seven basic commodities.

Agricultural Marketing Act Proposed by President Hoover in April 1929, it established the first major government program to help farmers maintain prices.

AIDS Acquired immune deficiency syndrome, the set of symptoms and illnesses caused by the HIV virus that killed many Americans in the late twentieth century.

Al Qaeda Network of Islamic extremists responsible for the 9/11 attacks as well as other terrorist acts.

Alamo A Catholic mission in San Antonio that was the site of a major battle in the Texas Revolution in which Mexican forces put down insurgents seeking Texas independence.

Albany Plan Benjamin Franklin's 1754 proposal for a "general government" to manage relations between the colonies and Indians; rejected by the colonies at the beginning of the French and Indian War.

Alexander H. Stephens Vice president of the Confederacy.

Alexander Hamilton One of the country's founders, Hamilton championed a strong central government as a Federalist and was influential in Washington's cabinet.

Alexis de Tocqueville French aristocrat who toured the United States in the early 1830s and wrote *Democracy in America*.

Alger Hiss A high-ranking member of the State Department accused in 1948 of passing classified documents to a communist agent; eventually convicted of perjury.

Alice Paul Head of the National Woman's Party.

Alien and Sedition Acts A group of laws passed under President John Adams that limited new immigrants' access to citizenship and gave the federal government broad powers to limit criticism of the government.

Allies One of the two sides in the First World War, comprised of Britain, France, Russia, and in 1917, the United States.

American Federation of Labor (AFL) Union of skilled workers, formed in 1881 and led by Samuel Gompers, that used strikes to gain concessions from management.

American Indian Movement (AIM) Organization of Native American activists formed in 1968 to promote Indian self-determination.

American Patriots Term for supporters of American independence during the Revolutionary War.

American Plan A euphemism for the open shop; the crusade for this became a pretext for a harsh campaign of union-busting.

American Socialist Party Political party for economic reform created in 1901 that was closely aligned with organized labor.

American System Henry Clay's economic plan to bolster and unify the American economy by raising protective tariffs, developing the transportation system, and establishing a strong national bank.

Amistad Ship at the center of an 1841 Supreme Court case over the foreign slave trade; the Court decided that the Africans who had commandeered the ship had been illegally captured and sold and were granted freedom.

Andrew Carnegie Scottish immigrant who became a steel magnate and then philanthropist during the Gilded Age.

Andrew Jackson Seventh president of the United States; had distinguished himself at the Battle of New Orleans in the War of 1812 and as an Indian fighter.

Andrew Johnson Democrat from Tennessee who served as Lincoln's vice president and, upon Lincoln's assassination, became the seventeenth president; opposed Radical Republican policies on Reconstruction.

Anne Hutchinson Critic of the clerical doctrine of grace who sparked the Antinomian heresy that challenged the spiritual authority of established clergy.

antebellum The period before a war; in U.S. history, the term is commonly used to describe the pre-Civil War period.

Antietam Site of a Union victory on September 17, 1862, that stands as the single bloodiest day in American military history, blunted Confederate progress northward, and prompted Lincoln to issue the preliminary Emancipation Proclamation.

Antifederalists Term used by Federalists to describe those who were against ratification of the Constitution.

Antinomianism A belief that salvation comes from God's grace alone and not from good works.

Antonio Lopez de Santa Anna Politician and general who served multiple stints as president of Mexico and led Mexico in the war with the United States, 1846–1848.

Apollo program A NASA program to land an astronaut on the moon in the 1960s.

appeasement A foreign policy that accepts (rather than opposes) the aggressive moves of another state or actor.

Appomattox Court House Site of Lee's surrender to Grant.

Armory Show An event in New York City that displayed works of the French postimpressionists and of some American modern artists; supported by the Ashcan artists.

Army-McCarthy hearings One of the earliest televised hearings of Congress, the spectacle of Joseph McCarthy demeaning and bullying witnesses whom he accused of communist sympathies led to his loss of public support and official censure for unbecoming conduct.

Articles of Confederation The first adopted plan for union by the states that established a federal Congress with the power to tax and issue money; each state had one vote.

artisan An independent, skilled craftsperson.

Ashcan school Art movement whose members produced work startling in its naturalism and stark in its portrayal of the social realities of the era.

Atlanta Compromise This term describes Booker T. Washington's philosophy, stated in an 1895 speech, that blacks should forgo agitation for political rights and concentrate on self-improvement and preparation for equality.

Atlantic Charter Statement of shared aims issued by America and Britain in August 1941; the two nations called for a new world order based on self-determination, economic cooperation, and antimilitarism.

Atlantic World The peoples and empires around the Atlantic Ocean rim that became interconnected in the sixteenth century.

Ayatollah Ruhollah Khomeini Anti-American religious leader of Iran who took control in 1979 after the previous leader was deposed.

Baby Boom A period of increased birthrate; the term is used most often to describe such a demographic trend from 1946 to 1964.

Bacon's Rebellion A major conflict in Virginia pitting the ruling gentry class against black and white laborers and black slaves seeking greater freedoms and opportunities that resulted in a sharper definition between Indian and white spheres of influence.

Baltimore and Ohio Railroad The oldest railroad in the United States, originally built to help Maryland compete with canals in other states.

Bank War Term used for President Andrew Jackson's fight against Nicholas Biddle and supporters of the Bank of the United States; Jackson ultimately succeeded in eliminating the Bank.

Barack Obama Former U.S. senator from Illinois and first African American elected president who set a progressive agenda during his eight years in office.

Bartolomé de Las Casas Dominican friar who fought for fairer treatment of indigenous people in Spanish colonies.

Battle of Fallen Timbers The 1794 defeat of Indian group the Miami in the Ohio Valley, which forced the defeated Miami to agree to a treaty that ceded Indian lands to the United States.

Battle of the Bulge The last major battle on the Western Front during World War II, as the Germans were finally stopped at Bastogne.

Bay of Pigs Failed invasion of Cuban exiles supported by the United States to overthrow the Castro regime in 1961.

Beats Term used to describe artists and authors, like Jack Kerouac, who were critics of middle-class society and conformity.

Benedict Arnold Military hero early in the Revolution; he lost hope as the war progressed and ultimately conspired with the British.

Benito Mussolini Leader of Italy's Fascist Party before and during World War II.

Benjamin Franklin Inventor, author, diplomat, and one of the most famous people of the 1700s; served as a colonial agent in England during the early part of the conflict between the colonies and England.

Benjamin Harrison Republican senator who was elected president in 1888 in one of the most corrupt elections in American history.

Betty Friedan Author of the 1963 *The Feminine Mystique* who described the frustration of many women who found themselves limited socially, economically, and intellectually in postwar America.

Bill Clinton Former governor of Arkansas and forty-second president during a period of economic prosperity in the 1990s; impeached but acquitted on charges of obstructing justice and lying about an extramarital affair.

Bill of Rights First ten amendments to the U.S. Constitution; limited the new government's ability to infringe upon certain fundamental rights.

Black Codes State laws that developed after the Civil War in the former Confederate states to limit the political power and mobility of black Americans.

Black Hawk War Attack by Sauk (or Sac) and Fox Indians against white settlers from 1831 to 1832 that ended after a brutal response by American forces.

black power A philosophy of racial empowerment and distinctiveness as opposed to assimilation into white culture.

Bonus Army The group of more than 20,000 World War I veterans who marched in 1932 into Washington demanding payment of owed monies from the federal government.

Booker T. Washington The chief spokesman for a commitment to black education and the founder and president of Tuskegee University.

Boston Massacre Inflammatory description of a deadly clash between a mob and British soldiers on March 5, 1770, that became a symbol of British oppression for many colonists.

Boston Tea Party Dramatic attempt by Boston leaders to show colonial contempt for the Tea Act; they dumped British tea into Boston harbor and triggered similar acts of resistance in colonial cities.

Boxer Rebellion A revolt begun by Chinese nationalists against foreigners in China.

braceros Contract laborers from Mexico allowed into the United States during World War II in response to wartime labor shortages.

brinksmanship The attempt to gain a negotiating advantage by pushing a situation to the edge of war or other disaster.

Brotherhood of Sleeping Car Porters An important union dominated and led by African Americans, including A. Philip Randolph.

Browder v. Gayle The 1956 district court decision affirmed by the Supreme Court that ruled that Montgomery's bus segregation laws were unconstitutional.

Brown v. Board of Education of Topeka The 1954 Supreme Court Decision that overturned "separate but equal" opinion of *Plessy v. Ferguson* and provided federal support for the civil rights movement.

Bull Moose Party Also known as the Progressive Party, launched by Theodore Roosevelt ahead of the 1912 presidential election.

Cahokia Major trading center in the Mississippi River valley near modern-day St. Louis, Missouri, from the seventh to the thirteenth centuries.

Californios Hispanic residents of California.

Calvin Coolidge Former governor of Massachusetts and vice president under Warren Harding; became president when Harding died in office; elected to the office of president in 1924 but did not run again in 1928.

Camp David accords Peace treaty between Israel and Egypt brokered by President Carter in 1978.

Cane Ridge Kentucky site of the 1801 religious revival that lasted a number of days with thousands of attendees.

capitalist Owner of material or financial assets useful for the accumulation of additional wealth.

carpetbaggers Slang term used by white Southern Democrats to describe white men from the North, many of them veterans, who settled in the South as hopeful planters, businessmen, and professionals and supported Republican policies.

Cecilius Calvert The second Lord Baltimore who, with his father George Calvert, was instrumental in the founding of Baltimore.

Central Intelligence Agency (CIA) Replaced the World War II-era Office of Strategic Services in 1947; tasked with the collection of information related to national security from around the world through open and covert methods.

Central Powers One of the sides in the First World War, comprised of Germany, Austria-Hungary, and the Ottoman Empire.

César Chávez Leader of the mostly Hispanic United Farm Workers (UFW) in the 1970s.

Charles E. Coughlin A Catholic priest famous for his national radio broadcasts; he proposed a series of monetary reforms that he insisted would restore prosperity and ensure economic justice.

Charles Sumner United States Senator from Massachusetts who was a leading voice against slavery and for black liberties.

charter A formal order from a governmental leader or body, like the king of a court, often granting the recipient power over a body of land, a business, or a people.

checks and balances A system that grants the various branches of government the power to oversee or constrain other branches, so that no part grows too powerful.

Chester A. Arthur Became president when Garfield was assassinated.

Chief Joseph Leader of the Nez Percé tribe in the Pacific Northwest during the late 1870s who fought efforts to force the tribe onto a reservation in the Idaho territory.

Chinese Exclusion Act The federal law of 1882 that blocked Chinese immigration and prevented those Chinese already living in America from becoming citizens for ten years.

Christian Coalition A religious political coalition formed in the 1970s to elect candidates supportive of its evangelical values.

Christopher Columbus Sea captain working for the Spanish crown whose trans-Atlantic voyages helped introduce the "New World" to Europeans.

citizenship The legal recognition of a person's inclusion in a body politic by the extension of various rights and privileges and the expectation of various duties and obligations.

city beautiful movement Led by architect Daniel Burnham, the movement sought to impose order and symmetry on the disordered life of American cities.

Civilian Conservation Corps (CCC) Agency that created camps in national parks and forests for young unemployed men from the cities to work in a semi-military environment; projects included planting trees, building reservoirs, and improving agricultural irrigation.

Claudette Colvin An early leader in the civil rights movement who was arrested at the age of fifteen for not giving up her seat on a Montgomery bus nine months before Rosa Parks.

Clovis people Term used for the oldest inhabitants of the Americas most probably from modern-day Siberia who would have traveled the Bering Strait some 11,000 years ago.

Coercive Acts Parliament's retaliation against the Boston Tea Party that was meant to coerce Boston colonists by reducing the colony's self-government.

Cold War A simmering conflict between the United States and Soviet Union that emerged at the end of World War II, expressed in ideological terms of difference between capitalism and communism but often executed as a competition for power and security; tensions took many forms, including espionage, an arms race, and proxy wars around the world.

colonization A process by which a country or territory falls, usually by force, under the control of a hostile country or territory.

colony A geographic area in one nation under control by another nation and typically occupied at least partly by settlers from that other nation.

committees of correspondence First called for by Samuel Adams, the committees formed in Boston and other parts of the colonies to share information about British abuses of power.

Common Sense Thomas Paine's popular pamphlet that encouraged independence from England by arguing that colonists could never be truly free under the English constitution.

Commonwealth v. Hunt Massachusetts Supreme Court decision (1842) that established the legality of unions in Massachusetts.

Community Action programs Part of Johnson's "war on poverty," programs that employed members of poor communities in designing and administering local services.

Compromise of 1850 Seeking to diffuse tensions over slavery, this series of bills admitted California

as a free state, abolished slavery in Washington, D.C., and established the Fugitive Slave Act.

Compromise of 1877 Rutherford B. Hayes's promise to withdraw federal troops from the South, effectively ending Reconstruction, in exchange for the support of Southern delegates in the disputed election of 1876 presidential election.

concentration policy U.S. government policy introduced in 1851 that forced Indian tribes to live in specific regions, thereby opening up new areas for settlement by non-Indians.

Coney Island The famous and popular amusement park located on a Brooklyn beach.

Confederate States of America Also known as the Confederacy, those slave states that seceded from the Union and declared an independent nation.

Confiscation Acts Two laws passed by the federal government during the Civil War, in 1861 and 1862, designed to free slaves held by Confederates.

Congress of Industrial Organizations (CIO) Led by John L. Lewis, this committee expanded the constituency of the American labor movement.

Congress of Racial Equality (CORE) Established in 1942, black organization that mobilized popular resistance to discrimination in new ways such as sit-ins and "Freedom Rides."

conquistador A European (especially Spanish and Portuguese) conqueror of the Americas (particularly Mexico and Peru) during the fifteenth and sixteenth centuries.

conscription The practice of requiring citizens to serve in the military or other national service; the draft.

conservationist A proponent of the protection of land for carefully managed development, as opposed to a preservationist, who seeks to protect nature from development altogether.

Constitution The legal framework of the United States created to resolve limitations of the Articles of Confederation.

consumerism An increased focus on purchasing goods for personal use; the protection or promotion of consumer interests.

containment The Cold War strategy that called for preventing the spread of communism, by force or by other means.

coolies Derogatory term for Chinese indentured servants whose conditions were close to slavery.

cotton kingdom Term used for the lower South to describe the economy and culture built on cotton production.

Cotton Mather Puritan theologian who, drawing from the knowledge of his slave, Onesimus, helped introduce smallpox immunizations to America.

counterculture A way of life opposed to the prevailing culture; the term typically refers to the revolution in lifestyles, values, and behavior among some young people of the 1960s.

Court-packing plan Derogatory nickname for one aspect of President Roosevelt's proposal to overhaul the federal court system.

covenant A Puritan belief that an individual's relationship with God and with others rested on mutual respect, duty, and consent.

Coxey's Army A group of unemployed who marched on Washington, led by an Ohio Populist, to demand relief from the depression.

Creole A person of European or African ancestry born in the Americas; also, a person of mixed European and African ancestry.

crop-lien system A credit system widely used in the South after the Civil War in which farmers promised a portion of their future crops in exchange for supplies from local merchants.

Cuban missile crisis A thirteen-day standoff between the USSR and the United States over Soviet nuclear missiles in Cuba that ended with the Kennedy–Khrushchev Pact.

cult of domesticity The early-nineteenth-century belief that women were the guardians of family and religious virtue within the home.

cult of honor A set of beliefs, associated with white southern males of the nineteenth century, that emphasized respect, reputation, and the protection of women.

D-Day The Allied attack of June 6, 1944, across the English Channel against Hitler's forces in France.

Dale Carnegie Author of the best-selling self-help manual *How to Win Friends and Influence People*, published in 1936.

Daniel Webster Prominent diplomat and politician of the early republic, serving as senator, representative, and secretary of state; regularly championed issues in defense of the Union.

Darwinism The argument that the human species had evolved from earlier forms of life through a process of "natural selection."

Daughters of Liberty Organization of women in the colonies that led the boycott against the Tea Act.

David Walker Black abolitionist who encouraged blacks to unite and take any necessary measures to fight slavery and other forms of discrimination.

Dawes Plan A 1924 agreement in which American banks would provide loans to Germany that would then be used to pay war reparations to Britain and France.

Dawes Severalty Act Legislation that provided for the gradual elimination of most tribal ownership of land and the allotment of tracts to individual owners.

Declaration of Independence A founding document of the United States, the declaration explained why the colonies were breaking away from England. Drafted by Thomas Jefferson who borrowed concepts from other works and edited by the Second Continental Congress, the declaration also appealed to foreign countries and spurred colonies to reform themselves as states.

Defense of Marriage Act (DOMA) A 1996 federal law that allowed states to decide whether or not to recognize same-sex marriages.

deism The belief that God created but does not actively control the universe.

Denmark Vesey A freed black living in Charleston, South Carolina, who in 1822 planned a thwarted slave rebellion that may have numbered over 9,000.

deregulation The process of removing government controls over industries such as airlines, trucking, electricity supply, and banking, with the intention of stimulating competition and innovation.

détente The easing of hostilities between countries, used especially in connection with the Cold War in the 1970s.

Dollar Diplomacy Foreign policies, especially those of the Taft administration in Latin America, that privileged American economic interests.

Dominion of New England Colonial entity formed when James II combined the government of Massachusetts with the government of the rest of the New England colonies and, later, also included New York and New Jersey.

Donald Trump New York Republican business-man and billionaire elected forty-fifth president in a surprising victory over Democrat Hillary Clinton.

Dorothea Dix Advocate for individuals with mental illness in America and Europe.

Dorr Rebellion Named after the leader, Thomas L. Dorr, the Dorr Rebellion was a failed attempt by a group in Rhode Island to set up a new state government with expanded voting rights.

Douglas MacArthur American general who headed the occupation of a conquered Japan at the end of World War II; also led UN forces against the North Koreans in the Korean War until relieved by President Truman for making insubordinate statements.

Dred Scott decision The 1857 Supreme Court ruling that effectively stated that a slave was not a citizen but was, instead, property and therefore could not bring a suit in the federal courts.

Dust Bowl A region that stretched north from Texas into the Dakotas and experienced a decade-long drought that began in 1930.

Dwight D. Eisenhower U.S. general in charge of the invasion of France across the English Channel, later the supreme Allied commander and then president of the United States elected in 1952.

Earth Day First started in 1970, a day of events meant to heighten public awareness of environmental issues.

Echo Park A national park on the border between Utah and Colorado that was threatened by development in the 1950s; environmental organizations rallied to block the dam project.

Edward Bellamy Author of the utopian novel _Looking Backward_ (1888) in which government monopolies created an equitable society.

Eleanor Roosevelt Outspoken supporter of racial justice and source of continuous pressure on the federal government to ease discrimination against blacks; wife of Franklin Roosevelt.

Eli Whitney American inventor best known for developing the cotton gin.

Elizabeth Cady Stanton Abolitionist and women's rights advocate who co-organized the Seneca Falls Convention.

Elizabeth I Protestant Queen of England for the latter half of the 1500s who presided over the beginnings of English colonial enterprises in America.

Elizabeth Keckley Personal seamstress of Mary Todd Lincoln who bought freedom for herself and her son through sewing.

Emancipation Proclamation Lincoln's executive order of 1863 declaring that the slaves held in the Confederate states were forever free.

embargo A ban on trade with another country, especially the refusal to allow foreign ships to unload goods at port.

encomienda The right to extract tribute and labor from the natives on large tracts of land in Spanish America; also the name given to the land and village in such tracts.

Enforcement Acts Also known as the Ku Klux Klan Acts, these congressional acts in 1870 and 1871 prohibited states from discriminating against voters on the basis of race and gave the national government authority to prosecute crimes by individuals under federal law.

Enlightenment An intellectual movement that stressed the importance of science and reason in the pursuit of truth.

Erie Canal A constructed waterway that connected the Great Lakes to the Hudson River and transformed New York into an economic powerhouse of the young United States.

Eugene V. Debs Leader of the American Railway Union in the Pullman strike of 1894; presidential candidate for the Socialist Party.

eugenics The pseudo-scientific movement that attributed genetic weakness to various races and ethnicities; also describes efforts to control or isolate supposed hereditary traits through selective breeding, sterilization, immigration restriction, and other forms of social engineering.

evangelist A devout person who aims to convert others to the faith through preaching and missionary work.

Factory Girls Association The 1834 union originally formed by Lowell workers to protest pay cuts.

factory system A method of manufacturing involving powered machinery, usually run by water, that allowed the use of unskilled labor and greater output than in the artisan tradition.

Fair Deal Harry Truman's twenty-one-point domestic program supporting expansion of Social Security, an increase of the minimum wage, public housing, and environmental/public works planning.

Farm Security Administration Created in 1937, this agency provided loans to help famers cultivating submarginal soil to relocate to better lands; in the end, it moved no more than a few thousand.

Farmers' Alliances Began among southern farmers in 1875 but spread nationwide; formed cooperatives and other marketing mechanisms.

fascism A term originating with Mussolini's Fascist Party and applying to any antidemocratic regime with a supreme leader, intolerance of dissent, faith in militarism over diplomacy, and a belief in national or ethnic superiority.

Federal Deposit Insurance Corporation (FDIC) Established by the Glass-Steagall Act of June 1933, this guaranteed all bank deposits up to $2,500.

Federal Highway Act of 1956 Massive ten-year federal project to build over 40,000 miles of interstate highways initiated under President Eisenhower.

federalism A political system dividing powers between state and federal governments that together constitute a federation.

Federalists Term for supporters of the Constitution and later a political party that favored a strong central government.

Fidel Castro One of the leaders against Fulgencio Batista's dictatorship of Cuba, Fidel Castro took control of Cuba in 1959 and turned Cuba into a communist state with support from the Soviet Union.

Fifteenth Amendment An 1870 constitutional amendment that forbade the states and the federal government from denying suffrage to any male citizen on account of race, color, or previous condition of servitude.

fireside chats President Franklin Roosevelt's regular radio addresses during which he explained in simple terms his programs and plans to the people, helping build public confidence in the administration.

First Battle of Bull Run The first major battle of the Civil War; also known as First Battle of Manassas.

First Continental Congress Early gathering of colonial delegates in 1774 that called for the repeal of all oppressive laws of Parliament since 1763.

Five Civilized Tribes Term used for the five tribes of the American South that had adopted some Euro-American social structures and institutions by the 1830s.

flappers Young women who challenged traditional expectations in the mid-1920s.

Fort Necessity Site of the opening skirmish in the French and Indian War, this stockade in the Ohio Valley was unsuccessfully protected by Militia Colonel George Washington.

Fort Sumter Fort in Charleston, South Carolina, that was shelled by Confederate forces on April 12, 1861, forcing its surrender and marking the start of armed conflict in the Civil War.

Forty-niners A slang term for people who flocked to California in 1849 in search of gold.

Fourteen Points President Woodrow Wilson's list of principles for which he believed the nation should be fighting during the First World War.

Fourteenth Amendment An 1868 constitutional amendment that granted citizenship to all persons born in the United States and prohibited states from denying "life, liberty, or property, without due process of law" or equal protection under the law.

Frances Perkins First female member of the cabinet; appointed by Roosevelt as secretary of labor.

Francis Cabot Lowell Pioneer of American textile manufacturing who created one of the first complete mills in Waltham, Massachusetts.

Frank Capra Italian-born director whose films presented social messages; films included *Mr. Deeds Goes to Town*.

Franklin Delano Roosevelt Assistant secretary of the navy, governor of New York, and president from 1933 until his death in office in 1945; his campaign and subsequent administrations offered Americans "a new deal."

Frederick Douglass African American abolitionist and reformer who was a major voice against slavery in both his writings and in public speeches throughout America and Europe.

free silver Economic philosophy that advocated for the coining of silver; farmers and others believed that expanding the money supply in this way would increase prices for their products and ease their debt payments.

Free-Soil Party The antislavery party that emerged during the 1848 presidential and congressional elections.

Freedmen's Bureau U.S. bureau established in 1858 that aimed to help former enslaved people forge independent lives.

freedom rides Civil rights initiative in which groups of interracial students traveled by bus through segregated states.

Freedom Summer Attempt by civil rights activists in the summer of 1964 to encourage black voter registration mostly in segregated states like Alabama and Mississippi.

French and Indian War Colonists' name given to the Seven Years' War in the colonies that strained the relationship of England to its colonies and marked the decline of relationships between Native Americans and Europeans.

Gabriel Prosser Leader of a thwarted large-scale slave revolt outside Richmond, Virginia, in 1800.

Gadsden Purchase The 1853 American acquisition from Mexico of nearly 30,000 acres of land that now form modern southern Arizona and southwestern New Mexico.

George B. McClennan Union general who ran unsuccessfully as a Northern Democrat in the 1864 presidential election against Lincoln.

George Calvert The first Lord Baltimore who, with his son Cecilius, the second Lord Baltimore, was instrumental in the founding of Maryland.

George Grenville Prime Minister to King George III who increased troops and taxes in the colonies after the French and Indian War and made many colonists believe colonial self-rule was under attack.

George H. W. Bush Vice president under Reagan who served as the forty-first president during the first Gulf War and several years of economic downturn.

George III King of England in 1760 who wanted to reassert the crown's authority; he was mentally unstable for most of his reign.

George W. Bush Son of the forty-first president and former governor of Texas, he pushed through broad tax cuts and led the country after the 9/11 attacks, initiating an aggressive war against terror.

George Washington Military leader and one of the founders of the United States; served as first president.

Gerald R. Ford Vice president appointed by Richard Nixon in 1973 who took over the presidency in 1974 after Nixon's resignation.

Geronimo Apache chief and medicine man who led the fight against resettlement efforts by Mexico and then the United States.

Gettysburg Pennsylvania town that was the site of a major Civil War battle on July 1–3, 1863, in which the Union Army turned back the Confederate march northward.

GI Bill Officially known as the Servicemen's Readjustment Act of 1944; provided housing, education, and job-training subsidies to veterans.

Gibbons v. Ogden Supreme Court case of 1824 that strengthened federal authority over interstate commerce.

globalization The process of interaction and exchange between peoples and ideas from different parts of the globe.

Good Neighbor Policy Franklin Roosevelt's position regarding the countries of Latin America, marking a departure from traditional American intervention.

gospel of wealth Term popularized by Andrew Carnegie to argue that those with immense wealth carry a greater burden to use that wealth for social progress.

Grangers Founded in 1867, the first major farm organization in the country to mobilize against railroads and other special interests; predecessor to the farmers' alliances of the late nineteenth century.

Great Awakening The first major American religious revival, begun in earnest in the 1730s.

Great Depression The major economic downturn of the 1930s that ended with American entrance into World War II.

Great Migration The movement of nearly half a million black people from the rural South to industrial cities in the North in the era of the First World War.

Great Recession of 2008 Economic crisis fueled by the collapse of the housing market and poor regulation of financial industries.

Great Society LBJ's legislative initiatives that focused on addressing the social problems of poverty, decaying cities, and poor schools.

greenbacks Paper currency not backed by gold or silver.

Grover Cleveland Reform governor of New York who was elected president in 1884 and again in 1892.

Guadalcanal One of the southern Solomon Islands, American forces assaulted a Japanese garrison here for six months in 1942–1943 before successfully driving them out.

Guantánamo U.S. naval base in Cuba where suspected terrorists from the war on terror have been interrogated and detained since 2002.

Gulf of Tonkin Resolution Act of Congress in 1964 that gave President Johnson the authority to escalate the conflict in Vietnam based on questionable accounts of attacks made on American ships by the North Vietnamese.

Half-Breeds Political group within the Republican Party led by James G. Blaine of Maine, who favored reform.

Handsome Lake Seneca native and revivalist of the Second Great Awakening who called for a return to native traditions among the Iroquois tribes.

Harlem Renaissance Term used to describe the flourishing artistic life created by a new generation of black intellectuals in New York who focused on the richness of their own racial heritage.

Harpers Ferry Site of the federal arsenal raided by John Brown in 1859.

Harriet Beecher Stowe Abolitionist, best known for her novel *Uncle Tom's Cabin*.

Harry Hopkins Former director of New York State relief agency; appointed by Roosevelt to administer New Deal agencies FERA and the WPA.

Harry S. Truman Democratic senator from Missouri, then Franklin Roosevelt's vice presidential candidate in the 1944 election, and president of the United States from 1945 to 1953.

Hartford Convention Meeting of New Englanders, many of them Federalists, that denounced the War of 1812; they had just adjourned when news of Jackson's victory in New Orleans and the peace treaty became known.

Hawley-Smoot Tariff This 1930 act established the highest import duties in history and stifled global commerce; it contributed to the dramatic contraction of international trade leading up to the Great Depression.

Haymarket bombing In a clash between striking laborers and police in Chicago on May 1, 1886, an unknown person threw a bomb into a crowd killing seven police and injuring nearly seventy others.

headright system A grant system that allowed new settlers to acquire fifty acres of land in a variety of ways.

Henry Cabot Lodge The Republican senator and chair of the Foreign Relations Committee who obstructed and opposed the ratification of the Treaty of Versailles after the First World War.

Henry Clay Prominent politician from Kentucky, serving as Speaker of the House, senator, and secretary of state and running unsuccessfully for president three times; one of the founders of the Whig Party; helped bring about the Missouri Compromise of 1820 while Speaker.

Henry David Thoreau Transcendentalist who urged Americans to resist both social conformity and unjust laws.

Henry Ford Early leader of the automobile industry who stressed the standardization of parts and assembly lines.

Henry George Author of *Progress and Poverty* (1879), which argued for tax reform on land as a way to break the power of monopolies.

Herbert Hoover Elected president in 1928, he personified the modern, prosperous, middle-class society of the New Era, but also came to be associated with the failure to adequately respond to the Great Depression.

Herman Melville Author of the 1851 classic *Moby Dick* that captured harsh aspects of nineteenth-century American culture.

Hessians German mercenaries hired by England during the American Revolutionary War.

Hetch Hetchy Valley that was the object of a 1906 controversy that brought the contending views of the early conservation movement to a head.

Hideki Tojo General and leader of the war party in Japan; replaced more moderate prime minister in 1941.

Hillary Rodham Clinton Former first lady, senator of New York, secretary of state, and in 2016 the first woman to earn the presidential nomination of a major political party.

Hindenburg German dirigible that crashed in flames in Lakehurst, New Jersey, in 1937, broadcast live over the radio.

Hiroshima Japanese site of the first detonation of an atomic bomb against an enemy nation, dropped by the United States in 1945.

Ho Chi Minh Longtime supporter of Vietnamese independence who later became the leader of the communists of Vietnam.

Holocaust Systematic Nazi campaign of the 1930s and 1940s to exterminate Jews and other "undesirable" groups of Europe.

Homestead Act Federal legislation permitting any citizen or prospective citizen, including freed slaves, to purchase 160 acres of public land in the western United States for a small fee after living on it for five years.

Homestead Strike A strike of the steel mill union in 1892 that led to armed conflict and the involvement of state militia.

Hoovervilles The term used to describe the shantytowns that unemployed people established on the outskirts of cities during the Depression.

Horace Mann Educational reformer who promoted education as essential to a strong democracy.

Horatio Alger Author of Gilded Age books whose hardworking heroes go from "rags to riches."

horizontal integration A corporate combination where a group of businesses that do the same thing are consolidated.

House Un-American Activities Committee (HUAC) Congressional committee that held widely publicized investigations into communist subversion within the American government.

Hudson River school New York landscape painters known for their depictions of spectacular vistas.

Huey P. Long Senator from Louisiana known as "the Kingfish" who initially supported Roosevelt but broke with him; champion of the Share-Our-Wealth

Plan, which would have guaranteed every American a home and income.

Hull House The most famous of the settlement houses, opened in Chicago in 1889.

Ida B. Wells African American journalist whose reporting in the late nineteenth century on racial violence launched what became an international antilynching movement.

Immigration Act of 1965 Legislation that revised laws from the 1920s, allowing for greater immigration from most areas and removing preferences for northern European immigrants.

impeachment The process of charging a public official with misconduct, with the potential for punishment including loss of office.

imperialism The process whereby an empire or nation pursues military, political, or economic advantage by extending its rule over external territories and peoples.

impressment The act of forcing people to serve in a navy or other military operation; the term is most commonly used in connection with the actions of British fleets against American sailors in the early 1800s.

indentured servitude The condition of being bound to an employer for a specific period of time, usually in exchange for the cost of passage to a new land. The labor practice was most commonly used in Britain's American colonies.

Indian Civil Rights Act Law passed by Congress in 1968 that extended Bill of Rights protection to reservation Indians and accepted Indian legal authority inside reservations.

Indian Removal Act An 1830 act that allowed the federal government to negotiate with American Indians to relocate them west of the Mississippi River.

Indian Territory Present-day Oklahoma, the land designated for American Indians forced to relocate west of the Mississippi River by the Indian Removal Act.

Industrial Revolution The transformation of the economy from manual to mechanized forms of production; started in Britain in the eighteenth century and later spread to other places, including in the United States in the nineteenth century.

Industrial Workers of the World (IWW) Known to its opponents as the "Wobblies," the radical labor organization led by "Big Bill" Haywood; advocated a single union for all workers.

Industrialization The process of a society changing from predominately agricultural production to a society based on factory production.

intercontinental ballistic missile (ICBM) Missile capable of traveling over oceans and into space to deliver nuclear strikes.

Interstate Commerce Act The first effective federal railroad regulation, passed in 1887; administered by a five-person agency.

Iran–Contra scandal Covert and illegal operation by members of the Reagan administration who funneled money gained from selling arms to the anti-American government of Iran to the anticommunist rebels or "Contras" in Nicaragua.

Iraq War An armed conflict (2003–2011) of Western countries led by the United States to depose Iraq leader Saddam Hussein, set up a more democratic government, and defend it against local insurgents.

Iroquois Confederacy Organization of five Indian nations that traded regularly with the French and English in the early colonial period, but their relationships with the colonists deteriorated during the mid to late 1700s.

isolationism A foreign policy that avoids forging alliances or lending support to other nations, especially in wartime.

Issei Japanese immigrants.

J. P. Morgan Banker and creator of U.S. Steel.

Jacob Leisler Colonist who raised a militia in 1689 and proclaimed himself the head of government in New York.

Jacob Riis New York newspaper photographer who wrote *How the Other Half Lives*, which used photos and words to expose the harshness of tenement life.

James A. Garfield Veteran Republican congressman from Ohio and a Half-Breed; won the presidency in the 1880 election; assassinated in 1881.

James Henry Hammond South Carolina senator who coined the expression "cotton is king."

James K. Polk North Carolinian and 11th president of the United States who served from 1845 to 1849.

James Madison Fourth president of the United States; instrumental in the creation of the U.S. Constitution.

James Oglethorpe Veteran British general who spearheaded the founding of Georgia.

Jamestown First colonial settlement of the London Company in North America.

Jane Addams Influential social worker and advocate of the settlement house movement.

Jarena Lee An African American woman who preached in public in contrast to rules and customs that prohibited her from doing so during the first half of the nineteenth century.

Jay's Treaty Crafted in response to continued British seizure of American ships in 1794 by the chief justice of the Supreme Court, John Jay; resolved the dispute by acknowledging American supremacy over the Northwest territory and producing a commercial relationship with Britain.

Jefferson Davis President of the Confederacy.

jeremiad A sermon of despair at society's lost moral virtue, usually warning about dire consequences in the world and the afterlife.

Jim Crow laws A dense network of state and local statutes that institutionalized an elaborate system of racial hierarchy.

Jimmy Carter Former governor of Georgia who served as the thirty-ninth president of the United States during a period of rising oil prices, economic recession, and the Iran hostage crisis.

jingoes A term coined in the late nineteenth century to refer to advocates for expanded U.S. economic, political, and military power in the world.

John Adams One of the country's founders; first vice president of the United States and the second president of the United States.

John Birch Society Ultra-conservative organization led by Robert Welch, who was convinced communism had infiltrated all levels of the American government.

John Brown Radical abolitionist who aimed to foment a slave insurrection in the South.

John Burgoyne General for British northern forces, defeated at Saratoga.

John C. Calhoun Prominent South Carolinian politician serving as senator, secretary of state, vice president, and secretary of war; supporter of slavery and of nullification, or the states' rights to nullify federal laws if they found them unconstitutional.

John Collier Commissioner of Indian affairs whose goal was to reverse the pressures of assimilation and instead champion Indian rights.

John D. Rockefeller Founder of Standard Oil, famous for horizontal and vertical integration, and the wealthiest man of the Gilded Age.

John Dos Passos Author of the *U.S.A.* trilogy in the 1930s, which attacked materialistic American culture.

John Foster Dulles Secretary of state under Eisenhower who advocated for aggressive action against communism, as well as brinksmanship as a strategy to gain concessions from foreign powers.

John J. Pershing The American general who led the expedition chasing Pancho Villa in 1916 and later commanded the American forces in the First World War.

John Kennedy First Catholic to be elected president after defeating Richard Nixon in 1960; assassinated in 1963.

John L. Lewis Leader of the United Mine Workers, champion of industrial unionism, and first president of the CIO.

John Marshall Chief Justice of the United States Supreme Court for over thirty years and a Federalist, Marshall most famously rendered the opinion in *Marbury v. Madison*.

John Muir The leading preservationist in the United States and founder of the Sierra Club.

John Peter Zenger New York publisher tried for libel whose case expanded free speech.

John Quincy Adams Son of John Adams, he served as secretary of state under James Monroe, president from 1825 to 1829, and later as a member of the House of Representatives.

John Smith World traveler and writer whose leadership helped the Jamestown colony survive.

John Steinbeck Author of *The Grapes of Wrath*, perhaps the best-known depiction of Depression-era American life.

John Tyler Virginian who became the tenth president after the death of William Henry Harrison only a month into his administration; regularly clashed with his fellow Whigs and was not nominated for reelection by his party.

John Winthrop Governor of the Massachusetts Bay Company who dominated colonial politics.

Jonathan Edwards New England Congregationalist preacher who was famous for vivid descriptions of hell and damnation.

Josef Stalin Communist dictator of the Soviet Union from the 1920s until his death in 1953; responsible for the death or exile of millions of Soviet citizens.

Joseph and Mary Brant Mohawk brother and sister who allied with the British, thus harming the unity of the Iroquois Confederacy's neutrality during the Revolutionary War.

Joseph Smith Founder of the Mormon faith.

Judith Sargent Murray Essayist of the early republic who argued for a larger role for women in the new country.

Julius and Ethel Rosenberg New York couple accused, convicted, and executed for passing secret information regarding America's atomic bomb to the Soviets; Julius was likely guilty, Ethel likely innocent.

Kansas-Nebraska Act Passed by Congress in May 1854, it allowed residents of the territories of Kansas and Nebraska to decide whether slavery would be permitted there.

Kate Chopin A southern writer who explored the oppressive features of traditional marriage; known for her shocking novel *The Awakening*.

King Philip's War The most prolonged and deadly encounter between whites and Indians in the seventeenth century.

Knights of Labor Short-lived early national labor union that championed eight-hour workdays and the end of child labor, open to almost all workers.

Know-Nothings Name used for the anti-immigrant, anti-Catholic group that formed in 1850 and organized as the American Party.

Korematsu v. U.S. U.S. Supreme Court case that upheld the internment of more than 100,000 Japanese Americans to detention camps.

Ku Klux Klan One of many secret societies that used terrorism and physical violence to intimidate former slaves and undercut their constitutional rights, especially the right to vote.

Langston Hughes A leading writer of the Harlem Renaissance.

League of Nations The organization President Woodrow Wilson hoped would implement the principles of the Fourteen Points after the First World War; it ultimately came into being without the United States as a member.

lend-lease A system that allowed the Franklin Roosevelt administration to lend or lease arms to the British without explicitly violating the Neutrality Acts.

Levittowns Named after developer William Levitt, Levittowns were inexpensive suburban developments of similarly built homes.

Lewis and Clark On the direction of President Jefferson, Meriwether Lewis and William Clark led an expedition from Missouri to the Pacific in order to gather information on the lands acquired in the Louisiana Purchase.

Liberia African nation established in 1830 by freed blacks whose manumission and voyage was sponsored by the American Colonization Society (ACS).

Liberty League An organization founded by conservative business leaders, led by the Du Pont family, and focused on attacking the New Deal.

Life **magazine** New and enormously popular photographic journal, first published in 1936, it had the largest readership of any publication in the United States other than *Reader's Digest*.

Little Bighorn Site of the 1876 battle in which Colonel George Custer and his men were surprised and killed by a large army of Sioux warriors.

long drive A journey over grasslands that allowed western cattle ranchers to deliver their animals to railroad centers.

Lord Cornwallis British officer with early successes as leader of the Southern British forces but who was forced to surrender at Yorktown in 1781.

Lord Dunmore's Proclamation British promise of 1775 to grant freedom to people enslaved by Patriots in exchange for joining their military forces against the rebelling colonists.

Lost Generation Author Gertrude Stein used this term to describe the young Americans emerging from World War I.

Louis D. Brandeis Lawyer and Supreme Court justice; author of *Other People's Money*, which was about the "curse of bigness."

Louisa May Alcott Author of the *Little Women* series about an ambitious girl who fought conventional society to become a writer.

Lowell or Waltham system A factory system used to mass-produce textiles, primarily in New England, that relied on young women workers who lived in factory communities.

Loyalists (Tories) Supporters of England and the king, they may have represented a third of the white colonial population; many left America after the Revolution.

Lucretia Mott Abolitionist and women's rights advocate who co-organized the Seneca Falls Convention.

Lusitania The British passenger liner sunk by Germany in May 1915, killing almost 1,200 people, including 128 Americans.

Lyndon Johnson Often called LBJ, the president from 1963 to 1969 who promoted major social reform in his Great Society legislation and expanded America's military role in Vietnam.

Malcolm X Leader of the civil rights movement who promoted black power; assassinated in 1965.

Manhattan Project The American military's secret operation to develop an atomic bomb.

Manifest Destiny An ideology holding that God or fate intended the United States to expand its dominion across the North American continent.

manumission The act of freeing slaves.

Mao Zedong Leader of the communist armies of China in ongoing conflict with the nationalist government of Chiang Kai-shek in the 1930s and 1940s; won that battle and declared a communist China in 1949.

Marbury v. Madison Important decision of the United States Supreme Court that established the court's authority over the constitutionality of laws.

Marcus Garvey The African American leader who encouraged black people to reject assimilation into white society and develop pride in their own race and culture; he founded the Universal Negro Improvement Association (UNIA).

Margaret Sanger The pioneer of the American birth-control movement.

Mark Twain Pen name of Samuel Langhorne, nineteenth-century American author and humorist who wrote *The Adventures of Tom Sawyer* (1876) and *The Adventures of Huckleberry Finn* (1885).

Marshall Plan American program after World War II meant to spark economic recovery in Europe and thus cultivate economic ties and broader alliances between the Continent and the United States; eventually channeled $13 billion into the economies of sixteen participating countries.

Martin Luther King Jr. Baptist minister who came to prominence during the Montgomery bus boycott and went on to be the voice of the civil rights movement until his assassination in 1968.

Martin Van Buren Eighth president of the United States after serving as Andrew Jackson's vice president; nicknamed the little magician, but struggled as president during a difficult depression.

Massachusetts Bay Company Group of Puritan merchants in England who organized a new colonial venture in America.

Mayflower Compact Document that the Pilgrims signed to establish a government for themselves.

McCarthyism Name given to the anticommunist crusade of Senator Joseph McCarthy in the early 1950s, during which he recklessly persecuted alleged communists, often without evidence.

McCulloch v. Maryland Supreme Court case that confirmed the implied powers of Congress by upholding the constitutionality of the Bank of the United States.

Medicaid Social welfare program created during the Johnson administration that extended medical care to all ages in need.

Medicare Social welfare program created under the Johnson administration to provide health care to elderly Americans.

mercantilism An economic theory popular in Europe from the sixteenth through eighteenth centuries holding that nations were in competition with one another for wealth, and that the state should maximize its wealth by limiting imports and establishing new colonies that would provide access to precious minerals, spices, and slaves.

Mesoamerica Land area of the Archaic period including the lower portion of modern-day Mexico and the rest of Central America where many native societies flourished.

mestizo A person of mixed European and American descent, traditionally in Spanish-speaking territories and nations.

Metacom Leader of an attempt by Indians in seventeenth-century New England to drive out English settlers and resist encroachment on their lands.

middle grounds Places where European and Indian cultures interacted and where neither side had a military advantage.

middle passage The name given to the route used by slave ships between Africa and the Americas.

Mikhail Gorbachev Soviet leader who initiated broad economic reforms, government restructuring, and changes in military policy including a reduced Soviet presence in Eastern Europe and who resigned when the Soviet Union ceased to exist.

minstrel show Form of popular theater and entertainment from the early 1800s to the early 1900s that openly mocked and degraded African American culture.

Missouri Compromise Agreement of 1820 that defused sectional conflict by agreeing to admit Maine as a free state and Missouri as a slave state, and to henceforth prohibit slavery in the Louisiana Purchase territory in the regions north of the southern border of Missouri.

Molly Maguires A secret society of Irish-born coal miners willing to use violence to deal with management.

monopoly A business entity that controls an industry or market sector without competition.

Monroe Doctrine Articulated in 1823, the policy of the United States that warned against European interference in the American continents and promised the United States would stay out of European affairs.

Morse code System, designed by Samuel Morse, of long and short electrical bursts that made the telegraph system a viable, long-distance communication system.

muckraker A journalist who exposes scandal, corruption, and injustice; the term was especially popular during the progressive era.

My Lai massacre The deliberate killing of hundreds of Vietnamese villagers in the hamlet of My Lai in early 1968.

Nat Turner Leader of a slave revolt in 1831 in Southampton County, Virginia, that killed 60 white men, women, and children before being crushed.

Nathaniel Hawthorne Novelist, best known for *The Scarlet Letter* and *The House of the Seven Gables*, who wrote about the misery caused by egotism.

National Association for the Advancement of Colored People (NAACP) Founded in 1909 when the Niagara Movement joined with sympathetic white progressives; goal was equal rights.

National Consumers League (NCL) Formed in the 1890s under the leadership of Florence Kelley; goal was to force retailers and manufacturers to improve wages and working conditions.

National Labor Relations Board (NLRB) Part of the Wagner Act, this board was an enforcement mechanism that compelled employers to recognize and bargain with legitimate unions.

National Organization for Women A leading advocacy organization for women's rights, formed in 1966.

National Origins Act of 1924 Law that banned immigration from East Asia entirely and reduced the quota for European immigrants; the result was an immigration system that greatly favored northwestern Europeans.

National Recovery Administration (NRA) A federal agency that called on businesses to accept the regulation of wages, hours, prices, and other labor practices with the goal of stabilizing the economy, maintaining the workforce, and reducing competition; invalidated by the Supreme Court in 1935.

National Socialist (Nazi) Party Germany's National Socialist organization, headed by Adolf Hitler, that came to power in 1933.

nativism A belief in the superiority of native-born inhabitants over immigrants; in particular, an anti-immigrant movement that began in the early 1800s in the United States and crested with the passage of immigration restriction in 1924.

Navigation Acts Three acts that Parliament passed to regulate colonial commerce.

Nelson Mandela Leader of the African National Congress and force against apartheid who became the first black president of South Africa in 1994.

neoconservatives A small but influential group of conservative intellectuals who rejected liberalism after the turmoil of the 1960s.

Neutrality Acts Series of laws between 1935 and 1937 that created a mandatory arms embargo against both sides in any military conflict and legislated other inhibitors of American involvement in another foreign war.

New Deal The broad array of reform initiatives launched during the administration of Franklin Roosevelt in the 1930s that dramatically increased the impact of the federal government on economic life and the personal welfare of citizens.

New Freedom Presidential candidate Woodrow Wilson's 1912 program that supported a progressive agenda.

New Frontier JFK's campaign plan for progressive domestic reforms.

New Jersey Plan Plan presented by William Paterson of New Jersey during the Constitutional Convention to have a single legislative body with equal representation for all states regardless of population.

New Nationalism Presidential candidate Theodore Roosevelt's 1912 program supporting economic concentration and using government to regulate and control it.

New Right Conservative movement that began in the 1970s and culminated in the election of Ronald Reagan.

New South A term referring to the economic modernization and industrialization of the South after Reconstruction.

Nicholas Biddle Ran the Second Bank of the United States; fought ultimately unsuccessfully against President Andrew Jackson for the survival of the institution.

Nicola Sacco and Bartolomeo Vanzetti The two anarchists accused of murder who were eventually executed in the 1927 amid widespread nativist prejudices and fears.

Nineteenth Amendment The amendment to the constitution ratified in 1920 that guaranteed women the right to vote.

Nisei The American-born children of Japanese immigrants.

Nixon Doctrine Foreign policy plan under President Nixon to continue to support allies' military defense needs while cutting back on American forces.

Noah Webster Author, teacher, and promoter of the new American nation, best known for his dictionaries and spellers that helped standardize the American language.

North Atlantic Treaty Organization (NATO) The postwar alliance of the United States and many of the countries of Western Europe, unified against invasion by the Soviet Union.

Northwest Ordinance A 1787 decree that created a single political territory out of the land north of the Ohio River.

NSC-68 A 1950 report commissioned by the Truman administration and issued by the National Security Council; called for a major expansion of American military power to combat the threat of communism and the Soviet Union.

nullification The theory that individual states, as the original creators of the federal government, possess the right to invalidate federal laws if they find them unconstitutional.

Occupy Wall Street (OWS) Protest movement of 2011 against economic inequality that began as an encampment in a Wall Street area park.

Office of Price Administration (OPA) Unpopular federal organization during World War II tasked with fighting economic inflation.

Office of War Information (OWI) Agency charged with disseminating the official U.S. viewpoint and encouraging domestic war efforts during World War II.

Okies Collective term for families from the Dust Bowl (though not all came from Oklahoma) traveling to California in search of jobs.

Okinawa Fierce battle in the Pacific on an island 370 miles south of Japan; saw the use of kamikaze planes and the loss of over 100,000 Japanese troops.

Oneida "Perfectionists" Members of a Utopian experiment in upstate New York who rejected traditional notions of family and marriage in favor of communal bonds.

Open Door The metaphor Secretary of State John Hay used in 1898 to characterize the access to Chinese markets he desired for the United States; it was later expanded to refer to a policy of granting equal trade access to all countries.

Oregon Trail A 2,100-mile wagon route that linked the Missouri River to western Oregon and was a main passageway for white western settlers between the 1830s and early 1870s.

Osama bin Laden Leader of Al Qaeda from 1987 until 2011, when he was killed in Pakistan by U.S. military special forces.

Palmer Raids Led by U.S. Attorney General A. Mitchell Palmer, these 1919 and 1920 police actions targeted alleged radical centers throughout the country, often using extralegal means.

Panama Canal The canal finished in 1914 that linked the Atlantic and the Pacific by creating a channel through Central America.

Pancho Villa The Mexican revolutionary whom Gen. John Pershing unsuccessfully pursued into Mexico after Villa killed Americans along the border.

Panic of 1819 Six-year depression that began with a price collapse of American trade goods.

Panic of 1837 Triggered by an executive order that the government would accept payment for land only in gold or silver or a currency backed by one of the metals, this economic crisis included business failures, a spike in unemployment, falling prices, and even bread riots.

Panic of 1893 The beginning of the most severe depression the United States had experienced at the time; triggered by the Philadelphia and Reading Railroad bankruptcy.

parity A complicated formula for setting an adequate price for farm goods and ensuring that farmers would earn back at least their production costs no matter the fluctuations of national or world agricultural markets.

Patrick Henry Virginia politician who lead the fight against the Stamp Act and declared supporters of Parliament taxes were enemies of the colonies.

Paxton Boys A group of Pennsylvania frontiersmen who demanded tax relief and massacred Conestoga Indians.

Pearl Harbor American naval base in Hawaii and headquarters of the Pacific Fleet; attacked by Japanese on December 7, 1941.

peculiar institution Southern term for slavery as a special institution of the South.

Pendleton Act First national civil service measure, passed in 1883, that tested applicants' qualifications for federal jobs by a test rather than patronage connections; largely symbolic at first but grew in reach over time.

Pequot War War in Connecticut during 1637 between English settlers and Indians of the region.

Pinckney's Treaty Agreement between the United States and Spain that guaranteed access to the Mississippi River for American trade and protection from Native Americans in Spain's territories.

planter class Wealthy slaveholding planters of the South who dominated southern society despite their limited number.

Plessy v. Ferguson An 1896 Supreme Court decision that ruled that separate accommodations for blacks and whites were legal so long as they were equal.

Plymouth Plantation First Pilgrim settlement in Massachusetts.

Pontiac Ottawa chief who led a coalition of tribes to war against the British from 1763 to 1766; achieved some gains including pressuring the British to restrain their settlers from the trans-Appalachian west, but eventually undermined by internal divisions, disease, and the brutal violence of settlers and the British military.

Popé Indian religious leader who led a successful uprising against the Spanish in 1680.

Popular Front This was a broad coalition of anti-fascist groups on the left; communism was its driving force.

popular sovereignty A term coined by Stephen A. Douglas to adjudicate the expansion of slavery in the western territories by allowing settlers to decide the status of slavery for their territory.

Populism A reform movement of the 1890s that promoted federal government policies to redistribute wealth and power from national elites to common people; more generally, refers to a political doctrine that supports the rights of the people over the elite.

Powhatan Chief of the Powhatan Confederacy and father of Pocahontas.

preservationist Activist who believes in the protection of natural environments rather than their managed development.

Proclamation of 1763 Attempt by England to reduce violence between Native Indians and English colonists by legally barring settlement beyond the Appalachian Mountains.

progressivism The ideology that claimed that the nation's most pressing need was to impose order and justice on a society that seemed to be approaching chaos.

prohibition Complete ban on the sale and manufacture of alcoholic beverages; 1920 amendment put it into effect on a national level.

Protestant Reformation The schism in the Catholic Church that began in 1517 with Martin Luther and led to new forms of Christian denominations still recognizable today.

Public Health Service Organization created in 1912; goal was to prevent occupational diseases and create common health standards.

Puerto Rico Part of the Spanish Empire from 1508 until 1898, when it fell under the control of the United States; became an American territory in 1917.

Pullman strike A 1894 railroad strike that escalated to twenty-seven states and territories, ultimately broken by federal troops and resulting in management's victory.

Puritans A sect of Protestants of England that wished to "purify" the Church of England of its Catholic ceremonies and practices.

Quakers A Protestant sect that called themselves the Society of Friends and believed that all could attain salvation by cultivating their inherent divinity.

quasi war The name given to the undeclared war between the United States and France of 1798–1799.

Queen Liliuokalani Nationalist leader of Hawaii elevated to the throne in 1891.

Rachel Carson Author of the 1962 book *Silent Spring* who argued that overuse of pesticides was destroying the environment.

Radical Republicans A wing of the Republican Party in the mid nineteenth century that aggressively opposed slavery and, after the Civil War, fought to expand and protect African American civil rights.

Ralph Waldo Emerson Transcendentalist philosopher who urged individuals to find fulfillment and self-improvement in nature.

range wars Conflicts between sheepmen and cattlemen, ranchers, and farmers.

Reagan Doctrine President Reagan's policy to combat communism by supporting anticommunist regimes and revolutionaries with money and military aid.

Reaganomics Supply-side economic policy embraced by Reagan and based on the idea that reducing taxes on corporations and the wealthy would encourage new investment and social well-being.

Rebecca Cox Jackson Radical African American religious figure who broke with the free black church movement in Philadelphia and ultimately joined the Shaker movement during the mid-nineteenth century.

Reconstruction The process by which the federal government, between 1865 and 1877, controlled the former Confederate states and set the conditions for their readmission to the Union.

Reconstruction Finance Corporation (RFC) The bill established a government agency to provide federal loans to troubled banks, railroads, and other businesses.

Red Scare A period of intense popular fear and government repression of real or imagined leftist radicalism; usually associated with the years immediately following World War I.

Redeemers Coalition of white southern landowners, business interests, and professionals who sought to "redeem" the South after the Civil War by limiting the influence of the Republican Party and violently overthrowing federal reconstruction policies and African American citizenship rights.

relocation centers Euphemistic name for areas of detention for more than 100,000 Japanese Americans during World War II, rounded up and evacuated against their will.

republicanism A system of governance in which power derives from the people, rather than from a ruling family, aristocratic class, or some other supreme authority.

Republicans Name for those who wished to limit the new government's power, in opposition to the Federalists.

Revolution of 1800 Thomas Jefferson's term for his election in 1800 which saw the peaceful transfer of power between ideologically opposed parties.

Richard Nixon Vice president under Dwight D. Eisenhower and president from 1969 until his resignation in 1974 as a result of the Watergate scandal.

Richard Wright Author of *Native Son*, a story of a young African American man broken by the system of racial oppression.

Roanoke The first English colony attempted in the North America.

Robert E. Lee Superintendent of West Point and later general of the Northern Army of Virginia, he won a string of early victories during the Civil War and later presided over the official surrender of the Confederacy.

Robert Fulton American inventor of the first commercially successful steamboat, the *Clermont*.

Robert M. La Follette Wisconsin senator and nationally known progressive.

Rocky Mountain school Group of late-nineteenth-century painters known for large-scale depictions of western landscapes.

Roe v. Wade Supreme Court ruling that allowed for legal abortions as part of a woman's right to privacy (Fourteenth Amendment) while also establishing conditions under which states can regulate abortion after the first trimester.

Roger B. Taney Appointed secretary of the treasury under President Jackson to remove federal deposits from the Bank of the United States; he was later appointed by Jackson as chief justice of the Supreme Court and wrote the *Dred Scott v. Sanford* decision in 1857.

Roger Williams Controversial minister who established the Rhode Island colony where people of different faiths could worship without interference.

Ronald Reagan Former governor of California elected as fortieth president in 1982 who led a conservative reform of American politics during his two terms.

Roosevelt Corollary President Theodore Roosevelt's amendment to the Monroe Doctrine, stating that the United States had the right not only to oppose European intervention in the Western Hemisphere but also to intervene in the domestic affairs of its neighbors should they be unable to maintain order and sovereignty.

Rosa Parks Civil rights activist who was arrested for not giving up her seat to a white passenger on a bus in Montgomery, Alabama, in 1955; her arrest spurred the Montgomery bus boycott.

Rosie the Riveter Popular image of a woman performing industrial work during World War II in America; became a symbol of female contributions to the war effort.

Rutherford B. Hayes Elected president in 1876 but largely ineffectual in office; the deals that led to his election are often described as marking the end of Reconstruction.

Saddam Hussein Iraqi leader whose invasion of Kuwait led to the first Gulf War; deposed by the United States in the second Gulf War.

Sagebrush Rebellion A late 1970s movement by western conservatives who opposed federal environmental regulations and restrictions on development.

Salem witchcraft trials An instance of the widespread hysteria in the 1680s regarding supposed satanic influences in New England that often targeted women.

Sam Houston A soldier, lawyer, congressman, and governor of Tennessee, he eventually moved to Texas where he commanded the Texas armies in their successful battle for independence from Mexico in 1836.

Samuel Gompers Union organizer under whose leadership the American Federation of Labor (AFL) grew by combining similar skilled unions together.

Sarah Bagley Creator of the Female Labor Reform Association that promoted better working conditions and shorter workdays in the mid-1840s.

Saratoga Site in New York where, with the help of Benedict Arnold, General Horatio Gates surrounded British General John Burgoyne and forced his surrender.

scalawags Slang term referring to Southern whites who supported the Republican Party and federal Reconstruction policies after the Civil War.

Scopes trial Tennessee case that attracted intense national attention to the debate over whether to teach evolution or creationism in the schools.

Scotch-Irish Scottish Presbyterians who had settled in northern Ireland in the early seventeenth century.

Scottsboro case A 1931 case that was among the most notorious examples of racism in the United States; an all-white jury convicted nine black teenagers of raping two white women despite overwhelming evidence of their innocence.

secession The act of asserting independence by withdrawing membership from a political state; it refers in particular to the South's departure from the United States in 1861.

Second Continental Congress Body of colonial representatives formed after the battles of Lexington and Concord to help resolve the conflict with Great Britain.

Second Great Awakening A wave of Protestant revival in the early 1800s signified by large congregations and dynamic sermons.

second middle passage Term coined by historian Ira Berlin to describe the forced movement of slaves with the United States, primarily from the upper South to the cotton states.

Second New Deal Launched in the spring of 1935 in response both to growing political pressures and continuing economic crisis, these new proposals represented a shift toward more openly anticorporate initiatives; this wave also included more long-term reforms including Social Security.

Securities and Exchange Commission (SEC) A federal government agency established in 1934 to police the stock market.

Selective Service Act The 1917 law that created a national draft to provide men to fight the First World War.

Seminole Wars Term used to describe a series of conflicts between United States forces and the Seminole, a mixture of Native Americans and black settlers in Florida; the first one, in 1816–1819, saw Andrew Jackson lead an invasion of Spanish Florida, during which Jackson's troops chased Seminole raiders and seized Spanish forts.

Seneca Falls Convention The 1848 meeting that produced the Declaration of Sentiments and Resolutions arguing for women's inalienable rights.

separation of powers The partitioning of authority to distinct branches of a government.

Seven Years' War Called the French and Indian War in the American colonies, the Seven Years' War was a global conflict between England and France ultimately won by England in 1763.

Shakers Utopian religious society committed to complete celibacy, equality of the sexes, and a simple ordered life.

sharecropping A farming system in which large landowners rent their fields to farmers, usually families, in return for a share of the crop's production.

Shays's Rebellion A 1786 uprising of poor Massachusetts farmers demanding relief from their debts.

Sherman Antitrust Act Aimed at prohibiting corporate combinations that restrained competition, and passed in 1890, it was largely ineffective.

Shiloh Name of battle site in southwestern Tennessee where, on April 6–7, 1862, Union forces won control of the upper Mississippi River.

silent majority Phrase coined by Richard Nixon to refer to conservative voters, as opposed to the more vocal counterculture.

sit-down strike A planned labor stoppage in which workers assume their positions in a factory or other workplace but refuse to perform their duties, thus preventing the use of strikebreakers.

slave codes Laws passed in the British colonies or in American states granting white masters absolute authority over the enslaved; these included laws depriving slaves of property, free movement, and legal defenses.

Social Darwinism The belief that societies are subject to the laws of natural selection and that some societies or peoples are innately superior to others.

Social Gospel The effort to make faith a tool of social reform; the movement was chiefly concerned with redeeming the nation's cities.

social justice A movement that seeks justice for whole groups or societies rather than individuals.

Social Security Act Passed in 1935; established several distinct programs including a pension program for workers (though many were excluded); also established a system of unemployment insurance and aid to people with disabilities as well to dependent children.

socialism A political theory that advocates government (rather than private) ownership and management of the means of production and distribution.

Sojourner Truth Former slave who lectured extensively on behalf of equal rights for blacks and women.

Sons of Liberty Groups of male colonists who organized against England's enforcement of the Stamp Act and who terrorized British officials.

sovereignty The authority to govern; popular sovereignty refers to the idea that the source of this authority is the people, who confer authority through elections.

Spanish Civil War The 1936–1939 war between Spain's liberal republican government and the conservative forces of General Francisco Franco.

Spanish-American War War of 1898 between the United States and Spain; took place in Cuba and the Philippines and resulted in American possession of or great influence over those areas and others.

specie circular Executive order issued by President Jackson that required gold or silver to buy public lands.

spoils system The process whereby elected officials give out government jobs as reward for political favors.

Sputnik The first earth-orbiting satellite launched by the Soviet Union in 1957.

stagflation An economic condition in which inflation is high, unemployment is high, and growth is low.

Stalwarts Political group within the Republican Party led by Roscoe Conkling of New York that favored traditional, professional machine politics.

Stamp Act Hated act passed by Prime Minister Grenville of England that required an official stamp on all paper documents in the colonies and united the colonies against England.

Stephen A. Douglas Democratic senator from Illinois who brokered the Compromise of 1850 and ran unsuccessfully against Lincoln and others in the presidential election of 1860.

Stephen F. Austin Immigrant from Missouri who established the first legal American settlement in the Mexican territory of Texas in 1822.

Stephen H. Long Dispatched by the United States government, he explored the Platte and South Platte Rivers in present-day Nebraska and Colorado.

Stonewall Riot Landmark 1969 event in the gay liberation movement that began as patrons of the Stonewall Inn, a gay nightclub, reacted violently against a police raid.

Stono Rebellion A slave revolt in South Carolina during the colonial period.

Strategic Defense Initiative (SDI) President Reagan's missile defense plan, which included ground and space-based antimissile defense weapons.

Students for a Democratic Society (SDS) Leading organization of student radicalism in the 1960s.

Sugar Act British act of 1764 designed to stop sugar smuggling in the colonies by lowering taxes on molasses but enforcing their payment and forcing compliance with trade laws.

Sunbelt The southeastern and southwestern regions of the United States.

Susan B. Anthony Abolitionist and one of the most iconic and active leaders of the early women's right movement.

Syngman Rhee Pro-Western though not reliably democratic leader of South Korea in 1950.

Taft-Hartley Act Officially known as the Labor-Management Relations Act of 1947; made it illegal to operate a business in which no worker could be hired without first being a member of a union.

Tallmadge Amendment Proposed amendment to Missouri's admission to statehood that would have gradually turned it from a slave state to a free state.

Tammany Hall Urban machine led by famously corrupt city boss William M. Tweed.

Taylorism Named for Frederick Winslow Taylor, an attempt to use scientific management to improve factory production.

Tea Act A 1773 act passed by England that gave the British East India Company the right to export tea to the colonies without paying the same taxes that were imposed on colonial merchants; the act enraged American merchants and colonists boycotted tea.

Tea Party movement Conservative political movement begun in 2009 to reduce taxes, government regulations, and federal efforts to implement universal health care.

Teapot Dome The location of rich naval oil reserves in Wyoming and part of a national scandal during the Harding administration.

Tecumseh A chief of the Shawnees who worked to unite native peoples against the threat of white expansion; died fighting for Britain in the War of 1812.

Tejanos The Mexican residents of Texas.

Teller Amendment The 1898 amendment to the war declaration against Spain that promised no American intention to occupy or control Cuba in the wake of an American victory.

temperance Self-restraint, especially concerning drink; the temperance movement pushed for bans on the sale and consumption of alcohol.

tenements By the late nineteenth century, this was a descriptor used for slum dwellings.

Tennessee Valley Authority (TVA) A regional planning program focused on water resources as a source of cheap electric power.

terrorism The use of violence as a form of intimidation against peoples and governments.

Tet offensive Large coordinated attack on January 31, 1968, of American strongholds in South Vietnam by communists forces that led to lost support for the Vietnam War in America.

Thaddeus Stevens U.S Representative from Pennsylvania who was an abolitionist and a leader of the Radical Republicans.

The Federalist Papers A collection of essays written by Alexander Hamilton, James Madison, and John Jay that supported ratification of the Constitution.

The Jazz Singer The first feature-length film with spoken dialogue, or "talkie."

The Other America Title of Michael Harrington's 1962 about the chronic problem of poverty in America.

the Prophet Also known as Tenskwatawa, the Shawnee prophet was a charismatic speaker, leader, and younger brother of Tecumseh; the Battle of Tippecanoe disillusioned many of his followers.

theocracy A form of government in which political power is believed to derive from a deity, and in which religious and government structures are intertwined.

Theodore Dreiser Author of *Sister Carrie*, which focused on the plight of single women.

Theodore Roosevelt Rough Rider during the Spanish-American War, governor of New York, Republican Party and progressive leader, vice president, and president of the United States from 1901 to 1909.

Thirteenth Amendment Passed on January 31, 1865, this constitutional amendment formally abolished slavery.

Thomas J. ("Stonewall") Jackson Confederate general who commanded troops in major Civil War engagements in the first half of war before being mortally wounded in the Battle of Chancellorsville in May 1863.

Thomas Jefferson One of the founders of the United States, he wrote most of the Declaration of Independence and served in all levels of government, both locally and nationally, in his long career.

Tiananmen Square Location in China of the 1989 student uprising that was brutally put down by Chinese authorities.

Townsend Plan Created by a California physician, this proposal focused on federal pensions for older adults.

Townshend Duties External taxes passed by England's Charles Townshend that taxed goods imported to the colonies; hated by the colonists, the taxes were later repealed after a colonial boycott of English goods.

Trail of Tears Term for the forced journey made by Native Americans to the Indian Territory that began in the winter of 1838, killing perhaps a quarter or more of the migrants.

transcendentalism A philosophical and literary movement of the early nineteenth century that sought beauty and truth in nature and the individual, rather than in formalized education, politics, or religion.

Treaty of Guadalupe Hidalgo Agreement to end the Mexican War in which the United States gained California and New Mexico and the Texas boundary was drawn at the Rio Grande.

trench warfare A common form of fighting in the First World War, whereby armies sought cover below ground from artillery bombardment, machine guns, and other military technologies.

Triangle Shirtwaist Company fire This disastrous event in New York was influential in finally passing a series of pioneering labor laws.

triangular trade A simplified description of the complex trade networks of the Atlantic World; the triangle metaphor refers to the trade in rum, slaves, and sugar among New England, Africa, and the West Indies.

Truman Doctrine Expressed policy of the United States, articulated in 1947, to support groups or governments fighting against communists around the world.

Turner thesis The theory articulated by Frederick Jackson Turner in 1893 that westward expansion into the frontier had defined and continually renewed American ideas about democracy and individualism.

U-2 Crisis A 1960 diplomatic incident between the United States and the Soviet Union when a U.S. U-2 spy plane was shot down by the Soviets after crossing Soviet air space.

U.S.S. *Maine* American vessel sunk in Havana harbor in February 1898; explosion was blamed on a Spanish mine and used by popular press to urge war; likely a mechanical error.

Ulysses S. Grant Chief of the Union armies (at the beginning of 1864) and eighteenth president who supervised much of Reconstruction.

United Nations An international organization, established in the peace talks after World War II, that contained a General Assembly and a Security Council of the five major powers.

United Service Organization (USO) Organization that recruited thousands of young women during World War II to serve as hostesses and sustain the morale of servicemen.

United States Sanitary Commission An organization of Northern civilian volunteers who raised money and support for the care of the sick and wounded during the Civil War; organized large numbers of female nurses to serve in field hospitals.

vaudeville A form of theater adapted from French models; the most popular urban entertainment into the first decades of the twentieth century.

vertical integration The arrangement by which a company takes ownership of businesses in various stages of production and distribution within the same industry.

Viet Cong Military arm of the National Liberation Front (NLF); communists in South Vietnam who fought against South Vietnamese rule and the American military with the support of the North Vietnamese.

Vietnamization Term used by President Nixon to describe transferring the responsibility for fighting the Vietnam War to the South Vietnamese.

Virginia and Kentucky Resolutions Written by Jefferson and Madison, respectively, in response to the Alien and Sedition Acts, the resolutions argued that states had the right to nullify federal laws.

Virginia House of Burgesses The first elected legislature in what would become the United States.

Virginia Plan James Madison's proposal during the Constitutional Convention for a two-house legislature where states would be represented in both bodies in proportion to their population.

Virginia Resolves Term used for a group of resolutions passed by the Virginia legislature declaring only the colonies' governments had the right to tax colonists.

virtual representation British political theory holding that members of Parliament represented all British subjects, not just those from the specific region that had elected them.

Vladimir Putin Political leader of Russia since 1999.

Voting Rights Act of 1965 Legislation that expanded the right to vote by providing federal protections to African Americans who had previously been barred by local and state regulations.

W. E. B. Du Bois Sociologist, historian, one of the first African Americans to receive a degree from Harvard, author of *The Souls of Black Folk*, chief spokesman for fighting for black civil rights, founding member of the Niagara Movement and the NAACP.

Wade-Davis Bill The 1864 bill stipulating that all Confederate states seeking readmission to the Union have a majority of its voters take a loyalty oath to the federal government; it never passed because Lincoln refused to sign it.

Walt Whitman Writer who helped define American literature with his book of poems, *Leaves of Grass*, and his focus on individual freedom.

War Hawks Term given to a group of congressmen who argued for war with Britain in 1812.

War Industries Board The 1917 agency created to coordinate government purchases of military supplies.

Warren G. Harding Senator from Ohio who was elected president in 1920; generally remembered as ill-suited for the office.

Warsaw Pact A Soviet-led alliance of its Eastern European satellite nations created in 1955.

Washington Irving Successful author in the early 1800s of historical works and short stories including "The Legend of Sleepy Hollow."

Washington, D.C. The capital of the United States designed by French engineer Pierre L'Enfant; took many years to develop into a major city.

Watergate Named after the site where Nixon's operatives were first arrested, the scandal involving Nixon's use of illegal campaign tactics and attempts to cover up those tactics.

Webster-Ashburton Treaty This 1842 treaty helped defined the northern border between British colonies (now Canada) and the United States and soothed American anger at British actions in the Caroline and Creole affairs.

Webster-Hayne debate Senate exchange between Daniel Webster and Robert Hayne that focused on the issue of states' rights versus national power, pitting the nullification advocate Hayne against the nationalist Webster.

welfare capitalism A corporate strategy for discouraging labor unrest by improving working conditions, hours, wages, and other elements of workers' lives.

Western Union Telegraph Company The dominant telegraph company by 1860, formed by a combination of smaller telegraph companies.

Whigs Political party formed during the presidency of Andrew Jackson to oppose Jackson and to support a more active federal government; favored industrial, commercial, and infrastructural development to promote economic growth.

Whiskey Rebellion A 1794 uprising of western Pennsylvania farmers opposed to a new federal whiskey tax; put down by troops led by President Washington.

Wilbur and Orville Wright Builders of the first self-powered airplane, successfully flown in 1903.

William Berkeley The royal governor of Virginia during Bacon's Rebellion.

William H. Seward Secretary of state in both President Lincoln's and President Johnson's administrations who negotiated purchase of Alaska from Russia in 1867.

William Henry Harrison Ninth president of the United States who died shortly after taking office; experienced Indian fighter at an early age and later governor of Indian Territory; defeated Tecumseh at the Battle of Tippecanoe.

William Howard Taft Theodore Roosevelt's most trusted lieutenant and his handpicked successor, who was elected president in 1908.

William Howe British commander who led troops in capturing New York in 1776 and Philadelphia in 1777, but who was largely seen as ineffective until replaced in 1778.

William James Harvard psychologist and most prominent publicist of pragmatism.

William Jennings Bryan Congressman from Nebraska, tireless 1896 presidential candidate, and author of the "Cross of Gold" speech; also later secretary of state under President Woodrow Wilson and a Christian fundamentalist witness in the Scopes trial.

William Lloyd Garrison Founder of *The Liberator*, a newspaper that focused on the harsh truths of slavery and argued for the immediate release of the enslaved and extension of citizenship to all.

William M. Tweed The famously corrupt boss of New York's political machine Tammany Hall.

William McKinley Governor of Ohio and former congressman who was elected president in 1896 and 1900; assassinated in 1901.

William Penn Outspoken Quaker who led the colony of Pennsylvania after receiving a royal land grant.

William Pitt Leading English secretary of state and prime minister who ran England's war effort during the Sevens Years' War.

William Randolph Hearst The most powerful U.S. newspaper chain owner; by 1914, he controlled nine newspapers and two magazines.

William T. Sherman Union general who captured Atlanta and in late 1864 marched his troops across Georgia and the Carolinas, burning crops and buildings as he went and crippling the Confederacy.

Wilmot Proviso Failed congressional plan to prohibit slavery in any territory acquired from Mexico.

Winston Churchill Outspoken British prime minister in power during most of World War II.

Women's Christian Temperance Union (WCTU) Led by Frances Willard after 1879 and advocate for abstinence from the consumption of alcohol; single largest women's organization in American history by 1911.

Woodrow Wilson Native Virginian, president of Princeton University, governor of New Jersey, Democratic Party and progressive leader, and president of the United States from 1913 to 1921.

Woodstock Music festival held in upstate New York in August of 1969 that became a symbol of the counterculture.

Worcester v. Georgia Supreme Court case of 1832 that affirmed federal authority over individual states' authority concerning the affairs of Indian tribes.

Works Progress Administration (WPA) Established in 1935, this was a system of work relief for the unemployed, but on a larger scale than earlier, similar endeavors; it included such programs as the Federal Art Project, the Federal Music Project, and the Federal Writers' Project.

Wounded Knee Located on the Pine Ridge Indian Reservation in South Dakota, it was the site of a massacre of between 150 and 300 Sioux, including women and children, by the U.S. Army on December 29, 1890.

XYZ Affair Name given to an international incident between U.S. and French diplomats that sparked the quasi war between France and the United States.

Yalta Conference A 1945 meeting between Roosevelt, Churchill, and Stalin that laid the groundwork for the United Nations, but otherwise established only murky or soon-violated agreements on the partition of Germany and the question of who would rule Poland.

yellow journalism Sensationalist reporting, particularly in newspapers of the late nineteenth and early twentieth centuries, so named for the color of a character in one of the papers' comic strips.

yeoman farmer Small farmer who worked his own soil and possessed no slave labor.

Yorktown Virginia site of the last major battle of the American Revolution, where Lord Cornwallis surrendered to George Washington and French forces in 1781.

Young America A political movement supporting free trade and territorial expansion in America during the late 1840s and 1850s.

Zachary Taylor American hero of the Mexican War who was elected president in 1848.

Zimmermann Telegram The communication intercepted in early 1917 from the German foreign secretary to the German ambassador in Mexico outlining a deal to draw the Mexicans into the war against the United States.

zoot suits Style of dress among Mexican American youths during World War II that featured padded shoulders and baggy pants; led to attacks by whites for flaunting wartime protocols to conserve clothing materials.

INDEX

AAA. *See* Agricultural Adjustment Administration
Abortion, 740, 741, 769, 804–805
Abraham Lincoln Brigade, 577
ACLU. *See* American Civil Liberties Union
ADA. *See* Americans for Democratic Action
Adams, Charles Francis, Jr., 489
Addams, Jane, 490
Adjustable rate mortgages (ARM), 792
Advanced Research Projects Agency (ARPA), 800
Advertising
  in 1920s, 548, 552–553
  in 1950s, 678
  railroad, 399
  television, 678
AEF. *See* American Expeditionary Forces
Affirmative action, 711, 740, 804
Affordable Care Act, 793, 797
Afghan War, 817
Afghanistan, Soviets in, 749
AFL. *See* American Federation of Labor
AFL-CIO. *See* American Federation of Labor and Congress of
  Industrial Organizations
Africa
  former colonies in, 749
  WWII in, 618, 619
African American women
  in cities, 427
  clubs, 493
  employment of, 366, 571
  during Reconstruction, 366
  teachers, 493
African Americans. *See also* Civil rights; Civil War; Voting
  rights
  Black Cabinet, 606
  black nationalism, 536–537
  black power, 714–715
  in cities, 427, 536–537, 545, 624, 685–686
  citizenship rights of, 352, 361, 368
  in Congress, 364, 379, 703
  education, 365, 375, 449, 803
  employment, 359, 568, 686, 711
  families, 366–367, 677–678
  free, 363
  in Great Depression, 567–568
  Harlem Renaissance, 537, 553
  incomes, 365–366
  land ownership, 365
  in legal system, 624, 707
  lynchings, 378–379, 536, 555, 656
  middle class of, 689, 803
  migration to cities, 427, 536–537, 545, 624
  military service, 474, 517, 525, 621, 688
  music, 684
  New Deal and, 606
  in New South, 360–361, 374–375
  performers, 376–377, 445
  police shootings, 711, 804
  populism and, 462–463
  post-civil rights era, 803–804
  poverty of, 366
  reformers, 500–501

  religion of, 363, 380
  in Spanish-American War, 474–475, 476
  union members, 424, 463
  workers, 545–546
  writers, 553–554
  WWI and, 525, 536–537
  WWII and, 621, 624–625
African National Congress (ANC), 779
Agency for International Development (AID), 715
Agnew, Spiro, 757
Agrarian revolt
  Farmers' Alliances in, 459–461
  Grangers in, 459
Agricultural Adjustment Act, 588
Agricultural Adjustment Administration (AAA), 588–589
Agricultural Marketing Act, 580
Agriculture, 403. *See also* Plantations; Rural life
  child labor, 421
  commercial, 402
  dryland farming, 401
  in Great Depression, 566, 567, 580
  irrigation, 401
  migrant workers, 384, 685, 737, 738
  New Deal and, 588–589
  in 1920s, 547
  in 1950s, 685, 690
  organizations, 459–461
  overproduction of, 402
  parity, 547
  research, 547
  sharecropping, 365, 374, 380, 567, 685
  technology, 547
  tenant farmers, 365, 374, 380, 578, 685
  in West, 391, 398–403
Aguinaldo, Emilio, 482, 483
AID. *See* Agency for International Development
AIDS disease, 738, 805–806
AIM. *See* American Indian Movement
Airplanes
  bombers, 620, 623–624
  early, 409
  mail delivery by, 543
  manufacturing of, 623
  in 1920s, 543
  in WWI, 409, 529
  in WWII, 614, 623–624, 632
Al Qaeda terrorists, 814, 818
Alabama
  civil rights movement in, 687–688, 704–705
  Montgomery bus boycott in, 688, 706
  same-sex marriage case in, 808–809
  Scottsboro case in, 567–568, 578
  voting rights march in, 710
Alaska, 481
al-Assad, Bashar, 817
Alcatraz, 736
Alcott, Louisa May, 414–415, 446
Aldrich, Nelson W., 458
Aldrin, Edwin "Buzz," 676
Alexander, Michelle, 707
Alger, Horatio, 414, 418–419

Algerian War, 749
Allen, Harvey, 575
Alliance system, 522
Allies
  in WWI, 522
  in WWII, 614–616, 618–619, 623–624, 631, 633–634
Alperovitz, Gar, 639
Altgeld, John Peter, 424
AMA. *See* American Medical Association
America First Committee, 615
American Broadcasting Company, 678
American Civil Liberties Union (ACLU), 538, 555–556
American Communist Party (CPUSA), 577–578
American Expeditionary Forces (AEF), 527
American Federation of Labor (AFL), 422–423, 497, 536, 544, 545, 597–598
American Federation of Labor and Congress of Industrial Organizations (AFL-CIO), 671
American Indian Movement (AIM), 736
American League, 443
American Medical Association (AMA), 491, 553
American Plan, 544
American Protective Association, 433
American Socialist Party, 415
American Telephone and Telegraph (AT&T), 447
Americans for Democratic Action (ADA), 655
Anaconda copper mine, 391
ANC. *See* African National Congress
Anderson, Carol, 707
Antiaircraft technology, 623
Antibiotics, 672
Anticommunism
  historians' views of, 644–645
  HUAC and, 663
  John Birch Society, 650
  liberals, 655
  McCarthyism, 664–665
  in 1930s, 579
  Red Scare, 538, 690
  suspected subversives, 662–666
Anti-imperialism, 479
Anti-Imperialist League, 479, 480–481
Antimonopoly, 487
Anti-Saloon League, 501
Antitrust laws, 458
  Clayton Antitrust Act, 513
  Federal Trade Commission Act, 513
A&P. *See* Atlantic and Pacific Tea Company
Apache Indians, 396–397
Apache Wars, 397
Apartheid, 779
Apollo program, 676
Appeasement, 605–606
Apple Computer Company, 800
Arab oil embargo, of 1973, 763
Arapaho Indians, 395
Arkansas, 355
  school desegregation, 687
ARM. *See* Adjustable rate mortgages
Armory Show, 448
Arms control treaties, 765
Arms embargo, 613
Armstrong, Neil, 676
Army, U.S. *See also* Military; World War II
  Indian wars with, 394–397
  WWI, 525, 527

Army-McCarthy hearings, 690
Arnaz, Desi, 680–681
ARPA. *See* Advanced Research Projects Agency
ARPANET, 800–801
Art
  Ashcan school, 447–448
  Rocky Mountain school, 387
  in urban age, 447–448
Arthur, Chester A., 456–457
Artisans, 420
Ashcan school, 447–448
Asia. *See also specific countries*
  Open Door, 518
Asian Americans. *See also* Chinese Americans; Japanese Americans
  discrimination toward, 386, 433, 627
  in Great Depression, 569
  migrant workers, 685
Assembly lines, 410, 623
Assimilation
  of immigrants, 432–433
  of Indians, 397, 525, 735
Associated Press. *See* Newspapers
Associationalism, in business, 559
Atlanta Compromise, 375
Atlantic and Pacific Tea Company (A&P), 441
Atlantic Charter, 616, 691
Atomic bombs. *See also* Nuclear weapons
  development of, 636–637
  Soviet, 662
  survivors of, 638
  Truman's decision to use, 637, 638–639
Atomic Energy Commission, 651
AT&T. *See* American Telephone and Telegraph
Attorneys, 491
Attrition, war of, Vietnam, 719
Auschwitz, 620, 633
Austro-Hungarian Empire, 516, 522
Automobile industry. *See also* Ford, Henry
  assembly lines in, 410, 544, 623
  growth and history of, 408–409
  unions for, 598
Automobiles
  in 1920s, 542, 548
  development of, 408–409
  economic impact of, 408–409
  interstate highways and, 690
Avery, Oswald, 801

Baby Boom, postwar, 630, 670, 696, 724
Back Bay, in Boston, 434
Bacterial infections, 672–673
Badoglio, Pietro, 618
Bakke v. Board of Regents of California, 753
Balkans, 813
Ball, Lucille, 680–681
Ballinger, Richard A., 508–509
Banks
  failures of, 565–566, 571
  FDIC for, 588
  Federal Reserves system of, 512–513, 566, 588
  in Great Depression, 563, 564, 565–566, 571
  national, 461
  New Deal and, 587
Barnum, P. T., 377
Barton, Bruce, 548

Baruch, Bernard, 530–531
Baseball
    during Civil War, 443
    professional, 443–444
Basketball, 444
Battle of the Bulge, 634
Battles. *See specific battles and wars*
Bay of Pigs, 715
Beard, Charles A., 405, 449
Beard, Mary, 405
Beatles, 734
Beats, 682–683
Beck, David, 671
Beckwith, Byron De La, 705
Begin, Menachem, 765
Belknap, William W., 368
Bell, Alexander Graham, 406, 446
Bell, Derrick, 708
Bell system, 446–447
Bell Trade Act, 748
Bellamy, Edward, 415
Bellow, Saul, 682
Bellows, George, 447, 448
Berlin crisis, 651–652
Berlin Wall, 716, 778–779
Bernstein, Barton, 594
Berryman, Clifford, 590
Bessemer, Henry, 407
Bierstadt, Albert, 387
Billington, Ray Allen, 388
Bimetallism, 463, 603
bin Laden, Osama, 815, 817
The Birth of a Nation film, 445, 555
Birth rates, in 1950s, 670
Birth-control movement, 549
Bissell, George, 408
Black Codes, 359
Black Lives Movement, 804
Black Panthers, 714–715
Black power, 714–715
Black Tuesday, 562
Blackett, P. M. S., 639
Blackfeet Indians, 394
Blackmun, Harry, 752
Blaine, James G., 456, 457
Blitzkrieg, of Nazi Germany, 613
Bloody Sunday, 710
Boland Amendment, 779–780
Bolshevik Revolution, 525, 603
Bonds, during WWII, 623, 628
Bonus Army, 581–582
Booth, John Wilkes, 358
Borah, William, 499
Bosch, Juan, 716
Bosnia, 786
Boss Tweed. *See* Tweed, William M.
Boston, Massachusetts
    Back Bay, 434
    police strike, 536, 558
    subway, 436
Boston marriages, 492
Bourbons. *See* Redeemers
Bourke-White, Margaret, 531
Bowers, Henry, 433
Boxer Rebellion, in China, 483–484
Bozeman Trail, 395

Braceros, 625
Bradley, Omar, 633, 634, 662
Branch, Taylor, 706
Brandeis, Louis D., 503, 511, 514, 538
Brezhnev, Leonid, 763
Briand, Aristide, 557
Brinkley, Alan, 595
Brinkmanship, 691
Bristow, Benjamin H., 368
Britain. *See* England
British Empire
    dissolution of, 748–749
    imperialism, 468
British Raj, 469
Brotherhood of Sleeping Car Porters, 545–546, 624
Browder v. Gayle, 688
Brown v. Board of Education of Topeka, 686–687, 706, 707, 708
Bruce, Louis, 736
Brush, Charles F., 406
Bryan, William Jennings
    anti-imperialism of, 473, 479
    Cross of Gold speech, 464–465
    presidential candidacies of, 453, 464, 465, 485, 508
    Scopes trial, 555–556
Buffalo, 382, 394, 395
Buffalo Bill. *See* Cody, Buffalo Bill
Bull Moose Party, 510–511
Bunau-Varilla, Philippe, 519
Burchard, Samuel, 457
Bureau of Indian Affairs, 397, 625, 736
Bureau of Reclamation, 679
Bureaucracies, 682
Burger, Warren, 752
Burnham, Daniel, 434
Burns, James MacGregor, 594
Burroughs, William S., 406
Bush, George H. W.
    foreign policy of, 780–781
    presidency of, 780
Bush, George W.
    cabinet of, 791
    domestic policies of, 790
    foreign policy of, 790
    Iraq War and, 790
    presidency of, 790
    religious beliefs of, 767
    war on terror of, 815
Bush v. Gore, 789
Business. *See also* Corporations; Industry
    associationalism, 559
    monopolies, 413, 419, 504, 513
    national organizations of, 491
    in 1950s, 689–690
    regulation of, 424, 503, 739
    trusts, 458, 459, 504, 513

California. *See also* San Francisco
    Alcatraz in, 736
    film industry, 575
    Gold Rush, 383–384, 391
    Indians and, 396
    labor laws in, 497
    Mexican residents, 383–384
    military contracts in, 671
    Proposition 13 in, 769–770

Californios, 383–384
Calley, William, 744
Camp David accords, 765
Canada Act, 749
Canals, Panama, 468, 519–520, 765, 769
Cannon, Joseph, 508
Capitalism
    critics of, 413–417
    progressive reforms in, 415
    welfare, 543–544
Capitalists, 402, 415
Capra, Frank, 550, 573
Caribbean islands
    colonies, 749
    U.S. influence on, 520, 614
Carlisle Indian School, 398, 449
Carnegie, Andrew, 411–412, 414, 416–417, 423–424, 479
Carnegie, Dale, 572
Carpetbaggers, 363
Carranza, Venustiano, 521
Carson, Rachel, 742
Carter, Jimmy, 770–771
    economic policies of, 764
    presidency, 764
    religious beliefs, 767
Castro, Fidel, 693
Catholic Church
    abortion issue, 769, 804
    conservative causes of, 768–769
    Democratic supporters of, 455
    missions in California, 383
Catt, Carrie Chapman, 493
Cattle ranching, 383, 392–393, 400–401
CCC. *See* Civilian Conservation Corps
Centers for Disease Control and Prevention (CDC), 806
Central Intelligence Agency (CIA), 651, 692, 693
Central Park, New York City, 433, 443, 445
Central Powers, of Germany and Austria-Hungary, 522
Cervera, Pascual, 475
Chafe, William, 706
Chain, Ernest, 673
Chain stores, 441
Chamber of Commerce, United States, 491
Chamberlain, Joseph, 489
Chamberlain, Neville, 606
Chambers, Whittaker, 663
Chaney, James, 710
Chávez, César, 737, 738
Checkers speech, of Nixon, 665
Chernobyl disaster, in Soviet Union, 810
Cheyenne Indians, 383, 395
Chiang Kai-shek, 583, 604, 634, 653
Chicago
    Columbian Exposition of 1893 in, 434
    Democratic convention riot, 726–727
    Haymarket bombing in, 423
    Hull House in, 490
    Memorial Day Massacre in, 598–599
    race riots in, 537
    skyscrapers in, 436
    suburbs of, 434
Chicanos. *See* Mexican Americans
Chief Joseph, 396
Child labor
    in agriculture, 421
    in industry, 421, 602

in mining, 504
    regulation of, 514, 602
    wages for, 421
Children
    mortality rates for, 673
    during WWII, 630
Children's Bureau, 493
China
    Boxer Rebellion in, 483–484
    communist government in, 691
    Korean War and, 661–662
    Trump and, 819
    U.S. relations with, 483, 648, 660
    in WWII, 634
China Lobby, 653
Chinatowns, 384–385, 569
Chinese Americans
    anti- sentiments toward, 386, 433, 627
    in Great Depression, 569
    immigrants, 384–387, 431, 546
    laundry workers, 385, 569
    workers, 384–385
    WWII and, 621, 627
Chinese Exclusion Act, 386, 546, 627
Chivington, J. M., 395
Chopin, Kate, 447
Christian Coalition, 768
Christianity. *See also* Catholic Church; Protestants
    evangelical, 767–769
    Social Gospel and, 490
Chuh Jan Yut, 385
Chun Duck Chin, 385
Church of Jesus Christ of Latter-day Saints (Mormons), 387, 769
Churchill, Winston
    Atlantic Charter and, 616
    Potsdam conference of, 644, 647–648
    Tehran Conference, 645
    WWII and, 614, 616, 619
    Yalta Conference and, 644, 646–647, 816–817
CIA. *See* Central Intelligence Agency
Cinema. *See* Films
CIO. *See* Congress of Industrial Organization
Cities
    African Americans and, 427, 536–537, 545, 685–686
    African Americans migration to, 427, 536–537, 545, 624
    chain stores, mail-order houses, and department stores in, 441–442
    Chinatowns, 384–385
    crime in, 437–438
    culture in, 447–451
    ethnic groups in, 429–432
    federal programs in, 703
    fire departments in, 436
    "ghettoes" in, 431
    growth of, 428–429
    health and safety in, 436–437
    housing in, 434–435
    immigrants in, 428–429, 431–432
    industries in, 425
    leisure activities in, 442–447
    middle class in, 437–438, 439
    migration to, 427
    municipal reform for, 495–496
    political machines and bosses in, 385, 439
    pollution in, 437
    poverty, 437–438

Cities—(*Cont.*)
 public spaces in, 433–434, 443
 race riots in, 536–537, 621, 624, 625, 711
 racial discrimination in, 710–711
 settlement houses in, 490
 Social Gospel in, 490
 technologies, 435–436
 violence in, 437–438, 711
Citizenship
 of African Americans, 352, 361, 368
 Fourteenth Amendment and, 361, 362, 372, 375
 of Indians, 397
City beautiful movement, 434
City manager plan, 495
Civil rights
 Carter on, 764
 of Indians, 735–736
 Roosevelt, E., on, 608–609
 Truman on, 655, 656–657
Civil Rights Act of 1866, 359
Civil Rights Act of 1964, 706, 708
Civil Rights Cases (1883), 375, 378
Civil rights movement
 causes of, 688–689
 Freedom Summer in, 710
 historians' views on, 706–708
 King's leadership in, 688, 689
 March on Washington in, 706, 708
 in 1940s, 655–657
 in 1950s, 686–689
 in 1960s, 704–711, 735–736
Civil service reform, 456–457
Civil War
 aftermath of, 352
 casualties in, 352
 veterans' pensions and, 455
Civil Works Administration (CWA), 592
Civilian Advisory Commission, 530
Civilian Conservation Corps (CCC), 592, 606, 630
Civilization, Roosevelt, T., on, 517–518
Clark, Dick, 684
Clark, William, 391
Clayton Antitrust Act, 513
Clean Air Act, 743
Clean Water Act, 743
Clemenceau, Georges, 534
Cleveland, Grover
 presidency of, 424, 458, 462, 463, 464, 473
 presidential elections of, 457–458
Clifford, Clark, 721
Climate, 401, 671
Clinton, Hillary Rodham
 as First Lady, 786
 presidential candidacy of, 797–798
 as secretary of state, 796, 818–819
 as senator, 791
Clinton, William "Bill," 781–782
 domestic policies of, 785–786, 787
 foreign policy of, 786, 789
 presidency of, 785–786
 presidential elections of, 785
 religious beliefs of, 767
Clubs, women, 492–493
Coal, 407, 685
Cochise, 396–397
Cody, Buffalo Bill, 387

Cody's Wild West show, 387
Cohan, George M., 532–533
Cold War. *See also* Anticommunism; Nuclear weapons
 alliances in, 645–646
 China fall and, 653
 containment policy of, 642, 648–650
 Cuban missile crisis in, 716
 Eisenhower policies in, 691–693
 end of, 777–780
 Europe division from, 653
 historians' views on, 644–645
 Korean War and, 660–662
 Middle East crises and, 692–693
 new, 819
 in 1950s, 644
 in 1960s, 715–717
 origins of, 643, 645
Colfax, Schuyler, 368
Colleges. *See* Universities
Collier, John, 607, 625
Collins, Michael, 676
Colombia, 519–520
Colonialism, end of, 748–749
Colorado
 mining, 391
 statehood, 386
Colored Farmers' National Alliance, 459
Columbia Broadcasting System, 678
Columbian Exposition, in Chicago, 434
Colvin, Claudette, 688
Comey, James, 798
Comic books, 574–575
Comintern. *See* Communist International
Command of the Army Act, 363
Commercial agriculture, 402
Commission on Civil Disorders, 711
Commission plan, for municipal reform, 495
Committee on Public Information (CPI), 531
Communications technology, 406, 548, 724
Communism, 649. *See also* Anticommunism
 fear of, 668–669
 Korean War and, 660–662
 massive retaliation for, 691
 NSC-68 and, 653
 Soviet Union and Eastern Europe, 644
 Soviet Union collapse of, 778–779
 subversion fears, 662–666
Communist International (Comintern), 538
Communist Party, 663–664, 706
Community Action programs, 703, 735
Compromise of 1877, 370–371
Computer technology, 543, 624, 674–675
Computers, 543, 624, 674–675
Comstock, Henry, 391
Comstock Lode, 391
Concentration policy, 394
Coney Island, 445–446
Congress, 458, 464, 665
 African American members of, 364, 379, 703
 HUAC in, 663
 Reconstruction and, 355, 357, 361–362
 Watergate investigations by, 757
 women in, 740
Congress of Industrial Organization (CIO), 598
Congress of Racial Equality (CORE), 624–625, 704–705, 714

Conkling, Roscoe, 456
Connally, John, 701
Connor, Eugene "Bull," 705
Conscription
    during Vietnam War, 733
    during WWI, 517
    in WWII, 614
Conservatives
    abortion issues of, 804–805
    capitalists as, 413–414
    free-market, 773–774
    grassroots, 773
    John Birch Society and, 630
    neo-, 771, 773–774
    on New Deal, 586–587, 592–593, 595, 630
    in 1960s, 700–701, 727–728
    in 1970s, 766–770
    religious, 766–769
    rise of movement of, 766–770
    Sagebrush Rebellion and, 766, 775
    as silent majority, 728, 751
    Tea Party and, 793–794
    during WWII, 624, 630–631
Consolidation, of corporations, 412–413, 543
Constitution, U.S. See specific amendments
Consumerism
    mass consumption and, 439, 441
    in 1920s, 548
    in 1950s, 677
    of women, 442
    during WWII, 627, 628
Containment policy, of Cold War, 642, 648–650
Contract Labor Law, 424
Conwell, Russell H., 414
Coolidge, Calvin
    Boston police strike and, 536, 558
    presidency of, 547, 556, 558
Coolies, 384
Coral Sea, Battle of, 618
CORE. See Congress of Racial Equality
Corporations
    consolidation of, 412–413, 543
    history of, 411–413
    holding companies of, 413
    power of, 411–412
    R&D laboratories, 409
Corruption
    in Agnew case, 757
    in business, 489
    in Grant administration, 368
    in payola scandals, 684
    of political machines and bosses, 439
    in Reconstruction governments, 364
    Teapot Dome and, 557
    in unions, 671
Cortina, Juan, 383
Coughlin, Charles E., 595–596, 604
Council of National Defense, 530
Counterculture, 733–734
Court-packing plan, 602
Cowboys, 387
Cox, Archibald, 755
Cox, James M., 539, 583
Coxey, Jacob S., 462, 463
Coxey's Army, 462–463

CPI. See Committee on Public Information
CPUSA. See American Communist Party
Crane, Stephen, 447
Crazy Horse, 396
Crédit Mobilier, 368
Credit system, 365–366, 402–503
Crile, G. W., 450
Crime
    in cities, 437–438
    during WWII, 630
"Crime of '73," 464
Criminal justice system. See Legal system
The Crisis magazine, 500
Cronon, William, 388
Crop-lien system, 366, 374
Cuba
    Bay of Pigs in, 715
    Castro government in, 693
    economy of, 471
    Maine incident, 473
    migration from, 431, 737–738
    missile crisis, 716
    revolution in, 475–476, 693
    Spanish-American War in, 453–454, 475–476,
        477, 485
    U.S. occupation of, 481
    war of independence in, 471, 473
Cuban missile crisis, 716
Cultural relativism, 607
Culture. See also Art; Music; Popular culture
    of Great Depression, 572–576
    in 1920s, 547–551, 554–556
    in 1950s, 677, 680–684
Cumming v. County Board of Education, 375
Custer, George A., 396
CWA. See Civil Works Administration
Czechoslovakia, Prague Spring, 724
Czolgosz, Leon, 503

Daimler, Gottfried, 408
Dakota Territory
    Black Hills gold rush, 391
    reservations, 394, 396
Darrow, Clarence, 556
Darwin, Charles, 448, 467, 555
Darwinism
    evolution and, 448, 555
    imperialism and, 448–449
    Scopes trial and, 555–556
    Social, 413–414, 448–449
Daugherty, Harry, 557
Davis, David, 370
Davis, Henry, 357
Davis, John W., 556, 558
Dawes, Charles G., 558
Dawes Plan, 558
Dawes Severalty Act, 397–398
Dawley, Alan, 499
Days, Drew, 764
D-Day, 632
DDT, 673–674
de Gaulle, Charles, 724
De Leon, Daniel, 415
Dean, James, 682, 755
Debs, Eugene V., 424, 502, 511, 512, 533

Debt, during WWII, 622–623
Decentralization, 503
Declaration of Indian Purpose, 735–736
Defense of Marriage Act (DOMA), 806, 809
Democratic Party
    in late nineteenth century, 454–455
    New Deal and, 586–587, 593, 601, 606, 610
    in 1920s, 556
Democratization, of government, 778–779
Deng Xiaoping, 765
Denning, Richard, 680
Department of Defense, 651
Department of Housing and Urban Development, 703
Department stores, 440–442
Depressions. *See also* Great Depression
    of 1873, 459
    of 1893, 453, 467
Deregulation, 775, 779
Desert Land Act, 386
Détente, Soviet-American, 747, 750–751, 769
Detroit, race riots in, 624
DeVoto, Bernard, 679
Dewey, George, 475
Dewey, John, 449
Dewey, Thomas E., 631, 655
Diaz, Porfirio, 521
Diem, Ngo Dinh, 692, 717
Dies, Martin, 579
Digital revolution, 799–800
Dillingham, William P., 502
Dime novels, 446
Dingley Tariff, 466
Diplomacy. *See also* Treaties
    Dollar Diplomacy, 520–521
    East Asia and threats to, 818–819
    morality and, 521–522
    in 1960s and 1970s, 715
    in 1980s, 776–777
    Open Door, 483–484, 518
    Republican, 369
    of Roosevelt, F., 603–604
    of Roosevelt, T., 518–520
    during WWII, 639, 645–646
Disarmament, 695
Discrimination. *See also* Racial discrimination
    toward Asian Americans, 386, 433, 627
    toward women, 711
Diseases
    AIDS, 738
    antibiotics for, 672
    bacterial infections and, 672–673
    in cities, 436
    germ theory, 450
    infectious, brought by Europeans, 383
    influenza, polio and viral, 673
    malaria, 673–674
    medical science and, 671–672
Disk jockeys, in radio, 684
Disney, Walt, 573
Dittmer, John, 706
Divorces, 492, 571–572
DNA discovery, 801
Dole, Robert, 760, 787
Dollar Diplomacy, 520–521
DOMA. *See* Defense of Marriage Act

Dominican Republic, 519, 521, 716
Dos Pasos, John, 576
Douglas, Lewis, 593
Dower, John, 639
Draft laws. *See* Conscription
Drake, Edwin L., 408
Dreiser, Theodore, 438, 447
Drones, 818
Du Bois, W. E. B., 356, 500–501
Duck and Cover film, 658–659
Dudziak, Mary, 707
Dukakis, Michael, 780
Dulles, John Foster, 650, 691, 692
Dunning, William A., 356
Duryea, Charles, 409
Duryea, Frank, 409
Dust Bowl, 566, 568, 576, 578
Dyson, Michael Eric, 707

Earth Day, 743, 807
Eastern Europe, 644. *See also* Cold War; *specific countries*
Echo Park, 679, 682
Eckford, Elizabeth, 687
Ecology, 741–742
Economic Cooperation Administration, 651
Economics. *See also* Depressions; Industry
    Keynesian policies in, 565, 566, 595, 689
    mass consumption and, 439, 441
    New Deal, 609–610
    in 1920s, 535–536, 543–544, 562
    in 1930s, 563
    in 1950s, 668, 669–671
    in 1960s and 1970s, 671, 698, 700, 704, 753–754
    in 1980s, 775–776
Economy Act, 588
Edison, Thomas A., 406, 445
Education
    of African Americans, 365, 375, 449, 803
    desegregation in, 686, 687, 740
    federal aid for, 703
    of Indians, 398, 449
    No Child Left Behind, 790
    professional, 491
    public schools, 365, 432, 451
    Reconstruction and Southern, 365
    reform of, 449, 703
    school shootings and, 797
    universal, 449
    of women, 451, 493
Egypt, 763
Eighteenth Amendment, 501, 554
Einstein, Albert, 636
Eisenhower, Dwight D.
    election of 1948 and, 655
    farewell address, 694–695
    McCarthyism and, 665
    presidency of, 687, 689–690, 692
    presidential elections, 665–666, 690
    Republicanism, 689–690
    in WWII, 618
Elections. *See also* Voting rights
    municipal, 495–496
    secret ballots for, 494, 496
    turnout for, 496–497
    UNIVAC on, 674

Elections, by year
  1860, 455
  1868, 367
  1872, 368
  1876, 370–371
  1880, 456–457
  1884, 457
  1888, 457–458
  1892, 458
  1896, 453, 465, 466, 484–485
  1900, 479–480
  1904, 508
  1908, 508
  1912, 511–512
  1916, 514, 524
  1920, 539, 557
  1924, 558
  1928, 556, 559
  1932, 583–584
  1936, 593
  1940, 615
  1944, 631
  1948, 655–656
  1952, 650, 665–666
  1956, 690
  1960, 699–700
  1964, 769
  1968, 726–728, 730, 759
  1972, 753
  1976, 763–764, 769
  1980, 770–771
  1984, 777
  1988, 780
  1996, 787–788
  2000, 789–790
  2004, 791
  2008, 791–793
  2012, 797
  2016, 797–798
Electoral College, election of 1876, 370–371
Electricity, 406–407, 589, 591–592, 609
Electronic technology, 674
Elementary and Secondary Education Act, 703
Ellington, Duke, 628
Ellis Island, 429
Ellsberg, Daniel, 744
Ellwood, I. L., 401
Emancipation, 352
Emergency Banking Act, 588
Employment. *See also* Unemployment
  of African American women, 366, 571
  of African Americans, 359, 568, 686, 711
  racial discrimination in, 359, 568, 686, 711
Energy source
  electricity, 406–407, 589, 591–592, 609
  nuclear, 810–811
Enforcement Acts of 1870 and 1871, 370
Engel v. Vitale, 752
England. *See also* British Empire; World War I; World War II
  blockade by, 522
  naval power of, 615
  Suez crisis and, 618, 692–693
  U.S. Civil War and, 369
Entitlement programs, 776
Environmental Protection Agency, 743, 775, 812
Environmentalism

conservation, 507–508
contemporary movement, 807
ecology and, 741–742
global movement for, 810–811, 813
historic roots of, 437
in 1960s and later, 741–743
organizations of, 507, 679, 742
Roosevelt, T., and, 505
Equal Pay Act, 739
Equal Rights Amendment (ERA), 551, 740–741, 804
Equality. *See also* Inequality
  Reconstruction and, 372
ERA. *See* Equal Rights Amendment
Ervin, Sam J., 755
Escobedo v. Illinois, 752
Espionage Act of 1917, 533
Ethnicity, in West labor, 390
Eugenics, 502
Europe. *See also* World War I; World War II;
      specific countries
  alliances of, 522
  Cold War division of, 652
  imperialism of, 468–469
  industrialization in, 564
  Marshall Plan and, 650–651
  population growth, 430
  social democracy in, 488
  trade and, 563
European Marxists, 502
Evangelical Christianity, 767–769
Evers, Medgar, 705
Ex parte Milligan, 363

F. W. Woolworth, 441
Factory system, 425
Fair Deal, 654–657
Fair Employment Practices Commission (FEPC),
      624, 656
Fair Labor Standards Act, 602
Fall, Albert B., 557
Falwell, Jerry, 768
Families
  African American, 366–367, 677–678
  in Great Depression, 571–572, 578
  of slaves, 366–367
  suburban, 670–671, 677, 678
  in WWII, 628–630
Family and Medical Leave Act, 786
Family Assistance Plan (FAP), 752
Far West. *See* West
Farm Credit Administration, 592
Farm Security Administration, 579, 589
Farmer, James, 624
Farmers' Alliances, 459–461
Farmers' Holiday Association, 580
Fascism, 577, 583, 748
Faubus, Orval, 687
Faulkner, William, 553
FCC. *See* Federal Communications Commission
FDIC. *See* Federal Deposit Insurance Corporation
Federal Art Project, of New Deal, 579, 601
Federal Communications Commission (FCC), 548
Federal Deposit Insurance Corporation (FDIC), 588
Federal Emergency Relief Administration
      (FERA), 592
Federal Employee Loyalty Program, 663–664

Federal government. *See also* Congress; Supreme Court
  budgets of, 704, 775, 787
  deficits, 776
  expansion of, 467
  in late nineteenth century, 455
  in 1920s, 541, 547, 556–558
  on racial segregation, 567–568
  Reagan on role of, 772–773
Federal Highway Act of 1956, 690
Federal Music Project, of New Deal, 601
Federal Reserve Act, 512–513
Federal Reserve Board, 775
Federal Trade Commission Act, 513
Federal Writers' Project (FWP), 570–571
Feis, Herbert, 638
The Feminine Mystique (Friedan), 739
Feminism, 805. *See also* Women's rights
  in 1960s and later, 725, 739–740
FEPC. *See* Fair Employment Practices Commission
FERA. *See* Federal Emergency Relief Administration
Ferber, Edna, 553
Ferdinand, Franz (archduke), 522
Ferraro, Geraldine, 740, 777
Ferrell, Robert H., 639
Fessenden, Reginald, 542
Field, Cyrus W., 406
Fifteenth Amendment, 362, 370, 372, 375
Film noir, 657
Films
  American industry, 550
  The Birth of a Nation, 445, 555
  film noir, 657
  in Great Depression, 573
  in 1920s, 548, 550–551
  in 1950s, 657, 683, 684
  during WWII, 632
Fireside chats, 587
Fish, Hamilton, 367–369, 579, 593
Fitzgerald, F. Scott, 553
Five-Power Pact, 557
Flappers, 549, 551
Fleming, Alexander, 673
Florey, Howard, 673
Foch, Ferdinand, 527
Folk music, 722–723
Folsom, Burton, 595
Foner, Eric, 356
Food, consumerism and, 441
Football, 443–444
Foraker Act, 476
Ford, Gerald, 762, 770–771
  presidency of, 745, 757, 769
Ford, Henry, 409, 410, 543–544
Foreign relations. *See* Diplomacy; Imperialism
Foreign Relations Committee, 535
Forest Service, U.S., 509
Foster, Vince, 786
Fourteen Points, of Wilson, 533–534
Fourteenth Amendment, 361, 362, 372, 375, 806, 808
France
  Allied invasion of, 618, 633–634
  D-Day invasion in, 632
  Paris Expositions in, 488
  social democracy in, 488
  Suez crisis in, 618, 692–693
  in Vietnam, 691–692

Franco, Francisco, 577
Frank, Leo, 555
Franklin, John Hope, 356
Frazier-Lemke Farm Bankruptcy Act, 592
Free African Americans, 363
Free silver, 464
Free Speech Movement, 732–733
Free trade, 786
Freedmen's Bureau, 355, 356, 365
Freedom of Access to Clinic Entrances Act, 805
Freedom rides, 704–705
Free-market conservatives, 773–774
Free-silver movement, 466–467
Frick, Henry Clay, 412, 423–424
Friedan, Betty, 739
Fulbright, J. William, 721
Furman v. Georgia, 752
FWP. *See* Federal Writers' Project

Gaddis, John Lewis, 644, 645
Gagarin, Yuri, 676
Garfield, James A., 456–457
Garfield, James R., 508–509
Garland, Hamlin, 403
Garrow, David, 706
Garvey, Marcus, 537
Gasoline technology, 408
Gast, John, 389
GATT. *See* General Agreement on Tariffs and Trade
Gay liberation, 738. *See also* Homosexuals
Gay Liberation Front, 738
Gender relations. *See also* Families
  in African American families, 366
  feminism and, 739–740
  in Great Depression, 575
  in 1920s, 548–549
  in suburban families, 670–671
General Agreement on Tariffs and Trade (GATT) treaties, 813
General Federation of Women's Clubs, 493
General Motors, 410, 689–690
Genetic research, 543, 801
Geneva accords, on Vietnam, 691, 692, 717
George, David Lloyd, 534
George, Henry, 415
Germ theory of disease, 450
German Americans, 533
Germany. *See also* Nazi Germany; World War I
  division in, 651–652, 716
  fascism in, 577
  Great Depression and, 564–565
  social democracy in, 488
  zone of occupation in, 646
Geronimo, 396–397
"Ghettoes," 431
Ghost Dance, 397
GI Bill, 654
Gideon v. Wainwright, 752
Gingrich, Newt, 787
Glass-Steagall Act, 588, 792
Glavis, Louis, 509
Glenn, John, 676
Glidden, Joseph H., 401
Global media, 724–725
Global warming, 807, 809, 811–812
Globalization. *See also* Trade
  age of, 784–820
  labor unions and, 813

Gold rushes
 Black Hills, 391
 California, 383-384, 391
Gold standard, 464-465
Gold Standard Act, 466
Goldwater, Barry, 701, 769
Gompers, Samuel, 422-423, 479, 497, 544
Good Neighbor Policy, 603-604
Goodman, Andrew, 710
Goodman, Benny, 628
Gorbachev, Mikhail, 777-779
Gordon, Linda, 499
Gore, Al, 789, 809, 811
Gorsuch, Anne, 775
Gospel of wealth, 414-415, 416-417
Grady, Henry, 373
Graham, Billy, 767
Granger Laws, 459
Grangers. *See* National Grange of the Patrons of Husbandry
Grant, Ulysses S., presidency of, 364, 367-369
The Grapes of Wrath (Steinbeck), 576
Grassroots conservatives, 773
Great Depression. *See also* New Deal
 African Americans and, 567-568
 bank failures during, 563, 564, 565-566, 571
 causes of, 562-563
 culture in, 572-576
 Hoover's policies in, 561, 579-580
 immigrants in, 568-569
 impact of, 580-582, 670
 politics during, 577-579
 progress of, 565-566
 public relief in, 566, 579-580
 responses to, 580-582
 stock market crash and, 562, 565
 unemployment in, 561, 564-565, 566, 567, 568, 569, 571-572
 values and, 572
 women and families in, 571-572, 578
 worldwide, 564-565
Great Lakes region, steel production in, 407
Great Migration, 545
Great Migration, of African Americans to cities, 427, 536-537, 545, 624
Great Plains. *See also* West
 climate in, 401
 Dust Bowl in, 566, 568, 576, 578
 Plains Indians, 382-383, 394
Great Railroad Strike, 422
Great Recession of 2008, 792
Great Society reforms, 701-702, 704, 721, 751
Great War. *See* World War I
Greeley, Horace, 368
Green, William, 544
Greenbacks, 368-369, 461, 495
Griffith, D. W., 445, 555
Griswold v. Connecticut, 741
Guadalcanal, 618
Guantánamo Bay, 815
Gulf of Tonkin Resolution, 718-719, 744
Gulf War, 780-781

Haley, Alex, 707
Haley, Bill, 683-684
Half-Breeds, 456
Hamby, Alonzo L., 639

Hamer, Fannie Lou, 710, 712-713
Hampton Institute, 449
Hancock, Winfield Scott, 456-457
Hanna, Marcus A., 464, 465, 503
Harding, Warren G., 533, 539
 death of, 557
 presidency of, 557
 Teapot Dome and, 557
Harlem Renaissance, 537, 553
Harrington, Michael, 684-685
Harris, Patricia Roberts, 764
Harrison, Benjamin, 457-458
Harrison, William Henry, grandson of, 457-458
Hawaii
 annexation to U.S., 471
 native population in, 470-471
 Pearl Harbor, 470, 616-617
 as territory, 470-471, 481
Hawley-Smoot Tariff, 580
Hay, John, 483, 484, 519
Hayes, Rutherford B., 370, 422
 presidency of, 456
Haymarket bombing, 423
Hays, Samuel, 498
Hays, Will, 575
Haywood, William "Big Bill," 502, 533
Hearst, William Randolph, 446, 472-473, 604
Hemingway, Ernest, 553, 577
Hepburn Railroad Regulation Act, 505
Herrán, Tomás, 519
Hetch Hetchy Valley, in Yosemite National Park, 507, 679
Hewitt, Abram S., 407
Hideki Tojo, 616, 626
Higher education. *See* Universities
Hill, James J., 411
Hindenburg, 575
Hine, Lewis, 421
Hiroshima, 637, 639, 657
Hispanics
 in Great Depression, 568
 migration to cities by, 737
 New Deal and, 606
 in West, 383-384
Hiss, Alger, 663, 665
Historians
 on anticommunism, 644-645
 on civil rights movement, 706-708
 on Cold War, 644-645
 on New Deal, 594-595
 on progressivism, 496-497
 on Reconstruction, 356-357
 on Truman's atom bomb decision, 638-639
 on Watergate, 756-757
 on West, 388-389
Hitchcock, Alfred, 550-551
Hitler, Adolf, 565, 577, 582, 615. *See also* Nazi Germany
 beliefs of, 604
 in comic books, 574-575
 death of, 634
 eastern offensive and, 618
 German invasion by, 613
 at Munich conference, 605-606
 rise of, 583
Ho Chi Minh, 691-692, 718
Ho Chi Minh trail, 719, 720

Hoffa, Jimmy, 671
Hofstadter, Richard, 498, 594
Holbrooke, Richard, 786
Holding companies, of corporations, 413
Holding Company Act, 597
Holly, Buddy, 683
Holmes, Oliver Wendell, 538
Holocaust, 619–620, 633
Home Owners' Loan Corporation, 592
Homelessness, 776
Homer, Winslow, 447
Homestead Act, 355, 386
Homestead Strike, 423–424, 463
Homosexuals
   AIDS epidemic, 738, 805–806
   marriages of, 806–807
   mental illness category deleted for, 738
   in military, 629, 786, 807
Hood, James, 705
Hooper, William, 470
Hoover, Herbert, 530
   as commerce secretary, 559
   foreign policy of, 582–583
   Great Depression and, 561, 579–580
   presidency of, 559, 561, 584
   WWI and, 530
Hoover, J. Edgar, 538, 663–664
Hoovervilles, 580
Hopkins, Harry, 592, 600, 606
Hopper, Edward, 447–448
Horizontal integration, in industry, 412
House Un-American Activities Committee (HUAC), 663
Housing
   in cities, 434–435
   in 1950s, 670–671, 686
Housing Act, 703
Howard, Oliver O., 355
Howells, William Dean, 447
HUAC. See House Un-American Activities Committee
Hubble Space Telescope, 676
Huerta, Victoriano, 521
Hughes, Charles Evans, 524, 602
Hughes, Langston, 553
Hull, Cordell, 604
Hull House, 490
Human Genome Project, 801
Humphrey, Hubert, 655, 726–728
Hungarian Revolution, 695
Huntington, Collis P., 411
Hurricane Katrina, 791
Hussein, Saddam, 781, 815, 816
Hydrogen bomb, 651, 674

"I Have a Dream" speech, of King, M. L.,
   706, 708
I Love Lucy, 680–681
IBM. See International Business Machines
ICBM. See Intercontinental ballistic missiles
ICC. See Interstate Commerce Commission
Ickes, Harold, 606
Idaho, statehood of, 387
Idealism, retreat from, 539
Immigrant labor force
   Chinese, 384–386
   indentured servants, 384, 431

   in late nineteenth century, 420
   need for, 547
Immigrants
   assimilation of, 432–433
   Chinese, 384–387
   in cities, 428–429, 431–432
   countries of origin, 703
   ethnic communities, 431–432
   military service of, 517, 525
   poverty, 420
   quotas for, 554, 627
Immigration
   indentured servants and, 384, 431
   nativism, 554–555
   population, 802–803
   quotas, 554, 627
   reforms for, 502
   restrictions for, 502
Immigration Act of 1965, 703
Immigration Restriction League, 433
Immunization, 673
Impeachment
   investigation of Nixon, 757–759
   of Johnson, A., 363, 379
Imperialism
   American, 467–470
   British Empire system of, 468
   of Europe, 468–469
Income taxes, 512
Incomes
   of African Americans, 365–366
   of middle class, 439
   in 1920s, 544, 547
   in 1930s, 566
   in Reconstruction South, 365–366
   during WWII, 622
Indentured servants
   Chinese, 384
   immigration and, 384, 431
Independent Republicans, 495
Indian Civil Rights Act, 736
Indian Civil Rights movement, 735–736
Indian Peace Commission, 394
Indian policies
   of assimilation, 397, 525, 735
   of concentration, 394
   in New Deal, 607
   of reservations, 394
   of termination, 735
Indian Reorganization Act, 625
Indian Territory
   reservations in, 394
   tribes removed to, 394
Indians. See also specific tribes
   assimilated, 397, 735
   code-talkers, 527, 621
   education of, 398, 449
   Plains, 382–383, 394
   religions of, 397
   rights movement, 735–736
   treaties with, 396
   tribal sovereignty, 394
   wars with U.S., 394–397
   Western lands and, 382–383
   WWII and, 625

Individualism, 413, 561
Indochina, defeat in, 745–746
Industrial Workers of the World (IWW) "Wobblies," 502
Industrialization, New South and, 373–374
Industry. *See also* Business; Corporations; *specific industries*
    assembly lines, 410
    decentralization and regulation of, 503
    factory system, 425
    growth, 405, 406–413
    horizontal integration in, 412
    labor force, 420–425
    meat-packing, 505
    New Deal and, 589–590
    in 1920s, 405
    production techniques, 409–410
    R&D, 409
    restructuring of, 754
    technologies, 406–413
    vertical integration in, 412, 419
    wages in, 420–421, 424, 671
    in WWI, 516, 531, 533
    in WWII, 622, 625, 630
Inequality. *See also* poverty
    of capitalism, 413–417
Inflation, 464
    in 1920s, 535–536
    in 1950s, 670
    in 1960s and 1970s, 721, 754
    in 1980s, 764, 775
    in postwar period, 654, 655
    during WWII, 622–623
Initiative, 496
Inouye, Daniel, 621
Insull, Samuel, 591
Intelligence
    CIA, 651
    U-2 crisis, 695–696
    Vietnam War, 745
    in WWII, 616, 624
Interchangeable parts, 410
Intercontinental ballistic missiles (ICBMs), 675
Internal combustion engine, 408
International Business Machines (IBM) Company, 674–675, 800
International Labor Defense, 568
Internet, 800–801
Interregnum, 584
Interstate Commerce Act, 458–459, 505
Interstate Commerce Commission (ICC), 459, 505
Inventions. *See* Technology
Iran, nuclear program in, 817
Iran-Contra scandal, 779–780
Iranian Revolution of 1979, 813
Iraq War, 815–817
Iron industry, 407
ISIS. *See* Islamic State of Iraq and Syria
Islamic State of Iraq and Syria (ISIS), 818
Isolationism, 603–606
Israel
    Egypt relations with, 692–693
    founding of, 692
Issei, 547, 627
Italy
    Tripartite Pact, 616
    in WWII, 613, 616, 619
IWW. *See* Industrial Workers of the World

James, William, 449
Japan. *See also* World War II
    alliance with Germany and Italy, 616
    atomic bombings, 637–639
    Great Depression and, 565, 583
    military technology in, 623
    surrender of, 637
    Tokyo firebombing, 636
    U.S. relations with, 518, 603
Japanese Americans
    in Great Depression, 569
    internment of, 625–627
    Issei and Nisei, 547, 627
    workers, 546–547
Jaworski, Leon, 757
Jay Cooke and Company, 368
The Jazz Singer, 548
Jeffries, Hassan, 707
Jews
    anti-Semitism, 555
    comic book writers, 574–575
    Holocaust and, 619–620, 633
    Reform Judaism, 433
Jim Crow laws, 375, 378–379, 687–688, 730
Jingoes, 467, 479
John Birch Society, 650
John Paul II (pope), 645
Johnson, Andrew
    impeachment of, 363, 379
    presidency, 359, 361, 365, 369
    as vice president, 358
Johnson, Hiram, 499
Johnson, Hugh S., 589
Johnson, Lady Bird, 742
Johnson, Lyndon B.
    Great Society of, 701–702, 704, 721
    presidency of, 704–705
    as vice president, 701
Joint Chiefs of Staff, 484
Joint Committee on Reconstruction, 359, 361
Jones, Paula, 787–788
Jones Act, 476
Jordan, Barbara, 758
Joubert, Jules-Francois, 672
Journalism. *See* Muckrakers; News media; Newspapers
Judaism. *See* Jews
Judd, G. P., 470

Kamehameha I of Hawaii (king), 470
Kearny, Stephen W., 383
Keating-Owen Act, 514
Kelley, Florence, 442
Kellogg, Frank, 557
Kelly, William, 407
Kennan, George F., 649, 717
Kennedy, Anthony, 807
Kennedy, David, 595
Kennedy, Edward, 770
Kennedy, Jacqueline Bouvier, 699
Kennedy, John F.
    assassination of, 701, 709
    foreign policy of, 715–716
    New Frontier policy of, 700
    presidential election of, 699–700
Kennedy, Joseph P., 699

Kennedy, Randall, 707
Kennedy, Robert, 705, 710, 721, 726, 737
  assassination of, 724, 726
Kennedy-Khrushchev Pact, 716
Keppler, Joseph, 490
Kerouac, Jack, 682
Keynes, John Maynard, 565, 566, 595, 689
Keynesianism, 565, 566, 595, 689
Khomeini, Ayatollah Ruhollah, 765
Khrushchev, Nikita, 695
Kim II Sung, 660
Kim Jong-un, 819
King, Martin Luther, Jr., 688, 689, 701, 704, 709
  assassination of, 724, 726
  as evangelical Christian, 767
  "I Have a Dream" speech, 706, 708
Kissinger, Henry, 763
  foreign policy and, 747–751
  Vietnam War and, 743–746
Klan. See Ku Klux Klan
Klarman, Michael, 708
Kluger, Richard, 707
Knights of Labor, 422, 461
Knox, Philander C., 520
Kolko, Gabriel, 498
Korean War, 670
  divided peninsula in, 660–661
  end to, 691
  limited mobilization during, 662
  MacArthur invasion and, 660–662
Korematsu v. U.S., 627
Kosovo, 789
Kruse, Kevin, 595
Ku Klux Klan, 369, 554–555, 556, 704–705, 710
Kyoto Protocol, 812

Labor force. See also Child labor; Immigrant labor force;
    Indentured servants; Strikes; Unemployment; Unions;
    Wages; Women, in workforce
  agricultural, 547
  factory system and, 425
  immigrant, 420
  leisure time, 442–447
  in 1920s, 545–547
  in postwar period, 671–672
  regulations for, 424, 503, 739
  weakness of, 424–425
  in West, 390–391
  working conditions, 420–421
Labor-Management Relations Act, 654–655
LaFeber, Walter, 644
LaFollette, Robert M., 496, 510
Laird, Melvin, 744
Lamar, Howard, 388
Land policies, in Reconstruction South, 365
Land-grant institutions, 449, 451
Landon, Alf M., 601
Latin America. See also specific countries
  immigration from, 703
  Roosevelt Corollary, 519, 520, 582
  U.S. policies and, 603–604
Latino activism, 737–738
Latter-Day Saints. See Church of Jesus Christ of Latter-day Saints
Lawyers, 491
Le Duc Tho, 745

League of Nations, 612
  covenant in, 534–535
  Japan and, 557
  opponents to, 534
  proposal of, 534
  replacing, 646
  Wilson's support of, 534
League of Women Voters, 551
Lease, Mary E., 460
Leffler, Melvyn, 644
Legal system. See also Regulations; Supreme Court
  African Americans in, 624, 707
Leisure activities
  in consumer society, 442–447
  gender differences in, 443
  in 1950s, 678–682
  public and private patterns for, 445–446
  of spectator sports, 443–444
Lend-lease program, 615–616
Leopold, Aldo, 741
Leuchtenburg, William, 594
Levitt, William, 677
Levittowns, 677
Lewinsky, Monica, 788
Lewis, John, 708–709
Lewis, John L., 577, 598, 654
Lewis, Sinclair, 553
Liberalism
  New Deal, 586, 594–595, 608–609
  in 1960s, 699–704
Liberty League, 593
Libraries, 434
Life magazine, 575–576, 628
Liliuokalani of Hawaii (queen), 470–471
Limerick, Patricia, 388
Limited liability corporations, 411
Lincoln, Abraham
  assassination of, 358, 405
  Civil War and, 354
  portrait of, 358
  Reconstruction and, 355, 357–358
Lindbergh, Charles, 409, 615
Lippman, Walter, 593
Literacy, voting rights and, 378, 709–710
Literature
  in Great Depression, 575–576
  Harlem Renaissance, 537, 553
  in 1920s, 548
  in 1950s, 682
  in urban age, 446, 447
  women writers, 414–415
Little Bighorn, Battle of, 396
Little Crow, 395
Little Steel formula, 622
Litwack, Leon, 356
Lodge, Henry Cabot, 535
Long, Huey P., 596, 601
Long drives, in cattle ranching, 392, 393
Lorentz, Pare, 579
Los Angeles
  growth in, 671
  Hispanics in, 625, 737
  industry in, 622
  Watts riots in, 711
  zoot-suit riots in, 625

Lost Generation, of WWI, 553
Louisiana, 355. *See also* New Orleans
Lucas, Sam, 377
Lucy and Desi television show, 680–681
Lusitania (ship), 523
Lynchings, 378–379, 536, 555, 656

MacArthur, Douglas, 482, 646, 665
  Bonus Army and, 581–582
  Korean War and, 660–662
  in WWII, 617–618, 634–635
MacLeod, Colin, 801
Madero, Francisco, 521
Madison, James, 758
Mahan, Alfred Thayer, 470
Mail-order houses, 441
Maine incident. *See* U.S.S. *Maine* incident
Malcolm X, 714–715
Malone, Vivian, 705
Mandela, Nelson, 779
Mangas Colorados, 396–397
Manhattan Project, 636–637
Manifest Destiny, New, 467
Manufacturing. *See* Industry
Mao Zedong, 604, 646, 653
Marable, Manning, 707
March on Washington, 706, 708
Marconi, Guglielmo, 406
Marielitos, 737
Marriage
  Boston, 492
  companionate, 549
  same-sex, 808–809
  during WWII, 630
Marshall, George C., 618, 651
Marshall Islands, 634
Marshall Plan, 650–651, 666
Martin, Joseph W., 662
Mass consumption, 439, 441
Massachusetts Institute of Technology, 450
Mass-circulation magazines, 548
Massive retaliation, for communism, 691
May, Elain Tyler, 499
May, Ernest, 644
MBSs. *See* Mortgage-backed securities
McAdoo, William, 556
McCain, John, 791, 792
McCarran Internal Security Act, 663
McCarthy, Eugene, 726
McCarthy, Joseph, 664–665, 666, 690
McCarthyism, 665, 666
  decline of, 690
McCarty, Maclyn, 801
McCord, James W., 755
McCormick, Richard, 498–499
McCormick Harvester Company, 423
McGerr, Michael, 499
McGovern, George S., 753
McKay, Claude, 537
McKeand, Kimberly, 808–809
McKinley, William
  assassination of, 503
  cartoon of, 478
  in Congress, 458, 464
  presidency of, 466–467, 473, 484

presidential elections of, 453, 464, 465, 479–480
  Spanish-American War and, 478
McKinley Tariff, 458, 464
McNair, Ronald, 676
McNamara, Robert, 721
McNary-Haugen Bill, 547
McVeigh, Timothy, 814
Meany, George, 671
Meat-packing industry, 505
Medicaid, 702–703
Medicare, 702–703, 787
Medicine. *See also* Diseases
  advances in, 450
  as profession, 491
  science and, 450
  vaccines, 673
Mellon, Andrew, 558–559
Memorial Day Massacre, 598–599
Men. *See* Gender relations
Mencken, H. L., 553
Mendel, Gregor, 543, 801
Mercedes-Benz vehicles, 408
Metropolitan Museum of Art, 433–434
Mexican Americans. *See also* Hispanics
  braceros, 625
  in California and Texas, 383–384, 547
  cattle ranching by, 392
  in cities, 625
  in Great Depression, 568
  immigrants, 383, 547
  as migrant workers, 384, 685, 738
  Texas territory, 383–384
  WWII workers of, 625
Mexican War, 383
Mexico
  Pershing expedition, 521
  Wilson and, 521
  Zimmermann Telegram and, 523
MFDP. *See* Mississippi Freedom Democratic Party
Mickey Mouse, 573
Middle class
  African Americans, 689, 803
  in cities, 437–438, 439
  in 1920s, 549
  in 1950s, 677, 679, 684, 689
  professionals, 491
  progressivism, 497
  as silent majority, 728, 751
Middle East, 765. *See also specific countries*
  conflicts in, 750–751, 817–818
  new challenges in, 817–818
  terrorism, 813–815, 817–818
Migrant workers, 384, 685, 737, 738
Migration
  to cities, 427, 624
  global, 427–428, 430–431
  to North, 566, 567
  reverse, 402
Miles, Nelson, 396, 475, 476
Military, 671. *See also* Veterans
  African Americans, 474, 517, 525, 621, 688
  Civil War veterans pension system, 455
  homosexuals in, 629, 786, 807
  immigrants in, 517, 525
  -industrial complex, 694–695

Military, 671. *See also* Veterans—(*Cont.*)
  Joint Chiefs of Staff in, 484
  modernization of, 484
  segregation in, 656
  technology, 528–530, 623
  women in, 525, 629, 630
Military-industrial complex, Eisenhower on, 694–695
Milliken v. Bradley, 753
Milosevic, Slobodan, 789
Minimum wages, 602, 656
Mining
  child labor in, 504
  gold rushes, 384, 391–392
Minstrel shows, 375, 376–377
Miranda v. Arizona, 752
Miscamble, Wilson, 639
Mississippi Freedom Democratic Party (MFDP), 710
Mitchell, Margaret, 575
Molly Maguires, 422
Mondale, Walter, 777
Monetary policy
  bimetallism, 463, 603
  gold standard, 464–465, 603
  in 1930s, 563
  in 1980s, 775–776
  silver question, 463–464
Monopolies. *See also* Antitrust laws
  critics of, 415, 419
  railroad, 504
  Wilson on, 513
Monroe Doctrine, 473
  Roosevelt Corollary to, 519, 582
Montana
  mining in, 391
  statehood of, 387
Montgomery, Bernard, 618
Montgomery bus boycott, 688, 706
Montreal Protocol, 775
Moral Majority, 768
Moran, Thomas, 387
Morgan, J. P., 412, 413, 504, 508
Morgan, Thomas Hunt, 543, 801
Mormons. *See* Church of Jesus Christ of Latter-day Saints
Morrill Land Grant Act, 449
Mortgage-backed securities (MBSs), 792
Mossadegh, Mohammed, 692
Motherhood, 549, 678
Motion Picture Association, 548
Movies. *See* Films
Mowry, George, 498
Muckrakers, Social Gospel and, 489–490
Mueller, Robert S., 819
Muir, John, 506–507
Mukden Incident, 583
Muller, Paul, 675
Munich conference, 605–606
Municipal reform, 496
  city manager plan, 495
  commission plan, 495
Murphy, Charles Francis, 497
Mushet, Robert, 407
Music
  folk, 722–723
  minstrel shows, 375, 376–377
  rap, 792, 794–796
  rock, 734–735
  rock n' roll, 683–684

Mussolini, Benito, 565, 577, 582, 583, 604, 619
My Lai massacre, 719

NAACP. *See* National Association for the Advancement of
  Colored People
NAFTA. *See* North American Free Trade Agreement
Nagasaki, 637, 638, 639, 657
NASA. *See* National Aeronautics and Space Administration
Nasser, Gamal Abdel, 692
National Advisory Committee on Aeronautics, 409
National Aeronautics and Space Administration (NASA), 675–676
National American Woman Suffrage Association (NAWSA), 493
National Association for the Advancement of Colored People
  (NAACP), 500, 501, 537, 688, 714
National Association of Colored Women, 493, 501
National Association of Manufacturers, 491
National bank, 461
National Broadcasting Company, 548, 678
National Civil Liberties Bureau, 538
National Consumers League (NCL), 442
National Cordage Company, 462–463
National Defense Research Committee, 623
National Environmental Protection Act, 743
National Farm Bureau Federation, 491
National Grange of the Patrons of Husbandry (Grangers), 459
National Greenback Party, 369
National Guard units, 474, 536, 687, 711
National Housing Act, 656
National Industrial Recovery Act, 589, 597
National Labor Relations Act, 597
National Labor Relations Board (NLRB), 597
National League, 443
National Liberation Front (NLF), 718
National Organization for Women (NOW), 739–740
National Origins Act of 1924, 554
National parks and forests, 505–507, 679
National Recovery Administration (NRA), 589–590, 606
National Rifle Association, 797
National Security Act, 651
National Security Administration, 815
National Security Council (NSC), 651
National Socialist Party, 583, 605
National War Labor Board, 531
National Woman's Party, 494, 551
National Youth Administration (NYA), 601
Nationalism, 415
  black, 536–537
  New, 510
Native Americans. *See* Indians
Native Sun (Wright, R.), 576
Nativism, 554–555
NATO. *See* North Atlantic Treaty Organization
Navy, U.S.
  Pacific bases of, 470
  Pearl Harbor base, 470, 616–617
  in WWI, 529–530
  in WWII, 630, 634–636
NAWSA. *See* National American Woman Suffrage Association
Nazi Germany, 565. *See also* World War II
  atomic bomb research in, 636
  blitzkrieg of, 613
  expansion of, 613–614
  Holocaust in, 619–620, 633
  military technology of, 623
  Stalin nonaggression pact with, 578
  Tripartite Pact in, 616

Nazi Party. *See* National Socialist Party
NCL. *See* National Consumers League
Nebraska, statehood of, 386
Nelson, Gaylord, 743
Neoconservatives, 771, 773–774
Neutrality, Roosevelt, F., on, 613–616
Neutrality Acts, 513, 604, 614, 615
Nevada
  mining in, 391
  statehood of, 386
New Deal
  African Americans and, 606
  conservative criticism of, 586–587, 592–593, 595, 630
  Democratic Party and, 586–587, 593, 601, 606, 610
  end of, 603, 609–610
  Farm Security Administration of, 579
  Federal Art Project of, 579, 601
  FWP of, 570–571
  historians' views of, 594–595
  Indian policies in, 607
  industrial recovery in, 589–590
  launching of, 587–592
  legacy of, 606–607, 609–610
  liberalism and, 586, 594–595, 608–609
  political realignment in, 601
  populist criticism of, 595–597
  recession and, 602–603
  regional planning for, 590–592
  relief programs of, 579–580, 592, 600–601
  Second, 597
  Social Security Act, 599–600
  Supreme Court cases, 589–590, 597, 601–602
  women and, 607–609
New Frontier policy, 700, 751
New Mexico
  American settlers, 383
  Hispanic residents, 383
  Indians, 383
  Mexican War, 383
New Nationalism, 510
New Orleans, 361
New Right, tax revolt of, 769–770
New South
  African Americans in, 360–361, 374–375
  industrialization and, 373–374
  Redeemers in, 372–373
New World Order, 650, 812–813
New York City
  Central Park, 433, 443, 445
  skyscrapers, 436
  Stonewall Riot, 738
  Tammany Hall in, 439, 457, 497
New York Journal, 472–473
New York Times, 659, 744
New York Tribune, 368
New York World, 472–483
News media, television, 678–681, 684, 689
Newspapers. *See also specific newspapers*
  chains, 548
  mass-circulation, 446
  yellow journalism, 472–473
Newton, Huey, 714
Nez Percé Indians, 396
Nguyen Van Thieu, 745
Nicaragua

  contras, 779–780
  treaty, 521
  U.S. troops in, 520
Nimitz, Chester, 617, 634
9/11 attacks, 784, 790, 814
1920s
  advertising in, 548, 552–553
  culture, 548–551, 554–556
  economy, 535–536, 543–544, 562
  federal government in, 541, 547, 556–558
  gender relations, 548–549
  industry in, 405
  labor force in, 545–547
  as New Era, 543, 548–549, 560
  politics, 556–559
  technology, 542–543, 547
1950s. *See also* Postwar period
  affluence, 668
  business in, 689–690
  civil rights movement in, 686–689
  Cold War, 644
  economic miracle in, 668, 669–671
  films in, 657, 683, 684
  Korean War, 660–662
  margins of society, 684–686
  middle class in, 677, 679, 684, 689
  politics, 669–670, 696
  popular culture, 677, 680–681, 683–684
  poverty, 684–685
  science and technology, 672–676
  youth culture, 682–683
1960s and 1970s. *See also* Vietnam War
  economy, 671, 698, 700, 704, 753–754
  environmentalism, 741–743
  events of 1968, 723–728
  foreign relations, 715–717, 747, 750–751
  liberalism in, 699–704
  New Left in, 731–733
  politics, 726–728, 761
  rights movements, 704–711, 730–740, 735–736. 725
  youth culture, 721, 724–725, 731–735
1980s
  economy, 775–776
  foreign relations, 776–777
  politics, 777
Nineteenth Amendment, 494, 539
Nisei, 547, 627
Nixon, Richard M., 699
  Checkers speech of, 665
  China visit, 747
  in Congress, 663, 665
  domestic policies, 751–752
  Ford, G., pardon of, 762
  foreign policy of, 747, 750–751
  impeachment investigation of, 757–759
  presidential election of, 726–728
  resignation of, 758, 759
  Supreme Court appointments by, 752–753
  as vice president, 692
  Vietnam War and, 743–745
  Watergate of, 755–759, 762–766
Nixon Doctrine, 750
NLF. *See* National Liberation Front
NLRB. *See* National Labor Relations Board
No Child Left Behind bill, 790

Noriega, Manuel, 781
Normandy invasion, 624, 631
Norris, Frank, 447
Norris, George, 499
North Africa, WWII in, 618, 619
North American Free Trade Agreement (NAFTA), 786
North Atlantic Treaty Organization (NATO), 595, 652–653, 817
North Carolina, Kitty Hawk at, 409
North Dakota, statehood of, 386
No-strike pledge, of unions, 621
NOW. *See* National Organization for Women
Noyce, Florence, 494
NRA. *See* National Recovery Administration
NSC. *See* National Security Council
NSC-68, 653
Nuclear energy, 810–811
Nuclear weapons. *See also* Atomic bombs
   arms control treaties, 765
   fears, 657, 658–659
   ICBMs, 675
NYA. *See* National Youth Administration
Nye, Gerald, 604, 615

Oakley, Annie, 387
Obama, Barack
   Affordable Care Act of, 793, 797
   domestic policies of, 794, 797, 812
   foreign policy of, 817, 819
   presidential elections of, 791
Obergefell v. Hodges, 807
O'Brien, Gail, 707
Ocala Demands, 460, 461
Occupational Safety and Health Administration, 437
Occupy Wall Street (OWS), 796
O'Connor, Sandra Day, 740
OEO. *See* Office of Economic Opportunity
Office of Defense Mobilization, 662
Office of Economic Opportunity (OEO), 703, 735, 751
Office of Price Administration (OPA), 622
Office of Scientific Research and Development, 623
Office of War Information (OWI), 628
Office of War Mobilization (OWM), 623
Ogletree, Charles, 708
Ohio, steel production in, 407
Oil industry, 408
   Teapot Dome scandal, 557
Okies, 566
Okinawa, 635–636
Old Guard Republicans, 509, 510
Olmsted, Frederick Law, 433
OPA. *See* Office of Price Administration
OPEC. *See* Organization of the Petroleum Exporting Companies
Open Door policies, 483–484, 644
   in Asia, 518
Open shop, 544
Oppenheimer, J. Robert, 636–637
Organization of the Petroleum Exporting Companies (OPEC), 751, 754, 764, 775
Orlando, Vittorio, 534
Oswald, Lee Harvey, 701
The Other America (Harrington), 684–685
Otto, Nicolaus August, 408
OWI. *See* Office of War Information

OWM. *See* Office of War Mobilization
OWS. *See* Occupy Wall Street

Pacific Islands. *See also* Hawaii
   Samoa, 470–471
   in WWII, 617–618, 634–636
Pacification program, in Vietnam War, 719–720
Pacifism, 523
Palmer, A. Mitchell, 538
Palmer Raids, 538
Panama Canal, 468, 519–520, 765, 769
Panic of 1873, 368–369, 370
Panic of 1893, 462–463
Panic of 1907, 508, 510
Paris Accord, 812
Paris Expositions, 488
Paris Peace Accord, 745
Paris Peace Conference, 534
Parity, 547
Parks, Rosa, 687–688
Partial Birth Abortion Ban Act, 804
Partisanship, resurgence of, 784–790
Pascoe, Peggy, 388
Pasteur, Louis, 672
Paterson, Thomas G., 644
Patronage, 439, 456–457
Patten, Simon, 443
Patterson, James T., 707
Patton, George S., 618, 633
Paul, Alice, 494, 551
Paulson, Henry, 792
Pawnee Indians, 383
Payne, Charles, 706
Payola scandals, in radio, 684
Peace Corps, 715
Peirce, Charles S., 449
Pendleton Act, 457
Pennsylvania, steel industry in, 407
Pennsylvania Railroad, 407–408
Pennsylvania Steel Company, 407–408
Pentagon Papers, 744
People's Party, 458, 461, 464–466, 484–485
Perkins, Frances, 607
Perot, Ross, 781–782, 786
Pershing, John J., 521, 527
Pesticides, 673–674
Pharmaceutical research, 450
Philadelphia and Reading Railroad, 462
Philippines
   immigrants, in California, 547
   independence of, 480–481, 748
   revolt against U.S. rule of, 481–483
   as Spanish colony, 478
   Spanish-American War, 475, 485
   U.S. occupation of, 478–479
   in WWII, 617–618, 634–635
Phillips, Sam, 683–684
Phillips-Fein, Kim, 595
Photography, 446
Pinchot, Gifford, 507, 509
Pink-collar jobs, 545
Plains Indians, 382–383, 394
Plantations, sugar, 478, 481
Platt Amendment, 481
Plessy v. Ferguson, 375, 686

Pocket veto, 357
Poland
    Auschwitz, 620, 633
    Soviets and, 648
    WWII, 613, 619–620, 624
Political machine, 439, 455, 489–490
Political parties. *See also specific parties*
    in late nineteenth century, 454–455
    New Deal realignment, 601
    in 1950s, 669–670, 696
    People's Party, 458, 461, 464–466, 484–485
Pollution. *See also* Environmentalism
    oil spills, 742–743
Pomeroy, Earl, 388
Popular culture
    Alger's novels, 418–419
    comic books, 574–575
    dime novels, 446
    in Great Depression, 574–575
    minstrel shows, 376–377
    in 1950s, 677, 680–681, 683–684
    television, 680–681
    Wild West shows, 387
    in WWI, 532–533
    in WWII, 628
    yellow journalism, 472–473
Popular Front, 577, 578, 722–723
Population growth, in 1950s, 670
Populism
    Coxey's Army, 462–463
    of farmers, 459, 461
    ideas, 453, 461–462
    New Deal and, 595–597
    People's Party and, 458, 461, 464–466, 484–485
    reformers, 459–461
Port Royal Experiment, 354
Postwar period. *See also* Cold War; 1950s
    economy during, 653–655, 671
    electronic research, 674
    families in, 670–671
    Marshall Plan and, 650–651
    popular culture of, 657
    Red Scare, 538, 690
Potsdam conference, 644, 647–648
Potter, David, 677
Poverty
    of African Americans, 366
    aid programs, 702–703
    of immigrants, 420
    in 1930s, 564, 566, 568
    in 1950s, 684–685
    reducing, 702–703, 704
    in rural areas, 685
    urban, 437–438
Powderly, Terence V., 422
Powell, Lewis F., Jr., 752
Pragmatism, 449
Prague Spring, in Czechoslovakia, 724
Preservationists, 507
Presidents. *See also* Elections; *specific presidents*
    patronage and, 456–457
    war powers, 363
President's Commission on the Status of Women, 739
Presley, Elvis, 683–684
Press. *See* Newspapers

Pro-choice movement, 741, 804–805
Professions
    middle class, 491
    women in, 492, 548, 740
Profiteering, 604
Progressive Party, 510–511, 655
Progressivism. *See also* Social democracy
    African Americans and, 500–501
    beliefs, 486, 487
    on decentralization and regulation, 503
    economic reforms, 491, 503
    historians' views, 496–497
    immigration restrictions, 502
    labor laws, 496, 499
    political reforms, 495–497
    of Roosevelt, T., 487
    settlement houses, 490
    Social Gospel, 489–490
    social justice, 490
    socialism and, 502–503
    sources of, 497, 499–501
    Taft and, 508–509
    temperance movement, 501
    western, 499–500
    woman suffrage, 493–494, 514
Prohibition, 501, 554
Proposition 13, 769–770
Prostitutes, 386, 392
Protestants
    fundamentalists, 448, 555–556
    Republican Party supporters of, 455
Public Health Service, 437
Public schools, 365, 432, 451
Public space, in cities, 433–434, 443
Public Works Administration (PWA), 589
Puck magazine, 438, 456, 518
Pueblo Indians, 382
Puerto Rico
    migration from, 737–738
    Spanish colony in, 476
    as territory, 476–477, 481
    U.S. annexation of, 476–478
Pulitzer, Joseph, 472–473
Pullman, George M., 424
Pullman strike, 424, 463
Pure Food and Drug Act, 505
Putin, Vladimir, 819
PWA. *See* Public Works Administration
Pyle, Ernie, 621, 628

Race relations. *See also* African Americans
    police shootings of blacks, 711, 804
Race riots, 536–537
    Commission on Civil Disorders on, 711
    in 1960s, 711
    during WWII, 621, 624, 625
Racial discrimination. *See also* Civil rights movement
    in cities, 710–711
    in employment, 359, 568, 686, 711
    in government employment, 656
    in New Deal, 606
    toward Asian Americans, 386, 433, 627
Racial segregation
    challenges to, 706–707
    desegregated schools, 686
    of federal government, 567–568

Racial segregation—(*Cont.*)
  Jim Crow laws, 375, 378–379, 687–688
  of military, 656
  of New Deal programs, 606
  prohibition of, 705
Racism
  anti-Chinese, 386
  in popular culture, 689
Radical Republicans, 355, 356, 359
Radio
  commercial, 548
  disk jockeys, 684
  in Great Depression, 572–573
  Marconi invention of, 406
  ownership of, 543
  payola scandals, 684
  Roosevelt, F., use of, 587
  shortwave, 542–543
Radio Act, 548
Railroads
  advertising, 399
  Chinese workers, 384
  combinations, 411
  expansion of, 410–412
  failures of, 462–463
  farmers and, 399, 402
  industry and, 407–408, 410–411
  monopolies, 504
  in New South, 373
  Pennsylvania, 407–408
  Philadelphia and Reading, 462
  regulation of, 458–459, 461, 505
  strikes, 422, 654
  transcontinental, 384, 386, 401
  tycoons, 411
  Union Pacific Railroad Company, 368
  in West, 384, 386, 402, 410
Ranching, 383, 392–393, 400–401
Randolph, A. Philip, 545–546, 624
Range wars, 392
Rap music, 792, 794–796
Raskob, John Jacob, 593
Ray, James Earl, 726
Reagan, Nancy, 774
Reagan, Ronald, 645, 740
  as California governor, 763, 769
  coalition, 771, 773–774
  fiscal crisis of, 776
  foreign policy of, 776–777
  on government role, 772–773
  presidency of, 774
  presidential elections of, 769, 770–771
  Reaganomics of, 775–776
Reagan Doctrine, 777
Reaganomics, 775
Recessions. *See also* Depressions
  in 1920s, 535–536
  of 1937, 602–603
  in 1980s, 775–776
  of 2008, 792
Reconstruction
  congressional, 355, 357, 361–362
  end of, 367–372
  Freedmen's Bureau and, 355, 356
  historians' views on, 356–357
  land redistribution, 354, 355, 365, 372

  legacy of, 352, 372
  loyalty oaths in, 355, 359
  plans for, 355, 357, 361–362
  politics of, 355
  Radical, 355, 357, 359–363
  readmission to Union, 359, 362
  South in, 363–367
  state governments, 355, 359, 363–364
  views of, 353–355
Reconstruction Finance Corporation (RFC), 580
Red Army, 618
Red Cloud, 395
Red Scare, 538, 690
Redeemers (Bourbons), 372–373
Referendum, 496
Reform Judaism, 433
Reformers. *See also* Populism; Progressivism
  African American, 500–501
  women, 492–494
Regulations
  business, 424, 503, 739
  of child labor, 514, 602
  deregulation, 775, 779
  progressivism labor laws, 496, 499
  railroad, 458–459, 461, 505
  stock market, 588
Rehnquist, William, 752
Religions. *See also* Catholic Church; Christianity; Jews; Protestants
  of African Americans, 363, 380
  of Indian tribes, 397
  of 1920s, 556–557
Religious fundamentalism, 448, 555–556
Relocation centers, 627
Remington, Frederic, 389–390
Republican Party
  Clinton administration and, 786–787
  in late nineteenth century, 453, 454–455
  in 1920s, 556–557
  Radical, 355, 356, 359
  in South, 379
Republicanism, Eisenhower, 689–690
Republicans, Reconstruction and, 355
Research and development (R&D) laboratories, 409
Reverse migration, 402
Revisionism, 644
RFC. *See* Reconstruction Finance Corporation
Rhodes, Cecil, 469
Richardson, Elliot, 757
Richmond, Virginia, 354
Riesman, David, 682
Right to life movement, 769
Rights. *See also* Civil rights; Voting rights; Women's rights
  human, 765
  movements in 1960s and 1970s, 704–711, 725, 735–736,
    739–740
Right-to-work laws, 655
Riis, Jacob, 435
Ritty, James, 406
Roberts, Oral, 767
Roberts, Owen J., 602
Robertson, Pat, 768, 769
Robinson, Joanne, 688
Rock music, 734–735
Rock n' roll music, 683–684
Rockefeller, John D., 412–413
Rockefeller, Nelson, 769

Rockefeller Institute for Medical Research, 450
Rocky Mountain school, 387
Rodgers, Daniel, 499
Roe v. Wade, 741, 753, 804
Roebling, John A., 436
Rogers, William, 744
Rolling Stones, 734–735
Roman Catholic Church. *See* Catholic Church
Romantic novels, 414–415, 446
Rommel, Erwin, 618
Romney, Mitt, 797
Roosevelt, Eleanor, 606, 607
    on civil rights, 608–609
Roosevelt, Franklin Delano, 539
    Atlantic Charter, 616
    Black Cabinet, 606
    career, 583–584
    death of, 637, 647
    election of 1920 and, 539
    foreign policy of, 612–613
    health, 583, 631
    judicial reforms of, 602
    on neutrality, 613–616
    presidency of, 612–616
    presidential elections of, 583, 615, 631
    Tehran Conference, 645
    WWII and, 612–616, 618–619, 622, 624, 630–631
    Yalta Conference, 644, 646–647, 816–817
Roosevelt, Theodore "Teddy"
    Bull Moose Party, 510–511
    cartoon of, 518
    on civilization, 517–518
    environmental policies of, 505
    foreign policy of, 517–520
    on immigration, 502
    imperialism and, 469, 473, 479
    muckrakers and, 489
    Panama Canal, 519–520
    post-presidency of, 509–510
    presidency of, 503
    presidential election of, 510, 512
    progressivism of, 503–505, 507–508
    Spanish-American War, 475, 476
    Square Deal of, 504–505
    as vice president, 503–504
    The Winning of the West, 390
Roosevelt Corollary, 519, 582
Root, Elihu, 484
Rosen, Ruth, 499
Rosenberg, Ethel, 663–664
Rosenberg, Julius, 663–664
Rosie the Riveter, 630
Ross, Edward A., 449
Roth v. United States, 752
Rough Riders, 476
Rove, Karl, 791
Ruby, Jack, 701
Rudolph, Eric Robert, 814
Rural Electrification Administration, 589
Rural life, poverty in, 685
Russia. *See also* Soviet Union
    economic sanctions on, 766
    presidential election tampering by, 798, 819
    WWI and, 518, 522, 530, 534
Rustin, Bayard, 624

Sabin, Albert, 673
Sabotage Act, 533
Sacco, Nicola, 538
Sadat, Anwar, 765
Sagebrush Rebellion, 766, 775
Saint-Lô, Battle of, 633
Salinger, J. D., 682
Salk, Jonas, 673
SALT I. *See* Strategic Arms Limitation Treaty
SALT II. *See* Strategic Arms Limitation Treaty II
Salvation Army, 437, 490
Samoa, 470–471
San Francisco
    Chinatown, 384–385
    Chinese immigrants, 384–385
    earthquake, 507
Sand Creek massacre, 395
Sandy Hook Elementary School shooting, 797
Sanger, Margaret, 549
Sargent, John Singer, 447
Satellite communication, 724
Scalawags, 363
Schlaes, Amity, 595
Schlesinger, Arthur M., 594
Schools. *See* Education
Schwarzkopf, Norman, 781
Schwerner, Michael, 710
Science. *See also* Medicine
    atomic bomb research, 636–637
    genetics, 543, 801
    research, 674
    space program, 675–676
    universities for technology and, 449–450
    during WWII, 623–624
SCLC. *See* Southern Christian Leadership Conference
Scopes, John T., 555–556
Scottsboro case, 567–568, 578
SDI. *See* Strategic Defense Initiative
SDS. *See* Students for a Democratic Society
Seale, Bobby, 714
Searcy, Cari, 808–809
Sears and Roebuck, 441
SEC. *See* Securities and Exchange Commission
Second New Deal, 597
Secret ballots, 495
Securities and Exchange Commission (SEC), 588
Security Council, of United Nations, 646, 660
Sedition Act of 1918, 533
Selective Service Act, 525, 651
Senate War Investigating Committee, 631
Serbia, 786
    Austria-Hungary invasion of, 516
    civil war in, 789
Servicemen's Readjustment Act of 1944, 654
Settlement house movement, 490
Seventeenth Amendment, 496
Seward, William H., 358, 369
Seward's Folly, 369
Seymour, Horatio, 367
Shafter, William R., 475–476
Sharecropping, 365, 374, 380, 567, 685
Share-Our-Wealth Plan, 596–597
Shaw, Anna Howard, 493
Sheep ranching, 383, 392
Sheldon, Charles, 490

Shelley v. Kraemer, 657
Shepard, Alan, 675
Sheppard-Towner Act, 553
Sherman, John, 479
Sherman, William T., 354
Sherman Antitrust Act, 458, 459, 504
Sherman Silver Purchase Act, 464
Sherwin, Martin, 639
Sholes, Christopher L., 406
Sierra Club, 507, 679, 742
Silent majority, 751
Silent Spring (Carson), 742
Silver question, 463–464
Sinai, 763
Sinclair, Upton, 447
Singer, Isaac, 412
Sioux Indians, 383, 395–396
Sirhan, Sirhan, 726
Sit-down strikes, 598
Sitting Bull, 396
Six Companies, 385
Sixteenth Amendment, 512
Sklar, Kathryn, 499
Skocpol, Theda, 594
Skyscrapers, 436
Sloan, John, 447
Smallpox, epidemics of, 383
Smith, Alfred E., 499, 556, 559, 583
Smith, Henry Nash, 379, 388
Smith-Connally Act, 622
SNCC. *See* Student Nonviolent Coordinating Committee
Snowden, Edward, 815
Social Darwinism, 413–414, 448–449, 487
Social Democracy, 488–489
Social Gospel, muckrakers and, 489–490
Social Security Act, 599–600
Social Security system, 493, 656
Social work, 490, 491
Socialism, 502–503, 660
Socialist Labor Party, 415, 533
Socialist Party of America, 502, 578
Soil Conservation and Domestic Allotment Act, 589
Somalia, 813
South. *See also* Reconstruction; *specific states*
    in Reconstruction, 363–367
    Sunbelt, 766
South America. *See specific countries*
South Dakota, statehood of, 386
Southern Christian Leadership Conference (SCLC),
    688, 714
Southern Tenant Farmers Union (STFU), 578
Sovereignty, tribal, 394
Soviet Union. *See also* Cold War; Russia
    Afghanistan invasion by, 765–766
    atomic and nuclear weapons, 662
    Chernobyl disaster, 810
    collapse of, 644–645, 778–779
    colonialism end, 749
    Germany invasion of, 615
    space programs of, 675
    U-2 crisis, 695–696
    U.S. relations with, 518, 602, 642, 643–645, 695–696, 716,
        776–777
    in WWII, 615, 618, 632, 637, 639
Space program, 675–676

Spanish Civil War, 577, 604
Spanish colony, in Puerto Rico, 476
Spanish-American War, 516, 748
    African American troops in, 474–475, 476
    background of, 473–474
    in Cuba, 453–454, 475–476, 477, 485
    in Philippines, 475, 485
Specie Resumption Act, 368–369
Spencer, Herbert, 413–414
Spock, Benjamin, 678
Sports
    baseball, 443–444
    professional, 443–444
Sputnik, 675
Square Deal, of Roosevelt, T., 504–505
St. Louis, 620
Stagflation, 763
Stalin, Josef
    Atlantic Charter, 616
    Cold War and, 642
    CPUSA and, 577
    death of, 695
    Korea and, 660
    Munich Conference and, 606
    Potsdam conference, 644, 647–648
    Roosevelt and, 603
    Tehran Conference, 645
    WWII and, 618, 642
    Yalta Conference, 644, 646–647,
        816–817
Stalwarts, 456
Stampp, Kenneth, 356
Standard Oil Company, 412–413, 419
Stanton, Edwin M., 362–363
Stanton, Elizabeth Cady, 493
Starr, Kenneth, 788
State governments
    as agent for reform, 496
    referendum and initiative of, 496
States' Rights Democratic Party ("Dixiecrat"), 655
Steam engines, 407
Steel industry, 662
    in Great Lakes region, 407
    in 1920s, 542, 543, 558
    strikes, 423–424
    technology, 407
    unions, 422–424
Steel Workers Organizing Committee (SWOC), 598
Steffens, Lincoln, 489–490
Stein, Gertrude, 553
Steinbeck, John, 576
Stephens, Alexander H., 359
Stephens, Uriah S., 422
Stevens, Thaddeus, 355
Stevenson, Adlai E., 665, 690
Stevenson, Bryan, 707
STFU. *See* Southern Tenant Farmers Union
Stilwell, Joseph W., 634
Stimson, Henry, 583, 638
Stock market
    in 1920s, 562
    regulation, 588
Stone v. Powell, 753
Stonewall Riot, 738
Strategic Arms Limitation Treaty (SALT I), 750

Strategic Arms Limitation Treaty II (SALT II), 765, 766, 777
Strategic Defense Initiative (SDI), 777
Strikes
  Boston police, 536, 558
  cooling off periods of, 655
  failed, 580, 598
  by farmers, 580
  Haymarket bombing, 423
  Homestead, 423–424
  mining, 654
  in postwar period, 654, 662
  Pullman, 424
  railroad, 422, 654
  sit-down, 598
  steel industry, 423–424, 662
  violence in, 423, 453
  after WWI, 536
  during WWII, 622
Student Nonviolent Coordinating Committee (SNCC), 704, 708
Students for a Democratic Society (SDS), 732
Submarines
  in WWI, 523–525
  in WWII, 615–616, 623, 634
Suburbs
  families, 670–671, 677, 678
  growth of, 670
  housing, 434, 542
  integration, 677–678
  politics and, 766
Suez Canal, 468, 618, 692–693, 749
Sugar plantations, 478, 481
Sugrue, Thomas, 707
Sumner, Charles, 355
Sumner, William Graham, 413–414, 448–449
Sun Myung Moon, 767
Sunbelt, politics and, 766
  growth of, 767
Supreme Court. *See also specific cases*
  Court-packing plan, 602
  Ex parte Milligan, 363
  on Fifteenth Amendment, 375
  on Fourteenth Amendment, 375
  New Deal cases, 589–590, 597, 601–602
  Scottsboro case, 567–568, 578
  Watergate case, 758
Survival of the fittest, 413–414
Swann v. Charlotte-Mecklenburg Board of Education, 752
Swift, Gustavus, 412
SWOC. *See* Steel Workers Organizing Committee
Syngman Rhee, 660
Syria, 817
Szyk, Arthur, 626

Taft, Robert, 665
Taft, William Howard
  as Philippines governor, 483
  presidency of, 508–509, 520–521
  presidential elections of, 508, 511–512
Taft-Hartley Act, 655
Tammany Hall, 439, 457, 497
Tammany Society, 438
Tarbell, Ida, 489
Tariffs
  Cleveland on reductions to, 457–458
  McKinley, 458, 466

  in 1920s, 547, 558
  protective, 512
  reduction of, 457–458
TARP. *See* Troubled Asset Relief Program
Tarver, W. W., 570–571
Taubman, William, 644
Taxes
  credits to, 786
  income, 512
  in 1920s, 558–559
  reduction in, 704, 786
Taylor, Frederick Winslow, 409–410
Taylorism, 409–410
Tea Party movement, 793–794
Teamsters Union, 671
Teapot Dome, 557
Technology
  agricultural, 547
  antiaircraft, 623
  barbed wire, 401
  communications, 406
  computers, 543, 624, 674–675
  digital revolution, 799–800
  electricity, 406–407
  electronic, 674
  of global media, 724–725
  industrial, 406–407
  Internet, 800–801
  iron and steel production, 407–408
  medical, 450
  military, 528–530, 623
  in 1920s, 542–543, 547
  in 1950s, 672–676
  R&D, 409
  in WWI, 528–530
  in WWII, 623–624
Tehran Conference, 645
Tehran hostage crisis, 765–766, 770
Telegraph, 461
Telephone, 406, 446, 461, 543
Television
  advertising, 678
  broadcasting, 684, 689
  development of, 678–679
  Lucy and Desi show, 680–681
  news, 678–681, 684, 689
  programming in 1950s, 678–679
  The Twilight Zone, 659
Teller, Henry T., 474
Teller Amendment, 474
Temperance
  prohibition and, 501
  supporters, 494
  WCTU on, 501
Temporary National Economic Committee (TNEC), 602
Ten Percent Plan, 355, 357
Ten Point program, 714
Tenant farmers, 365, 374, 380, 578, 685
Tenements, 435
Tennessee, 355
  Scopes trial, 555–556
Tennessee Coal and Iron Company, 508, 510
Tennessee Valley Authority (TVA), 591–592, 609
Tenure of Office Act, 362, 363
Termination, as Indian policy, 735

Terrorism
  in Middle East, 813–814
  in 1920s, 554–555, 556
  rise of, 813–815
  war on, 815
Tet offensive, in Vietnam War, 725
Texas
  cattle ranching in, 383
  Hispanic residents, 383–384
  military contracts in, 671
Textile industry, in New South, 373
Thatcher, Margaret, 645
Theater, 444–445
Theory of evolution, 448, 555
Third World, Nixon Doctrine, 750
Thirteenth Amendment, 359
Thomas, Norman, 578
Three Mile Island, 811
Thurmond, Strom, 655
Tiananmen Square, in Beijing, 778
Tilden, Samuel J., 370, 371
Timber Culture Act, 386
Time magazine, 663, 672, 795
TNEC. *See* Temporary National Economic Committee
Tokyo firebombing, 636
Tong wars, 385
Townsend Plan, 595
Trade
  free-trade agreements, 786, 813
  in 1920s, 558
  in 1930s, 563
Trade unions. *See* Unions
Transcontinental railroads, 384, 386, 401
Transmission Control Protocol/Internet Protocol (TCP/IP), 800
Transportation. *See also* Automobiles; Railroads
  public mass, 435–436
Travel
  air, 543
  by automobile, 690
  Trump ban on, 627
  vacations, 679
Treaties
  arms control, 765
  with Indians, 396
Treaty of Paris, 478–479
Treaty of Portsmouth, 518
Treaty of Versailles, 534–535, 564
Treaty of Washington, 369
Trench warfare, in WWI, 527–528
Triangle Shirtwaist Fire, 497, 499
Tribal sovereignty, 394
Tripartite Pact, 616
Troubled Asset Relief Program (TARP), 792
Trujillo, Rafael, 716
Truman, Harry S.
  atom bomb decisions, 637, 638–639
  on civil rights, 655, 656
  Fair Deal, 654–657
  Korean War and, 660, 662
  Potsdam conference, 644, 647–648
  presidency of, 637, 647–649, 692
  presidential election of, 655
  as vice-president, 631
Truman Doctrine, 649
Trump, Donald, 774
  Affordable Care Act replace and repeal, 797
  on China, 819
  on immigration, 798
  presidency of, 817
  presidential election of, 797
  Russian election tampering and, 798, 819
  travel ban of, 627
Truth in Securities Act, 588
Tuck, Stephen, 708
Turing, Alan, 624
Turkey, 649–650
Turner, Frederick Jackson, 388–389, 390, 449
Turner thesis, 390
TVA. *See* Tennessee Valley Authority
Twain, Mark, 389, 479
Tweed, William M., 439
21st Century Cures Act, 801
Twenty-First Amendment, 588
The Twilight Zone, 659
Tydings, Millard, 748
Typewriter, 406

U-2 crisis, of Soviet Union, 695–696
UAW. *See* United Auto Workers
UFW. *See* United Farm Workers
Unemployment
  in Great Depression, 561, 564–565, 566, 567, 568, 569, 571–572
  in 1950s, 670, 690
  in 1980s, 775–776
  in Panic of 1893, 462–463
  in recession, 535–536
UNIA. *See* Universal Negro Improvement Association
Union Labor Party, 497
Union Pacific Railroad Company, 368
Unions. *See also* Strikes
  AFL, 422–423, 497, 536, 544, 545, 597–598
  AFL-CIO, 671
  African American, 424, 463
  company, 544
  corruption, 671
  craft, 421, 597
  establishment of, 421–422
  globalization and, 813
  membership, 544, 622, 672
  migrant workers, 737, 738
  militancy in 1930s, 577
  Molly Maguires and, 422
  New Deal and, 597–599
  in 1920s, 544
  in 1950s, 671–672
  no-strike pledge of, 622
  right-to-work laws, 655
  Teamsters, 671
  women in, 493, 630
  WWI and, 536
  WWII and, 622
United Auto Workers (UAW), 598
United Farm Workers (UFW), 738
United Mine Workers, 504, 654, 671
United Nations, 646, 650, 660
United Service Organizations (USO), 629
United States. *See specific branches of military; specific departments; specific divisions of government*
United States v. Richard M. Nixon, 758
UNIVAC. *See* Universal Automatic Computer

Universal Automatic Computer (UNIVAC), 674–675
Universal Negro Improvement Association (UNIA), 537
Universal schooling, 449
Universities
    African American, 365, 375, 449
    coeducational, 451
    desegregation, 740
    land-grant institutions, 449, 451
    private, 449
    state, 449–450, 671
    for women, 451, 492, 548
Urban. *See* Cities
Urban League, 714
U.S. Steel Corporation, 412, 508, 510
U.S.A trilogy (Passo), 576
USO. *See* United Service Organizations
U.S.S. *Maine* incident, 473, 475
Utah, statehood of, 387

Valentino, Rudolph, 551
Vanderbilt, Cornelius, 411
Vanzetti, Bartolomeo, 538
Vaudeville, 444–445
Vaux, Calvert, 433
Veblen, Thorstein, 491
Vertical integration, in industry, 412, 419
Veterans
    Civil War pension system, 455
    WWI, 535–536, 580–582
    WWII, 689
Viet Cong, 718, 719
Vietnam
    Diem assassination, 718
    division in, 717–718
    French colony, 691–692, 749
    Geneva accords on, 691, 692, 718
Vietnam War, 698
    atrocities, 719
    Christmas bombing, 745
    cost of, 746
    Easter offensive, 745
    fall of Saigon, 745–746
    Gulf of Tonkin Resolution, 718–719, 744
    My Lai massacre in, 719, 744
    Nixon's policies, 743–745
    pacification program in, 719–720
    peace accords, 691, 692, 718, 745
    protests, 721, 722–723, 724–725, 733, 744
    Tet offensive, 725
    U.S. strategies in, 718–721
    U.S. troops in, 719
Vietnamization, 743–744
Villa, Pancho, 521
Violence. *See also* Race riots
    in cities, 437–438, 711
    against Indians, 396
    police, 711
    school shootings, 797
    in strikes, 423, 453
Virginia, freed slaves in, 360–361
The Virginian (Wister), 387, 390
Von Richthofen, Walter Baron, 400–401
Voting rights
    of African Americans, 355, 369, 375, 378, 379, 709–710, 712–713
    Fifteenth Amendment, 362, 370, 372, 375
    limits of, 378, 709–710
    literacy requirements, 378, 709–710

restrictions for, 374–375, 709–710
    of women, 493–494
Voting Rights Act of 1965, 710

Wabash, St. Louis, and Pacific Railway Co. v. Illinois, 458
Wade, Benjamin E., 357
Wade-Davis Bill, 357, 359
Wages
    of African Americans, 439
    in industry, 420–421, 424, 671
    minimum, 602, 656
    in 1920s, 544
    in 1950s, 671, 690
    of women, 421, 571, 739
Wagner, Robert F., 499, 597
Wagner Act, 602, 654
Wallace, George, 705, 727–728, 753
Wallace, Henry A., 615, 631, 655
Wanamaker, John, 440–441
War Industries Board, 530
War on poverty, of Johnson, L., 702–703
War on terror, 815
War Production Board (WPB), 623
Ward, Lester Frank, 415, 449
Warren, Earl, 626, 686, 701, 752
Wars. *See specific wars*
Warsaw Pact, 653
Washington, Booker T., 375, 500
Washington, statehood of, 387
Washington Conference of 1921, 557
Water pollution, 752
Watergate, 755, 759
    Congress investigations of, 757
    historians on, 756–757
    politics and diplomacy after, 762–766
    Supreme Court case on, 758
Watson, John B., 549
Watts riot, 711
WCTU. *See* Women's Christian Temperance Union
Wealth. *See also* Capitalists
    Gospel of, 414–415, 416–417
    self-made men, 412–413, 418–419
Weapons
    drones, 818
    gun control, 797
    ICBMs, 675
    of mass destruction, 816
    in WWI, 528–529
    in WWII, 623
Weaver, James B., 458, 461
Weaver, Robert, 703
Webb, Walter Prescott, 388
Weisbrot, Robert, 706
Welch, Robert, 650
Welfare capitalism, 543–544
Welles, Orson, 575
Wells-Barnett, Ida B., 378, 501
West
    agriculture in, 391, 398–403
    economy of, 390–393
    ethnic groups in, 390
    as frontier, 381
    Indian lands and, 382–383
    labor force in, 390
    New Deal and, 609
    paintings, 387
    Plains Indians, 394

West–(*Cont.*)
  progressivism in, 499–500
  railroads in, 384, 386, 402, 410
  ranching in, 383, 392–393, 400–401
  rise of modern, 671
  romantic images of, 387–390
  rural life in, 403
  Sunbelt, 766
West, settlement of
  Chinese migration to, 384–386
  farmers, 398–403
  historians' views, 388–389
  Homestead Act, 355, 386
  Indian resistance to, 395–397
  trails, 395
West Coast Hotel v. Parrish, 602
Westad, Odd Arne, 645
Weyler, Valeriano, 471
Wheeler, Burton, 615
Wheeler, Joseph, 475
Wheeler-Nicholson, Malcolm, 574
Whistler, James McNeil, 447
White, Richard, 388
White supremacy, 455, 461
Whitewater affair, 786, 787
Whyte, William H., Jr., 682
Wiebe, Robert, 498
Wild West shows, 387
Willard, Frances, 501
Williams, William Appleman, 644
Willkie, Wendell, 615
Wilson, Woodrow
  foreign policy of, 521
  Fourteen Points, 533–534
  on graduated income tax, 512
  international vision of, 521, 524, 534
  on monopolies, 513
  neutrality of, 522–523
  New Freedom program of, 511, 514
  presidency of, 511–513
  presidential elections of, 511–512
  progressivism, 487
  on protective tariff, 511–512
  stroke of, 535
  Treaty of Versailles, 534–535
  WWI and, 522–525
Wilson-Gorman Tariff, 458
The Winning of the West (Roosevelt, T.), 390
Wister, Owen, 387, 390
The Wizard of Oz, 576
Woman's Political Committee, 688
Women. *See also* Abortion; Gender relations
  clubs, 492–493
  in Congress, 740
  as consumers, 442
  discrimination against, 711
  divorces and, 492
  domestic roles of, 421, 571
  education of, 451, 492, 493
  feminism, 739–740
  flappers, 549, 551
  in Great Depression, 571–572, 578
  lesbians, 738
  military service of, 525, 629, 630
  motherhood, 549, 678
  New Deal and, 607–609
  professional, 492, 548, 740

  reformers, 492–494
  romantic novels and, 414–415, 446
  settlement houses, 490
  single, 492
  sports, 444
  suffrage, 493–494, 514
  union members, 493, 630
  in USO, 629
  in West, 391–392
  writers, 414–415
  in WWII, 629
Women, in workforce
  African Americans, 366, 571
  equal pay regulations and, 739
  increased participation, 630
  in industry, 373, 410, 421
  in 1920s, 545–547
  in 1930s, 571
  in postwar period, 654, 678
  telephone operators, 446
  Triangle Shirtwaist Company Fire, 497, 499
  wages, 421, 571, 739
  in WWI, 531
  in WWII, 622, 630
Women's Christian Temperance Union (WCTU), 501
Women's March on Washington, 805
Women's rights
  Equal Rights Amendment, 551, 740–741, 804
  in 1920s, 549
  in 1960s and later, 725, 739–740
  voting, 493–494
Women's Trade Union League (WTUL), 493
Wood, Leonard, 481
Woodstock, 734–735
Working classes, 420, 445
Works Progress Administration (WPA), 600–601, 602, 626, 630
World Court, 612
World Series, 443
World Trade Center attacks, 814, 816
World Trade Organization (WTO), 786
World War I (WWI)
  African Americans and, 525, 536–537
  airplanes in, 409, 529
  alliances, 522
  Allies in, 522
  armistice, 527, 533–535, 539
  casualties, 516, 525, 527, 530
  Central Powers in, 522
  disenchantment with, 553–554
  dissent, 524, 531, 533
  financing, 530–531
  global instability after, 517
  Lost Generation after, 553
  organizing economy, 530–531
  Paris Peace Conference, 534
  posters, 526
  preparedness, 523
  profiteering, 604
  propaganda, 531
  reparations, 558, 563, 564, 603
  songs, 532–533
  Treaty of Versailles, 534–535
  trench warfare in, 527–528
  U.S. and, 522–525
  veterans, 535–536, 580–582
  Western Front, 528
  Wilson and, 522–525

World War II (WWII)
  African Americans and, 621, 624–625
  airplanes in, 614, 623–624, 632
  Allies in, 614–616, 618–619, 623–624, 631, 633–634
  atomic warfare in, 636–639
  beginning of, 606
  casualties, 616, 636, 637
  cultural impact, 627–631
  D-Day, 632
  end of, 634, 637, 642
  in Europe, 618–619, 631–634
  German invasions, 613–614
  intelligence, 616, 621
  London bombings, 614
  minority group experiences, 624–625
  Normandy invasion, 624, 631
  in North Africa, 618, 619
  in Pacific, 634–636
  Pearl Harbor attack, 616–617
  science and technology, 623–624
  U.S. economy, 621–623
  U.S. entry into, 616
  veterans, 689
Worster, Donald, 388
Wounded Knee massacre, 397, 736
Wovoka, 397

WPA. *See* Works Progress Administration
WPB. *See* War Production Board
Wright, Almroth, 673
Wright, Orville, 409
Wright, Richard, 576
Wright, Wilbur, 409
WTO. *See* World Trade Organization
WTUL. *See* Women's Trade Union League
WWI. *See* World War I
WWII. *See* World War II
Wyoming, statehood of, 387

Yalta Conference, 644, 646–647, 816–817
Yankee imperialism, 481
Yellow journalism, 472–473
Yom Kippur War, 751, 754
Yosemite National Park, 507, 679
Young, Andrew, 764
Youth culture
  in 1950s, 682–683
  in 1960s and 1970s, 721, 724–725, 731–735
Yugoslavia, 786, 789

Zimmermann Telegram, 523
Zone of occupation, in Germany, 646
Zoot suits, 625